Criminal Law
3rd Edition

John Schmolesky

Acknowledgements

I am indebted to the many students who have been in my first-year Criminal Law course at St. Mary's University School of Law. I have learned from them, and their comments and questions have been helpful to me in developing this book. This work benefitted from the many discussions and ideas that my erstwhile colleague, Professor Geary Reamey, has shared with me for more than 30 years. I am also indebted to my colleague at St. Mary's, Professor Dorie Klein, who generously shared her work on her own Criminal Law text, which greatly enhanced this book. I also want to acknowledge the essential support and encouragement of our law school dean, Steve Sheppard, and St. Mary's University. Finally, I am very grateful for the help of my research assistants Brian Nesbit and Karly Houchin on the original edition and Gary Hillier and Zoe Russell on the revised editions.

Criminal Law
Summary Table of Contents

Criminal Law
Table of Contents

Chapter 1: Mental State and Intent

Introduction

Def. of crim. law

The first year law school course entitled "Criminal Law" is a study of conduct deemed threatening to public and personal safety and/or morally reprehensible by society. This course will examine the component parts that are necessary for criminal liability and recognized defenses to allegations of criminality. Other important doctrines will be examined, including: when criminal sanctions can be imposed vicariously upon persons whose conduct did not personally cause the harms proscribed by statute, when criminal sanctions can be imposed for criminality that was not completed but manifested a dangerous intent on the part of actors who attempted or conspired to engage in criminal acts, and constitutional limitations on the use of criminal sanctions.

The closest cousin to criminal law in the traditional first-year law school curriculum is tort law. A crime may also be a tort. Thus, for example, the former football star O.J. Simpson was tried (but acquitted) of a criminal charge of murder, but the same wrongful deaths were the basis of civil liability in tort. The differing outcomes in the criminal and civil Simpson cases illustrate important differences between tort and criminal law. (A tort action generally involves private parties, and the measure of civil liability is money damages that are granted to a successful tort plaintiff.) In contrast, a criminal case is a matter of public law. In a criminal proceeding, a public prosecutor represents the state or government, not the victim of the crime. The prosecutor often works closely with a victim, who may be a witness at a criminal trial, but the wishes of the victim concerning whether and what charges to file are not binding on the prosecutor. For example, many prosecutor offices have a policy of presenting criminal charges for acts of domestic violence even if the victim of the violence has reconciled with the domestic partner and opposes criminal prosecution of the accused.

The acquittal in the Simpson criminal case was not *res judicata* as to the wrongful death civil suit because different parties were involved (the state instead of the victim), but also because different standards of proof applied. The criminal acquittal was a finding that the alleged criminal offense was not proved to the satisfaction of the jury beyond a reasonable doubt. The civil verdict was a jury finding of liability for the wrongful death by the lower standard of a preponderance of the evidence. The more onerous standard in a criminal case is a reflection of the greater certainty of guilt required in light of the consequences of a criminal conviction. Unlike the economic adjustment in a tort case, a criminal conviction represents the stigma of societal condemnation and the potential loss of liberty or even life.

Proof beyond reasonable doubt Crim. v. Civil law

The requirement of proof beyond a reasonable doubt is only one of the significant differences between criminal and civil law. Although this course deals primarily with the substantive law of crime, a number of procedural issues will be discussed in order to place the substantive law in a meaningful context. There are important procedural differences between criminal and civil law. A criminal defendant cannot be required to testify or present any defense due to the Fifth Amendment right against self-incrimination. The existence of a criminal defendant's Fifth Amendment right against self-incrimination has the effect of narrowing the range of discovery in criminal cases. Typically, there is little surprise to either party at the point a civil case comes to trial because of the extensive right of each party to depose and send interrogatories to the other. However, a defendant cannot be required to submit to a deposition, and a refusal to testify at trial cannot be the subject of argument or instruction to the jury that the defendant's unwillingness is an indication of guilt. No matter how much evidence is presented against a defendant, a trial court may not direct a verdict in favor of the prosecution in a criminal case due to the criminal defendant's absolute right to go to a jury in serious criminal cases. No felony conviction can be returned against a criminal defendant without representation of counsel at state expense if the defendant is indigent. No conviction is possible without a jury verdict unless the right to counsel and a jury is knowingly and voluntarily waived.

[handwritten note in left margin: must go to jury unless waived.]

Unlike civil law that is largely the product of centuries of common law development in our legal tradition, criminal law has almost entirely abandoned common law crimes. In Texas, for example, all common law crimes have been explicitly abolished, and only conduct or circumstances proscribed by a statute may be the subject of criminal prosecution. *See* TEX. PENAL CODE art. 1.03. Thus, this criminal law course is a statutory code course that will provide many opportunities to construe criminal statutes. The emphasis on statutory law is a reflection of the heightened concern with fair notice that is characteristic of criminal law. This does not mean the common law traditions of criminal law are unimportant. Many statutory provisions reflect common law doctrines, and courts often rely upon common law traditions in construing the meaning of statutes. Nonetheless, it is fair to say that criminal law is the subject in the typical first-year criminal law curriculum that is most grounded in statute.

[handwritten note in left margin: No common law for crime in TX]

Because of the code-based nature of substantive criminal law, this course will be based upon the Texas Penal Code and many Texas cases interpreting that code. However, the course is not about Texas Criminal Law. Rather, Texas cases and statutes are used to illustrate general principles of criminal law that are at issue in all American jurisdictions—state and federal. Federal cases and cases from other jurisdictions will be included. However, because of the paramount importance of a penal code in criminal law, this course and this text will use as its foundation the penal law in the jurisdiction of this law school: the state of Texas. Frequent mention will be made to the Model Penal Code of the American Law Institute. This seminal work of the 1950's and 60's is not the law in any American jurisdiction, but it has been highly influential. In the decades after the completion of the Model Penal Code, nearly every American jurisdiction re-drafted its penal code, and portions of the model code were frequently lifted virtually verbatim. Even if the Model Penal Code was not followed in an area of criminal law, the discussion in the text and commentary of the model code informed the debate in state legislatures.

Mental State in Criminal Law

Our legal practice in criminal law has traditionally been to inquire into the mental state of the actor rather than merely the objective conduct or results caused by the defendant's conduct. It is a bedrock axiom that criminal liability usually depends upon more than causing harmful results or engaging in behavior that society regards as unacceptable. Rather, a *mens rea*, or guilty mind, must accompany a guilty act in order for there to be criminal liability. This is another important distinction between criminal law and its tort law cousin. Mere negligence is usually not sufficient for criminal liability as it is for civil tort liability. The central importance of mental state in criminal law reflects the central difference between allocation of costs that are the primary concern of tort law as opposed to societal condemnation and potential deprivation of life or liberty in criminal law. It may be appropriate to make a tortfeasor pay for the costs created by his or her negligent conduct, but the stigma and penalty associated with criminal law violations requires a moral culpability associated with a guilty mind.

Culpability + Guilty mind (mens rea)

The importance of mental state in criminal law is matched by the difficulties associated with it. The type of mental state that is sufficient for criminality is hard to define in general and difficult to discern in many specific cases. Objective conduct and results may be the subject of dispute, but these issues are far more accessible and certain than what was in a person's mind. A person's subjective state of mind must be inferred from objective circumstances. The difficulties associated with mental state were often compounded by criminal statutes that used a variety of unenlightening terms to signal a requirement of *mens rea*, such as "feloniously," "maliciously," "fraudulently," "willfully," or "corruptly." These terms were used in various statutes without a definition, and different jurisdictions—even different courts within the same jurisdiction—sometimes used these ambiguous terms in an inconsistent manner.

One of the areas in which the Model Penal Code has had the greatest influence is with the mental state requirements for crime. Most of the major penal code recodifications that occurred in the second half of the 20th century used the four-part division of mental states and their relatively clear and consistent definitions provided in the Model Penal Code. Texas was part of the trend to adopt the approach of the model code in the major recodification of 1974, which is still the basic code that we use today in Texas (although amended many times since 1974). The Texas Penal Code adopted a general listing of four differing mental states with definitions almost verbatim from the Model Penal Code. The Texas Penal Code refers to them as four "culpable mental states":

- Intent;
- Knowledge;
- Recklessness; and
- Criminal negligence.

See TEX. PENAL CODE art. 6.02.

Article 6.03 of the Texas Penal Code adopts, in a nearly verbatim manner, the following definitions of these culpable mental states taken from the Model Penal Code (with emphasis added):

(a) A person acts **intentionally,** or with intent, with respect to the nature of his conduct or to a result of his conduct when it is his **conscious objective or desire** to engage in the conduct or cause the result.

(b) A person acts **knowingly**, or with knowledge, with respect to the nature of his conduct or to circumstances surrounding his conduct when he is **aware of the nature of his conduct or that the circumstances exist.** A person acts knowingly, or with knowledge, with respect to a result of his conduct **when he is aware that his conduct is reasonably certain to cause the result**.

he is aware

(c) A person acts **recklessly**, or is reckless, with respect to circumstances surrounding his conduct or the result of his conduct **when he is aware of but consciously disregards a substantial and unjustifiable risk that the circumstances exist or the result will occur.** The risk must be **of such a nature and degree that its disregard constitutes a gross deviation from the standard of care that an ordinary person would exercise** under all the circumstances as viewed from the actor's standpoint.

he should be aware

(d) A person acts with criminal negligence, or is **criminally negligent**, with respect to circumstances surrounding his conduct or the result of his conduct **when he ought to be aware of a substantial and unjustifiable risk that the circumstances exist or the result will occur. The risk must be of such a nature and degree that the failure to perceive it constitutes a gross deviation from the standard of care that an ordinary person would exercise** under all the circumstances as viewed from the actor's standpoint.

These four culpable mental states are hierarchical. That is, they are listed in the order of greatest culpability to lowest. Article 6.02(e) of the Texas Penal Code states that proof of a higher culpable mental state suffices to establish proof of a lower mental state. The first chapter of the text will deal with the highest mental states of intent and knowledge. Chapter II will discuss the lower level culpable mental states of recklessness and criminal negligence. Frequently, the Texas Penal Code—like the penal code in many jurisdictions—provides statutes stating that "intent or knowledge" is required. Thus, a defendant who put a bomb on a private plane that he owned in order to collect insurance monies would not be able to win an acquittal of murder charges because he only desired to damage the plane. The defendant's knowledge of the collateral damage to the pilot and others on board would be sufficient. However, some statutes require the specific intent to engage in certain conduct or to achieve a certain result or create an intent requirement as to some elements and a differing requirement as to others. The *Godfrey* case, which follows, has an atypical use of intent or knowledge. Rather than a disjunctive use of intent or knowledge, the statute employs an intent and knowledge requirement applicable to different statutory elements.

Godfrey v. State

No. 14-13-00100-CR, 2014 WL 309381
(Tex. App.—Houston [14th Dist.] Jan. 28, 2014, no pet.)

Sharon McCally, Justice

A jury convicted appellant Orlando Dewan Godfrey of evading arrest or detention with a motor vehicle, and the trial court assessed punishment at two years' confinement, probated for two years.

[A]ppellant contends the evidence is "insufficient to prove intent to evade arrest." We hold that there is sufficient evidence for a jury to find beyond a reasonable doubt that appellant intentionally fled from a person he knew was a peace officer attempting to lawfully arrest or detain him.

The State and appellant each presented one witness at trial. First, Houston Metro Police Officer Robert Smith testified that he was driving in his marked patrol car south on State Highway 288 when he observed two cars—a Chevrolet Corvette and a Chevrolet Camaro convertible with its top down—speeding and racing. Appellant was driving the Camaro.

Smith pursued the cars from a distance; he kept track of the cars by watching their taillights. Eventually, he got within fifty or seventy-five feet of the Camaro, with his car's siren and flashing lights activated. Using his car's P.A. system, Smith told the driver of the Camaro, "You better pull it over." He saw appellant look in the rearview mirror. The car in front of the Camaro pulled over, and then the Camaro sped off at a high rate of speed. Smith pursued. Without signaling, the Camaro moved to the left across three lanes of traffic at a high rate of speed, passed some more vehicles, and then changed lanes to its right. Eventually the brake lights of the Camaro came on, and it slowed down. Officer Smith pulled up behind the Camaro, and the Camaro stopped on the right shoulder.

Smith arrested appellant. At some point, Smith asked appellant why he did not stop, and appellant said it was because he did not see Smith. Appellant's girlfriend, Delta Scott, was a passenger in the Camaro. Smith testified that Scott told him she was telling appellant to stop and that she was scared. Scott testified at trial that she did not say anything to Officer Smith. She testified that the music in the Camaro was loud, and she could not hear very well. She testified that appellant pulled over as soon as they noticed the police car behind them. A video camera in Officer Smith's car recorded the incident, and a redacted version of the video was played for the jury.

Section 38.04 of the Texas Penal Code establishes the elements of the offense of evading arrest or detention: "A person commits an offense if he intentionally flees from a person he knows is a peace officer or federal special investigator attempting to arrest or detain him." TEX. PEN. CODE ANN. § 38.04(a) (West 2015). The offense is a third degree felony if "the actor uses a vehicle while the actor is in flight." TEX. PEN. CODE ANN. § 38.04(b)(2) (West 2015). Thus, to convict appellant of the charged offense, "the State had to prove appellant, while using a vehicle,

13

intentionally fled from a person he knew to be a peace officer attempting lawfully to arrest or detain him." *Redwine v. State*, 305 S.W.3d 360, 362 (Tex. App.—Houston [14th Dist.] 2010, pet. ref'd). A person violates § 38.04 "only if he knows a police officer is attempting to arrest him but nevertheless refuses to yield to a police show of authority." *Id.*

When evaluating the sufficiency of the evidence to prove an appellant's intent for evading arrest in a vehicle, the speed, distance, and duration of the pursuit may be factors to consider. *Griego v. State*, 345 S.W.3d 742, 751 & n.10 (Tex. App.—Amarillo 2011, no pet.). But "no particular speed, distance, or duration is required to show the requisite intent if other evidence establishes such intent." In *Griego*, for example, the court of appeals found the evidence insufficient when the speed of the pursuit was unremarkable; the duration was mere seconds; the route of the pursuit, given the parties' locations and the characteristics of the roads, would have made it "physically unlikely or impossible that appellant could have seen the officers turn around to pursue him"; and the defendant's conduct and statements upon exiting his car at his destination (a residence) were not necessarily consistent with guilt.

This court also found the evidence insufficient in *Redwine*, even though the defendant admitted to turning onto a county road to avoid contact with a patrol vehicle, because there was only equivocal testimony from one of the officers about whether the patrol vehicle's lights were flashing during the pursuit. *See Redwine* at 364, 368. Thus, there was no "show of authority" for a jury to rationally conclude that the defendant knew the officers were trying to arrest or detain him.

On the other hand, in *Hobyl v. State*, the First Court of Appeals found the evidence legally and factually sufficient to support a conviction for evading arrest in a vehicle. *Hobyl v. State*, 152 S.W.3d 624, 627–28 (Tex. App.—Houston [1st Dist.] 2004, pet. dism'd). The arresting officer testified that he was pacing Hobyl, who was on a motorcycle traveling at about seventy-five miles per hour in the left lane of Highway 61. At about the same time the officer turned on his emergency lights and siren, Hobyl increased his speed to 110 miles per hour. The officer testified that Hobyl looked in his side mirrors during the pursuit, which lasted about three miles. Then, the officer pulled up next to Hobyl in an adjacent lane and motioned for Hobyl to stop. Soon thereafter, Hobyl stopped on the right-hand shoulder. Hobyl testified that he could not see the patrol vehicle because he was in a crouched position, and he could not hear the siren due to noise from his motorcycle, the wind, and flapping from his rain suit.

This case is most similar to *Hobyl*. Officer Smith activated the flashing lights of his patrol vehicle, blasted the siren, and instructed appellant to "pull over" through the P.A. system while Smith was within fifty feet of appellant's top-down convertible. Smith testified that appellant looked in the rearview mirror, so appellant would have known that Smith was attempting to pull him over. In response to Smith's shows of authority, however, appellant sped away and traversed multiple lanes of traffic without signaling. Although appellant indeed pulled over within a minute of this encounter, the duration factor is not dispositive and certainly not as favorable as it was in *Griego*. Further, we note that the jury could have disbelieved appellant's self-serving statement that he did not see Smith. The totality of the circumstantial evidence would have enabled a rational jury to find beyond a reasonable doubt that appellant intentionally fled from a person he knew to be a police officer attempting lawfully to arrest him.

14

Accordingly, the evidence is sufficient to sustain appellant's conviction.

Notes

1.   The evading arrest statute in *Godfrey* requires an intent to evade, but with a knowledge requirement as to the police officer's identity during the evasion. This appears to make little difference to the defendant's claim that he did not see the officer and was making no effort to evade anyone. Suppose, however, a defendant claimed she was trying to evade another car driving erratically and aggressively. Unbeknownst the defendant, the other car was an unmarked police car, and the officer driver was attempting to pull the defendant over. Such a defendant might claim that, while there was an intentional evasion, she lacked the required knowledge that the person evaded was a police officer. The difference among the four mental states creates subtle issues that the parties may raise and the jury must resolve. The difficulty is increased by the fact that the mental state words are sometimes defined differently by different jurisdictions and courts. In some jurisdictions, the term intent is used, but the term is defined more broadly to include what Texas and the Model Penal Code would define as knowledge. Words in statutes mean what legislatures writing the statute say that they mean or, more precisely, what courts interpreting what legislatures meant the words to mean.

2.   In addition to the ambiguity of language, the difficulty of mental state issues is increased by the tendency to slip from one mental state concept to another because of the inherent relationship among the various culpable mental states. For example, in *Godfrey*, did the jury find that the defendant was in fact aware of the arresting officer or only that he should have paid more attention and should have been aware of the officer's attempted arrest? Could the defendant support his insufficient evidence claim by getting affidavits from jurors stating they found the defendant guilty because he should have been aware of the attempted arrest but the jury did not unanimously agree that he was aware of it? What if the defendant's claim was not one of insufficient evidence but a claim that there was an improper jury instruction in a case in which the jury was instructed that it should find the defendant guilty if he or she should have known that a police officer was attempting to arrest him? *instructions to jury, what were they asked to do*

3.   Consider another possible scenario based on facts similar to *Godfrey*. The defendant who evaded the driver of another car testifies she knew the driver was a police officer from personal experience, but believed the officer, who was not in uniform, was not acting in an official capacity. Suppose the defendant testifies this officer had been seeking a personal relationship with the defendant when he was off-duty, and the defendant believed the officer's aggressive driving was another act of personal bravado rather than a police official attempting to make an arrest. Would the defendant be guilty under the statute, which requires the actor intentionally evade a person known to be a police officer <u>acting</u> in his or her official capacity as a police officer in making an arrest? The answer may depend in part on whether the knowledge requirement applies only to the immediately proximate element of police officer status or whether it also applies to the requirement of an official arrest.

Intent As to Which Elements?

The question of how far down the line the mental state requirement applies is an important and persistent problem of statutory interpretation in criminal law. For example, what if an aggravated assault statute states: "It is an offense intentionally to assault a person, who is a police officer, acting in the official performance of his or her duties." Is the actor who assaults a person—say a non-uniformed police officer on an undercover detail—guilty of just simple assault (any victim) or aggravated assault (a heightened penalty applicable to police officer victims)? As a matter of logic and grammar, the word intentionally could modify *police office* and *official performance* requirements, or could only apply to the immediately proximate assault element. The answer is a matter of deciding what the legislature intended. In reality, few, if any, legislators probably consider such questions in deliberating and voting upon the statute. More realistically, the question that courts usually decide is, if the issue had been considered by the legislature, what would be the legislative intent?

In reading the *Peek* case, which follows, do you agree the legislative purpose of adding higher penalties to drug distribution offenses that occur near public schools is furthered by the decision finding that the intent required by the statute applies to possession with intent to deliver but not the location in a drug-free-zone?

Peek v. State

No. 11-12-00319-CR, 2015 WL 1778952
(Tex. App.—Eastland Apr. 16, 2015, pet ref'd.)

Opinion by Justice John M. Bailey

The jury convicted Kevin Royce Peek of possession of four grams or more but less than 200 grams of methamphetamine with the intent to deliver in a drug-free zone. Appellant pleaded true to two enhancement allegations. The jury found both enhancement allegations to be true, and it assessed Appellant's punishment at confinement for life in the Institutional Division of the Texas Department of Criminal Justice.

Appellant does not challenge the sufficiency of the evidence to support his conviction for possession of four grams or more but less than 200 grams of methamphetamine with intent to deliver. He does challenge the sufficiency of the evidence to establish that he committed the offense in a drug-free zone.

Specifically, Appellant contends that the evidence was insufficient to support the jury's finding that he committed the offense within 1,000 feet of Early High School. We review a challenge to the sufficiency of the evidence under the standard of review set forth in *Jackson v. Virginia*, 443 U.S. 307, 319 (1979). Under that standard, we examine all of the evidence in the light most favorable to the verdict and determine whether, based on that evidence and any reasonable inferences from it, any rational trier of fact could have found the essential elements of the offense beyond a reasonable doubt. In conducting a sufficiency review, we defer to the jury's role as the sole judge of the witnesses' credibility and the weight their testimony is to be afforded.

Detective Dibrell testified regarding the location where he stopped Appellant's vehicle. He said that the stop occurred on Early Boulevard, "directly across from the high school." He then testified as follows in answer to the prosecutor's questions:

Q. And, so, when we say directly across from the high school, can you give the jury an estimation of approximately how far away they would have been from the school property?

A. 50 foot maybe – four lines, including the left turn lane. Then right on the other side of that is school property.

Q. All right.

A. Or – I don't know if it actually belongs to the school, because you have some occupied space between it and the school, but.

Q. Well, can you safely say that it was fairly close to the school?

A. Oh, yes, yes, for sure. I mean, just right there across the street. There may have been like a building or something else, but right behind that is the school.

Q. All right. So, if I was to ask you specifically about, you know, from where they were stopped to where the school was located or school property, the edge of the school property and so forth, would it have been less than a thousand feet?

A. Oh, yes, definitely.

Q. No doubt about that?

A. No, no question about it.

Q. Okay. Now, the school we are talking about, that is the one that is located there at the 115 Sudderth Drive in Early, Texas?

A. Yes, sir.

Kirby testified that Detective Dibrell pulled Appellant over by Early High School. Kirby said that Appellant stopped the vehicle right by Early High School.

Based on the evidence, we conclude that a rational trier of fact could have found that Appellant committed the offense within 1,000 feet of the premises of a school. Therefore, the evidence is sufficient to support the finding that Appellant committed the offense in a drug-free zone.

We affirm the judgment of the trial court.

– evidence was sufficient

Motive Versus Intent

It is important to distinguish motive from intent. Generally, motive is relevant, but not required in criminal prosecutions. The fact the defendant is the beneficiary of a life insurance policy on the life of the victim of an alleged murder is relevant because it makes it more likely that the defendant committed the crime due to the motive to commit it. However, that does not mean an individual who opens fire on strangers in a movie theater is immune from prosecution because the person lacks a conventional motive. Thus, while there is much attention devoted to the motive of the accused in criminal cases, it is not usually a required element of proof.

A *good* motive is not a defense to criminal liability. Robin Hood does not have a good defense to robbery charges on the theory his crimes are not committed for personal aggrandizement, but rather to redistribute wealth from the rich to the poor. The nature of the defendant's motive may be relevant to some discretionary decisions, such as the sentence to be imposed upon conviction. A judge might be moved to give Bob Cratchet probation instead of prison if he embezzles money from Scrooge to get an operation for Tiny Tim rather than to obtain money for a beach vacation, but it does not affect Bob's guilt of the criminal offense.

Even if the crime is for "good" guilt of A is not affected

Special Intent Crimes

Motive is sometimes relevant to substantive guilt itself with special intent crimes. The term "special intent" has been applied in a number of different ways that has caused confusion. The drafters of the Model Penal Code made a conscious decision to avoid the term because of the difficulties associated with it, including different rules concerning the defenses of mistake of fact and voluntary intoxication in special intent cases (which will be discussed later). The State of Texas chose to follow the approach of the Model Penal Code in eschewing different rules for special intent crimes. However, criminal law decisions are replete with references to the concept, and the general rule concerning motive is often inapplicable in special intent cases.

The most common definition of special intent, and the meaning that will be intended when it is used in these materials, is that a special intent is a particular desire of the defendant that goes beyond the conduct or circumstances that are the focus of the criminal statute. For example, burglary is one of the most common special intent crimes. The act forbidden is the entry into a home or building without the consent of the owner. However, to be guilty of the crime of burglary the prosecution must also prove a special intent—an intent beyond the act of unpermitted entry itself; an intent to enter for the purpose of committing a crime or theft. *See, e.g.* TEX. PENAL CODE § 30.02. Motive refers to why a person does something (*i.e.* the defendant killed the victim to get the insurance money or Robin Hood robbed to get money for the poor) and is ordinarily irrelevant to the defendant's guilt or innocence. However, motive is made relevant in many strict liability crimes. For example, a person who breaks into a home on a cold night to get warm is not guilty of burglary because he or she lacks the special intent (or motive) of committing theft or another crime. This person would be guilty of criminal trespass, a general intent crime of entering without the consent of the owner, *see* TEX. PEN. CODE § 30.05, because the actor's motive is irrelevant to substantive guilt (although it may be taken into account with regard to disposition).

Like general intent, specific intent must be proved circumstantially, but the additional requirement of a special intent crime makes the prosecution's task more difficult as it may well require circumstantial proof of a criminal motive. Consider the case of *State v. Rocker*, 475 P.2d 684 (1970), which involved a conviction of an offense "against common decency" based upon an indictment alleging the defendant, Rocker, indecently exposed himself by sunbathing in the nude on a public beach. Although the statute did not specify there was any mental state, the appellate court reviewing the conviction read in a requirement of intent, as courts often do in construing statutes that do not use an explicit *mens rea* word like intent. The Hawaii Supreme Court stated,

> Sunbathing in the nude is not per se illegal. It must be coupled with the intent to indecently expose oneself. The intent necessary is a general intent, not a specific intent.... [T]he intent may be inferred from the conduct of the accused and the circumstances and environment of the occurrence.

The Hawaii Supreme Court affirmed the conviction, although nobody but the defendant and his friend were on the beach when they first arrived and removed their swimming trunks. Police officers who arrested the defendants observed the nude defendants with binoculars. Clearly the defendants had knowingly exposed themselves, but such exposure only becomes "indecent" if it is done with an intent that others observe or at least knowledge that others will or might observe and be offended. Despite the isolated nature of the beach, the appellate court ruled that the jury could have inferred the necessary intent from the existence of a well-worn path to the beach and testimony that it was a favorite spot for fishing.

The *Rocker* case illustrates a version of "intent" broader than the narrow Texas definition of intent that is equated only with what the defendant desires. No actions of the defendants in *Rocker* suggested they intended (desired) to show themselves naked to other observers. The *Rocker* Court used the word "intentionally" in a broader sense to include what Texas statutes describe as knowledge. Remember, words mean what the legislature say they mean (as interpreted by a court), and not what a dictionary or the Model Penal Code proclaims. The dissenting judge in *Rocker*, Judge Levinson, complained the majority approach was erroneous even under a broader definition of intent because it allowed a conviction on the basis of only recklessness or negligence. Levinson reasoned that because there was no proof from which it could be shown the defendants were aware of the well-worn path—the beach was accessible from a less worn direction as well—or the popularity of fishing at the location, the evidence failed to show the defendants knew others could be present who might be offended.

Consider how the defendants in *Rocker* would have fared under an equivalent Texas statute proscribing "indecent exposure." Texas Penal Code Section 21.08 provides:

> A person commits an offense if he exposes his anus or any part of his genitals with intent
> to arouse or gratify the sexual desire of any person, and he is reckless about whether
> another is present who will be offended or alarmed by his act.

An absent minded jogger who removed his sweat pants thinking that he had short gym trunks underneath would not be guilty under either the Texas or Hawaiin statutes because of a lack of intent to expose (if the jury believes such testimony). However, *Rocker* is much less likely to be prosecuted or convicted in Texas under Section 21.08. Note the Texas statute has differing mental states for different elements in the statute. While Article 21.08 specifies the recklessness standard for the presence of other people that the dissenting judge in *Rocker* claimed was the real standard being applied by the majority, it would seem unlikely a jury could find the quietly isolated nude sunbathers had the special intent (or motive) of arousing or gratifying the sexual desire of any person.

One should not conclude from examining *Rocker* and the Texas Indecent Exposure Statute that Texas is soft on public nudity. Texas prosecutors have avoided the difficult special intent requirements of Section 21.08, while finding an easier way of prosecuting nude sunbathers. The Texas Disorderly Conduct statute, Article 42.01 of the Texas Penal Code, provides a large array of options for prosecuting annoying, loud, obscene, and mildly threatening conduct at the level of a class B or C misdemeanor. One of the options under this statute is Subsection (10), which makes it an offense if a person "exposes his anus or genitals in a public place and is reckless about whether another may be present who will be offended or alarmed by his act."

It is not uncommon for penal codes to have overlapping offenses. The legal issues raised by the prospect of multiple criminality will be examined in a later chapter. Because the disorderly conduct statute provides a very similar offense to indecent exposure, without the difficulty of the special intent requirement, it has been used far more frequently than the indecent exposure statute to combat the perceived threat of public nudity. We will revisit the disorderly conduct issue of public nudity in the chapter examining the lower end of the mental state hierarchy—recklessness and criminal negligence—and interpretations of the statute in the Court of Criminal Appeals.

We will encounter more specific intent statutes particularly when we discuss inchoate offenses at the end of the materials. Inchoate crimes are incomplete crimes where criminal liability is imposed even though the harm that is the subject of the statute has not occurred. The actor must specifically intend the harm and act in some way in furtherance of that specific intent. Thus, the inchoate crimes of attempt, conspiracy and solicitation provide for criminal liability based upon the defendant's specific intent to commit the incomplete offense.

Chapter 2: Knowledge

Although common law crimes have been abolished in Texas and most American jurisdictions, the common law heritage often informs the interpretation courts give to the intent of the legislature in interpreting statutes. The tradition of requiring a guilty mind or *mens rea* as well as a culpable act is a good example. Statutes that omit a mental state requirement completely are often interpreted to include such a requirement because of the common law tradition of *mens rea*, as was illustrated by the *Rocker* case in the last chapter. The *Elonis* case is another example of an implied mental state requirement where none is specified by statute.

[handwritten top margin: Implied mental State requirement]

[handwritten: guilty mind= Mens Rea + Culpable Act]

Elonis v. United States

135 S. Ct. 2001 (2015)

Chief Justice Roberts delivered the opinion of the Court.

[handwritten: Statute used]

Federal law makes it a crime to transmit in interstate commerce "any communication containing any threat . . . to injure the person of another." 18 U.S.C. § 875(c). Petitioner was convicted of violating this provision under instructions that required the jury to find that he communicated what a reasonable person would regard as a threat. The question is whether the statute also requires that the defendant be aware of the threatening nature of the communication, and—if not—whether the First Amendment requires such a showing. *[handwritten: Issue]*

I

A

Anthony Douglas Elonis was an active user of the social networking website Facebook. Users of that website may post items on their Facebook page that are accessible to other users, including Facebook "friends" who are notified when new content is posted. In May 2010, Elonis's wife of nearly seven years left him, taking with her their two young children. Elonis began "listening to more violent music" and posting self-styled "rap" lyrics inspired by the music. Eventually, Elonis changed the user name on his Facebook page from his actual name to a rap-style nom de plume, "Tone Dougie," to distinguish himself from his "on-line persona." The lyrics Elonis posted as "Tone Dougie" included graphically violent language and imagery. This material was often interspersed with disclaimers that the lyrics were "fictitious," with no intentional "resemblance to real persons." Elonis posted an explanation to another Facebook user that "I'm doing this for me. My writing is therapeutic."

Around Halloween of 2010, Elonis posted a photograph of himself and a co-worker at a "Halloween Haunt" event at the amusement park where they worked. In the photograph, Elonis was holding a toy knife against his co-worker's neck, and in the caption Elonis wrote, "I wish." Elonis was not Facebook friends with the co-worker and did not "tag" her, a Facebook feature that would have alerted her to the posting. But the chief of park security was a Facebook "friend" of Elonis, saw the photograph, and fired him.

In response, Elonis posted a new entry on his Facebook page:

Moles! Didn't I tell y'all I had several? Y'all sayin' I had access to keys for all the f***in' gates. That I have sinister plans for all my friends and must have taken home a couple. Y'all think it's too dark and foggy to secure your facility from a man as mad as me? You see, even without a paycheck, I'm still the main attraction. Whoever thought the Halloween Haunt could be so f***in' scary?

This post became the basis for Count One of Elonis's subsequent indictment, threatening park patrons and employees.

23

Elonis's posts frequently included crude, degrading, and violent material about his soon-to-be ex-wife. Shortly after he was fired, Elonis posted an adaptation of a satirical sketch that he and his wife had watched together. In the actual sketch, called "It's Illegal to Say . . ." a comedian explains that it is illegal for a person to say he wishes to kill the President, but not illegal to explain that it is illegal for him to say that. When Elonis posted the script of the sketch, however, he substituted his wife for the President. The posting was part of the basis for Count Two of the indictment, threatening his wife:

Hi, I'm Tone Elonis.

Did you know that it's illegal for me to say I want to kill my wife? . . .

It's one of the only sentences that I'm not allowed to say. . . .

Now it was okay for me to say it right then because I was just telling you that it's illegal for me to say I want to kill my wife. . . .

Um, but what's interesting is that it's very illegal to say I really, really think someone out there should kill my wife. . . .

But not illegal to say with a mortar launcher.

Because that's its own sentence. . . .

I also found out that it's incredibly illegal, extremely illegal to go on Facebook and say something like the best place to fire a mortar launcher at her house would be from the cornfield behind it because of easy access to a getaway road and you'd have a clear line of sight through the sun room. . . .

Yet even more illegal to show an illustrated diagram. [diagram of the house] . . . .

The details about the home were accurate. At the bottom of the post, Elonis included a link to the video of the original skit, and wrote, "Art is about pushing limits. I'm willing to go to jail for my Constitutional rights. Are you?"

After viewing some of Elonis's posts, his wife felt "extremely afraid for [her] life." A state court granted her a three-year protection-from-abuse order against Elonis (essentially, a restraining order). Elonis referred to the order in another post on his "Tone Dougie" page, also included in Count Two of the indictment:

Fold up your [protection-from-abuse] order and put it in your pocket

Is it thick enough to stop a bullet?

Try to enforce an Order

that was improperly granted in the first place

Me thinks the Judge needs an education

on true threat jurisprudence

And prison time'll add zeros to my settlement . . .

And if worse comes to worse

I've got enough explosives to take care of the State Police and the Sheriff's Department.

At the bottom of this post was a link to the Wikipedia article on "Freedom of speech." Elonis's reference to the police was the basis for Count Three of his indictment, threatening law enforcement officers.

That same month, interspersed with posts about a movie Elonis liked and observations on a comedian's social commentary, Elonis posted an entry that gave rise to Count Four of his indictment:

That's it, I've had about enough

I'm checking out and making a name for myself

Enough elementary schools in a ten mile radius to initiate the most heinous school shooting ever imagined

And hell hath no fury like a crazy man in a Kindergarten class

The only question is . . . which one?

Meanwhile, park security had informed both local police and the Federal Bureau of Investigation about Elonis's posts, and FBI Agent Denise Stevens had created a Facebook account to monitor his online activity. After the post about a school shooting, Agent Stevens and her partner visited Elonis at his house. Following their visit, during which Elonis was polite but uncooperative, Elonis posted another entry on his Facebook page, called "Little Agent Lady," which led to Count Five:

"You know your s***'s ridiculous

when you have the FBI knockin' at yo' door

Little Agent lady stood so close

Took all the strength I had not to turn the b**** ghost

Pull my knife, flick my wrist, and slit her throat

Leave her bleedin' from her jugular in the arms of her partner

[laughter]

So the next time you knock, you best be serving a warrant

And bring yo' SWAT and an explosives expert while you're at it

Cause little did y'all know, I was strapped wit' a bomb

Why do you think it took me so long to get dressed with no shoes on?

I was jus' waitin' for y'all to handcuff me and pat me down

Touch the detonator in my pocket and we're all goin'

[BOOM!]

Are all the pieces comin' together?

S***, I'm just a crazy sociopath

that gets off playin' you stupid f***s like a fiddle

And if y'all didn't hear, I'm gonna be famous

Cause I'm just an aspiring rapper who likes the attention

who happens to be under investigation for terrorism

cause y'all think I'm ready to turn the Valley into Fallujah

But I ain't gonna tell you which bridge is gonna fall

into which river or road

And if you really believe this s***

I'll have some bridge rubble to sell you tomorrow

[BOOM!][BOOM!][BOOM!].

B

A grand jury indicted Elonis for making threats to injure patrons and employees of the park, his estranged wife, police officers, a kindergarten class, and an FBI agent, all in violation of 18 U.S.C. § 875(c). In the District Court, Elonis moved to dismiss the indictment for failing to allege that he had intended to threaten anyone. The District Court denied the motion, holding that Third Circuit precedent required only that Elonis "intentionally made the communication, not that he intended to make a threat." At trial, Elonis testified that his posts emulated the rap lyrics of the well-known performer Eminem, some of which involve fantasies about killing his ex-wife. In Elonis's view, he had posted "nothing . . . that hasn't been said already." The Government presented as witnesses Elonis's wife and co-workers, all of whom said they felt afraid and viewed Elonis's posts as serious threats. Elonis requested a jury instruction that "the government

26

must prove that he intended to communicate a true threat." The District Court denied that request. The jury instructions instead informed the jury that

> A statement is a true threat when a defendant intentionally makes a statement in a context or under such circumstances wherein a reasonable person would foresee that the statement would be interpreted by those to whom the maker communicates the statement as a serious expression of an intention to inflict bodily injury or take the life of an individual.

The Government's closing argument emphasized that it was irrelevant whether Elonis intended the postings to be threats—"it doesn't matter what he thinks." A jury convicted Elonis on four of the five counts against him, acquitting only on the charge of threatening park patrons and employees. Elonis was sentenced to three years, eight months' imprisonment and three years' supervised release.

Elonis renewed his challenge to the jury instructions in the Court of Appeals, contending that the jury should have been required to find that he intended his posts to be threats. The Court of Appeals disagreed, holding that the intent required by Section 875(c) is only the intent to communicate words that the defendant understands, and that a reasonable person would view as a threat. We granted certiorari.

II

A

An individual who "transmits in interstate or foreign commerce any communication containing any threat to kidnap any person or any threat to injure the person of another" is guilty of a felony and faces up to five years' imprisonment. 18 U.S.C. § 875(c). This statute requires that a communication be transmitted and that the communication contain a threat. It does not specify that the defendant must have any mental state with respect to these elements. In particular, it does not indicate whether the defendant must intend that his communication contain a threat.

Elonis argues that the word "threat" itself in Section 875(c) imposes such a requirement. According to Elonis, every definition of "threat" or "threaten" conveys the notion of an intent to inflict harm.

For its part, the Government argues that Section 875(c) should be read in light of its neighboring provisions, Sections 875(b) and 875(d). Those provisions also prohibit certain types of threats, but expressly include a mental state requirement of an "intent to extort." *See* 18 U. S. C. § 875(b) (proscribing threats to injure or kidnap made "with intent to extort"); § 875(d) (proscribing threats to property or reputation made "with intent to extort"). According to the Government, the express "intent to extort" requirements in Sections 875(b) and (d) should preclude courts from implying an unexpressed "intent to threaten" requirement in Section 875(c). *See Russello v. United States*, 464 U.S. 16, 23 (1983) ("[W]here Congress includes particular language in one section of a statute but omits it in another section of the same Act, it is generally presumed that Congress acts intentionally and purposely in the disparate inclusion or exclusion.").

The Government takes this *expressio unius est exclusio alterius* canon too far. The fact that Congress excluded the requirement of an "intent to extort" from Section 875(c) is strong evidence that Congress did not mean to confine Section 875(c) to crimes of extortion. But that does not suggest that Congress, at the same time, also meant to exclude a requirement that a defendant act with a certain mental state in communicating a threat. The most we can conclude from the language of Section 875(c) and its neighboring provisions is that Congress meant to proscribe a broad class of threats in Section 875(c), but did not identify what mental state, if any, a defendant must have to be convicted.

In sum, neither Elonis nor the Government has identified any indication of a particular mental state requirement in the text of Section 875(c).

B

The fact that the statute does not specify any required mental state, however, does not mean that none exists. We have repeatedly held that "mere omission from a criminal enactment of any mention of criminal intent" should not be read "as dispensing with it." This rule of construction reflects the basic principle that "wrongdoing must be conscious to be criminal." As Justice Jackson explained, this principle is "as universal and persistent in mature systems of law as belief in freedom of the human will and a consequent ability and duty of the normal individual to choose between good and evil." The "central thought" is that a defendant must be "blameworthy in mind" before he can be found guilty, a concept courts have expressed over time through various terms such as *mens rea*, scienter, malice aforethought, guilty knowledge, and the like. Although there are exceptions, the "general rule" is that a guilty mind is "a necessary element in the indictment and proof of every crime." We therefore generally "interpret criminal statutes to include broadly applicable scienter requirements, even where the statute by its terms does not contain them." *United States v. X-Citement Video, Inc.*, 513 U.S. 64, 70 (1994).

This is not to say that a defendant must know that his conduct is illegal before he may be found guilty. The familiar maxim "ignorance of the law is no excuse" typically holds true. Instead, our cases have explained that a defendant generally must "know the facts that make his conduct fit the definition of the offense," even if he does not know that those facts give rise to a crime.

[I]n *Liparota v. United States*, we considered a statute making it a crime to knowingly possess or use food stamps in an unauthorized manner. 471 U.S. 419, 420 (1985). The Government's argument, similar to its position in this case, was that a defendant's conviction could be upheld if he knowingly possessed or used the food stamps, and in fact his possession or use was unauthorized. But this Court rejected that interpretation of the statute, because it would have criminalized "a broad range of apparently innocent conduct" and swept in individuals who had no knowledge of the facts that made their conduct blameworthy. For example, the statute made it illegal to use food stamps at a store that charged higher prices to food stamp customers. Without a mental state requirement in the statute, an individual who unwittingly paid higher prices would be guilty under the Government's interpretation. The Court noted that Congress *could* have intended to cover such a "broad range of conduct," but declined "to adopt such a

28

sweeping interpretation" in the absence of a clear indication that Congress intended that result. The Court instead construed the statute to require knowledge of the facts that made the use of the food stamps unauthorized.

To take another example, in *Posters 'N' Things, Ltd. v. United States*, this Court interpreted a federal statute prohibiting the sale of drug paraphernalia. 511 U.S. 513 (1994). Whether the items in question qualified as drug paraphernalia was an objective question that did not depend on the defendant's state of mind. But, we held, an individual could not be convicted of selling such paraphernalia unless he "knew that the items at issue [were] likely to be used with illegal drugs." Such a showing was necessary to establish the defendant's culpable state of mind. And again, in *X-Citement Video*, we considered a statute criminalizing the distribution of visual depictions of minors engaged in sexually explicit conduct. We rejected a reading of the statute which would have required only that a defendant knowingly send the prohibited materials, regardless of whether he knew the age of the performers. We held instead that a defendant must also know that those depicted were minors, because that was "the crucial element separating legal innocence from wrongful conduct." *See also Staples v. United States*, 511 U.S. 600, 619 (1994) (defendant must know that his weapon had automatic firing capability to be convicted of possession of such a weapon).

When interpreting federal criminal statutes that are silent on the required mental state, we read into the statute "only that *mens rea* which is necessary to separate wrongful conduct from 'otherwise innocent conduct.'" *Carter v. United States*, 530 U. S. 255, 269 (2000) (quoting *X-Citement Video*, 513 U.S. at 72). In some cases, a general requirement that a defendant *act* knowingly is itself an adequate safeguard. For example, in *Carter*, we considered whether a conviction under 18 U.S.C. § 2113(a), for taking "by force and violence" items of value belonging to or in the care of a bank, requires that a defendant have the intent to steal. We held that once the Government proves the defendant forcibly took the money, "the concerns underlying the presumption in favor of scienter are fully satisfied, for a forceful taking—even by a defendant who takes under a good-faith claim of right—falls outside the realm of . . . 'otherwise innocent'" conduct. In other instances, however, requiring only that the defendant act knowingly "would fail to protect the innocent actor." A statute similar to Section 2113(a) that did not require a forcible taking or the intent to steal "would run the risk of punishing seemingly innocent conduct in the case of a defendant who peaceably takes money believing it to be his." In such a case, the Court explained, the statute "would need to be read to require . . . that the defendant take the money with 'intent to steal or purloin.'"

C

Section 875(c), as noted, requires proof that a communication was transmitted and that it contained a threat. The "presumption in favor of a scienter requirement should apply to *each* of the statutory elements that criminalize otherwise innocent conduct." The parties agree that a defendant under Section 875(c) must know that he is transmitting a communication. But communicating *something* is not what makes the conduct "wrongful." Here "the crucial element separating legal innocence from wrongful conduct" is the (threatening nature of the communication.) The mental state requirement must therefore apply to the fact that the communication contains a threat. ✗

Does it have threat? v. other ppl understood it to be a threat

Elonis's conviction, however, was premised solely on (how his posts) would be understood by a reasonable person. Such a "reasonable person" standard is a familiar feature of civil liability in tort law, but is inconsistent with "the conventional requirement for criminal conduct—*awareness* of some wrongdoing." Having liability turn on whether a "reasonable person" regards the communication as a threat—regardless of what the defendant thinks—"reduces culpability on the all-important element of the crime to negligence." *Cochran v. United States*, 157 U. S. 286, 294 (1895) (defendant could face "liability in a civil action for negligence, but he could only be held criminally for an evil intent actually existing in his mind"). Under these principles, "what [Elonis] thinks" does matter.

The Government is at pains to characterize its position as something other than a negligence standard, emphasizing that its approach would require proof that a defendant "comprehended [the] contents and context" of the communication. The Government gives two examples of individuals who, in its view, would lack this necessary mental state—a "foreigner, ignorant of the English language," who would not know the meaning of the words at issue, or an individual mailing a sealed envelope without knowing its contents. But the fact that the Government would require a defendant to actually know the words of and circumstances surrounding a communication does not amount to a rejection of negligence. Criminal negligence standards often incorporate "the circumstances known" to a defendant. Courts then ask, however, whether a reasonable person equipped with that knowledge, not the actual defendant, would have recognized the harmfulness of his conduct. That is precisely the Government's position here: Elonis can be convicted, the Government contends, if he himself knew the contents and context of his posts, and a reasonable person would have recognized that the posts would be read as genuine threats. That is a negligence standard.

Negligence Rule:

In support of its position the Government relies most heavily on *Hamling v. United States*, 418 U.S. 87 (1974). In that case, the Court rejected the argument that individuals could be convicted of mailing obscene material only if they knew the "legal status of the materials" distributed. Absolving a defendant of liability because he lacked the knowledge that the materials were legally obscene "would permit the defendant to avoid prosecution by simply claiming that he had not brushed up on the law." It was instead enough for liability that "a defendant had knowledge of the contents of the materials he distributed, and that he knew the character and nature of the materials."

This holding does not help the Government. In fact, the Court in *Hamling* approved a state court's conclusion that requiring a defendant to know the character of the material incorporated a "vital element of scienter" so that "not innocent but *calculated purveyance* of filth . . . is exorcised." In this case, "calculated purveyance" of a threat would require that Elonis know the threatening nature of his communication. Put simply, the mental state requirement the Court approved in *Hamling* turns on whether a defendant knew the *character* of what was sent, not simply its contents and context.

Elonis's conviction cannot stand. The jury was instructed that the Government need prove only that a reasonable person would regard Elonis's communications as threats, and that was error. Federal criminal liability generally does not turn solely on the results of an act without considering the defendant's mental state. That understanding "took deep and early root in American soil" and Congress left it intact here: under Section 875(c), "wrongdoing must be conscious to be criminal." There is no dispute that the mental state requirement in Section 875(c) is satisfied if the defendant transmits a communication for the purpose of issuing a threat, or with knowledge that the communication will be viewed as a threat. In response to a question at oral argument, Elonis stated that a finding of recklessness would not be sufficient. Neither Elonis nor the Government has briefed or argued that point, and we accordingly decline to address it. Given our disposition, it is not necessary to consider any First Amendment issues. *Recklessness not addressed*

Both Justice Alito and Justice Thomas complain about our not deciding whether recklessness suffices for liability under Section 875(c). Justice Alito also suggests that we have not clarified confusion in the lower courts. That is wrong. Our holding makes clear that *Holding* negligence is not sufficient to support a conviction under Section 875(c), contrary to the view of nine Courts of Appeals. There was and is no circuit conflict over the question Justice Alito and Justice Thomas would have us decide—whether recklessness suffices for liability under Section 875(c). No Court of Appeals has even addressed that question. We think that is more than sufficient "justification," for us to decline to be the first appellate tribunal to do so.

The judgment of the United States Court of Appeals for the Third Circuit is reversed, and the case is remanded for further proceedings consistent with this opinion.

Justice Alito, concurring in part and dissenting in part. *Confusion bc only partial answer* *to mental state requirement*

The Court's disposition of this case is certain to cause confusion and serious problems. Attorneys and judges need to know which mental state is required for conviction under 18 U.S.C. § 875(c), an important criminal statute. This case squarely presents that issue, but the Court provides only a partial answer. The Court holds that the jury instructions in this case were defective because they required only negligence in conveying a threat. But the Court refuses to explain what type of intent was necessary. Did the jury need to find that Elonis had the *purpose* of conveying a true threat? Was it enough if he *knew* that his words conveyed such a threat? Would *recklessness* suffice? The Court declines to say. Attorneys and judges are left to guess.

This will have regrettable consequences. While this Court has the luxury of choosing its docket, lower courts and juries are not so fortunate. They must actually decide cases, and this means applying a standard. If purpose or knowledge is needed and a district court instructs the jury that recklessness suffices, a defendant may be wrongly convicted. On the other hand, if recklessness is enough, and the jury is told that conviction requires proof of more, a guilty defendant may go free. We granted review in this case to resolve a disagreement among the Circuits. But the Court has compounded—not clarified—the confusion. *Consequences & confusion*

Why is recklessness enough? My analysis of the *mens rea* issue follows the same track as the Court's, as far as it goes. I agree with the Court that we should presume that criminal statutes require some sort of *mens rea* for conviction. To be sure, this presumption marks a departure from the way in which we generally interpret statutes. We "ordinarily resist reading words or elements into a statute that do not appear on its face." But this step is justified by a well-established pattern in our criminal laws. "For several centuries (at least since 1600) the different

No determination for Recklessness

common law crimes have been so defined as to require, for guilt, that the defendant's acts or omissions be accompanied by one or more of the various types of fault (intention, knowledge, recklessness or—more rarely—negligence)." Based on these "background rules of the common law, in which the requirement of some *mens rea* for a crime is firmly embedded," we require "some indication of congressional intent, express or implied, . . . to dispense with *mens rea* as an element of a crime." *Staples v. United States*, 511 U.S. 600, 605–606 (1994).

For a similar reason, I agree with the Court that we should presume that an offense like that created by § 875(c) requires more than negligence with respect to a critical element like the one at issue here. As the Court states, "[w]hen interpreting federal criminal statutes that are silent on the required mental state, we read into the statute 'only that *mens rea* which is necessary to separate wrongful conduct from 'otherwise innocent conduct.'" Whether negligence is morally culpable is an interesting philosophical question, but the answer is at least sufficiently debatable to justify the presumption that a serious offense against the person that lacks any clear common-law counterpart should be presumed to require more.

Once we have passed negligence, however, no further presumptions are defensible. In the hierarchy of mental states that may be required as a condition for criminal liability, the *mens rea* just above negligence is recklessness. Negligence requires only that the defendant "should have been aware of a substantial and unjustifiable risk." And when Congress does not specify a *mens rea* in a criminal statute, we have no justification for inferring that anything more than recklessness is needed. It is quite unusual for us to interpret a statute to contain a requirement that is nowhere set out in the text. Once we have reached recklessness, we have gone as far as we can without stepping over the line that separates interpretation from amendment.

There can be no real dispute that recklessness regarding a risk of serious harm is wrongful conduct. In a wide variety of contexts, we have described reckless conduct as morally culpable.

Accordingly, I would hold that a defendant may be convicted under § 875(c) if he or she consciously disregards the risk that the communication transmitted will be interpreted as a true threat. Nothing in the Court's noncommittal opinion prevents lower courts from adopting that standard.

There remains the question whether interpreting § 875(c) to require no more than recklessness with respect to the element at issue here would violate the First Amendment. Elonis contends that it would. I would reject that argument. It is settled that the Constitution does not protect true threats. And there are good reasons for that rule: True threats inflict great harm and have little if any social value.

Justice Thomas, dissenting.

We granted certiorari to resolve a conflict in the lower courts over the appropriate mental state for threat prosecutions under 18 U.S.C. § 875(c). Save two, every Circuit to have considered the issue—11 in total—has held that this provision demands proof only of general intent, which here requires no more than that a defendant knew he transmitted a communication,

This Ct over turns other9

is intent required?
Recklessness sufficient?

knew the words used in that communication, and understood the ordinary meaning of those words in the relevant context. The outliers are the Ninth and Tenth Circuits, which have concluded that proof of an intent to threaten was necessary for conviction.

Rather than resolve the conflict, the Court casts aside the approach used in nine Circuits and leaves nothing in its place. Lower courts are thus left to guess at the appropriate mental state for § 875(c). All they know after today's decision is that a requirement of general intent will not do. But they can safely infer that a majority of this Court would not adopt an intent-to-threaten requirement, as the opinion carefully leaves open the possibility that recklessness may be enough.

This failure to decide throws everyone from appellate judges to everyday Facebook users into a state of uncertainty. This uncertainty could have been avoided had we simply adhered to the background rule of the common law favoring general intent.

Enacted in 1939, § 875(c) provides, "Whoever transmits in interstate or foreign commerce any communication containing any threat to kidnap any person or any threat to injure the person of another, shall be fined under this title or imprisoned not more than five years, or both." Because § 875(c) criminalizes speech, the First Amendment requires that the term "threat" be limited to a narrow class of historically unprotected communications called "true threats." To qualify as a true threat, a communication must be a serious expression of an intention to commit unlawful physical violence, not merely "political hyperbole;" "vehement, caustic, and sometimes unpleasantly sharp attacks;" or "vituperative, abusive, and inexact" statements. It also cannot be determined solely by the reaction of the recipient, but must instead be "determined by the interpretation of a *reasonable* recipient familiar with the context of the communication.

There is thus no dispute that, at a minimum, § 875(c) requires an objective showing: The communication must be one that "a reasonable observer would construe as a true threat to another." And there is no dispute that the posts at issue here meet that objective standard.

The only dispute in this case is about the state of mind necessary to convict Elonis for making those posts. On its face, § 875(c) does not demand any particular mental state. As the Court correctly explains, the word "threat" does not itself contain a *mens rea* requirement. But because we read criminal statutes "in light of the background rules of the common law, in which the requirement of some *mens rea* for a crime is firmly embedded," we require "some indication of congressional intent, express or implied, . . . to dispense with *mens rea* as an element of a crime." Absent such indicia, we ordinarily apply the "presumption in favor of scienter" to require only "proof of *general intent*—that is, that the defendant [must] posses[s] knowledge with respect to the *actus reus* of the crime."

Under this "conventional *mens rea* element," "the defendant [must] know the facts that make his conduct illegal," but he need not know *that* those facts make his conduct illegal. It has long been settled that "the knowledge requisite to knowing violation of a statute is factual knowledge as distinguished from knowledge of the law."

Simply posting threat should be enough to establish intent.

33

Our default rule in favor of general intent applies with full force to criminal statutes addressing speech. Well over 100 years ago, this Court considered a conviction under a federal obscenity statute that punished anyone "who shall knowingly deposit, or cause to be deposited, for mailing or delivery," any "obscene, lewd, or lascivious book, pamphlet, picture, paper, writing, print, or other publication of an indecent character." *Rosen v. United States*, 161 U.S. 29, 30 (1896). In that case, as here, the defendant argued that, even if "he may have had . . . actual knowledge or notice of [the paper's] contents" when he put it in the mail, he could not "be convicted of the offence . . . unless he knew or believed that such paper could be properly or justly characterized as obscene, lewd, and lascivious." The Court rejected that theory, concluding that if the material was actually obscene and "deposited in the mail by one who knew or had notice at the time of its contents, the offence is complete, although the defendant himself did not regard the paper as one that the statute forbade to be carried in the mails." As the Court explained, "Congress did not intend that the question as to the character of the paper should depend upon the opinion or belief of the person who, with knowledge or notice of [the paper's] contents, assumed the responsibility of putting it in the mails of the United States," because "[e]very one who uses the mails of the United States for carrying papers or publications must take notice of . . . what must be deemed obscene, lewd, and lascivious."

This Court reaffirmed *Rosen*'s holding in *Hamling v. United States*, 418 U.S. 87 (1974), when it considered a challenge to convictions under the successor federal statute, *see id.* at 98, n.8 (citing 18 U.S.C. § 1461 (1970 ed.)). Relying on *Rosen*, the Court rejected the argument that the statute required "proof both of knowledge of the contents of the material and awareness of the obscene character of the material." In approving the jury instruction that the defendants' "belief as to the obscenity or non-obscenity of the material is irrelevant," the Court declined to hold "that the prosecution must prove a defendant's knowledge of the legal status of the materials he distributes." To rule otherwise, the Court observed, "would permit the defendant to avoid prosecution by simply claiming that he had not brushed up on the law."

Decades before § 875(c)'s enactment, courts took the same approach to the first federal threat statute, which prohibited threats against the President. In 1917, Congress enacted a law punishing anyone

> who knowingly and willfully deposits or causes to be deposited for conveyance in the mail . . . any letter, paper, writing, print, missive, or document containing any threat to take the life of or to inflict bodily harm upon the President of the United States, or who knowingly and willfully otherwise makes any such threat against the President.

Courts applying this statute shortly after its enactment appeared to require proof of only general intent. In *Ragansky v. United States*, 253 F. 643 (7th Cir. 1918), for instance, a Court of Appeals held that "[a] threat is knowingly made, if the maker of it comprehends the meaning of the words uttered by him," and "is willfully made, if in addition to comprehending the meaning of his words, the maker voluntarily and intentionally utters them as the declaration of an apparent determination to carry them into execution." The court consequently rejected the defendant's argument that he could not be convicted when his language "[c]oncededly . . . constituted such a threat" but was meant only "as a joke." Likewise, in *United States v. Stobo*, 251 F. 689 (Del. 1918), a District Court rejected the defendant's objection that there was no allegation "of any facts . . . indicating any intention . . . on the part of the defendant . . . to menace the President of the United States." As it explained, the defendant "is punishable under the act whether he uses the words lightly or with a set purpose to kill," as "[t]he effect upon the minds of the hearers, who cannot read his inward thoughts, is precisely the same." At a minimum, there is no historical practice requiring more than general intent when a statute regulates speech.

Applying ordinary rules of statutory construction, I would read § 875(c) to require proof of general intent. To "know the facts that make his conduct illegal" under § 875(c), *see Staples*, 511 U.S. at 605, a defendant must know that he transmitted a communication in interstate or foreign commerce that contained a threat. Knowing that the communication contains a "threat"—a serious expression of an intention to engage in unlawful physical violence—does not, however, require knowing that a jury will conclude that the communication contains a threat as a matter of law. Instead, like one who mails an "obscene" publication and is prosecuted under the federal obscenity statute, a defendant prosecuted under § 875(c) must know only the words used in that communication, along with their ordinary meaning in context.

General intent divides those who know the facts constituting the *actus reus* of this crime from those who do not. For example, someone who transmits a threat who does not know English—or who knows English, but perhaps does not know a threatening idiom—lacks the general intent required under § 875(c). *See Ragansky, supra*, at 645 ("[A] foreigner, ignorant of the English language, repeating [threatening] words without knowledge of their meaning, may not knowingly have made a threat."). Likewise, the hapless mailman who delivers a threatening letter, ignorant of its contents, should not fear prosecution. A defendant like Elonis, however, who admits that he "knew that what [he] was saying was violent" but supposedly "just wanted to express [him]self," acted with the general intent required under § 875(c), even if he did not know that a jury would conclude that his communication constituted a "threat" as a matter of law.

The majority refuses to apply these ordinary background principles. Instead, it casts my application of general intent as a negligence standard disfavored in the criminal law. But that characterization misses the mark. Requiring general intent in this context is not the same as requiring mere negligence. Like the mental-state requirements adopted in many of the cases cited by the Court, general intent under § 875(c) prevents a defendant from being convicted on the basis of any *fact* beyond his awareness. *See, e.g., United States v. X-Citement Video, Inc.*, 513 U.S. 64, 73 (1994) (knowledge of age of persons depicted in explicit materials); *Staples, supra,* at 614–615 (knowledge of firing capability of weapon); *Morissette v. United States*, 342 U.S. 246, 270–271 (1952) (knowledge that property belonged to another). In other words, the defendant must *know*—not merely be reckless or negligent with respect to the fact—that he is committing the acts that constitute the *actus reus* of the offense. But general intent requires *no* mental state (not even a negligent one) concerning the "fact" that certain words meet the *legal* definition of a threat. That approach is particularly appropriate where, as here, that legal status is determined by a jury's application of the legal standard of a "threat" to the contents of a communication. And convicting a defendant despite his ignorance of the legal—or objective— status of his conduct does not mean that he is being punished for negligent conduct. By way of example, a defendant who is convicted of murder despite claiming that he acted in self-defense has not been penalized under a negligence standard merely because he does not know that the jury will reject his argument that his "belief in the necessity of using force to prevent harm to himself [was] a reasonable one."

The Court apparently does not believe that our traditional approach to the federal obscenity statute involved a negligence standard. It asserts that *Hamling* "approved a state court's conclusion that requiring a defendant to know the character of the material incorporated a 'vital element of scienter' so that 'not innocent but *calculated purveyance* of filth . . . is exorcised.'" According to the Court, the mental state approved in *Hamling* thus "turns on whether a defendant knew the *character* of what was sent, not simply its contents and context." It is unclear what the Court means by its distinction between "character" and "contents and context." "Character" cannot mean *legal* obscenity, as *Hamling* rejected the argument that a defendant must have "awareness of the obscene character of the material." Moreover, this discussion was not part of *Hamling*'s holding, which was primarily a reaffirmation of *Rosen*. *See Hamling*, 418 U.S. at 120–21; *see also Posters 'N' Things*, 511 U.S. at 524–25 (characterizing *Hamling* as holding that a "statute prohibiting mailing of obscene materials does not require proof that [the] defendant knew the materials at issue met the legal definition of 'obscenity'").

The majority's treatment of *Rosen* is even less persuasive. To shore up its position, it asserts that the critical portion of *Rosen* rejected an "'ignorance of the law' defense," and claims that "no such contention is at issue here." But the thrust of Elonis' challenge is that a § 875(c) conviction cannot stand if the defendant's subjective belief of what constitutes a "threat" differs from that of a reasonable jury. That is akin to the argument the defendant made—and lost—in *Rosen*. That defendant insisted that he could not be convicted for mailing the paper "unless he knew or believed that such paper could be properly or justly characterized as obscene." The Court, however, held that the Government did not need to show that the defendant "regard[ed] the paper as one that the statute forbade to be carried in the mails," because the obscene character of the material did not "depend upon the opinion or belief of the person who . . . assumed the responsibility of putting it in the mails." The majority's muddying of the waters cannot obscure the fact that today's decision is irreconcilable with *Rosen* and *Hamling*.

In light of my conclusion that Elonis was properly convicted under the requirements of § 875(c), I must address his argument that his threatening posts were nevertheless protected by the First Amendment.

Adopting Elonis' view [that only communication intended by the sender to be a threat may be the basis of a criminal conviction] would make threats one of the most protected categories of unprotected speech, thereby sowing tension throughout our First Amendment doctrine. We generally have not required a heightened mental state under the First Amendment for historically unprotected categories of speech. For instance, the Court has indicated that a legislature may constitutionally prohibit "'fighting words,' those personally abusive epithets which, when addressed to the ordinary citizen, are, as a matter of common knowledge, inherently likely to provoke violent reaction," *Cohen v. California*, 403 U.S. 15, 20 (1971), without proof of an intent to provoke a violent reaction. Because the definition of "fighting words" turns on how the "ordinary citizen" would react to the language, this Court has observed that a defendant may be guilty of a breach of the peace if he "makes statements likely to provoke violence and disturbance of good order, even though no such eventuality be intended," and that the punishment of such statements "as a criminal act would raise no question under [the Constitution]," *Cantwell v. Connecticut*, 310 U.S. 296, 309–310 (1940); *see also Chaplinsky v.*

New Hampshire, 315 U.S. 568, 572–573 (1942) (rejecting a First Amendment challenge to a general-intent construction of a state statute punishing "'fighting' words"); *State v. Chaplinsky*, 18 A. 2d 754, 758 (1941) ("[T]he only intent required for conviction . . . was an intent to speak the words."). And our precedents allow liability in tort for false statements about private persons on matters of private concern even if the speaker acted negligently with respect to the falsity of those statements. *See Philadelphia Newspapers, Inc. v. Hepps*, 475 U.S. 767, 770, 773–75 (1986). I see no reason why we should give threats pride of place among unprotected speech.

* * *

There is always a risk that a criminal threat statute may be deployed by the Government to suppress legitimate speech. But the proper response to that risk is to adhere to our traditional rule that only a narrow class of true threats, historically unprotected, may be constitutionally proscribed.

The solution is not to abandon a mental-state requirement compelled by text, history, and precedent. Not only does such a decision warp our traditional approach to *mens rea*, it results in an arbitrary distinction between threats and other forms of unprotected speech. Had Elonis mailed obscene materials to his wife and a kindergarten class, he could have been prosecuted irrespective of whether he intended to offend those recipients or recklessly disregarded that possibility. Yet when he threatened to kill his wife and a kindergarten class, his intent to terrify those recipients (or reckless disregard of that risk) suddenly becomes highly relevant.

I respectfully dissent.

Notes

1.   If the jury in this case had been instructed that the defendant could be found guilty only if the jury found beyond a reasonable doubt that the defendant knew (not that a reasonable person would know) that the messages would create fear for the recipients, and the jury had returned a verdict of guilty on all counts, how would an appellate court rule on a claim by the defendant that the evidence was insufficient?

2.   One of the complaints of the concurring and dissenting judges in *Elonis* is that the majority is incorporating a mental state that requires the prosecution to prove the defendant must know the law of assault rather than the nature of his conduct. The concurring and dissenting judges point out that, in the pornography cases, the knowledge requirement goes to the nature of the material that the defendant possesses and not whether the law considers the material illegal and outside of the protection of the First Amendment. They argue the defendant in *Elonis* knew the nature of his communication, and it should be irrelevant whether he knew the legal standard for determining whether a reasonable person would be put in fear from his communication. In other words, the mental state requirement applies to the relevant circumstances in the case and not the fact that the conduct or circumstances in question are illegal. For example, a visitor from Colorado to Texas who mistakenly thinks that recreational possession of marijuana is legal here,

as it is in Colorado, has no defense based upon his mistake of law as long as he knew what he had.

The *Elonis* majority agrees with the traditional rule but finds knowledge of the character of the communication to include awareness that the communication will be viewed fearfully by the recipients. The line between fact and law is often hazy, and whether the mistake is one of fact or law is an issue that we will explore in more detail later. An important line of relatively recent cases has created exceptions to the ignorance of the law is no excuse dogma when the law in question is complex, administrative, and *mala prohibita* rather than *mala in se*. That is, if the conduct in question is criminal because it has been made so when it is not intrinsically evil.

3.   The majority in *Elonis* does not reach the First Amendment issue addressed by the concurring and dissenting opinions because the majority decides the case on the basis of statutory interpretation. Although the statute is silent about a mental state requirement, the court interprets the statute in light of the common law tradition of *mens rea* in criminal cases. Thus, the trial court erred in not including in the jury instruction some type of subjective knowledge or awareness requirement. Therefore, it became unnecessary to address the constitutional question. Courts often avoid finding a statute unconstitutional or even considering constitutional challenges if a decision can be reached on narrower grounds such as statutory interpretation or mere procedural error, such as an improper jury instruction. (The concurring and dissenting judges would find no error in the jury instruction and, therefore, address the First Amendment claim, finding no violation.)

The First Amendment challenge that was avoided in *Elonis* has been raised successfully in some cases that demonstrate there are constitutional limits to criminal police power of the state. An example of a case finding a criminal statute unconstitutional on First Amendment grounds is *Texas v. Johnson*, 491 U.S. 397 (1989), which invalidated a Texas statute, similar to statutes in 48 statutes, prohibiting desecration of the American flag. The case arose from a protest at the 1984 Republican Convention in Dallas, Texas, during which the defendant poured kerosene on an American flag and set it on fire. The defendant was charged and convicted under a Texas law that prohibits vandalizing or desecrating a venerated object. The conviction was affirmed by the Fifth Court of Appeals of Texas, but the Texas Court of Criminal Appeals reversed holding the First Amendment protects flag burning as symbolic speech, a holding that was later affirmed by a five-person majority of the United States Supreme Court.

Although successful constitutional challenges to substantive penal statutes are rare, *Johnson* is not the only case finding limits on the state authority to create criminal laws. The state has broad inherent "police powers" to legislate to protect the safety, health, and morals of the community. However, the authority is not unlimited. In addition to the First Amendment limits on the police power, traditional criminal law sanctions on abortion and private, consenting homosexual conduct have been held to violate constitutional protections of the right to privacy. *See Lawrence v. Texas*, 539 U.S. 558 (2003); *Roe v. Wade*, 410 U.S. 179 (1973). Statutes that would apply retroactively to conduct committed prior to the promulgation of the law would run afoul of the constitutional protections against *ex post facto* laws. *See, e.g., Papachristou v. City of Jacksonville*, 405 U.S. 156 (1972). Statutes that are so vague they fail to provide fair notice of the prohibited conduct are contrary to the due process protection and known as the void for vagueness doctrine. *See, e.g., Beazell v. Ohio*, 269 U.S. 167 (1925).

<u>Rule:</u> the mental State Of negligence is insufficient for a statute Criminalizing the making of a threat. The required mental State is whether the Δ had the purpose to issue a threat OR had knowledge that the communication be viewed as a threat.

• Statute does not contain a mental State element. The Statute must be read to include a mental State necessary to separate wrong & innocent behavior.

• negligence Standard is not sufficient "reasonable ^{RP} person" bc RP Standard does not rule out the possibility of innocent conduct on the Person who transmitted the communication.

• Mental State element should be whether Δ had the purpose to threaten someone or if Δ knew that the communication will be viewed as threat (NOT used at trial)

Willful Blindness

What if a person suspects there may be criminal activity, but the actor avoids learning facts that would confirm these suspicions? If the individual continues with conduct that he or she suspects might be criminal but avoids certainty in order to be able to claim lack of knowledge, is a conviction under a statute requiring knowledge appropriate? If the law wishes to avoid rewarding such studied efforts at ignorance, how can this principle be articulated to maintain requirements of subjective knowledge? The federal courts have been active in maintaining that "deliberate blindness" should be regarded as equivalent to knowledge. The *Jewell* case that follows is an example.

deliberate blindness = knowledge

United States v. Jewell

532 F.2d 697 (9th Cir. 1976)

Browning, Circuit Judge.

Appellant defines "knowingly" in 21 U.S.C. §§ 841 and 960 to require that positive knowledge that a controlled substance is involved be established as an element of each offense. On the basis of this interpretation, appellant argues that it was reversible error to instruct the jury that the defendant could be convicted upon proof beyond a reasonable doubt that if he did not have positive knowledge that a controlled substance was concealed in the automobile he drove over the border, it was solely and entirely because of the conscious purpose on his part to avoid learning the truth. The majority concludes that this contention is wrong in principle, and has no support in authority or in the language or legislative history of the statute.

It is undisputed that appellant entered the United States driving an automobile in which 110 pounds of marihuana worth $6,250 had been concealed in a secret compartment between the trunk and rear seat. Appellant testified that he did not know the marijuana was present. There was circumstantial evidence from which the jury could infer that appellant had positive knowledge of the presence of the marihuana, and that his contrary testimony was false.[1] On the other hand there was evidence from which the jury could conclude that appellant spoke the truth that although appellant knew of the presence of the secret compartment and had knowledge of facts indicating that it contained marijuana, he deliberately avoided positive knowledge of the presence of the contraband to avoid responsibility in the event of discovery.[2] If the jury

---

1. Appellant testified that a week before the incident in question he sold his car for $100 to obtain funds "to have a good time." He then rented a car for about $100, and he and a friend drove the rented car to Mexico. Appellant and his friend were unable to adequately explain their whereabouts during the period of about 11 hours between the time they left Los Angeles and the time they admitted arriving in Mexico.

Their testimony regarding acquisition of the load car follows a pattern common in these cases: they were approached in a Tijuana bar by a stranger who identified himself only by his first name "Ray." He asked them if they wanted to buy marihuana, and offered to pay them $100 for driving a car north across the border. Appellant accepted the offer and drove the load car back, alone. Appellant's friend drove appellant's rented car back to Los Angeles.

Appellant testified that the stranger instructed him to leave the load car at the address on the car registration slip with the keys in the ashtray. The person living at that address testified that he had sold the car a year earlier and had not seen it since. When the Customs agent asked appellant about the secret compartment in the car, appellant did not deny knowledge of its existence, but stated that it was in the car when he got it.

2. Both appellant and his companion testified that the stranger identified as "Ray" offered to sell them marihuana and, when they declined, asked if they wanted to drive a car back to Los Angeles for $100. Appellant's companion "wanted no part of driving the vehicle." He testified, "It didn't sound right to me." Appellant accepted the offer. The Drug Enforcement Administration agent testified that appellant stated "he thought there was probably something wrong and something illegal in the vehicle, but that he checked it over. He looked in the glove box and under the front seat and in the trunk, prior to driving it. He didn't find anything, and, therefore, he assumed that the people at the border wouldn't find anything either (emphasis added). Appellant was asked at trial whether he had seen the special compartment when he opened the trunk. He responded, "Well, you know, I saw a void there, but I didn't know what it was." He testified that he did not investigate further. The Customs agent testified that when he opened the trunk and saw the partition he asked appellant "when he had that put in." Appellant told the agent "that it was in the car when he got it."

41

concluded the latter was indeed the situation, and if positive knowledge is required to convict, the jury would have no choice consistent with its oath but to find appellant not guilty even though he deliberately contrived his lack of positive knowledge. Appellant urges this view. The trial court rejected the premise that only positive knowledge would suffice, and properly so.

Appellant tendered an instruction that to return a guilty verdict the jury must find that the defendant knew he was in possession of marihuana. The trial judge rejected the instruction because it suggested that "absolutely, positively, he has to know that it's there." The court said, "I think, in this case, it's not too sound an instruction because we have evidence that if the jury believes it, they'd be justified in finding he actually didn't know what it was he didn't because he didn't want to find it."

The court instructed the jury that "knowingly" meant voluntarily and intentionally and not by accident or mistake. The court told the jury that the government must prove beyond a reasonable doubt that the defendant "knowingly" brought the marihuana into the United States (count 1: 21 U.S.C. § 952(a)), and that he "knowingly" possessed the marihuana (count 2: 21 U.S.C. § 841(a)(1)). The court continued:

> The Government can complete their burden of proof by proving, beyond a reasonable doubt, that if the defendant was not actually aware that there was marijuana in the vehicle he was driving when he entered the United States his ignorance in that regard was solely and entirely a result of his having made a conscious purpose to disregard the nature of that which was in the vehicle, with a conscious purpose to avoid learning the truth.

The legal premise of these instructions is firmly supported by leading commentators here and in England. Professor Rollin M. Perkins writes, "One with a deliberate antisocial purpose in mind . . . may deliberately 'shut his eyes' to avoid knowing what would otherwise be obvious to view. In such cases, so far as criminal law is concerned, the person acts at his peril in this regard, and is treated as having 'knowledge' of the facts as they are ultimately discovered to be." John Ll. J. Edwards, writing in 1954, introduced a survey of English cases with the statement, "For well-nigh a hundred years, it has been clear from the authorities that a person who deliberately shuts his eyes to an obvious means of knowledge has sufficient *mens rea* for an offence based on such words as . . . 'knowingly.'" Professor Glanville Williams states, on the basis both English and American authorities, "To the requirement of actual knowledge there is one strictly limited exception. . . . [T]he rule is that if a party has his suspicion aroused but then deliberately omits to make further enquiries, because he wishes to remain in ignorance, he is deemed to have knowledge." Professor Williams concludes, "The rule that willful blindness is equivalent to knowledge is essential, and is found throughout the criminal law."[3]

---

3. Mr. Williams' concluding paragraph reads in its entirety: "The rule that willful blindness is equivalent to knowledge is essential, and is found throughout the criminal law. It is, at the same time, an unstable rule, because judges are apt to forget its very limited scope. A court can properly find willful blindness only where it can almost be said that the defendant actually knew. He suspected the fact; he realized its probability; but he refrained from obtaining the final confirmation because he wanted in the event to be able to deny knowledge. This, and this alone, is willful blindness. It requires in effect a finding that the defendant intended to cheat the administration of justice. Any wider definition would make the doctrine of willful blindness indistinguishable from the civil doctrine of negligence in not obtaining knowledge."

The substantive justification for the rule is that deliberate ignorance and positive knowledge are equally culpable. The textual justification is that in common understanding one "knows" facts of which he is less than absolutely certain. To act "knowingly," therefore, is not necessarily to act only with positive knowledge, but also to act with an awareness of the high probability of the existence of the fact in question. When such awareness is present, "positive" knowledge is not required.

This is the analysis adopted in the Model Penal Code § 2.02(7) states: "When knowledge of the existence of a particular fact is an element of an offense, such knowledge is established if a person is aware of a high probability of its existence, unless he actually believes that it does not exist." As the Comment to this provision explains, "Paragraph (7) deals with the situation British commentators have denominated 'willful blindness' or 'connivance,' the case of the actor who is aware of the probable existence of a material fact but does not satisfy himself that it does not in fact exist."

Appellant's narrow interpretation of "knowingly" is inconsistent with the Drug Control Act's general purpose to deal more effectively "with the growing menace of drug abuse in the United States." Holding that this term introduces a requirement of positive knowledge would make deliberate ignorance a defense. It cannot be doubted that those who traffic in drugs would make the most of it. This is evident from the number of appellate decisions reflecting conscious avoidance of positive knowledge of the presence of contraband in the car driven by the defendant or in which he is a passenger, in the suitcase or package he carries, in the parcel concealed in his clothing.

It is no answer to say that in such cases the fact finder may infer positive knowledge. It is probable that many who performed the transportation function, essential to the drug traffic, can truthfully testify that they have no positive knowledge of the load they carry. Under appellant's interpretation of the statute, such persons will be convicted only if the fact finder errs in evaluating the credibility of the witness or deliberately disregards the law.

It is worth emphasizing that the required state of mind differs from positive knowledge only so far as necessary to encompass a calculated effort to avoid the sanctions of the statute while violating its substance. "A court can properly find willful blindness only where it can almost be said that the defendant actually knew." In the language of the instruction in this case, the government must prove, "beyond a reasonable doubt, that if the defendant was not actually aware . . . his ignorance in that regard was solely and entirely a result of . . . a conscious purpose to avoid learning the truth."[4]

---

4. We do not suggest that the instruction given in this case was a model in all respects. The jury should have been instructed more directly (1) that the required knowledge is established if the accused is aware of a high probability of the existence of the fact in question, (2) unless he actually believes it does not exist.

The deficiency in the instruction does not require reversal, however. Appellant did not object to the instruction on this ground either below or in this court. Since both of the elements referred to are implied in the instruction, the deficiency in the instructions is not so substantial as to justify reversal for plain error.

Appellant did not argue below or in this court that the instruction did not require an awareness of a high probability that the controlled substance was present. An objection on this ground would have little merit. The instruction given

To act knowingly is not necessarily to act w/only positive knowledge but to act w/awareness of the highest probability of the existence of the fact in question.

No legitimate interest of an accused is prejudiced by such a standard, and society's interest in a system of criminal law that is enforceable and that imposes sanctions upon all who are equally culpable requires it.

Holding → The conviction is affirmed.

Anthony M. Kennedy, Circuit Judge, dissenting, with whom Ely, Hufstedler and Wallace, Circuit Judges, join.

English authorities seem to consider willful blindness a state of mind distinct from, but equally culpable as, "actual" knowledge. When a statute specifically requires knowledge as an element of a crime, however, the substitution of some other state of mind cannot be justified even if the court deems that both are equally blameworthy.[5]

The willful blindness doctrine is uncertain in scope. There is disagreement as to whether reckless disregard for the existence of a fact constitutes willful blindness or some lesser degree of culpability. Some cases have held that a statute's scienter requirement is satisfied by the constructive knowledge imputed to one who simply fails to discharge a duty to inform himself.

(that "[appellant's] ignorance in that regard was solely and entirely the result of his having made a conscious purpose to disregard the nature of that which was in the vehicle") suggests that the accused must be aware of facts making the presence of the contraband all but certain. Only if the accused were aware of such facts could his ignorance of the presence of the marihuana be "solely and entirely "the result of his conscious purpose to avoid the truth. Under this instruction, neither reckless disregard nor suspicion followed by failure to make full inquiry would be enough.

Nor did appellant suggest in the court below or in this court that the instruction given was deficient because it failed to state specifically (as we think would have been preferable) that appellant could not be convicted if he actually believed there was no controlled substance in the car. The reason appellant does not raise this objection may be, again, that the instruction given includes the limitation by reasonable inference. If appellant were ignorant of the presence of contraband solely and entirely because he "made a conscious purpose to disregard the nature of that which was in the vehicle," as the instruction given requires, it would hardly be a realistic possibility that he might at the same time have entertained a good faith belief that there was no contraband present. Nor did the instruction permit the jury to convict on an "objective" rather than "subjective" theory of the knowledge requirement; that is, on the theory that appellant was chargeable with knowledge because a reasonable man would have inspected the car more thoroughly and discovered the contraband inside. The negligence theory was advanced by the government but was rejected by the trial court. The instruction given by the trial court required the jury to find that appellant had a deliberate purpose to avoid the truth. Moreover, the jury was expressly informed that an act was not done "knowingly" within the meaning of the statute if it was done by "mistake or accident or other innocent purpose."

5. This case does not present the question of how far Congress could reduce the requirement of a *mens rea* for possession of drugs. The statutes use the terms "knowingly or intentionally." It is true that a strict interpretation of the scienter requirement may produce fewer convictions in combating "the growing menace of drug abuse." But the Supreme Court has cautioned that "the purpose of every statute would be 'obstructed' by requiring a finding of intent, if we assume that it had a purpose to convict without it." Here it is clear that Congress intended to require knowledge as an element of these offenses.

The spirit of the doctrine which denies to the federal judiciary power to create crimes forthrightly admonishes that we should not enlarge the reach of enacted crimes by constituting them from anything less than the incriminating components contemplated by the words used in the statute.

There is also the question of whether to use an "objective" test based on the reasonable man, or to consider the defendant's subjective belief as dispositive.

The approach adopted in § 2.02(7) of the Model Penal Code clarifies, and, in important ways restricts, the English doctrine:

> When knowledge of the existence of a particular fact is an element of an offense, such knowledge is established if a person is aware of a high probability of its existence, unless he actually believes that it does not exist.

This provision requires an awareness of a high probability that a fact exists, not merely a reckless disregard, or a suspicion followed by a failure to make further inquiry. It also establishes knowledge as a matter of subjective belief, an important safeguard against diluting the guilty state of mind required for conviction. It is important to note that § 2.02(7) is a definition of knowledge, not a substitute for it; as such, it has been cited with approval by the Supreme Court.

In light of the Model Penal Code's definition, the "conscious purpose" jury instruction is defective in three respects. First, it fails to mention the requirement that Jewell have been aware of a high probability that a controlled substance was in the car. It is not culpable to form "a conscious purpose to avoid learning the truth" unless one is aware of facts indicating a high probability of that truth. To illustrate, a child given a gift-wrapped package by his mother while on vacation in Mexico may form a conscious purpose to take it home without learning what is inside; yet his state of mind is totally innocent unless he is aware of a high probability that the package contains a controlled substance. Thus, a conscious purpose instruction is only proper when coupled with a requirement that one be aware of a high probability of the truth.

The second defect in the instruction as given is that it did not alert the jury that Jewell could not be convicted if he "actually believed" there was no controlled substance in the car. The failure to emphasize, as does the Model Penal Code, that subjective belief is the determinative factor, may allow a jury to convict on an objective theory of knowledge that a reasonable man should have inspected the car and would have discovered what was hidden inside. One recent decision reversed a jury instruction for this very deficiency failure to balance a conscious purpose instruction with a warning that the defendant could not be convicted if he actually believed to the contrary.

Third, the jury instruction clearly states that Jewell could have been convicted even if found ignorant or "not actually aware" that the car contained a controlled substance. This is unacceptable because true ignorance, no matter how unreasonable, cannot provide a basis for criminal liability when the statute requires knowledge. A proper jury instruction based on the Model Penal Code would be presented as a way of defining knowledge, and not as an alternative to it.

We do not agree with the majority that we can only reverse if the conscious purpose instruction constituted "plain error." Before the instruction was given, the defense counsel objected "strenuously" on the basis that the jury could convict Jewell for failure to make an adequate attempt to check out the car. When the trial judge rejected this argument, the defense counsel further requested that he "add an addendum" to the charge so the jury would understand it properly. The trial court rejected this suggestion as well, and cut off further argument, saying "The record may show your objection."

Although the defense counsel did not fully anticipate our analysis of the conscious purpose instruction, he came close. (1) He gave a reason for his objection that the instruction would allow conviction without proof of the scienter element. (2) He further suggested adding "an addendum" to warn the jury against misinterpreting the instruction. We believe these objections were sufficient to require reversal on appeal unless the deficiencies in the instruction were harmless error.

We do not question the sufficiency of the evidence in this case to support conviction by a properly-instructed jury. As with all states of mind, knowledge must normally be proven by circumstantial evidence. There is evidence which could support a conclusion that Jewell was aware of a high probability that the car contained a controlled substance and that he had no belief to the contrary. However, we cannot say that the evidence was so overwhelming that the erroneous jury instruction was harmless. Accordingly, we would reverse the judgment on this appeal.

Can't just substitute another state of mind is "statute requires knowledge. A's arguement = he had to check car for **Notes.** *proper jury instruction = define "knowingly" not give subs to it.* *drugs*

1.   The dissenting opinion is by Justice Kennedy when he sat on the Ninth Circuit before his elevation to the United States Supreme Court. Justice Kennedy is famous for being the deciding vote in a number of important Supreme Court cases decided by a 5-4 vote. Kennedy's is a reputed centrist, but is also generally regarded as being a center-right vote. The designation of liberal and conservative is often cloudy and misleading, but many criminal law commentators commonly regard judges who tend to favor the prosecution to be conservative and those who are more likely to regard defense arguments favorably as liberal. Is this opinion by Justice Kennedy a liberal decision? Is there a traditional conservative theory evident in this opinion?

2.   All federal circuits allow the use of jury instructions on the doctrine of "willful blindness." Only a handful of states have recognized the doctrine. The Supreme Court of North Carolina has rejected the deliberate ignorance doctrine, stating it "does not comport with the law of North Carolina." *State v. Bogle*, 376 S.E.2d 745 (N.C. 1989). Texas courts have not explicitly rejected or accepted the doctrine.

3.   One old Texas case appears to have implicitly accepted the concept of deliberate blindness. *Johnson v. State* involved a conviction for keeping a disorderly house—a statute aimed at combatting prostitution—that forbade knowingly permitting "lewd, lascivious, or indecent" conduct manner. *Johnson v. State*, 24 S.W. 410 (Tex. Crim. App. 1893). Would such a statute survive a void for vagueness challenge in the present era?

4.   The opinion by Presiding Judge Hurt stated that the evidence conclusively established the owner of the establishment in question had "employed in his theater women of bad reputation for chastity, and that some of them conducted themselves in a lewd, lascivious, and indecent manner." The question was whether the defendant knew of this conduct. At trial, the defendant

presented the testimony of one Phillips, an employee who had acted as watchman at the theater, to the effect that he had seen no improper conduct by any of the women engaged at the theater. Upon cross–examination, however, Phillips stated, from what he saw, "it was not a place where he would take his wife and daughter." The Court concluded the conviction should be affirmed despite the refusal of the trial court to give an instruction that would have informed the jury that actual knowledge was required. The Court stated:

> Did appellant know of the character and conduct of his female employees? We are of opinion that the circumstances show that he did, or that he blindly and willfully refused to observe that which was evident. The court charged the jury that they must believe from the evidence, beyond a reasonable doubt, that appellant knowingly employed or had in his service such women, or that he knowingly permitted them to conduct themselves in the forbidden manner, and it was not required that they should be further instructed on the question of knowledge. There was no error in refusing the requested instructions.

Court: Appellant tried to avoid knowledge of drugs to avoid sanctions of statute while violating its substance. Appellant noticed conceled compartment. These facts show that, although appellant did not see actual drugs, he was trying to remain ignorant but knew something was wrong. A Δ could not allege he was deliberately ignorant bc this mental state with respect to this crime = culpable as positive knowledge.

Chapter 3: Recklessness and Criminal Negligence

Introduction

Determining the mental state of the accused at the time of the crime is as difficult as it is crucial in the criminal law. Certainty concerning the internal thoughts of another is impossible, and the lines between the four identified mental states in the Texas Penal Code are often obscure. For example, the key to "knowledge" is the defendant's awareness that a certain harmful result will likely occur or that some forbidden circumstance likely exists. The lower culpable mental state of recklessness also requires proof of awareness of a "substantial and unjustifiable" risk that a harmful result will occur or some circumstance exists that is consciously disregarded. The thin distinction between these two definitions is shaved even closer by the willful ignorance doctrine. Didn't the defendant in *Jewell* consciously disregard a substantial and unjustifiable risk that the car he agreed to drive across the border contained contraband?

Recklessness and criminal negligence definitions also contain much in common. Both involve risk creation that is both substantial and unjustifiable. The critical difference is that the three mental states of intent, knowledge, and recklessness are all subjective states of mind. The tort law standard of negligence—what a reasonable person **would have known** or what the defendant **should have known** if he or she was acting with reasonable caution—is not enough in most criminal cases. If the jury had concluded Jewell did not actually know of the contraband in the car, the jury instructions stated that the jury should return a verdict of not guilty even if this belief was foolish, careless, or stupid. If a person's foolish or stupid belief or decision causes harm, civil law may allocate the costs of the consequences to the defendant who negligently caused the damage that a more reasonable person would have avoided. We do not *usually* stigmatize a person as a criminal and deprive the person of liberty under the criminal law for being stupider or more careless than a reasonable person. Except, sometimes we do in strict liability crimes, which we examine in the next chapter, and under the relatively rare criminal statutes that impose criminal liability on the basis of negligence.

The determination of grossly unacceptable risk creation must be made by considering all of the circumstances. Driving a car very fast in a crowded urban area can create great risk, but what if the driver is trying to win a drag race or trying to transport a heart attack victim quickly to the hospital? The presence or absence of social utility affects the judgment rather than a mathematical probability of harm.

A person who acts recklessly is aware of, but consciously disregards, a substantial and unjustifiable risk. A person who acts negligently is not aware, but ought to be, of a substantial and unjustifiable risk. Proving that someone was or was not aware of a risk can present similar difficulties to proving whether someone acted intentionally or knowingly. Additionally, the culpable mental states of recklessness and negligence require a further determination that the risk that the defendant either was aware of but consciously disregarded, or ought to have been aware of but was not, was a substantial and unjustifiable risk.

The determination of the degree of deviation from what is reasonable can be affected by the magnitude of the harm risked. The dissent by Judge Keller in the criminal negligence case of *Williams*, which follows, weighs heavily the fact that the risk involved concerned vulnerable children rather than a more trivial risk. Other relevant factors are the circumstances known to the defendant. In the criminal negligence case of *Hookie*, that appears after *Williams*, what indications were there that the brakes of the truck were defective?

Williams v. State

235 S.W.3d 742 (Tex. Crim. App. 2007)

Cochran, J., delivered the opinion of the Court in which, Price, Womack, Johnson, Keasler, Hervey and Holcomb, JJ., joined.

We granted appellant's petition for discretionary review to examine the culpable mental state of recklessness.

Appellant was convicted of injury to a child and sentenced to fifteen years' imprisonment after her two children died in an accidental house fire while her boyfriend was babysitting them. We hold that the evidence in this case was legally insufficient to support her conviction under Section 22.04 of the Texas Penal Code. The court of appeals erred in concluding that the State proved the criminal offense of reckless injury to a child when the evidence showed that appellant took her children from their grandmother's house (which had working utilities) to her boyfriend's temporary home (which did not have working utilities) and left them under her boyfriend's care with a lit candle in the bedroom. The State's proof of these facts—proof beyond a reasonable doubt—did not establish a criminally culpable reckless state of mind.

I.

Two of appellant's children, Ujeana, age seven, and Precious, age eight, died in a house fire in the early morning hours of October 5, 2002. Ujeana, Precious, and appellant lived with appellant's mother, Zula Mae Scott, who routinely cared for the young girls. Occasionally the girls stayed with their father, Charles Leon Williams, Jr. Sometimes they stayed with appellant and her boyfriend, Herbert Ronald Bowden, in his "home." Bowden lived in an altered duplex with both halves of the house combined into a single unit. It was a four-room structure, but it had no kitchen or bathroom, no working utilities, and very little furniture. In Bowden's bedroom there was a bed, as well as a dresser under the window, and a chair in front of the nailed-up door to the outside. There was a couch in the living room. The house was, according to Bowden, "somewhat trashy." There was indeed trash on the floor, mainly in the living room.

Bowden lived in this makeshift home with permission, and he paid a nominal rent. He intended to live there until he saved enough money from his new job at Bennigan's restaurant to afford a proper apartment. About two weeks before the fire, Zula Mae learned that appellant and Bowden were taking the children to the duplex. She warned them both that "it was too dangerous to be taking them down there and burning candles," in part because of the risk of a house fire.

Nevertheless, after he got off work on October 4, 2002, Bowden went to Zula Mae's house to pick up appellant and her girls. Zula Mae was not yet home from work. The four walked to his duplex. Appellant went out to get cigarettes and ran into the girls' father, Charles Leon Williams, Jr., in the parking lot of the store. He asked appellant where the girls were. She told him that they were "at home," which meant, to Mr. Williams, "with Zula Mae."

When appellant returned to the duplex, she told Bowden that she wanted to go out with friends, and he agreed to watch the girls. He dressed them in his sweatshirts to keep them warm, and then he and appellant put the girls to bed in his bedroom. They placed a burning candle in an aluminum pie plate for light because Bowden did not want the girls to be left "in the dark." Bowden said that he and appellant "were sitting there talking and um, and uh, soon as we got through talking I took the candle and sat it over there in the corner at the edge of the bed. I sat it there." The candle was closer to the wall than the bed. After appellant left, Bowden checked on the girls who were asleep with the candle still lit. "I don't know why I didn't think to blow the candle out, I just didn't want them to be in the dark."

Bowden said that he left the house only once—around 9:30—to get a cigarette from his neighbor Preston. Then he "ran on back down the street and went on back in the house and went and checked on 'em and they were still sleep. And I went and sat in the living room on the couch. And then I went and got up and checked on 'em again and that was I'm saying that was about 10 o'clock or so."

Bowden finally fell asleep on the living-room couch. Around 1:00 a.m., Bowden woke up to loud screams and saw that the bedroom where the girls were sleeping was on fire. When he looked in the "open" door all he could see "was flames and smoke." He said he got down close to the floor, but he "could barely even see the bottom of the bed you know? And it was that much smoke in there." He could still hear the girls screaming, and he was "hollering, calling their names, but they wasn't responding like they heard my voice." He ran out of the front door, and "I went around to the side window and uh, knocked it out. But flames were coming out of it." When he could not get in the window, he ran around to the boarded-up exterior bedroom door and tried to pull it open, but again he could not get inside.

Wichita Falls Police Officer Jonathan Lindsay was the first emergency responder. When he arrived, he saw Bowden with a towel wrapped around one of his hands, crying "my babies are inside, my babies are inside." Bowden was "frantic." By the time the fire department arrived, the house was "fully involved" with flames, and the firemen were unable to enter it. The children never got out.

Appellant, who had been told about the fire, arrived back at the scene as the fire department was extinguishing the blaze. Bowden—who had cut his hand when he broke the window trying to get to the children—was briefly checked out by medical personnel. He had no burns or cough.

Jim Graham, the Assistant Fire Marshal for the Wichita Falls Fire Department, talked to Bowden at the scene. Bowden told him about the candle, about waking up to find the bedroom on fire, and about how he tried to enter the room first through the open bedroom door, then through the outside window, and finally through the boarded-up back door.

Officer Ginger Harrill took statements from both Bowden (who was still in his socks) and appellant. They were both cooperative.

Appellant's statement related her activities that night. For the most part, her statement did not make much sense. It was fractured and incoherent. She stated that as soon as she, Bowden, and the girls arrived at the duplex, she went out to buy cigarettes. When she returned, she "hung out" for a while with the girls and Bowden. Then she lit a candle in the bedroom and put the girls to bed. Around 8:30 p.m., she went out to buy chips and Little Debbies for the girls—something she was supposed to have done on her first trip to the store. She mentioned a cast of characters that she saw or talked to during the evening: Paul Taylor, who gave her change for the girls' snacks; Judy, the owner of Lucky One Stop; a "young Spanish guy" who gave her a ride in a blue van; Christine, who lives down the street; Preston, from whose house she called Jerry, Christine's cousin; Easy B (AKA Anita Gibson) and Dee, who live at the Budget Motel; Shewe, who "got into it" with Easy B at the Budget Motel; an unknown man in a van, "I don't know his name, he just gave me a ride"; BL (AKA Lewis) and Pine, who told her the "girls just got burned up." Investigator Harrill asked appellant about Ujeana and Precious staying at Bowden's place:

Harrill: Ok. Uh, how often do you and the girls stay down there?

Williams: Uh, Uh, We go down there sometimes. . . . We don't stay down there, we slept down there a couple of times.

Harrill: Um hmm.

Williams: 2 or 3 times. But we don't. . . . Um, Like Mama said, we should've brought 'em home.

Harrill: Well I'm not trying to be harsh but that's gonna come up. Why didn't you just leave 'em at your mom's?

Williams: Well at the time Mama wasn't there.

Harrill: Ok.

Williams: Mama wasn't there. 'Cause Mama don't make it home until after 5:30.

Both appellant and Bowden denied drinking or getting high that night.

Assistant Fire Marshal Graham investigated the fire and concluded that it was an accident:

There was absolutely nothing in this room that would lead me, as an investigator, to believe that this fire was in any way intentionally set. We're looking at the accidental introduction by a human of some—some open flame. Take that with Mr. Bowden's statement of having a candle placed in there, that's exactly what we would have seen. Some material got too close to the candle. As the girls were described sleeping on the bed, changing places, moving over, it's quite likely—the most likely scenario was a sheet, maybe clothing, material used for—wrapped under their head for a pillow gets knocked—either knocked off the bed or hangs off the bed. At this point the candle can ignite it.

The cause of the fire was, without question, the introduction of an open flame to the combustible material in the corner of that room. The only known open flame or alleged open flame to be there was the candle that was put there for light that night.

Bowden and appellant were each indicted for two counts of reckless injury to a child. Bowden was alleged to have committed the two offenses "by leaving [each girl] in a room without adult supervision with a candle burning." Appellant was alleged to have committed the offenses by either (1) taking the girls from a house with working utilities to a building without them and leaving the children in a room with a lit candle, or (2) leaving them asleep in a building without utilities with a burning candle instead of taking them to a house with working utilities. These were the specific acts that the State relied upon to prove recklessness.

The two cases were consolidated for trial, and both Bowden and appellant were convicted. Bowden was sentenced to ten years' imprisonment on each count, and appellant was sentenced to fifteen years' imprisonment on each count.

On appeal, appellant claimed that the evidence was legally and factually insufficient to prove her guilt. The court of appeals rejected this claim and held, in essence, that a rational trier of fact could conclude that the act of taking children from a home with utilities to one without utilities and leaving them in a bedroom with a lit candle is sufficient to create the known risk of death or serious bodily injury to those children, even if another adult caretaker is present.

II.

To sustain a conviction for reckless injury to a child the evidence must prove that a defendant recklessly, by act or omission, caused serious bodily injury to a child.

Was she aware of risk & ignored it?

Criminal recklessness must not be confused with (or blended into) criminal negligence, a lesser culpable mental state. With criminal negligence, the defendant *ought* to have been aware of a substantial and unjustifiable risk that his conduct could result in the type of harm that did occur, and that this risk was of such a nature that the failure to perceive it was a gross deviation from the reasonable standard of care exercised by ordinary people. Criminal negligence depends upon a morally blameworthy failure to appreciate a substantial and unjustifiable risk while recklessness depends upon a more serious (moral blameworthiness)—the actual disregard of a known substantial and unjustifiable risk.

Definition/ Rule of CN

How could you not have known abt risk?

Thus, "at the heart of reckless conduct is conscious disregard of the risk created by the actor's conduct." As has often been noted, "mere lack of foresight, stupidity, irresponsibility, thoughtlessness, ordinary carelessness, however serious the consequences may happen to be," do not suffice to constitute either culpable negligence or criminal recklessness. Recklessness requires the defendant to actually foresee the risk involved and to consciously decide to ignore it. Such a "devil may care" or "not giving a damn" attitude toward the risk distinguishes the culpable mental state of criminal recklessness from that of criminal negligence, which assesses blame for the failure to foresee the risk that an objectively reasonable person would have foreseen. "Those who are subjectively aware of a significant danger to life and choose, without justification, to engage in actions (or in some cases inactions) that threaten to bring about that danger have made a calculated decision to gamble with other people's lives." This combination of an awareness of the magnitude of the risk and the conscious disregard for consequences is crucial.

Rule of Recklessness

what make an act reckless

53

juaged on conduct Not outcome

Whether a defendant's conduct involves "an extreme degree of risk" must be determined by the conduct itself and not by the resultant harm. Nor can criminal liability be predicated on every careless act merely because its carelessness results in death or injury to another.

Numerous Texas cases have addressed factual scenarios in which the jury could conclude that the defendant consciously disregarded a substantial and unjustified risk of serious injury to a child. These include holding a child's feet under extremely hot water; ramming a parked car that had an 18–month–old child in it; twisting and pulling a baby's leg; letting a 350–pound lion, which was neither muzzled nor declawed, out of its cage at a flea market populated by children; and speeding and running through stop signs with a child passenger. These cases involved an actor committing a highly dangerous act whose substantial and unjustifiable risks were known to, but disregarded by, the actor, and that act led directly to serious harm to a child. In other reckless injury cases, the defendant failed to perform an act that directly resulted in the injury. In one case the defendant was held to have recklessly caused bodily injury to her children by failing to report to the authorities that her boyfriend had violently kidnaped them. In still other cases the actors have left a disabled victim lying in bleach for at least an hour; failed to immediately seek medical help for a lethargic child; and left four-year-old twins unsupervised and wandering around an apartment complex.

In sum, in addressing the culpable mental state of recklessness under section 6.03(c), the factfinder (and a reviewing court) must examine the defendant's conduct to determine whether

Statute to be applied to determine Risk

(1)   the alleged act or omission, viewed objectively at the time of its commission, created a "substantial and unjustifiable" risk of the type of harm that occurred;

(2)   that risk was of such a magnitude that disregard of it constituted a gross deviation from the standard of care that a reasonable person would have exercised in the same situation (i.e., it involved an "extreme degree of risk, considering the probability and magnitude of the potential harm to others");

(3)   the defendant was consciously aware of that "substantial and unjustifiable" risk at the time of the conduct; and

(4)   the defendant consciously disregarded that risk.

With that background of the pertinent law concerning a reckless state of mind, the level of risk required, and causation for the harm suffered, we turn to the present case.

III.

The court of appeals held the evidence legally sufficient to prove that appellant recklessly, by act or omission, caused serious bodily injury to her two children. The court of appeals found, in essence, that a rational trier of fact could conclude that

(1)   taking children from a home with utilities to one without utilities, and
(2)   leaving them in a bedroom with a lit candle,
(3)   creates the foreseeable risk of death or serious bodily injury to those children,

54

(4)   even if another adult caretaker is present.

Furthermore, the court concluded that there was legally sufficient evidence to support a finding that appellant was consciously aware of this risk and that she disregarded it. The court of appeals stated,

> As the girls' mother, Appellant was at least as responsible as Bowden for the decision to take them from Zula Mae's house to the structure, and she, herself, "knew that room," had placed the dresser in front of the window and the chair in front of the locked door. Appellant lit the candle and made sure the girls were in bed in the room with the candle burning before she left for several hours. From the evidence that she always made sure to extinguish the candle, the jury could have inferred that Appellant assumed the role of making sure of extinguishing the candles in that house. This is supported by her statement to Sergeant Harrill that she had no idea what Bowden may have done with the candle after she left. The jury could have inferred that Appellant was aware of but disregarded the risk that Bowden would not know what to do with the candle, specifically that he should extinguish it before leaving the room with the girls asleep. Moreover, Appellant acknowledged that she did not expect the girls to be awake when she returned hours later. Thus, the jury could have further inferred that she was aware of but disregarded the fact that they would fall asleep with the candle burning.

Appellant contends that there is legally insufficient evidence that she consciously disregarded a substantial or unjustifiable risk that her girls would suffer grievous harm. *Holding*

We agree [that] there is legally insufficient evidence that appellant consciously disregarded a substantial or unjustifiable risk that her children would suffer serious bodily injury in a house fire if she took them from a house with utilities to one without utilities. Viewed objectively, this act, either by itself or in combination with the State's second act of alleged recklessness—leaving the girls in a room with a lit candle—does not involve a "substantial and unjustifiable" risk of serious bodily injury or death. There is nothing inherently dangerous about staying or sleeping in a structure that does not have utilities. Staying in a structure without utilities does not increase the likelihood of dying in a fire. Indeed, as noted by the court of appeals, the evidence shows the opposite:

evidence of house fires in favor of △

> As to the lack of utilities, Battalion Chief Holzer testified that the majority of home fires the department responds to are in homes with utilities and that a major concern for them is to make sure the utilities are turned off. And the fire investigator agreed that electrical distribution equipment such as wiring, outlets, and cords are the second leading cause of fire death and the third leading cause of fires in the United States. Cooking fires are "number one." Only 15 percent of fires in 2001 were attributable to open flames or embers. Fires can occur in homes that have utilities; lack of utilities does not create an immediate chance that there will be a fire. Sammy Beatty did not believe candles were inherently dangerous and believed his girlfriend had some. Zula Mae admitted she had scented candles in her house that she used sometimes even when children were around.

If taking children to spend the night in a structure without utilities is conduct that involves an extreme risk of danger for which one may be subject to criminal prosecution for injury to a child should harm befall that child, the backwoods campers of the world are in serious jeopardy. Any adult who lights a campfire that emits a spark that lands on a child's pajamas and severely burns the child can be prosecuted as a felon. Scoutmasters beware. If a Coleman gas lantern tips over and sets the children's pup tent ablaze, they might suffer the same fate. The parent who uses a candle to read a bedtime story to the weary little camper may rue the reading hour if the candle tips over and burns the child. Any of these harms might befall a camper's child, but the act of camping in a site without utilities does not create such a foreseeable substantial and unjustifiable risk of serious bodily injury or death that it suffices to hold the camper's parent criminally liable should injury occur. Yet this act is precisely the same as that alleged by the State in this case: taking a child from a house with working utilities to one without them.

One could also pose the legal issue in the opposite manner: Would appellant have been free from criminal liability had she done everything that she did do, but Bowden's duplex had working utilities? After all, people who have electricity frequently use candles as well as, or instead of, electric lights on various occasions. Zula Mae used candles even though her house had light bulbs. But the law does not predicate a finding of criminal liability for creating an unjustifiable and substantial risk of injury upon whether the actor used a candle out of necessity (an act that purportedly creates a substantial and unjustifiable risk) or for aesthetic purposes (a purportedly blameless act).

The State argues that appellant's act of taking the children from Zula Mae's house to Bowden's was a reckless one because appellant ignored her mother's sage advice: "It was too dangerous to be taking them down there and burning candles." Alas, who among us has not been guilty, from time to time, of ignoring our mother's wise words. In hindsight, of course, Zula Mae proved to be a prescient Cassandra; the very harm that she had predicted did, in fact, occur. But merely because appellant failed to heed her mother's words does not mean that the act of taking the children to Bowden's house (or camping outdoors for that matter) created a substantial and unjustified risk of serious bodily injury to the girls. Appellant's "stupidity, irresponsibility, thoughtlessness, or ordinary negligence" do not constitute reckless disregard of a substantial and unjustified risk. A number of judicial decisions involving criminal "gross negligence" or "recklessness" have held that warnings like that given to appellant by Zula Mae do not suffice to establish the existence of a severe risk of injury or the defendant's conscious disregard of such a risk. The importance of such warnings must be viewed in light of the likelihood of their occurrence and magnitude of the danger posed at the time the defendant acted, not in post-event hindsight.

Because we cannot conclude that the act of taking a child from a house with working utilities to one without working utilities is the type of conduct that, by its nature, raises a substantial and unjustifiable risk of injury, we hold that it cannot support a finding of reckless injury to a child. Thus, even if the State proved beyond all possible doubt that appellant did take her children from a house with working utilities to one without, that fact cannot, either by itself or in combination with other acts, support a finding of criminal recklessness under these circumstances.

Therefore, we must consider whether appellant's act of leaving her two girls in a room with a lit candle under Bowden's supervision could support a finding that she was criminally reckless in causing her children's death. This is an act that, by its nature and depending upon the circumstances, could support a finding of recklessness—the conscious disregard of a substantial and unjustifiable risk of injury. Were there such circumstances shown in this case? The court of appeals correctly stated, "It was undisputed that Appellant did not leave the girls alone to sleep in the room with the candle burning but left them awake with Bowden in the room to care for them, and there was evidence that he was trustworthy to care for the children." In fact, there was absolutely no evidence that Bowden was an incompetent or uncaring babysitter. All of the evidence indicated that, in fact, he was a considerably more responsible caretaker than appellant herself. It is, as appellant asserts, "mere speculation by the appellate court that the jury could have inferred that Bowden would not know what to do with the candle or that Appellant assumed the role of making sure of extinguishing the candles in that house." There is nothing in the record to support this supposition that Bowden did not know what to do with a lit candle. Blowing out a candle is not rocket science. And there is nothing in the record to suggest that Bowden could not handle the task or did not care enough to handle it. Quite the reverse. In hindsight, Bowden expressed great remorse and regret that he did not blow out the candle when he went back in to check on the sleeping girls. He had left it burning so that the girls would not be in the dark. In hindsight, this was obviously an unwise decision; even at the time this was, perhaps, an unwise decision, but it does not prove he was an incompetent caretaker or that appellant was actually aware that he was an incompetent caretaker. A parade of State's witnesses had nothing bad to say about Bowden and much that showed his conscientious character. There is simply no evidence to suggest that Bowden, the "Johnny-on-the-Spot" babysitter, was in any way incompetent. But the oddity of this case—the fact that appellant left the children in the care of Bowden, who was not shown to be an unsuitable caregiver—makes it one of a kind. That difference takes this case out of the norm of reported fatal neglect cases. On this record, we cannot agree that appellant's leaving her children with Bowden in a room with a lit candle represents a gross deviation from the standard of conduct that a law-abiding person in appellant's situation would observe. The Texas Supreme Court has enunciated an appropriate standard for civil cases involving reckless conduct which, applied here, asks: "viewed objectively" from appellant's viewpoint, did her act or omission "involve an extreme degree of risk, considering the probability and magnitude of the potential harm" to her two daughters? The acts that the State alleged and proved do not meet that threshold. This factual situation—leaving Ujeana and Precious, 7–and 8–year–old girls, in bed with a lit candle upright in a metal pan with Bowden nearby watching over the girls—is not one so inherently fraught with danger as to create, in the mind of the objectively reasonable person, the awareness of a substantial and unjustifiable risk of serious bodily injury. If appellant's conduct would not suffice to raise a jury issue for imposition of punitive damages in a civil case, it is hardly sufficient to raise a jury issue for a criminal conviction. *if not enough for civil case not enough for crim.*

The State's allegations of the purportedly reckless acts committed by appellant are simply not acts that, viewed objectively under these particular circumstances, involved "an extreme degree of risk, considering the probability and magnitude of the potential harm to others." Appellant may have been a "bad" mother, unworthy of her mother, her children, and her boyfriend, but she did not commit the crime of reckless injury to a child merely because she took her children from a house with utilities to one without utilities, and left them, under the care of a responsible adult, with a lit candle in the bedroom.

In this case, the evidence of a criminally reckless *mens rea* [was] legally insufficient to sustain appellant's conviction. We thus reverse the court of appeals and order an acquittal.

Keller, P.J., filed a dissenting opinion in which Meyers, J., joined.

This case is not about a family camping trip gone wrong. It's not about a poor family doing the best it could with the little they had. This case is about two little girls who died a horrible death because their mother, for no good reason, took them from a safe home and left them in a place that she knew was a fire hazard. She left them there with a lit candle, telling them she was going to the store to get them snacks and that she would be back, but she didn't come back. The jury had no trouble deciding that appellant's behavior on the night of October 4, 2002, was criminal. After three days of trial, it took them just an hour and a half to come to that conclusion, which the Court today undoes.

There are two aspects of this case that I believe the Court overlooks. First, for an act to be reckless, the risk that it creates must be unjustifiable. What differentiates this case from the scenarios posited by the Court is that here, leaving the children with a lit candle was—for so many reasons—unjustifiable. Appellant could have left the girls at the home where they lived with their grandmother. She could have left them with their father, who had come by the house expecting to pick them up for the weekend. There was no pressing need to move them to a dangerous house. But even if one were to conclude that appellant's wish to be with her children at her boyfriend's house justified taking them there, there was no need to light the candle. There was normally enough light in the bedroom from the streetlight in the alley. And finally, of course, there was no justification for failing to blow out the candle. Appellant's mother testified that appellant probably would have put out the candle if she had been there. This, again, is evidence of recklessness in that it shows appellant knew it was important to blow out the candle, yet failed to do so. Instead of returning from the store with chips and Little Debbies, as she had told her boyfriend and her children she would, she stayed out for hours, not returning until she heard that the girls had died, the snacks discarded in the van where she was when she heard the news.

The fact that appellant failed to return when she said she would is the second aspect of the case that the Court's analysis seems to overlook. Bowden assumed responsibility for the girls while appellant went to the store, but he expected her back hours before the fire. The Court states that "there is nothing to suggest that . . . appellant, had she been there, would have prevented this tragedy." But there is evidence in the record that directly suggests it. Appellant had told her mother she always made sure the candles were out when she went to sleep. Her mother testified that she believed appellant, if she had been there, probably would have put out the candle. Had she returned and blown out the candle, the fire would not have happened. Had she returned and failed to blow out the candle, no one would be arguing that she was not responsible. Either way, she is responsible for the fire because she failed to return when she said she would.

Moreover, the Court discounts the evidence that appellant knew the risk because people sometimes disregard a mother's advice. But the jury wasn't bound to believe that appellant did so. There was plenty of evidence from which the jury could conclude that appellant knew that it was risky to take the girls to Bowden's house to spend the night. First, appellant's mother had

58

told her that it was dangerous precisely because of the fire hazard. Appellant did hear this warning—she later told police that she should have brought them home, "like mama said." Second, when appellant happened upon the girls' father that night, she told him the girls were "at grandma's," which was untrue. It is in no way unreasonable for the jury to take all this as evidence that appellant was aware of the risk of fire and, because of this awareness, thought she needed to hide the truth about where the girls were from their father. No other explanation for the lie presents itself from the record.

In my opinion, these two aspects of the case—the unjustifiability of the risk and the failure to return—are sufficient to rebut the Court's conclusion.

The court of appeals carefully examined the evidence, applied the appropriate standard for reviewing sufficiency of the evidence, and gave proper deference to the jury's implied credibility decisions. I agree with that court's reasoning and its conclusion, and I respectfully dissent to the reversal of appellant's conviction.

Notes

1.   The basic facts of this case are undisputed: Williams left her daughters in bed in a house without electricity, with a lit candle in the bedroom, in the care of another adult unfit to care for them. Do these facts establish that she acted recklessly with regard to the children's lives, in other words that she consciously disregarded a substantial and unjustifiable risk that her daughters would suffer serious injury or die?

The majority thought the evidence was insufficient to establish recklessness—focusing on the "substantial" part of "substantial and unjustifiable"—explaining the risk that children would suffer serious harm in this case was not quantitatively high because, for example, house fires are less common in houses without electricity than in houses with electricity. The dissenting opinion seems to focus on the "unjustifiable" part, stating that Williams had "no good reason" to leave her daughters at Bowden's house. Should these two parts be considered separately or together?

2.   What if Williams had at least a *more important* reason for leaving her daughters, such as she was going to school, work, or attending to her mother in a medical emergency? Do you think that factor would change the opinion of the dissenters? What if Williams left the children with their father or her mother, and one of them forgot to blow out a candle, leading to the same catastrophe in a house with utilities? If the fire had started in Bowden's house because a gang member threw a Molotov Cocktail through the window from a passing car, would Williams and Bowden be reckless because the children were left in a house in a dangerous neighborhood? If, instead of a fire, a wall had collapsed in Bowden's ramshackle house, crushing the children, would Williams be reckless for leaving the children there?

3.   The majority found the evidence insufficient. Which, if any, of the following hypothetical facts would have changed the opinion of the majority judges?
   • Bowden and Williams "got high" and had several drinks before Williams left.

- Williams said that she would only be gone for a few minutes but she met friends who persuaded her to party all night.
- Bowden's house had been condemned as a fire hazard and he had been warned not to live there by the Fire Marshall.
- Williams was unaware of what the Fire Marshall had communicated to Bowden.

Criminal Negligence

The majority opinion at one point seems to suggest Williams might have acted negligently, stating: "Appellant's stupidity, irresponsibility, thoughtlessness, or ordinary negligence" do not constitute reckless disregard of a substantial and unjustified risk. Should Williams have been charged with criminally negligent homicide? Would the question of whether Williams acted negligently be any easier to answer than the question of whether she acted recklessly?

The culpable mental states in the Texas Penal Code have a hierarchical relationship. Thus, under 6.02(e) Texas Penal Code, "Proof of a higher degree of culpability than that charged constitutes proof of the culpability charged." This is sensible because otherwise it would be theoretically possible for someone like Bowden to defend against a criminal charge alleging recklessness by claiming to have set the fire intentionally in the hope of killing the children. The close hierarchical relationship between culpable mental states prevents such fanciful claims of being too guilty to be convicted of the charged offense. It also creates the possibility of submitting for the jury's consideration a lesser offense than the one charged as an option where the only difference between the charged offense and the lesser-included offense is that there is a lesser mental state requirement. (The subject of lesser-included offenses will be discussed in greater detail later.) If the jury finds that there was recklessness, but not knowledge, there may be an acquittal if there is no lesser offense available. However, in many areas of the law, there are cascading statutes with a similar objective but vary in some way by the degree of harm or the type of culpable mental state.

When otherwise similar or identical offenses differ only in having different mental states, the statutes share the relationship of greater and lesser-included offenses. The crimes of manslaughter and criminally negligent homicide share this relationship. Both crimes deal with criminal acts that cause the death of the victim. The defendant in *Williams* was charged with injury to a child. As with mental states, proof of more harm than needed is a poor defense. Death certainly qualifies as an injury. The charge in *Williams* certainly could have been one of manslaughter, which consists of recklessly causing the death of the children. If this had occurred, the lesser-included offense of criminally negligent homicide might have been submitted. If you were a juror for Williams, would you be more comfortable finding her guilty of criminally negligent homicide rather than a higher offense requiring recklessness? Or would you find her not guilty because what occurred was merely an accident (without a culpable mental state)?

In attempting to answer this question, consider how recklessness and criminal negligence differ. Both require a substantial and unjustifiable risk of harm, but recklessness requires subjective awareness of the risk that is disregarded by the actor. Because the actor subjectively perceives the risk but consciously chooses to ignore it, recklessness is part of the criminal law tradition of requiring a guilty mind as well as a guilty act. By contrast, the actor's failure to perceive any risk created by dangerous conduct that creates a substantial and unjustifiable risk is the essence of criminal negligence. It matters not that a defendant convicted of a criminal negligence offense did not desire to cause harm or know or be aware of a substantial risk of harm. If a reasonable person would have perceived the risk and the defendant should have but did not, there can be criminal liability under a criminal negligence statute. Thus, for the first time with criminal negligence, we cross the line of requiring subjective fault on the part of the defendant and allowing a criminal conviction based on what the defendant should have known. Negligence is a controversial basis for imposing criminal liability because it deviates from the doctrine that a guilty mind rather than a merely a guilty act is required for criminal liability. Others maintain that the complete failure to pay attention to substantial risk is can be equally culpable to disregarding a known risk, and the law should prod people to pay attention to substantial risks.

Texas follows the Model Penal Code in providing that criminal liability may not be predicated on mere negligence; the deviation from the standard of care that we would expect of a reasonable person must be gross or substantial for criminal liability. Recklessness requires a conscious disregard of a foreseeable risk. Is there a precise measure of this required greater degree of negligence? Precise measurement is neither possible nor desirable. Whether the standard has been met is a jury question, and the guidance provided to the jury about how to gauge the level of deviation from a reasonable standard of care in jury instructions is neither precise nor mechanical.

This compromise between allowing negligence as a basis for criminal liability and requiring something more than ordinary tort negligence has not been followed in all states. Some states have adopted ordinary negligence as the *mens rea* requirement for criminal liability. Other states have gone further than Texas in the other direction by making recklessness the minimum mental state for criminal liability. The *Hookie* case, which follows, is an application of the Texas standard.

Hookie v. State

136 S.W.3d 671 (Tex. App.—Texarkana 2004, no pet.)

Opinion by Chief Justice Morriss.

One week after being cited for maladjusted brakes on his log truck and promising to adjust them properly, Ronald Gene Hookie was unable to stop the truck at a red light and collided with a pickup truck in which Laurie Ann Davis was a passenger, killing her. A jury found Hookie guilty of criminally negligent homicide, and he was sentenced to one year in a state jail facility. On appeal, Hookie asserts the evidence was legally and factually insufficient to sustain his conviction.

<u>Background</u>

On October 15, 2002, Trooper Dennis Jones of the Texas Department of Public Safety (DPS) License and Weight Division stopped Hookie, who was transporting a load of logs from a job site to the mill. During the thirty-minute inspection, Jones found twelve violations for which he issued two citations to Hookie. For the first axle brake that was out of adjustment, Jones declared the truck out of service, meaning that the vehicle could not be operated until measures were taken to remedy the deviation. Hookie told Jones he could properly adjust the brakes on site, which is a common practice in the trucking industry according to the testimony of both Hookie and Jones. Jones believed Hookie would adjust the brakes, so Jones continued on his way. Hookie testified that, as Jones was leaving, Hookie was already beginning to adjust the brakes. Between October 15 and October 22, there were no DPS inspections of Hookie's truck.

One week later, on October 22, 2002, friends Laurie Davis and Davina Russom were returning from a trip to Longview after having portraits made of Laurie's daughter and Davina's son. On their way home, the four stopped at a fast food restaurant on Highway 80, ate, and continued on their way. Shortly thereafter, their pickup truck approached and, on a green light, entered the intersection of Highway 80 and Loop 485. Laurie warned Davina to "Watch that truck," referring to Hookie's loaded log truck. The warning came too late. The log truck collided with the pickup and sent it spinning and flipping high into the air. By the time the pickup landed, it was upside down and had ejected Laurie. The children crawled out the now-broken back window, suffering only minor injuries. Davina also escaped with minor injuries. Laurie was airlifted to a hospital, but died in transit due to massive head injuries.

After the collision, Hookie stopped his truck approximately 100 feet past the intersection on Loop 485. Several people talked to Hookie during the moments after the collision. DPS Trooper Adam Bell was the first to arrive at the scene. Not considering the accident investigation a criminal one, he interviewed Hookie, who admitted his "brakes didn't hold." The conversation is recorded by Bell's in-car camera. Hookie said the same to investigating officer Jason Weeks of the Gladewater Police Department. Weeks called Jones to inspect the truck. Jones learned the truck was the same one he had inspected one week earlier. This inspection revealed that the brakes were even further out of adjustment than they had been one week before and that only two of the ten brakes on the truck complied with safety regulations. For instance, the left front axle brake which had, only one week before, been two and one-eighth inches out of

63

adjustment—and had been the cause Jones had declared the truck "out of service"—was determined after the accident to be out of adjustment by two and one-fourth inches.[1] The inspection also revealed several other safety violations.

Hookie admitted he had no brakes when he came to the intersection. He stated that, as soon as he discovered the brakes had failed, he tried to gear down the truck in order to stop it. Trooper Carl Davis, who arrived to assist at the scene, testified Hookie told him that the brakes did not work and that he geared down to stop the truck. Davis testified he passed this information along to Weeks. Weeks testified that the accident investigation turned into a criminal one when he learned the truck had been declared out of service for violations which remained evident one week later—on the day of the accident.

Sufficiency of Evidence

A person commits criminally negligent homicide if he or she causes the death of an individual by criminal negligence. TEX. PEN. CODE ANN. § 19.05(a) (West 2015). The Code defines criminal negligence as follows:

> A person acts with criminal negligence, or is criminally negligent, with respect to circumstances surrounding his conduct or the result of his conduct when he ought to be aware of a substantial and unjustifiable risk that the circumstances exist or the result will occur. The risk must be of such a nature and degree that the failure to perceive it constitutes a gross deviation from the standard of care that an ordinary person would exercise under all the circumstances as viewed from the actor's standpoint.

TEX. PEN. CODE ANN. § 6.03(d) (West 2015).

The failure to perceive the risk distinguishes criminal negligence from reckless conduct. Criminal negligence requires that the person should have been aware of the risk surrounding the conduct or the results of the conduct. Thus, the State must prove that a defendant ought to have been aware of a substantial and unjustifiable risk. Also, the State must establish that the failure to perceive this risk was a gross deviation from the standard of care that an ordinary person in those circumstances would exercise.

No one argues that the collision did not cause the death of Laurie Davis. Beyond that, however, to convict, the State must have established (1) that Hookie should have been aware his conduct posed a substantial and unjustifiable risk and (2) that Hookie's failure to perceive the risk constituted a gross deviation from the standard of care an ordinary person would have exercised under similar circumstances. The record shows, through Hookie's testimony, he has operated a truck for approximately thirty years and has driven a log truck for five years. From this evidence, the jury could have reasonably concluded Hookie should have been aware of the substantial and unjustifiable risk posed by operation of the truck with maladjusted brakes. Further, since Jones had issued citations for the brakes and had declared the truck out of service due to the poor adjustment of the brakes, that should have made Hookie realize the substantial risk posed by operation of the vehicle without making the proper adjustments or without careful daily inspections of those brakes.

---

1. The maximum allowable movement in brakes of this type is one and three-fourths inches.

From the evidence, a jury could have reasonably concluded Hookie's continued operation of the truck with the brakes out of adjustment constituted a gross deviation from the standard of care an ordinary person would have exercised under those circumstances. Hookie, as the driver of the truck, had a statutory duty to conduct a daily inspection of the truck, including the condition of the brakes.[2] Further, having heard that brake adjustment is a common concern, the jury could conclude a reasonable person in those circumstances would have made the repairs after citations were issued for the safety violations and would have been especially vigilant about the brakes during his or her daily inspections. Hookie testified he did a visual inspection of the truck the morning of October 22 in which he looked to see if anything was out of the ordinary. The jury either disbelieved him or determined that, even if he had done as he said and walked around the truck, his cursory inspection was insufficient to guard against the substantial risk posed under these circumstances. Jones also testified, based on his experience as a trooper in the License and Weight Division, that a reasonable person would not have operated a truck under such conditions.

Hookie contends that, since he made the repairs October 15, he did not fail to perceive the risk that poorly adjusted brakes would pose. He argues that the brakes had gone out of adjustment again by October 22 and that this collision was an unavoidable accident. Hookie readily admits that the brakes went out and that the light was red when he entered the intersection. After having compared the violations found October 15 with those found one week later, on the day of the collision, Jones testified that, in his opinion, Hookie simply had not made the adjustments he claimed. Further, the jury could have determined from the measurements taken during the two inspections that the repairs were not made. The left front axle brake was out of adjustment by two and one-eighth inches October 15; on October 22 the same brake was two and one-quarter inches out of adjustment. Since the condition of the brakes had worsened, the jury could have reasonably concluded the repairs were not performed within one week of the accident.

Further, ten out of twelve brakes on the truck were out of adjustment October 22. One brake on axle number four showed so much rust it appeared to have been inoperable for some time, a defect Hookie would certainly have noticed had he adjusted all the brakes on October 15 as he testified or had carefully inspected the truck each day. Finally, Davis' testimony that Hookie indicated to him he regularly used the "gearing down" method to stop the truck due to its faulty brakes weighs in favor of the jury's verdict. Such conditions lend themselves to a conclusion that the necessary adjustments were not made October 15 as Hookie stated, or between then and the time of the accident.

The jury could also rely on the testimony of Davis, who testified Hookie told him the truck's "brakes don't work." From this, the jury could conclude Hookie did not make the repairs and, thus, did act with the requisite state of mind. The jury could have reasonably concluded from the evidence presented to it at trial that Hookie continued to operate the truck after it was declared out of service, that he should have been aware that doing so created a substantial and

---

2. 49 C.F.R. §§ 396.11–396.13. Texas has adopted federal regulations regarding motor carrier safety. TEX. TRANSP. CODE ANN. § 644.051 (West 2015); 26 Tex. Reg. 9754 (2001) (codified at 37 TEX. ADMIN. CODE § 4.11) (in effect at time of accident).

unjustifiable risk, and that such operation was a gross deviation from the standard of care that an ordinary person would exercise under those circumstances.

The evidence to the contrary, that is, supporting Hookie's contention the collision resulted from an accident, consists largely of Hookie's testimony. Again, he concedes that the light was red and that the brakes were gone. He maintains, however, he made the repairs necessary to get the brakes back into compliance with safety regulations on October 15, immediately after having been cited for the safety concerns and being notified the truck was declared out of service until the adjustments were made. He claims to have adjusted every one of the brakes. There is some evidence which supports this position. Jones and Hookie both testified that brakes going out of adjustment is a common mechanical problem in the trucking industry and that it is also common for an experienced truck driver to adjust the brakes on site. Reconciliations of conflicts in the evidence is the exclusive province of the jury. We are not to substitute our opinion for that of the jury. Rather, we recognize that the determination of weight to be given to conflicting evidence often depends on an evaluation of credibility. Therefore, the jury was free to disbelieve or give less weight to Hookie's testimony that he made the necessary adjustments to the brakes October 15. We defer to that finding.

We overrule Hookie's points of error regarding evidentiary sufficiency.

Notes

1.   *Hookie* does not involve a lesser-included offense situation because the defendant is charged with criminally negligent homicide. While in some circumstances lesser offenses can be submitted (such as criminally negligent homicide when the charge is manslaughter—also known as reckless homicide), a defendant is at risk of conviction only of the charged offense and of lesser crimes. One indicted for criminally negligent homicide, like Hookie, could not be convicted of the greater crimes of manslaughter or murder. However, the key factual issue that the jury in *Hookie* apparently found in favor of the State was whether the defendant had repaired the brakes of the truck. If, in fact, the brakes had not been repaired, Hookie would have been in no position to argue he was not aware of the defective brakes because of the clear warning he'd been given by the state inspector. Would the result in *Hookie* have been the same if the conviction had been for manslaughter? If the charge had been manslaughter and criminally negligent homicide had been submitted as a lesser-included offense, which is the more appropriate offense of conviction?

2.   If a defendant who is cleaning a gun "accidently" shoots and kills a person nearby and the defendant claims that he or she thought the gun was unloaded, what is the more appropriate charge—manslaughter or criminally negligent homicide? The defendant may argue criminally negligent homicide is appropriate because he/she did not disregard the risk created by the loaded gun; the defendant honestly but mistakenly believed the gun to be unloaded. The prosecution might argue the defendant had training in the handling of a gun, and the first rule of gun safety is never point a gun at another person (regardless of whether you believe the gun to be loaded or unloaded). The prosecutor argues the defendant's disregard of this known rule resulting in death establishes manslaughter. Assume you are a juror who finds the defendant mistakenly but

honestly believed the gun was unloaded. Would you vote to convict of manslaughter, criminally negligent homicide, or would you find this to be an accident and acquit?

Chapter 4: Strict Liability Offenses

Introduction

The common law tradition of requiring a guilty mind as well as a guilty act for criminal liability has continued in the 20th and 21st centuries for traditional crimes codified in statute and for a large number of more modern crimes. However, there are a large number of crimes for which there is no mental state requirement. These offenses are known as strict liability crimes. Strict liability offenses make up an exception to the common law because they provide for a criminal penalty for engaging in a criminal act or causing a forbidden result even if the defendant did not act intentionally, knowingly, recklessly, or without negligence.

These statutes are a by-product of the industrial revolution and the development of complex interdependent societies. A good example of typical strict liability offenses are those defined by the Federal Food, Drug, and Cosmetic Act, which prohibits such conduct as the "adulteration or misbranding of any food, drug, device, tobacco product, or cosmetic in interstate commerce." These offenses do not require proof of any mental state at all so long as the defendant (a real person or a corporation) committed the prohibited conduct. The justification for this departure from cornerstone principles of criminal culpability is that public welfare requires strict liability. Unlike an individual, traditional crime where a single victim or a small group of victims are harmed, impure food and drugs can endanger thousands. Thus, many strict liability offenses are referred to as "public welfare offenses."

Many strict liability offenses are part of complex administrative schemes designed to regulate potentially hazardous activities that affect the public generally. Often there is a broad legislative mandate stating the public interest in preventing harms in a whole industry or public activity. The task of developing specific rules is delegated to an administrative agency that will enforce the code it develops. Consider this statute from the state of Wisconsin dealing with business practices:

> 100.20 **Methods of competition and trade practices.** (1) Methods of competition in business and trade practices in business shall be fair. Unfair methods of competition in business and unfair trade practices in business are hereby prohibited.

It was certainly a good day's work when the Wisconsin Legislature made unfair business practices illegal, but it left the heavy lifting of defining what is unfair and subject to prosecution to a large administrative agency that would promulgate and enforce rules. Many agencies administer the their rules in a manner that provides warnings of possible violations and prosecution only of those who refuse to comply or continue to repeat the offense. Many of these defendants could be convicted of regulations requiring *mens rea* because of the warnings provided, but the ability to warn, threaten, and prosecute without the *mens rea* requirement expedites enforcement and strengthens the enforcement clout of the agency. Of course, because no mental state is required, there is no guarantee that strict liability statutes will be administered in the "regular" manner.

Traffic offenses are generally strict liability offenses in part because of the high volume of anticipated prosecution. Proof of intentional speeding would complicate the enforcement and prosecution of traffic offenses that are usually processed in an assembly-line fashion with almost no trace of due process protections.

Two important justifications for criminal liability without fault in convictions for traffic and public welfare offenses are (1) that they are not as stigmatizing as convictions for more traditional crimes and (2) the penalty is usually relatively low. Many strict liability offenses provide only fines as penalties. The Model Penal Code advocated limiting strict liability offenses to those carrying fines only, but that proposal has not been widely adopted in the United States. It is certainly unusual for a felony offense to be strict liability, but the United States Supreme Court has upheld strict liability offenses carrying potential sentences of up to five years.

One of the impediments to a clearer delineation of what can be considered strict liability is that courts often duck the issue by reading a mental state into a statute that is silent as to any *mens rea* requirement. This approach has allowed courts to avoid answering a more difficult question[are there constitutional limits to the type of crimes and penalties that can be imposed without proof of a culpable mental state?]Texas is not an exception to this practice. In fact, the Texas Legislature has provided a default setting in a general statute that declares that the omission of one of the four magic terms (intent, knowledge, recklessness, or criminal negligence) does not mean a statute calls for strict liability. Article 6.02(b) of the Texas Penal Code provides:

> If the definition of an offense does not prescribe a culpable mental state, a culpable mental state is nevertheless required unless the definition plainly dispenses with any mental element.

As for which mental state to require, subsection (c) of the same statute provides:

> If the definition of an offense does not prescribe a culpable mental state, but one is nevertheless required under Subsection (b), intent, knowledge, or recklessness suffices to establish criminal responsibility.

Notice the statute does not authorize reading-in criminal negligence. Thus, the court must choose recklessness or a higher mental state that requires subjective fault on the part of the defendant. The *Walker* case, which follows, is an example of a Texas court reading in a mental state to a statute that does not provide one explicitly.

State v. Walker

195 S.W.3d 293 (Tex. App.—Tyler 2006, no pet.)

Sam Griffith, Justice.

[handwritten: quash to render a previous decision invalid.]

The State of Texas appeals the trial court's grant of Appellee Dennis Howard Walker's motion to quash the indictment. In its sole issue, the State contends that the trial court erred in quashing the indictment because no culpable mental state is required for the offense. We affirm.

[handwritten: Issue →]   [handwritten: Holding]

Background

Appellee was charged by indictment for violating section 12.002(b) of the Texas Property Code. More specifically, the indictment alleged that, on or about February 24, 2004, Appellee recorded West Oaks Subdivision Units II and III plat and subdivision of real property in the Smith County Clerk's office without approval by the appropriate authority, to wit: City of Tyler Planning and Zoning.

On July 5, 2005, Appellee filed a motion to quash the indictment. After a hearing on August 31, the trial court stated its ruling on the motion and its reasoning in a letter to counsel for both parties. The court's analysis began with the presumption that a culpable mental state is required unless case law allows a prosecutor to pursue a strict liability prosecution. The court stated that the presumption against a strict liability prosecution strengthens if the offense is punishable by confinement. The court also noted that there had never been a prosecution of this offense in the state. Viewing the severity of the possible punishment and the gravity of the expected harm to the public, the trial court concluded that the motion to quash the indictment should be granted. On October 5, the trial court signed an order quashing the indictment. This appeal followed.

[handwritten: procedural History]

Culpable Mental State

[handwritten: Statute does not require culpable mental state]

In its sole issue, the State argues that the trial court erred in quashing the indictment because the law does not require that the State allege a culpable mental state for the offense. Further, the State contends that the trial court failed to consider all of the relevant factors mandating a conclusion that the statute is one of strict liability. Appellee disagrees, arguing that the State failed to rebut the presumption requiring a culpable mental state for the offense.

Statute Violated

The State alleged that Appellee violated section 12.002(b) of the Texas Property Code. This statute states as follows:

> A person may not file for record or have recorded in the county clerk's office a plat or replat of a subdivision of real property unless it is approved as provided by law by the appropriate authority and unless the plat or replat has attached to it the documents required by Section 212.0105 or 232.023, Local Government Code, if applicable.

A violation of this statute is a misdemeanor, punishable by a fine of not less than $10 or more than $1,000, confinement in the county jail for a term not to exceed ninety days, or both.

[handwritten at top: Statute does not provide for one explicit mental state so the court reads IN the mental state]

Applicable Law

[handwritten: state as a Rule]

If the definition of an offense does not prescribe a culpable mental state, one is nevertheless required unless the definition plainly dispenses with any mental element. TEX. PEN. CODE ANN. § 6.02(b) (West 2015). A trial court must look for a manifest intent to dispense with the requirement of a culpable mental state. Silence of a statute about whether a culpable mental state is an element of the offense leaves a presumption that one is required. In the absence of an express intent to dispense with the requirement of a culpable mental state, we must inquire whether such an intent is manifested by other features of the statute. These features include the language of the statute; the nature of the offense as either *malum prohibitum* or *malum in se*; the subject of the statute; the legislative history of the statute; the seriousness of harm to the public; the defendant's opportunity to ascertain the true facts; the difficulty in proving a culpable mental state; the number of prosecutions expected; and the severity of the punishment.

[handwritten: Other factors to consider if silent on mental state]

If, in fact, the statute plainly dispenses with a culpable mental state as an element of the offense, it is a strict liability statute. A strict liability statute is based upon the principle that "a person who commits an act in violation of the law may be held criminally liable even though he might be innocent of any criminal intent."

[handwritten: plainly manages w/o]

Analysis

We begin by observing that section 12.002(b) of the Texas Property Code does not include a culpable mental state as an element of the offense. Because the statute is silent regarding a culpable mental state, we presume that culpability is required. In order to determine whether the statute manifests an intent to dispense with a culpability requirement, we examine other features of the statute.

[handwritten: Look to other things if no mention of mental state]

Language of the statute. If any section of the statute prescribes a mental state while another section omits a mental state, we presume the legislature intended to dispense with a mental element in that section. In this case, the section regulating the filing of a subdivision plat or replat is silent as to mental state. As such, we do not presume the drafters of the statute intended to dispense with a culpable mental state as an element of the offense. *See id.* Therefore, this factor weighs in favor of requiring a culpable mental state.

Nature of the offense as malum prohibitum *or* malum in se. Traditionally, *malum in se* offenses include acts that are inherently immoral such as murder, arson, or rape. However, a *malum prohibitum* offense is defined as an act that is a crime merely because it is prohibited by statute, although the act itself is not necessarily immoral. *Malum prohibitum* offenses include speeding, illegal dumping of trash, and possession of a firearm while under a domestic restraining order. The implication is that a strict liability offense must be *malum prohibitum*. Because violation of this statute cannot be considered inherently immoral, it is a *malum prohibitum* offense. Thus, this factor weighs against requiring a culpable mental state.

Subject of the statute. Strict liability statutes are traditionally associated with the protection of public health, safety, or welfare. The court of criminal appeals has upheld statutes that impose strict liability for offenses including air and water pollution, driving while intoxicated, sale of horse meat for human consumption, adulteration of food, and speeding. The statute in this case regulates the proper filing of a subdivision plat or replat with the county clerk.

[handwritten: Requires culpability]

71

The State argues that this statute affects public welfare or safety because the general public is endangered by purchasing home lots while unaware that a future highway may be built on their lots. The class of public safety statutes that appellate courts have found to impose strict liability comprises statutes that punish dangerous activities which may result in serious physical injury or death to members of the public. The potential harm from the offense charged in this case is not of that nature. As such, this factor weighs in favor of requiring a culpable mental state.

Legislative history of the statute. The only significant legislative history of this statute is that fines and criminal penalties were added in 1987. However, this statute never included a culpable mental state. The State contends that such an omission after several amendments indicates that the legislature intended a violation of the statute to be a strict liability offense. However, we cannot find any authority or legislative history to support this contention, nor has the State cited any. Moreover, the amending of the statute without adding a mental state does not rise to the level of "a manifest intent to dispense with the requirement of a culpable mental state." Therefore, this factor is, at most, neutral.

Seriousness of harm to the public. Again, it is proper to consider whether this statute relates to public health, safety, or welfare. Generally, the more serious the consequences to the public, the more likely the legislature meant to impose liability without regard to fault. In most strict liability offenses, the statutes protect unwitting and unwilling members of the public from the noxious and harmful behavior of others in situations in which it would be difficult for members of the public to protect themselves. *Id.* The State argues that the harm to the public is the increased cost to build the proposed highway and the cost of eminent domain proceedings. However, the monetary harm that could result from this offense is not of the same nature as the harm contemplated by strict liability statutes such as speeding, driving while intoxicated, adulteration of food, and air and water pollution. Such statutes involve serious risks to the public, including serious physical injury or death. Thus, this factor weighs in <u>favor of requiring</u> a culpable mental state.

Defendant's opportunity to ascertain the true facts. This factor should be viewed in the context of who, as between one in a business or an ordinary citizen, would have greater knowledge of the accepted standards of conducting the activity out of which the offense arose. In other words, we must consider who is in the best position to prevent the violation. The State contends that knowledge was imputed to Appellee, as a developer of real estate, regarding the plat filing requirements for developing a subdivision. Nonetheless, there is nothing in the statute indicating that it only applies to those whose business is real estate or property. As Appellee pointed out in oral argument, the statute could apply to an ordinary citizen who desires to subdivide a family farm. Unlike a person involved in the business of real estate or property, an ordinary citizen is not in a position to know that such a law exists. *See id.* As such, this factor weighs in favor of requiring a culpable mental state.

Difficulty in proving a mental state. The greater the difficulty in proving a mental state, the more likely legislators intended to create a strict liability offense to ensure more effective law enforcement. The State argues that the difficulty in proving a mental state in this statute is high because the statute does not mandate that the actual recording of a particular plat be done by the person charged with the offense. Intent is a matter of fact to be determined from all of the

[handwritten margin note (left): Comparison to]

[handwritten note (bottom): Harder to prove mental state = Strict liability]

circumstances. A defendant's intentions or culpable mental state can be inferred from circumstantial evidence, such as his words, acts, and conduct. Because intent may be inferred from a defendant's words, actions, and conduct, proving a mental state in this statute is no more difficult than proving a mental state in another offense, such as murder or robbery. Thus, this factor weighs in favor of requiring a culpable mental state.

Number of prosecutions expected. The fewer the expected prosecutions for commission of an offense, the more likely the legislature meant to require prosecuting officials to delve into the issue of fault. The State argues that this factor should be treated as neutral because the record is silent on this factor. At oral argument, the State admitted that it could find no prosecutions of this statute. In his brief, Appellee pointed out that there have been no reported prosecutions in twenty-three years since the statute's enactment. Both parties stated that reported appellate cases are the only source from which this information would be available to them. Because neither the State nor Appellee could find any prosecutions of this statute, this factor weighs in favor of requiring a culpable mental state.

Severity of the punishment. = Most important The greater the possible punishment, the more likely some fault is required. Strict liability is generally associated with civil violations that are punishable by fine only. Conversely, if the offense is punishable by confinement, the presumption against strict liability strengthens. A violation of this section is punishable by a fine, confinement not to exceed ninety days, or both. Possible confinement of up to ninety days for violation of this statute is a strong indication that a culpable mental state is required. Therefore, this factor weighs in favor of requiring a culpable mental state.

A majority of the factors we have considered weigh in favor of requiring a culpable mental state. However, these factors are not equally important. In our analysis, we consider the seriousness of the possible punishment, ninety days in jail, as a particularly important factor that weighs against strict liability. Because the majority of the factors weigh in favor of requiring a culpable mental state and the punishment includes ninety days of confinement, we cannot say that the statute manifests an intent to dispense with a culpable mental state sufficient to overcome the presumption that one was required. Thus, we must conclude that a culpable mental state was required in the indictment. Accordingly, the State's sole issue is overruled.

Disposition Δwins

The judgment of the trial court is affirmed.

Notes

Strict liability offenses have been challenged as violating constitutional guarantees, such as the Fifth and Fourteenth Amendments' guarantee of due process and the Eighth Amendment's prohibition on cruel and unusual punishment, but these challenges have been largely unsuccessful. Eighth Amendment challenges—based upon a theory the punishment provided is so grossly disproportionate to the criminal act as to be cruel and unusual—have generally failed.

In *Harmelin v. Michigan*, 501 U.S. 957 (1961), for example, the United States Supreme Court rejected a disproportionality claim under the Eighth Amendment in the case of a defendant who received a sentence of life imprisonment without the possibility of parole for possession of about two pounds of cocaine, though he had no prior criminal record. Upholding such an astonishing penalty for a non-violent crime is indicative of judicial reluctance to interfere with substantive legislative choices with regard to what to make criminal and how severely to punish it.

This same reluctance explains why a substantive due process claim is unlikely to succeed. Due process claims may be either procedural or substantive, but courts are much more comfortable striking down laws passed by a democratically elected legislature if fair process has not been provided. Courts constantly deal with the fairness of process: notice, opportunity to be heard, confrontation and cross-examination, the assistance of counsel, and the imperative of an impartial tribunal, to mention a few. However, a substantive due process ruling that it is not within the legitimate power of the legislature to make an act criminal without proof of a culpable mental state is a much more sensitive intrusion into the domain of the legislative branch—one that bears the historical stigma of the New Deal era conflict between FDR and the nine old men of the United States Supreme Court that brought the country to the brink of a constitutional crisis.

It is not surprising, therefore, that most courts decide to avoid the issue in many cases by reading in a mental state requirement that obviates the need for a constitutional decision. A rare contrary example is the decision of the Alaska Supreme Court in *Speidel v. State*, 460 P. 2d 77 (Alaska 1969), which held that a state statute penalizing the failure to return a rental car could only be read as providing criminal liability for simple negligence. The Alaska Court held that the lack of a subjective mental state was unconstitutional for an offense carrying a penalty and stigma similar to common law theft. *Speidel* is a rare example of a court refusing to read-in a subjective mental state requirement and then finding that a criminal statute without such a requirement violates substantive due process and is beyond the power of the legislature. The much more common method is to avoid the constitutional issue by dealing with a statute—silent as to a subjective mental state—by interpreting it to include one.

While the read-in of mental state provision of 6.02(b) strongly supports Texas courts in finding implied mental states, the statute provides an exception when a court finds the legislature "plainly dispensed" with *mens rea*. The *Exxon* case that follows is an example of a case in which the court finds the legislative silence concerning a culpable mental state was intended.

Ct finds the leg. silence concerning a culpable mental state was intended

Exxon Co. v. State

Strict Liability

646 S.W.2d 536 (Tex. App.—Houston [1st Dist.] 1982)

Price, Justice.

This is an appeal from a conviction for the offense of air pollution under the provisions of Article 4477-5b of Vernon's Ann. Civ. Stat. The evidence was presented to the trial court by way of an agreed stipulation. Punishment was a $1,000.00 fine. *No mention of Culpability*

This prosecution was initiated by a complaint signed by A.R. Peirce, the director of the Harris County Pollution Control Department. The pollutant was a catalytic dust released into the air from the Exxon refinery located in Baytown, Texas on February 27, 1981. This dust settled over a wide area of Baytown, interfering with other persons' use and enjoyment of their property. The appellant had no permit to emit the discharged dust.

Prior to trial, the appellant filed a motion to quash the information and two motions to dismiss the prosecution. The contention on appeal is that the trial court erred in overruling these motions. The appellant contends here, as it did in the motion to quash, that the information is defective because it fails to allege a culpable mental state in violation of the TEX. PENAL CODE ANN. § 6.02(b) (West 2015). *Issue?*

Article 4477-5b of Vernon's Ann.Civ.Stat., entitled *Air Pollution,* provides in part:

Section 1. In this article:

(1) "Air contaminant" means particulate matter, dust, fumes, gas, mist, smoke, vapor, or odor, or any combination thereof, produced by processes other than natural.

(2) "Person" means an individual or a private corporation.

(3) "Air pollution" means the presence in the atmosphere of one or more air contaminants or combinations thereof, in such concentration and of such duration as are or may tend to be injurious to or to adversely affect humans, animal life, vegetation or property, or as to interfere with the normal use and enjoyment of animal life, vegetation or property.

(4) "Source" means any point of origin of an air contaminant, whether privately or publicly owned or operated.

Sec. 2. No person may cause or permit the emission of any air contaminant which causes or which will cause air pollution unless the emission is made in compliance with a variance or other order issued by the Texas Air Control Board.

. . . .

Sec. 4. Any person who violates any of the provisions of Sections 2 or 3 of this article is guilty of a misdemeanor and upon conviction is punishable by a fine of not less than $10 nor more than $1,000. Each day that a violation occurs constitutes a separate offense.

75

Omitting the formal parts, the information alleges that:

Exxon Company U.S.A. . . . on or about February 27, 1981, did then and there unlawfully cause and permit the emission of an air contaminant, to-wit: dust produced by an unnatural process, from a catalytic unit at a refinery in Baytown, Texas, which emission caused air pollution, namely the presence in the atmosphere of the aforesaid air contaminant in such concentration and of such duration as to adversely affect property and to interfere with the normal use and enjoyment of property, the said emission of the air contaminant not being made in compliance with a variance or other order issued by the Texas Air Control Board.

Sections 6.02 and 6.03 of the Penal Code establish the requirements and definitions of culpability for the Penal Code, and Section 1.03(b) makes it clear that these provisions, as well as the other provisions of Title 1, 2, and 3 of the Code, apply to offenses defined by the civil statutes "unless the statute defining the offense provides otherwise." Since nothing in Article 4477-5b provides otherwise, it is clear that Sections 6.02 and 6.03 apply to this statute.

Section 6.02 of the Penal Code provides in part:

(a) Except as provided in Subsection (b) of this section, a person does not commit an offense unless he intentionally, knowingly, recklessly, or with criminal negligence engages in conduct as the definition of the offense requires.

(b) If the definition of an offense does not prescribe a culpable mental state, a culpable mental state is nevertheless required unless the definition plainly dispenses with any mental element.

(c) If the definition of an offense does not prescribe a culpable mental state, but one is nevertheless required under Subsection (b) of this section, intent, knowledge, or recklessness suffices to establish criminal responsibility.

In determining whether the Legislature, through enactment of Sections 6.02 and 1.03(b) of the Penal Code, intended to require proof of a culpable mental state in the offense of air pollution, we must first examine the legislative history of the statute. The present air pollution statute was transferred without change from Article 698d, Sections 1 through 6 of the Penal Code of 1925, pursuant to the authority granted by Section 5 of Acts, 63rd Legislature, Ch. 399.

In *Ex parte Ross*, 522 S.W.2d 214 (Tex. Crim. App. 1975), the defendant claimed that a complaint charging him with the offense of driving while intoxicated was defective because it failed to allege a culpable mental state. The court, after noting that the DWI statute had been transferred verbatim from the criminal statutes to the civil statutes, held that a culpable mental state was not required. The court reasoned that if the Legislature had intended to require proof of a culpable mental state, it could have done so easily when it amended the statute and transferred it from the Penal Code to the civil statutes. Thus, to allow Section 6.02 to supply the missing *mens rea* would be an awkward analysis of the legislature's intent.

The reasoning of the Court of Criminal Appeals in the *Ross* decision was likewise applied in *American Plant Food Corp. v. State*, 587 S.W.2d 679 (Tex. Crim. App. 1979), holding that there was no *mens rea* requirement in the water pollution statute. This concept of strict liability is founded on the premise that the mere doing of the act constitutes the offense and the lack of intent will not exonerate the party nor does this make the prohibited act any less harmful to society.

The appellant cites numerous cases holding that Section 6.02 has been applied to a variety of offenses defined outside the Penal Code to require a culpable mental state. We agree with the State's analysis of these cases in their brief. In each case, the nature of the offense required that an identifiable person be aware of a situation that presented a choice between right and wrong conduct, and the person consciously chose to do the wrong conduct.

In contrast, cases involving air pollution, especially where corporations are involved, would be difficult to prosecute because of the difficulty in charging one person with the responsibility of causing the problem. Considering the risks to public health, to require anything other than a strict liability standard would be to deny the public the right to be protected from hazardous activities.

We overrule the first ground of error.

Notes

Suppose a defendant has been charged with an offense under Section 48.01 of the Texas Penal Code, which provides:

Smoking Tobacco

(a-1) A person commits an offense if the person is in possession of a burning tobacco product, smokes tobacco, or operates an e-cigarette in a facility of a public primary or secondary school or an elevator, enclosed theater or movie house, library, museum, hospital, transit system bus, or intrastate bus, plane, or train which is a public place.

(b) It is a defense to prosecution under this section that the conveyance or public place in which the offense takes place does not have prominently displayed a reasonably sized notice that smoking is prohibited by state law in such conveyance or public place and that an offense is punishable by a fine not to exceed $500.

(c) All conveyances and public places set out in Subsection (a-1) shall be equipped with facilities for extinguishment of smoking materials and it shall be a defense to prosecution under this section if the conveyance or public place within which the offense takes place is not so equipped.

(d) It is an exception to the application of Subsection (a-1) if the person is in possession of the burning tobacco product, smokes tobacco, or operates the e-cigarette exclusively within an area designated for smoking tobacco or operating an e-cigarette or as a participant in an authorized theatrical performance.

. . . .

(f) An offense under this section is punishable as a Class C misdemeanor.

At trial, the defendant testifies on his own behalf and states:

I was at the San Antonio Museum of Art waiting to take the large freight elevator when the doors opened. There were two men and a very large painting inside. One of the men was smoking a cigarette. This man walked out and said: "Hold this please," as he handed me the lit cigarette. It happened so fast, I didn't say yes or know, I just took the cigarette from him and he picked up the painting with this companion and walked away. I never saw him again. A moment later, a security guard came around the corner and told me that I was violating the Texas law against possessing burning tobacco products. I told the guard that it wasn't my cigarette but he wouldn't listen.

The brief testimony at trial included only the defendant's testimony and the testimony of the security guard. The security guard testified he found the defendant in the museum with a burning cigarette in his hand. A sign above the elevator stated smoking was prohibited in the museum, and there was an ashtray near an outside door about ten feet from where the defendant was standing. The guard testified that when he informed the defendant of his violation, the defendant stated that the cigarette was not his own, but the guard informed the defendant that anyone in possession of burning tobacco was guilty whether or not he owned the product.

At the close of the evidence, the defense requested a jury instruction to the effect that the jury should be told a defendant can be found guilty under the statute "only if he intentionally or knowingly possessed the burning tobacco product." The prosecutor argued the proposed instruction misstated the law because 48.01 of the Texas Penal Code is a strict liability offense. The judge overruled the defendant's request and informed the jury it should return a verdict of guilty "if the jurors found beyond a reasonable doubt that the defendant possessed a burning tobacco product in the museum." The jury returned a verdict of guilty. The judge imposed the sentence of a $500 fine.

The defendant appealed to the Fourth Court of Appeals, arguing the trial court erroneously overruled his requested jury instruction. What arguments will the prosecution and defense make on appeal?

Strict Liability Elements

In some cases, an issue may arise as to whether the mental state requirement applies to a particular element or whether it is a strict liability element. The *Gardner* case that follows is a classic example of such an issue in which restricting the mental state requirement to the immediately adjacent element would essentially rob the mental state requirement of any meaning.

Gardner v. State

780 S.W.2d 259 (Tex. Crim. App. 1989)

Campbell, Judge.

Appellant was convicted of the offense of unauthorized use of a motor vehicle. V.T.C.A. Penal Code, § 31.07. Punishment was assessed at three years confinement in the Texas Department of Corrections. In a published opinion, the Fifth Court of Appeals reversed the judgment of the trial court and entered a judgment of acquittal, finding that there was insufficient evidence to support the conviction. *Gardner v. State*, 736 S.W.2d 179 (Tex. App.—Dallas 1987). We granted the State's petition for discretionary review to determine whether the "Court of Appeals erred in holding that the State must prove that the defendant knew that he did not have the owner's consent to drive an automobile before obtaining a conviction for unauthorized use of a motor vehicle." We will affirm. Holding for Δ [handwritten annotations: "ISSUE →" and "Holding for Δ"]

On August 23, 1986, appellant drove from Emory, Texas to Dallas, Texas to visit his father and to go on a date. He stopped at a friend's, "David's," where he met his date. After thirty to forty-five minutes appellant and his date left for Lake Ray Hubbard.

Appellant returned to Dallas the next morning to take his date home. After dropping his date off, he began experiencing engine trouble. Since he lived in Emory, Texas, some ninety miles away, he stopped at "David's" to try to fix his truck sometime around 5:00 a.m. Appellant testified that David loaned him a Camaro to go to an auto parts store and he further testified that he believed that David owned the car.

Officer David Alan Durica testified that, at approximately 5:30 a.m. on August 24th, 1986, appellant was stopped in Dallas County, Texas after failing to use his turn signal indicator. Appellant was driving a stolen 1986 Chevrolet Camaro at the time. The Camaro's license plates had been removed and replaced with paper license tags.

When questioned about the car, the appellant told Durica that he had borrowed the car from a friend named "David." Appellant gave David's phone number to the officer. Durica then had his dispatcher call the telephone number. The dispatcher asked the person at that number whether or not a person at that number owned a vehicle like the one appellant was driving, and whether or not that person knew the appellant. The person at that number denied knowing the appellant or giving him the car. After the person at that telephone number denied knowing him, appellant informed the officer that his truck was parked in the front yard of that address.

Durica testified that he then drove to the address of the appellant's alleged friend. Appellant remained handcuffed in the backseat of the police car while Durica investigated appellant's story. Durica discovered the appellant's truck parked in the backyard. The doors of the truck were unlocked. Inside the truck were the license plates that had been removed from the Camaro. The person at that address denied knowing the appellant. Durica recalled asking the person at that address for the keys to the truck, but did not recall being given any keys. Appellant testified that he did not give the officers the truck keys. He testified that he had given David a set of keys. He retained an ignition key in his pocket. At appellant's request, his truck was impounded.

Durica was later called to testify by the appellant. Although he was not positive, Durica testified that he now recalled that he had gotten the keys to appellant's truck from the appellant. Durica was the officer who drove the truck from the backyard to the front yard to be towed. He stated he could not figure out the gear pattern at first and had trouble moving the truck. Durica also testified that the appellant was travelling in the opposite direction from the parts store for which he was allegedly destined when stopped by police. At trial, appellant waived his right to a trial by jury. Appellant also stipulated as to the ownership of the vehicle and the fact that he did not have the owner's permission to drive the car.

State had to prove A knew he couldn't drive car

The Fifth Court of Appeals reversed appellant's conviction, holding that V.T.C.A. Penal Code, § 31.07 required the State to prove that the defendant knew that he did not have the owner's consent to drive an automobile before obtaining a conviction for unauthorized use of a motor vehicle. The Court of Appeals purported to follow this Court's holding in *Musgrave*.

The State contends that there is no requirement under *Musgrave* that the State prove that the defendant knew he did not have the owner's consent to drive an automobile to support a conviction under Penal Code, § 31.07. The appellant apparently concedes this argument by asking this Court to re-examine our decision in *Musgrave*.

As this Court noted in *Musgrave*, the unauthorized use of a motor vehicle prohibition contained in Section 31.07 is carried over from prior Penal Code art. 1341. In *Musgrave*, this Court was asked to determine the scope of V.T.C.A. Penal Code, § 31.07, which provides that:

> (a) A person commits an offense if he intentionally or knowingly operates another's boat, airplane, or motor-propelled vehicle without the effective consent of the owner.

Must meet elements

This Court held that the State was required to prove that: (1) a person (2) intentionally or knowingly (3) operates an airplane, boat, or motor-propelled vehicle (4) without the effective consent of the owner. Further, the *Musgrave* Court held that the mistaken belief that one has the consent of one authorized to give such consent does not create an additional element of the offense. Thus, under *Musgrave*, the State was not required to prove the defendant knew he did not have the consent of the owner to operate a vehicle to sustain a conviction.

Issue + element

The question before this Court is whether a culpable mental state is applicable to the fourth element under Section 31.07, to wit: "without the effective consent of the owner."

Penal Code, § 6.03 recognizes that the material elements of offenses vary in that they may involve (1) the nature of the forbidden conduct or (2) the attendant circumstances or (3) the result of the conduct. As Judge Roberts aptly stated in his concurrence in *Musgrave*, the majority opinion, while giving effect to the state of mind requirement as it relates to the conduct, ignored that requirement as it relates to the circumstances surrounding the conduct. Judge Roberts reasoned:

81

The offense of unauthorized use of a motor vehicle requires proof of the forbidden conduct and the attendant circumstances of the crime. The State had to show at a minimum that the appellant knowingly operated the motor vehicle of another (the conduct element) without the effective consent of the owner (the attendant circumstances element). Under the approach adopted by Section 6.03 the mental state requirement applies to the attendant circumstances element as well as to the conduct element of the offense. A person acts knowingly with respect to circumstances surrounding his conduct when he is aware that the circumstances exist. In other words, knowledge that the requisite external circumstances exist is an element of the instant offense.

Section 31.07 is not a strict liability offense. The so-called "forbidden conduct"—operating a motor-vehicle—is made unlawful only when the defendant is aware of the attendant circumstances—that the operation of the vehicle is without the owner's consent.

This requirement is implicitly recognized in this Court's decisions in *Woodfox v. State*, 742 S.W.2d 408 (Tex. Crim. App. 1987), and *Lynch, supra*. Both cases involved the defense of mistake of fact in a prosecution for unauthorized use of a motor-vehicle. A mistake of fact defense is authorized under V.T.C.A. Penal Code, § 8.02(a) which provides that:

> (a) It is a defense to prosecution that the actor through mistake formed a reasonable belief about a matter of fact if his mistaken belief negated the kind of culpability required for commission of the offense.

It would be counter-intuitive to allow for a defense that would negate a defendant's mental culpability, yet not require that the State prove that the defendant was aware of the attendant circumstances that would trigger guilt under the statute.

We therefore hold that, in a prosecution under Section 31.07, *supra*, one of the elements to be proven by the State is the knowledge of the defendant that he did not have the consent of the owner to operate the boat, airplane or motor-propelled vehicle in question. To the extent that *Musgrave* is inconsistent with this holding, it is overruled.

The judgment of the Court of Appeals is affirmed.

McCormick, P.J., and Davis, J., concur in the result.

Berchelmann, Judge, dissenting.

I dissent. I agree, however, with the majority that the State must establish a defendant's knowledge of the owner's lack of consent as an element of the offense in unauthorized use of a motor vehicle prosecutions. TEX. PENAL CODE ANN. § 31.07 (West 2015). I likewise agree with the majority that § 31.07 is not a "strict liability" statute.

The record is replete with evidence that appellant knew he did not have the owner's consent to operate the motor vehicle. First, appellant did not, in fact, have the owner's consent. I would characterize this alone as circumstantial evidence sufficient to support that appellant knew he did not have the owner's consent. Such an analysis does not make § 31.07 a strict liability statute, however, for the defendant is entitled to submission and consideration of a defensive charge where supported by the record. This distinction is clearly stated in *Lynch v. State*, 643 S.W.2d 737, 738 (Tex. Crim. App. 1983), wherein we stated that a defendant is entitled to a mistake of fact defense in § 31.07 prosecutions for "to hold such innocent use is no defense would be to make § 31.07 a strict liability offense." Were § 31.07 a strict liability statute, mistake of fact regarding an element of the offense would be irrelevant, as in, for example, a statutory rape prosecution.

In the case at bar, there is additional evidence, beyond that which I would require to find evidentiary sufficiency, that appellant knew he did not have the owner's consent. The stolen vehicle's license plates were found in appellant's vehicle. Appellant's story that he was "borrowing" the stolen car for transportation to an auto parts store is contradicted by the direction in which appellant was traveling. There is, undoubtedly, ample evidence upon which a rational trier of fact could have found the element of knowledge of lack of consent beyond a reasonable doubt.

Notes

RULING

A ruling in *Gardner*—that the mental state only applies to the operation of an automobile—and the circumstance of consent would effectively make the entire statute strict liability because it is hard to imagine being able to operate a motor vehicle unknowingly. In some cases, a policy decision is made that strict liability is appropriate as to the only meaningful element. The *Aviles* case that follows involves the classic example of sex offenses with a minor. What makes the offense a serious felony is the age of the victim, but knowledge or even a lack of negligence as to the age of the minor is irrelevant as a matter of policy. No mental state applies to the question of age because of a policy decision to protect minors from sexual predators and to warn potential defendants to exercise great care.

Reading too broad = SLC

Sexual assault of child [handwritten]

Aviles v. State

No. 04-13-00490-CR, 2014 WL 3339611 (Tex. App.—San Antonio July 9, 2014, no pet.)

Opinion by Sandee Bryan Marion, Justice.

Issue [handwritten]

In a single issue on appeal, appellant asserts the trial court erred by refusing his request to instruct the jury on the defense of "mistake of fact." We affirm. *Holding* [handwritten]

Background

The State indicted appellant for aggravated sexual assault of a child under section 22.021 of the Texas Penal Code. The relevant portion of the indictment alleged appellant "did intentionally and knowingly cause the penetration of the sexual organ of M.R., a child who was younger than fourteen years, by [appellant's] sexual organ." During the jury charge conference, the defense requested a mistake of fact instruction with respect to M.R.'s age, which the trial court denied. A jury subsequently found appellant guilty of aggravated sexual assault of a child under the age of fourteen, and the trial court assessed punishment at fifteen years' confinement.

Discussion

On appeal, appellant asserts he was entitled to a mistake of fact instruction with respect to M.R.'s age. Appellant acknowledges mistake of fact is not an applicable defense in offenses prosecuted under section 22.011 (sexual assault) and section 21.11 (indecency with a child) of the Texas Penal Code. However, appellant asserts that because he was prosecuted under section 22.021 (aggravated sexual assault), those cases holding that mistake of fact is not a defense do not apply to him. We disagree.

A person commits the offense of aggravated sexual assault if the person intentionally or knowingly causes the penetration of the anus or sexual organ of a child by any means if the victim is younger than fourteen years of age. *See* TEX. PENAL CODE ANN. § 22.021(a)(1)(B)(i), (2)(B) (West 2015). When a charge of any sexual offense against a child is made, mistake of fact or the accused's ignorance of the victim's age is not a defense. Recently, the Court of Criminal Appeals reaffirmed this position, stating:

> In prosecutions for sexual assault and aggravated sexual assault the defendant need not know that the victim is a child, and a child cannot consent to sexual acts. These are all strict liability offenses when it comes to child victims. Therefore, we have long held that even a very reasonable mistake of fact with respect to the child victim's age is not a defense to sex offenses. *Child victims SLC* [handwritten]

Ex parte Burns, No. WR–69222–03, 2012 WL 243686, at *4 (Tex. Crim. App. Jan. 25, 2012) (J. Cochran, concurring).

Therefore, we affirm the trial court's judgment.

SLC → doesn't matter if you knew/didn't know (harder to defend self)

Notes

Both the *Gardner* and *Aviles* cases deal the defense of mistake of fact. This defense will be discussed soon in the part of the text that deals with elements the State must prove to win a conviction. Other defenses that can be raised to avoid a conviction will be dealt with later. *Gardner* and *Aviles* explain why this defense is seemingly being taken out of order. Some defenses are independent of the elements of the crime. A person who harms or kills another in self-defense is not claiming a lack of intent or denying that his or her act caused the harm. Rather, the self-defense doctrine justifies conduct that otherwise would be a crime because of factors independent of the elements of the charged criminal offense (the reasonable belief in the necessity to use a reasonable degree of force to combat an unprovoked assaultive threat).

Negation

A mistake of fact defense in contrast is not an independent defense but a negating defense. A person who picks up an umbrella thinking it is hers lacks the mental state required for the crime of theft, even if the umbrella in fact belongs to another. A defendant seeking to avoid a theft conviction can take the counter-punching approach of arguing the state has not proved all of the elements of the offense because of the failure to prove the necessary mental state. Alternatively, the defendant can take the affirmative approach of arguing she has the defense of mistake of fact.

Under age kids → by law deemed unable to give consent

Chapter 5: Transferred Intent

Introduction

Having looked at the culpable mental states provided by the Texas Penal Code from the highest level—intent—to the lowest level—criminal negligence—this chapter returns to the top of the mental state hierarchy, but with a twist. What if there is a discrepancy between the defendant's criminal intent and the result? Unlike the next chapter dealing with mistake of fact, which generally involves a non-criminal intent but an act or result which violates a penal statute, in transferred intent cases, the defendant intends a criminal act or result but accomplishes something different. Is any evil purpose sufficient? The answer is the same as that usually given for legal questions: it depends. The answer depends upon the type of required mental state and the difference between what was intended and what actually occurred. In all of the cases that follow, the required mental state is intent (or intent <u>and</u> knowledge). The doctrine of transferred intent may prevent the conviction of a defendant for a crime requiring intent, but may fail to prevent conviction under a statute that requires the mental state of recklessness or negligence.

Even if the statute is one that requires intent, not all differences between what was intended and what occurred prevent a conviction. Three categories are important with regard to a divergence of the defendant's intent and the actual occurrence:

1. Defendant intends one type of harm but actually causes another type;
2. Defendant intends to harm one victim but causes harm to a different victim;
3. Defendant intends to cause some harm but actually causes greater harm.

The legal rules differ depending upon which category of divergence between intent and result is involved. The following English cases of *Cunningham* and *Faulkner* deal with the first category. These cases deal with long-standing principles of Anglo-American law that reaffirm the principal of *mens rea* in criminal law.

Transferred intent: different type of harm

The Crown **Regina v. Cunningham** "in the name of the people"

41 Court of Criminal Appeal 155 (1957).

theft & suffocating MIL

Byrne, J.

The appellant was convicted . . . upon an indictment framed under § 28 of the Offences against the Person Act which . . . charged that he unlawfully and maliciously caused to be taken by Sarah Wade a certain noxious thing, namely, coal gas, so as thereby to endanger the life of the said Sarah Wade.

The facts were that the appellant was engaged to be married and his prospective mother-in-law was the tenant of a house, No. 7A, Bakes Street, Bradford, which was unoccupied, but which was to be occupied by the appellant after his marriage. Mrs. Wade and her husband, an elderly couple, lived in the house next door. At one time the two houses had been one, but when the building was converted into two houses a wall had been erected to divide the cellars of the two houses, and that wall was composed of rubble loosely cemented.

Stole gas meter

On the evening of January 17, 1957, the appellant went to the cellar of No. 7A, Bakes Street, wrenched the gas meter from the gas pipes and stole it, together with its contents, and in a second indictment he was charged with the larceny of the gas meter and its contents. To that indictment he pleaded guilty and was sentenced to six months' imprisonment. In respect of that matter he does not appeal.

The facts were not really in dispute, and in a statement to a police officer the appellant said: "All right, I will tell you. I was short of money, I had been off work for three days, I got eight shillings from the gas meter. I tore it off the wall and threw it away." Although there was a stop tap within two feet of the meter the appellant did not turn off the gas, with the result that a very considerable volume of gas escaped, some of which seeped through the wall of the cellar and partially asphyxiated Mrs. Wade, who was asleep in her bedroom next door, with the result that her life was endangered.

Lawyer

At the close of the case for the prosecution, Mr. Brodie, who appeared for the appellant at the trial and who has appeared for him again in this court, submitted that there was no case to go to the jury, but the judge, quite rightly in our opinion, rejected this submission. The appellant did not give evidence.

The act of the appellant was clearly unlawful and therefore the real question for the jury was whether it was also malicious within the meaning of section 23 of the Offences against the Person Act, 1861. Issue intent?

Before this court Mr. Brodie has taken three points, all dependent upon the construction of that section. Section 23 provides: "Whosoever shall unlawfully and maliciously administer to or cause to be administered to or taken by any other person any poison or other destructive or noxious thing, so as thereby to endanger the life of such person, or so as thereby to inflict upon such person any grievous bodily harm, shall be guilty of felony. . . ."

Issues Δ argued

Mr. Brodie argued, first, that *mens rea* of some kind is necessary. Secondly, that the nature of the *mens rea* required is that the appellant must intend to do the particular kind of harm that was done, or, alternatively, that he must foresee that that harm may occur yet nevertheless continue recklessly to do the act. Thirdly, that the judge misdirected the jury as to the meaning of the word "maliciously."

malice def.

We have considered . . . the following principles: . . . In any statutory definition of a crime, malice must be taken not in the old vague sense of wickedness in general but as requiring either (1) an actual intention to do the particular kind of harm that in fact was done; or (2) recklessness as to whether such harm should occur or not (i.e., the accused has foreseen that the particular kind of harm might be done and yet has gone on to take the risk of it). It is neither limited to nor does it indeed require any ill will towards the person injured.

We think that this is an accurate statement of the law. In our opinion the word "maliciously" in a statutory crime postulates foresight of consequence.

In his summing-up Oliver J. directed the jury as follows:

"Unlawful" does not need any definition. It is something forbidden by law. What about "malicious"? "Malicious" for this purpose means wicked; something which he has no business to do and perfectly well knows it. "Wicked" is as good a definition as any other which you would get.

Jury should have decided if intent to harm MIL

With the utmost respect to the learned judge, we think it is incorrect to say that the word "malicious" in a statutory offence merely means wicked. We think the judge was, in effect, telling the jury that if they were satisfied that the appellant acted wickedly, and he had clearly acted wickedly in stealing the gas meter and its contents, they ought to find that he had acted maliciously in causing the gas to be taken by Mrs. Wade so as thereby to endanger her life.

In our view it should have been left to the jury to decide whether, even if the appellant did not intend the injury to Mrs. Wade, he foresaw that the removal of the gas meter might cause injury to someone but nevertheless removed it. We are unable to say that a reasonable jury, properly directed as to the meaning of the word "maliciously" in the context of section 23, would without doubt have convicted.

In these circumstances this court has no alternative but to allow the appeal and quash the conviction.

Notes

The defendant's conviction in the *Cunningham* case under a statute requiring proof the defendant "unlawfully and maliciously" endangered the safety of his mother-in-law was overturned because of the improper jury instruction. Could the defendant be tried again for this offense? If there is a second trial, what should the jury instruction say? If the jury returns a guilty verdict after being given a proper instruction, would the conviction be affirmed on a second appeal?

If Cunningham is tried again and the prosecutor merely charges theft of the coins taken from the gas meter, there doesn't seem to be any question of the defendant's guilt of this offense in light of the defendant's admission. Unlike the *Cunningham* case, in *Faulkner*, which follows in the text, the rum, which is the larcenous object of the defendant's desire, is never stolen.

Rule: Malice requires actual intention to do a particular kind of harm or recklessness as to whether such harm should occur or not.

Issue: whether Apellant's actions were also malicious and constituted the crime of felony for malicious administrating of gas to an individual

question of malicious actions should have been determined by jury.
Malice is not limited to nor does it require any ill will toward one person injured.
A foreseeable consequence of his actions could be sufficient
Malice does not require wickedness
Foresteability or recklessness enough to prove malice

Regina v. Faulkner

13 Cox. Crim. Cas. 550 (Crown Cas. Res. Ireland, 1877)

At the Cork Summer Assizes, 1876, the prisoner was indicted for setting fire to the ship Zemindar, on the high seas, on the 26th day of June, 1876. It was proved that the Zemindar was on her voyage home with a cargo of rum, sugar, and cotton, worth 50,000. That the prisoner was a seaman on board, that he went into the bulk head, and forecastle hold, opened the sliding door in the bulk head, and so got into the hold where the rum was stored; he had no business there, and no authority to go there and went for the purpose of stealing some rum . . . that when . . . he had a lighted match in his hand; that the rum caught fire; that the prisoner himself was burned on the arms and neck; and that the ship caught fire and was completely destroyed. At the close of the case for the Crown, counsel for the prisoner asked for a direction of an acquittal on the ground that on the facts proved the indictment was not sustained, nor the allegation that the prisoner had unlawfully and maliciously set fire to the ship proved. The Crown contended that inasmuch as the prisoner was at the time engaged in the commission of a felony, the indictment was sustained, and the allegation of the intent was immaterial.

At the second hearing of the case before the Court for Crown Cases Reserved, the learned judge made the addition of the following paragraph to the case stated by him for the court: "It was conceded that the prisoner had no actual intention of burning the vessel." The learned judge told the jury that although the prisoner had no actual intention of burning the vessel, still if they found he was engaged in stealing the rum, and that the fire took place in the manner above stated, they ought to find him guilty. The jury found the prisoner guilty on both counts, and he was sentenced to seven years penal servitude. The question for the court was whether the direction of the learned judge was right, if not, the conviction should be quashed.

Issue

Barry, J.

A very broad proposition has been contended for by the Crown, namely, that if, while a person is engaged in committing a felony, or, having committed it, is endeavoring to conceal his act, he accidently does some collateral act which if done willfully would be another felony either at common law or by statute, he is guilty of the latter felony. I am by no means anxious to throw any doubt upon, or limit in any way, the legal responsibility of those who engage in the commission of felony, or acts *mala in se*; but I am not prepared without more consideration to give my assent to so wide a proposition. No express authority either by way of decision or dictum from judge or text writer has been cited in support of it. I shall consider myself bound for the purpose of this case by the authority of *Reg. v. Pembliton* (12 Cox C. C. 607). That case must be taken as deciding that to constitute an offence under the Malicious Injuries to Property Act, sect. 51, the act done must be in fact intentional and willful, although the intention and will may (perhaps) be held to exist in, or be proved by, the fact that the accused knew that the injury would be the probable result of his unlawful act, and yet did the act reckless of such consequences. The present indictment charges the offence to be under the 42nd section of the same Act, and it is not disputed that the same construction must be applied to both sections. The jury were directed to give a verdict of guilty upon the simple ground that the firing of the ship, though accidental, was caused by an act done in the course of, or immediately consequent upon,

No malice?

a felonious operation, and no question of the prisoner's malice, constructive or otherwise, was left to the jury. I am of opinion that, according to *Reg. v. Pembliton*, that direction was erroneous, and that the conviction should be quashed. ~~are~~ *Lower ct wrong in jury charge*

Fitzgerald, J.

I concur in opinion with my brother Barry, and for the reasons he has given, that the direction of the learned judge cannot be sustained in law, and that therefore the conviction should be quashed. I am further of opinion that in order to establish the charge of felony under sect. 42, the intention of the accused forms an element in the crime to the extent that it should appear that the defendant intended to do the very act with which he is charged, or that it was the necessary consequence of some other felonious or criminal act in which he was engaged, or that having a probable result which the defendant foresaw, or ought to have foreseen, he, nevertheless, persevered in such other felonious or criminal act. The prisoner did not intend to set fire to the ship; the fire was not the necessary result of the felony he was attempting; and if it was a probable result, which he ought to have foreseen, of the felonious transaction on which he was engaged, and from which a malicious design to commit the injurious act with which he is charged might have been fairly imputed to him, that view of the case was not submitted to the jury. On the contrary, it was excluded from their consideration on the requisition of the counsel for the prosecution. Counsel for the prosecution in effect insisted that the defendant, being engaged in the commission of, or in an attempt to commit a felony, was criminally responsible for every result that was occasioned thereby, even though it was not a probable consequence of his act or such as he could have reasonably foreseen or intended. No authority has been cited for a proposition so extensive, and I am of opinion that it is not warranted by law. Conviction quashed.

Notes

1.   In *Faulkner* there are two incomplete crimes. The defendant had the mental state required for theft but not the act of taking or the result of the owner losing the property. The arson conviction was overturned because the trial judge's instruction allowed the jury to convict based only upon the result needed for arson without proof that the defendant had the mental state required for this offense. Is the state unable to obtain any criminal conviction despite the fact that the defendant clearly had a criminal intent and caused a significant harm? What, if any, possible charges are available to a prosecutor?

2.   Faulkner is a 19th century case that demonstrates the concept of *mens rea* is a long-standing cornerstone of our legal tradition. Not only must the defendant have a guilty mind rather than just a guilty act; the guilty mind must coincide with the criminal act. If Faulkner had accidently kicked over a lantern and burned down the ship, he would not be guilty of arson. There is no different result merely because the defendant had a "wicked" intent to commit a crime (to use the terminology of the judge in *Cunningham*). The *Pembliton* case, referred to in *Faulkner*, goes even further in maintaining this rule. There, the defendant's intent was to harm a person by throwing a stone at the intended victim. The stone missed the intended victim but broke a window. Because we generally regard harm to a person as a more serious type of crime,

the defendant had a worse intent than what he accomplished, unlike Cunningham and Faulkner who caused results worse than their intentions. Nonetheless, the *Pembliton* Court overturned the conviction on the basis of the same refusal to make any type of evil intent satisfy the mental state requirement.

Issue: Were jury's instructions correct, in holding out the element of intent of the prisoner?
If a person commits a felony and in the process of that felony unintentionally commits what would otherwise be considered a felony, is that person guilty of the 2nd felony?

Holding: NO

Rule: Seperate felonies for different charges. Felon should be charged for very act he committed
Intent element not presented at bar.

Reasoning: Differing views of intent not shown to jury.
Jury did not decide if it was necessary result ot theft or if it was probable

Transferred Intent: Different Victim

In contrast to the refusal to transfer intent from one intended crime to an unintended result, the rules of transferred intent are different when the discrepancy between what was intended and what occurred is a (different victim.) The Texas case of *Castillo* demonstrates the Texas rule, which is consistent with the common law tradition of allowable transferred intent.

Castillo v. State

71 S.W.3d 812 (Tex. App.—Amarillo 2002, pet. struck)

Brian Quinn, Justice.

Roy Castillo (appellant) was convicted by a jury of murder. He alleges that the jury charge was improper. We affirm the judgment. *Holding*

Background

After being involved in a fight at a local pool hall and its adjacent parking lot, appellant and a friend drove to appellant's home to obtain firearms, namely a pistol-grip shotgun and a 9mm pistol. Then they returned, with the weapons, to the scene of the fight. Upon arriving at same, the two exited their vehicle and began shooting at a black car. Inside the car sat various people including Ambrose Bustos, one of the participants in the earlier fight, and Julian Moreno. The latter was struck in the head by a bullet and killed. *killed*

When appellant later discovered that someone had died as a result of the shooting, he threw the shotgun, the pistol, and its ammunition clip in the Anchor Lake. In his confession to police, appellant admitted firing his pistol at the car and throwing the weapons in the lake. The weapons were later recovered from the lake.

The State indicted appellant for murdering Moreno. One of its theories at trial involved the concept of transferred intent. That is, the State attempted to show that though appellant and his friend intended to kill Bustos, they succeeded in murdering Moreno. When both litigants rested their respective cases, the court charged the jury. Included therein were paragraphs informing the jury that they could convict appellant for murder if they found he intentionally or knowingly caused the death of Moreno or if he intended to kill Bustos but actually killed Moreno. So too did it instruct the jury on the lesser included offense of manslaughter. The jury eventually found appellant guilty of murder.

Improper Jury Charge

Initial Issue! Appellant initially contends that the trial court's instruction concerning transferred intent was improper.

Regarding the supposed need to instruct the jury that the "acts taken by appellant to show transferred intent must be done knowingly or intentionally," we see two possible interpretations of the appellant's contention. The first is that the court must inform the jury that it can convict only if the actions directed towards the individual whom appellant actually wanted to kill were taken with the requisite *mens rea*. Here, the trial court did just that. It informed the jurors that they could convict only if appellant caused the death of Moreno while "*intending* to cause the death of an individual, Ambrose Leon Bustos. . . ."

The second interpretation of appellant's argument involves the supposed need to state that appellant acted with a particular *mens rea* towards Moreno as he caused the death of Moreno while actually trying to kill Bustos. We find this proposition meritless based upon a plain reading

94

[handwritten annotations: "says+mentions nothing abt intent / what the code actually says"]

of § 6.04(b) of the Penal Code. Though euphemistically called "transferred intent," the concept espoused in that section of the Code does not deal with intent or any other *mens rea*. Rather, it depicts an effort by the legislature to criminalize an act which resulted in injury or harm to someone other than the person to whom the injury or harm was actually directed. As much can be garnered from the wording of the statute. In stating that one "is nevertheless criminally responsible for causing a result if the only difference between what actually occurred and what he [intended, knew or risked] is that a different person was" harmed or injured, the legislature was addressing the results of the conduct. TEX. PENAL CODE ANN. § 6.04(b)(2) (West 2015). That is, it was telling the public that it did not matter who was hurt or affected by the act. As long as the accused intended, knew or risked hurting or affecting a particular person and someone was affected, the accused would be culpable for the crime he tried to commit. So, acting with a particular *mens rea vis-a-vis* the actual victim was and is unimportant, and such a *mens rea* need not be alleged nor proved. Indeed, if this were not so, and if the State were required to allege and prove that the accused acted with a particular mens rea towards the ultimate victim, then their concept of transferred intent would be superfluous. *[handwritten: (unnecessary)]*

[handwritten annotation right margin: "This code doesn't say / (+matters who was affected) / who was affected"]

Accordingly, we affirm the judgment of the trial court. *[handwritten: Holding/Result]*

Notes

[handwritten: Doesn't matter who the victim is]

1.   Another way of looking at the problem of a variance between the victim intended and the victim harmed is that it is irrelevant to the statutory offense. The Texas assault and homicide statutes refer to causing bodily injury or death to "another." A person who shoots at X with intent to kill X but misses and kills Y has both the mental state needed, an intent to kill another, and the forbidden result of causing the death of another. The statute does not require an identity between the victim intended and the victim harmed or killed. This analysis reaches the same result as *Castillo* without transferred intent.

2.   If X shoots at Y and misses, X cannot be convicted of murder because no death was caused—an essential element of murder. If Y is aware of the shot, it might be some form of assault because firing a bullet in the victim's direction would reasonably cause fear in the victim. If X shoots at Y and misses, but hits and kills Z, can X be convicted of attempted murder of Y and the completed murder of Z? In part, this is a multiple criminality issue that will be examined in greater detail in a later chapter. Courts and commentators have differed with regard to this issue. One school of thought is that the transferred intent doctrine is designed to allow a completed crime of two differing parts: the intent to kill Y and the killing of Z (in our example). However, the doctrine should be used only to create a single crime and not to multiply criminality under this theory. Others argue that there are two victims that are described by two differing statutes and the harm created for both should be allowed if the prosecution alleges and proves both offenses.

3.   Should there be some kind of limit on the extent to which transferred intent can be used? Suppose a defendant fires a gun above the heads of a large crowd. Should that be considered an attempted murder or assault of everyone present?

Transferred Intent: Degree of Harm and Mistake of Fact

diff harm or diff victim

The law of transferred intent is substantially similar in all American jurisdictions with regard to a difference between the defendant's intent and the actual results of a different type of harm or a different victim. The approach varies by jurisdiction in the third category—a difference between the degree of harm intended and that actually inflicted. If the defendant intends greater harm than that inflicted, there is no difficulty. If X intends serious bodily injury but only succeeds in causing bodily injury, the mental state is more than sufficient for battery.

A more perplexing problem is the situation where the jury finds the defendant intended bodily injury, but the defendant actually causes serious bodily injury. For example, suppose the defendant testifies she wanted to hit the victim, and she wanted it to hurt, but she didn't want the blow with her fist to cause the victim to fall against the curb, causing serious bodily injury. If the jury believes the testimony, should the defendant's criminal liability be limited to the extent of the defendant's intent or should the defendant be held responsible for the harm actually caused?

When harm more serious is caused which unintended jury is left to decide

The common law approach in criminal law was the same as with tort law. You take your victim as you find him or her. The defendant does not come to court with clean hands. Regardless of the actor's intent, the harm inflicted is the same. In tort law, the victim's compensation is not to be limited to the harm intended, and a defendant's criminal liability is also so limited under the common law approach. Some jurisdictions have softened this outcome in criminal cases where the issue is not compensation for the victim but the condemnation of society and the possible loss of liberty.

The drafters of the Model Penal Code opted to soften the common law rule to the extent of making the issue a jury question. If there is evidence raising the issue of divergence between the harm intended and that caused, the jury is informed that the defendant is nonetheless responsible for the harm actually inflicted, "unless the result is too remote or accidental to justly holding the defendant responsible." Thus, the matter becomes a factual determination for the jury to resolve under the unique facts of the particular case.

Although the drafters of the revised Texas Penal Code in 1974 followed many aspects of the Model Penal Code, they drafted a statute with different and ambiguous language concerning transferred intent. The *Thompson* case that follows deals with a defendant that claimed he did not intend to cause the degree of harm he caused. The trial court instructed the jury in a manner that tracks the confusing language of the relevant Texas statute. *Thompson* is the most recent attempt by the Texas Court of Criminal Appeals to construe the Texas statute, and it joins the issue with another question that is the subject of the next section of the text: the defense of mistake of fact.

negates (nullify)

We have already touched on the subject of mistake of fact because of its close relationship to mental state. If one is mistaken in a way that negates the mental state required for the crime, there is no *mens rea*. Viewed in this way, mistake of fact is merely a more specific and defensive way of referring to the mental state required for the crime. In an area that Presiding Judge Keller describes as one of the most difficult in Texas criminal law, the Court comingles the related questions of mental state, transferred intent, and mistake of fact.

[handwritten top margin: Mistake of fact: a defense to a crime where the mistaken belief, if it were true, would negate a mental state that's an element of the crime. Usually the mistake must be reasonable.]

Thompson v. State

236 S.W.3d 787 (Tex. Crim. App. 2007)

Keller, P.J., delivered the opinion of the Court

In this case we consider the scope of one of the more difficult penal code provisions, which deals with one variant of the law of "transferred intent" in Texas. Texas Penal Code § 6.04(b)(1) provides:

> A person is nevertheless criminally responsible for causing a result if the only difference between what actually occurred and what he desired, contemplated, or risked is that . . . a different offense was committed.

We conclude that the provision can be used under certain circumstances to transfer intent from a lesser offense to a greater offense, even when those offenses are contained within the same penal code section. That conclusion comes with caveats, which we will discuss below. Perhaps the most important caveat is that a defendant subject to this type of transferred intent instruction is entitled (upon request) to a mistake of fact instruction. Finding that the trial court's "transferred intent" instruction was not erroneous, we affirm the judgments of the courts below.

[handwritten: Holding]

I. BACKGROUND
A. The Incident

[handwritten: what actually happened] *[handwritten: brother]*

Appellant was an associate pastor at a Baptist church. His twin brother, Caleb Thompson, was also active in the church. The victim was an eleven-year-old boy who attended a children's Bible-study program at the church. On July 3, 2002, the victim's Bible-study teacher reported to appellant that the child was misbehaving. Appellant drove the child to Caleb's nearby residence. At some point, Caleb joined them. Appellant beat the child with a tree branch. He struck the victim more than 100 times during a period estimated by the child at one-and-a-half hours. During at least part of that time, Caleb helped hold the child down. As a result of the beating, the victim's back was one huge bruise from his neck to his buttocks. A paramedic testified that it was the worst bruising he had ever seen. The victim's blood pressure was low, his heart rate was fast, and he appeared to be undergoing hypovolemic shock, which is an indication that he was losing blood. A doctor testified that the bruising was severe and palpable, indicative of deep tissue bruising, and that the victim's urine was "Coca-Cola colored," indicating collection in the kidneys of a substance called myoglobin, which is released into the blood as a result of the death of muscle cells. The doctor further testified that, as a result of this condition, the child would have died from renal failure if he had not received prompt medical attention.

B. Trial

The injury to a child offenses at issue here are:
(1) intentionally or knowingly causing serious bodily injury, a first-degree felony, and
(2) intentionally or knowingly causing bodily injury, a third-degree felony.[1]

[handwritten bottom margin: Pastor beat child]

Appellant was charged with the first-degree felony of injury to a child and the second-degree felony of aggravated assault.

The charge also contained two sets of instructions, to which appellant objected, that applied the doctrine of "transferred intent" found in Texas Penal Code § 6.04(b)(1). First, the charge contained an abstract instruction tracking the language of that provision. Second, with respect to the injury to a child offense, the charge contained an application paragraph that permitted the jury to find appellant guilty of the first-degree felony if he merely intended to cause *bodily injury*, so long as he actually caused *serious bodily injury*:

> Now, bearing in mind the foregoing instructions, if you believe from the evidence, beyond a reasonable doubt that the defendant . . . intending to cause bodily injury to [L.G.], a child 14 years of age or younger, by striking [L.G.] with a stick, branch, or an object unknown to the Grand Jury, did then and there cause serious bodily injury to [L.G.], a child 14 years of age or younger, by striking [L.G.] with a stick, branch or object unknown to the Grand Jury, and [the defendant] did then and there use or exhibit a deadly weapon, to wit: a stick, a branch, or an object unknown to the Grand Jury, during the commission of this offense, in that the manner of its use or intended use was capable of causing death or serious bodily injury, then you will find the defendant . . . guilty as alleged in Count I. . . .

Appellant was convicted of both offenses and sentenced to confinement for twenty-six years for the offense of injury to a child and for twenty years for the offense of aggravated assault.

C. Appeal

On appeal, appellant contended that the jury charge improperly allowed the jury to elevate the third-degree offense of injury to a child (intentionally or knowingly causing *bodily injury*) to the first-degree offense of injury to a child (intentionally or knowingly causing *serious bodily injury*). The State agreed that the "transferred intent" instructions should not have been given but argued that the error was harmless. The court of appeals, however, relying primarily upon *Honea v. State*, 585 S.W.2d 681 (Tex. Crim. App. 1979), held that no error occurred. After addressing the arguments of both parties, the court of appeals held that "appellant's intent to cause bodily injury to L.G. 'transferred' to the serious bodily injury that actually resulted from appellant's conduct."

D. Discretionary Review

Appellant contends that *Honea* was wrongly decided, and he criticizes the opinion for failing to seriously analyze the issue. He complains that a literal application of § 6.04(b)(1)

---

[1] TEX. PENAL CODE ANN. § 22.04(a) (West 2015) ("A person commits an offense if he intentionally [or] knowingly . . . by act . . . causes to a child . . . (1) serious bodily injury . . . or (3) bodily injury."), (e)-(f) (offense classifications); *see also* § 1.07(a)(46)("'Serious bodily injury' means bodily injury that creates a substantial risk of death or that causes death, serious permanent disfigurement, or protracted loss or impairment of the function of any bodily member or organ").

would result in an extraordinarily broad expansion of criminal liability that the legislature could not possibly have intended.

II. ANALYSIS
A. Precedent

In *Honea*, we construed § 6.04(b)(1). The defendant in that case bound and gagged the victim in a barn and stole $1,200 from his shirt pocket. As a result of lying bound and gagged on the barn floor, the victim inhaled dust, which caused him to cough, vomit, and eventually suffocate. The defendant contended that there was a fatal variance between the allegations in the aggravated robbery indictment and the proof at trial because he did not intentionally and knowingly cause serious bodily injury. Relying upon § 6.04, this Court held that, because the defendant clearly intended to rob the victim and his acts resulted in the offense of aggravated robbery, his intent to rob transferred to the aggravated robbery. In arriving at this conclusion, the Court also cited former Article 42 (a predecessor to § 6.04(b)) and two cases that construed that statute.

only in that a diff. offense was committed

The defendant also complained of the trial court's denial of his request for a mistake of fact instruction. Paraphrasing the predecessor statute, the Court summarily held that "no mistake of fact issue was raised."

In addressing appellant's contention that *Honea* was wrongly decided, we turn to principles of statutory construction. In doing so, we keep in mind that the "doctrine of *stare decisis* indicates a preference for maintaining consistency" with past decisions, especially those that interpret statutory enactments.

B. Statutory Construction

. . . .

2. *Statutory Language*

We begin with the statutory language. Texas Penal Code § 6.04 provides, in its entirety:

(a) A person is criminally responsible if the result would not have occurred but for his conduct, operating either alone or concurrently with another cause, unless the concurrent cause was clearly sufficient to produce the result and the conduct of the actor clearly insufficient.

(b) A person is nevertheless criminally responsible for causing a result if the only difference between what actually occurred and what he desired, contemplated, or risked is that:

(1) a different offense was committed; or

(2) a different person or property was injured, harmed, or otherwise affected.

While the present case involves the construction of subsection (b)(1), the remainder of the statute provides some useful context from which to determine the meaning of that subsection. We make two observations about the statutory language. First, subsection (b) is worded to *discount the significance* of certain types of differences. That is, the subsection makes the difference legally irrelevant, at least for causation purposes. Second, the statute contains two "transferred intent" provisions that use parallel language. They both turn on the "only difference" being a particular type of fact. In subsection (b)(1), that different fact is a different offense while, in subsection (b)(2), that different fact is a different victim or object of the crime.

Although the parties have not raised an issue with respect to the mistake of fact defense found in Texas Penal Code § 8.02, consideration of that section is necessary to our interpretation of § 6.04(b)(1). The mistake of fact defense provides:

> (a) It is a defense to prosecution that the actor through mistake formed a reasonable belief about a matter of fact if his mistaken belief negated the kind of culpability required for commission of the offense.

> (b) Although an actor's mistake of fact may constitute a defense to the offense charged, he may nevertheless be convicted of any lesser included offense of which he would be guilty if the fact were as he believed.

In this case, a mistake of fact regarding the seriousness of L.G.'s injury would seem to negate the charged mental state of intent to cause serious bodily injury. Because appellant intended to commit bodily injury, which is also an offense, the intentional culpable mental state would "transfer" to the serious bodily injury actually committed, but he would have a defense, so long as his mistaken belief about the type of injury he was inflicting was *reasonable*. Of course, he would still be guilty of the lesser-included offense of intending to cause bodily injury.

So, a plain meaning construction of the relevant statutes seems to support *Honea*'s interpretation of the transferred intent provision but appears to conflict with its related holding that the mistake of fact defense is inapplicable.

3. *Extratextual Sources*

In 1962, the American Law Institute issued its official draft of the Model Penal Code, which became highly influential throughout the United States, including in Texas. The Model Penal Code set forth its proposed law of transferred intent in § 2.03:

> (2) When purposely or knowingly causing a particular result is an element of an offense, the element is not established if the actual result is not within the purpose or the contemplation of the actor unless:

> > (a) the actual result differs from that designed or contemplated, as the case may be, only in the respect that a different person or property is injured or affected or that the injury or harm designed or contemplated would have been more serious or more extensive than that caused; or

> > (b) the actual result involves the same kind of injury or harm as that designed or

contemplated and is not too remote or accidental in its occurrence to have a [just] bearing on the actor's liability or on the gravity of his offense.

The Model Penal Code thus recognized that all culpable mental states were subject to being transferred, and it contained "different person or property" provisions similar to the ones in the current Texas Penal Code. But § 2.03 contained no provision transferring culpability between *offenses*. It did contain a provision extending liability to "the same kind of injury" so long as that injury was not "too remote or accidental" to have a "just bearing" on the actor's liability or the gravity of the offense. But the Model Penal Code contained another provision that more explicitly addressed liability for the commission of an unintended offense. That provision was found in the section titled "Ignorance or Mistake," § 2.04:

(1) Ignorance or mistake as to a matter of fact or law is a defense if:

(a) the ignorance or mistake negatives the purpose, knowledge, belief, recklessness or negligence required to establish a material element of the offense;

(b) the law provides that the state of mind established by such ignorance or mistake constitutes a defense.

(2) *Although ignorance or mistake would otherwise afford a defense to the offense charged, the defense is not available if the defendant would be guilty of another offense had the situation been as he supposed.* In such case, however, the ignorance or mistake of the defendant shall reduce the grade and degree of the offense of which he may be convicted to those of the offense of which he would be guilty had the situation been as he supposed.

The Model Penal Code's mistake defense contained no requirement that the mistake be "reasonable." Indeed, the explanatory note indicated that the mistake "defense" was simply an application of the general principles of culpability inherent in any offense containing a culpable mental state:

The matter is conceived as a function of the culpability otherwise required for commission of the offense. Such ignorance or mistake is a defense to the extent that it negatives a required level of culpability or establishes a state of mind that the law provides as a defense. The effect of this section therefore turns upon the culpability level for each element of the offense, established according to its definition and the general principles set forth in Section 2.02.

The Model Penal Code commentary viewed "mistake of fact" as being a mere evidentiary issue:

In other words, ignorance or mistake has only evidential import; it is significant whenever it is logically relevant, and it may be logically relevant to negate the required mode of culpability or to establish a special defense.

In his treatise on criminal law defenses, Robinson explains: "§ 2.04(1) does not provide a general mistake defense but simply states the obvious: If a culpable state of mind is required by an offense definition and cannot be proven because of the defendant's ignorance or mistake, then the defendant cannot be convicted of the offense."[2]

The [Texas] Legislature rejected the proposed provisions [of the proposed Penal Code drawing from Model Penal Code language] that made liability contingent upon whether an accidental occurrence had "a just bearing on the actor's criminal responsibility or the gravity of his offense." Instead, the Legislature created § 6.04(b)(1), which extended liability where the "only difference" with respect to the actor's culpability was that a "different offense was committed."

Although the proposed version simply required that the defendant's mistake be an "honest" one, the enacted version requires that the mistaken belief be "reasonable." This requirement reflects language found in the prior version of the statute. As with the transferred intent provision, then, the mistake of fact defense appears to incorporate elements from both the Model Penal Code and the prior version of the Texas Penal Code.

The history of these two provisions reveals that the law of transferred intent with respect to offenses has been entwined with the law of mistake. Given that history, it seems probable that the Legislature intended in its enactment of the current Penal Code that these two aspects of the law go hand-in-hand. A codified, specialized example of this interaction may be found in the current Penal Code in the offense of murder. The murder statute describes three methods of committing the offense: (1) intentionally or knowingly causing the death of an individual, (2) intending to cause serious bodily and committing an act clearly dangerous to human life that causes the death of an individual, and (3) felony murder. The first method is the traditional form of murder, while the third is the new (in 1974) offense of felony murder. But the second method is a straightforward application of the doctrine of the transferred intent of offenses, along with conditions that negate a mistake of fact defense. A person who "intends to commit serious bodily injury" intends thereby to commit the offense of aggravated assault. By actually causing death, the person commits the unintended offense of murder. And committing "an act clearly dangerous to human life" negates the reasonableness requirement found in the mistake of fact defense. By contrast, the offense of *capital* murder contains what appears to be a sort of anti-transfer element: the offense specifically requires that a murder be committed "as defined under Section 19.02(b)(1)," the provision proscribing intentional and knowing murders.

We also observe that applying the mistake of fact defense to the transfer of intent between offenses mitigates greatly the concern that a person could be penalized far beyond his actual culpability. At the same time, it has the salutary effect of placing some onus on the person who intends to commit a lesser offense to exercise care that a greater one is not in fact committed. Our interpretation seems to be the only one that gives meaning and effect both to § 6.04(b)(1) and to § 8.02.

4. *Conclusion*

Given the plain language and the history of the provisions at issue, we conclude that § 6.04(b)(1) does indeed authorize the transfer of a culpable mental state between offenses contained in the same statute and also between greater and lesser included offenses. That

---

2. PAUL H. ROBINSON, CRIMINAL LAW DEFENSES, Vol. 1, Ch. 3, § 62(d), p. 262 (1984).

authorization may be overridden by language defining a particular offense, as in the offense of capital murder, but no such impediment arises with respect to the injury-to-a-child offense. Where § 6.04(b)(1) permits the transfer of a culpable mental state, mistake of fact may be raised as a defense. The mistake must be reasonable for it to constitute a circumstance that exculpates the defendant of the offense charged, and of course, the defendant would still be guilty of any lesser included offense that would be applicable if the facts were as the defendant believed. Given our holding, we overrule *Honea* to the limited extent that it held that a defendant is not entitled to a mistake-of-fact instruction. A is entitled to mistake of fact inst.

C. Jury Charge

A didn't request MoF so no error

The trial court correctly submitted the law of transferred intent in the jury charge. The charge contained no instruction regarding the mistake of fact defense, but appellant failed to request its submission, and as a result, no error occurred with respect to the absence of that defensive instruction. Although our holding regarding the mistake of fact defense constitutes a new proposition of law, that does not relieve appellant of the obligation to preserve such a claim. Even new rules that are held to be retroactive can be forfeited by a party's failure to complain at trial.

We affirm the judgment of the court of appeals. Holding

Notes

1.   Note the importance of preserving issues for appellate review. Because no request was made for a mistake of fact jury instruction, the defendant is not able to have this claim considered on the merits. Of course, in light of the fact that *Honea* was the prevailing law at the time of Thompson's trial, it is not surprising his trial attorney did not think to ask for such an instruction. Even if the attorney was prescient enough to see a connection between mistake of law and transferred intent, counsel likely would have decided that a mistake of fact jury instruction request would be futile because the trial judge would have had to violate the law as it then existed in order to grant the instruction. However, futility does not excuse the procedural default of failing to make a contemporaneous objection. A wise attorney litigates for the future as well as the present. It is important to ask even if you know the answer may be "no." Otherwise, you will not have presented a record that might be the basis for changing the law.

2.   Are you persuaded by Judge Keller's compromise? The prosecution is entitled to an instruction stating the intent to cause some injury (transient pain) may be transferred to the serious bodily injury caused (severe bruising and near death). In effect, this means if the defendant intended a little harm, the jury should infer he or she intended the greater harm caused. In other words, no mental state is required as to the greater harm if the jury finds an intent to cause the lesser harm.

On the other hand, the defense is given a method to present the defense of, "I didn't mean to cause so much harm" by presenting a mistake of fact defense and seeking an instruction to that effect. In other words, the defendant will claim, "I was reasonably mistaken about the severity of the injury that I intentionally caused." At first blush, this seems to mean if there is intent to cause any injury, the defendant can be guilty of any degree of harm caused if the defendant was negligent in failing to prevent the greater degree of harm. This reads a negligence standard into a statutory offense that says nothing about negligence. If the justification is that a negligence standard is better for the defendant than no argument being allowed about a mistake, consider that the defensive instruction will tell the jury the reasonable mistake must negate the mental state required for the crime, which is intent or knowledge. Is this shotgun marriage of transferred intent and mistake of fact destined to live happily ever after, or will it end badly?

3.   The confusion in this area of Texas criminal law is in part due to the poorly worded Texas statute. Section 6.04(b) states: "A person is nevertheless criminally responsible for causing a result if the only difference between what actually occurred and what he desired, contemplated, or risked is that: (1) a different offense was committed; or (2) a different person or property was injured, harmed, or otherwise affected." Subsection (2) is a codification of the common law as expressed in cases like *Castillo*. If X intends to shoot Y, but misses and instead kills Z, then X is guilty of the murder of Z.

However subsection (1) is problematic. What is meant by a different "offense"? One could interpret this to mean that if Faulkner intended to steal rum, but by igniting the rum and burning the ship, he committed arson and is nonetheless guilty. Of course, arson requires a mental state of intending to burn the property, which Faulkner lacks. The statute is unclear, and it might be unconstitutional for the legislature to require a mental state, but then to relieve the State of the obligation to prove it. *See Mullaney v. Wilbur* later in the text. In fact, Texas cases have followed the approach of *Faulkner* and *Cunningham* in holding that intent does not transfer to a different type of harm. However, the poorly-worded statute is no help in deciding these cases, and it offers no clue as to legislative intent as to the severity of harm question in cases like *Thompson*.

Chapter 6: Mistake of Fact

Introduction

The first part of this text deals primarily with what the state must prove in order to win a criminal conviction—elements like mental state, an act, and causation. After a brief detour into the particular subject of homicide offenses, we will then delve into defenses. Unlike necessary statutory elements of the offense that the state must allege and prove, defenses require the defendant's participation in raising and perhaps shouldering a burden of persuasion in order to win an acquittal on defensive grounds. As we will see when we discuss the matter more deeply later in the text, it is the requirement that the defendant bear some burden that makes an issue a defense rather than an element. The burden on the defendant is a burden of production (some evidence to put the matter into the case) and, sometimes, a burden of persuasion (the defendant must convince the jury typically by a preponderance of the evidence of the veracity of the defense claim)

With many defenses there is only a burden of production. Once met, the defensive matter is at issue, but the State must disprove the defense beyond a reasonable doubt. Even though the State has the same burden as with elements, the defense differs because the defendant must take the initiative to inject issue into the case. If this burden is not met, the State has no burden to disprove a potential defense. Elements are different. The state must allege all essential elements in a charging instrument (an indictment or information in most criminal cases) and must convince the jury (or the judge in a bench trial) that the elements have been shown beyond a reasonable doubt.

The reason we are taking up the defense of mistake of fact now instead of with other defenses is the close relationship between the required mental state for the crime and the defensive claim of a lack of a culpable mental state due to a mistake that negates the required mental element for the crime. For example, a person who picks up an umbrella, thinking that it is hers, lacks the mental state required for the crime of theft, even if the umbrella in fact belongs to another. A defendant seeking to avoid a theft conviction can take the counter-punching approach of arguing the state has not proved all the elements of the offense because of the failure to prove the necessary mental state. Alternatively, the defendant can take the affirmative approach of arguing she has a defense of mistake of fact.

Mistake of fact is the opposite side of the mental state coin because the defense only applies if the mistake negates the required mental element for the crime. Thus, the defense is established only if the mistake is relevant. A mistake with regard to a strict liability element is not relevant. We saw that previously with *Aviles*, a mistake as to the age of the person with whom Aviles had sexual relations is irrelevant under traditional statutory rape offenses because the mental state does not extend to the critical factor of the victim's age.

If the legislature redefined theft as an offense when a person intentionally takes property that in fact belongs to another, the mental state requirement might be interpreted as applying only to the act of taking and not to the issue of ownership. You may recall that the *Musgrave* case (which was overruled in *Gardner*) took this approach. The intent was interpreted to apply only to the operation of an automobile and not to the issue of ownership, which was a strict liability element. *Gardner* changed the rule, which now permits an instruction based upon a defense of, "I thought I had the permission of the owner." Under the *Musgrave* view of the offense, that claim was irrelevant. The *Ingram* case that follows illustrates the need to have a relevant mistake in order to claim the defense of mistake of fact.

Mistake of fact had nothing to do w/ culpability

Ingram v. State *burglary of habitation*

261 S.W.3d 749 (Tex. App.—Tyler 2008, no pet.)

Brian Hoyle, Justice.

On November 19, 2006, Appellant burglarized a home in Lindale, Texas. Appellant was arrested and charged by indictment with burglary of a habitation. The jury found Appellant guilty and assessed his punishment at thirty-six years of imprisonment and a $4,000 fine. This appeal followed.

Appellant argues that the trial court erred by failing to give an instruction for the jury to consider evidence that Appellant did not believe the structure he entered was a habitation. We have assumed, without deciding, that sufficient evidence was presented to warrant a mistake of fact instruction if such an instruction was otherwise proper under the law. Therefore, we determine whether such an instruction was otherwise proper.

Appellant has asserted that his belief that the structure in question was not a habitation was relevant to a defense of mistake of fact. For evidence to relate to a mistake of fact defense under section 8.02(a), the mistaken belief asserted must "negate the kind of culpability required for the commission of the offense." TEX. PENAL CODE ANN. § 8.02(a) (West 2015). Section 30.02 of the penal code, which sets forth the relevant offense, prescribes the culpable mental state in regard to the actor's purpose for entering the habitation. *See* TEX. PENAL CODE ANN. § 30.02 (West 2015). It does not require a culpable mental state in regard to the habitation element of the offense. *See* TEX. PENAL CODE ANN. § 30.02 (West 2015); *see also Mabra v. State*, 997 S.W.2d 770, 774 (Tex. App.—Amarillo 1999, pet. ref'd) ("The elements of burglary of a habitation are (1) a person (2) without the effective consent of the owner (3) entering a habitation (4) with intent to commit felony or theft."). Therefore, Appellant's alleged belief that the structure was abandoned did not relate to the culpable mental state to commit the offense. As such, Appellant was not entitled to a mistake of fact instruction regarding his belief that the structure was not a habitation.

Notes

The need for a relevant mistake and the lack of applicability of a mistake of fact claim to a strict liability element is a reflection of the element-matching approach of the mistake of fact defense, as envisioned by the drafters of the Model Penal Code. As the Texas Court of Criminal Appeals put it, "[t]he drafters of the proposed [revised Texas] penal code viewed the mistake-of-fact defense as essentially redundant of the requirement that the State prove the mental element of an offense, but they included the defense as a method of placing upon the defendant the burden of producing evidence so that a mistake of fact is something the prosecution does not have to negate unless raised." *Celis v. State*, 416 S.W.3d 419, 431 (Tex. Crim. App. 2013).

Under this redundant mental state approach, the type of mistaken belief needed for a mistake of fact defense depends upon the mental state element or elements of the statutory offense. If there is a subjective mental state element, a defendant's honest mistaken belief inconsistent with the mental state provides either a defense or an absence of required proof as to an element. If the mental state requirement is one of the rare statutes providing that negligence is enough for criminal liability, the defendant's mistaken belief to negate the required mental state must be relevant, honestly held, and reasonable. If the statutory offense is strict liability, a mistake of fact is irrelevant because there is no mental state to be negated. The following chart, phrased in terms of the umbrella hypothetical example, summarizes this element matching aspect of mistake of fact.

If the defendant claims she thought she owned the umbrella, her mistaken belief provides a defense if the jury finds the defendant:

Nature of the Defendant's Belief	Statutory Mental State as to Ownership
Honestly believed it was his umbrella	Intentionally, knowingly, recklessly
Reasonably believed it was his umbrella	Negligently
No defense regardless of belief	Strict liability

The Model Penal Code approach to mistake of fact constituted a repudiation of a common law rule that had been much criticized. The common law of mistake of fact made the type of belief that was required for a mistake of fact defense depend upon whether the crime was one with a general intent or a specific intent. If the offense required a specific intent, then an honest or good faith mistake that negates the specific intent required for commission of the offense constituted a mistake of fact defense, even if the mistake was unreasonable. Under the common law, for general intent crimes, a mistake of fact defense required a relevant mistake that was both honest and reasonable.

The Model Penal Code advocated eliminating the confusing and inconsistently defined terms of general and specific intent and criticized what it regarded as an inconsistent approach that resulted from its application to the problem of mistake of fact. If the defendant committed theft by taking an umbrella that she thought she owned, the jury could only acquit if the jury found the defendant's mistaken belief to be reasonable. (Although the defendant could be acquitted if the prosecution failed to prove that the defendant intended to take another's property.) If, on the other hand, the indictment charged the defendant with burglary by intentionally entering the property of the owner with intent to take the same umbrella, the defendant's belief only had to be honestly held for the jury to find in the defendant's favor on a mistake of fact claim. *I.e.,* I only recently moved into the row of identically appearing townhouses and I opened the unlocked door to take what I thought was my own umbrella.

This distinction made no sense to the drafters of the Model Penal Code. Either the jury should disbelieve the defendant's claim of an honestly held belief that negates the mental state or the jury should acquit because the defendant lacked the required mental state (assuming jurors believed the defendant's mistake claim). To require a reasonable belief reduced the mental state to one of objective negligence when the statute requires the defendant possess a subjective *mens rea*.

Although a number of states adopted this part of the Model Penal Code, Texas took a different approach in drafting Article 8.02 of the Texas Penal Code:

> (a) It is a defense to prosecution that the actor through mistake formed a reasonable belief about a matter of fact if his mistaken belief negated the kind of culpability required for commission of the offense.

The statute does not distinguish between general and specific intent crimes and seems to allow a mistake of fact defense only when the mistake is reasonable. The *Moore* case that follows is an example of one in which the mistake of fact instruction tracks the requirements of 8.02.

Moore v. State

No. 2-08-039-CR, 2009 WL 1996290
(Tex. App.—Fort Worth, July 9, 2009, no pet.)

Sue Walker, Justice.

Appellant Casey J. Moore appeals his conviction for theft of property with a value of more than $1,500 but less than $20,000, arguing that the evidence at trial was both legally and factually insufficient to sustain the conviction. We will affirm. *Holding*

Moore's grandmother, Eloise Parmes, received widow's benefits from the Department of Veteran's Affairs ("VA"). The VA directly deposited $935 per month into a Bank of America checking account held jointly by Mrs. Parmes and Moore. The direct deposits from the VA were the only deposits made into this joint checking account. By law, Mrs. Parmes's widow's benefits were to cease upon her death.

Mrs. Parmes died on November 18, 2002. No one informed the VA of her death, and for approximately a year and a half the VA continued to directly deposit the benefits into the joint checking account. The VA deposited a total of $15,212 into Mrs. Parmes's and Moore's joint account between the time of her death and the termination of the account. After Mrs. Parmes's death, Moore wrote checks totaling $14,100 from the joint checking account to Texas Express Movers, a business owned by him and his wife.

The VA eventually learned of Mrs. Parmes's death and ceased making the benefit payments. The VA then began an investigation into the benefits it had paid after Mrs. Parmes's death that were no longer in the joint account. During that investigation, Moore informed Agent Bryan Sewell that Mrs. Parmes had told him that he could use the benefit payments to pay for moving and storing her household goods. Moore claimed that he wrote checks from the joint checking account to Texas Express Movers and used cash or credit cards to pay a third party moving company, Deluxe Movers, to move and store Mrs. Parmes's belongings. Texas Express Movers paid $2,000 to Deluxe Movers between the time of Mrs. Parmes's death and the termination of the joint checking account.

Following the investigation, Moore was indicted for theft of property from Agent Sewell. A jury found Moore guilty of theft of more than $1,500 but less than $20,000. The trial court assessed his punishment at two years' confinement, probated for five years, and $13,329 in restitution. This appeal followed.

 Moore argues that the evidence at trial was legally and factually insufficient to support the jury's finding that he intended to unlawfully appropriate the money deposited by the VA into the joint checking account.

Under Texas law, a theft is committed when a person unlawfully appropriates property with intent to deprive the owner of that property. TEX. PENAL CODE ANN. § 31.03(a) (West 2015). Appropriation of property is unlawful when it is without the owner's effective consent.

110

TEX. PENAL CODE ANN. § 31.03(b)(1) (West 2015). "Appropriate" means to acquire or otherwise exercise control over property other than real property. *Id.* § 31.01(4)(B). "Deprive" means to withhold property from the owner permanently or for so extended a period of time that a major portion of the value or enjoyment is lost to the owners. *Id.* § 31.01(2)(A). "Effective consent" includes consent by a person legally authorized to act for the owner. *Id.* § 31.01(3).

For a person to act with intent, it must be his conscious objective or desire to engage in a particular conduct or a particular result. *Id.* § 6.03(a). Intent is most often proved through the circumstantial evidence surrounding the crime, rather than through direct evidence. In determining whether the defendant had criminal intent to commit theft, we may consider whether the defendant experienced personal gain from the property obtained from the owner. *See King v. State*, 17 S.W.3d 7, 17 (Tex. App.—Houston [14th Dist.] 2000, pet. ref'd) (noting that evidence that King had criminal intent was shown in part by his use of complainant's money for sole purpose of paying personal expenses and purchasing items for personal benefit). *Use of money for personal use → can lead to intent*

Here, Moore transferred approximately $15,000 from the joint checking account into an account for his business, Texas Express Movers. Although Moore told Agent Sewell that he then used the funds to pay Deluxe Movers—using cash and credit cards—to move and store his grandmother's household items, the evidence showed that he paid Deluxe Movers only $2,000, leaving approximately $13,000 of the monies Moore took unaccounted for by this explanation. The record reflects that Moore spent funds from the Texas Express Movers account at various establishments, including a pub, grocery stores, and restaurants.

A's arguement says π did not show intent

Moore argues that the State failed to prove that he appropriated the property with the requisite intent because Mrs. Parmes gave him permission to use the funds to move and store her goods. But by law after Mrs. Parmes died she was not entitled to receive and did not own any of the VA benefits deposited into the joint checking account. Agent Sewell testified that he was the de facto owner of all VA funds deposited in the joint checking account following the death of Mrs. Parmes. And no evidence exists that Moore at any point acquired the effective consent of either the VA or Agent Sewell to take the VA widow's benefits deposited in the joint checking account. He simply removed the funds from the joint checking account and deposited them into his own business account.

Moore also contends that he did not know he had a duty to inform the VA of Mrs. Parmes's death and did not know that he was not entitled to spend the VA funds after her death. Consequently, he argues that these mistakes of fact negated the requisite mental state for theft.

Mistake-of-fact instructions were included in the jury charge. The jury was instructed that "it is a defense to prosecution that a person through mistake formed a reasonable belief about a matter of fact if his mistaken belief negated the kind of culpability required for commission of the offense charged." The jury charge also included an application paragraph on mistake of fact and instructed the jury to find Moore not guilty if they found that Moore, "through mistake, formed a reasonable belief that he was entitled to receive and disburse monies received, if any, from the Veteran's Administration."

Whether Moore's purported mistake of fact was reasonable and negated the requisite criminal intent was for the jury to decide. Although Moore claimed a purported mistake of fact and offered an explanation for his conduct, the jury was not required to believe him. The jury could have reasonably concluded that an ordinary and prudent person in Moore's position would have understood that he was not entitled to his deceased grandmother's widow's benefits from the VA. The jury could have inferred that Moore possessed the specific intent to commit theft based on the facts that he never informed the VA of his grandmother's death, never applied to receive her benefit funds, and removed the entirety of those funds from her account and placed them in his own business account. *See Coronado v. State*, 508 S.W.2d 373, 374 (Tex. Crim. App. 1974) ("Specific intent to commit theft can be inferred from the surrounding circumstances.").

Viewing all of the evidence in the light most favorable to the prosecution and resolving all conflicting inferences in favor of the prosecution, we hold that a rational trier of fact could have found the essential elements of theft of more than $1,500 but less than $20,000 beyond a reasonable doubt, including that Moore intended to deprive the VA of its funds and that Moore's explanation for his actions was merely part of a ruse to accomplish the theft.

We affirm the judgment of the trial court.

Holding

Notes

1.   Could the defendant claim the jury instruction requiring a reasonable belief is inconsistent with the statutory requirement of the intent required for conviction? Given the Texas statutory requirement of a reasonable mistaken belief, was the mistake of fact claim the best manner for presenting the defendant's theory that he had the permission of the owner and he was unaware of a notification to the government requirement? Do you think a different manner of presenting the same claim would have mattered to the jury?

2.   What if the defense argued his mistake negated the mental state, but did not ask for an instruction on mistake of fact? Would that prevent the defendant from presenting his claim that he had the permission of the owner and he was unaware of a notification requirement? Could the prosecution ask for a mistake-of-fact defense instruction because it decreases the mental state with regard to the crucial disputed issue from intent to negligence?

3.   What if the defendant requested an instruction on the defense of mistake of fact, and it was refused by the trial court? Despite not following the Model Penal Code approach of the redundant mistake-of-fact defense, the close identity of mental state and mistake of fact has influenced Texas courts in cases in which a trial court has refused to give a jury instruction on the statutory mistake-of-fact defense. In cases where a jury instruction is erroneously refused because, on appeal, the defense was ruled to have met the production burden, the courts have held that no error occurred because jury instructions concerning mental state adequately addressed the issue or, alternatively, the error in refusing the instruction was harmless for the same reason.

Another line of cases dealing with claims of ineffective assistance of counsel also supports the conclusion that Texas courts regard the mistake-of-fact statute as superfluous because the State must prove *mens rea* beyond a reasonable doubt (unless the statute or the element in question is strict liability, which would also prevent a valid claim of mistake of fact). In a case in which the defendant was charged with forgery of a writing, TEX. PENAL CODE sec. 32.21(b), the State was required to prove he acted "with intent to defraud or harm another." The defendant claimed he mistakenly believed the bills he passed were authentic. The appellate court found that defense counsel did not provide ineffective assistance by failing to request a jury instruction on mistake of fact because "proof of the culpable mental state necessarily proves lack of mistake regarding the authenticity of the bills." *Okonkwo v. State*, 398 S.W.3d 689, 695 (Tex. Crim. App. 2013).

if culpability is there cannot raise mistake of fact defense

In a similar case, the court ruled a mistake-of-fact instruction was unnecessary because "the jury could not have convicted the defendant under the charge the jury was given if they believed his story that he did not know" the person he assaulted was a police officer. The jury charge instructed the jury they had to find the defendant knew the victim was a public servant in order to convict him of "Assault of a Public Servant." The appellate court held that the trial court did not err in failing to submit the "didn't know the police were police" mistake-of-fact instruction because the instruction was not necessary. *Traylor v. State*, 43 S.W.3d 725, 730 (Tex. App.—Beaumont 2001, no pet.) (citing *Bruno v. State*, 845 S.W.2d 910 (Tex. Crim. App. 1993) ("The jury heard both stories. As they would have necessarily been required to disbelieve appellant's story before they could find sufficient evidence to convict, the instruction need not have been given in the instant case.")).

Not all claims of mistake of fact arise in such a benign setting as the wrong umbrella taken by an absent-minded person. The *Morgan* case that follows in the text has attracted a great deal of controversy and commentary. The English House of Lords resulted in a split decision, with the majority finding the trial court erred by requiring the jury to find the defendants had a reasonable mistaken belief, rather than just an honestly held negating belief. Despite the error, the judges essentially found the error harmless because the jury's verdict was not affected by the erroneous instruction. This was based in part upon the fact that some of the defendants claimed not to have participated in the events that were the subject of trial and then changed their story in order to claim an honest belief there was consent. Does the *Morgan* case convince you the Texas Legislature had good reason to retain the requirement of a reasonable mistaken belief?

Director of Public Prosecutions v. Morgan

House of Lords, 1975 [1976] A.C. 182, [1975] 2 W.L.R. 913, [1975] 2 All E.R. 347.

Appeal by the defendants from an order of the Court of Appeal (Criminal Division) dismissing their appeals against conviction.

The appellants were convicted at Stafford Crown Court on January 24, 1974; Morgan of aiding and abetting rape, Parker of aiding and abetting rape and of rape; McLarty of aiding and abetting rape and of rape; McDonald of rape and of aiding and abetting rape. They were sentenced to concurrent terms of four years' imprisonment and Morgan to concurrent terms of 10 years' imprisonment.

Morgan was a senior N.C.O. in the Royal Air Force. He was 37 years old, his wife 34, and they had been married for about 13 years and had boys of 11 and 12. For some time husband and wife had been on poor terms, and she had engaged in two love affairs, at least one of them being (as Mrs. Morgan alleged) at her husband's instigation. Of the other three accused, one was nearly 20, the other two were in their twenties, all three of them serving in the Royal Air Force. It was common ground that Morgan invited the other three accused, all complete strangers to him, that night to go back to his house and have intercourse with his wife and that as he drove them from Wolverhampton to his home at Cosford he supplied each of them with a contraceptive. The only issue between the various accused relating to this part of the case was that Morgan denied the assertion of the others that during the car journey he told them that his wife might put up a show of struggling, but that this would only be a charade stimulating her sexual excitement, as in reality she would welcome intercourse with them. They claimed that, although they were at first incredulous, Morgan finally persuaded them that he was serious and that their behavior thereafter was throughout based on their belief that Mrs. Morgan was indeed only play-acting. Certainly she could have done nothing more than she did to resist the attacks made upon her, and before the House of Lords counsel for the appellants accepted that in fact she never did consent to what transpired from the moment the four men reached Morgan's home. She was awakened from sleep in a bedroom which she shared with her 11-year-old son and her evidence was that all four accused in part dragged and in part carried her into another room which contained a double bed. She claimed that she struggled violently and shouted "Police!" several times until a hand was placed over her mouth, that both children were awakened and that thereafter each of the four accused had sexual intercourse with her. It was established that, as soon as the three strangers had departed and Morgan had gone to bed, Mrs. Morgan drove off to Cosford Hospital and complained of having been raped, her case being that she did all she could to resist but that she was throughout held down on the bed by three men while the fourth had intercourse with her.

Lord Cross of Chelsea: The question of law which is raised by the appeal is whether the judge was right in telling the jury that, if they came to the conclusion that Mrs. Morgan had not consented to the intercourse in question but that the defendants believed or may have believed that she was consenting to it, they must nevertheless find the defendants guilty of rape if they were satisfied that they had no reasonable grounds for so believing.

Rape Case

The Sexual Offences Act 1956, which provides by section 1(1) that it is an offence *Statute to abide by* "for a man to rape a woman," contains no definition of the word "rape." No one suggests that rape is an "absolute" offence to the commission of which the state of mind of the defendant with regard to the woman's consent is wholly irrelevant. The point in dispute is as to the quality of belief which entitles the defendant to be acquitted and as to the "evidential" burden of proof with regard to it.

Was As belief qualified

Rape is not a word in the use of which lawyers have a monopoly and the question to be answered in this case, as I see it, is whether according to the ordinary use of the English language a man can be said to have committed rape if he believed that the woman was consenting to the intercourse and would not have attempted to have it but for his belief, whatever his grounds for so believing. I do not think that he can.

Lord Hailsham of St. Marylebone: Bridge J., in giving the judgment of the Court of Appeal, attempted to do so by three propositions which, again, I quote in extensor. He said:

The relevant principles can perhaps be restated in the following propositions:

1. In all crimes the Crown has both the evidential and the probative burden of showing that the accused did the prohibited act.

2. Wherever the definition of a crime includes as one of its express ingredients a specific mental element both the evidential and the probative burden lie upon the Crown with respect to that element. In seeking to rebut the Crown's case against him in reference to his state of mind the accused may and frequently does assert his mistaken belief in non-existent facts. Of course it is right that in this context the question whether there were reasonable grounds for the belief is only a factor for the jury's consideration in deciding whether the Crown has established the necessary mental element of the crime. This is because the issue is already before the jury and no evidential burden rests upon the accused.

3. But where the definition of the crime includes no specific mental element beyond the intention to do the prohibited act, the accused may show that though he did the prohibited act intentionally he lacked *mens rea* because he mistakenly but honestly and reasonably, believed facts which, if true, would have made his act innocent. Here the evidential burden lies upon the accused but once evidence sufficient to raise the issue is before the jury the probative burden lies upon the Crown to negative the mistaken belief. The rationale of requiring reasonable grounds for the mistaken belief must lie in the law's consideration that a bald assertion of belief for which the accused can indicate no reasonable ground is evidence of insufficient substance to raise any issue requiring the jury's consideration. Thus, for example, a person charged with assault upon a victim shown to have been entirely passive throughout who said he had believed himself to be under imminent threat of attack by the victim but could indicate no circumstance giving cause for such a belief would not discharge the evidential burden of showing a mistaken belief that he was acting lawfully in self-defense.

In the event Bridge J. then went on to subsume rape under the third and not the second heading and so to reach the conclusion:

115

The correct view, we think, is that, on proof of the fact of absence of consent from circumstances in the nature of the case must have come to the notice of the defendant, he may be presumed to have appreciated their significance, and it is this presumption which casts upon the defendant the evidential burden of showing an honest and reasonable belief in consent before any issue as to his state of mind can arise for the jury's consideration.

He goes on to say that, once the "evidential" burden is discharged the "probative burden" is cast once more on the Crown.

With due respect, I do not believe the conclusion follows. I can see no reason why the class of case to which his second proposition applies should be limited to cases where the mental ingredient is limited to a "specific mental element."

I believe the law on this point to have been correctly stated by Lord Goddard C.J. in *Steane* (1947) 32 Cr.App.R. 61, 66; [1947] K.B. 997, 1004, when he said:

> If on the totality of the evidence there is room for more than one view as to the intent of the prisoner, the jury should be directed that it is for the prosecution to prove the intent to the jury's satisfaction, and if, on review of the whole evidence, they either think the intent did not exist or they are left in doubt as to the intent, the prisoner is entitled to be acquitted.

Once one has accepted, what seems to me abundantly clear, that the prohibited act in rape is non-consensual sexual intercourse, and that the guilty state of mind is an intention to commit it, it seems to me to follow as a matter of inexorable logic that there is no room either for a "defence" of honest belief or mistake, or of a defence of honest and reasonable belief and mistake. Either the prosecution proves that the accused had the requisite intent, or it does not. In the former case it succeeds, and in the latter it fails. Since honest belief clearly negatives intent, the reasonableness or otherwise of that belief can only be evidence for or against the view that the belief and therefore the intent was actually held, and it matters not whether, to quote Bridge J. in the passage cited above: "the definition of a crime includes no specific element beyond the prohibited act." If the mental element be primarily an intention and not a state of belief it comes within his second proposition and not his third. Any other view, as for insertion of the word "reasonable" can only have the effect of saying that a man intends something which he does not.

Lord Simon of Glaisdale: [A]greeing as I do with the judgment of Bridge J. in the Court of Appeals, I feel no reluctance in coming to this conclusion, which seems to me to accord with legal principle and with good sense.

The common law seems to be the same in the U.S.A.

It remains to consider why the law requires, in such circumstances, that the belief in a state of affairs whereby the *actus* would not be *reus* should be held on reasonable grounds. One reason was given by Bridge J. in the Court of Appeal:

> The rationale of requiring reasonable grounds for the mistaken belief must lie in the law's consideration that a bald assertion of belief for which the accused can indicate no

116

reasonable ground is evidence of insufficient substance to raise any issue requiring the jury's consideration.

I agree; but I think there is also another reason. The policy of the law in this regard could well derive from its concern to hold a fair balance between victim and accused. It would hardly seem just to fob off a victim of a savage assault with such comfort as he could derive from knowing that his injury was caused by a belief, however absurd, that he was about to attack the accused. A respectable woman who has been ravished would hardly feel that she was vindicated by being told that her assailant must go unpunished because he believed, quite unreasonably, that she was consenting to sexual intercourse with him.

Lord Edmund Davies: The parties to these appeals are at one in regarding the offence of rape as falling within the third of Bridge J.'s propositions, but they differ widely in relation to what is involved in "the intention to do the prohibited act." Before this House, learned prosecuting counsel submitted that rape consists simply in having sexual intercourse with a woman who does not in fact consent, and that more than this the Crown need not establish in order to secure a conviction. This simplistic approach is reminiscent of the minority judgments in *Tolson* (1889) 23 Q.B.D. 168, of which more hereafter, that a man commits bigamy if he goes through a marriage ceremony while his wife is alive, even though he honestly and reasonably believes she is dead. Indeed, it would mean that rape involved no mental element save the intention to have intercourse.

It was rightly submitted for the appellants that such an approach involves a fundamentally wrong conception of what constitutes rape. The offence lacks statutory definition, the Sexual Offences Act 1956, s. 1(1) merely declaring it an offence for a man to rape a woman. [But all the definitions in the treatises] indicate that knowledge by the accused of the woman's unwillingness to have intercourse is essential to the crime of rape.

Notes

1.   Mr. Morgan was charged only with aiding and abetting the others in the commission of the offense but not as a principal? Why?

2.   Lord Cross uses the English terms of the evidential and probative burdens. The American terminology is the burden of production and the burden of persuasion. The production burden is relatively low—"some evidence." "Some evidence" is enough evidence of a factor (such as mistake of fact) to put the matter at issue in the case. The trial judge decides if the burden or production has been met by granting or denying a jury instruction on the issue. Unless the jury has been waived and the proceeding is a bench trial, the judge is the neutral referee who does not weigh the credibility of the evidence. Rather, the judge decides if the evidence raises the issue, assuming the evidence presenting the issue would be believed.

The burden of persuasion, on the other hand, is a credibility question for the jury. The jury must decide, in light of the law as instructed by the judge, whether it is persuaded by the evidence of the issue, such as mistake of fact. Usually, the standard is proof beyond a reasonable doubt if the burden is on the prosecution and by a preponderance of the evidence if the burden is on the defendant. The burden of persuasion prevents ties in the justice system. If the jury is in "equipoise" concerning the evidence, the party who has the burden to persuade loses.

Who should have the burden of production and persuasion with regard to mistake of fact? We will return to the subject of burdens of proof when we discuss criminal defenses later in the text.

3.   The *Morgan* opinion cites an American case providing that a rape offense is committed if, in fact, there is not effective consent and it is not necessary that the defendant know there was no consent. This stance would appear to offer more protection for women and to prevent the situation that would allow Mr. Morgan to consent to rough sex on Mrs. Morgan's behalf if the gullible junior airmen honestly believed Morgan's story. In practice, however, many commentators argued that by making consent a strict liability issue, the law compensated by requiring "the utmost resistance" by the victim of sexual assaults as a proxy for the mental state requirement, increasing the danger to rape victims.

4.   Many investigative and legal practices with regard to sexual assault offenses have changed. One notable change is the adoption of rape shield laws in nearly every American jurisdiction. These laws generally make the past sexual history of the victim inadmissible subject to certain exceptions, typically for prior sexual activity between the accused and the victim or for the purpose of impeachment. Despite a more welcoming environment for rape victims, the offense remains the most under-reported personal violence offense.

Gen. Rule: Δ must possess a reasonable belief to assert mistake of fact as negating the intent required for the crime.

Issue: what is the appropriate standard for a Δ to successfully assert mistake of fact to negate the intent necessary for the crime

Holding: ~~Affirmed~~ Reversed. No reasonable jury could have failed to convict all 4 Δs. when an accused challenges the intent or state of mind requirements of the crime alleged under a MOF claim, the belief must have been reasonable.

Reasoning: Each Justice based opinion on whether Δ could have believed that the victim was a voluntary participant. No justice focused on the woman's state of mind or actions she took to manifest a lack of consent. The instruction to the jury was erroneous, No reasonable jury could have found anything other than conviction.

118

Chapter 7: Mistake of Law

Introduction

We took up the question of mistake of fact because the nature of the defense makes it merely a variation of the question concerning mental states. It has been recognized in our legal tradition for centuries that an appropriate mistaken belief negating the required mental state can be a valid defense. The tradition with regard to mistake of law is just the reverse. The prevailing common law principle that has been codified in every American jurisdiction is that "ignorance of the law is no excuse." Why interrupt our discussion of the elements that the prosecution generally must prove to deal with this subject? The answer is that the distinction between fact and law is not always clear.

Assume someone flies into San Antonio from Denver carrying a pouch of legally purchased marijuana from Colorado. His defense will fail if he claims he did not intend to carry a controlled substance because he thought marijuana was legal in Texas. The defendant is not mistaken about what he possesses. He knows what he has. His mistake is about the law in Texas, and ignorance of the law is no excuse. However, some legal issues are a hybrid of a fact and law.

Consider the case of a person who takes his car to a mechanic to have it repaired. When the bill arrives, the defendant is unable to pay. Under the law of the state, the holder of a mechanic's lien is considered to be the owner of the car. Suppose the defendant sneaks into the garage after closing and drives away with what he believes is his car.

If the defendant is charged with intentionally operating the motor vehicle without the consent of the owner, what legal claims could be presented? The defendant might argue lack of the required mental state, mistake of fact, or mistake of law. Given the tradition that ignorance of the law is no excuse, either of the first two would be preferable.

When the mistake concerns non-criminal law, such as who is the owner in the hypothetical car repair case, or whether someone is in fact legally married in a bigamy case, the law is more accepting of the mistake excuse because it often allows the claim to be one of the more broadly-accepted mistake-of-fact claims. Whether someone is married or is the owner of property may be facts, but they are facts that depend on civil law concepts from family and property law.

Recognizing that mistakes of non-criminal law are akin to mistakes of fact can create some fascinating and perplexing issues that defy easy categorization as fact or law. The question of whether defendants had a valid mistake defense was at the heart of the interesting case of *Barker v. United States*, which involved one of the Watergate break-ins. In *Barker*, several members of the "Special Investigations" unit were prosecuted for conspiracy to violate the Fourth Amendment rights of Dr. Lewis J. Fielding. The conspirators included John D. Ehrlichman and G. Gordon Liddy, who were tried separately, while Barker and his associates were what the Court of Appeals called "the foot soldiers of the Watergate break-in." The Fourth Amendment violation occurred when the defendants in *Barker* burglarized Dr. Fielding's office for the purpose of obtaining records on his patient, Daniel Ellsberg, who had leaked the "Pentagon Papers" to The New York Times.

In *Barker*, the defendants sought to present a defense of good faith reliance on apparent authority, based on their belief that E. Howard Hunt, who was their White House superior, had the authority to order the break-in of Dr. Fielding's office. The defendants characterized this as a combined mistake-of-fact and mistake-of-law defense. Specifically, the defendants argued: "The mistake of fact was the belief that Hunt was a duly authorized government agent; the mistake of law was that Hunt possessed the legal prerequisites to conduct a search [without] either probable cause or a warrant." *United States v. Barker*, 546 F.2d 940, 946 (D.C. Cir. 1976).

The district court did not allow the defense, ruling it was a mistake-of-law defense. The defendants were convicted. On appeal, the D.C. Circuit Court of Appeals ruled the trial judge should have allowed the defense, reversed the convictions, and ordered a new trial. The appellate judges disagreed, however, about why the defendants should have been allowed to present their apparent authority defense. Among the rationales offered were that the defendants had reasonably relied on Hunt's expressions of authority, which were equivalent to an official interpretation of the law; that it could be "peculiarly unjust" and "counterproductive" not to recognize orders of high-ranking White House officials as warranting an exception to the rule that ignorance of the law is no excuse; and that the defendants' mistaken belief in Hunt's authority was "close enough" to a mistake of non-criminal law. As Judge Bazelon explained in a companion case:

> The defendants' mistake of law is largely a mistake as to Hunt's authority, *i.e.* whether he had reasonable grounds for ordering the burglary.... [A] mistake as to the lawful authority of a government official, which is what Hunt allegedly presented himself as, is sufficiently close to a mistake of fact and sufficiently similar to a mistake as to civil law . . . that exculpation should be permitted.

United States v. Barker, 514 F.2d 208, 236 n.38 (D.C. Cir. 1975) (Bazelon, C.J., concurring).

The *Barker* case could be called a mistake-of-fact case with regard to non-criminal law, or it could be construed to be a mistake-of-law defense of the type that has been recognized in limited circumstances in which the defendant relies upon some official statement of the law. These statutes represent a very limited exception to the doctrine that ignorance of the law is no excuse. The Texas version, codified at Article 8.03 of the Texas Penal Code provides:

> (a) It is no defense to prosecution that the actor was ignorant of the provisions of any law after the law has taken effect.

> (b) It is an affirmative defense to prosecution that the actor reasonably believed the conduct charged did not constitute a crime and that he acted in reasonable reliance upon:

>> (1) an official statement of the law contained in a written order or grant of permission by an administrative agency charged by law with responsibility for interpreting the law in question; or

(2) a written interpretation of the law contained in an opinion of a court of record or made by a public official charged by law with responsibility for interpreting the law in question.

Although 8.03 is entitled "Mistake of Law," it would be more accurately described as a much more limited defense of reasonable reliance on a written statement of law by an official with the authority to interpret the law. The drafters of the Model Penal Code included a similar defense to the one that Texas adopted. The difficulties of interpreting one of these limited reliance statutes is illustrated by the following *Marrero* case, which deals with the meaning of the term "peace officer," a factual question based upon legal interpretation.

Cop Carrying gun

People v. Marrero

507 N.E.2d 1068 (Court of Appeals of New York, 1987)

Bellacosa, Judge.

The defense of mistake of law is not available to a Federal corrections officer arrested in a Manhattan social club for possession of a loaded .38 caliber semi-automatic pistol who claimed he mistakenly believed he was entitled, pursuant to the interplay of Criminal Procedure Law 2.10, Criminal Procedure Law 1.20 and Penal Law § 265.20,[1] to carry a handgun without a permit as a peace officer.

On the trial of the case, the court rejected the defendant's argument that his personal misunderstanding of the statutory definition of a peace officer is enough to excuse him from criminal liability under New York's mistake of law statute (Penal Law § 15.20).[2] The court refused to charge the jury on this issue and defendant was convicted of criminal possession of a weapon in the third degree. We affirm the Appellate Division order upholding the conviction.

Holding

Defendant was a Federal corrections officer in Danbury, Connecticut, and asserted that status at the time of his arrest in 1977. He claimed at trial that there were various interpretations of fellow officers and teachers, as well as the peace officer statute itself, upon which he relied for his mistaken belief that he could carry a weapon with legal impunity.

The starting point for our analysis is the New York mistake statute as an outgrowth of the dogmatic common-law maxim that ignorance of the law is no excuse. The central issue is whether defendant's personal misreading or misunderstanding of a statute may excuse criminal conduct in the circumstances of this case. *Issue*

The defendant claims as a first prong of his defense that he is entitled to raise the defense of mistake of law under section 15.20(2)(a) because his mistaken belief that his conduct was legal was founded upon an official statement of the law contained in the statute itself. Defendant argues that his mistaken interpretation of the statute was reasonable in view of the alleged ambiguous wording of the peace officer exemption statute, and that his "reasonable" interpretation of an "official statement" is enough to satisfy the requirements of subdivision (2)(a). However, the whole thrust of this exceptional exculpatory concept, in derogation of the

---

1. Penal Law § 265.02 decreed that "A person is guilty of criminal possession of a weapon in the third degree when . . . [s]uch person possesses any loaded firearm." Penal Law § 265.20 provided that among those exempted from § 265.02 are "[p]eace officers as defined by section 2.10 of the criminal procedure law." Criminal Procedure Law §§ 2.10 and 1.20(33) specified that "peace officer" included "[a]n attendant, or an official, or guard of any state prison or of any penal correction institution."

2. Penal Law § 15.20 provided that:

> A person is not relieved of criminal liability for conduct because he engages in such conduct under a mistaken belief that it does not, as a matter of law, constitute an offense, unless such mistaken belief is founded upon an official statement of the law contained in (a) a statute or other enactment . . . or (d) an interpretation of the statute or law relating to the offense, officially made or issued by a public servant, agency, or body legally charged or empowered with the responsibility or privilege of administering, enforcing or interpreting such statute or law.

traditional and common-law principle, was intended to be a very narrow escape valve. ~~Δ read & applied statute too broadly~~

(handwritten, top margin): Δ read & applied statute too broadly

Application in this case would invert that thrust and make mistake of law a generally applied or available defense instead of an unusual exception which the very opening words of the mistake statute make so clear, i.e., "A person is not relieved of criminal liability for conduct . . . unless" (Penal Law § 15.20). The momentarily enticing argument by defendant that his view of the statute would only allow a defendant to get the issue generally before a jury further supports the contrary view because that consequence is precisely what would give the defense the unintended broad practical application.

It was early recognized that the "official statement" mistake of law defense was a statutory protection against prosecution based on reliance of a statute that did in fact authorize certain conduct. "It seems obvious that society must rely on some statement of the law, and that conduct which is in fact 'authorized' . . . should not be subsequently condemned. The threat of punishment under these circumstances can have no deterrent effect unless the actor doubts the validity of the official pronouncement—a questioning of authority that is itself undesirable." (Note, _Proposed Penal Law of New York_, 64 COLUM. L. REV. 1469, 1486). While providing a narrow escape hatch, the idea was simultaneously to encourage the public to read and rely on official statements of the law, not to have individuals conveniently and personally question the validity and interpretation of the law and act on that basis. If later the statute was invalidated, one who mistakenly acted in reliance on the authorizing statute would be relieved of criminal liability. That makes sense and is fair. To go further does not make sense and would create a legal chaos based on individual selectivity.

In the case before us, the underlying statute never in fact authorized the defendant's conduct; the defendant only thought that the statutory exemptions permitted his conduct when, in fact, the primary statute clearly forbade his conduct. Moreover, by adjudication of the final court to speak on the subject in this very case, it turned out that even the exemption statute did not permit this defendant to possess the weapon. It would be ironic at best and an odd perversion at worst for this court now to declare that the same defendant is nevertheless free of criminal responsibility.

(handwritten, right margin): of formal judgement or disputed matter; legal threats & compelling someone to actually going for law suit

Strong public policy reasons underlie the legislative mandate and intent which we perceive in rejecting defendant's construction of New York's mistake of law defense statute. If defendant's argument were accepted, the exception would swallow the rule. Mistakes about the law would be encouraged, rather than respect for and adherence to law. There would be an infinite number of mistake of law defenses which could be devised from a good-faith, perhaps reasonable but mistaken, interpretation of criminal statutes, many of which are concededly complex. Even more troublesome are the opportunities for wrongminded individuals to contrive in bad faith solely to get an exculpatory notion before the jury. These are not _in terrorem_ arguments disrespectful of appropriate adjudicative procedures; rather, they are the realistic and practical consequences were the dissenters' views to prevail. Our holding comports with a statutory scheme which was not designed to allow false and diversionary stratagems to be provided for many more cases than the statutes contemplated. This would not serve the ends of justice but rather would serve game playing and evasion from properly imposed criminal responsibility.

Accordingly, the order of the Appellate Division should be affirmed.

Wachtler, C.J., and Simons and Titone, JJ., concur with Bellacosa, J.

Hancock, J., dissents and votes to reverse in a separate opinion in which Kaye and Alexander, JJ., concur.

Notes

1.   The dissenting judge argues Marrero should not be punished for a crime that is not *malum in se* (intrinsically wrong) but *malum prohibitum* (wrong only because it has been made a crime) when he has a valid interpretation of the law. To punish someone on the basis of what later turns out to be the law is not in keeping with the goal of the penal system to punish subjective wrongdoing. The dissent argues the result here can only be justified on utilitarian grounds that are insufficient for a criminal conviction. Do you agree?

2.   The dissenting judge also points out that the statute had not been interpreted contrary to the defendant's reasonable interpretation. Does the application of the statute by the *Marrero* Court applied to earlier conduct violate the spirit if not the substance of *ex post facto* and other fair notice doctrines? Is Marrero's interpretation of the statute clearly wrong?

3.   Consider that the trial judge initially granted Marrero's motion to dismiss, agreeing with Marrero that the statute allowed him to carry a loaded firearm. The court of appeals reversed in a 3-2 decision. Far from being someone who is disregardful of the law, Marrero is someone who appears to have carefully considered the law. Why does the court fail to give him the benefit of the doubt?

Marrero has inspired a good deal of scholarly debate. Some commentators have suggested that facts about *Marrero* that were not mentioned in the court's opinion caused the court to view Marrero as someone trying to evade the law rather than rely upon it. For example, the federal prison at which Marrero worked forbade guards to carry guns either on or off duty; Marrero had supplied his girlfriend and another companion with guns, even though they clearly had no grounds for believing their possession to be lawful; and Marrero menacingly reached for his weapon when the police approached him in the Manhattan club. Should Marrero's personal motivations be relevant to determining whether he should be allowed to present a mistake of law defense?

Fair Notice

The grudging exception to the doctrine that ignorance of the law is no excuse for reasonable reliance on official statements, as evidenced by cases like *Marrero*, indicate that mistake of law claims are not favored. However, the venerable principle that ignorance of the law is no excuse has undergone some considerable strain in recent years in cases that suggest that, sometimes, the mental state requirement applies to the fact of illegality rather than merely the surrounding circumstances or the desired or likely result of a defendant's conduct.

The first case in this relatively recent line of cases, *Lambert v. California*, was a decision from a divided court that remained the sole incursion on the "ignorance of the law is no excuse" fortress for many years. *Lambert* involved a local ordinance requirement of felons to register with the police. Thus, the statute punished not an affirmative crime, but the failure to act. As we will see when we discuss the act requirement for liability, omissions can be the basis for criminal conviction. Nonetheless the *Lambert* Court was concerned with the lack of notice involved in the registration statute when combined with a statute penalizing an omission. Following *Lambert* is a Texas registration case that avoids a ruling of unconstitutionality on *Lambert* grounds.

failure to register as convict

Lambert v. California

355 U.S. 225 (1957)

Justice Douglas delivered the opinion of the Court.

Section 52.38(a) of the Los Angeles Municipal Code defines "convicted person" as follows:

Any person who, subsequent to January 1, 1921, has been or hereafter is convicted of an offense punishable as a felony in the State of California, or who has been or who is hereafter convicted of any offense in any place other than the State of California, which offense, if committed in the State of California, would have been punishable as a felony.

Section 52.39 provides that it shall be unlawful for "any convicted person" to be or remain in Los Angeles for a period of more than five days without registering; it requires any person having a place of abode outside the city to register if he comes into the city on five occasions or more during a 30-day period; and it prescribes the information to be furnished the Chief of Police on registering.

Section 52.43(b) makes the failure to register a continuing offense, each day's failure constituting a separate offense.

Appellant, arrested on suspicion of another offense, was charged with a violation of this registration law. The evidence showed that she had been at the time of her arrest a resident of Los Angeles for over seven years. Within that period she had been convicted in Los Angeles of the crime of forgery, an offense which California punishes as a felony. Though convicted of a crime punishable as a felony, she had not at the time of her arrest registered under the Municipal Code. At the trial, appellant asserted that § 52.39 of the Code denies her due process of law and other rights under the Federal Constitution, unnecessary to enumerate. The trial court denied this objection. The case was tried to a jury which found appellant guilty. The court fined her $250 and placed her on probation for three years. Appellant, renewing her constitutional objection, moved for arrest of judgment and a new trial. This motion was denied. On appeal the constitutionality of the Code was again challenged. The Appellate Department of the Superior Court affirmed the judgment, holding there was no merit to the claim that the ordinance was unconstitutional. The case is here on appeal. The case having been argued and reargued, we now hold that the registration provisions of the Code as sought to be applied here violate the Due Process requirement of the Fourteenth Amendment.

Procedural History

Holding
Violation of 14th Amend

The registration provision, carrying criminal penalties, applies if a person has been convicted "of an offense punishable as a felony in the State of California" or, in case he has been convicted in another State, if the offense "would have been punishable as a felony" had it been committed in California. No element of willfulness is by terms included in the ordinance nor read into it by the California court as a condition necessary for a conviction.

We must assume that appellant had no actual knowledge of the requirement that she register under this ordinance, as she offered proof of this defense which was refused. The

126

question is whether a registration act of this character violates due process where it is applied to a person who has no actual knowledge of his duty to register, and where no showing is made of the probability of such knowledge.

No vicious will necessary for crime

We do not go with *Blackstone* in saying that "a vicious will" is necessary to constitute a crime, 4 for conduct alone without regard to the intent of the doer is often sufficient. There is wide latitude in the lawmakers to declare an offense and to exclude elements of knowledge and diligence from its definition. But we deal here with conduct that is wholly passive—mere failure to register. It is unlike the commission of acts, or the failure to act under circumstances that should alert the doer to the consequences of his deed. The rule that "ignorance of the law will not excuse," *Shevlin-Carpenter Co. v. State of Minnesota*, 218 U.S. 57, 68 (1910), is deep in our law, as is the principle that of all the powers of local government, the police power is "one of the least limitable." *District of Columbia v. Brooke*, 214 U.S. 138, 149 (1909). On the other hand, due process places some limits on its exercise. Engrained in our concept of due process is the requirement of notice. Notice is sometimes essential so that the citizen has the chance to defend charges. Notice is required before property interests are disturbed, before assessments are made, before penalties are assessed. Notice is required in a myriad of situations where a penalty or forfeiture might be suffered for mere failure to act. Recent cases illustrating the point are *Mullane v. Central Hanover Bank & Trust Co.*, 339 U.S. 306 (1950); *Covey v. Town of Somers*, 351 U.S. 141 (2009); *Walker v. City of Hutchinson*, 352 U.S. 112 (1956). These cases involved only property interests in civil litigation. But the principle is equally appropriate where a person, wholly passive and unaware of any wrongdoing, is brought to the bar of justice for condemnation in a criminal case.

Registration laws are common and their range is wide. Many such laws are akin to licensing statutes in that they pertain to the regulation of business activities. But the present ordinance is entirely different. Violation of its provisions is unaccompanied by any activity whatever, mere presence in the city being the test. Moreover, circumstances which might move one to inquire as to the necessity of registration are completely lacking. At most the ordinance is but a law enforcement technique designed for the convenience of law enforcement agencies through which a list of the names and addresses of felons then residing in a given community is compiled. The disclosure is merely a compilation of former convictions already publicly recorded in the jurisdiction where obtained. Nevertheless, this appellant on first becoming aware of her duty to register was given no opportunity to comply with the law and avoid its penalty, even though her default was entirely innocent. She could but suffer the consequences of the ordinance, namely, conviction with the imposition of heavy criminal penalties thereunder. We believe that actual knowledge of the duty to register or proof of the probability of such knowledge and subsequent failure to comply are necessary before a conviction under the ordinance can stand. As Holmes wrote in The Common Law, "A law which punished conduct which would not be blameworthy in the average member of the community would be too severe for that community to bear." Its severity lies in the absence of an opportunity either to avoid the consequences of the law or to defend any prosecution brought under it. Where a person did not know of the duty to register and where there was no proof of the probability of such knowledge, he may not be convicted consistently with due process. Were it otherwise, the evil would be as great as it is when the law is written in print too fine to read or in a language foreign to the community.

The recording system

127

Reversed.

Justice Burton dissents because he believes that, as applied to this appellant, the ordinance does not violate her constitutional rights.

Mr. Justice Frankfurter, whom Mr. Justice Harlan and Mr. Justice Whittaker join, dissenting.

The present laws of the United States and of the forty-eight States are thick with provisions that command that some things not be done and others be done, although persons convicted under such provisions may have had no awareness of what the law required or that what they did was wrongdoing. The body of decisions sustaining such legislation, including innumerable registration laws, is almost as voluminous as the legislation itself. The matter is summarized in *United States v. Balint*, 258 U.S. 250, 252 (1922):

> Many instances of this are to be found in regulatory measures in the exercise of what is called the police power where the emphasis of the statute is evidently upon achievement of some social betterment rather than the punishment of the crimes as in cases of *mala in se*.

Surely there can hardly be a difference as a matter of fairness, of hardship, or of justice, if one may invoke it, between the case of a person wholly innocent of wrongdoing, in the sense that he was not remotely conscious of violating any law, who is imprisoned for five years for conduct relating to narcotics, and the case of another person who is placed on probation for three years on condition that she pay $250, for failure, as a local resident, convicted under local law of a felony, to register under a law passed as an exercise of the State's "police power." Considerations of hardship often lead courts, naturally enough, to attribute to a statute the requirement of a certain mental element—some consciousness of wrongdoing and knowledge of the law's command—as a matter of statutory construction. Then, too, a cruelly disproportionate relation between what the law requires and the sanction for its disobedience may constitute a violation of the Eighth Amendment as a cruel and unusual punishment, and, in respect to the States, even offend the Due Process Clause of the Fourteenth Amendment.

But what the Court here does is to draw a constitutional line between a State's requirement of doing and not doing. . . . If the generalization that underlies, and alone can justify, this decision were to be given its relevant scope, a whole volume of the United States Reports would be required to document in detail the legislation in this country that would fall or be impaired. I abstain from entering upon a consideration of such legislation, and adjudications upon it, because I feel confident that the present decision will turn out to be an isolated deviation from the strong current of precedents—a derelict on the waters of the law. Accordingly, I content myself with dissenting.

Rule: In order for a conviction to stand for failure to reg. D must have actual knowledge of a duty to register or proof of such knowledge (probability of)

Issue: Was ordinance unconstitutional for violating due process? YES

Holding: Reversed. Bc ordinance violated due process requirement 14th Amend. when it was applied to a person who had no actual knowledge of her duty to register + where no showing was made of the probability of such knowledge.

Varnes v. State

63 S.W.3d 824 (Tex. App.—Houston [14th Dist.] 2001, no pet.)

Don Wittig, Senior Justice (Assigned).

Jimmy Dean Varnes appeals from his felony conviction for failing to register as a sex offender. A jury found him guilty, found an enhancement paragraph in the indictment to be true, and assessed his punishment at twenty years' imprisonment. On appeal, Varnes contends that the statute requiring registration is unconstitutional. We affirm. *Holding*

Background

After serving most of his sentence on a conviction for indecency with a child, Varnes was offered parole. At trial in the present case, Ruth Potts, a state parole officer, testified that in a March 3, 1999, pre-release interview she read to Varnes all of the requirements placed on his parole, including registration as a sex offender. She also specifically stated that she told him that he would have to register with local law enforcement after release regardless of his parole status. Steven McCune, a surveillance officer for the Board of Pardons and Parole, testified that he was present at the pre-release interview and that Potts did, in fact, go over "each and every term" of the Sex Offender Registration Program. Varnes, however, refused to agree to the conditions of parole, and remained incarcerated for six more weeks until the expiration of his sentence, sometime in April 1999.

On October 1, 1999, Varnes was stopped and questioned by Deputy Glenn Madux of the Galveston County Sheriff's Department. Deputy Madux instigated an investigation that ultimately discovered that Varnes had been convicted of a sexual offense but was not registered in Galveston County, or anywhere, as a sex offender. Varnes was then arrested for failing to register. Deputy Michael Henson testified that he interviewed Varnes after the arrest. Henson stated that Varnes told him that he left Seadrift, Texas, in Calhoun County, to come to Galveston County in August 1999. Henson further testified that Varnes told him that he had been living in the Crystal Beach area, in Galveston County, but then he was injured and moved in with his daughter for three weeks, also in Galveston County.

Varnes was specifically charged as follows:

> Jimmy Dean Varnes . . . having resided and intended to reside for more than seven days in the County of Galveston, Texas, [did] intentionally and knowingly fail to register a reportable conviction with the local law enforcement authority in the County of Galveston County, Texas, not later than the seventh day after the defendant's arrival in Galveston County, Texas. . . .

The jury found him guilty and assessed punishment, with enhancement, at twenty years' imprisonment.

Constitutional Analysis

Varnes attacks the constitutionality of the Sex Offender Registration Program, contained in Chapter 62 of the Texas Code of Criminal Procedure. *See* TEX. CODE CRIM. PROC. ANN. arts.

62.01–.12 (Vernon Supp. 2001). Chapter 62 specifies a number of duties required of both state officials and persons convicted of certain sexual crimes. For example, the statute requires a person convicted of a "qualifying offense" to initially register upon leaving a correctional facility, to verify such registration with the local authorities, and to register or verify registration in any locale where the person resides or intends to reside for more than seven days. *Id.* art. 62.02. For further example, the statute requires state officials to notify the prospective registrant of his duties under the statute, to actually complete the initial registration for the registrant, and to send the completed form to the local authorities where the registrant is to reside immediately following release. *Id.* art. 62.03. If a convicted sex offender fails to meet any of his or her requirements under the statute, the statute imposes criminal liability upon him or her for that failure. *Id.* art. 62.10. The statute does not, however, impose any penalties on the State for failing to meet any of its requirements under the statute, nor does it make the convicted offender's duties contingent on the State's fulfillment of its duties. In other words, the statute does not expressly provide the convicted sex offender with a defense to prosecution under the statute based on the State's failure to act. SLC?? No defense?

Due Process

Varnes contends Chapter 62 violates the Due Process Clause of the United States Constitution and the due course clause of the Texas Constitution. *See* U.S. CONST. amends. V, XIV; TEX. CONST. art. I, § 19. Because Varnes has not separately briefed his state and federal constitutional claims, we assume that he claims no greater protection under the state constitution than that provided by the federal constitution. *See Johnson v. State*, 47 S.W.3d 701, 706 (Tex. App.—Houston [14th Dist.] 2001, pet. filed).

Specifically, Varnes argues that because the State failed to fulfill its duties under the registration statute, it is unconstitutional to prosecute him for his own failure under the statute. We begin by noting that our analysis might be different if Varnes was convicted of initially failing to register. It was at that time that each of the requirements cited by Varnes was to have been performed by the State. Varnes, however, was convicted of failing to register in Galveston County after having resided there for seven days (and after having apparently moved from Calhoun County). The state officials had no independent duties specifically related to this move, and hence the State's earlier failure to perform such functions as completing and filing the initial registration are not implicated in this case.

Varnes also argues, however, that the State failed to properly apprise him of all of his obligations under the statute. Article 62.03 specifically requires that prior to release an institution official must inform the prospective registrant of each of his duties under the statute. However, as discussed above, the statute does not expressly create a defense to prosecution based upon the State's failure to meet the exact requirements of the statutory language. Nor has Varnes cited us to any textual references or precedent suggesting that such a defense should be read into the statute. We decline to hold that a technical violation of the State's duties under the statute necessarily nullifies prosecution under the statute, particularly since the statute expressly makes the prospective registrant responsible for verifying the State's actions and liable for his own failure to act under the statute. *See* TEX. CODE CRIM. PROC. ANN. arts. 62.02(a), 62.10 (West 2015); *see also People v. Garcia*, 25 Cal.4th 744 (2001) (holding that technical omissions concerning notice do not require reversal under similar registration statute).

However, this does not complete our analysis. The requirement of notice in the statute appears to be aimed at meeting existing constitutional due process requirements. Such due process notice requirements are necessary because of the very nature of a criminal registration statute. As the Supreme Court stated in *Lambert v. California*, 355 U.S. 225 (1958):

> The question is whether a registration act of this character violates due process where it is applied to a person who has no actual knowledge of his duty to register, and where no showing is made of the probability of such knowledge. . . . [W]e deal here with conduct that is wholly passive—mere failure to register. It is unlike the commission of acts, or the failure to act under circumstances that should alert the doer to the consequences of his deed. The rule that "ignorance of the law will not excuse" is deep in our law, as is the principle that of all the powers of local government, the police power is "one of the least limitable." On the other hand, due process places some limits on its exercise. Engrained in our concept of due process is the requirement of notice. Notice is sometimes essential so that the citizen has the chance to defend charges. . . . Notice is required in a myriad of situations where a penalty or forfeiture might be suffered for mere failure to act. Violation of [the registration statute] is unaccompanied by any activity whatever, mere presence in the city being the test. Moreover, circumstances which might move one to inquire as to the necessity of registration are completely lacking. . . . *We believe that actual knowledge of the duty to register or proof of the probability of such knowledge and subsequent failure to comply are necessary before a conviction under the ordinance can stand.* . . . Where a person did not know of the duty to register and where there was no proof of the probability of such knowledge, he may not be convicted consistently with due process.

Id. at 227–30 (citations omitted, emphasis added); *see also Billingslea v. State*, 780 S.W.2d 271, 275 (Tex. Crim. App. 1989) (citing *Lambert*, 355 U.S. at 229). Hence, due process requires actual notice or the reasonable probability of actual notice before violation of a registration statute can be prosecuted against an individual. The Texas sex offender registration statute requires a showing of nothing more than this.

The notice requirement under the *Lambert* opinion, however, has been very narrowly applied by subsequent courts. In fact, it has frequently been said that the prediction in Justice Frankfurter's dissent has been rendered true: that *Lambert* will stand as "an isolated deviation from the strong current of precedent—a derelict on the waters of the law."

Given the limited scope of *Lambert*, we find that the record ^found for state sufficiently proves that Varnes received actual notice, or the reasonable probability of notice, of his duties under the statute. Ruth Potts testified that in his parole pre-release interview, she read to Varnes all of the requirements placed on his parole, including registration as a sex offender. She also specifically stated that she told him that he would have to register with local law enforcement after release regardless of his parole status. She further explained, at trial, that in saying this she meant that he would still have to register even if he was not under parole supervision. Steven McCune testified that he was present at the pre-release interview and that Potts did, in fact, go over "each and every term" of the sex offender registration program. Also in the record, the judgment from Varnes's last conviction states that: "The defendant is required under Article 62.02 C.C.P. to register as a Sex Offender with the appropriate law enforcement agency." Although this language is not direct proof of actual knowledge, absent proof that Varnes read the judgment, it is some additional evidence tending to show a reasonable probability of notice. The presence of Varnes's thumbprint just below the statement adds further weight to the inference.

Varnes stresses that, to the extent notification occurred, it was during a parole release interview and not in relation to his ultimate release. He further maintains that the State's witnesses on the issue exhibited a certain degree of confusion themselves regarding the requirements of the act. Although we agree in part with each of these contentions, they do not alter our conclusion regarding the existence of actual notice or the reasonable probability of actual notice. Although the State unquestionably failed to inform Varnes of his duties in the precise manner and at the precise time as directed under the statute, we find that the evidence supports the conclusion that Varnes did receive actual notice or the reasonable probability of actual notice. *Lambert*, 355 U.S. at 227–30. Most importantly, he was told that he would have to follow the registration requirements regardless of his parole status. Accordingly, we find that Varnes's constitutional right to due process was not violated by his prosecution in this case.

The judgment of the trial court is affirmed.

The Knowledge of Illegality as Part of Mental State

Lambert involves constitutional concerns with fair notice. Another way of dealing with issues of notice is to interpret statutes in a way that expands the mental state requirement to apply not merely to the typical subjects of the relevant circumstances or the likely result of the defendant's conduct, but to the very fact of illegality. This interpretation makes a defendant's mistake of law exculpatory, not as an independent affirmative defense, but as a failure-of-proof defense. The traditional doctrine concerning ignorance of the law spares the state this burden. It also rests on the premise that it is desirable to encourage citizens to know the law and to discourage tactical evasions of the law based on claims of ignorance. However, the doctrine of ignorance of the law is no excuse developed at a time when there were a limited number of criminal offenses and in which society punished offenses regarded as evil or sinful in the Judeo-Christian tradition.

In the 20th and 21st centuries, however, criminal statutes have appeared in a host of areas far removed from the traditional list of common law crimes. Tax codes, environmental laws, occupational health and safety and numerous other complex and comprehensive schemes have developed in the administrative state. The typical case in which the mental state has expanded to the fact of regulations involves a highly technical statute often promulgated on the basis of legislative delegation to an administrative agency rather than a direct legislative enactment. Such provisions are often *malum prohibitum* crimes that would not be obvious violations of criminal statutes or a shared moral tradition. Two examples of this important trend follow. The *Ratzlaff* case, Justice Ginsberg's first opinion for the court, is an example of a financial crime the court interpreted as requiring knowledge. The regulation in question prohibited structuring a financial transaction to avoid the mandatory reporting requirement for cash transactions in an amount greater than $10,000. Clearly Ratzlaff knew he was structuring his cash withdrawals to avoid the reporting requirement. Thus, he would be guilty under a traditional *mens rea*. However, the Court reads in a mental state requirement as applying to the fact of illegality.

The *Bryan* case that follows *Ratlaff* is an interesting policy compromise that finds a particularized knowledge of federal regulation is not required, but that general knowledge of illegality is, at least when "highly technical" statutes are at issue.

CTR

Ratzlaf v. U.S.

510 U.S. 135 (1994)

Justice Ginsburg delivered the opinion of the Court.

Federal law requires banks and other financial institutions to file reports with the Secretary of the Treasury whenever they are involved in a cash transaction that exceeds $10,000. 31 U.S.C. § 5313; 31 CFR § 103.22(a) (1993). It is illegal to "structure" transactions—i.e., to break up a single transaction above the reporting threshold into two or more separate transactions—for the purpose of evading a financial institution's reporting requirement. 31 U.S.C. § 5324. "A person willfully violating" this antistructuring provision is subject to criminal penalties. § 5322. This case presents a question on which Courts of Appeals have divided: Does a defendant's purpose to circumvent a bank's reporting obligation suffice to sustain a conviction for "willfully violating" the antistructuring provision? We hold that the "willfulness" requirement mandates something more. To establish that a defendant "willfully violat[ed]" the antistructuring law, the Government must prove that the defendant acted with knowledge that his conduct was unlawful. *Burden of Proof on State or Govt.*

Issue →
Holding

On the evening of October 20, 1988, defendant-petitioner Waldemar Ratzlaf ran up a debt of $160,000 playing blackjack at the High Sierra Casino in Reno, Nevada. The casino gave him one week to pay. On the due date, Ratzlaf returned to the casino with cash of $100,000 in hand. A casino official informed Ratzlaf that all transactions involving more than $10,000 in cash had to be reported to state and federal authorities. The official added that the casino could accept a cashier's check for the full amount due without triggering any reporting requirement. The casino helpfully placed a limousine at Ratzlaf's disposal, and assigned an employee to accompany him to banks in the vicinity. Informed that banks, too, are required to report cash transactions in excess of $10,000, Ratzlaf purchased cashier's checks, each for less than $10,000 and each from a different bank. He delivered these checks to the High Sierra Casino.

He avoided CTR → (knowingly)

Based on this endeavor, Ratzlaf was charged with "structuring transactions" to evade the banks' obligation to report cash transactions exceeding $10,000; this conduct, the indictment alleged, violated 31 U.S.C. §§ 5322(a) and 5324(3). The trial judge instructed the jury that the Government had to prove defendant's knowledge of the banks' reporting obligation and his attempt to evade that obligation, but did not have to prove defendant knew the structuring was unlawful. Ratzlaf was convicted, fined, and sentenced to prison.

It had to show Δ knew of CTR + avoid it But no proof direct Δ knew structuring was illegal.

Ratzlaf maintained on appeal that he could not be convicted of "willfully violating" the antistructuring law solely on the basis of his knowledge that a financial institution must report currency transactions in excess of $10,000 and his intention to avoid such reporting. To gain a conviction for "willful" conduct, he asserted, the Government must prove he was aware of the illegality of the "structuring" in which he engaged. The Ninth Circuit upheld the trial court's construction of the legislation and affirmed Ratzlaf's conviction. We granted certiorari, and now conclude that, to give effect to the statutory "willfulness" specification, the Government had to prove Ratzlaf knew the structuring he undertook was unlawful. We therefore reverse the judgment of the Court of Appeals. *Holding*

Congress enacted the Currency and Foreign Transactions Reporting Act (Bank Secrecy Act) in 1970 in response to increasing use of banks and other institutions as financial intermediaries by persons engaged in criminal activity. The Act imposes a variety of reporting requirements on individuals and institutions regarding foreign and domestic financial transactions.

The criminal enforcement provision at issue, 31 U.S.C. § 5322(a), sets out penalties for "[a] person willfully violating," inter alia, the antistructuring provision. Section 5322(a) reads:

> A person willfully violating this subchapter [31 U.S.C. § 5311 *et seq.*] or a regulation prescribed under this subchapter (except section 5315 of this title or a regulation prescribed under section 5315) shall be fined not more than $250,000, or [imprisoned] for not more than five years, or both.

Ratzlaf admits that he structured cash transactions, and that he did so with knowledge of, and a purpose to avoid, the banks' duty to report currency transactions in excess of $10,000. The statutory formulation (§ 5322) under which Ratzlaf was prosecuted, however, calls for proof of "willful[ness]" on the actor's part.

"Willful," this Court has recognized, is a "word of many meanings," and "its construction [is] often . . . influenced by its context."

The United States urges . . . that §5324 violators, by their very conduct, exhibit a purpose to do wrong, which suffices to show "willfulness":

> On occasion, criminal statutes—including some requiring proof of "willfulness"—have been understood to require proof of an intentional violation of a known legal duty, *i.e.*, specific knowledge by the defendant that his conduct is unlawful. But where that construction has been adopted, it has been invoked only to ensure that the defendant acted with a wrongful purpose.

Brief for the United States 23–25.

"[S]tructuring is not the kind of activity that an ordinary person would engage in innocently," the United States asserts. It is therefore "reasonable," the Government concludes, *a reasonable person would not structure* "to hold a structurer responsible for evading the reporting requirements without the need to prove specific knowledge that such evasion is unlawful." Brief for the United States 29.

Undoubtedly there are bad men who attempt to elude official reporting requirements in order to hide from Government inspectors such criminal activity as laundering drug money or tax evasion. But currency structuring is not inevitably nefarious. Consider, for example, the small business operator who knows that reports filed under 31 U.S.C. § 5313(a) are available to the Internal Revenue Service. To reduce the risk of an IRS audit, she brings $9,500 in cash to the bank twice each week, in lieu of transporting over $10,000 once each week. That person, if the United States is right, has committed a criminal offense, because she structured cash transactions "for the specific purpose of depriving the Government of the information that Section 5313(a) is

135

designed to obtain." Nor is a person who structures a currency transaction invariably motivated by a desire to keep the Government in the dark. But under the Government's construction an individual would commit a felony against the United States by making cash deposits in small doses, fearful that the bank's reports would increase the likelihood of burglary, or in an endeavor to keep a former spouse unaware of his wealth.

Courts have noted "many occasions" on which persons, without violating any law, may structure transactions "in order to avoid the impact of some regulation or tax." This Court, over a century ago, supplied an illustration:

> The Stamp Act of 1862 imposed a duty of two cents upon a bank-check, when drawn for an amount not less than twenty dollars. A careful individual, having the amount of twenty dollars to pay, pays the same by handing to his creditor two checks of ten dollars each. He thus draws checks in payment of his debt to the amount of twenty dollars, and yet pays no stamp duty.... While his operations deprive the government of the duties it might reasonably expect to receive, it is not perceived that the practice is open to the charge of fraud. He resorts to devices to avoid the payment of duties, but they are not illegal. He has the legal right to split up his evidences of payment, and thus to avoid the tax.

United States v. Isham, 84 U.S. 496, 506 (1873).

In current days, as an amicus noted, countless taxpayers each year give a gift of $10,000 on December 31 and an identical gift the next day, thereby legitimately avoiding the taxable gifts reporting required by 26 U.S.C. § 2503(b).

In light of these examples, we are unpersuaded by the argument that structuring is so obviously "evil" or inherently "bad" that the "willfulness" requirement is satisfied irrespective of the defendant's knowledge of the illegality of structuring. Had Congress wished to dispense with the requirement, it could have furnished the appropriate instruction.

We do not dishonor the venerable principle that ignorance of the law generally is no defense to a criminal charge. In particular contexts, however, Congress may decree otherwise. That, we hold, is what Congress has done with respect to 31 U.S.C. § 5322(a) and the provisions it controls. To convict Ratzlaf of the crime with which he was charged, violation of 31 U.S.C. §§ 5322(a) and 5324(3), the jury had to find he knew the structuring in which he engaged was unlawful. Because the jury was not properly instructed in this regard, we reverse the judgment of the Ninth Circuit and remand this case for further proceedings consistent with this opinion.

Reversed & remanded b/c jury charge was incorrect

It is so ordered.

Rule: To establish that a Δ "willfully violated" the anti structuring law, the gov't must prove the Δ acted w/ knowledge that his conduct was unlawful.

Jury was improperly instructed. It must also prove Δ acted w/ knowledge that his conduct was unlawful.

Bryan v. United States

524 U.S. 184 (1998)

Stevens, J., delivered the opinion of the Court, in which O'Connor; Kennedy, Souter, Thomas, and Breyer, JJ., joined. Scalia, J., filed a dissenting opinion, in which Rehnquist, CJ. and Ginsburg, J, joined.

[The defendant was convicted under 18 U.S.C. § 924(a)(1)(D), prohibiting anyone from "willfully" violating, inter alia, § 922(a)(1)(A), which forbids dealing in firearms without a federal license. The evidence at the unlicensed dealing trial was adequate to prove that Bryan was dealing in firearms and knew his conduct was unlawful, but there was no evidence he was aware of the federal licensing requirement. The trial judge refused to instruct there could be no conviction absent such awareness, and instructed the jury to the contrary. Bryan was found guilty. The Supreme Court, in a majority opinion by Justice Stevens, J., concluded:]

defining willful w/ precedent

As a general matter, when used in the criminal context, a "willful" act is one undertaken with a "bad purpose." In other words, in order to establish a "willful" violation of a statute, "the Government must prove that the defendant acted with knowledge that his conduct was unlawful." *Ratzlaf*.

A's arguments on appeal

Petitioner argues that a more particularized showing is required in this case for two principal reasons. First, he argues that the fact that Congress used the adverb "knowingly" to authorize punishment of three categories of acts made unlawful by § 922 and the word "willfully" when it referred to unlicensed dealing in firearms demonstrates that the Government must shoulder a special burden in cases like this. This argument is not persuasive because the term "knowingly" does not necessarily have any reference to a culpable state of mind or to knowledge of the law. As Justice Jackson correctly observed, "the knowledge requisite to knowing violation of a statute is factual knowledge as distinguished from knowledge of the law." *distinction bt fact & law*

With respect to the three categories of conduct that are made punishable by § 924 if performed "knowingly," the background presumption that every citizen knows the law makes it unnecessary to adduce specific evidence to prove that "an evil-meaning mind" directed the "evil-doing hand." More is required, however, with respect to the conduct in the fourth category that is only criminal when done "willfully." The jury must find that the defendant acted with an evil-meaning mind, that is to say, that he acted with knowledge that his conduct was unlawful.

Petitioner next argues that we must read § 924(a)(1)(D) to require knowledge of the law because of our interpretation of "willfully" in two other contexts. In certain cases involving willful violations of the tax laws, we have concluded that the jury must find that the defendant was aware of the specific provision of the tax code that he was charged with violating. *See, e.g., Cheek*. Similarly, in order to satisfy a willful violation in *Ratzlaf*, we concluded that the jury had to find that the defendant knew that his structuring of cash transactions to avoid a reporting requirement was unlawful. Those cases, however, are readily distinguishable. Both the tax cases and *Ratzlaf* involved highly technical statutes that presented the danger of ensnaring individuals engaged in apparently innocent conduct. As a result, we held that these statutes "carve out an

137

exception to the traditional rule" that ignorance of the law is no excuse and require that the defendant have knowledge of the law. The danger of convicting individuals engaged in apparently innocent activity that motivated our decisions in the tax cases and *Ratzlaf* is not present here because the jury found that this petitioner knew that his conduct was unlawful."

Justice Scalia, J., for the three dissenters, stated:

It is enough, in my view, if the defendant is generally aware that the *actus reus* punished by the statute—dealing in firearms without a license—is illegal. But the Court is willing to accept a *mens rea* so "general" that it is entirely divorced from the *actus reus* this statute was enacted to punish. That approach turns § 924(a)(1)(D) into a strange and unlikely creature. Bryan would be guilty of "willfully" dealing in firearms without a federal license even if, for example, he had never heard of the licensing requirement but was aware that he had violated the law by using straw purchasers or filing the serial numbers off the pistols. The Court does not even limit (for there is no rational basis to limit) the universe of relevant laws to federal firearms statutes. Bryan would also be "act[ing] with an evil-meaning mind," and hence presumably be guilty of "willfully" dealing in firearms without a license, if he knew that his street-corner transactions violated New York City's business licensing or sales tax ordinances."

Notes

1.   Is it wise to develop a doctrine of "ignorance of the law is an excuse"? The bedrock contrary principle recognized that harsh individual cases might occur, but it is in the public interest to prosecute those who are unaware of the law. The rule encouraged knowledge of the law and caution in engaging in activity that might violate it. It prevented rational calculators from finding ways to violate the law secure in the knowledge that intentional evasion would be hard to prove. Is this new development a laudable attempt to reign in the scope of criminal prosecution or a threat to the public interest?

2.   The rulings in cases like *Ratzlaff* and *Bryan* are merely statutory construction. As Justice Ginsberg puts it in *Ratzlaff*: "Had Congress wished to dispense with the requirement [of knowledge of the regulation], it could have furnished the appropriate instruction." What if Congress does provide clear instruction that the law can be enforced without regard to the defendant's knowledge of the regulation? Are there constitutional principles derived from *Lambert* or other sources that should cause a court to strike down such a statute as unconstitutional?

3.   The movement to recognize that ignorance of the law can be an excuse has occurred primarily in federal courts. The number of statutes in which federal courts have interpreted mental state requirements as including knowledge of illegality include numerous federal tax provisions, the federal false statement provisions, the federal anti-structuring provisions, the federal firearms provisions, the Medicare and Medicaid anti-kickback provisions, the Occupational Safety and Health Act, the Child Support Recovery Act, and the Trading With the Enemy Act. Proof of knowledge of illegality has also been required to support a conviction for willfully misapplying student loan funds, willfully exporting an aircraft,

138

willfully attempting to export weapons or ammunition, willfully transporting monetary instruments in excess of $5,000 into the United States, willfully neglecting to submit for induction into the Army, intentionally using the contents of telephone conversations recorded in violation of Title III of the Omnibus Crime Control and Safe Streets Act of 1968, and knowingly acquiring or possessing food coupons in a manner not authorized by law. Conspiring or causing another to commit one of these substantive offenses has also been found to require proof that the accused knew she was violating the law. Thus, ignorance or mistake of law has already become an acceptable excuse in a number of federal cases, particularly in prosecutions brought under statutes requiring proof of "willful" conduct on the part of the accused.

Rule of Law: An individual can be convicted of "willfully" violating a Fed statute if the individual knows his actions are unlawful.

Issue: Whether △ can be convicted of violating the firearm statute for willfully selling firearms w/o evidence of his knowledge of the federal licensing requirements set out in the statute.

Holding: YES. △ need not be aware or "know" which individual statute he was violating in order for his actions to be considered "willful."

A △ satisfies a "willful" act under mens rea requirement if △ acted w/ knowledge that his actions were unlawful. Ignorance of the law cannot overcome a △'s conviction for violating a Fed stat. △ knew his actions violated the law (just not specific subsection)

Dissent: Mens rea requirement of statute is ambiguous bc def of willful is determined differently w/ every statute

139

Chapter 8: Voluntary Act, Possession and Omissions

Voluntary Act

The requirement of a guilty mind has been the focus of our attention thus far. As crucial as the culpable mental state concept is in the criminal law, guilty thoughts are not enough for criminal liability. Rather, some type of voluntary act is needed. However, any sense of relief that we have at last escaped the mental aspect of crime would be premature. The three sub-topics we will address in this chapter dealing with the act requirement have a significant overlap with the mental state requirement.

The three topics we will address under the rubric of the criminal law are set out in Texas Penal Code Section 6.01, entitled "Requirement of a Voluntary Act or Omission." It states:

> (a) A person commits an offense only if he voluntarily engages in conduct, including an act, an omission, or possession.
>
> (b) Possession is a voluntary act if the possessor knowingly obtains or receives the thing possessed or is aware of his control of the thing for a sufficient time to permit him to terminate his control.
>
> (c) A person who omits to perform an act does not commit an offense unless a law as defined by Section 1.07 provides that the omission is an offense or otherwise provides that he has a duty to perform the act

All three topics will be addressed in this chapter in the order of the statute. What constitutes a sufficiently voluntary act for criminal liability? What constitutes "possession" that will qualify as a voluntary "act" for criminal liability? When can the failure to act be the basis of a criminal conviction?

Requiring a voluntary act for a criminal conviction is consistent with the purpose of the mental state requirement to punish people in accordance with their culpability and to deter people from committing crimes. The justification for imposing criminal sanctions is premised on the idea that people with free will have chosen to act in ways that society condemns. Actions that are beyond the control of the actor are not blameworthy, and the concept of deterrence assumes people have the freedom to make choices that can be influenced by penal sanctions. These same ideas pervade of the law of *mens rea* and many cases that raise issues of a lack of a voluntary act could also be analyzed on the basis of mental state. Arguably, the voluntary act requirement is an even more fundamental cornerstone of criminal law than *mens rea*. After all, there are strict liability offenses that dispense with a mental state, but some type of act (or the failure to act when there is a legal duty) is the required atomic particle for any crime and cannot be eliminated. The case of *Robinson v. California*, which follows after *Martin* and *Farmer*, makes this point by striking down a statute that punishes a status rather than an act.

The easiest voluntariness cases are those in which the actor has no physical control over his or her action. Consider the following classic case involving public intoxication.

drunkguy

Martin v. State

17 So. 2d 427 (Ala. Ct. App. 1944)

Simpson, Judge.

Appellant was convicted of being drunk on a public highway, and appeals. Officers of the law arrested him at his home and took him onto the highway, where he allegedly committed the proscribed acts, viz., manifested a drunken condition by using loud and profane language.

The pertinent provisions of our statute are: "Any person who, while intoxicated or drunk, appears in any public place where one or more persons are present, . . . and manifests a drunken condition by boisterous or indecent conduct, or loud and profane discourse, shall, on conviction, be fined," etc. Code 1940, Title 14, Section 120.1. Under the plain terms of this statute, a voluntary appearance is presupposed. The rule has been declared, and we think it sound, that an accusation of drunkenness in a designated public place cannot be established by proof that the accused, while in an intoxicated condition, was involuntarily and forcibly carried to that place by the arresting officer.

Conviction of appellant was contrary to this announced principle and, in our view, erroneous. It appears that no legal conviction can be sustained under the evidence, so, consonant with the prevailing rule, the judgment of the trial court is reversed and one here rendered discharging appellant.

No voluntary choice ≠ act requirement

Notes

1.   *Martin* demonstrates that a lack of voluntary choice can negate the act requirement for conviction. However, the typical scope of the voluntary act is quite narrow. For example, if X forces Y at gun point to assist in the commission of a crime, does Y have a valid claim of a lack of a voluntary act? Surprisingly, the answer is no. Y made a choice to assist X (if we assume that Y knew of X's purpose). Of course, Y's choice is not voluntary in the sense of having only bad choices (commit a crime or be shot), but it is not involuntary in the sense of having no physical control, as in *Martin*. Y's defense is not to argue that the State did not show a voluntary act, but rather, to argue a defense of duress (discussed later in the text). The difference in theory may be small in some cases, but there are significant differences. For example, duress has been held not to provide a defense to homicide, and the defensive claim requires a defendant meet a burden of production and possibly also persuasion.

The limited view of the concept of a voluntary act is also demonstrated by the following Texas case of *Farmer v. State*. Although the defendant in *Farmer* might have an involuntary intoxication claim (a defense discussed later in the text), the limited nature of the voluntariness required for a voluntary criminal act dooms this line of attack.

Farmer v. State

411 S.W.3d 901 (Tex. Crim. App. 2013)

Hervey, J., delivered the opinion of the Court in which Keller, P.J., Meyers, Price, Womack, Keasler, and Alcala, JJ., joined.

Appellant, Kody William Farmer, was convicted of driving while intoxicated and sentenced to 90 days' confinement and to pay a $200 fine. His sentence of confinement was suspended for one year of community supervision. The question presented in this case is whether *[issue]* there was sufficient evidence adduced at trial to entitle Appellant to a jury-charge instruction on voluntariness. The court of appeals held that Appellant was entitled to a voluntariness instruction. We will reverse the judgment of the court of appeals and affirm the judgment of the trial court.

[Holding → does not get voluntariness instruction]

I. Facts

Appellant suffered from chronic back pain due to a work-related injury. As a result, he had taken different medications on and off for more than 10 years, including Ultram, a painkiller, and Soma, a muscle relaxer. Also, four days prior to the incidents in question, Appellant was prescribed Ambien, a sleep aid, for the first time to assist with his insomnia. Ambien and Soma are considered controlled substances by the Federal Government, and all three drugs come with warnings that they may cause drowsiness.

In the morning, Appellant would usually take his Ultram, and sometimes his Soma, before getting in the shower. To help Appellant make sure he took his medication, Appellant's wife would lay out Appellant's medicine for him to take. The morning of the incident in question, Appellant's wife laid out his Ultram and Ambien on their microwave, but she separated the pills so that Appellant would take the Ambien at night because "both his doctor and his pharmacist recommended that he be within minutes of going to bed before taking Ambien."

During questioning following the accident, Appellant stated that he did not remember taking any of his medication. But he did admit after watching a video of his actions that he did not have the normal use of his mental or physical faculties. Appellant testified that he took Ultram that morning and "I guess Soma. I thought—is what I thought I was taking." He also testified that he did not intentionally or voluntarily take Ambien, and that he does not know how it was introduced into his body because he had never taken Ambien before. However, in response to the question of how Ambien was found in his blood if he had never taken the medication before, he answered, "I don't know. I don't know. I guess it was taken by mistake." Appellant's wife did not remember seeing Appellant take his medication that morning, but she remembered that "the Ambien I laid out for the night that was on the other side of [the] microwave was gone." She also testified that she was a hundred percent certain that "he took what I had laid out."

II. Procedural Posture

Appellant was charged with driving while intoxicated. At the close of evidence, the defense requested three jury-charge instructions. Specifically, the defense argued that Appellant

Δ arguments

involuntarily took the Ambien because he thought that the Ambien was his muscle-relaxant medication, Soma. The trial judge discussed the possibility of including an instruction on voluntariness that "would encompass involuntary intoxication," but ultimately the trial judge overruled Appellant's objections and declined to charge the jury on any of the requested instructions. Appellant was found guilty and punishment was assessed at one year of confinement and a $200 fine. His confinement was probated for a term of twelve months.

Trial ct for state Appellate ct reversed & remanded

Procedural History

Appellant appealed his conviction to the Fort Worth Court of Appeals, and the court reversed Appellant's conviction and remanded to the trial court. It held that the facts of this case are "most closely akin to an involuntary act because the evidence suggests that although Farmer voluntarily took the pills laid out for him by his wife, he involuntarily took the Ambien pill because of his wife's act." As a result, Appellant was denied a defense that could have resulted in an acquittal, and he suffered some harm because of that error. *Id.* The court of appeals did not review the State's claim on appeal that the trial court correctly excluded the instructions because they improperly commented on the weight of the evidence.

Not reviewed

III. Arguments

State's arguments

The State argues that no evidence was offered at trial to entitle Appellant to a jury instruction on voluntariness. Therefore, the trial judge correctly denied Appellant's request for such an instruction. However, the State does not dispute that Appellant preserved his jury-charge objection under our case law and, as a result, would need to show that he suffered some harm if the trial judge erred, rather than egregious harm.

IV. The Law

SL no culpability required

Under Texas law, a person commits an offense if the person is intoxicated while operating a motor vehicle in a public place. TEX. PENAL CODE ANN. § 49.04(a) (West 2015). A person is intoxicated if he or she has a blood alcohol concentration of .08 or higher or does not have the normal use of his mental or physical faculties. In cases not involving alcohol, such as this case, the latter standard must be proven. The offense of driving while intoxicated is a strict liability crime meaning that it does not require a specific mental state (*e.g.*, intentionally, knowingly, or recklessly intending to operate a motor vehicle while intoxicated), only a person on a public roadway voluntarily operating a motor vehicle while intoxicated.

Because Appellant's jury-instruction arguments touched on the defenses of "accident" and "involuntary act," we think it is also helpful to address those issues. We have previously discussed the relationship between the two theories. *See Rogers v. State*, 105 S.W.3d 630 (Tex. Crim. App. 2003). In Rogers, we held that the claim of "accident" was not interchangeable with the claim of "involuntary act" because the defense of "accident" was applicable only to offenses committed under the former Penal Code. We explained that, when the Texas Penal Code of 1974 was adopted, the Legislature abandoned the "accident" approach as a catch-all, in favor of the more precise approach taken by the American Law Institute in the Model Penal Code. Part of that new approach included a rejection of the defense of "accident," which ambiguously addressed the physical actions and the mental state of a criminal defendant. Instead, the drafters adopted two separate defenses to replace the defensive theory of "accident." The first, and relevant one here, is "involuntary act," which focuses solely on physical acts of the accused and is now found in Section 6.01(a) of the Texas Penal Code. The second defense, which focuses on the defendant's state of mind at the time of the incident, requires a culpable mental state, the absence of which can be used to defend oneself from criminal liability. Thus, to avoid ambiguity in the law, the old defense of "accident" was divided into its constituent parts—the defense of "involuntary act" and the defense that a defendant lacked the requisite mental state to commit the crime. *Id.* at 638; *see also* 43 GEORGE E. DIX & JOHN M. SCHMOLESKY, TEXAS PRACTICE: CRIMINAL PRACTICE AND PROCEDURE § 43:34 (3d ed. 2011).

Section 6.01(a) of the Texas Penal Code places a restriction on offenses listed in the Penal Code. In relevant part, it states that "a person commits an offense only if he voluntarily engages in conduct, including an act" or "an omission." Thus, to be guilty of driving while intoxicated, the accused must meet the requirements of the driving-while-intoxicated statute and have voluntarily engaged in an act or omission. *See* TEX. PENAL CODE ANN. §§ 6.01(a), 49.04(a) (West 2015). In discussing what is meant by the requirement of a voluntary act, we have stated that

> before criminal responsibility may be imposed, the actor's conduct must "include[ ] either a voluntary act or an omission when the defendant was capable of action." The operative word under Section 6.01(a), for present purposes, is "include." Both the Model Penal Code comments and the Practice Commentary to the 1974 Texas Penal Code stress that the "voluntary act" requirement does not necessarily go to the ultimate act (e.g., pulling the trigger), but only that criminal responsibility for the harm must "include an act" that is voluntary (e.g., pulling the gun, pointing the gun, or cocking the hammer).

Rogers, 105 S.W.3d at 638 (footnotes omitted). We have also stated that voluntariness, as described by Section 6.01(a), "refers only to one's own physical body movements[,]" and that a movement is considered involuntary only if that movement is "the nonvolitional result of someone else's act, [was] set in motion by some independent non-human force, [was] caused by a physical reflex or convulsion, or [was] the product of unconsciousness, hypnosis or other nonvolitional impetus . . . ." *Id.* Thus, a voluntary act that comprised a portion of the commission of the offense is sufficient to satisfy the requirement of Section 6.01(a), even if that voluntary act was accidental or the consequences of that act were unintended.

With respect to when a defendant is entitled to a jury instruction on a defensive issue, this Court has long held that a defendant is entitled to a jury instruction on a defensive issue if it is raised by the evidence, regardless of the strength or credibility of that evidence. Thus, viewing the evidence in the light most favorable to Appellant, we must decide if there was some evidence adduced at trial to warrant a jury instruction on the defensive issue of voluntariness.

V. Discussion

Viewed in the light most favorable to Appellant, the record reflects that Appellant's wife laid out the medication that Appellant was supposed to take the day of the accidents. Likewise, the record also reflects that Appellant's wife testified that one of the medications was Ambien, and that later, she saw that both pills she had set out for her husband were gone. Presumably, Appellant ingested both pills by mistake, including the Ambien. That theory is supported by the blood-test results that showed Appellant had Ambien in his system at, or near, the time of the incident, although he had testified that he had never taken Ambien before.

this is/what is important

Appellant's argument on discretionary review is limited to asserting that Appellant did not voluntarily take the Ambien pill. Thus, we do not address any other conduct on the part of Appellant

The court of appeals focused on whether the action of Appellant's wife's in placing the Ambien on the microwave caused Appellant to involuntarily take the Ambien because he thought it was a different prescription medication. However, whether Appellant took Ambien by mistake or on purpose is irrelevant to our analysis when determining if there was a voluntary act under Section 6.01(a) of the Texas Penal Code. The proper inquiry in this case is whether Appellant voluntarily picked up and ingested prescription medication. *Rogers*, 105 S.W.3d at 637–38 (stating that "[v]oluntary conduct 'focuses upon conduct that is within the control of the actor'"). Even Appellant admitted that he thought that he took the Ambien by mistake, and no evidence contradicted that testimony. To the contrary, as we noted, the blood test supported that hypothesis.

Δshould have taken time to check pills

All that is necessary to satisfy Section 6.01(a) of the Texas Penal Code is that the commission of the offense included a voluntary act. Appellant makes no allegation that his arm movement to pick up and ingest the medication was the result of anything other than his own conscious action, and no other evidence at trial supported Appellant's request for a jury instruction on voluntariness. Appellant may have mistakenly taken the wrong prescription medication, but the evidence supports the conclusion that he voluntarily picked up the prescription medication from the microwave and ingested it. Stated another way, this is not a case of unknowingly or unwillingly taking pharmaceutical medication; this is a case of knowingly taking pharmaceutical medication but mistakenly taking the wrong one. While we may be sympathetic to a "mistake," Appellant was involved in two accidents because of his "mistake." Even if Appellant took the medication in error, that error was made because Appellant did not take the time to verify the medication he was taking, although he knew that he was prescribed medications that could have an intoxicating effect. Based on the foregoing analysis, we hold that the trial court properly denied Appellant's request to include a defensive instruction on voluntariness, even when the evidence is viewed in the light most favorable to Appellant.

VI. Conclusion

Holding

We conclude that Appellant's action in taking the Ambien pill was a voluntary act because Appellant, of his own volition, picked up and ingested the Ambien pill. It is of no consequence that Appellant mistakenly took the wrong prescription medication when he knew that he was taking a prescription medication and was aware that he was prescribed medications with intoxicating effects. Moreover, because no other evidence at trial raised an issue of Appellant's voluntariness in taking that medication, the trial court properly denied Appellant's request. As a result, the court of appeals erred when it reversed the judgment of the trial court. We reverse the judgment of the court of appeals and affirm the judgment of the trial court.

Notes

1.   Does the *Farmer* case take too narrow a view of what is voluntary? Does the criminal law lose some of its grounding by punishing people who are not morally blameworthy? The two cases that follow raise important issues concerning what should be the proper scope of the concept of voluntariness. The first case, *Robinson v. California*, produced a good deal of commentary and speculation about whether criminal conduct that is related to what the court seemed to be calling the illness of drug addiction could still be punished. Did the opinion prevent criminal conviction of anyone whose crime was a product of an illness or addiction, and how would those concepts be defined? Six years after *Robinson*, the court examined these issues again in *Powell*, a case that arose in Texas. The limited view of *Robinson* as a case dealing with an unusual status offense caused *Robinson* to be regarded as an isolated and limited decision instead of case of revolutionary significance.

Robinson v. State of California

370 U.S. 660 (1962)

Stewart, J., delivered the opinion of the Court. Douglas, J., and Harlan, J., concur.

A California statute makes it a criminal offense for a person to "be addicted to the use of narcotics." This appeal draws into question the constitutionality of that provision of the state law, as construed by the California courts in the present case.

[handwritten: Issue: Is this unconstitutional]

The appellant was convicted after a jury trial in the Municipal Court of Los Angeles. The evidence against him was given by two Los Angeles police officers. Officer Brown testified that he had had occasion to examine the appellant's arms one evening on a street in Los Angeles some four months before the trial. The officer testified that at that time he had observed "scar tissue and discoloration on the inside" of the appellant's right arm, and "what appeared to be numerous needle marks and a scab which was approximately three inches below the crook of the elbow" on the appellant's left arm. The officer also testified that the appellant under questioning had admitted to the occasional use of narcotics.

[handwritten: Facts:]

The appellant testified in his own behalf, denying the alleged conversations with the police officers and denying that he had ever used narcotics or been addicted to their use. He explained the marks on his arms as resulting from an allergic condition contracted during his military service. His testimony was corroborated by two witnesses.

It would be possible to construe the statute under which the appellant was convicted as one which is operative only upon proof of the actual use of narcotics within the State's jurisdiction. But the California courts have not so construed this law. Although there was evidence in the present case that the appellant had used narcotics in Los Angeles, the jury was instructed that they could convict him even if they disbelieved that evidence. The appellant could be convicted, they were told, if they found simply that the appellant's "status" or "chronic condition" was that of being "addicted to the use of narcotics." And it is impossible to know from the jury's verdict that the defendant was not convicted upon precisely such a finding.

This statute, therefore, is not one which punishes a person for the use of narcotics, for their purchase, sale or possession, or for antisocial or disorderly behavior resulting from their administration. It is not a law which even purports to provide or require medical treatment. Rather, we deal with a statute which makes the "status" of narcotic addiction a criminal offense, for which the offender may be prosecuted "at any time before he reforms." California has said that a person can be continuously guilty of this offense, whether or not he has ever used or possessed any narcotics within the State, and whether or not he has been guilty of any antisocial behavior there.

It is unlikely that any State at this moment in history would attempt to make it a criminal offense for a person to be mentally ill, or a leper, or to be afflicted with a venereal disease. A State might determine that the general health and welfare require that the victims of these and other human afflictions be dealt with by compulsory treatment, involving quarantine,

Comparison of drug addicts to mentally ill → require treatment

confinement, or sequestration. But, in the light of contemporary human knowledge, a law which made a criminal offense of such a disease would doubtless be universally thought to be an infliction of cruel and unusual punishment in violation of the Eighth and Fourteenth Amendments.

We cannot but consider the statute before us as of the same category. In this Court counsel for the State recognized that narcotic addiction is an illness. Indeed, it is apparently an illness which may be contracted innocently or involuntarily. We hold that a state law which imprisons a person thus afflicted as a criminal, even though he has never touched any narcotic drug within the State or been guilty of any irregular behavior there, inflicts a cruel and unusual punishment in violation of the Fourteenth Amendment. To be sure, imprisonment for ninety days is not, in the abstract, a punishment which is either cruel or unusual. But the question cannot be considered in the abstract. Even one day in prison would be a cruel and unusual punishment for the "crime" of having a common cold.

We are not unmindful that the vicious evils of the narcotics traffic have occasioned the grave concern of government. There are, as we have said, countless fronts on which those evils may be legitimately attacked. We deal in this case only with an individual provision of a particularized local law as it has so far been interpreted by the California courts.

Reversed. *Holding*
Statute unlawful

Notes

1.   Allowing criminal liability on the basis of a status might subvert traditional notions of appropriate jurisdictional limitations. For example, if a person became addicted to narcotics in Canada and then came to Texas, any acts of possession, purchase, and use that occurred in Canada would not be within the territorial jurisdiction of the state of Texas.

2.   If a child is born an addict through in vitro transmission from her mother, would it be constitutional or fair to hold the child responsible? How far does this principle go? What if the child was born an addict, but is prosecuted 20 years later without ever having been free of addiction? Would the crime of drug possession be excused via involuntary addiction?

Rule: a state law that imprisons as a criminal a person afflicted w/ a narcotic addiction, even though he has never touched a narcotic drug within the state or been guilty of any irregular behavior there, inflicts a cruel & unusual punishment

Holding: Yes, unconstitutional bc cruel & unusual punishment for a sick person.

Powell v. Texas

392 U.S. 514 (1968)

Justice Marshall announced the judgment of the Court and delivered an opinion in which Chief Justice Black and Justice Harlan join.

In late December 1966, appellant was arrested and charged with being found in a state of intoxication in a public place, in violation of TEX. PENAL CODE ANN. art. 477 (1952), which reads as follows:

> Whoever shall get drunk or be found in a state of intoxication in any public place, or at any private house except his own, shall be fined not exceeding one hundred dollars.

Appellant was tried in the Corporation Court of Austin, Texas, found guilty, and fined $20. He appealed to the County Court at Law No. 1 of Travis County, Texas, where a trial de novo was held. His counsel urged that appellant was "afflicted with the disease of chronic alcoholism," that "his appearance in public (while drunk was) . . . not of his own volition," and therefore that to punish him criminally for that conduct would be cruel and unusual, in violation of the Eighth and Fourteenth Amendments to the United States Constitution.

The trial judge in the county court, sitting without a jury, made certain findings of fact, but ruled as a matter of law that chronic alcoholism was not a defense to the charge. He found appellant guilty, and fined him $50. There being no further right to appeal within the Texas judicial system, appellant appealed to this Court.

Appellant testified concerning the history of his drinking problem. He reviewed his many arrests for drunkenness; testified that he was unable to stop drinking; stated that when he was intoxicated he had no control over his actions and could not remember them later, but that he did not become violent; and admitted that he did not remember his arrest on the occasion for which he was being tried. On cross-examination, appellant admitted that he had had one drink on the morning of the trial and had been able to discontinue drinking. In relevant part, the cross-examination went as follows:

> Q. You took that one at eight o'clock because you wanted to drink?
>
> A. Yes, sir.
>
> Q. And you knew that if you drank it, you could keep on drinking and get drunk?
>
> A. Well, I was supposed to be here on trial, and I didn't take but that one drink.
>
> Q. You knew you had to be here this afternoon, but this morning you took one drink and then you knew that you couldn't afford to drink any more and come to court; is that right?
>
> A. Yes, sir, that's right.

Q. So you exercised your will power and kept from drinking anything today except that one drink?

A. Yes, sir, that's right.

Q. Because you knew what you would do if you kept drinking that you would finally pass out or be picked up?

A. Yes, sir.

Q. And you didn't want that to happen to you today?

A. No, sir.

Q. Not today?

A. No, sir.

Q. So you only had one drink today?

A. Yes, sir.

On redirect examination, appellant's lawyer elicited the following:

Q. Leroy, isn't the real reason why you just had one drink today because you just had enough money to buy one drink?

A. Well, that was just give to me.

Q. In other words, you didn't have any money with which you could buy any drinks yourself?

A. No, sir, that was give to me.

Q. And that's really what controlled the amount you drank this morning, isn't it?

A. Yes, sir.

Q. Leroy, when you start drinking, do you have any control over how many drinks you can take?

A. No, sir.

Appellant claims that his conviction on the facts of this case would violate the Cruel and Unusual Punishment Clause of the Eighth Amendment as applied to the States through the Fourteenth Amendment. The primary purpose of that clause has always been considered, and properly so, to be directed at the method or kind of punishment imposed for the violation of criminal statutes; the nature of the conduct made criminal is ordinarily relevant only to the fitness of the punishment imposed.

Appellant, however, seeks to come within the application of the Cruel and Unusual Punishment Clause announced in *Robinson v. California*, 370 U.S. 660 (1962), which involved a state statute making it a crime to "be addicted to the use of narcotics." This Court held there that "a state law which imprisons a person thus afflicted (with narcotic addiction) as a criminal, even though he has never touched any narcotic drug within the State or been guilty of any irregular behavior there, inflicts a cruel and unusual punishment . . . ."

On its face the present case does not fall within that holding, since appellant was convicted, not for being a chronic alcoholic, but for being in public while drunk on a particular occasion. The State of Texas thus has not sought to punish a mere status, as California did in *Robinson*; nor has it attempted to regulate appellant's behavior in the privacy of his own home. Rather, it has imposed upon appellant a criminal sanction for public behavior which may create substantial health and safety hazards, both for appellant and for members of the general public, and which offends the moral and esthetic sensibilities of a large segment of the community.

It is suggested in dissent that *Robinson* stands for the "simple" but "subtle" principle that "criminal penalties may not be inflicted upon a person for being in a condition he is powerless to change." In that view, appellant's "condition" of public intoxication was "occasioned by a compulsion symptomatic of the disease" of chronic alcoholism, and thus, apparently, his behavior lacked the critical element of *mens rea*. Whatever may be the merits of such a doctrine of criminal responsibility, it surely cannot be said to follow from Robinson. The entire thrust of Robinson's interpretation of the Cruel and Unusual Punishment Clause is that criminal penalties may be inflicted only if the accused has committed some act, has engaged in some behavior, which society has an interest in preventing, or perhaps in historical common law terms, has committed some *actus reus*. It thus does not deal with the question of whether certain conduct cannot constitutionally be punished because it is, in some sense, "involuntary" or "occasioned by a compulsion."

Affirmed.

Justice Black, whom Justice Harlan joins, concurring (opinion omitted).

Justice White, concurring in the result.

If it cannot be a crime to have an irresistible compulsion to use narcotics, *Robinson v. California*, 370 U.S. 660 (1962), I do not see how it can constitutionally be a crime to yield to such a compulsion. Punishing an addict for using drugs convicts for addiction under a different name. Distinguishing between the two crimes is like forbidding criminal conviction for being sick with flu or epilepsy but permitting punishment for running a fever or having a convulsion. Unless *Robinson* is to be abandoned, the use of narcotics by an addict must be beyond the reach of the criminal law. Similarly, the chronic alcoholic with an irresistible urge to consume alcohol should not be punishable for drinking or for being drunk.

Powell's conviction was for the different crime of being drunk in a public place. Thus even if Powell was compelled to drink, and so could not constitutionally be convicted for drinking, his conviction in this case can be invalidated only if there is a constitutional basis for saying that he may not be punished for being in public while drunk. The statute involved here, which aims at keeping drunks off the street for their own welfare and that of others, is not

152

challenged on the ground that it interferes unconstitutionally with the right to frequent public places.

It is unnecessary to pursue at this point the further definition of the circumstances or the state of intoxication which might bar conviction of a chronic alcoholic for being drunk in a public place. For the purposes of this case, it is necessary to say only that Powell showed nothing more than that he was to some degree compelled to drink and that he was drunk at the time of his arrest. He made no showing that he was unable to stay off the streets on the night in question.

Because Powell did not show that his conviction offended the Constitution, I concur in the judgment affirming the Travis County court.

Justice Fortas, with whom Justice Douglas, Justice Brennan, and Justice Stewart join, dissenting.

The issue posed in this case is a narrow one. There is no challenge here to the validity of public intoxication statutes in general or to the Texas public intoxication statute in particular. This case does not concern the infliction of punishment upon the "social" drinker—or upon anyone other than a "chronic alcoholic" who, as the trier of fact here found, cannot "resist the constant, excessive consumption of alcohol." Nor does it relate to any offense other than the crime of public intoxication.

It is settled that the Federal Constitution places some substantive limitation upon the power of state legislatures to define crimes for which the imposition of punishment is ordered. In *Robinson v. California*, 370 U.S. 660 (1962), the Court considered a conviction under a California statute making it a criminal offense for a person "(t)o be addicted to the use of narcotics." At Robinson's trial, it was developed that the defendant had been a user of narcotics. The trial court instructed the jury that "to be addicted to the use of narcotics is said to be a status or condition and not an act. It is a continuing offense and differs from most other offenses in the fact that (it) is chronic rather than acute; that it continues after it is complete and subjects the offender to arrest at any time before he reforms." *Id.* at 662–663.

This Court reversed Robinson's conviction on the ground that punishment under the law in question was cruel and unusual, in violation of the Eighth Amendment of the Constitution as applied to the States through the Fourteenth Amendment. The Court noted that narcotic addiction is considered to be an illness and that California had recognized it as such. It held that the State could not make it a crime for a person to be ill. Although Robinson had been sentenced to only 90 days in prison for his offense, it was beyond the power of the State to prescribe such punishment. As Mr. Justice Stewart, speaking for the Court, said: "even one day in prison would be a cruel and unusual punishment for the 'crime' of having a common cold." *Id.* at 667.

Robinson stands upon a principle which, despite its subtlety, must be simply stated and respectfully applied because it is the foundation of individual liberty and the cornerstone of the relations between a civilized state and its citizens: Criminal penalties may not be inflicted upon a person for being in a condition he is powerless to change. In all probability, Robinson at some time before his conviction elected to take narcotics. But the crime as defined did not punish this conduct. The statute imposed a penalty for the offense of "addiction"—a condition which Robinson could not control. Once Robinson had become an addict, he was utterly powerless to avoid criminal guilt. He was powerless to choose not to violate the law.

In the present case, appellant is charged with a crime composed of two elements—being intoxicated and being found in a public place while in that condition. The crime, so defined, differs from that in *Robinson*. The statute covers more than a mere status. But the essential constitutional defect here is the same as in *Robinson*, for in both cases the particular defendant was accused of being in a condition which he had no capacity to change or avoid. The trial judge sitting as trier of fact found upon the medical and other relevant testimony, that Powell is a "chronic alcoholic." He defined appellant's "chronic alcoholism" as "a disease which destroys the afflicted person's will power to resist the constant, excessive consumption of alcohol." He also found that "a chronic alcoholic does not appear in public by his own volition but under a compulsion symptomatic of the disease of chronic alcoholism." I read these findings to mean that appellant was powerless to avoid drinking; that having taken his first drink, he had "an uncontrollable compulsion to drink" to the point of intoxication; and that, once intoxicated, he could not prevent himself from appearing in public places.

The findings in this case . . . compel the conclusion that the infliction upon appellant of a criminal penalty for being intoxicated in a public place would be "cruel and inhuman punishment" within the prohibition of the Eighth Amendment. This conclusion follows because appellant is a "chronic alcoholic" who, according to the trier of fact, cannot resist the "constant excessive consumption of alcohol" and does not appear in public by his own volition but under a compulsion' which is part of his condition.

I would reverse the judgment below.

Notes

1.   Is punishing Powell consistent with the goals of the criminal law? Does Powell deserve to be punished? Will punishing him deter Powell or others from committing the same crime? Are there methods other than criminal conviction whereby society can deal with problems caused by those who abuse alcohol?

2.   Is there an "irresistible compulsion to use narcotics" for some? If an addict can avoid using drugs or an alcoholic can refrain from drinking while a police officer is present, is that a sufficient degree of control to demonstrate a person is choosing to engage in the behavior? Note the defendant in *Powell* testified he only had one drink that morning.

3.   Although *Powell* reduced the apparent significance of *Robinson*, that decision has recently been resurrected by advocates for the homeless. A 2010 Alabama case invalidated a statute that criminalized the failure of sex offenders to provide a stable mailing address on the theory that applying the law to people who did not have a stable mailing address criminalized the status of being homeless. *State v. Adams*, 91 So. 3d 724 (Ala. Crim. App. 2010). A Los Angeles statute that made it a crime to sleep in public was successfully attacked on the basis of *Robinson*

because the statute, as applied to people who did not have anywhere else to sleep, criminalized the status of being homeless. The Ninth Circuit Court of Appeals explained:

> The City could not expressly criminalize the status of homelessness by making it a crime to be homeless without violating the Eighth Amendment, nor can it criminalize acts that are an integral aspect of that status. Because there is substantial and undisputed evidence that the number of homeless persons in Los Angeles far exceeds the number of available shelter beds at all times, including on the nights of their arrest or citation, Los Angeles has encroached upon Appellants' Eighth Amendment protections by criminalizing the unavoidable act of sitting, lying, or sleeping at night while being involuntarily homeless. A closer analysis of *Robinson* and *Powell* instructs that the involuntariness of the act or condition the City criminalizes is the critical factor delineating a constitutionally cognizable status, and incidental conduct which is integral to and an unavoidable result of that status, from acts or conditions that can be criminalized consistent with the Eighth Amendment.

Jones v. City of Los Angeles, 444 F.3d 1118 (9th Cir. 2006).

4.   The defense in a number of cases has attempted to raise a claim of an involuntary act due to mental or physical conditions that allegedly prevented conscious control of the defendant's actions. These claims include sleepwalking, post-traumatic stress disorder, brainwashing, and hypnosis. Although there is scientific evidence to support that sleepwalkers, for example, can and do engage in complex behaviors without being conscious, such claims rarely succeed with juries, even when courts allowed testimony on such claims and jury instructions about the legal requirement of a voluntary act.

5.   If a defendant is unconscious at the time the harm described in a criminal statute occurs, the prosecutorial strategy may track back to an earlier time when the defendant consciously did something that set the stage for the later harmful act. For example, in *People v. Decina*, 138 N.E.2d 799 (1956), the defendant had an epileptic seizure while driving. The defendant's loss of control of the car killed four children. Although there was no voluntary act when car hit children, the conviction for negligent homicide was upheld based upon the voluntary negligent act of the defendant beginning to drive knowing he was subject to seizures.

A similar theory was used in the Texas case of *George v. State*, 681 S.W.2d 43 (1984). The defendant's argument—that because the hammer of a gun slipped, the death of his wife was an involuntary accident—was rejected because the evidence of his earlier voluntary act of holding the gun to head of victim and drawing the hammer back was reckless.

Rule: a state law that imprisons a person afflicted w/ narcotic addiction as a criminal, even though he has never touched a narcotic drug within one state or been guilty of any irregular behavior there, inflicts a cruel & unusual punishment.

Issue: Was Δ's conviction violative of the right against Cruel & Unusual punishment.

Holding: NO. Dist. cts finding that Δ was afflicted w/ chronic alcoholism was problematic bc Dist ct. failed to articulate symptoms. Dist Ct didn't seek to punish a status but impose a criminal sanction for public behavior

155

Possession

If X slips a bag of marijuana into the pocket of Y's coat, and the bag is discovered by a police officer who stopped Y on the basis of a speeding ticket before X has discovered it, is Y guilty of possession of a controlled substance? If the jury believes the evidence that Y did not know he had the bag in his pocket, the answer is no, because the possession is not considered voluntary unless the defendant is aware of having a choice about whether to take control or custody of the item.

What if Y knowingly took the bag from X, but X had informed Y the bag contained oregano for the pasta dish that he was going to repair? This too fails to constitute voluntary possession because Y lacks knowledge of the nature of the thing that he controls (assuming that the jury believes the oregano story). Is this also a voluntary act claim, or is it instead a lack of a mental state? The following Texas case raises difficult questions concerning the requirement of knowing the character of the item possessed.

handwritten: Credit card Skimming device

Ramirez-Memije v. State

444 S.W.3d 624 (Tex. Crim. App. 2014)

Meyers, J., delivered the opinion of the Court in which Keasler, Hervey, Cochran, and Alcala, JJ, joined.

Appellant, Roman Ramirez–Memije, was charged with fraudulent possession of identifying information under Texas Penal Code Section 32.51(b). A jury found him guilty and sentenced him to three years' imprisonment. He appealed, arguing that the trial court erred in *handwritten: Procedural* failing to instruct the jury on voluntary conduct under Section 6.01. The court of appeals *handwritten: History* reversed the trial court's judgment and remanded the case for further proceedings. *Ramirez–Memije v. State*, 397 S.W.3d 293 (Tex. App.—Houston [14th Dist.] 2013). The State filed a petition for discretionary review, which we granted to consider the following question:

> Is a defendant entitled to an instruction on voluntary possession when he claims he did not know the forbidden nature of the thing he possessed, or is his defense merely a negation of his knowledge of surrounding circumstances that is required by Section 6.03(b)?

handwritten: Issue:

We hold that Appellant was not entitled to the requested instruction, and we reverse the decision of the court of appeals. We remand the case to the court of appeals for consideration of Appellant's remaining issues. *handwritten: Holding for State → not entitled to instruction*

Facts

Appellant received a credit-card skimming device from Dante Salazar and delivered it to Antonio Cercen, who worked as a waiter at a restaurant. Cercen used the skimmer to collect restaurant customers' identifying information and credit-card numbers and then returned the skimmer to Appellant. Several customers reported unauthorized credit-card purchases after dining at the restaurant, and an investigation revealed that all of the complaining customers had been waited on by Cercen. Cercen agreed to assist in the investigation, and agents set up a sting operation. The next time Appellant delivered the skimmer to Cercen, agents found identifying information on the skimmer and arrested Appellant. Appellant then agreed to help agents and set up delivery of the skimmer to Salazar.

Appellant was indicted for fraudulent possession of identifying information. At trial, Appellant claimed that he did not know what the skimming device was and did not know what information it contained. He said that he did not receive any benefits from participating in the credit-card skimming operation. Appellant requested a jury charge regarding the requirement of a voluntary act or omission under Penal Code section 6.01. The trial court denied his request. The instructions to the jury included the statutory language defining intent and knowledge found in Section 6.03. The jury found Appellant guilty and sentenced him to three years' confinement.

Court of Appeals

Appellant appealed his conviction, claiming that the trial court erred by refusing to include his requested jury instruction on voluntary conduct under Section 6.01. The court of appeals looked to the plain language of Section 6.01(b) and determined that "the thing possessed" referred to the item of contraband prohibited by the statute. The court reasoned that, because there is no offense for possession of the skimmer, "the thing possessed" here must mean the identifying information. The court of appeals stated that, although Section 6.01(b) contains an element of *mens rea* because it says "knowingly" and "aware of," the concepts of *actus reus* and *mens rea* are separate. The court of appeals concluded that Appellant was entitled to a jury charge on voluntary act under Section 6.01(b) because there was evidence that he did not know that the skimmer contained identifying information, thus the evidence raised the issue of whether his possession was voluntary. Finding some harm to Appellant, the court of appeals reversed the trial court's judgment.

Arguments of the Parties

State's Argument

The State argues that the court of appeals erred in concluding that Appellant was entitled to an instruction on voluntary possession. The State contends that, to establish unlawful possession, the State has always had to show that the accused knew that what he possessed was contraband. Thus, according to the State, the question here is whether the requirement that the State prove a defendant's knowledge of the forbidden nature of the thing possessed is a function of *mens rea* or the general requirement of voluntariness. The State says that knowing you possess something is different from knowing that what you possess is contraband. According to the State, the Model Penal Code says that the "thing possessed" refers to "the physical object, not to its specific quality or properties" and that "the extent to which the defendant must be aware of such specific qualities or properties is a problem of *mens rea*."

The State concludes that the knowledge of the nature of the thing possessed is a required culpable mental state and is different from voluntary conduct. Because it was undisputed that Appellant knowingly obtained or received the skimmer from Cercen, he was not entitled to an instruction on voluntariness.

Appellant's Argument

Appellant states that the court of appeals correctly determined that the requirement of a voluntary act under Section 6.01 is not subsumed by the *mens rea* requirement. Appellant argues that he was entitled to an instruction on voluntary conduct under Section 6.01(b) because the evidence raised the issue of whether his possession was voluntary. Appellant states that "if evidence raises a fact issue as to an accused's possession of contraband, the jury must be instructed on what constitutes possession under the law, which includes a § 6.01(b) instruction, as well as a *mens rea* instruction." Appellant argues that if the issue is raised, both instructions must be given.

Appellant states that the court of appeals correctly interpreted the "thing possessed" as the contraband alleged in the indictment and notes that the indictment charged him with possession of identifying information, not with possession of the skimmer. Appellant concludes that the "trial court did not instruct the jury regarding the law of possession as enacted by the legislature in TEX. PENAL CODE ANN. § 6.01 (West 2015), either in its abstract portion or in the application section of the jury charge. Therefore, the jury was induced to believe that appellant

158

was guilty, if he possessed the skimmer, whether he knew that the skimmer contained illegally obtained identifying information."

hes saying contraband important

Caselaw and Statutes

Penal Code Section 32.51(b) states that "A person commits an offense if the person, with the intent to harm or defraud another, obtains, possesses, transfers, or uses an item of: (1) identifying information of another person without the other person's consent; . . . (b–1) For the purposes of Subsection (b), the actor is presumed to have the intent to harm or defraud another if the actor possesses: (1) the identifying information of three or more other persons." The jury charge here tracked the language from the statute and said, "You are instructed that the defendant is presumed to have the intent to harm or defraud another if the defendant possesses the identifying information of three or more other persons."

During the jury charge conference, Appellant cited *Evans v. State*, 202 S.W.3d 158 (Tex. Crim. App. 2006). Appellant said that the proper law to apply to possession is the law that has been established in drug cases and wanted the court to add a sentence to the jury charge stating that Appellant knew that the matter possessed was identifying information. Appellant focused on the part of *Evans* that said that the State must prove "that the accused knew the matter possessed was contraband" and wanted the trial court to instruct the jury that the State must prove that Appellant knew that the matter possessed was identifying information. After reviewing *Evans*, the trial court refused to include Appellant's requested instruction.

Evans discussed the necessity of linking the contraband to the accused to protect innocent bystanders, relatives, roommates, or friends from being convicted for possession due merely to their proximity to another's contraband. *Evans* analyzed the sufficiency of the evidence linking the defendant to drugs found during a police search of a house. We did not discuss Section 6.01(b) in that case because the issue in Evans was whether the defendant exercised care, custody, control, or management of the substance. Thus, the question in *Evans* was whether he actually possessed the contraband, not whether his possession of the contraband was a voluntary act.

We did discuss Section 6.01 in *Farmer v. State*, 411 S.W.3d 901 (Tex. Crim. App. 2013), in which we considered whether the trial court erred in failing to give an instruction on voluntary act. Farmer was convicted of driving while intoxicated. He argued that the jury should have been instructed on voluntary act under Section 6.01(a) because he presented evidence at trial that he believed that he was taking a different medication when he mistakenly took a sleeping pill. We concluded that Farmer was not entitled to an instruction on voluntary act because he voluntarily took a pill. We reasoned that the proper inquiry was whether Farmer voluntarily picked up and ingested prescription medication prior to driving. The consequences of Farmer's voluntary act of taking a pill may have been unintended because he accidently took the wrong pill, but the ingestion of a pill was a voluntary act.

Analysis

The general requirements for an offense to have been committed are an *actus reus* and a *mens rea*. Penal Code Section 6.01 covers *actus reus* and requires that a person voluntarily engage in an act, omission, or possession. Criminal responsibility is established if the person voluntarily engaged in the act, omission, or possession with the mental state required for the specific offense. While a voluntary act is usually some sort of bodily movement, possession is shown by care, custody, control, or management. Thus, knowingly receiving an object is a voluntary act under Section 6.01(b); knowing the forbidden nature of the object that is knowingly possessed is the culpable mental state under Section 6.03.

Appellant's argument is that the possession was not a voluntary act because he did not know that the skimmer contained identifying information. We disagree. If there was evidence that the skimmer had been slipped into Appellant's bag without his knowledge, then there may be a question of voluntary possession and Appellant may have been entitled to an instruction regarding the requirement of a voluntary act. But here it is undisputed that Appellant knowingly had the skimming device, which contained the identifying information, in his possession. Appellant knowingly received the skimming device and knew that he was transferring the device. This satisfies the requirement of a voluntary act under Section 6.01.

Appellant said that he did not know that his conduct was illegal or that the device was contraband because he did not know what the device was or what was on the device. He said he did not receive anything in return for transferring the device between Cercen and Dante Salazar. The jury heard this testimony and the testimony of agents who said that Appellant told them that he was given cash and electronics for transferring the device. This evidence goes to the mens rea of intent to harm or defraud, upon which the jury was properly instructed.

For example, if a defendant were arrested while transporting a package for a friend and police determined that the package contained marijuana, the defendant could claim at trial that he did not know what the package contained, that he did not know the package contained marijuana, or that he thought the package contained oregano, and that he did not knowingly or intentionally possess marijuana. The jury would then have to decide whether to believe his claim that he did not have the requisite *mens rea* for the possession of marijuana offense. *See* TEX. HEALTH & SAFETY CODE ANN. § 481.121(a) (West 2015). The defendant could not, however, claim that his possession of the package filled with marijuana was an involuntary act because he knowingly accepted the package from his friend.

Conclusion

Appellant was not entitled to an instruction on voluntary conduct and the trial court did not err in denying Appellant's motion to include a 6.01 instruction. The judgment of the court of appeals is reversed, and the case is remanded for consideration of Appellant's remaining issues.

Price, J., filed a dissenting opinion in which Keller, P.J., and Womack and Johnson, JJ., joined.

The Court holds that, because it is undisputed that the appellant knowingly possessed the skimmer, he is not entitled to an instruction under Section 6.01(b), which depicts the circumstances under which "possession" may constitute a "voluntary act" under the Texas Penal Code. But, as the court of appeals took great pains to emphasize in its opinion, the indictment in this case did not allege that the appellant possessed the skimmer. It alleged that he possessed more than ten items of "identifying information," those being the "electronic identification *thing possessed was CC information*

number [s]" of a dozen individuals—credit card numbers. The appellant admitted possessing the skimmer, but he testified that he did not even know what a skimmer was, much less that it contained such "identifying information." Because the skimmer was not "the thing possessed" in contemplation of Section 6.01(b), the court of appeals rejected the State's argument that no voluntary act instruction was necessary because the evidence showed he "knowingly obtained" the skimmer, asking itself, rather, whether it was contested that the appellant "knowingly obtained" the identifying information. Today the Court entirely ignores this distinction, though it was the linchpin in the court of appeal's analysis. *did A know what he obtained*

The Court observes that the appellant might have been entitled to an instruction on possession as a voluntary act under Section 6.01(b) if there had been evidence that he did not knowingly obtain the skimmer—if it had been slipped into his bag unbeknownst to him, for example. I do not disagree that, under those circumstances, the appellant would have been entitled to such an instruction, since he would not have been aware of possessing either the skimmer or the identifying information contained therein. But I disagree that this would be the only set of circumstances that could justify submitting the Section 6.01(b) instruction. The Court seems to rely on our recent opinion in *Farmer v. State* for the proposition that the appellant need not be aware of the contents of the skimmer in order for his possession of it to constitute a voluntary act for purposes of Section 6.01(b). But *Farmer* involved a prosecution for driving while intoxicated, so the concept of possession as a voluntary act, and therefore Section 6.01(b), was not implicated there. *Farmer* is largely inapposite here.

The Court concludes that the appellant's testimony that "he did not know what the device was or what was on the device" entitles him to no more than an ordinary jury instruction regarding the culpable mental state for the offense in question—that he must have possessed the identifying information in this case with the specific "intent to harm or defraud another." Again, I do not disagree that, if the jury believed that the appellant was unaware that the skimmer even contained any identifying information, it would almost certainly conclude that he lacked the requisite specific intent to harm or defraud anyone. But while this circumstance might properly inform a some-harm analysis under *Almanza v. State*, it does not necessarily resolve the question of whether it was error for the trial court to refuse the appellant's request for a possession-as-a-voluntary-act instruction under Section 6.01(b). The answer to that question turns on an exegesis of Section 6.01(b) itself, which—unlike the court of appeals—the Court today does not undertake.

In its treatment of the issue, the court of appeals observed that "the 'voluntary act' of possession seemingly involves an overlap between *actus reus* and *mens rea*." I think this is undoubtedly correct. Under Section 6.01(a) of the Penal Code, a person commits an offense only if he voluntarily engages in "conduct," including "an act, an omission, or possession." An "act" "means bodily movement, whether voluntary or involuntary." An "omission" is a "failure to act." And Section 6.01(b), in turn, defines "possession" as a "voluntary act if the possessor knowingly obtains or receives the thing possessed or is aware of his control of the thing for a sufficient time to permit him to terminate his control." Thus, *actus reus* and *mens rea* seemingly merge.

As the practice commentary to Section 6.01 of the 1974 Penal Code noted, "although possession is often treated in the criminal law as the equivalent of an act, it is not strictly

speaking a bodily movement so subsection (b) [of Section 6.01] is necessary to treat it as such."
And as the court of appeals aptly observed, "the unique character of 'possessory' offenses has
always plagued and confounded the bench and bar, for it defies analysis by the general
methodology of viewing the major components of offenses as 'conduct' distinct from 'intent.'"
Given this hybridization of conduct and intent as reflected in Section 6.01(b), it does not suffice
for the Court today simply to conclude that a proper jury instruction with respect to *mens rea*
wholly obviates the need to also instruct the jury with respect to the possession-as-a-voluntary-
act component of the *actus reus*. The appellant may be legally entitled to both instructions.
While failing to submit one to the jury under appropriate circumstances may not always prove
even to generate "some harm" in light of submission of the other, that does not mean that the
failure did not constitute error in the first place.

So what exactly does Section 6.01(b) require, then, in the way of an instruction in
possession-related offenses? An accused is guilty of such an offense "only if" he voluntarily
engages in the conduct of possession, and such conduct is voluntary "if the possessor knowingly
obtains or receives the thing possessed." I think it is clear enough that, in order to voluntarily
possess "the thing possessed" for purposes of this provision, the accused need not be aware of
"the nature of the thing possessed" so long as he knows that, whatever it is, he does indeed
possess it. What if he does not know he possesses it? One clear example of this would be the
Court's slipping-the-skimmer-into-the-appellant's-bag hypothetical. Under these circumstances,
the appellant does not even realize he possesses the skimmer, much less any identifying
information contained therein. But does that reflect the only circumstance in which it can be said
that an accused may possess a thing without knowing it?

Suppose "the thing possessed" were a box, and the evidence showed that the accused had
shaken the box so that he was aware that there was something inside it, though he was manifestly
unaware of the nature of "the thing possessed." Under these circumstances, I would agree that
the accused would know that he had "obtained" the contents of the box (whatever those contents
may be), and he would not be entitled to an instruction under Section 6.01(b). But suppose,
instead, that what the accused knowingly possessed was, by all available perception, simply a
solid cube; but that, unbeknownst to him, the solid cube contained contraband embedded in its
interior. The fact that the accused did not know that the content of the cube was contraband
would not entitle him to a Section 6.01(b) instruction-that would purely be a question of his
culpable mental state. But the fact that he cannot have been expected to know that anything
might be contained within a solid cube may well mean that he does not voluntarily possess what
is within it, for purposes of Section 6.01(b), regardless of whether he is aware of its nature.
Because the nature of the thing he knowingly possessed gave him no basis to infer that he also
possessed something in its interior, he cannot be said to have knowingly possessed "the thing
possessed" inside. Under these circumstances, in addition to those that the Court concedes, I
should think that the accused would be entitled to a Section 6.01(b) instruction.

In this case, the appellant's testimony raised the possibility that he simply did not have
any way to know that the skimmer contained "the thing possessed" under the indictment-the
identifying information. If the appellant genuinely did not know what a skimmer was, then the
situation is more like the solid cube in my hypothetical than the rattling box. The appellant
would have no basis to suspect that the skimmer was a container for holding anything, much less

162

identifying information, which was "the thing possessed" in contemplation of the indictment. This being so, I agree with the court of appeals that the appellant was entitled to his requested Section 6.01(b) instruction.

Because I believe the court of appeals correctly resolved this issue, and almost certainly reached the proper disposition of the case, I respectfully dissent.

Notes

1.   Does it matter whether we characterize the defendant's claim as a lack of knowledge, a mistake of fact, or a lack of a voluntary act? If we believe the defendant didn't know the nature of the skimming device, can he still be found guilty? If we don't believe the defendant, can he be innocent?

2.   A number of possession cases involve prosecution on a joint possession theory. This does not mean the possession of joints, although most of these cases involve drugs. Joint possession refers to the fact that things can be possessed simultaneously by more than one person. In the typical case, a controlled substance is found in shared premises. If drugs are found in an apartment shared by four roommates, does everyone possess? The state must prove more than presence in a place with drugs. One who knows her roommate possesses drug does not make that person a possessor.

The majority opinion in *Ramirez–Memije* was referred to *Evans v. State*, 202 S.W.3d 158 (Tex. Crim. App. 2006). In *Evans*, the issue was how to determine who is in possession of drugs found in a house occupied by more than one person. Evans's aunt, Priestly, had already been arrested for selling drugs. When the police arrived at her residence to search for more drugs, Evans was found sitting near a coffee table that contained baggies and pill bottles filled with cocaine. Priestly told the police the drugs were only hers and not Evans's. Evans's ex-wife, Jorden, testified on his behalf that the family had asked Evans to stop by Priestley's house to check on it while his grandmother, who usually also resided there, was temporarily away. A jury convicted Evans of possession of cocaine.

The Fourth Court of Appeals reversed the conviction, finding the evidence presented by the prosecution was insufficient to establish that Evans exercised care, custody, control, or management of the cocaine. This evidence consisted of the following: when the police arrived at the house, they found Evans in close proximity to the drugs; there was no one else in the house with Evans and the drugs; when asked by the police if he knew why they were there, Evans said, "Drugs;" Evans had received an item of mail, postmarked one month earlier, at the address where he and the drugs were found; men's clothes were found in the house; Evans was found with $160 on his person; and the street value of the cocaine found on the coffee table was $1300.

A majority of the Texas Court of Criminal Appeals ruled the Fourth Court of Appeals had not given proper deference to the jury's verdict. The Court did approve of the intermediate court's statement of the legal issues:

The court of appeals then noted that, in a possession of a controlled substance prosecution, "the State must prove that: (1) the accused exercised control, management, or care over the substance; and (2) the accused knew the matter possessed was contraband." Regardless of whether the evidence is direct or circumstantial, it must establish that the defendant's connection with the drug was more than fortuitous. This is the so-called "affirmative links" rule which protects the innocent bystander—a relative, friend, or even stranger to the actual possessor—from conviction merely because of his fortuitous proximity to someone else's drugs. Mere presence at the location where drugs are found is thus insufficient, by itself, to establish actual care, custody, or control of those drugs. However, presence or proximity, when combined with other evidence, either direct or circumstantial (e.g., "links"), may well be sufficient to establish that element beyond a reasonable doubt. It is, as the court of appeals correctly noted, not the number of links that is dispositive, but rather the logical force of all of the evidence, direct and circumstantial.

Evans v. State, 202 S.W.3d 158, 161-62 (Tex. Crim. App. 2006).

The court disagreed, however, that the evidence was insufficient to prove Evans possessed the drugs:

Appellant did offer evidence of a reasonable alternate hypothesis: he was merely "checking on" Ms. Priestley, who was known by her family to be involved with drugs, while his grandmother was in Oklahoma for a few days. He had just driven fifteen miles from his ex-wife's home, and the police serendipitously arrived at the very moment that he was calling his former wife at Fort Hood from his grandmother's phone. This is a plausible explanation for appellant's presence in the house and his proximity to the drugs, as well as his knowledge of their existence. This tidy explanation accounted nicely for almost all of the incriminating evidence. Also, Ms. Priestley's repeated statements to the police after appellant was arrested that all of the drugs were hers is consistent with Ms. Jorden's testimony. The jury was entitled to believe this evidence, but it was not required to do so. . . . A jury could have found that both Ms. Jorden (appellant's former wife and the mother of his children, with whom he was still very friendly) and Ms. Priestley had a motive to place all blame on Ms. Priestley (she was, after all, caught "red-handed"). The jury, by its verdict, rejected this alternate scenario.

We conclude that the circumstantial evidence, when viewed in combination and its sum total, constituted amply sufficient evidence connecting appellant to the actual care, custody, control or management of the cocaine in front of him. It is the logical force of the circumstantial evidence, not the number of links that supports a jury's verdict. The logical force of the combined pieces of circumstantial evidence in this case, coupled with reasonable inferences from them, is sufficient to establish, beyond a reasonable doubt, that appellant exercised actual care, custody, control, or management of the cocaine on the coffee table.

Evans v. State, 202 S.W.3d 158, 165 (Tex. Crim. App. 2006).

3.   Whether there are sufficient "affirmative links" between a defendant and contraband present at the scene is an issue that has been developed in hundreds of appellate cases. A summary of a number of the affirmative links that courts have considered can be derived from the decision of the Thirteenth Court of Appeals in *Myers v. State*, 665 S.W.2d 590 (Tex. App.—

Corpus Christi 1984, pet. ref'd). The fact scenario is a typical one—the discovery of a controlled substance, methamphetamine in an apartment where the defendant resided pursuant to a search with a warrant. The warrant was executed sometime between 8:00 and 9:00 o'clock in the morning. The defendant and a companion were ordered out of bed and escorted to the living room where the search warrant and their rights were read to them. A detective found a hypodermic syringe filled with a liquid, a bag containing two small packets of powdery substance, several empty syringes, and, on top of the refrigerator, a bottle containing a liquid substance. All of these substances were positively identified as methamphetamine.

At the trial on the merits, the defendant's companion testified the methamphetamine was hers, that she pled guilty to the offense, and that she was assessed a prison sentence of five years. Aside from the evidence of the contraband found in the apartment, the evidence linking the defendant to the contraband was his presence and the presence of some of his clothing and bills for utilities in his name at the apartment. The Court of Appeals examined the evidence in light of a number of "affirmative link" cases:

> We begin with the evidence linking appellant to the motel apartment. In *Rhyne v. State*, 620 S.W.2d 599 (Tex. Crim. App. 1981), the defendant testified that he rented the apartment and the utilities were billed to him. There, the Court of Criminal Appeals wrote: "Further, the fact that a defendant has rented the premises upon which narcotics are found, if also occupied by others, is not usually sufficient in and of itself to justify a finding of joint possession." It is undisputed that [defendant's companion] occupied the premises with appellant. Since appellant did not have sole access to the premises, we must look for other affirmative links to the contraband.

> In *Guitierrez v. State*, 533 S.W.2d 14 (Tex. Crim. App. 1976), wherein a conviction for possession of heroin where the sufficiency of the evidence to show possession was successfully challenged, the dissent pointed out that needle marks were on both of the arms of defendant. However, the majority noted the needle marks were not shown to be recent. In the instant case, numerous syringes were found, one was even full of methamphetamine, but there was no evidence of any needle marks on appellant's body. In *Hernandez v. State*, 517 S.W.2d 782 (Tex. Crim. App. 1975), the court again pointed out that even if the testimony concerning needle marks was about the defendant, there was no showing whether the needle marks were recent or old scars.

> Another affirmative link appearing in the cases is whether the defendant was under the influence of the controlled substance. Here, there was no evidence suggesting that appellant was under the influence of methamphetamine. In *Woods*, 533 S.W.2d at 18, it was noted that no contraband was discovered on the defendant. That was also true of appellant.

> Often, the "close proximity" of the defendant to the contraband is listed as a factor to be considered in determining whether the defendant possessed the contraband. In *Hernandez*, evidence showing that defendant had been sleeping on a mattress under which officers discovered four needles and a syringe was not sufficient in and of itself to support the conviction. *Hernandez*, 517 S.W.2d at 784. The Court in *Hernandez* observed that the circumstances in *Hausman v. State*, 480 S.W.2d 721 (Tex. Crim. App. 1972), were even "more incriminating." But in *Hausman*, where the defendant was discovered apparently asleep or at least in a "tranquil" state, the question was asked (and answered in

defendant's favor) whether the close proximity of defendant to a bag of marijuana (one foot from his head) was sufficient to bring the case within an exception to the rule that mere presence at the scene of the crime does not of itself justify drawing an inference that the defendant was a participant therein. *Hausman*, 480 S.W.2d at 723–24. *Hausman* is distinguishable in that "Unlike the cases where the accused is the owner of the car or dwelling where the narcotic is discovered, appellant did not have dominion and control of the place where the marijuana was found."

In *Oaks v. State*, 642 S.W.2d 174 (Tex. Crim. App. 1982), an acquittal for possession of heroin was ordered where the question was: how close is close? Writing that the issue presented was a "close question," the Court, in reversing the Court of Appeals, held: "'Close' is a matter of degree and close proximity alone would, under the circumstances, hardly be an affirmative link to the heroin but only a factor to be considered in the totality of the circumstances."

In the instant case, appellant was discovered in the bedroom. All the contraband was discovered in either the living area or kitchen. The evidence is therefore insufficient to support a finding of close proximity.

Closely related to the question of close proximity is whether the contraband is in plain view. It would appear the two are inversely proportional; the farther away the contraband is, the more open and obvious it must be before the affirmative link is established. In our case, the evidence is unclear whether the contraband was in plain view. The packets on the table were in a "little plastic bag or pouch." Officer Rose testified he discovered the bottle of methamphetamine in the kitchen on the refrigerator but offered no further information. [Defendant's companion] testified the small bottle was behind a canister. Concerning the syringe, Officer Rose discovered it on the air conditioner; he pointed out that he saw it because he was tall or eye level with it. Officer Wright saw the syringe when his attention was directed to it. On this testimony, we find that the evidence is insufficient to hold the contraband was in such plain view as to characterize it as in close proximity to appellant.

. . . .

Other factors to be considered are incriminating statements, furtive gestures, or attempts to escape.

The term "possession" is statutorily defined as actual care, custody, control or management. This term describes a relationship to property. Possession is not an act nor is it an omission, but it is defined as something distinct from both act and omission.

As previously noted, the prosecution sought only to establish a relationship between appellant and the apartment. No further attempt was made to link appellant to the contraband. On the facts and circumstances of this case, we cannot say the evidence is sufficient to affirmatively link appellant to the contraband. Control of the apartment is not synonymous with control of the contraband when the appellant does not have sole access. No other link was shown. . . .

The judgment of the trial court is reversed, and appellant is ordered acquitted.

Omission

Most crimes involve a prohibited affirmative act that proscribes engaging in conduct such as killing, injuring, or taking another person's property. Some statutes, however, create a duty to act, and the failure to perform the duty can be the basis of criminal liability. Examples in the Texas Penal Code include Article 25.05, which makes it a crime to fail to provide support for a dependent child, and Article 38.08, which provides that prison employees who fail to take any action to prevent a prison escape are guilty of a crime. Statutes like these present few difficulties because the statute itself delineates those who have a legal duty that can be breached through inaction. A more challenging question is whether a crime *not* defined in a manner that makes inaction culpable can be committed by omission.

The common law tradition has been to avoid creating universal duties to aid people in distress. A person who continues to sip a cocktail by a swimming pool while a swimmer with a cramp in the deep end of the pool cries out for help is not guilty of a crime, even though the cocktail-drinker is within easy reach of a floatation device. Such a person may be behaving immorally by doing nothing, but, unless that person has a legal duty, the behavior is not illegal. Good Samaritan statutes, which require people to provide aid to those in physical danger if the aid can be accomplished without risk to the rescuer, have been passed in some jurisdictions. The less-communal approach of the common law has been explained on the ground that the criminal sanction should not be used merely for falling short of saintliness. Perhaps a more compelling reason is that it is difficult to draw a fair consistent causal line. Does responsibility for a death caused by not getting an accident victim to the hospital extend to those who voted to spend public money on a new football stadium instead of more ambulances and better roads?

While a broad community duty of care does not exist, the common law developed a number of well recognized categories of public duty including:

- *Special relationship.* Examples include parents, who have a duty to provide food, shelter, and other necessities to their children. Thus, if the cocktail drinker next to the pool is the parent of a drowning child, the failure to do anything could be a crime.

- *Contract.* Examples include operators of nursing homes, homecare nurses, and babysitters, who have a duty to provide food and medical care. Thus, if the cocktail drinker next to the pool has been hired to be the lifeguard for the pool, the failure to do anything could be a crime.

- *Statutory duty.* Examples include the duty of certain professionals to report suspected child abuse and the duty of innkeepers to refuse to serve alcohol to obviously intoxicated patrons. Thus, if the cocktail drinker next to the pool is the owner of a commercial swimming pool subject to regulatory statutes designed to enhance the safety of swimmers, the failure to do anything could be a crime.

- *Creation of the risk.* Examples include the duty of those involved in automobile accidents to stop and provide aid. Thus, if the cocktail drinker next to the pool was a person who urged the person who is now drowning to climb over a fence to swim in a pool after hours when no one else was present, the failure to do anything could be a crime.

- *Voluntary assumption of care.* Examples include the duty to continue providing food or medical care to people unable to care for themselves. Thus, if the person by the pool put down his drink and began to try to help the drowning person but then abandons the effort because the water is too cold, the failure to continue the voluntary rescue could be a crime.

Until recently, Texas took an extreme position by refusing to recognize common law duties. Instead, only legal duties expressly imposed by statute could create criminal liability for a failure to act. This was the state of the law at the time of the *Billingslea* case, which follows. The opinion in *Billingslea* was cited in the floor debate of a bill that became law and changed Texas law for omissions.

Billingslea v. State

734 S.W.2d 422 (Tex. App.—Dallas 1987) aff'd,
780 S.W.2d 271 (Tex. Crim. App. 1989)

Baker, Justice

Ray Edwin Billingslea was convicted of injury to an elderly individual by failing to obtain medical care for his mother. A jury found appellant guilty and assessed punishment at 99 years' confinement in the Texas Department of Corrections.

Appellant was charged by indictment with the offense of injury to an elderly individual. Appellant, his wife and son lived with appellant's 94–year old mother (decedent) in her home. Decedent became bedridden during March of 1984. Appellant, his wife and son cared for the decedent, including cooking for her and changing her linens. Appellant's son testified that decedent refused medical help. The granddaughter of the decedent testified that she made several attempts in April of 1984 to telephone decedent, but appellant always answered and told her that decedent was asleep, and on one occasion told her to stay out of his and his mother's business or he would kill her (granddaughter). On another occasion, appellant refused to let granddaughter and her son into the home to see decedent because he said she was asleep.

The daughter of decedent (Ms. Jefferson) testified that she received a call on April 19, 1984, from her daughter, which caused her to become concerned about decedent's health. Ms. Jefferson called the Social Security office in Dallas and asked them to investigate. An investigator (Mosley) with the Texas Department of Human Resources received a report from the local Social Security office and went to appellant's home on April 24, 1984, accompanied by a Dallas Police Department social service worker and two Dallas police officers. Appellant let them in the house and upon entering, Mosley noticed a strong odor as of rotten flesh. They found decedent in an upstairs bedroom. When asked if she was in pain, decedent moaned in response. Because of the odor, Mosley had to cover her face in order to continue the conversation. One of the officers had to leave the room because of the odor when Mosley pulled back the covers. Decedent was lying in her own urine and excrement and had a large bedsore on her heel which had eaten away part of the heel. Bedsores on the hip and back were ulcerated and had eaten to the bone. Paramedics were called to the home and decedent was transferred to Parkland Memorial Hospital. At the hospital it was further determined that decedent suffered from significant muscle loss and advanced bedsores which had some maggots in them. A doctor indicated that these bedsores probably had taken four to six weeks to develop into their current state. Decedent also had second-degree burns on her inner thighs from lying in her own urine. There was no evidence that decedent had been given any medical care during this period nor could she have secured medical care for herself. Decedent died on May 5, 1984.

Δ's argument

Appellant contends in his first point of error that the indictment failed to allege any statutory duty to act. Section 22.04 of the Texas Penal Code provides in part:

(a) A person commits an offense if he intentionally, knowingly, recklessly, or with criminal negligence, by act or omission, engages in conduct that causes to a child who is 14 years of age or younger or to an individual who is 65 years of age or older:

Can base case on this statute.

169

(1) serious bodily injury;

Omitting the formal parts, the indictment charged that appellant committed the offense as follows:

> (that the defendant did) then and there intentionally and knowingly engage in conduct that caused serious bodily injury to [decedent], an individual over 65 years of age, said conduct being by the following act and omission, to wit: the said defendant failed to obtain medical care for [decedent], the natural mother of the said defendant, who lived in the same house as defendant, and the said [decedent] was at said time physically unable to secure medical care for herself.

The important determination is whether the duty to act is an essential element of the offense that must be alleged in the indictment.

In *Ronk v. State*, 544 S.W.2d 123 (Tex. Crim. App. 1976), the mother and father of a child were prosecuted under section 22.04. The decision before the Court was whether the indictments, which failed to allege a relationship which would place the defendants under a statutory duty to secure medical treatment for a child, were missing a necessary element to constitute an offense. The court held that an essential element to an offense arising out of the failure to provide medical care for a child is the duty to provide care. Therefore, failure to allege a statutory duty or a relationship which would place a defendant under a statutory duty to perform the omitted act is a fundamental defect. The State responds to appellant's first point of error by arguing that section 22.04 does not by its terms limit itself to omissions involving statutory duties. Admitting that there are no explicit statutory duties resting upon children which require support of elderly parents, the State asserts that section 22.04 also includes the common law duties that would arise according to the factual, not necessarily familial, relationship of the parties. The State's basic theory of criminal responsibility in this case was that appellant owed a duty of care to the decedent because he had voluntarily assumed the primary responsibility for caring for the decedent, who could not care for herself; and the appellant also, by that responsibility, prevented others from coming to the decedent's aid. We disagree.

Although we perceive appellant was obviously under a moral duty to care for his elderly mother, and in those jurisdictions that recognize common law duties as a basis for criminal liability he would be held responsible for his failure to act, such is not the law in Texas.

It is clear, and regrettably so, in cases of this nature, that a statutory duty to act is required. Such duty and its omission must be alleged in the indictment and proved.

Alternatively, the State argues that Section 22.04 satisfies the Section 6.01(c) requirement that an omission is an offense if the statute so provides. Section 6.01 provides in part:

> (a) A person commits an offense only if he voluntarily engages in conduct, including an act, an omission or possession.

> . . . .

(c) A person who omits to perform an act does not commit an offense unless a statute provides that the omission is an offense or otherwise provides that he has a duty to perform the act.

Section 22.04 . . . does not contain or allude to a legal duty to act as a basis for making an omission an offense. Of course, there is a statutory duty for parents to support their children which is found in the Texas Family Code sections 4.02 and 12.04. However, no such statutory duty of a child to support a parent can be found and the State admits this in its brief. Therefore, we conclude that section 22.04 does not make an omission an offense within the meaning of section 6.01(c), and hold that since the State has not alleged a statutory duty to act in the indictment, the indictment is fundamentally defective and the conviction void. Point of error number one is sustained. *Statute does not have omission & no duty to act alleged*

Appellant's second point of error attacks the sufficiency of the evidence asserting the State failed to establish any criminal responsibility.

When viewed in a light most favorable to the verdict, the evidence shows that the State has failed to prove an essential element of the offense, namely, the duty to act. There is no evidence in the record that appellant had a statutory duty to act because no such duty exists under Texas law.

Although the facts in this case are extreme, and the conduct of the appellant reprehensible, the evidence is insufficient for failure to allege and prove a statutory duty to act. As recognized earlier in the opinion, only the legislature can impose statutory duties so that failure to act can be the basis of criminal liability. While an appellate court may properly write in areas traditionally reserved to the judicial branch of government, it would be a usurpation of our powers to add language to a statute where the legislature has failed to do so. Intrusion into the legislative arena without regard for traditional, constitutional, and legal safeguards of legislative power would violate a fundamental judicial rule. The court should carefully search out a statute's intent, giving full effect to all of its terms. But the court must find the legislative intent in the language of the statute and not elsewhere. The court is not a lawmaking body and it is not responsible for omissions in legislation. Since the legislature has not statutorily imposed a duty to cover the situation in this case, we must sustain appellant's second point of error.

Since our conclusions with respect to the appellant's first and second points of error are dispositive of this appeal, we do not address appellant's third, fourth, and fifth points of error.

The trial court's judgment is reversed and a judgment of acquittal is rendered. *Holding*

Notes

1.   The offense of conviction in *Billingslea* provided that "a person commits an offense if he intentionally, knowingly, recklessly, or with criminal negligence, by act **or omission**, engages in conduct that causes to . . . an individual who is 65 years of age or older: (1) serious bodily

injury . . . ." Why wasn't it sufficient that the explicit statutory language stated the offense could be committed by omission?

2.   After the events in *Billingslea*, the Texas legislature revised section 22.04, apparently expanding the bases for criminal liability for omissions. Under the current statute, "an omission . . . is conduct constituting an offense under this section if: (1) the actor has a legal or statutory duty to act; or (2) the actor has assumed care, custody, or control of a child, elderly individual, or disabled individual." The statute further specifies that "the actor has assumed care, custody, or control if he has by act, words, or course of conduct acted so as to cause a reasonable person to conclude that he has accepted responsibility for protection, food, shelter, and medical care for a child, elderly individual, or disabled individual."

This statute was in effect by the time of the appeal to the Texas Court of Criminal Appeals. It is undisputed that Billingslea voluntarily assumed care of his mother. Why didn't the court use the voluntary care duty to affirm the conviction?

3.   A more general revision of Texas statutes occurred when the legislature amended former Section 6.01(c) as it appeared in the *Billingslea* case. In place of the former statutory duty language, the statute now says: "a person who omits to perform an act does not commit an offense unless a law as defined by Section 1.07 provides that the omission is an offense or otherwise provides that he has a duty to perform the act." The term "law" in turn is defined in Section 1.07(30) as "the constitution or a statute of this state or of the United States, a written opinion of a court of record, a municipal ordinance, an order of a county commissioner's court, or a rule authorized by and lawfully adopted under a statute."

Although no Texas court has explicitly so held, a plausible interpretation of this statute is that by changing the statute to "law" and defining the word "law" to include courts, Texas has now joined the mainstream, and will recognize court-created common law duties. An indication of the new communal attitude was the promulgation of another statute creating a legal duty to act—a limited Good Samaritan statute.

Section 38.171 of the Texas Penal Code, entitled "Failure to Report Felony," provides:

(a) A person commits an offense if the person:
    (1) observes the commission of a felony under circumstances in which a reasonable person would believe that an offense had been committed in which serious bodily injury or death may have resulted; and
    (2) fails to immediately report the commission of the offense to a peace officer or law enforcement agency under circumstances in which:
        (A) a reasonable person would believe that the commission of the offense had not been reported; and
        (B) the person could immediately report the commission of the offense without placing himself or herself in danger of suffering serious bodily injury or death.
(b) An offense under this section is a Class A misdemeanor.

Chapter 9: Lesser Included Offense

Introduction

The next two chapters deal with an important aspect of the requirement of a criminal act. One physical act or transaction may violate more than one statute. Two different but closely related questions will be addressed. If multiple statutory offenses are implicated by a single act, may the defendant be convicted of all of them? Or is criminal liability limited to a single offense? This is a question that involves constitutional issues related to the protection against double jeopardy, and these issues will be addressed in the next chapter. In this chapter, we will deal with an issue that involves another constitutional concern: the requirement of fair notice.

Although the constitutional right to notice involves many aspects that are beyond the scope of our discussion, this chapter will deal with an important notice question—when may a defendant be charged with one offense, but convicted of another? It would clearly violate the right to fair notice to the criminally accused if the indictment or information charged the defendant with embezzlement, but all of the proof presented at trial was about an unrelated arson. Defendants are often convicted of offenses other than the offense charged, but the different offense of conviction bears a sufficient relationship to the charged offense in order to avoid notice problems. The procedural rules dealing with what is known as lesser-included offenses reveals an important understanding about substantive offenses in a penal code. Statutes are often not isolated, but are grouped in clusters of similar offenses.

Lesser-offense instructions are equally available to the prosecution and the defense, and neither side can prevent the other from requesting such an instruction when circumstances make it appropriate to submit these options to the jury. However, if both sides refrain from requesting a lesser-included offense instruction, the case may be submitted to the jury on the all-or-nothing basis of guilty or not guilty of the charged offense. Such a result may be preferred if both parties believe providing the middle-ground option of a lesser offense of conviction will induce a compromise result less favorable than the defendant's wish for an acquittal or the prosecution's desire for a conviction of the charged offense. Because of the strategic nature of the decision, it is appropriate for a trial court to defer to the implied strategic decisions of the parties by refraining from submitting lesser-offense instructions without a party's request, although there is Texas authority upholding *sua sponte* submission of lesser offense instructions by the trial court. It is clear the defense may not claim error successfully on appeal due to the omission of a lesser-included offense if the defense refrained from requesting one. Likewise, any error in the improper submission of a lesser-included instruction is waived if the defense fails to object to the instruction.

Lesser-included offense instructions are given in a cascading sequence. A lesser-included offense instruction informs the jurors to consider a lesser offense if they have reasonable doubt concerning the charged offense, and to only consider further lesser-included offenses if they have a reasonable doubt about the prior lesser-included offense if more than one such instruction is given. This sequential style of instruction, sometimes referred to as a "stair-step" charge, that requires the jury unanimously to decide guilt or innocence as to the greater offense before even considering whether the defendant should be found guilty of any lesser offense has been criticized as being overly restrictive by forbidding consideration of the lesser offense without an acquittal of the greater. Some courts have softened the stair-step approach by instructing the jury to give the defendant the benefit of the doubt in deciding which of two or more options to choose, which encourages a consideration of all possible verdicts.

In Texas, a statutory definition of a "lesser included offense" is provided by Article 37.09 of the Texas Code of Criminal Procedure, which states an offense is considered a lesser included of the charged offense if:

(1) It is established by proof of the same facts or less than all the facts that establish the offense charged.

(2) It differs from the offense charged only in that a less serious injury or risk of injury is involved

(3) It differs from the offense charged only in that it requires a less culpable mental state.

(4) It is an attempt to commit the offense charged or to commit another included offense of the offense charged.

The second through fourth definitions above are relatively clear and could be subsumed by the first definition, which is the broadest and most ambiguous. Thus, an offense requiring proof only of "bodily injury" is a lesser-included offense of an otherwise identical offense requiring "serious bodily injury" (i.e. aggravated assault and assault); an offense requiring "recklessness" is a lesser-included offense of an otherwise identical offense requiring "intent or knowledge" (i.e. murder and manslaughter); and an uncompleted crime is a lesser included offense of the same completed crime (i.e. robbery and attempted robbery).

The situation can be more complex if the issue is whether the offense for which an instruction is requested is established "by the same or less than all of the facts of the charged offense." The simple case is one in which the lesser statute contains all of the elements of the greater, except that the greater contains an additional element not found in the lesser. The issue becomes more debatable when elements differ and it must be determined whether the elements of the lesser offense are implied by the greater.

Perhaps the most important ambiguity in determining whether a requested offense qualifies as a lesser-included offense of that charged is whether the determination is based upon an abstract consideration of the statutory elements as they appear in the penal code or other statute, or whether the analysis may rely on facts alleged in the particular charging instrument or the facts proved at trial. In other words, must the lesser offense be considered included within the elements of the charged offense in all cases from the face of the statutes without resort to particular facts? Or is it sufficient that the requested offense is within allegations of the offense as charged in the indictment or as presented by the proof in the case?

The standard used to determine whether offenses have the relationship of greater and lesser included vary by jurisdiction. Consider the facts and allegations in the Texas case of

174

Bartholomew v. State, 871 S.W.2d 210 (Tex. Crim. App. 1994). The defendant in *Bartholomew*, who was charged with reckless driving, sought lesser-included offense instructions for two less serious traffic offenses: speeding and racing. Because a driver may be reckless in myriad ways having nothing to do with racing or speeding, these offenses would appear not to be necessarily included within the proof necessary to establish the charged offense based solely on a consideration of the statutory elements. This would preclude a lesser-offense instruction in jurisdictions using the strict statutory elements approach. However, the Court of Criminal Appeals reversed the reckless driving conviction because of the trial court's failure to submit the requested racing and speeding alternatives to the jury because the indictment alleged the State would attempt to prove that the defendant drove recklessly by "racing" and "speeding."

Is there is a limit to the extent that indictment allegations or proof at trial may result in instructions concerning offenses not intrinsically related to the primary offense alleged by the State? For example, after alleging or proving that a burglar happened to have a controlled substance in his pocket when he (1) entered a dwelling (2) without the permission of the owner (3) with an intent to steal, could the prosecution successfully request a drug possession offense as a lesser included offense?

After issuing rules that gave conflicting indications about whether the court was using a strict statutory elements approach or whether a broader approach grounded in allegations in a charging instrument or based on any evidence adduced at trial, the court of Criminal Appeals appears to have resolved the issue in the *Hall* case that follows.

Hall v. State

225 S.W.3d 524 (Tex. Crim. App. 2007)

Womack, J., delivered the opinion of the Court.

An important issue in this case was whether the offense of aggravated assault by threat is a lesser-included offense of murder. We granted review to resolve ambiguities and conflicts in our decisions about the method of determining whether the allegation of a greater offense includes a lesser offense. We hold that the determination should be made by comparing the elements of the greater offense, as the State pled it in the indictment, with the elements in the statute that defines the lesser offense. We decide that aggravated assault was not a lesser offense included in the offense of murder that was alleged in the indictment in this case.

I.

The laws in our nation have taken four approaches to lesser-included offenses, which have been labeled "strict-statutory," "cognate-pleadings," "cognate-evidence," and "inherently related."

Some states permit a lesser included-offense instruction only when all of the statutory elements of the lesser offense are contained within the statutory elements of the greater offense. This has been called the strict statutory approach.

Many states have found this approach to be inflexible, and have adopted standards that permit an instruction even when the lesser offense is not composed of a subset of the statutory elements of the greater crime. This approach is known as the "cognate" theory, and it is the majority approach. There are two significantly different versions of the cognate theory, which mirror the two divergent lines of authority in our own cases.

One is known as the "cognate-pleadings" approach, in which the court looks to the facts and elements as alleged in the charging instrument, and not just to the statutory elements of the offense, to determine whether there exists a lesser-included offense of the greater charged offense.

The other cognate approach is known as the "cognate-evidence" approach, a more liberal approach in which the court includes the facts adduced at trial in its lesser-included offense analysis.

The fourth, and most liberal, view is the one reflected in the Model Penal Code, which permits a lesser-included offense instruction on any offense that is "inherently related" to the greater offense. At least one state permits lesser-included offenses to be determined solely from the evidence without reference to relationship or the elements of the crime, taking the most expansive portions of the cognate evidence approach and the inherent relationship approach.

II. Article 37.09

In this state, the answers to questions about lesser-included offenses must be based on Article 37.09 of the Code of Criminal Procedure, which was Texas' first general statute that defined lesser-included offenses.

Before the enactment of Article 37.09 in 1973, the Code of Criminal Procedure did not contain a generally applicable rule for lesser-included offenses. Instead, it specified that certain offenses included certain lesser offenses.

Article 37.09 became effective on January 1, 1974, as a conforming amendment in the new Penal Code Act. Rather than providing a list of greater and lesser offenses, it set out general definitions of a lesser-included offense that apply to all offenses:

An offense is a lesser included offense if:

(1) it is established by proof of the same or less than all the facts required to establish the commission of the offense charged;

(2) it differs from the offense charged only in the respect that a less serious injury or risk of injury to the same person, property, or public interest suffices to establish its commission;

(3) it differs from the offense charged only in the respect that a less culpable mental state suffices to establish its commission; or

(4) it consists of an attempt to commit the offense charged or an otherwise included offense.

The problematic definition is in Article 37.09(1)—specifically the term "facts required to establish."

III. *Day v. State*

We gave the term "facts required to establish" two different interpretations in the very first case in which we construed Article 37.09(1): *Day v. State*, 532 S.W.2d 302 (Tex. Crim. App. 1976). One interpretation was in our opinion on original submission, on which we shall rely in this case. The other interpretation was in the opinion on rehearing, which we shall modify and correct.

Day was charged with, and convicted of, burglary with intent to commit theft. He appealed, complaining of the trial court's refusal to charge the jury on a lesser-included offense of criminal trespass. The evidence was that police found Day inside a restaurant, which was not open, at 3 a.m. The front window was broken, a cigarette machine had been broken into, a box containing property from the manager's office was near the cigarette machine, and Day had a letter opener from the office in his pocket.

> [Day,] testifying in his own behalf, stated that at approximately 3 a.m. on the date in question he was proceeding past [the restaurant] on the way home from a girlfriend's house. He stated that he observed a man come out of the restaurant and then noticed that

177

a window had been broken out. [He] entered the restaurant through the broken window intending to telephone the police to report the broken window. He stated that the cigarette machine was already overturned and the cigarette packs already scattered on the floor at the time of his entry. [He] testified that he stepped on the letter opener and then put it in his pocket as a "reflex action." By his testimony, he was unable to find a light switch or telephone and was apprehended by the police approximately two minutes after entry.

In our opinion on original submission in *Day* we established the method of analysis under the new statute. There are two steps in the analysis of whether there may be a conviction for a lesser offense in a particular case. "Our initial inquiry concerns whether criminal trespass is, as the appellant contends, a lesser included offense of burglary." After we determined that it was a lesser-included offense, "Our next inquiry concerns whether there was sufficient evidence at trial to have required the court to submit to the jury the issue of criminal trespass."

We also demonstrated the methods and standards to be used in the two-step analysis. The first step was to determine whether criminal trespass was a lesser-included offense of burglary. We began by setting out the four definitions of a lesser-included offense in Article 37.09. Then we set out the statutory elements of burglary and criminal trespass. Then we compared the elements of the charged offense and the lesser offense and construed some terms in the statutes. We concluded, "Therefore, the elements of criminal trespass, including 'notice,' could be established by proof of the same facts necessary to prove the offense of burglary. The proof of additional facts would not be necessary, and the requirement of Article 37.09(1), Vernon's Ann. C.C.P., would be satisfied. Therefore, we hold that the offense of criminal trespass is a lesser included offense of all three types of burglary."

The first step of the analysis was completed by comparing the elements of the greater offense and the lesser offense without any reference to the facts or evidence of the particular case.

On rehearing, the Court's opinion incorrectly said the opposite.

The *Day* Court took up two issues on rehearing. One was the State's argument "that the requested charge was properly denied because the indictment would not support a conviction for criminal trespass. The State cites numerous authorities for the proposition that an indictment will not support conviction for what otherwise would be a lesser included offense unless the indictment pleads all of the necessary allegations to charge such other offense." After surveying the law of lesser-included offenses before 1973, we said, "With respect to the State's challenge raised against the power of the court to enter judgment for criminal trespass upon the indictment in this case, we hold that the new statutory scheme of lesser included offenses, as contrasted with the old statutory scheme of offenses with degrees, did not create such a restriction upon the jurisdiction of the trial court once properly invoked to try the offense charged, to proceed to judgment upon the lesser included offense . . . ."

Just before that holding, the Court made the statement, "On original submission we held that *on the facts of this case* criminal trespass was a lesser included offense to the burglary charged under the terms of Art. 37.09(1), V.A.C.C.P." This was a misstatement of the holding on original submission, which had made no reference to the facts of the case.

We made a similar statement in connection with the next issue, which was our *sua sponte* decision to consider the constitutionality of the new statute. Some aspects of the lesser included-offense statutes before 1973 fell short of the constitutional requirements for due process of law. If an offense was listed in the former statute as a lesser-included offense, we held that the elements of the lesser offense need not be pleaded in the indictment for the greater offense.

To dispense with the need for pleading all the constituent elements of the lesser offense, which applies in other cases . . . the relationship between the offense charged and the other offense not only must be within the terms of the statute specifying offenses with degrees, but also that relationship between the two offenses must be such that the other offense is in fact not repugnant to the offense charged. To state that the Legislature by statute may authorize conviction for any offense so designated upon trial for some other offense regardless of the relationship between the two is to state an obvious absurdity violative of basic principles of due process. A statute within such absurd principle might authorize upon the trial of A for the murder of B a conviction for the murder of C, or the rape of D, or the possession of contraband, or any other offense. The violations of due process that would occur are manifest.

Although the parties had not raised the question, the Court held that the 1973 revision of Article 37.09 did not violate the constitution in this way.

> The careful reader will observe that each definition in Art. 37.09 is stated with reference to "the offense charged," and moreover, each such definition specifically states the manner in which the lesser included offense differs from the offense charged. The enumerated variations in the statute do not enlarge upon the offense charged, but instead vary in a manner that either is restrictive or reduces culpability as compared to the offense charged. In view of those restrictions, we hold Arts. 37.08 and 37.09, *supra*, are constitutional insofar as they authorize, as did the prior scheme of degrees of offenses, conviction upon an indictment charging one offense for a lesser included offense of the offense charged.

Then our opinion on rehearing made a second troublesome statement. "We must add, however, that whether one offense bears such a relationship to the offense charged is an issue which must await a case by case determination, both because the statute defines lesser included offenses in terms of the offense charged and because it defines lesser included offenses in terms of the *facts of the case*."

The trouble with the statement is that Article 37.09(1) does not speak of the facts of the case; it speaks of "the facts required to establish the commission of the offense charged." The opinion on rehearing, without analysis, said this meant the evidence in the case. The opinion on original submission used the elements of the offense charged, without reference to the evidence in the case.

Thus, in our first case to construe Article 37.09, a majority of the Court took conflicting positions.

When it said that the question of whether one offense was included in another depended on the evidence, the opinion on rehearing in *Day* was misreading both the opinion on original submission and Article 37.09. This view is somewhat bolstered by the fact that only eight weeks after the Court delivered the opinion on rehearing in *Day*, the author of that opinion denied that his opinion should be read to authorize consideration of the evidence on the issue of whether one offense was included within the allegation of another. Until today, this court has frequently ignored his protestations, and continued to say that Article 37.09 as interpreted in the opinion on rehearing in *Day* requires consideration of the evidence in making the decision.

The conflict has persisted, with some of the Court's opinions determining whether one offense is a lesser-included offense of another by comparing the elements of the offenses, and others by comparing the evidence in the case to the elements of the lesser offense.

The question to be resolved is whether "the facts required" in Article 37.09(1) are determined by the evidence adduced at trial, or whether the determination is a question of law that can be answered before the trial begins by looking at the elements and facts alleged in the charging instrument.

The statement in the opinion on rehearing in *Day* that "the statute defines lesser included offenses in terms of the offense charged and it defines lesser included offenses in terms of the facts of the case," is based on a misreading of the statute. Instead of seeing the statute as providing alternate definitions of lesser-included offenses, the proper reading follows the bulk of the court's analysis in *Day*: the statute sets out the two-step process of first looking at the charging instrument to discern the lesser-included offenses and next determining whether the evidence at trial supports giving one of these predetermined lesser-included offense instructions.

III. Constitutional Implications

This court has said on a number of occasions that when the greater offense may be committed in more than one manner, the manner alleged will determine the availability of lesser-included offenses. For example, aggravated assault may be committed by threat with a deadly weapon or by inflicting serious bodily injury. Assault by committing bodily injury is a lesser-included offense of aggravated assault by inflicting serious bodily injury, but not of aggravated assault by threat with a deadly weapon. . . . If the evidence determines whether an offense is included within the alleged offense, the results would be different.

The United States Supreme Court referred to this problem in *Schmuck v. United States*, 489 U.S. 705 (1989). The Court construed Federal Rule of Criminal Procedure 31(c), which speaks in terms of a lesser-included offense's being "necessarily included in the offense charged." The Court indicated that there might be a constitutional violation if the relationship were base don evidence rather than the pleaded elements:

. . . .

It is ancient doctrine of both the common law and of our Constitution that a defendant cannot be held to answer a charge not contained in the indictment brought against him . . . . This stricture is based at least in part on the right of the defendant to notice of the charge brought against him . . . . Were the prosecutor able to request an instruction on an offense whose elements were not charged in the indictment, this right to notice would be placed in jeopardy.

Other courts have remarked on the lack of notice when the evidence test is used. For example, the Florida Supreme Court said:

> The accusatory pleading must apprise the defendant of all offenses of which he may be convicted. This . . . means that he may be convicted of any lesser offense, which, although not an essential ingredient of the major crime, is spelled out in the accusatory pleading in that it alleges all of the elements of the lesser offense and the proof at trial supports the charge. The gist is not what the defendant would like to persuade a jury he may be guilty of, but that the accusatory pleading apprise him of all offenses of which he may be convicted.

Our Code of Criminal Procedure also recognizes that the charging instrument should include all of the elements of the offenses with which the defendant is charged. Article 21.03 commands, "Everything should be stated in an indictment which is necessary to be proved." Determining lesser-included offenses from the evidence at trial instead of from the elements of the offense listed on the charging instrument fails to adhere to this directive.

Another problem with the evidence approach is that the Supreme Court compares elements of offenses, rather than conduct or evidence, to decide when successive prosecutions violate the Double Jeopardy Clause of the Fifth Amendment. In the absence of a contrary expression of legislative intent, the elements of offenses, as they are pleaded in the indictment, also are compared to decide whether multiple punishments violate the Double Jeopardy Clause. Problems could result if lesser-included offenses were determined by a comparison of evidence at trial, while jeopardy issues were determined by a comparison of the statutory elements as alleged in the charging instrument, for conviction bars prosecution for a greater or lesser-included offense.

IV.

Article 37.09, as it was applied in the Court's opinion on original submission in Day, is compatible with the cognate-pleadings approach to lesser-included offenses, although this label was not adopted in the opinion. When the Court evaluated the burglary statute to see, as a matter of law, whether trespass was a lesser-included offense, it held that although burglary of a building does not include an element of notice, which is a requirement of the offense of trespass, that element is satisfied by proof of a "fencing or other enclosure obviously designed to exclude intruders."

However, if the factual allegations in the charging instrument did not reflect that the building's exterior served as such a barrier, then "additional facts" would be necessary to support trespass as a lesser-included offense. The opinion on original submission in Day used the pleadings approach to find that trespass is a lesser-included offense of burglary.

We now hold that the pleadings approach is the sole test for determining in the first step whether a party may be entitled to a lesser-included-offense instruction. The availability of a lesser-included instruction in a given case still would depend on the second step, whether there is some evidence adduced at trial to support such an instruction.

The first step in the lesser-included-offense analysis, determining whether an offense is a lesser-included offense of the alleged offense, is a question of law. It does not depend on the evidence to be produced at the trial. It may be, and to provide notice to the defendant must be, capable of being performed before trial by comparing the elements of the offense as they are alleged in the indictment or information with the elements of the potential lesser-included offense.

The evidence adduced at trial should remain an important part of the court's decision whether to charge the jury on lesser-included offenses. The second step in the analysis should ask whether there is evidence that supports giving the instruction to the jury." A defendant is entitled to an instruction on a lesser-included offense where the proof for the offense charged includes the proof necessary to establish the lesser-included offense and there is some evidence in the record that would permit a jury rationally to find that if the defendant is guilty, he is guilty only of the lesser-included offense." In this step of the analysis, anything more than a scintilla of evidence may be sufficient to entitle a defendant to a lesser charge. In other words, the evidence must establish the lesser-included offense as "a valid, rational alternative to the charged offense."

Applying the first step of the lesser included-offense analysis in the instant case, we do not consider the evidence that was presented at trial. Instead, we consider only the statutory elements of murder as they were modified by the particular allegations in the indictment:

(1) the appellant

(2) caused the death of an individual

(3) by shooting the individual with a gun

(4) (a) with intent to cause the individual's death or

　　(b) (1) with intent to cause the individual serious bodily injury and

　　(2) committing an act clearly dangerous to human life.

We then compare them with the elements of the lesser offense of aggravated assault by threat that could be included in that offense:

(1) the appellant

(2) threatened another individual with imminent bodily injury

(3) intentionally, knowingly, or recklessly

(4) by displaying a deadly weapon, namely a gun.

We then ask the question that Article 37.09(a) poses: are the elements of the lesser offense "established by proof of the same or less than all the facts required to established the commission of the offense charged"?

The answer is that they are not. The facts required to prove the lesser offense include two that are not the same as, or less than, those required to establish the offense charged: threatening and display.

It is true that the evidence may show threatening and display. The evidence may show a number of other lesser offenses as well, such as disorderly conduct by discharging a firearm in a public place or across a public road or by displaying a firearm in a public place in a manner calculated to alarm, unlawful carrying of weapon, or unlawful possession of weapon. But those offenses likewise are not established by the same or less than the proof required to prove the allegations in the indictment for murder. Aggravated assault by threat, like the other offenses mentioned, requires proof of additional facts.

The Court made this clear in *Day*. Burglary can be committed by unlawfully entering a building with intent to commit theft, or by unlawfully entering and thereafter committing theft. The evidence in the case would have supported a verdict for either theory of burglary, but the indictment did not allege the element of committing theft after entry.

The cognate-pleadings analysis that we used in the opinion on original submission in *Day* requires us to reason that, although the evidence may have supported a verdict of aggravated assault by the threat of displaying a gun, the indictment did not allege threats or display. By analyzing the statutory elements of the offense as they were modified in the indictment, the assault by threats was not included within the allegation of murder.

To hold otherwise would be contrary to the better analysis of the statute and might run afoul of the requirements of due process by making it impossible to know before trial what lesser offenses are included within the indictment, yet making it possible at the end of the trial to convict for any offense that was incidentally shown by the evidence.

We disapprove the statements in the opinion on rehearing in *Day* that implied the contrary, and (like the author of those statements) we disapprove the decisions that have held the contrary.

The judgment of the Court of Appeals is affirmed.

Evidentiary Support

A finding that a requested offense qualifies as being "included" within the proof required for the charged offense is a necessary, but not a sufficient, condition for granting a requested lesser-offense instruction. Thus, an instruction on a lesser offense requested by the defense is required only if both of the following conditions are fulfilled:

- The lesser offense is included within the proof necessary to establish the offense charged; and
- Some evidence exists in the record that would permit a jury rationally to find that, if guilty, the defendant is guilty only of the lesser-included offense.

Thus, under this two-part standard, merely because manslaughter and criminally-negligent homicide are lesser-included offenses of murder does not mean that it is appropriate to submit an instruction on these offenses at every murder trial, even though they are offenses identical to murder except for a less-culpable mental state. Whether the lesser-offense instructions should be given depends on the evidence that was presented at trial. For example, if the sole defense of a murder defendant is an alibi, so that the only contested issue is the identity of the perpetrator, it would make no sense to give the jury the option of finding the defendant was out of town for purposes of murder, but was present for purposes of the same homicide, submitted as a lesser offense of murder. However, an instruction on manslaughter or criminally-negligent homicide might well be appropriate if there is testimony the defendant recklessly discharged a gun or allowed a gun to fire accidentally because of a failure to take adequate safety precautions. It would not matter that there is evidence contrary to this theory because a lesser-included-offense instruction is appropriate when requested by a party if "some" evidence of unsafe firearm handling suggested recklessness or criminal negligence.

There is equal treatment of defense and prosecution requests for lesser-included offenses with regard to the first step of the analysis in which it is determined whether the requested offense is included within the charged offense. If the offense qualifies as a lesser included, either party may request the instruction, and neither party can veto the other's entitlement to such a jury charge. Neither party is entitled to an instruction if the offense does not qualify as a lesser included.

Equality of treatment for the parties ends with the second step. The requirement of evidence to support the lesser offense applies only to the defendant but not the State. Presiding Judge Keller gave an explanation of the lack of symmetry in *Grey v. State*, which follows.

Grey v. State

298 S.W.3d 644 (Tex. Crim. App. 2009)

Keller, P.J., delivered the opinion of the Court.

In the *Royster-Rousseau* line of cases [*Royster v. State*, 622 S.W.2d 442 (Tex. Crim. App. 1981) and *Rousseau v. State*, 855 S.W.2d 666 (Tex. Crim. App. 1993)], we established a two-pronged test for determining when a trial judge should submit to the jury a lesser-included offense that is requested by the defendant. Under the second prong of the test, "some evidence must exist in the record that would permit a jury rationally to find that if the defendant is guilty, he is guilty only of the lesser offense." In *Arevalo v. State*, this Court held that the second prong applies equally to the submission of lesser-included offenses that are requested by the State. We granted review in this case to determine the following ground presented by the State: "*Arevalo v. State* should be overruled." Agreeing with the State, we overrule *Arevalo* and hold that the State is not bound by the second prong of the *Royster-Rousseau* test.

I. Background

Appellant was indicted for aggravated assault by causing bodily injury and using a deadly weapon. The alleged deadly weapon was appellant's hand, used to strangle the victim. In addition to instructions about the indicted offense, the jury charge contained an instruction on the lesser-included offense of simple assault by causing bodily injury. The jury charge was prepared by the prosecutor's office, and one of the prosecutors stated on the record that she had no objection to it and thought it was sufficient. But defense counsel objected to the lesser-included-offense instruction. The jury found appellant guilty of the lesser-included offense of simple assault.

On appeal, appellant claimed that the submission of the lesser-included offense was error. The court of appeals agreed and reversed the conviction.

II. Analysis

One obvious flaw in the rule laid down by *Arevalo* and its progeny, one that produces inconsistent and unjust results in every single case in which the rule is applied, is the remedy. When a lesser-included offense is submitted in violation of *Arevalo*, and the defendant is convicted of that offense, the remedy this Court has imposed is a remand for a new trial on the very same lesser-included offense that the defendant has just claimed should never have been submitted. Such a result is "illogical," but we fashioned this remedy because alternative remedies seemed unavailable or worse. Because a conviction on the lesser offense operates as an acquittal of the greater offense, retrial on the greater offense is not possible. But an outright acquittal of the criminal charge would be absurd where the evidence was in fact legally sufficient to support a conviction for the lesser-included offense.

So where did the rule in *Arevalo* come from, and what is the legal basis for its existence? *Arevalo*'s holding was based upon the "guilty only" requirement that is the second prong of the *Royster-Rousseau* test. In dissents in *Arevalo*, Presiding Judge McCormick and Judge Meyers both suggested that the "guilty only" requirement has constitutional underpinnings, describing when a lesser-included-offense instruction is *required*, but not necessarily describing all the circumstances under which such an instruction is *permitted*. In *Rousseau*, we had clarified the "guilty only" prong (but did not change existing law) by borrowing language from the federal standard, which we observed was stated in the Supreme Court decision of *Hopper v. Evans*. *Evans* discussed *Beck v. Alabama*, in which the Supreme Court concluded that a failure in a capital case to submit a lesser-included offense when raised by the evidence violates the constitution because there is an unwarranted risk that "a jury might convict a defendant of a capital offense because it found that the defendant was guilty of a serious [but lesser] crime."

The Supreme Court expressly reserved the question of whether the federal constitution can require the submission of a lesser-included offense in a non-capital case, and more recently it has suggested that *Beck*'s holding may be limited to cases in which the death penalty was automatic upon conviction for the greater offense. We have assumed that the erroneous failure to submit a lesser-included-offense instruction requested by the defense in a non-capital case constitutes ordinary jury charge error.

Though the Court's opinion in *Arevalo* cited to articles 37.08 and 37.09, neither statute contains any language that suggests the application of a "guilty only" requirement for determining when a lesser-included offense should be submitted. The propriety of the "guilty only" requirement appears to be a matter of common law, which will be discussed in more detail below.

In *Arevalo*, this Court conceded that we had "never stated a rationale for the second prong of the [*Royster-Rousseau*] test," but we "thought the rationale was obvious." We said that the "guilty only" rule was designed to preserve the integrity of the jury as a factfinder by ensuring that it was instructed on a lesser-included offense "only when that offense constitutes a valid, rational alternative to the charged offense."

The Court in *Arevalo* then made an inferential leap: It held that this rationale "is as applicable to the State's request for a lesser-included offense as it is to a defendant's request." Why? Because a lesser-included-offense instruction "must not constitute an invitation to the jury to reach an irrational verdict."

But the Court did not ask or answer the next obvious question: How does a lesser-included-offense instruction invite a jury to reach an irrational verdict? If the lesser offense is viewed in isolation, a jury's verdict would be rational so long as the lesser offense is included in the charging instrument and supported by legally sufficient evidence. The "guilty-only" prong of the *Royster-Rousseau* test requires, however, that we view the rationality of the lesser offense, not in isolation, but in comparison to the offense described in the charging instrument. But why should we make that comparison? The answer must be that the State is entitled to pursue the charged offense and, therefore, is entitled to receive a response from the jury on whether the defendant is guilty of the charged offense. Is the defendant similarly entitled to a response from the jury on the charged offense? The answer to that question is clearly no. It is the State, not the defendant, that chooses what offense is to be charged. In fact, the State can abandon an element of the charged offense without prior notice and proceed to prosecute a lesser-included offense. If the State can abandon the charged offense in favor of a lesser-included offense, there is no logical reason why the State could not abandon its unqualified pursuit of the charged offense in favor of a qualified pursuit that includes the prosecution of a lesser-included offense in the alternative.

We have already addressed one detrimental consequence of the rule in *Arevalo*: the remedy for the supposed error is illogical. Another detrimental consequence is that the prosecutor may be faced with a situation in which any decision he makes carries a high risk of error. If the prosecutor requests a lesser-included offense, he may run the risk of a reversal under *Arevalo*. But if the prosecutor fails to request a lesser-included offense, he may also run the risk of an outright acquittal by a jury or an acquittal for legal insufficiency on appeal.

The present case is illustrative. To convict appellant of aggravated assault in this case, the State had to prove that he used or exhibited a deadly weapon. The alleged deadly weapon in this case was appellant's hand. The court of appeals held that the evidence in this case does not show that the defendant was guilty only of a simple assault because the evidence shows only that the defendant's hand was a deadly weapon. But it is easy to see how a jury might not be willing to find that a person's hand is a deadly weapon, despite all the evidence in favor of that proposition. And at the time of trial, the State might have legitimately perceived the possibility (though unlikely) that an appellate court would decide that the evidence was legally insufficient to prove the deadly weapon element.

The cautious approach for the prosecutor to take would be—or at least should be—to request the lesser-included offense. Allowing submission of lesser offenses when requested by the prosecutor would serve at least two important interests. First, society has an interest in convicting and punishing people who are guilty of crimes. When, in the prosecutor's judgment, submission of the lesser-included offense will enhance the prospects of securing an appropriate criminal conviction for a defendant who is in fact guilty, society's interests are best served by allowing the submission. Second, the prosecutor has "the primary duty . . . not to convict, but to see that justice is done." Even if the prosecutor believes in a given case that he will secure a conviction on the charged offense if the only alternative is acquittal, he might also believe that the jury should be given the option to decide whether a conviction on the lesser offense is more appropriate.

Of course, the prosecutor could simply abandon the charged offense in favor of the lesser-included offense. But doing so would reflect not caution but capitulation. If the prosecutor believes the evidence for the charged offense is strong but also believes that the jury ought to be able to consider the lesser-included offense, then abandoning the charged offense as a remedy for the dilemma created by *Arevalo* would be overkill. And the decision on whether to abandon the charged offense would itself pose a dilemma because the prosecutor would not want to effectuate an abandonment unnecessarily.

F. Conclusion

The common-law rule established in *Arevalo* is based on flawed premises, places undue burdens on the prosecutor, and results in an illogical remedy. Consequently, we overrule *Arevalo*.

The judgment of the court of appeals is reversed, and the case is remanded to address appellant's remaining points of error.

Notes

1.   The "guilty only" language for evidentiary support, which after *Grey* applies only to the defense, does not mean the defendant must prove there is insufficient evidence for the charged offense in order to be entitled to an instruction on a lesser-included offense. The appropriate standard is similar to that for a defense instruction, which requires submission if there is "some evidence" of a defensive matter, like self-defense. The question with the partial defense of lesser-included offenses is whether there is some evidence that the defendant might be not guilty of the charged offense, but guilty of the requested lesser included. In deciding whether to give a charge on a lesser offense, as with defense instructions, the court must not consider either the credibility of evidence raising the lesser offense or whether it conflicts with other evidence.

2.   While the threshold showing required for a lesser-included-offense instruction is low, Texas courts have stated it is insufficient that the jury might disbelieve evidence pertaining to the greater offense; rather, there must be some evidence of the lesser-included offense for the jury to consider before an instruction on a lesser-included offense is warranted. For example, in *Enriquez v. State*, 21 S.W.3d 277 (Tex. Crim. App. 2000), a chemist affirmatively testified in a possession of a controlled substance trial that only one small sample of the total quantity seized had been analyzed. The Court of Criminal Appeals held that an instruction on a lesser offense involving possession of a smaller quantity was appropriate because this testimony would have been "some evidence directly germane" to the lesser-included offense. However, the *Enriquez* Court stated that, when a chemist testified her usual practice was to test a sample from each bundle of a controlled substance, and that her recollection was that "some type of sample" was analyzed from each bundle, the accused was not entitled to a lesser-included-offense instruction based upon the mere possibility that the jury would not believe the chemist's testimony.

3.   The distinction between the low threshold of "some evidence" versus the need for more than the possibility of disbelief has proved to be elusive, and suggests it is advisable for defense attorneys to seek lesser-included-offense instructions when in doubt in addition to arguing that any refusal of a request is reversible error on appeal. For example, in *Jones v. State*, 984 S.W.2d 254, 258 (Tex. Crim. App. 1998), the Court of Criminal Appeals seemed to say that the possibility of partial disbelief is sufficient to require a lesser-included-offense instruction—a standard that would appear to make lesser included offenses mandatory in all cases if taken to the limits of this logic. *Jones* involved a robbery case in which the trial court denied lesser-included-offense instructions for theft and assault when the defendant, in his testimony at trial, denied he took items from the store. While the defendant admitted participating in a fight with store employees, he claimed he acted in self-defense. In holding the trial court's refusal to instruct the jury of both lesser offenses on the grounds of the defendant's "blanket denial" of wrongdoing was erroneous, the Court of Criminal Appeals reasoned that such an approach

> neglects the fact that a jury is permitted to believe or disbelieve any part of a witness' testimony (including that of a defendant) and it disregards the fact that a lesser included

offense can be raised by any evidence from any source so long as a rational trier of fact could conclude from that evidence that a defendant is guilty only of that lesser included offense.

4.   An illustration of applying the affirmative proof test in meeting the "guilty only" standard for lesser-included offenses that was difficult for the State occurred in *Hampton v. State*, 109 S.W.3d 437, 441 (Tex. Crim. App. 2003). *Hampton* is an aggravated sexual assault case in which the State presented testimony from the victim that a knife was used. There was no contrary evidence on this point. The mere failure to find or retrieve a knife matching the description given by the victim was not affirmative evidence that no knife was used during the assault. Because the failure to find a knife could not properly be considered to be evidence to support the charge of the lesser-included offense of sexual assault, the submission of this offense over defense objection was reversible error in a case in which the defendant was convicted of the requested lesser-included offense. Cases such as *Hampton* are no longer valid in light of the decision of the Court of Criminal Appeals in *Grey*, which exempts the State from the evidentiary support requirement.

5.   As the *Grey* opinion noted, any error in a noncapital case pertaining to a lesser-included offense is a matter of state law and has no federal constitutional significance. It is only a constitutional imperative in the "death is different" jurisprudence of capital cases where the need for heightened reliability requires an instruction on a lesser-included offense when a jury rationally could convict on the lesser offense and acquit on the greater offense. *See Beck v. Alabama*, 447 U.S. 625 (1980).

Despite the non-constitutional nature of a lesser-included-offense claim, when error is properly preserved, reversible error routinely has been found when the trial court failed to submit a lesser-included offense that was requested by the defense and supported by the evidence. In *Saunders v. State*, 913 S.W.2d 564, 571 (Tex. Crim. App. 1995), the Court of Criminal Appeals stated that a finding of harm is "essentially automatic" when a lesser-included-offense instruction is improperly refused because the jury is denied the opportunity to convict the defendant for a lesser offense. However, *Saunders* referred to a situation in which a defense request for a lesser-offense instruction is erroneously refused, and only the options of guilty of the charged offense and acquittal were submitted to the jury. Harmless error is more likely to be found in cases in which there is an erroneous decision to instruct on a lesser-included offense, but the jury charge contains other proper lesser-included-offense instructions, particularly if the jury returns a verdict of guilty of the charged offense. The existence of such an intervening lesser-offense instruction does not automatically foreclose harm because, in some circumstances, the intervening lesser offense may be the least plausible theory under the evidence. However, in cases where a lesser-offense option provides a realistic option for a jury, the jury's return of a verdict for the charged offense rather the lesser-offense instruction that was given supports a harmless error determination.

6.   *Grey* overturned the prior decision in *Arevalo*, which held the requirement of evidence to support the submission of the lesser offense applies to both parties. *Grey* does not affect the part of *Arevalo* that found an erroneous submission of a lesser-included offense could be reversible error; it only redefined the circumstances in which the submission of a State request would be error. Thus, if at the behest of the State, a trial court improperly submits a lesser-included-

189

offense instruction for an offense that is not included within the elements of the charged offense, the error should result in a reversal unless the error is harmless. However, the defense's failure to object to the erroneous submission of a lesser-included offense will result in a waiver of the issue on appeal.

Chapter 10: Double Jeopardy

The Meaning of the Same Offense

The Double Jeopardy Clause of the Fifth Amendment of the United States Constitution states: "Nor shall any person be subject for the same offense to be twice put in jeopardy of life or limb." Article I, section 14 of the Texas Constitution provides a similar protection in similar language. TEX. CONST. art. I, § 14 ("No person, for the same offense, shall be twice put in jeopardy of life or liberty; nor shall a person be again put upon trial for the same offense after a verdict of not guilty in a court of competent jurisdiction."). Article 1.10 of the Texas Code of Criminal Procedure also states that no person shall be put in jeopardy of life or liberty twice for the same offense.

The primary value protected by the double jeopardy doctrine is that of the desire for finality, as is the case with the doctrine of *res judicata* applicable in civil cases. However, in the criminal context, the need for finality is particularly compelling in light of the enormous impact of criminal prosecution on the accused. The protections against double jeopardy help to limit the extraordinary embarrassment, expense, and ordeal of a criminal prosecution. A further aspect of the desire for finality is the prevention of unfair prosecutorial manipulation of the criminal process. Double jeopardy protections help to prevent the State from continued empaneling of juries until it finds one favorably disposed to conviction.

The defendant's finality interest in limiting the ordeal of criminal accusation and in preventing unfair prosecutorial manipulation through multiple proceedings is not unlimited. The defendant's interest in finality must be weighed against the State's legitimate interest in law enforcement. For example, a defendant who gets their conviction reversed on appeal is not immunized against a second prosecution by double jeopardy protections because the State's countervailing interest in law enforcement outweighs the defendant's interest in finality. The balance is different, however, if the appellate reversal is on the grounds of insufficient evidence because, while the state is entitled to one error-free attempt to prove criminal accusations, the defendant's interest in finality prevents retrial when the state simply has failed in its efforts to prove its case.

The United States Supreme Court has stated the Double Jeopardy Clause contains three protections: it protects against a second prosecution for the same offense after an acquittal; it protects against a second prosecution for the same offense after a conviction; and it protects against multiple punishments for the same offense. The core concept of "same offense" critical to all three protections has proved to be difficult to define and is dependent on the specific facts of the case as well as the terms of the statutory offense.

Of the two primary approaches taken in different jurisdictions for the problem of defining the "same offense," a focus on the actions of the defendant predominate in a minority of states while the particular elements of the offense charged is of preeminent importance in the approach now taken in Texas and the majority of American jurisdictions. Under the federal standard enunciated by the United States Supreme Court and a majority of the states, the fact that the defendant broke into a home with a gun to rob a victim may result in convictions for carrying the gun, burglary for the entry into the home with an intent to commit a crime, and robbery. For over one hundred years, Texas followed the minority approach, providing greater protection by determining the concept of the "same offense" by reference to the defendant's single connected acts. Additionally, the approach allowed the prosecution to choose any of the offenses committed, but it could only obtain one conviction and penalty for what was regarded as a single act or transaction.

Under either approach, the facts and the elements are important. For example, even if the same statutory offense is involved, the defendant clearly does not obtain a license to commit a criminal act on Tuesday because of the commission of the same criminal act on Monday. If only one act is committed at a discrete time, but more than one victim is injured, has one criminal act been committed or two? If a murderer simultaneously kills two people with one bomb, it is not surprising that most jurisdictions would regard that as two crimes because two victims were killed. However, is the result the same if a defendant steals one suitcase in which four people have packed personal belongings? Are four theft prosecutions appropriate because of the fortuity of four people being victimized by the single theft? Even in the murder situation, if the murderer was unaware of the presence of multiple victims, is the result the same? For example, the number of victims is a fortuity when a drunk driver strikes another car and kills all of the occupants. Should the number of manslaughter convictions depend upon the single incident or the number of people who happen to be in the vehicle?

The Court of Criminal Appeals answered this particular question by holding in *Ex parte Rathmell*, 717 S.W.2d 33 (Tex. Crim. App. 1986), that the legislative unit of the offense of DWI manslaughter is the number of victims, despite the defendant's lack of knowledge or control over the number of occupants in a car. It is not necessarily the case that the number of victims control in the context of other crimes. Such difficulties in defining what constitutes the same offense causes the answer to be specific to the facts of the particular crime and the elements of the offenses, as well as by the method of defining what is the same offense under the applicable legal doctrine of the jurisdiction.

The starting point in determining the troublesome question of what constitutes the "same offense" in most jurisdictions, including Texas, is taken from the decision of the United States Supreme Court in *Blockburger v. United States*, 284 U.S. 299 (1932), which focuses upon the statutory language creating the criminal offense. Under *Blockburger*, for a single act that violates more than one criminal statute, each of the proposed statutory offenses is examined to determine if each requires proof of an element or elements that the other does not. If so, the statutory offense is presumably not the same, and both offenses generally may be prosecuted. This approach often allows multiple convictions for offenses committed in the same transaction, even though the statutory offenses contain many common elements, so long as they differ in at least one respect. The *Gore* case that follows in the text illustrates the application of the *Blockburger* rule, which determines the meaning of the crucial term "offense" primarily on the basis of the elements of the statutory offense rather than the conduct of the defendant.

Gore v. United States

357 U.S. 386 (1958)

Justice Frankfurter delivered the opinion of the Court.

This is a prosecution under an indictment containing six counts for narcotics offenses. Four counts were based on provisions of the Internal Revenue Code of 1954 and two counts on the Narcotic Drugs Import and Export Act, as amended. The first three counts derive from a sale on February 26, 1955, of twenty capsules of heroin and three capsules of cocaine; the last three counts derive from a sale of thirty-five capsules of heroin on February 28, 1955. Counts One and Four charged the sale of the drugs, on the respective dates, not "in pursuance of a written order" of the person to whom the drugs were sold on the requisite Treasury form, in violation of § 4705(a) of the Internal Revenue Code of 1954, 26 U.S.C.A. § 4705(a). Counts Two and Five charged the sale and distribution of the drugs on the respective dates not "in the original stamped package or from the original stamped package," in violation of § 4704(a) of the Internal Revenue Code of 1954, 26 U.S.C.A. § 4704(a). Counts Three and Six charged facilitating concealment and sale of the drugs on the respective dates, with knowledge that the drugs had been unlawfully imported, in violation of § 2(c) of the Narcotic Drugs Import and Export Act, as amended by the Act of November 2, 1951, 65 Stat. 767.

In short, Congress had made three distinct offenses in connection with the vending of illicit drugs, and the petitioner, having violated these three independent provisions, was prosecuted for all three as separate wrongdoings, despite the fact that these violations of what Congress had proscribed were compendiously committed in single transactions of vending. Duly tried before a jury, petitioner was convicted, and no question touching the conviction is before us. In controversy is the legality of the sentences imposed by the trial court. These were imprisonment for a term of one to five years, imposed on each count, the sentences on the first three counts to run consecutively, the sentences on the remaining three counts to run concurrently with those on the first three counts. Thus the total sentence was three to fifteen years. Petitioner moved to vacate the sentence, claiming that for all three counts a sentence as for only one count could be imposed. The motion was denied and the Court of Appeals affirmed, with expressions of doubt by two of the judges, who felt themselves bound by *Blockburger v. United States*, 284 U.S. 299 (1932). We brought the case here, in order to consider whether some of our more recent decisions, while not questioning *Blockburger* but moving in related areas may not have impaired its authority.

We adhere to the decision in *Blockburger v. United States, supra*.[1]

---

1. In *Blockburger*, the Court adopted this rule:

> A single act may be an offense against two statutes and if each statute requires proof of an additional fact which the other does not, an acquittal or conviction under either statute does not exempt the defendant from prosecution and punishment under the other.

Illustrative of *Blockburger* operating to the defendant's advantage is *Ball v. United States*, 470 U.S. 856 (1985), where the defendant was convicted of receipt of a firearm by a convicted felon and possession of the same firearm by a convicted felon. The Court held that, while the prosecutor could prosecute simultaneously for those two

The considerations advanced in support of the vigorous attack against it have left its justification undisturbed, nor have our later decisions generated counter currents.

We are strongly urged to reconsider *Blockburger* by reading the various specific enactments of Congress as reflecting a unitary congressional purpose to outlaw nonmedicinal sales of narcotics. From this the conclusion is sought to be drawn that since Congress had only a single purpose, no matter how numerous the violations by an offender, of the specific means for dealing with this unitary purpose, the desire should be attributed to Congress to punish only as for a single offense when these multiple infractions are committed through a single sale. We agree with the starting point, but it leads us to the opposite conclusion. Of course the various enactments by Congress extending over nearly half a century constitute a network of provisions, steadily tightened and enlarged, for grappling with a powerful, subtle and elusive enemy. If the legislation reveals anything, it reveals the determination of Congress to turn the screw of the criminal machinery—detection, prosecution and punishment—tighter and tighter. The three penal laws for which petitioner was convicted have different origins both in time and in design.

It seems more daring than convincing to suggest that three different enactments, each relating to a separate way of closing in on illicit distribution of narcotics, passed at three different periods, for each of which a separate punishment was declared by Congress, somehow or other ought to have carried with them an implied indication by Congress that if all these three different restrictions were disregarded but, forsooth, in the course of one transaction, the defendant should be treated as though he committed only one of these offenses.

This situation is *toto coelo* different from the one that led to our decision in *Bell v. United States*, 349 U.S. 81 (1955). That case involved application of the Mann Act, 18 U.S.C.A. § 2421,—a single provision making it a crime to transport a woman in interstate commerce for purposes of prostitution held that the transportation of more than one woman as a single transaction is to be dealt with as a single offense, for the reason that when Congress has not explicitly stated what the unit of offense is, the doubt will be judicially resolved in favor of lenity. It is one thing for a single transaction to include several units relating to proscribed conduct under a single provision of a statute. It is a wholly different thing to evolve a rule of lenity for three violations of three separate offenses created by Congress at three different times, all to the end of dealing more and more strictly with, and seeking to throttle more and more by different legal devices, the traffic in narcotics. Both in the unfolding of the substantive provisions of law and in the scale of punishments, Congress has manifested an attitude not of lenity but of severity toward violation of the narcotics laws.

Finally, we have had pressed upon us that the *Blockburger* doctrine offends the constitutional prohibition against double jeopardy. If there is anything to this claim it surely has long been disregarded in decisions of this Court.

Suppose Congress, instead of enacting the three provisions before us, had passed an enactment substantially in this form: "Anyone who sells drugs except from the original stamped package and who sells such drugs not in pursuance of a written order of the person to whom the

---

offenses, the defendant could be convicted and sentenced on only one.

194

drug is sold, and who does so by way of facilitating the concealment and sale of drugs knowing the same to have been unlawfully imported, shall be sentenced to not less than fifteen years' imprisonment: Provided, however, That if he makes such sale in pursuance of a written order of the person to whom the drug is sold he shall be sentenced to only ten years' imprisonment: *And provided further*, That if he sells such drugs in pursuance of a written order and from a stamped package, he shall be sentenced to only five years' imprisonment." Is it conceivable that such a statute would not be within the power of Congress? And is it rational to find such a statute constitutional but to strike down the *Blockburger* doctrine as violative of the double jeopardy clause?

In effect, we are asked to enter the domain of penology, and more particularly that tantalizing aspect of it, the proper apportionment of punishment. Whatever views may be entertained regarding severity of punishment, whether one believes in its efficacy or its futility, these are peculiarly questions of legislative policy.

Affirmed.

Chief Justice Warren, dissenting.

The problem of multiple punishment is a vexing and recurring one. It arises in one of two broad contexts: (a) a statute or a portion thereof proscribes designated conduct, and the question is whether the defendant's conduct constitutes more than one violation of this proscription. Thus, murdering two people simultaneously might well warrant two punishments but stealing two one-dollar bills might not. (b) Two statutes or two portions of a single statute proscribe certain conduct, and the question is whether the defendant can be punished twice because his conduct violates both proscriptions. Thus, selling liquor on a Sunday might warrant two punishments for violating a prohibition law and a blue law, but feloniously entering a bank and robbing a bank, though violative of two statutes, might warrant but a single punishment.

In every instance the problem is to ascertain what the legislature intended. Often the inquiry produces few if any enlightening results. Normally these are not problems that receive explicit legislative consideration. But this fact should not lead the judiciary, charged with the obligation of construing these statutes, to settle such questions by the easy application of stereotyped formulae. It is at the same time too easy and too arbitrary to apply a presumption for or against multiple punishment in all cases or even to do so one way in one class of cases or even to do so one way in one class of cases and the other way in another. Placing a case in the category of unit-of-offense problems or the category of overlapping-statute problems may point up the issue, but it does not resolve it.

Where the legislature has failed to make its intention manifest, courts should proceed cautiously, remaining sensitive to the interests of defendant and society alike. All relevant criteria must be considered and the most useful aid will often be common sense. In this case I am persuaded, on the basis of the origins of the three statutes involved, the test and background of recent amendments to these statutes, the scale of punishments prescribed for second and third offenders, and the evident legislative purpose to achieve uniformity in sentences, that the present purpose of these statutes is to make sure that a prosecutor has three avenues by which to

195

prosecute one who traffics in narcotics, and not to authorize three cumulative punishments for the defendant who consummates a single sale.

Notes

1.   A more generous approach, from the defense's point of view, to defining what constitutes the "same offense" focuses primarily upon the conduct of the accused rather than the particular language of the charged statutory offense. Such an approach is followed only in a minority of jurisdictions in the United States, which at one time included Texas. For over one hundred years, the Texas Court of Criminal Appeals followed what it called the "carving doctrine," which allowed the prosecutor to "carve" any offense that could be established under the same criminal act or episode with which the defendant was charged, but only one act in the transaction could be prosecuted. Under the carving doctrine, a defendant who entered the home of the victim to rob him with a gun and did so could be prosecuted for robbery, burglary, or the illegal carrying of the gun, but not all three, because the offenses occurred in the same transaction. Under the more permissive *Blockburger* rule, the prosecution is presumptively allowed to obtain a conviction for all three offenses because entry without the consent of the owner is not required for the robbery and the gun possession offense, the burglary statute does not require proof of the completed robbery or the possession of a gun, and the gun offense does not require an entry without permission or use of the gun to rob.

2.   Under the carving doctrine, defining the scope of a defendant's "act" often proved difficult. Is pointing a gun and threatening a victim a separate assault from the harm caused when the gun is fired? Or is it part of the same transaction? Is the result different if several minutes intervene between the threat and the killing? If the threat was close in time to a killing, but the threat was directed at a different victim than the individual killed, was it the same criminal act or transaction or a different one? The Court of Criminal appeals cited such difficulties as one of the reasons for abandoning the carving doctrine in *Ex parte McWilliams*, 634 S.W.2d 815, 822, 824 (Tex. Crim. App. 1982).

3.   The elimination of the carving doctrine, however, has not completely eliminated the need to decide difficult issues involving the component parts of a defendant's actions. If a defendant is charged with multiple violations of the same statute, the *Blockburger* same-elements test is not helpful in determining whether multiple convictions would violate double jeopardy protections. For example, in *Jones v. State*, 285 S.W.3d 501 (Tex. App.—Fort Worth 2009, pet. granted), the defendant made numerous false statements on applications for loans to purchase residential properties. The defendant falsely stated he owned two fictitious bank accounts and also submitted another person's credit report as his own. The State argued each material false or misleading statement in the loan application was a separate offense, but the court of appeals vacated some of the convictions on the theory the making of false or misleading statements to obtain property or credit was the gravamen of the offense, and that only one offense was committed per application despite the number of false statements made within the application. In reaching this result, the court of appeals rejected the state's analogy to the perjury statute, which allows for a conviction for each false statement made while under oath.

4.   Particular difficulties arise in determining how many offenses may be prosecuted with regard to continuing offenses. Is a prison inmate who escapes guilty of only one offense from the time of the escape until capture, or is each day the inmate fails to return a separate offense? The approach generally taken by the courts is to allow the legislature to define the permissible unit of prosecution in any way it chooses. However, often the problem before the courts is that the unit of the offense is not specified. Such difficulties cannot be resolved by resort to the *Blockburger* standard because only one statute is implicated.

Legislative Intent

The limited scope of the conception of the "same offense" related to statutory elements is closely related to the concept of lesser-included offenses that may be submitted to the jury along with the charged offense. The defendant can be convicted of a lesser-included offense without violating the constitutional right to notice because all of the elements of the lesser offense are necessarily subsumed into the greater offense. Thus, for example, a defendant indicted for auto theft—requiring proof the defendant intentionally took an automobile without permission of the owner with intent to permanently deprive the owner of the vehicle—is not deprived of fair notice of joyriding—requiring proof the defendant merely took the vehicle without permission. By this same logic, however, a conviction for both would be contrary to the *Blockburger* rule because, *each* statutory offense does not require proof of a fact that the other does not. In *Brown v. Ohio*, 432 U.S. 161 (1977), the United States Supreme Court so held, declaring it would violate double jeopardy for the defendant to be convicted in the county of Ohio where he initially stole the vehicle for joyriding and in the county where he was arrested several days later for auto theft because the two offenses are the same for double jeopardy purposes.

The limited protection afforded against convictions for greater and lesser-included offenses within the same jurisdiction can be eliminated if the legislature expressly authorizes multiple convictions and penalties. In *Missouri v. Hunter*, 459 U.S. 359 (1983), the Supreme Court held that the *Blockburger* test is simply a rule to help establish the presumptive legislative intent in the absence of a clear indication from the legislature. The protection of the Double Jeopardy Clause is limited to exceeding the punishment or number of convictions authorized by the legislature for a single offense. In *Hunter*, the defendant was convicted in one trial of both armed robbery and armed criminal action. Under Missouri law, armed criminal action is a lesser-included offense of armed robbery and, therefore, the two statutes are considered the "same offense" for double jeopardy purposes (because the elements of one are completely included within the other). Thus, *each* statutory offense does not include a fact that the other did not. However, because the Missouri Legislature had expressly provided that the punishment imposed for the crime of armed criminal action "shall be in addition to any punishment provided by law for the crime committed . . . with . . . a dangerous or deadly weapon," there was no double jeopardy violation.

The determination that multiple convictions or punishments are permissible despite the existence of statutes that fail to contain distinct elements, as in *Hunter*, has been found in some Texas cases on the basis of an express legislative authorization. For example, in *Jimenez v. State*, 240 S.W.3d 384 (Tex. App.—Austin 2007, pet. ref'd), convictions for felony murder and injury to a child occurring in the same transaction were upheld based upon section 22.04(h) penal code, which allows an accused who is charged with injury to a child, elderly individual, or disabled individual to be prosecuted for any other offense violated. A similar result was reached in *Garza v. State*, 213 S.W.3d 338 (Tex. Crim. App. 2007), in which the Court of Criminal Appeals upheld a conviction for capital murder and murder committed as a member of a criminal street gang because section 71.02(b) of the Texas Penal Code specifically provides that an offense committed as part of organized criminal activity can be charged under that specific provision as well as any substantive offense committed.

Because the *Blockburger* rule is merely a presumptive rule of legislative intent, the defense can also benefit if it is ruled the legislature did not intend to allow multiple convictions when there is only one physical act or transaction, even when the statutes pass the *Blockburger* test due to separate and distinct statutory elements. The *Irby* case that follows is an example of an unsuccessful attempt by the defense to invoke a more lenient result than would be suggested by *Blockburger* on the ground of legislative intent.

Irby v. United States

390 F.2d 432 (D.C. Cir. 1967)

McGowan, Circuit Judge, with whom Circuit Judges Danaher, Burger, and Tamm join.

In 1958 appellant, represented by counsel, pleaded guilty to the housebreaking and robbery counts of a 9-count indictment, and received consecutive sentences of two to eight years on the one, and four to twelve years on the other. The other counts were then dismissed. In 1965 he moved under 28 U.S.C. § 2255 to regain his liberty on the ground that the two sentences could not validly have been made to run consecutively. The District Court denied the motion in a long opinion which explored with care the single legal issue raised by the motion. Upon appeal, a panel of this court reversed, one judge dissenting. The Government's petition for rehearing *en banc* was granted; and, after rehearing, the District Court's judgment is herewith affirmed.

There are circumstances where it cannot safely be assumed that simply because the legislature had defined two separate crimes with differing elements and prescribed separate punishments for them, it contemplated that such punishments can be consecutively inflicted. The nature of the two criminal specifications, and of the course of conduct in which both crimes may be thought to have been committed, may be such as to raise a doubt as to a legislative purpose to encompass both punishments. In such a case, an aid to the divination of such purpose in the form of a so-called "rule of lenity" has been devised to the end of barring double punishment where there is substantial doubt as to whether Congress would have intended it to be imposed.

It is not novel that Congress has differentiated between housebreaking and robbery in terms of the one as an invasion of the security of the dwelling, and the other as an intrusion upon the security of the person. This was a distinction familiar to the common law, and it was perpetuated in the statutes found to have been violated here. Stealing something worth $1000 may be only an aggravation of the misdeed involved in stealing something worth $10. But taking something, whatever its worth, from another's person by force and putting in fear brings in a new and different interest which it has been though important to protect, namely the person threatened as distinct from the property taken.

One whom wrongfully goes into a house to pilfer what he can find may or may not start out with a purpose to rob, if necessary. If he consciously entertains both purposes from the beginning, it can be said that he sets out with an intent to commit both larceny and robbery, or crimes against both property and person, if the opportunity presents itself. In such circumstances, he will be guilty of housebreaking in either event once he crosses the threshold, but, if he retires upon finding the house occupied and without robbing the occupant, he has made the decision which saves him from punishment for robbery. The point is, of course, that his invasion of the premises to steal does not irrevocably commit him to rob from the person of anyone he finds there. The choice is still his up to the moment of confrontation.[1] If he decided to rob, consecutive

---

1. We do not think that the indictment can be characterized as asserting that appellant's course of conduct was motivated by a single criminal intent. In the housebreaking count, he was charged with entering a dwelling "with intent to steal property of another." In the robbery count, he was charged with taking two rings from the person and from the immediate possession of a named complainant "by force and violence and against resistance and by sudden

200

punishments are not made available solely as a means of exacting greater retribution. Congress could well have conceived of them as a deterrent to compromising the safety of the person as well as the security of the premises. They illuminate the differing dangers to society inherent in stealing what one finds in a vacant house, and robbing the occupant as well when he proves to be at home. We cannot, at any rate, say with confidence that Congress did not contemplate some additional disincentive for the latter.[2]

The judgment of the District Court is affirmed.

Leventhal, Circuit Judge (concurring).

I concur in the judgment, since I agree that it is possible that a combination at one scene of a housebreaking, with intent to commit larceny, and a robbery, may reflect sufficiently separate criminal purposes to permit consecutive punishment. While they may also, I think be so integrated as to preclude consecutive punishment, that objection is one that should ordinarily be put forward when sentence is imposed, or timely in a motion to reduce the sentence.

In the absence of other, specific legislative intention on the side of either lenity or harshness, we can only invoke a generalized legislative intent. This is more likely presumed than real, and embodies a large standard of reasonableness and fairness to offenders and society alike. The standard that best conforms to my estimate of a generalized legislative intention is this: A defendant guilty of a serious crime is subject to judgment of imprisonment. The sentencing judge is given latitude so that a heavier punishment will be appropriate for a crime that is aggravated in its particular facts. When the same act can be classified as different crimes, he may be punished with the most onerous penalty provided for the most extreme crime for which he was charged. But he is not to be given two or more consecutive punishments for what is essentially a single criminal episode—say a robbery, committed of course with intent to rob—merely because the law would also have punished him if he had stopped or been apprehended before completing the robbery, on the ground that his acts and intent constitute either an attempt to commit robbery or a substantive crime which is made punishable because it is a preliminary step taken with that ultimate intent.

If a defendant breaks into a house at night for the purpose of relieving the bejeweled guests at a dinner party of material encumbrances, the robbery is indeed a heinous offense that should be severely punished. There is not merely a robbery, but a robbery aggravated by housebreaking. But in my view the defendant is not subject to consecutive punishment on the theory that there are consecutive crimes even though it is the same intention—intention to

---

and stealthy seizure and snatching and by putting in fear." The two are not the same, and they are fully consistent with either concurrent or consecutive criminal purposes of a different order. The Supreme Court has, of course, been alert to prohibit double punishment for the commission of a federally-created crime and for the attempt to do so. *See Prince v. United States*, 352 U.S. 322, 77 S.Ct. 403, 1 L.Ed.2d 370 (1957).

2. The drafters of the American Law Institute's Model Penal Code were explicitly conscious of the unfairness involved in the imposition of "cumulative penalties . . . for entering with intent to steal and for stealing, although ordinarily attempt merges in the completed offense." Although proposing a burglary offense not essentially unlike our housebreaking statute, they added a ban on duplicate penalties in [§ 221.1].

commit the felony of robbery—which makes a felony of his preliminary housebreaking as well as of the robbery that completes the sequence of the criminal episode.

If at the scene of the crime the defendant can be said to have realized that he has come to a fork in the road, and nevertheless decides to invade a different interest, then his successive intentions make him subject to cumulative punishment, and he must be treated as accepting that risk, whether he in fact knows of it or not.

I think a rule that focuses on changes in the extent and direction of the defendant's criminal intention provides a basis for permitting cumulative punishment that is related to *mens rea*, and that this is sounder than a generalized approach that two or more consecutive punishments are proper for a single episode because criminality of the activity is established by more than one section of the code.

Chief Judge Bazelon, with whom Circuit Judge Skelly Wright, concurs (dissenting).

There are two questions before us. The first is whether, in some cases, the D.C. housebreaking and robbery statutes prohibit cumulative punishment. The second is whether Irby's is one of those cases.

The answer to the first question depends entirely upon statutory construction. The housebreaking statute reads as follows: "Whosoever shall, either in the night or in the daytime, break and enter, or enter without breaking, any dwelling whether at the time occupied or not with intent to commit any criminal offense, shall be imprisoned for not more than fifteen years." 22 D.C. CODE § 1801 (1961). Housebreaking, by the terms of the statute, is committed in preparation for some other criminal offense which is intended at the time of entry. It seems most likely that Congress, instead of desiring to punish for both the preparation and the completion, created two separate crimes in order to punish those housebreakers who are thwarted and who do not complete the intended crime.

The Supreme Court faced a similar situation in *Prince v. United States*, 352 U.S. 322 (1957). There the defendant was convicted of robbing a federally insured bank and entering the bank with intent to commit a felony. The Supreme Court reasoned that:

> It is a fair inference from the wording in the Act, uncontradicted by anything in the meager legislative history, that the unlawful entry provision was inserted to cover the situation where a person enters a bank for the purpose of committing a crime, but is frustrated for some reason before completing the crime. The gravamen of the offense is not in the act of entering, which satisfies the terms of the statute even if it is simply walking through an open, public door during normal business hours. Rather the heart of the crime is the intent to steal. This mental element merges into the completed crime if the robbery is consummated.

Therefore, the Supreme Court held that Congress did not intend to punish cumulatively for the preparation and the completed crime.

A similar inference is warranted here, since, as in *Prince*, our statute defines housebreaking as entry with intent to commit another crime. And, as in *Prince*, the gravamen of the offense is not simply the act of entering, which need not be forcible to satisfy the terms of the statute. Indeed, it is possible that a person may be guilty of housebreaking although he has not committed a criminal trespass as long as he enters the premises with the required criminal intent.

Even if a criminal trespass is a necessary prerequisite to a finding of housebreaking, it is evident that the illegal act of entry is not the gravamen of housebreaking. If nothing more than entering without permission were involved, a penalty in the order of six months would probably be thought enough by Congress. However, Congress provided a much stiffer penalty for housebreaking. And the likely reason is that Congress believed that entry with an intent to commit another crime would often, in fact, lead to that other crime. As in *Prince*, the intent to commit another crime is at the heart of the offense. By deterring housebreaking Congress meant also to deter the intended crime which might follow. If so, then the housebreaking statute punishes for the possibility or probability of the intended crime. We do not think Congress would have wanted to impose punishment of fifteen years of the probability of the intended crime and an additional fifteen years for the crime itself.

Under this analysis, however, cumulative punishment is prohibited only if the crime defendant in fact committed was the same as the crime he intended to commit when he entered the dwelling. This seems to be the question which divides the court. The majority does not think "the indictment can be characterized as asserting that appellant's course of conduct was motivated by a single criminal intent." Judge Leventhal thinks the record is unclear and would require more specific allegations of a single intent. We think the record is clear enough to show that Irby had only one criminal purpose when he committed the two crimes.

According to the indictment, Irby entered the complainant's dwelling with an "intent to steal [his] property." While in the house, Irby carried out his intention and stole two rings worth $2,200.

The fact that in order to steal he did things which made his crime robbery, as opposed, for example, to grand larceny or petit larceny, does not negate the fact that what he did within the house was motivated by the same criminal purpose ("to steal property of another") as his illegal entry.

Furthermore, it is significant that Irby was originally charged with carrying a dangerous weapon and assault with a dangerous weapon. If these charges are correct, they suggest that when Irby entered the dwelling he was already prepared to use "force and violence" (*i.e.*, to commit robbery) if necessary.

We think the record sufficiently shows that defendant entered the dwelling with the objective of stealing property, by force if necessary, and that he carried out this objective. Since there is substantial doubt that Congress intended cumulative punishment in this situation, the rule of lenity must be applied. Irby should have been punished for either housebreaking or robbery but not both consecutively.

Notes

1.   Determining legislative intent is notoriously difficult. Rarely does the legislature make clear its purpose with regard to technical questions, such as the number of prosecutions intended when one act or transaction violates a statute multiple times or violates multiple statutes simultaneously. As a result, the *Blockburger* rule remains an important component of the crucial double jeopardy question of what constitutes the same offense in the absence of an express legislative statement. However, successful arguments have been made that the default rule of *Blockburger* should not control because the legislature did not intend multiple convictions when there is a single act. For example, in *Bigon v. State*, 252 S.W.3d 360 (Tex. Crim. App. 2008), the Court of Criminal Appeals held that convictions for felony murder and intoxication manslaughter based upon the same incident and victims violated double jeopardy despite differences in the statutory elements on the theory that the legislature did not intend to impose multiple punishments for the same offense.

2.   In the absence of an express legislative statement, the Court of Criminal Appeals has applied a standard enunciated in *Ex parte Ervin*, 991 S.W.2d 804 (Tex. Crim. App. 1999), to determine the question of legislative intent with regard to whether multiple convictions are permitted for one physical act that violates more than one statutory provision. The nonexclusive list of factors suggested by *Ervin* include whether the statutory offenses are in the same statutory section; whether the offenses are phrased in the alternative; whether the offenses are named similarly; whether the offenses have common punishment ranges; whether the offenses have a common focus; whether the common focus tends to indicate a single instance of conduct; whether the elements that differ between the two offenses can be considered the same under an imputed theory of liability; and whether there is legislative history containing an articulation of an intent to treat the offenses the same or differently for double jeopardy purposes.

Double Jeopardy and Lesser Included Offenses

It has long been held that a conviction for both a greater and lesser-included offense violates double jeopardy. For example, in *Brown v. Ohio*, 432 U.S. 161 (1977), the United States Supreme Court held that prosecutions for (1) auto theft in one Ohio county, where the car was found, and (2) joyriding in the county in which the same car was taken, violated double jeopardy protections because joy riding is a lesser included of auto theft. Auto theft differed from joy riding only because of the addition of the element of an intent to permanently deprive the owner of the car. An indictment for auto theft could result in a conviction of the lesser offense of joyriding because the auto theft charge provided notice of the lesser offense of joyriding. However, with lesser-included offenses, the jury is instructed to choose between auto theft and joyriding (unless the jury acquits), but not to convict of both.

Two caveats to the holding in *Brown* should be pointed out. First, a clearly expressed legislative intent to allow one penalty for joyriding, which is committed as soon as the car is taken, and another for the auto theft if the defendant's later acts manifest an intention to deprive the owner of the car permanently, can override the presumed legislative intent to allow only one penalty. In the absence of such an express legislative intention, however, the default setting prohibition against multiple convictions and penalties for greater and lesser included offenses would apply.

A second exception to the *Brown* rule could occur if Brown drove the car out of Ohio and he was prosecuted in Ohio in addition to being prosecuted in another state or in federal court. Under the so called dual-sovereignty doctrine, prosecution for the same offense in another state or in federal court does not create a double jeopardy bar to additional prosecution, regardless of the similarity of the elements of the statutory offenses in the different jurisdictions. *See Heath v. Alabama*, 474 U.S. 82 (1985) (prosecution for criminal offense in Georgia did not bar prosecution for related events in Alabama); *Bartkus v. Illinois*, 359 U.S. 121 (1959) (state prosecution following federal prosecution does not violate double jeopardy because prosecution is by a different sovereign); *Abbate v. United States*, 359 U.S. 187 (1959) (federal prosecution following state criminal prosecution does not violate double jeopardy because of dual sovereignty doctrine). Two counties within the same state are not separate sovereigns because their authority derives from the law of the same state.

In the absence of express legislative authorization of conviction and punishment for both greater and lesser-included offenses or different jurisdictions, double jeopardy prevents a conviction for both a greater and lesser offense based upon a single incident. Jurisdictions vary in the approach taken to determine whether offenses are regarded as having the relationship of greater and lesser included. For example, the offenses of robbery and burglary are not presumptively the same for double jeopardy purposes, and the offenses do not share an intrinsic relationship of greater and lesser-included offenses. Robbery does not require proof of an unconsented entry into a home or building, and burglary requires such an entry with the intent to commit a theft of other crimes that may have nothing to do with the elements of robbery. If an inherent relationship is required, the two offenses cannot be greater and lesser included, and burglary could not be submitted as lesser included of robbery. However, if the allegations of the charging instrument or the proof at trial may be consulted, there is a possible relationship that might allow submission of one offense as a lesser included of another, with double jeopardy prohibitions against a conviction for both. If the robbery indictment alleges the defendant broke into the victim's home without permission to rob the victim, does this create a relationship of greater and lesser-included offenses despite the lack of an intrinsic statutory connection? If there is no such allegation, but the evidence at the robbery trial shows the entry into the victim's home without consent in order to commit the robbery, is that sufficient to create a greater and lesser-included-offense relationship?

In *Hall*, the Court of Criminal Appeals adopted what it called the cognate-pleadings test, which expands a consideration of the relatedness of the two offenses beyond the abstract statutory elements by allowing a consideration of the offenses alleged in the charging instrument. The court rejected moving to a "cognate evidence" approach—which would allow submission of burglary as a lesser included offense of robbery based upon a consideration of the facts proved at trial—in part because of concerns over fair notice and double jeopardy. To submit burglary on the basis of an indictment alleging merely robbery with no mention of an unpermitted entry might violate the defendant's constitutional right to notice and make it difficult to protect the defendant's right against double jeopardy.

Although the law of lesser-included offenses in Texas prior to *Hall* was not clear or consistent, many prior cases had limited the first step in determining whether an offense could be submitted as a lesser-included offense to a consideration of the statutory elements in the abstract. *Hall* broadened the scope of lesser-included-offense law. This does not mean that burglary is eligible to be submitted as a lesser-included offense in every aggravated assault case. For example, in an outdoor robbery, there is no issue or allegation of an unpermitted home entry. But if the indictment alleges the defendant entered a home without consent and committed a robbery, the potential relationship of greater and lesser-included offenses is established. The relationship is only potentially established because there must be some basis for the jury to believe the defendant could be not guilty of the aggravated assault but guilty of the burglary. For example, this occurs when it is undisputed that someone entered a home and committed robbery and the only evidence suggesting the defendant is not guilty of the offense is based upon alibi evidence presented by the defense. In this situation, the lesser offense should not be submitted because there is no basis for concluding the defendant is guilty only of the lesser offense; either the jurors believe beyond a reasonable doubt the defendant is the burglar and the robber, or they believe the defendant is neither the burglar nor the robber because they believe the defendant's alibi (or at least the alibi evidence raises a reasonable doubt). There is no reason to give instructions that would require the jury to find the defendant had an alibi for robbery but did not for the burglary committed at the same time and same place.

Is a collateral effect of *Hall* the expansion of double jeopardy protections? It appeared that the expansion of lesser-included-offense law had also expanded double jeopardy protections after the decision in *Girdy v. State*, 175 S.W.3d 877 (Tex. App.—Amarillo 2005, pet. ref'd). In *Girdy*, the defendant was charged in a single indictment with aggravated kidnapping and aggravated assault based upon an unbroken sequence in which the defendant obtained a knife, threatened the complainant and others with it, demanded car keys from the complainant, forced her into the car with a knife in his hand, drove the car to a new location while brandishing the knife, and held it against the victim while removing her from the car. A jury convicted the defendant of both offenses and sentenced him to 50 years in prison for the kidnapping and 10 years in prison for the assault. The Court of Appeals reversed, noting while it was not necessary for the State to prove abduction in order to convict the defendant of assault, in proving the abduction for purposes of kidnapping, the State had satisfied the elements for aggravated assault. Because the same evidence used to prove the kidnapping proved the assault, the lower court held the aggravated assault was a lesser-included offense of aggravated kidnapping, and convictions for both crimes violated double jeopardy.

On discretionary review, the State presented a *Blockburger* elements argument, pointing out that aggravated kidnapping contains an element not contained in aggravated assault— abducting another person—and, therefore, because there are elements of aggravated assault that are unique to that offense and not included in aggravated kidnapping, there was no double jeopardy violation in convicting the defendant of both offenses. The appellate court rejected the narrow statutory elements gauge urged by the State in light of the expanded cognate pleadings approach of *Hall* and the pleadings in the case alleging that the defendant committed the offense of aggravated kidnapping "by using and threatening to use deadly force" by his use of "a deadly weapon, to-wit: a knife, that in the manner of its use and intended use was capable of causing death and serious bodily injury." Although the aggravated kidnapping and aggravated assault offenses are not inherently related, under the indictment allegations, they were the same offense.

The *Girdy* Court not only referred to the indictment, it examined the proof at trial. The decision in *Girdy* suggested a broad rule of double jeopardy protection equal to, if not greater than, cognate pleading expansion of lesser included offenses. The court stated:

> If, as here, the prosecution, in proving the elements of one charged offense, also necessarily proves another charged offense, then that other offense is a lesser-included offense. In such a case, there must be clear legislative intent to punish the offenses separately. If no such intent is shown, multiple punishments for the criminal act that is the subject of the prosecution are barred.

Because no such legislative intent was shown, the decision of the Court of Appeals was affirmed on appeal by the Texas Court of Criminal Appeals. *Girdy v. State*, 213 S.W.3d 315, 317 (Tex. Crim. App. 2006).

Without overruling *Girdy* or even citing it, the Court of Criminal Appeals appears to have severed the connection between its expanded cognate-pleading approach to lesser-included offenses and the scope of double jeopardy protection in its opinion in *Ex parte Watson*, 306 S.W.3d 259 (Tex. Crim. App. 2009). That case involved an automobile accident in which the defendant failed to yield the right-of-way while attempting to make a left turn at an intersection and struck a motorcycle coming from the opposite direction. The defendant pled no contest to the failure-to-yield charge in a justice of the peace court. The court accepted the plea, placed the defendant on deferred adjudication for a period of sixty days, and ordered him to pay court costs and complete a driver safety course as a condition of his probation. About two years later, the defendant was indicted for intoxication assault based upon the same incident. He filed a pretrial application for writ of habeas corpus claiming his prosecution for intoxication assault was barred by the Double Jeopardy Clause. The trial court denied relief, as did the court of appeals, in an unpublished decision. The Court of Criminal Appeals affirmed, holding the defendant's argument had distorted the cognate-pleadings approach of *Hall* because it relied on the facts proved at trial to show the manner in which the intoxicated assault had occurred.

There were more than facts proved at trial to support the habeas applicant's argument in *Watson*, however. The indictment alleged that the defendant: "did then and there operate a motor vehicle in a public place while intoxicated . . . and did by reason of such intoxication cause serious bodily injury to another, . . . by accident or mistake, to-wit: failing to yield the right of way while turning left . . . ." This is the equivalent of the allegation of aggravated kidnapping in *Girdy* that alleged that in the course of the aggravated kidnapping, the defendant used a "deadly weapon; to wit a knife . . . that was capable of causing death or bodily injury." But, unlike *Girdy*, which found that the indictment allegations were crucial in determining both lesser-included-offense issues as well as the scope of double jeopardy, the *Watson* Court severed the connection forged in *Girdy* and returned double jeopardy law to a pure elements test under *Blockburger* and *Hunter*. Because the facts required to prove the alleged lesser offense of failure to yield right-of-way had several elements that are not the same as, or less than, those required to establish the alleged greater offense of intoxication assault, the analysis was at an end. The opinion in *Girdy* implicitly held that the scope of double jeopardy law is congruent with the expanded lesser included offense law of *Hall*. In *Watson*, the court denied this connection, stating:

> Nowhere in [*Hall*] did we say that the use of any language in the indictment that was not required by the statute transforms such language into additional elements of the charged offense. The State's mention of "failing to yield the right of way while turning left" in the indictment for intoxication assault describes the statutory element of "accident or mistake." While the use of such language in the indictment might be helpful in providing notice to appellant and later in proving to the jury as to how appellant was supposed to have caused the bodily injury in question, it does not increase or change the number of elements for the greater offense beyond that defined by the statute itself. . . . [T]he intoxication-assault statute merely requires a showing that the defendant in a given case "cause[d]" serious bodily injury to another "by reason of" his intoxicated state. *See* TEX. PEN. CODE § 49.07. It does not say anything about the specific *manner* in which such injury was caused, merely requiring such injury to be the result of an "accident or mistake" as opposed to being intentional.

Ex parte Watson, 306 S.W.3d 259, 264–265 (Tex. Crim. App. 2009).

Thus, the *Watson* Court returned to the statutory elements approach of *Blockburger* and *Hunter* in its analysis of the limited scope of double jeopardy protection rather than the expanded-pleadings approach used in the lesser-included-offense case of *Girdy* without expressly overruling that opinion. The court in *Watson* failed to address the inconsistency with *Girdy*, even though the habeas applicant in *Watson* had a more compelling circumstance of multiple convictions versus the multiple punishment issue involved in *Girdy*.

Double Jeopardy in Multiple Trials

The narrow presumptive definition of the term "same offense" provided by the *Blockburger* rule appears to provide little double jeopardy protection because the legislature can easily evade any prohibition by defining offenses in a manner that is essentially the same while including some independent element. The statutes in *Gore*, which relate to heroin sales, provide a good example. As a practical matter, one heroin sale would always violate all three statutes because each statutory offense required proof of a fact not required for another: knowledge that the heroin was imported, the lack of a prescription, and the lack of a stamped package for the heroin sale. Of course, one cannot obtain a prescription for heroin or a governmentally distributed stamped package for the substance, and the Supreme Court has conclusively presumed that all heroin is imported. Under the *Blockburger* rule, because each offense required proof of a fact that the others did not, a single heroin sale could become three convictions and separate penalties. If that doesn't create enough legislative flexibility to evade double jeopardy prohibitions, the legislature could pass statutes that do not meet the separate elements test of *Blockburger* but make it clear that consecutive penalties are permitted, as occurred in *Missouri v. Hunter*. This avoids double jeopardy strictures because the multiple penalty protection of the Double Jeopardy Clause consists only of exceeding the penalty authorized by the legislature.

Under *Blockburger* and *Hunter*, it appears that double jeopardy protections only limit the prosecution and the courts, but legislatures are virtually immune from constitutionally-based double jeopardy restrictions. An explanation for this diminished view of double jeopardy doctrine was provided in Justice Frankfurter's majority decision in *Gore*:

> Suppose that instead of passing three separate statutes all outlawing the sale of heroin and providing a five year penalty for each, Congress had passed a single statute making it a crime to sell heroin not in a stamped package and not pursuant to a prescription and knowing that the heroin was imported and providing a penalty of fifteen years. Suppose further that Congress provided that if any of the three elements of stamped package, absence of a prescription, or knowledge of importation were shown not to exist, that the penalty would be reduced by five years. So long as the fifteen year penalty for the single heroin sale is not constitutionally excessive, why shouldn't Congress be able to fragment the offense into three separate five year units and obtain a five-year conviction for each?

In light of the historic deference shown to legislative judgments about the appropriate penalty for a criminal conviction, it is clear that any constitutionally imposed ceiling will rarely, if ever, intrude upon legislative prerogative. In *Harmelin v. Michigan*, 501 U.S. 957 (1991), for example, the plurality opinion by Justice Scalia stated, outside the context of capital punishment, there is no constitutional review based upon a claim of a disproportionately harsh sentence. While the concurring opinion by Justice Kennedy, whose vote and the others joining him were needed to create a plurality, leaves the door open to an extremely narrow proportionality review under the auspices of the Cruel and Unusual Punishment Clause of the Eighth Amendment, the narrowness of that opening is underscored by the fact that Kennedy concurred in upholding a punishment of life in prison without the possibility of parole for a first-time offender found guilty of cocaine possession.

Given the traditional deference to legislative line-drawing with regard to criminal punishment, the virtually unlimited scope given to the legislature in creating multiple penalties that can be imposed in the context of a single criminal trial makes Justice Frankfurter's analysis compelling. It is difficult to see how Gore was harmed by three five-year consecutive sentences for one heroin sale imposed in a single trial, at least if that is what Congress intended, when

Congress clearly could have authorized life imprisonment in light of *Harmelin*. If it is appropriate to give the legislature such unreviewable authority with regard to the severity of the punishment, it is more understandable that the double jeopardy limitation on multiple punishment in one trial is confined to a sentence or sentences that exceed what the legislature has designated as the maximum penalty that may be imposed. Although a defendant might hope for a lower sentence or fewer consecutive sentences, the ordeal of criminal prosecution is not appreciably increased by multiple charges disposed of in a single criminal proceeding rather than one consolidated offense. Similarly, the defendant's interest in being free from unfair prosecutorial manipulation obtained through multiple proceedings is not threatened so long as the convictions are obtained in a single trial. In this setting, the prosecutor is not seeking a higher sentence because of dissatisfaction with a sentence imposed by the first tribunal. The defendant's finality interest is slight, and the State is merely exercising its interest in law enforcement in a more fragmentary manner if it obtains multiple punishments in a single proceeding.

To apply the same limited definition of the "same offense" based upon *Blockburger*, in the context of multiple proceedings rather than multiple penalties in a single proceeding, however, alters the calculus. In this situation, a prosecutor who is unhappy with the decision concerning the penalty imposed at one trial for an offense, such as heroin sale not in a stamped package, could seek a second prosecution and penalty for sale of heroin not pursuant to a prescription, or a third for a sale of heroin that the defendant knew was imported, each time hoping to find a more sympathetic judge or jury. The expense, anxiety, and ordeal of repeated prosecutions are different from the possibility of multiple punishments in one trial.

The United States Supreme Court briefly recognized the differing policy interests involved in multiple proceedings versus multiple penalties in a single proceeding. In *Grady v. Corbin*, 495 U.S. 508 (1990), a five to four majority found that the *Blockburger* view of the "same offense" might not be a sufficient definition in the context of multiple proceedings.

The Court in *Grady* held that a guilty plea to traffic offenses might create a double jeopardy bar to a more serious manslaughter charge based upon fatalities caused by the driving infractions, despite the fact the statutes in question had differing elements, because the *Blockburger* rule was limited to describing when multiple punishments could be imposed in a single criminal transaction. The *Grady* Court reasoned that greater constitutional protections were required when multiple trials were involved rather than multiple penalties at a single trial. This greater protection took the form of focusing on the defendant's conduct rather than merely the statutory elements of the offenses for which the defendant had been convicted. Under the *Grady* approach, if the same "conduct" alleged in a second criminal trial was the basis of a previous criminal conviction, the double jeopardy prohibition prevents the second proceeding, even though the defendant was not in actual jeopardy of being convicted of the manslaughter charge when pleading guilty to the relatively minor traffic offense.

The holding in *Grady*, by focusing on the defendant's conduct rather than the statutory elements, gave independent constitutional protection against multiple prosecution without regard to the intent of the legislature. In the one trial context, it was within the power of the legislature to determine how many punishments could be imposed subject only to the requirement of the clarity induced by the *Blockburger* presumption against multiple penalties when same or similar statutory elements were involved. However, under *Grady*, when the greater expense, anxiety, and ordeal of repeated prosecutions were involved as well as an increased risk of unfair prosecutorial manipulation, greater protections applied.

The disengagement of the limited *Blockburger* definition of "same offense" from the multiple trials context did not last long. Two justices who voted with the five-person majority in *Grady* retired and, less than four years later, one of the *Grady* dissenters, Justice Scalia, wrote an opinion in *United States v. Dixon*, 509 U.S. 688 (1993), repudiating *Grady* and re-establishing *Blockburger* as the sole definition of the crucial term "same offense." Unlike *Grady*, which focused on the defendant's conduct independent of the statutory definition of the offense, in *Dixon*, the legislative definition controlled the outcome of the double jeopardy case. For example, a conviction for criminal assault in a second proceeding was barred by a previous conviction for contempt of court based upon the same assault because the elements of the assault offense were completely subsumed within the more complex crime of contempt of court based upon assault. However, the same defendant's second conviction for assault with intent to kill was upheld because the contempt conviction did not require proof an attempt to kill, while proof of the violation of a court order, required for contempt, was not part of the proof needed to establish assault with intent to kill. Thus, applying the *Blockburger* rule, each statutory offense required proof of a fact that the other did not, and multiple convictions were permitted despite the fact the defendant's "conduct" resulting in the two convictions was the same, as was the time, place, and victim of the offense.

In dissent, Justice Souter complained that minor variations in the definition of the statutory offense should not control the scope of a defendant's double jeopardy protections when multiple criminal prosecutions are involved. Justice Souter thought it odd that a conviction for robbery would bar a second trial for robbery in a dwelling or robbery with a gun, but that a prior conviction for robbery with a gun would not bar a subsequent conviction for robbery in a dwelling under the *Blockburger* rule because the latter two statutory offenses each required proof of a fact that the other does not. According to Justice Souter, if the robbery was simultaneously committed with a gun in a dwelling against the same victim on the same date, the protection against double jeopardy should be made of sturdier stuff when the prosecution attempts to obtain multiple convictions in multiple trials. Justice Souter said the *Blockburger* rule was adequate in helping to determine when multiple penalties could be imposed within a single proceeding, permitting two consecutive sentences at one trial for robbery with a gun and robbery in a dwelling based on the same transaction. Justice Souter believed the definition of the "same offense" should be broader when the state attempts to make a defendant suffer the expense, ordeal, and anxiety of a second criminal trial.

Mixed messages have been sent by the Texas Court of Criminal Appeals with regard to whether Article I, Section 14 of the Texas Constitution provides that broader foundation to the concept of the "same offense" in the context of multiple prosecutions than has been required by the United States Supreme Court in *Dixon*. Two cases decided prior to *Grady* and *Dixon* appeared to adopt such an approach, both involving multiple prosecutions of driving while intoxicated and manslaughter by the operation of a motor vehicle by an intoxicated driver. In *May v. State*, 726 S.W.2d 573 (Tex. Crim. App. 1987), and *Ex Parte Peterson*, 738 S.W.2d 688 (Tex. Crim. App. 1987), a second prosecution was disallowed without regard to the sequence of the prosecution. Whether the manslaughter conviction was obtained first or second, two convictions were not permitted—not because the offenses were deemed the same, but because the same intoxicated driving incident was the subject of both the first conviction and the second attempted prosecution.

Although *May* and *Peterson* have not been expressly overruled, as the Austin Court of Appeals noted in *State v. Guzman*, 182 S.W.3d 389, 392 (Tex. App.—Austin 2005), their continuing vitality is questionable because both were decided before *Dixon* and both purported to interpret the Double Jeopardy Clause of the Fifth Amendment. The *May* and *Peterson* interpretations of that Clause appeared to be correct when *Grady* was later decided, but it became incorrect under the still later decision in *Dixon*.

Whether the Court of Criminal Appeals is willing to consider expanding the approach taken with multiple prosecutions beyond the minimum federal constitutional protection as a matter of Texas constitutional law has not been clear. In some cases, the court has appeared to foreclose any attempt to broaden the concept of "the same offense" for double jeopardy cases involving multiple prosecutions. For example, in *Ortega v State*, 171 S.W.3d 895, 896 (Tex. Crim. App. 2005), the defendant was indicted for assault of a public servant based upon an indictment alleging the defendant caused bodily injury to a police officer—a public servant who was lawfully discharging his official duty when he arrested the defendant. The defendant asserted a double jeopardy bar to this prosecution because of his prior conviction for resisting arrest by the same officer on the same occasion. After the trial court denied the defense motion, the defendant was convicted of the assault of a public servant offense, but the court of appeals reversed, holding that resisting arrest and assault of a police officer offenses were the same offense for double jeopardy purposes. The Court of Criminal Appeals reversed, holding the lower court's analysis had been based upon the fact that the same conduct was involved. The *Ortega* Court noted that, while a conduct approach had been used by the United States Supreme Court in *Grady v. Corbin*, the Supreme Court overruled *Grady* in *United States v. Dixon*, which held the critical factor in determining whether multiple convictions can be obtained is whether the same conduct is involved, regardless of whether the defendant is convicted of multiple charges in one trial or is convicted in multiple trials. The Court of Criminal Appeals in *Ortega* stated blandly, without further inquiry or discussion, that the courts of Texas are bound to follow the United States Supreme Court's rule that the Fifth Amendment jeopardy questions must be resolved by application of the test of *Blockburger*, which compares elements of offenses, not conduct.

Several intermediate appellate courts have applied *Dixon* while denying multiple prosecution double jeopardy claims. *See State v. Rios*, 861 S.W.2d 42, 43 (Tex. App.—Houston [14th Dist.] 1993, pet. ref'd); *State v. Jackson*, 75 S.W.3d 653, 657 (Tex. App.—Eastland 2002, pet. ref'd) (court of appeals reluctantly held that prior contempt finding bars conviction in light of apparent acceptance of *Dixon* by Court of Criminal Appeals, but suggested that issue be reconsidered because *Dixon* was only a plurality opinion). The unquestioning acceptance of the federal standard is particularly curious in light of the history of the former carving doctrine, which was part of Texas for over one hundred years, and used a conduct-based approach to double jeopardy issues for both multiple punishments and multiple prosecutions. The long history of a Texas standard that differed from the federal constitutional minimum makes it clear that Texas is free to have a more expansive view of double jeopardy protections under its state constitution.

Collateral Estoppel

The *Dixon* Court recognized that broader constitutional protections are available in the multiple trial context in one limited situation. If a defendant is acquitted in the first trial, the doctrine of collateral estoppel—which is a part of double jeopardy law—might be invoked successfully by the defendant in order to prevent the state from having a second opportunity to prove a crucial factual issue already decided adversely to the State in a trial before a competent tribunal. Collateral estoppel helps prevent the prosecution from empaneling repetitive juries in order to find the one most favorably disposed to the State's case and avoiding double jeopardy constraints by alleging offenses that, while factually very similar, differ with regard to some element that makes the statutory offense different under the *Blockburger* and *Hunter* test.

Thus, for example, a defendant acquitted of a sale of heroin that was not pursuant to a prescription might prevent a second prosecution alleging a sale of heroin that was not in a stamped package, despite the fact that convictions for both with consecutive sentences would be upheld if obtained in a single trial. Even though the first acquittal is not the for the same offense alleged in the second indictment under the narrow frame of reference of the *Blockburger* rule, a second attempt to prove the defendant was the person who sold the same heroin would not be allowed in a second trial because the State is not permitted to re-litigate the same fact that has been determined adversely to the State in the first trial. The collateral estoppel doctrine moves beyond the limited same elements test into the realm of which facts concerning the conduct were involved (and resolved) in the prior acquittal.

The United States Supreme Court first recognized this extension of the Double Jeopardy Clause in *Ashe v. Swenson*, 397 U.S. 436 (1970), a case in which the defendant was one of four men accused of robbery of six poker players. Ashe was brought to trial on a charge he helped rob one of the poker players, but he was acquitted. The prosecution then charged Ashe with the robbery of another victim, which would not have constituted the "same offense" under traditional double jeopardy doctrine because the different victim made the offense different from the charge brought in the first trial. The same witnesses who had identified Ashe as one of the robbers testified again at a second trial, although this time apparently with a greater assurance in his ability to identify Ashe, and Ashe was convicted. The United States Supreme Court held that the second conviction violated the concept of collateral estoppel because, when an issue of ultimate fact has been resolved in favor of the accused, the state should be precluded from bringing further charges against the accused that require proof of the same issue.

While the collateral estoppel doctrine creates an important principle recognizing greater protections when there are multiple prosecutions, the doctrine has serious limitations. The doctrine only applies when there has been an acquittal at the first trial. Thus, the doctrine does nothing to protect the double jeopardy rights of a defendant who has been convicted in a previous trial. If there has been a conviction in the first trial, only the State could benefit from it, and it is clear that collateral estoppel is part of the double jeopardy protection available only to the defendant. To allow the State to argue collateral estoppel in order to prevent a jury from possibly acquitting a defendant based upon a fact that has already been determined adversely to the defendant in a first conviction would undermine the defendant's right to have a jury determine guilt or innocence in every criminal case.

The ambiguity of general verdicts in criminal cases is one of the most important problems in the application of the collateral estoppel doctrine. In a case like *Ashe v. Swenson*, it was apparent that the only serious issue contested by the defense was the identity of the defendant as one of the robbers. However, in many cases, the basis of the acquittal could be due to a number of different reasons, such as whether the defendant caused the harm, whether the offense was committed with the requisite mental state, whether the defendant qualified for a statutory defense, or a host of other issues. When it is unclear what issue was actually determined adversely to the state at the first trial, collateral estoppel is unavailable. *See Bobby v. Bies*, 556 U.S. 825 (2009) (unclear whether issue of defendant's mental retardation was decided at first trial); *Ex parte Infante*, 151 S.W.3d 255 (Tex. App.—Texarkana 2004) (identity was not shown to be determinative issue in the acquittal the first sexual assault trial, and, even if it was, that finding would not preclude prosecution of any other offenses because they were alleged to have been committed on different occasions); *Ex parte Tarlton*, 105 S.W.3d 295 (Tex. App.—Houston [14th Dist.] 2003) (because the trial court rationally could have based its verdict on issues other than those that the defendant sought to foreclose, the second prosecution after the prior acquittal did not violate the collateral estoppel rule).

For collateral estoppel to apply, courts must first determine whether the jury resolved a specific, relevant fact, and how broad the scope of the finding was. The burden is on the defendant to demonstrate the issue the accused seeks to foreclose was actually decided in the first proceeding.

Meeting this burden is difficult because of the tradition of general verdicts in criminal cases. A case illustrating the opaque nature of the general verdict is *Hisey v. State*, 207 S.W.3d 383 (Tex. App.—Houston [1st Dist.] 2006), in which the defendant was indicted for capital murder based upon allegations he killed two different individuals in the same transaction—a factor that elevates simple murder to capital murder. The jury impliedly acquitted the defendant of *capital murder* by finding the defendant guilty of *murder* with a traditional general verdict that provided no further information. Because the jury charge authorized a conviction of murder if the jury found either that the defendant killed victim X or victim Y, the conviction was reversed because the jury charge erroneously failed to inform the jury it must be unanimous in its conclusion that one particular victim was killed by the defendant. The defendant could not be tried for capital murder because of the implied acquittal of this charge, but the Court of Appeals stated the defendant could be charged with the murder of either victim on retrial. The acquittal of capital murder suggests that the jury had a reasonable doubt about the murder of one of the victims by the defendant, but because the general verdict did not reveal for which victim the state failed to prove its case, a new charge naming either of the victims was not precluded.

Because collateral estoppel can only apply when there is a second prosecution that involves an issue of ultimate fact necessarily decided adversely to the State by a competent tribunal in the first trial, courts have consistently rebuffed collateral estoppel claims based upon inconsistent verdicts at a single trial. The fact the jury acquitted the defendant of one or more charges does not create a collateral estoppel prohibition against conviction of other counts in the same trial, even if the acquittal is logically inconsistent with the convictions. The jury's prerogative to be inconsistent within a single trial is explained in part on the desire to allow jury nullification, and the assumption that the acquittals are explained as possible nullifications will prevent invalidation of the convictions if supported by sufficient evidence under the deferential standard applied to insufficiency of evidence claims.

Collateral estoppel is also inapplicable when the prosecutions involve different defendants. Thus, an acquittal for one individual, in the same or separate trials, does not create a collateral estoppel opportunity for another, even if the individual is alleged to be a participant in the crime with the defendant who was acquitted.

Chapter 11: Homicide, Murder and Heat of Passion

Introduction

The approach taken in this text is to look at general questions like mental state, the act requirement, and causation, and to use cases dealing with various crimes to illustrate these principles rather than to discuss individual types of crimes and distill general principles from them. This chapter departs from that approach by discussing the generic crime of homicide and the particular manifestations of it, such as murder, felony murder, manslaughter, and criminally negligent homicide. One of the reasons for examining homicide is that there are doctrines related to homicide offenses that are unique in criminal law. The provocation discount that can reduce the penalty for murder, which is discussed in this chapter, is not duplicated elsewhere in the substantive criminal law. Felony murder allows the intent for a non-homicide felony to transfer to a resulting death that may have occurred by accident. Such a transference is contrary to the rules concerning transferred intent discussed earlier in the text.

In addition to these unique features of homicide, the cluster of homicide offenses are all *result* crimes. Unless the defendant's act causes the death of another, whatever else it may be, the crime cannot be a homicide. The requirement of a particular result does not exist in all criminal offenses. For example, a defendant can be convicted of perjury for testifying falsely under oath without any showing the false testimony was believed or caused any harm. Thus, homicide offenses provide a template for discussing the issue of causation.

The penalties that can be imposed upon a criminal conviction are generally beyond the scope of this text and course, but the penalty of death is a sanction of such severity that it deserves attention particularly in a text featuring Texas law, as the state of Texas imposes the death penalty more often than any other state. There is only one offense that can result in the penalty of death in the Texas Penal Code, and that is the highest of the homicide offenses: capital murder.

Finally, examining homicide allows review of some important problems we have discussed. Homicide is a concept that embodies a cluster of offenses with a common core of a criminal act that causes death. The highest grades of capital murder and murder are distinguished from the lower ranks of manslaughter and criminally negligent homicide by differences in the required mental state. Thus, homicide allows us to reconsider mental state and lesser-included offense problems in a particular setting.

Texas Homicide Statutes and the Common Law Tradition

The Texas homicide statutes are found in sections 19.01 through 19.05 of the Texas Penal Code. Section 19.01(a), "Types of Criminal Homicide," defines the generic crime of homicide as "(a) A person commits criminal homicide if he intentionally, knowingly, recklessly, or with criminal negligence causes the death of an individual."

Thus, the common core of all homicide offenses is the element of causing the death of an individual. The particular types of homicide are named in subsection (b) of 19.01: "(b) Criminal homicide is murder, capital murder, manslaughter, or criminally negligent homicide."

This same core offense of homicide is divided into particular categories depending upon the mental state accompanying the act that caused the death of another, ranging from intentional in capital murder down to criminally negligent homicide. There is a breathtaking range of penalties from the highest to the lowest: from death (or life imprisonment without the possibility of parole) to a two-year maximum sentence for the state-jail felony of criminally negligent homicide. Homicide offenses provide a dramatic example of the importance of mental state. Although the harm of the offense is the same, differences in what the defendant desired, knew, risked, or should have been aware of create different dispositions ranging from a two-year sentence (which could be suspended and the defendant placed upon probation) to the death penalty.

The offense of murder (Section 19.02) requires intent or knowledge; manslaughter (Section 19.04) requires proof of recklessness; and the offense of criminally negligent homicide (Section 19.05) describes the required mental state. Capital murder (Section 19.03) is premised on one form of murder, defined in Subsection 19.02(a), plus the existence of certain aggravating factors accompanying the intentional murder. The capital murder statute will be examined as part of capital punishment in a later chapter. The Texas homicide statutes (excluding capital murder) are set out below:

Sec. 19.02. Murder.

(a) In this section:

> (1) "Adequate cause" means cause that would commonly produce a degree of anger, rage, resentment, or terror in a person of ordinary temper, sufficient to render the mind incapable of cool reflection.

> (2) "Sudden passion" means passion directly caused by and arising out of provocation by the individual killed or another acting with the person killed which passion arises at the time of the offense and is not solely the result of former provocation.

(b) A person commits an offense if he:

> (1) intentionally or knowingly causes the death of an individual;

> (2) intends to cause serious bodily injury and commits an act clearly dangerous to human life that causes the death of an individual; or

> (3) commits or attempts to commit a felony, other than manslaughter, and in the course of and in furtherance of the commission or attempt, or in immediate flight

from the commission or attempt, he commits or attempts to commit an act clearly dangerous to human life that causes the death of an individual.

(c) Except as provided by Subsection (d), an offense under this section is a felony of the first degree.

(d) At the punishment stage of a trial, the defendant may raise the issue as to whether he caused the death under the immediate influence of sudden passion arising from an adequate cause. If the defendant proves the issue in the affirmative by a preponderance of the evidence, the offense is a felony of the second degree.

Sec. 19.04. Manslaughter.

(a) A person commits an offense if he recklessly causes the death of an individual.

(b) An offense under this section is a felony of the second degree.

Sec. 19.05. Criminally Negligent Homicide.

(a) A person commits an offense if he causes the death of an individual by criminal negligence.

(b) An offense under this section is a state jail felony.

The murder statute is subdivided into three types in Subsection 19.02(b). The first type is intentionally or knowingly causing the death of another; the second is intending serious bodily harm, but causing death; and the third is causing the death by a dangerous act during the commission of a felony. The third type is known as felony murder, and will be discussed more fully in the next chapter. Only the first type of murder—intentionally or knowingly—can be the predicate for capital murder.

Under the common law, murder was the intentional killing of another human being with malice aforethought. The Model Penal Code and the Texas Penal Code have dropped the malice aforethought requirement in favor of a more streamlined statute which requires only intent or knowledge. The justification for the deletion of malice aforethought has removed a confusing term that added little to administration of homicide law. Malice in the sense of ill will towards the victim was never required. A killer who simply opened fire on patrons at a movie theater or a restaurant after carefully preparing an arsenal of weapons is guilty of murder in Texas, and this is also true of in jurisdictions that continue to use the terminology of malice aforethought.

Aforethought was a more difficult concept that was often explained as involving premeditation. Some jurisdictions still retain the common law language, for example, the federal murder statute, codified at 18 U.S.C.A. § 1111:

> Murder is the unlawful killing of a human being with malice aforethought. Every murder perpetrated by poison, lying in wait, or any other kind of willful, deliberate, malicious,

and premeditated killing . . . is murder in the first degree. Any other murder is murder in the second degree.

The idea of premeditation suggested a difference in culpability between a person who carefully planned and executed a murder and a person who killed spontaneously in the heat of the moment. However, premeditation did not require much in the way of advanced planning. Jury instructions in states retaining malice aforethought usually inform the jury that malice aforethought can be formed at the moment of the commission of the unlawful act. All that is required is that the defendant has the ability to think about what he or she is doing. Since premeditation can occur in an instant, and malice is not required, the drafters of the Model Penal Code urged that the concept of malice aforethought was not helpful, and the revised Texas Penal Code that became effective in 1974 followed this approach.

Under the common law, homicide was divided into two general categories: (1) murder—which was the killing of another human being with malice aforethought, and (2) manslaughter—which was the killing of another human being without malice aforethought. Malice could be either *express* malice, which is an intent to kill, or *implied* malice, which is a form of recklessness so extreme as to elevate the offense from manslaughter to murder. A variety of terms continue to be used to describe the mental state of implied malice in jurisdictions that still follow the common law approach, but it is most frequently referred to as "depraved heart" or "depraved mind" murder. The criteria for when recklessness becomes so extreme that it should be treated as a variety of murder rather than a reckless or negligent homicide is unclear. Sometimes the concept related to the creation of an extremely high risk, and in other cases it was said that it required an act with an "abandoned and malignant heart" that showed no regard for the value of human life. Examples of depraved heart homicide include throwing large stones from the roof of a building onto crowded sidewalks, playing "Russian roulette," drag racing in a crowded urban area, and piloting a speed boat through a group of swimmers.

Texas does not have a form of extreme recklessness homicide, but the second type of murder described in Subsection 19.02(b)(2) is a specific type of homicide regarded as an example of depraved heart homicide in some other jurisdictions. If one lacks an intent to kill, but possesses an intent to cause serious bodily injury, and succeeds in causing death, it qualifies as murder under Subsection 19.02(b)(2) of the Texas Penal Code. This form of murder is a first-degree felony punishable by a range of imprisonment of five to ninety-nine years or life, but it cannot be the predicate for a capital murder conviction.

The Partial Defense of Provocation

Under the common law, the offense of manslaughter often had two forms: voluntary or involuntary. These terms were unfortunate because a truly involuntary act, such as an accident where the death was beyond the control of the actor, would be no crime at all. Involuntary manslaughter referred to a killing without malice aforethought, and voluntary manslaughter was a killing that occurred in the heat of passion. The heat of passion standard operated like a partial defense based upon the rationale that someone who kills in response to reasonably provoking conditions is not as culpable as someone who kills without such provocation. Although the killing is not justified in the way that a complete defense (such as a killing in self-defense) would be, the act of killing is less blameworthy if it is in response to circumstances that a reasonable person would find provoking. A conviction of voluntary manslaughter carries a lesser penalty than murder. Texas law has now discarded the separate offense of voluntary manslaughter, but it has retained a similar mitigation of punishment for killing in response to provocation that reduces the penalty level to the same extent that a conviction of voluntary manslaughter would have under the former homicide statutes—from a first-degree felony level to a second-degree felony. This is a significant partial defense because the maximum is reduced from a possible life sentence to a maximum of 20 years' imprisonment.

The common law regarded the partial defense of reasonable provocation as a concession to human weakness and was grudging with regard to the type of circumstances that would justify the reduction in penalty. There were four categories traditionally recognized as reasonably provoking: (1) being the victim of an aggravated assault or battery; (2) observing a serious crime committed against close relative; (3) engaging in mutual combat; and (4) observing a spouse in an act of adultery.

This restrictive list helped maintain the objective nature of the test of what was reasonable. It was not enough that the defendant was provoked; the provocation had to be sufficient for a reasonable person to be provoked. Of course, the partial defense required that the jury find the particular defendant must also have been provoked. A husband who is indifferent to the adultery of his wife cannot use the occasion of witnessing her adultery as an excuse to commit a murder at a discounted rate of punishment. In addition to the objective standard of the initial reasonable provocation, the jury also had to find that a reasonable person would not have "cooled off" in the interim between the provoking event and the killing.

The modern trend has been to move away from the strictures of the traditional common law heat-of-passion standard. Juries have been given more freedom to judge claims of provocation based upon individual facts without having to fit the events into a procrustean form. The cooling off period has also been liberalized in many jurisdictions with the recognition that passions can be rekindled by events that would be insufficient by themselves, but that represent a pattern of events that can be deemed to be adequately provoking. The *Berry* case from California, which follows, is representative of the modern trend with regard to partial defense of provocation.

People v. Berry

Choking wife

556 P.2d 777 (Cal. 1976)

Sullivan, Justice.

Defendant Albert Joseph Berry was charged by indictment with one count of murder and one count of assault by means of force likely to produce great bodily injury. The assault was allegedly committed on July 23, 1974, and the murder on July 26, 1974. In each count, the alleged victim was defendant's wife, Rachel Pessah Berry. A jury found defendant guilty as charged and determined that the murder was of the first degree.

Defendant contends that there is sufficient evidence in the record to show that he committed the homicide while in a state of uncontrollable rage caused by provocation and flowing from a condition of diminished capacity and therefore that it was error for the trial court to fail to instruct the jury on voluntary manslaughter as indeed he had requested. He claims: (1) that he was entitled to an instruction on voluntary manslaughter since the killing was done upon a sudden quarrel or heat of passion. *jury charge incorrect*

Defendant, a cook, 46 years old, and Rachel Pessah, a 20-year-old girl from Israel, were married on May 27, 1974. Three days later Rachel went to Israel by herself, returning on July 13, 1974. On July 23, 1974, defendant choked Rachel into unconsciousness. She was treated at a hospital where she reported her strangulation by defendant to an officer of the San Francisco Police Department. On July 25, Inspector Sammon, who had been assigned to the case, met with Rachel and as a result of the interview a warrant was issued for defendant's arrest.

While Rachel was at the hospital, defendant removed his clothes from their apartment and stored them in a Greyhound Bus Depot locker. He stayed overnight at the home of a friend, Mrs. Jean Berk, admitting to her that he had choked his wife. On July 26, he telephoned Mrs. Berk and informed her that he had killed Rachel with a telephone cord on that morning at their apartment. The next day Mrs. Berk and two others telephoned the police to report a possible homicide and met Officer Kelleher at defendant's apartment. They gained entry and found Rachel on the bathroom floor. A pathologist from the coroner's office concluded that the cause of Rachel's death was strangulation. Defendant was arrested on August 1, 1974, and confessed to the killing.

At trial defendant did not deny strangling his wife, but claimed through his own *Claiming voluntary manslaughter* testimony and the testimony of a psychiatrist, Dr. Martin Blinder, that he was provoked into killing her because of a sudden and uncontrollable rage so as to reduce the offense to one of voluntary manslaughter. He testified that upon her return from Israel, Rachel announced to him that while there she had fallen in love with another man, one Yako, and had enjoyed his sexual favors, that he was coming to this country to claim her and that she wished a divorce. Thus commenced a tormenting two weeks in which Rachel alternately taunted defendant with her involvement with Yako and at the same time sexually excited defendant, indicating her desire to remain with him. Defendant's detailed testimony, summarized below, chronicles this strange course of events.

221

After their marriage, Rachel lived with defendant for only three days and then left for Israel. Immediately upon her return to San Francisco she told defendant about her relationship with and love for Yako. This brought about further argument and a brawl that evening in which defendant choked Rachel and she responded by scratching him deeply many times. Nonetheless they continued to live together. Rachel kept taunting defendant with Yako and demanding a divorce. She claimed she thought she might be pregnant by Yako. She showed defendant pictures of herself with Yako. Nevertheless, during a return trip from Santa Rosa, Rachel demanded immediate sexual intercourse with defendant in the car, which was achieved; however upon reaching their apartment, she again stated that she loved Yako and that she would not have intercourse with defendant in the future.

On the evening of July 22nd defendant and Rachel went to a movie where they engaged in heavy petting. When they returned home and got into bed, Rachel announced that she had intended to make love with defendant, "But I am saving myself for this man Yako, so I don't think I will." Defendant got out of bed and prepared to leave the apartment whereupon Rachel screamed and yelled at him. Defendant choked her into unconsciousness.

Two hours later defendant called a taxi for his wife to take her to the hospital. He put his clothes in the Greyhound bus station and went to the home of his friend Mrs. Berk for the night. The next day he went to Reno and returned the day after. Rachel informed him by telephone that there was a warrant for his arrest as a result of her report to the police about the choking incident. On July 25th defendant returned to the apartment to talk to Rachel, but she was out. He slept there overnight. Rachel returned around 11 a.m. the next day. Upon seeing defendant there, she said, "I suppose you have come here to kill me." Defendant responded, "yes," changed his response to "no," and then again to "yes," and finally stated "I have really come to talk to you." Rachel began screaming. Defendant grabbed her by the shoulder and tried to stop her screaming. She continued. They struggled and finally defendant strangled her with a telephone cord.

Dr. Martin Blinder, a physician and psychiatrist, called by the defense, testified that Rachel was a depressed, suicidally inclined girl and that this suicidal impulse led her to involve herself ever more deeply in a dangerous situation with defendant. She did this by sexually arousing him and taunting him into jealous rages in an unconscious desire to provoke him into killing her and thus consummating her desire for suicide. Throughout the period commencing with her return from Israel until her death, that is from July 13 to July 26, Rachel continually provoked defendant with sexual taunts and incitements, alternating acceptance and rejection of him. This conduct was accompanied by repeated references to her involvement with another man; it led defendant to choke her on two occasions, until finally she achieved her unconscious desire and was strangled. Dr. Blinder testified that as a result of this cumulative series of provocations, defendant at the time he fatally strangled Rachel, was in a state of uncontrollable rage, completely under the sway of passion.

We first take up defendant's claim that on the basis of the foregoing evidence he was entitled to an instruction on voluntary manslaughter as defined by statute which is "the unlawful killing of a human being, without malice . . . upon a sudden quarrel or heat of passion."

precedent is persuasive ☆ **Rule of Law:**

We . . . held in [*People v.*] *Valentine*, 169 P.2d 1 (Cal. 1946), that there is no specific type of provocation required by section 192 and that verbal provocation may be sufficient. In *People v. Borchers*, 325 P.2d 97 (Cal. 1958), in the course of explaining the phrase "heat of passion" used in the statute defining manslaughter we pointed out that "passion" need not mean "rage" or "anger" but may be any "violent, intense, high-wrought or enthusiastic emotion" and concluded there "that defendant was aroused to a heat of 'passion' by a series of events over a considerable period of time . . . ." Accordingly we there declared that evidence of admissions of infidelity by the defendant's paramour, taunts directed to him and other conduct, "supports a finding that defendant killed in wild desperation induced by [the woman's] long continued provocatory conduct." We find this reasoning persuasive in the case now before us. Defendant's testimony chronicles a two-week period of provocatory conduct by his wife Rachel that could arouse a passion of jealousy, pain and sexual rage in an ordinary man of average disposition such as to cause him to act rashly from this passion. It is significant that both defendant and Dr. Blinder testified that the former was in the heat of passion under an uncontrollable rage when he killed Rachel. *this is important.*

The Attorney General contends that the killing could not have been done in the heat of passion because there was a cooling period, defendant having waited in the apartment for 20 hours. However, the long course of provocatory conduct, which had resulted in intermittent outbreaks of rage under specific provocation in the past, reached its final culmination in the apartment when Rachel began screaming. Both defendant and Dr. Blinder testified that defendant killed in a state of uncontrollable rage, of passion, and there is ample evidence in the record to support the conclusion that this passion was the result of the long course of provocatory conduct by Rachel.

Therefore we conclude that the jury's determination that defendant was guilty of murder of the first degree under the instructions given did not necessarily indicate that . . . the jury had found that defendant had not killed Rachel under a heat of passion. Since this theory of provocation constituted defendant's entire defense to the first count, we have no difficulty concluding that the failure to give such instruction was prejudicial error and requires us to reverse the conviction of murder of the first degree. *Holding: conviction reversed*

Notes

1. Prosecutors almost never charge the offense of voluntary manslaughter even if the case involves one of the classically recognized categories of provocation and no appreciable cooling off period. Why do you think this is?

2. Voluntary manslaughter usually enters the case as it did in *Berry* as a requested lesser-included-offense instruction. There is not much mystery about who killed Rachel. It was easy for the California Supreme Court to conclude that the error could not be regarded as harmless because it was the only defensive evidence that Berry had, although it related only to the partial defense of provocation. Of course, the court did not determine whether the conviction should be for murder or manslaughter, only that the jury should have been given the choice. If you were on

the jury on retrial, would you find Berry guilty of the charged offense of murder or the requested lesser included of voluntary manslaughter?

3.   What factors should be taken into account in deciding the provocation issue? Jury instructions usually say that the issue should be determined by jurors by placing yourself in the defendant's "situation," but then asking not only whether the defendant was provoked, but whether a reasonable person would have been provoked under the circumstances. If Berry was particularly jealous because of the age difference between him and his wife, is that an appropriate factor to take into account? Isn't it part of the defendant's situation? If Berry had a spouse that was unfaithful to him in a previous marriage that made him particularly sensitive to marital infidelity, is that part of his "situation"? Should jurors take into consideration that Berry has a "hot temper"? Would considering any of these things destroy the objective nature of the inquiry?

The drafters of the Model Penal Code recognized the tension between the objective character of required provocation and the fact that the decision of whether provocation is adequate to reduce the crime to manslaughter must be judged from the defendant's "circumstances," "situation," or point of view. The commentary to the Model Penal Code section 210.3 states:

> The word "situation" is designedly ambiguous. On the one hand, it is clear that personal handicaps and some external circumstances must be taken into account. Thus, blindness, shock from traumatic injury, and extreme grief are all easily read into the term "situation." On the other hand, it is equally plain that idiosyncratic moral values are not part of the actor's situation. An assassin who kills a political leader because he believes it is right to do so cannot ask that he be judged by the standard of a reasonable extremist. . . . In between these two extremes however, there are matters neither as clearly distinct from individual blameworthiness as blindness or handicap nor as integral a part of moral depravity as a belief in rightness of killing. . . . The proper role of such factors cannot be resolved satisfactorily by abstract definition of what may constitute adequate provocation. . . . There thus will be room for interpretation of the word "situation," and that is precisely the flexibility desired. . . . In the end, the question is whether the actor's loss of self-control can be understood in terms that arouse sympathy in the ordinary citizen. Section 210.3 faces this issue squarely and leaves the ultimate judgment to the ordinary citizen in the function of a juror assigned to resolve the specific case.

In 1993, the Texas legislature eliminated the separate offense of voluntary manslaughter and made provocation a mitigating factor to be considered at sentencing rather than an issue to be decided during the guilt-innocence phase of a trial. Under the revised statute, Subsection 19.02(d) of the Texas Penal Code states:

> At the punishment stage of a trial, the defendant may raise the issue as to whether he caused the death under the immediate influence of sudden passion arising from an adequate cause. If the defendant proves the issue in the affirmative by a preponderance of the evidence, the offense is a felony of the second degree.

Subsection 19.02(a) provides two key definitions:

(1) "Adequate cause" means cause that would commonly produce a degree of anger, rage, resentment, or terror in a person of ordinary temper, sufficient to render the mind incapable of cool reflection

(2) "Sudden passion" means passion directly caused by and arising out of provocation by the individual killed or another acting with the person killed which passion arises at the time of the offense and is not solely the result of former provocation.

The new statute moves the issue of provocation out of the guilt/innocence stage and into the punishment phase of trial. In most jurisdictions, this would eliminate the jury from the provocation decision because the jury has no role in sentencing in non-capital cases. In Texas, however, a defendant can elect to have the jury determine punishment if a pre-trial motion is filed requesting jury sentencing. In the absence of an affirmative request, the judge determines the sentence and, thus, the judge would determine the partial provocation defense. Under the former voluntary manslaughter system, the state had the burden of persuasion on the issue of lack of provocation. Under the amended statute, however, the defendant has the burden of persuasion to demonstrate "sudden passion" from an "adequate cause." The new Texas approach to the partial defense of provocation is discussed in the two *Trevino* cases that follow in the text.

Rule: No specific type of provocation required by this statute & verbal provocation maybe be sufficient.

Issue: Can murder be reduced to voluntary manslaughter where the heat of passion under which the offense was committed was the product of a continuous period of provocation resulting in the intermittent outbreaks of rage leading to the murder

Holding: Yes, trial ct erred in failing to instruct the jury on voluntary manslaughter bc evidence showed the killing was done upon sudden quarrel or heat of passion.

Trevino v. State

100 S.W.3d 232 (Tex. Crim. App. 2003)

Per curiam.

Tommy Trevino shot and killed his wife. He argued the shooting was in self-defense, but the jury rejected this argument and convicted him. At punishment, he requested and was denied a jury charge on sudden passion. We agree with the Court of Appeals that the judge erred in denying this charge, and that the judgment of conviction should be reversed.

I. Facts and Procedural History
A. Guilt/Innocence

The shooting occurred on the Monday after Thanksgiving, 1997. Exactly what happened that day between Trevino and his wife Michelle was the subject of heated debate at trial. The State's witnesses portrayed the incident as a cold-blooded murder by a controlling and abusive husband who, after the murder, staged the crime scene to look like self-defense. The defense argued that the shooting occurred in self-defense after a heated argument and struggle.

Members of Michelle's family testified that Trevino was controlling and Michelle was afraid of him. He would go to nightclubs without Michelle. Eventually Michelle asked Trevino for a divorce, and after that, Trevino would buy her flowers and take her out. But by the date of the offense, Michelle was gaining independence, and had a job interview that very afternoon.

Detective Thomas Boetcher, the lead detective in the case, testified that the crime scene he found did not match the story Trevino told him. Trevino told Detective Boetcher that he and Michelle had been having an argument because she found some phone numbers of some other women in his wallet. They were in the living room, and she confronted Trevino with a .38 caliber revolver. She pointed it at him and pulled the trigger twice, which scared Trevino, but the gun did not fire. Trevino then went to the bathroom and flushed the phone numbers down the toilet. At some point he retrieved his 9 millimeter pistol. As he was leaving the bathroom, Michelle fired a shot at him. According to Trevino, the shot was fired in the bathroom. At this point, the two began struggling over the two guns. Trevino said that Michelle got shot, but they continued to struggle, and then another shot was fired, and finally another.

But Boetcher testified that, while Trevino said that Michelle shot him in the bathroom, there was no bullet hole inside the bathroom. Boetcher also testified that he found a 9 millimeter in the living room and a .38 caliber revolver in the hallway near the bathroom, about five feet from Michelle's body. The 9 millimeter had been taken apart, with the clip removed, but Trevino had not told Boetcher that he had done that. Boetcher felt that the .38 caliber had no evidentiary value to the case—that it had not been a part of the shooting. Boetcher conceded that Trevino granted consent to search the house and made no attempts to flee.

Trevino's sister, Paula, was the first person Trevino called after the incident. She testified that when the initial phone call came from Trevino, Trevino "was freaking out and sounded like he was scared and panicked." She drove over to the house immediately and found Trevino "crying and shaking." Trevino knelt beside Michelle's body and "was upset and crying." He appeared to be "extremely upset," and he was "pacing." According to Paula, Trevino was "consistently upset and crying."

Sometime after Paula arrived at Trevino's house, she called 911. While she admitted that she had previously told the grand jury that she got the call from Trevino before noon and therefore would have been at his house by about 12:20, the 911 call was not made until 12:52. At trial, she testified that she had been mistaken before the grand jury. She explained that she could not have gotten to Trevino's house that soon because she was with her personal trainer until 11:30 and it takes her 30 minutes to get home from there. She testified that she knew she was watching the news when she got the call from Tommy and the news comes on at noon. The timing was important because the State argued that Paula had delayed in calling 911, implying that she had aided Trevino in staging the crime scene to look like self-defense.

While Paula told the firefighters that she had been there for 15 minutes by the time they had arrived, many of the personnel on the scene testified that it appeared that Michelle had been dead for longer than 15 minutes. Firefighter Stacy Banks testified that when he first arrived on the scene, he thought the shooting had just happened, but he then began to believe that Michelle had "been down for a while." The defense established on cross-examination that the police initially went to the wrong house, and that some of the firefighters walked to the house from their truck parked down the street.

Another firefighter testified that he saw dried blood on Michelle, which made him assume that it had been there for a while. A paramedic testified that when he arrived, he noticed that Michelle had dried blood on her face, indicating to him that she had been dead for a little while. She was ashen gray and cold to touch, and her pupils were large, more evidence that she had been dead for some time. Another firefighter-EMT testified that Paula told him Michelle had been down about 15 minutes by the time he arrived. But he noticed cyanosis, which indicates that the person has been down for more than several minutes.

Detective Kraus testified that he entered the home and saw Trevino kneeling over Michelle. Trevino said "you gotta help her, you gotta help her" and he "sounded distressed."

The gunshot residue tests from both Trevino and Michelle were inconclusive, and no fingerprints were identifiable from either weapon. Some witnesses testified that Trevino was calm and unemotional after the shooting, but the defense attempted to portray that as shock. The defense established during its cross-examination of the firearms examiner that the gun could have been fired accidentally.

Dr. Marc Krouse, the medical examiner, testified that he did the autopsy on Michelle. He found three bullet wounds and testified to their entry and exit points, trajectories, and the damage each caused. He said the pelvic wound came first, and the effect of that shot could have ranged from virtual immediate unconsciousness to almost no effect at all. Based on the blood smear on the wall, he felt that after this shot, Michelle had fallen to the floor.

The bullet through the head was the second shot fired and was a fatal wound that would produce death in seconds. He said Michelle could not have struggled after being shot in the head. The shot through her heart was the third shot. She was already dead when this shot hit her. Krouse testified that when this last shot was fired, Michelle's back was up against something. The time between the shots was not long—somewhere between seconds to a minute or two.

Trevino presented two defense witnesses. Ted Trevino, Trevino's brother, testified that several years before this incident, he had relayed to Trevino something that Michelle had told him—that she was angry at Trevino for coming home with hickeys on his neck; that while Trevino slept, she had pointed a gun at him; and that she would have shot him except that he had been holding their daughter in his arms while he slept. He admitted that Michelle had told him that Trevino had hit her once in the past, and he testified that he also saw Michelle strike Trevino.

Teresa Trull, Trevino's sister and a police officer, testified that she arrived at the scene and saw Trevino in the patrol car. Trevino "looked shocked." He had "a thousand-yard stare, which, to me, is symptomatic of battle fatigue or post-traumatic stress disorder." He "looked past, beyond me. I was trying to make eye contact with him, but due to the shock, he was looking past me." She also testified that Trevino is not an emotional person and rarely displays emotion.

In closing arguments, the State argued that Trevino was a controlling and abusive husband, that he hit Michelle and cheated on her, and that Michelle was afraid of him. She finally summoned the courage to leave and on the day of her death had a job interview. Trevino saw that he was losing control, so he killed her and then staged the crime scene to look like self-defense.

The defense replied that there was no evidence of an abusive relationship or a staged crime scene. They explained that the State wanted the jury to believe it was a staged crime scene "because if it's not staged, it's self-defense."

The jury was charged on both accident and self-defense, but rejected both defenses and found Trevino guilty of murder.

B. Punishment

At the punishment phase, Trevino requested the judge to instruct the jury pursuant to Penal Code Section 19.02(d). That section provides that if the defendant proves by a preponderance of the evidence that he caused the victim's death while under the immediate influence of sudden passion arising from an adequate cause, the offense is a second-degree felony rather than a first-degree felony. The judge rejected the proposed charge.

The defense presented 15 witnesses testifying that Trevino was a reliable and model employee with no temper, had no prior convictions, was a wonderful and supportive father, and could satisfy the conditions of probation. The State presented two rebuttal witnesses who testified that Trevino was an absentee father and a jealous husband.

The jury sentenced Trevino to 60 years in prison.

C. Court of Appeals

On appeal, Trevino argued the judge erred in denying him the sudden passion charge and that Trevino had been harmed. The court of appeals agreed. We granted the State's petition for discretionary review to address the appellate court's analysis.

II. Entitlement to Sudden Passion Charge

The State argues that "there was no evidence from which a jury could have rationally inferred that [Trevino] . . . acted in sudden passion." In support of this argument, the State points out evidence from the record that (1) Trevino destroyed the telephone numbers during the argument with Michelle, indicating that his mind was indeed capable of cool reflection; (2) Trevino "effectively" admitted to Detective Boetcher that he armed himself before going into the bathroom, and he did not state that he armed himself because he feared Michelle; (3) Trevino and Paula both told Detective Boetcher that Trevino "managed" to shoot Michelle, implying that it was an accident, and there can be no sudden passion if a shooting is accidental; and (4) Trevino never expressed remorse to Detective Boetcher, which "would certainly be expected" from someone who acted in sudden passion. The State contends that Trevino himself "apparently never felt any such passion arise and the record shows only calculation and reflection on his part."

The problem with the State's argument is that it addresses solely the evidence against sudden passion. While the evidence the State mentions was presented at trial, an appellate court's duty is to look at the evidence supporting that charge, not on the evidence refuting it. The evidence that supports the sudden passion instruction in this case consists of the following:

- Detective Boetcher testified that Trevino told him that there had been a verbal altercation between him and Michelle; that Michelle was angry because she found some phone numbers in his wallet of some other girls; that Trevino was in the living room when Michelle confronted him with a .38 pistol, pointed it at Trevino, and pulled the trigger twice; that Trevino was scared, but the gun did not fire, so he figured the gun was not loaded; that Trevino went to the bathroom and at some point got his 9 millimeter gun; that Michelle shot at Trevino in the bathroom; that the two then struggled over the guns; that Michelle got shot; that the struggle continued; and that Michelle was eventually shot three times.

- Paula testified that when the initial phone call came from Trevino, after the shooting, Trevino "was freaking out and sounded like he was scared and panicked." She drove over to the house immediately and found Trevino "crying and shaking." Trevino knelt beside Michelle's body and "was upset and crying." He appeared to be "extremely upset," and he was "pacing." According to Paula, Trevino was "consistently upset and crying."

- Detective Kraus testified that he entered the home and saw Trevino kneeling over Michelle. Trevino said, "You gotta help her, you gotta help her." He "sounded distressed."

229

• Teresa Trull, Trevino's sister and a police officer, testified that she arrived at scene and saw Trevino in the patrol car. Trevino "looked shocked." He had "a thousand-yard stare, which, to me, is symptomatic of battle fatigue or post-traumatic stress disorder." He "looked past, beyond me. I was trying to make eye contact with him, but due to the shock, he was looking past me."

This evidence may be weak and it arguably was impeached by the State's evidence. But a defendant is entitled to the sudden passion charge even if the evidence is weak and even if it is contradicted by the State's evidence. This evidence constitutes "some" evidence that Trevino acted in sudden passion.

We affirm the Court of Appeals' judgment, which reversed the trial court's judgment as to punishment and remanded the case to the trial court to conduct a new punishment hearing.

Holding

even if evidence is weak ahere is still evidence there for a crime ot sudden passion → jury still has to be charged w/ this defense.

Trevino v. State

157 S.W.3d 818 (Tex. App.—Fort Worth 2005, no pet.)

John Cayce, Chief Justice.

Appellant Tommy Trevino appeals his conviction for murder. In a single point, appellant contends that the evidence is factually insufficient to negate the defensive issue of sudden passion. We will affirm.

Appellant was tried for the murder of his wife, Michelle Trevino, in the fall of 1999. A jury found him guilty of murder and sentenced him to sixty years' confinement. Appellant appealed his sentence, contending that the trial court erred by failing to instruct the jury on sudden passion. We reversed the trial court and remanded the case for a new trial on punishment. The following facts were adduced on retrial.

At the time of her death, the deceased and appellant had been together for about nine years. Appellant admitted that he had been unfaithful to the deceased during their marriage. His infidelity had been a source of conflict between them. For instance, one time when appellant came home with hickeys on his neck, the deceased allegedly pointed a gun at him while he slept. She told appellant's brother that she would have shot appellant if he had not been holding their daughter. Despite their problems, appellant attended family events with the deceased and helped her raise their two children.

About three months before the murder, the deceased told appellant that she wanted a divorce. After that, appellant started paying more attention to her. He would take her out to lunch, buy her flowers, and take her to dance clubs, which the deceased enjoyed. Although their relationship improved for a while, the deceased indicated that they were having problems again just two days before her murder.

The deceased worked various jobs throughout their marriage. At the time of her death, she was earning minimum wage, and appellant was unemployed because of neck injuries he sustained in a car accident. The deceased completed some applications for higher paying jobs, though she did not submit them. On the day of her murder, however, the deceased told her employer that she had a job interview and arranged to work a later shift.

The State argued that appellant disapproved of the deceased's plan to find a higher paying job because it would increase her independence and ability to leave him. According to the State, appellant murdered the deceased because she was going to leave him and he did not want her to be with anyone else. Appellant disagreed with the State's proffered motive and testified that he shot the deceased because she shot at him.

According to appellant, he and the deceased were both at home around noon on December 1, 1997. As appellant sat on his living room sofa watching television, the deceased looked through his wallet and found a woman's phone number. She then pointed an empty revolver at him, demanded to know who the woman was, and pulled the trigger twice.

Appellant's heart "jumped in [his] chest." In a state of terror, appellant took a nine millimeter pistol out of the living room closet and went into the bathroom, closing the door behind him. He used the bathroom and flushed the phone numbers down the toilet. As he exited the bathroom into the dark hallway, he heard a gunshot "right in front of [his] face." At that point, he started shooting and tried to knock the revolver out of the deceased's hand. After the shooting, appellant called his sister, who went to his house and then called 911.

The first police officer to arrive on the scene saw appellant kneeling next to the deceased. Appellant appeared distraught and told him to help the deceased. The deceased was lying across the threshold of the bathroom, with her upper body in the bathroom and her legs extended into the hallway. The officer noticed a revolver lying in the hall. He asked appellant to move away from the deceased and come towards him; appellant complied. He was then handcuffed by a second police officer, who led him out of the house. Both the second officer and firefighters passing appellant as they entered the house testified that he looked calm.

Emergency personnel determined that the deceased was not breathing and did not have a pulse or heartbeat. The condition of her body led them to believe that she had "been down for a while." The deceased was pronounced dead at the scene.

The deceased had a total of six bullet wounds. The first bullet entered her left hip and exited through her right buttock, the second bullet entered the left side of her head and exited through the right side of her head, and the third bullet entered the center of the front of her chest and exited through her back. A blood smear on the hallway wall was consistent with the exit wound from the hip shot and indicated that the deceased had slid down against the wall to the floor. Although the deceased could have continued to struggle after the first shot, the shot to her head would have caused immediate shock and rendered the deceased incapable of any volitional movement. The lack of bleeding from the chest wound, which was inflicted as the deceased lay upon the floor, indicated that she had been in a state of shock when she sustained it. Appellant fired all three shots from the nine millimeter pistol within a short span of time.

A fourth shot, from the revolver found in the hallway, struck the upper part of the wall at the end of the hallway. Investigators found bullets for the revolver in the master bedroom's closet. To reach the closet from the living room, one would have to walk past the bathroom door. Although the revolver emits a cloud of gunpowder when fired, neither the deceased nor appellant had any measurable amounts of gunpowder on their hands. The revolver did not have any identifiable fingerprints on it. The deceased's manicured fingernails were in perfect condition and did not contain any traces of appellant's skin or blood.

After hearing the evidence, the jury failed to find that appellant acted under the influence of sudden passion and assessed punishment of life in prison.

In his sole point, appellant contends that the evidence is factually insufficient to negate the defensive issue of sudden passion.

In reviewing this point, we must consider all of the evidence relevant to the issue of sudden passion and determine whether the verdict is so against the great weight and preponderance of the evidence as to be manifestly unjust. We are to give deference to the fact finder's determinations, including determinations involving the credibility and demeanor of witnesses.

At the punishment stage of a murder trial, the defendant may raise the issue of whether he *cannot soley but past provocation* caused the death under the immediate influence of sudden passion arising from an adequate cause. "Sudden passion" means passion directly caused by and arising out of provocation by the individual killed or another acting with the person killed that passion arises at the time of the offense and is not solely the result of former provocation. "Adequate cause" means cause that would commonly produce a degree of anger, rage, resentment, or terror in a person of ordinary temper, sufficient to render the mind incapable of cool reflection. The accused may not rely upon a cause of his own making, such as precipitating a confrontation. If the defendant proves sudden passion by a preponderance of the evidence, the offense is punished as a second-degree felony.

Appellant's sudden passion argument was based on his testimony that he shot the deceased in a state of terror caused by the deceased's shooting the revolver at him. The jury was free to make its own determination of appellant's credibility and reject appellant's version of events if it did not believe he was telling the truth. The jury could have doubted appellant's story based on his strange response to the deceased's allegedly firing the pistol at him twice or the lack of physical evidence to support his contentions that she fired the revolver and struggled with him.

In addition to his testimony, appellant cites the presence of the revolver in the hallway and a bullet from that revolver in the hallway wall, his brother's testimony that the deceased previously pointed a gun at appellant when she was angry with him, and his demeanor as observed by the first police officer to arrive at the scene. None of this evidence, however, compelled the jury to find that appellant murdered the deceased under the influence of sudden passion.

The fact that the revolver had been fired did not prove that it had been fired by the deceased. Moreover, even if the jury believed appellant's brother's testimony about the deceased's pointing a gun at appellant in the past, it was not bound to conclude that she did so on the day of her murder. Without the deceased's fingerprints on the revolver or gun powder on her hands, the jury could have concluded that appellant fired the revolver after he murdered the deceased to make it look like self-defense.

Further, the fact that appellant appeared distraught to the police officer who first arrived on the scene did not require the jury to believe that he was in a state of terror when he committed the murder. The testimony merely showed that appellant acted like he wanted the officer to help the deceased after she was already dead. The jury could have weighed that testimony against the testimony that appellant seemed calm just minutes after he appeared distraught and the fact the appellant called his sister, rather than 911, after the shooting and concluded that his demeanor was contrived.

After weighing all of the evidence, we conclude that the jury's failure to find that appellant murdered his wife under the immediate influence of sudden passion was not so

not wrong or unjust enough

contrary to the great weight and preponderance of the evidence as to be clearly wrong and unjust. Accordingly, we overrule appellant's sole point and affirm the judgment of the trial court.

Notes

1.   The two *Trevino* opinions help to demonstrate the important difference between the specific types of burdens within the generic term of burden of proof. The burden of production is the burden of coming forward with "some" or "any" evidence. The judge determines whether this low standard has been met by deciding to give a jury instruction on the relevant issue, in this case the reasonable provocation question. Because there was some evidence, the failure to give the jury the option on the disputed issue was error.

On retrial of the punishment phase, the defendant was given the instruction that should have been granted in the first trial. However, the jury decided the defendant did not meet the burden of persuasion on provocation by a preponderance of the evidence standard. The appellate court deferred to the jury's decision and affirmed. Do you think it is likely an appellate court would ever overturn a jury decision on the partial defense of provocation?

2.   In several chapters, we will be examining the question of burden of proof as the method of allocating what is considered an element of the offense and what is considered a defense. In the case of *Mullaney v. Wilbur*, the United States Supreme Court reversed a murder conviction on due process grounds because state law had put the burden of persuasion on the defendant to show reasonable provocation. Has Texas violated the due process requirement that the State prove the guilt of a defendant beyond a reasonable doubt? You will want to revisit this question after you read *Mullaney* and the opinion that distinguished *Mullaney* in *Patterson v. New York*, which upheld a statute that placed a burden of persuasion on the defendant with regard to the issue of provocation. Is the Texas statute like the one in *Mullaney* or *Patterson*?

Homicide statutes are linked by a prohibition against the same result—causing the death of another. They differ primarily because of differences in a culpable mental state. Because proof of a higher mental state suffices for proof of a lower one, the homicide offenses carry a relationship of greater and lesser-included offenses. The *Gonzalez* case that follows is an example of the close relationship among homicide offenses and the difficulty in determining where within a range of statutes a conviction should fall. The defendant was indicted for murder (intentional or knowing murder), the jury found the defendant guilty of manslaughter (reckless homicide), and the defendant claimed on appeal that the evidence was insufficient to support the conviction because it showed only criminally negligent homicide.

Killing wife w/ shotgun

Gonzalez v. State

did he know risk?

No. 08-01-00451-CR, 2004 WL 100517 (Tex. App.—El Paso Jan. 22, 2004, no pet.)

David Wellington Chew, Justice.

Appellant Luis Gonzalez was indicted and tried for the murder *Crime* of Lorenza Orozco. The jury found Appellant guilty of the lesser-included offense of manslaughter and assessed punishment of 18 years' imprisonment and a fine of $10,000. On appeal, Appellant challenges *Issue* the sufficiency of the evidence to sustain his conviction. We affirm. *Holding*

On the evening of October 6, 2000, Appellant shot his wife Lorenza Orozco with a 12–gauge shotgun during an argument in their home. Ms. Orozco died as a result of the injuries she sustained. Appellant and the victim had been together for over three years and had a two-year-old son. They had a lot of problems in their relationship and financial disagreements. That evening, Appellant got out of work around 8:30 p.m. and went to the Lamplighter Bar, a strip club, and drank a couple of beers. About half an hour later, Ms. Orozco entered the club, went to Appellant's table, and started yelling at Appellant. The club's bouncer threw the couple out. Appellant arrived home first and as he got out of his vehicle, Ms. Orozco pulled up and almost ran him over. Appellant went to her vehicle, picked up their son from the back seat, and went into the house. Appellant recalled that while he was closing the door, Ms. Orozco hit him in the mouth. Appellant put his sleeping son on the sofa and he and Ms. Orozco continued arguing.

In his statement to police, Appellant stated that during the argument he grabbed Ms. Orozco and shook her from the arms and stated that she was getting out of hand. He then called her mother and told her what was happening and that he could not stand Ms. Orozco and did not want her there anymore. Ms. Orozco grabbed a lamp and Appellant hung up the phone and went upstairs. Appellant then went into his room, grabbed a shotgun that he kept loaded in his closet and went back downstairs. Appellant told Ms. Orozco to shut up and leave, but she kept going on and calling him names. Appellant pulled on the trigger and the shotgun went off. Ms. Orozco fell to the floor and he walked upstairs and put the shotgun away. Appellant returned and picked up his son who was crying. He then called 911 and told them to come quickly because he had shot his wife accidentally. Appellant stated that he did not want to shoot her, he just wanted to scare her.

At trial, Appellant offered contrary testimony concerning the immediate events leading up to the shooting. Appellant testified that after they returned home and during their argument, his brother-in-law called on the phone. Appellant gave the phone to Ms. Orozco and while she was on the phone, he went upstairs to take a shower. Ms. Orozco followed Appellant upstairs and came towards him, threw something at him, and started yelling at him and hitting him. Appellant then picked up the 12–gauge shotgun, which was behind the 9–millimeter gun, on the top shelf in the closet. Appellant stated that he wanted to scare her and calm her down. Appellant testified that he did not grab the 9–millimeter because he knew it was loaded, but knew the shotgun was not loaded. Appellant went downstairs, carrying the shotgun, and Ms. Orozco followed behind him. She kept on hitting him, so he called his mother-in-law. After he hung up the phone, Ms. Orozco swung at him and threw something at him. Appellant picked up the shotgun, which was on top of the counter and put it by his side. Appellant pointed the shotgun at Ms. Orozco. Ms. Orozco had something in her hand and swung at him and Appellant told her to stop. When she did it again, Appellant flinched and the gun went off. Ms. Orozco grabbed her arm and asked Appellant to call 911. At first, Appellant could not react and did not respond to her. Appellant testified that he was in shock because the gun should have never been loaded. Ms. Orozco then yelled at him to call 911 and he did.

In this case, Appellant was charged with murder, but at trial, the jury was also instructed on the lesser-included offenses of reckless manslaughter and criminally negligent homicide. The jury found Appellant guilty of manslaughter. A person commits manslaughter if he recklessly causes the death of an individual. To obtain a conviction for manslaughter, the State must prove that: (1) the risk that the defendant perceived was both substantial and unjustifiable; and (2) the defendant's disregard of the risk constituted a gross deviation from the ordinary standard of care. Under the Texas Penal Code, a person commits criminally negligent homicide by causing the death of an individual by criminal negligence.

On appeal, Appellant argues that if he is guilty, he is guilty of the lesser-included offense of criminally negligent homicide, rather than manslaughter, because he failed to perceive the injury or death that could result from his conduct because he thought the shotgun was unloaded. Therefore, the only disputed element on appeal is Appellant's mental state, that is, whether he was aware of a substantial and unjustifiable risk created by his conduct and consciously disregarded it, or whether he was unaware of the risk involved or failed to perceive that risk. Proof of a culpable mental state often relies on circumstantial evidence, and in comparing recklessness versus criminal negligence, is a conclusion to be drawn by the trier of fact through inference from all the circumstances.

In this case, according to his statement, Appellant and Ms. Orozco were in the middle of an argument when he went upstairs to his room and grabbed a shotgun that he kept loaded in the closet. Appellant then returned downstairs, continued arguing with Ms. Orozco, and then pulled on the trigger and the shotgun went off. Appellant stated that he did not want to shoot her, but only intended to "scare her." At trial, Appellant testified that he grabbed the shotgun because he knew it was not loaded, had never loaded the shotgun, did not know how the safety worked, and had never test fired the shotgun, which he had purchased used in December 1999. Appellant denied that he racked the shotgun and did not know who had racked it. Officer Garcia recovered assorted ammunition and other evidence at Appellant's residence, including a box of .38 caliber ammunition, a box of 9–millimeter ammunition, and an empty box of Federal brand shotgun ammunition from the upstairs bedroom closet. In addition to the loaded shotgun, Officer Garcia recovered a loaded 9–millimeter pistol. Firearms expert Joseph Correa testified that Appellant's shotgun was functioning properly, and in order to fire this type of shotgun, it would have had to have already been racked. Though Appellant testified that he had never taken a firearms safety course, he admitted that he had owned other guns before.

Based on the evidence viewed in a light most favorable to the verdict, the jury could reasonably infer that Appellant knew the shotgun was loaded when he pointed it at Ms. Orozco and knew the risk of potential injury created by his conduct given his familiarity with guns and his intention of scaring the victim. The evidence also supports the inference that Appellant

236

consciously disregarded the risk created by his conduct by pulling on the trigger while the gun was pointed at Ms. Orozco. We conclude that the evidence was legally sufficient to sustain Appellant's conviction for manslaughter. Further, we conclude the evidence is also factually sufficient because the proof of guilt was not so obviously weak nor was the contrary evidence so overwhelmingly outweighed by the supporting evidence as to render the conviction clearly wrong and manifestly unjust. Although at trial, Appellant denied knowing that the shotgun was loaded and testified that he did not know how the gun operated or how the safety worked, the jury was free to believe all, some, or none of Appellant's testimony. A decision is not manifestly unjust merely because the fact finder resolved conflicting evidence in favor of the State.

For the reasons stated above, we affirm the trial court's judgment. Holding

Notes

1.   What evidence supports the jury's finding that the defendant was aware of but consciously disregarded a substantial and unjustifiable risk? Would the evidence have supported a verdict that the defendant was guilty of negligent homicide or murder?

2.   In Texas, the issue of provocation is now a sentencing matter; thus, there is no offense of "voluntary manslaughter." What most jurisdictions call involuntary manslaughter is, in Texas, simply manslaughter, which is reckless homicide under Section 19.04 of the Texas Penal Code. The former involuntary manslaughter statute also included an intoxicated driver causing death branch that has been broken out into a separate strict liability offense called Intoxication Manslaughter.

Texas Penal Code Section 49.08, "Intoxication Manslaughter," provides:

(a) A person commits an offense if the person:

(1) operates a motor vehicle in a public place, operates an aircraft, a watercraft, or an amusement ride, or assembles a mobile amusement ride; and

(2) is intoxicated and by reason of that intoxication causes the death of another by accident or mistake.

(b) Except as provided by Section 49.09, an offense under this section is a felony of the second degree.

Chapter 12: Felony Murder – mental state

Introduction

The Texas felony murder rule is found in Texas Penal Code Section 19.02(b)(3):

A person commits an offense [of murder] if he . . . commits or attempts to commit a felony, other than manslaughter, and in the course of and in furtherance of the commission or attempt, or in immediate flight from the commission or attempt, he commits or attempts to commit an act clearly dangerous to human life that causes the death of an individual.

Under the felony murder rule, a killing that occurs during the commission or attempted commission of a felony is murder, even if the killing was accidental (that is, the defendant did not intend to kill, did not intend to cause serious bodily injury, and was not reckless regarding the risk of killing). This is an exception to the principle that intent to do one thing cannot serve as a substitute for intent to do another thing. Recall the *Faulkner* case, which held that the defendant's criminal intent to steal the rum could not be substituted for the unintended fire that started when the defendant accidently ignited the rum that he wanted to steal.

The early felony murder rule was an understandable doctrine because all felonies in England at the time were punishable by death. If a death occurred accidently in the course of an intended felony, the underlying felony became a murder because it did not matter whether the offender was hanged for one felony or the other. The doctrine has been abolished in England, the country from which we inherited it, and the drafters of the Model Penal Code recommended its abolition by reducing the role of the commission of a felony when a death occurs to a mere presumption of extreme recklessness. Despite the attacks on the felony murder rule, only a handful of states have eliminated it, and it remains a fixture of American criminal law.

The primary objection to felony murder in an era when only aggravated murders result in a possible death sentence is that it imposes strict liability for a death that occurs during the commission of a felony. Because the whole point of the gradations crafted in homicide offenses is to rank the crimes according to mental state, the felony murder doctrine threatens to undermine this effort by punishing someone who kills accidently as if the killing had been intentional. Critics of the felony murder rule argue that disproportionate punishments occur from imposing the same punishment level because either the intentional killer is punished too leniently or the accidental killer is punished too harshly.

The possible disproportionality of the felony murder rule is powerfully illustrated by the case *Enmund v. Florida*, 458 U.S. 782 (1982), in which the defendant agreed to drive the get-away car from what he thought was going to be a non-violent burglary. One of Enmund's co-defendants wrested a gun from one of the victims who tried to thwart the burglars, and the victim was killed by his own gun. Because Enmund was an accessory to a burglary in which a death occurred, he was convicted of murder and sentenced to death. (In Texas, by statute, only intentional or knowing killing can be the basis of a capital conviction.) The United States Supreme Court overturned the death sentence on disproportionate sentence grounds, but this kind

238

of disproportionality review typically applies only with death sentences, and a sentence of life imprisonment would be upheld in a case like this.

The *Lomax* case that follows raises an interesting question about how far the felony murder rule can go in reducing the importance of the defendant's mental state.

Felony: a crime typically one involving violence, regarded as more serious than a misdemeanor, and usually punishable by imprisonment for more than one year or by death.

Aggravated Murder: purposely causing the death of another w/ prior calculation and design, or purposely causing the death of another under the age of 13, cop, or in the course of committing certain serious felony offenses.

Manslaughter: killing another person w/o malice aforethought (less moral blame than murder 1st or 2nd)

Felony murder doctrine: harsh; some jx tightens gap on duration of crime; some jx does not apply to killings by someone other than one of the felons

Felony murder does not require culpability

Lomax v. State

233 S.W.3d 302 (Tex. Crim. App. 2007)

Hervey, J., delivered the opinion of the Court in which Keller, P.J., Meyers, Price, Keasler and Cochran, JJ., joined.

In this case, we decide that felony driving while intoxicated (felony DWI)[1] can be the underlying felony in a "felony-murder" prosecution under Section 19.02(b)(3) of the Texas Penal Code, which, among other things, provides that a person commits murder if he causes a person's death during the commission of a "felony, other than manslaughter." *no culpability.*

A jury convicted appellant of felony-murder and sentenced him, as an habitual offender with two prior felony convictions, to 55 years in prison. Viewed in the light most favorable to the jury's verdict, the evidence shows that appellant was committing felony DWI[2] on a crowded public street and also tailgating, speeding and weaving when his car collided with another car resulting in the death of a five-year-old girl.[3] Appellant's blood-alcohol content was about three times the legal limit at the time of the collision. Appellant was charged with felony-murder under Section 19.02(b)(3), with the felony DWI alleged as the underlying felony.[4]

 *Δ's argument*

Appellant claimed in the trial court and on direct appeal that felony DWI cannot be the underlying felony for felony-murder, because the underlying felony is what supplies the required culpable mental state for felony-murder and felony DWI cannot supply this culpable mental state since felony DWI does not require proof of a culpable mental state. The court of appeals rejected this claim. We granted review of the following ground:

 Issue

> Can a felony murder conviction be based on an underlying felony that expressly requires no *mens rea*, despite the fact that in a felony-murder conviction, the *mens rea* for the act of murder is supplied by the *mens rea* of the underlying felony?

The issue is whether Section 19.02(b)(3), which does not prescribe a culpable mental state, "plainly dispenses" with a culpable mental state. *See* § 6.02(b), TEX. PENAL CODE ANN. (West 2015) (if definition of offense "does not prescribe a culpable mental state," a culpable mental state "is nevertheless required unless the definition plainly dispenses with any mental

---

1. *See* TEX. PENAL CODE ANN. § 49.09(b)(2) (West 2015).

2. The record reflects that appellant had two prior DWI convictions, which made the underlying felony DWI a third-degree felony. *See* TEX. PENAL CODE ANN. § 49.09(b)(2) (West 2015).

3. The evidence, therefore, shows that the victim's death occurred "in the course of and in furtherance of" appellant's commission of an inherently dangerous felony DWI.

4. In relevant part, the indictment alleged that appellant

> while in the course of and the furtherance of the commission of [felony DWI] did commit an act clearly dangerous to human life, to wit: by operating his motor vehicle . . . at an unreasonable speed, by failing to maintain a proper lookout for traffic and road conditions, and by failing to take adequate evasive actions prior to striking a motor vehicle occupied by [the victim] and did thereby cause the death of [the victim].

element"). We must presume that a culpable mental state is required unless a contrary intent "is manifested by other features of the statute."

It is significant and largely dispositive that Section 19.02(b)(3) omits a culpable mental state while the other two subsections in Section 19.02(b) expressly require a culpable mental state. A person commits murder under Section 19.02(b)(1) when he "knowingly and intentionally" causes a person's death. A person commits murder under Section 19.02(b)(2) when he "intends to cause serious bodily injury" and commits an act clearly dangerous to human life that causes a person's death. The omission of a culpable mental state in Section 19.02(b)(3) is "a clear implication of the legislature's intent to dispense with a mental element in that [sub]section." *intended not to put it there* *plainly dispensed*

Appellant argues that interpreting Section 19.02(b)(3) to dispense with a culpable mental state renders murder under Section 19.02(b)(3) a "strict liability" offense and that "murder is never a strict liability crime in Texas." While Section 19.02(b)(3) might contain some features not normally associated with "strict liability" offenses, on balance these features do not overcome the clear legislative intent to plainly dispense with a culpable mental state. And, deciding that Section 19.02(b)(3) dispenses with a culpable mental state is consistent with the historical purpose of the felony-murder rule, the very essence of which is to make a person guilty of an "unintentional" murder when he causes another person's death during the commission of some type of a felony. We hold that Section 19.02(b)(3) plainly dispenses with a culpable mental state. *No need for culpability*

We also agree with the State that felony DWI is neither manslaughter nor a lesser included offense of manslaughter. In this case, therefore, we give effect to the plain language of Section 19.02(b)(3) exempting only manslaughter as the underlying felony for felony-murder.

The judgment of the Court of Appeals is affirmed. *Holding* *★ manslaughter can't be underlying felony*

Notes

No mens rea needed bc done while doing other crime

1.   Do you agree that the legislature intended to dispense with *mens rea* altogether by omitting the requirement from both the felony murder statute and the felony DWI statute?

2.   What if the defendant did not have prior DWI convictions? The underlying offense then would have been a misdemeanor. A few jurisdictions have a misdemeanor manslaughter rule that operates in a similar fashion to convert the underlying offense into a manslaughter conviction. Most states, including Texas do not.

If the defendant had no prior DWI convictions, does that mean that no homicide conviction would have been possible?

Limitations: Dangerous Felony

The felony murder doctrine has been the subject of efforts to place limits on its use by both courts and legislatures. One of the most common methods of limitation has been to restrict felony murder to certain dangerous crimes. In some states, this takes the form of enumerating certain felonies that are the only offenses that can give rise to felony murder liability. Some states require that the underlying felony be *malum in se* rather than *malum prohibitum*, and others require that the felony be dangerous. The dangerous felony rule sometimes requires a finding that the felony is inherently dangerous, while other states permit a wide range of felonies to serve as the potential predicate for a felony murder conviction, but require that the commission of the felony be dangerous under the facts of the case. The Texas statute does not restrict the offense to particular felonies, but it does require some type of act dangerous to human life. Thus, in Texas, the underlying felony must be dangerous under the facts of the case. The Texas dangerous felony rule is discussed in the *Torres* case, which follows.

applicable in TX

Torres v. State

No. 01-01-00999-CR, 2002 WL 31838694
(Tex. App.—Houston [1st Dist.] Dec. 19, 2002, pet. ref'd)

Elsa Alcala, Justice.

A jury convicted appellant, Juan M. Torres, for felony murder and arson, and assessed punishment for each offense at 40 years' confinement in prison. Appellant contends that the evidence at trial was factually insufficient to sustain his convictions.

Background

In the spring of 2000, appellant worked at a McDonald's restaurant. During the early morning hours on February 13, appellant, along with his brother and a co-worker, decided to break into the restaurant and steal money located in an office safe. After trying unsuccessfully to break into the safe for several hours, the trio used bolt-cutters and a blow torch to break into the safe, only to discover that the safe contained an inner-safe. Appellant and his accomplices left the restaurant after failing to open the inner-safe.

Before leaving the restaurant, appellant set fire to the office cabinets. As a result, the restaurant began to burn, and firefighters were called to the scene. Upon arriving at the scene, two firefighters entered the restaurant to ensure that no one was trapped inside. While searching the restaurant, both firefighters suffered asphyxia due to inhalation of smoke. Both died from asphyxia. Appellant was subsequently charged with felony murder and arson.

In his first point of error, appellant contends that the evidence was factually insufficient to sustain his felony murder conviction because the State failed to prove that appellant committed an "act clearly dangerous to human life." According to appellant, the act of starting a fire in an empty, freestanding building is not clearly dangerous to human life.

Texas has codified the felony murder rule in section 19.02(b)(3) of the Penal Code, which provides, as follows, that a person commits murder if he or she:

> commits or attempts to commit a felony, other than manslaughter, and in the course of and in furtherance of the commission or attempt, or in immediate flight from the commission or attempt, he commits or attempts to commit an act clearly dangerous to human life that causes the death of an individual.

Tex. Penal Code Ann. § 19.02(b)(3) (West 2015).

Appellant's felony-murder indictment alleged that, while committing the felony offense of burglary of a building, appellant committed acts clearly dangerous to human life, namely starting a fire and fleeing without extinguishing the fire. The indictment further alleged that these acts caused the death of Kimberly Smith, one of the firefighters killed in the restaurant.

Unlike some jurisdictions, the Texas Legislature has not enumerated specific [mentioned one by one] felonies that, in the abstract, can support a felony-murder charge. Instead, the Legislature required that the State prove that the specific actor, under the specifically articulated circumstances, committed some act that was clearly dangerous to human life. Acts that are clearly dangerous to human life are thus determined on a case-by-case basis.

Texas courts have found acts of arson sufficient to support felony-murder convictions. We, too, find appellant's act of arson sufficient to support his felony-murder conviction. The evidence shows that appellant intentionally set fire to wooden cabinets in the restaurant office causing the restaurant to burn down. It is clear that burning down a restaurant within the Houston city limits would trigger a rapid response from firefighters. It is also clear that a fire as severe as the one caused by appellant would place firefighters' lives in danger. We find that the State satisfied the "clearly dangerous to human life" element of section 19.02(b)(3).

Alternatively, appellant contends that his act of arson did not cause the firefighters' deaths. According to section 19.02(b)(3), an act clearly dangerous to human life must cause the death of an individual before the felony-murder rule applies. Appellant argues that the firefighters entered the restaurant on their own initiative without waiting for orders from their superiors. Appellant asserts that the firefighters took an unreasonable course of action that caused their deaths.

We disagree. Although some testimony suggested that the firefighters entered the restaurant without waiting for orders, other testimony suggested that the firefighters entered the restaurant with orders and that this course of action was proper under the circumstances. Additionally, the State presented testimony explaining that firefighters enter buildings under circumstances such as these to save the lives of persons who might be trapped in the flames. The jury heard the evidence and concluded that appellant's act of arson caused the death of Kimberly Smith. We decline to usurp the jury's function as factfinder in order to find that the firefighters acted in an unreasonable manner that resulted in their deaths. The facts appellant relies on do not so weaken or overwhelm the State's evidence as to render the judgment clearly wrong and manifestly unjust.

Reasonable interpretation

? **Merger** ?

One of the concerns with the felony-murder doctrine is that it could usurp all other forms of homicide. For example, most murders involve a prior or contemporaneous assault or battery. If the assaultive crime can be the underlying offense for felony murder, the result might be that the other forms of homicide created by the legislature would fall into disuse, except to provide a possible springboard to felony murder. It would subvert the effort to grade homicide offenses if every felonious homicide was converted to felony murder. To combat this problem, courts have developed a "merger rule" that requires that the underlying felony for felony murder must be separate and independent from the assaultive act that caused the death.

Under the merger doctrine, the felony-murder rule does not apply if the underlying felony is an integral part of the killing; the underlying felony "merges" and cannot be the basis for felony murder. The *Rodriguez* case that follows notes that Texas adopted a strong merger rule in *Garrett*, but later cases have held that the only offenses that "merge" with felony murder are manslaughter (which is explicitly precluded as a predicate felony in the felony murder statute) and lesser-included offenses of manslaughter.

Rodriguez v. State

953 S.W.2d 342 (Court of Appeals of Texas—Austin, 1997)

John F. Onion, Jr., Justice (Retired).

This appeal is taken from a conviction for felony murder. After finding appellant, Albert Ray Rodriguez, guilty, the jury assessed his punishment at fifty years' imprisonment and a fine of $4,000.

In his sole point of error, appellant contends that the trial court erred in overruling the objection to the court's jury charge regarding the offense of felony murder because the merger doctrine barred his conviction for felony murder.

The sufficiency of the evidence to sustain the conviction is not challenged. A brief recitation of the facts will place the point of error in proper perspective. The victim, James Beaty, was shot and killed while riding as a passenger in a red Pontiac Firebird on Francisco Street in Austin on the night of April 21, 1995. It was two days before Beaty's nineteenth birthday. Michelle Esquivel, Beaty's girlfriend, who was driving, was shot in the right thigh. Joseph Michael Gonzales, a passenger in the rear seat, escaped injury.

Appellant testified that he had purchased a .45 caliber handgun "off the street" the night before the shooting and had a friend purchase ammunition for the weapon on Friday morning, April 21st. That night the 17-year old appellant was in the back yard of his parent's home talking on a cordless telephone when he saw a red Pontiac Firebird drive past. He retrieved the pistol which he had concealed under a car and walked to the front of the house. There was testimony that the Firebird had driven past the house once or twice. When the Firebird appeared again after the appellant had obtained his pistol, he observed the Firebird "slow down." Appellant recognized Beaty as the front seat passenger. Appellant testified he then "panicked" and fired the pistol repeatedly at the Firebird, perhaps eight times. Appellant claimed he fired the pistol at the driver's door, despite the fact that Beaty, of whom he was putatively afraid, was seated in the passenger seat. Appellant explained that Beaty had threatened his life, that thereafter there had been a drive-by shooting at his parents' home where he lived, and that he had been shot at while in his own automobile only days before the fatal incident. Appellant could not connect Beaty with the two shootings, but believed the gang to which Beaty belonged was involved. Appellant related that at 2:00 or 3:00 a.m. on Friday before Easter Sunday 1995, he and a cousin had driven to a Jack-In-The-Box restaurant; that Beaty and Michelle Esquivel were working at the drive-thru window; that while he knew Beaty as Pollo Loco (Crazy Chicken) and knew he was a member of the Bros Gang, there had been no difficulty between them; that Beaty began to stare at him, threw gang signs at him, and then threatened his life. Appellant got his food order and left. He later saw Beaty on Easter Sunday in a park. Beaty again threw gang signs, but no trouble developed because appellant left the park. Appellant denied being in a gang and claimed the Outloz or Oz group to which he belonged was merely a graffiti group.

Michelle Esquivel testified that she and Beaty had been at the home of relatives nearby and had gone to a store and were returning to their relatives' house when they were fired upon. They had offered Gonzales a ride when they encountered him at the store.

Chief Medical Examiner, Dr. Roberto Bayardo, testified that Beaty died from "massive internal bleeding due to a gunshot wound that penetrated his body in the left upper back and exited through the right chest wall." The .45 caliber weapon was recovered and the bullets retrieved from the car and elsewhere were shown to have been fired from appellant's firearm.

Subsection (b) of section 19.02 of the Texas Penal Code under which appellant was charged provides:

> (b) A person commits an offense if he:
>
> > (1) intentionally or knowingly causes the death of an individual;
> >
> > (2) intends to cause serious bodily injury and commits an act clearly dangerous to human life that causes the death of an individual; or
> >
> > (3) commits or attempts to commit a felony, other than manslaughter, and in the course of and in furtherance of the commission or attempt, or in immediate flight from the commission or attempt, he attempts or attempts to commit an act clearly dangerous to human life that causes the death of an individual.

TEX. PENAL CODE ANN. § 19.02(b).

Section 22.05 (Deadly Conduct) of the Texas Penal Code provides:

> (a) A person commits an offense if he recklessly engages in conduct that places another in imminent danger of serious bodily injury.
>
> (b) A person commits an offense if he knowingly discharges a firearm at or in the direction of:
>
> > (1) one or more individuals; or
> >
> > (2) a habitation, building, or vehicle and is reckless as to whether the habitation, building, or vehicle is occupied.
>
> (c) Recklessness and danger are presumed if the actor knowingly pointed a firearm at or in the direction of another whether or not the actor believed the firearm to be loaded.
>
> (d) For purposes of this section, "building," "habitation," and "vehicle" have the meanings assigned those terms by Section 30.01.
>
> (e) An offense under Subsection (a) is a Class A misdemeanor. An offense under Subsection (b) is a felony of the third degree.

TEX. PENAL CODE ANN. § 22.05.

The instant indictment charged appellant under all three modes of committing first degree murder under section 19.02 in one count with three separate paragraphs. The third paragraph charged felony murder by alleging that appellant

> did then and there commit a felony, namely, deadly conduct, and in the course and furtherance of the commission of said felony commit an act clearly dangerous to human life, namely, knowingly discharge a firearm, a deadly weapon, at and in the direction of one or more individuals and at and in the direction of a motor vehicle and was reckless as to whether the said motor vehicle was occupied, thereby causing the death of James Beaty.

At the conclusion of the guilt/innocence phase of the trial, the proposed jury charge submitted all three modes of murder under section 19.02, as well as the offense of manslaughter. Appellant objected to the submission of felony murder because the charge boot strapped the offense of deadly conduct into felony murder, violating the merger doctrine. Appellant contended that the felony murder rule has no application where the underlying felony sought to be used as the basis for the operation of the rule is the very act which caused the homicide. The trial court overruled the objection and submitted the charge authorizing the jury to first consider murder under section 19.02(b)(1), then murder under section 19.02(b)(2), and then felony murder under section 19.02(b)(3). Lastly, the trial court submitted the offense of manslaughter.

The jury found appellant guilty of felony murder. It is appellant's contention that the trial court erred in charging on felony murder over timely objection and that any conviction resulting therefrom cannot stand.

Our research reveals that early on Texas limited felony murder to certain enumerated felonies but also permitted conviction on the theory of transferred intent. Article 1141 of the 1911 Penal Code provided: "All murder committed by poison, starving, torture, or with express malice, or committed in perpetration, or in the attempt at perpetration of arson, rape, robbery or burglary, is murder in the first degree; and all murder not of the first degree is murder of the second degree." With the language unchanged, this article was the successor to article 711 of 1895 Penal Code, to article 606 of the 1858 code, and to "Act of March 20, 1848, p. 219 (Hart. Dig. art. 501)." The 1911 code provision was not brought forward in the 1925 Penal Code or later codes. We do find that article 1325 of the 1925 Penal Code provided that when death was occasioned by any offense in the chapters on arson or willful burning, the offender was guilty of murder. This article was later amended to provide that in the absence of malice aforethought of the offender, the punishment shall be life imprisonment or any term of year not less than two years.

Article 42 of the 1925 Penal Code provided: "One intending to commit a felony and who in the act of preparing for or executing the same shall through mistake or accident do another act which, if voluntarily done, would be a felony, shall receive the punishment affixed to the felony actually committed." This provision was the successor unchanged from article 48 of both the 1911 and 1895 Penal Codes and traceable at least to 1858.

The 1974 Penal Code definitely made changes in statutes relating to murder in Texas. Section 19.02, a unique statute, simplified the definition of first degree murder by eliminating the concept of malice. Three separate and distinct statutory modes or ways of committing the offense were established. Then section 19.02(a)(1) used two carefully defined terms, "intentional" and "knowing," to describe the culpable mental state necessary under that subsection. Although section 6.01 of the 1974 code provided that a person commits an offense only if his conduct is voluntary, the term is subsumed in the terms of "intentional" and "knowing."

The second mode of first degree murder, under section 19.02(a)(2), applied to an unintended killing when there is an intent to cause serious bodily injury plus the commission of an act clearly dangerous to human life that causes death. A specific intent to kill was not an essential element of murder under this mode. A killing under this subsection was murder notwithstanding that no murder was intended. The third mode of committing first degree murder was found in section 19.02(a)(3), which codified the felony murder doctrine in a different manner than the earlier codes.

The legislature restricted the felony murder doctrine under this subsection to the commission or attempt to commit any felony (other than voluntary and involuntary manslaughter) but only when in the course of and in the furtherance of the commission or attempt to commit an act clearly dangerous to human life is committed that causes the death of an individual.

The legislature saw fit to expressly exempt only the offenses of voluntary and involuntary manslaughter from the application of section 19.02(a)(3). This is because, as voluntary manslaughter, it would be futile to recognize sudden passion arising from an adequate cause as sufficiently mitigating to reduce a voluntary killing to voluntary manslaughter under section 19.04 of the 1974 Penal Code, if in the next breath voluntary manslaughter may become first degree murder by virtue of section 19.03(a)(3) of the 1974 Penal Code.

It would seem clear that section 19.02(a)(3) was to replace, at least in the first part, the felony murder aspect of the former code. It was a separate mode of first degree murder, a distinct crime for which the killing did not have a separate *mens rea* element apart from the felony. No transferred intent was required. It was this change in the law of felony murder that has caused some confusion.

One of the first cases to come to grips with the third mode of murder under section 19.02 of the 1974 code was *Rodriquez v. State*, 548 S.W.2d 26 (Tex. Crim. App. 1977). The court observed that section 19.02(a)(3) was silent as to, and plainly did not dispense with, the culpable mental state required for the underlying felony committed or attempted, but held that the culpable mental state shall be one of intent, knowledge, or recklessness as required by section 6.0216 then in effect under such circumstances. The court then added:

> Thus, the culpable mental state for the act of murder is supplied by the mental state accompanying the underlying committed or attempted felony giving rise to the act. The transference of the mental element establishing criminal responsibility for the original act to the resulting act conforms to and preserves the traditional *mens rea* requirement of criminal law.

The court then rejected the defendant's claim that section 19.02(a)(3) was unconstitutional for its failure to specify the culpable mental state required for the act of murder.

Now, we enter the area of troublesome cases decided under the 1974 code. While *Rodriquez* declined to "add to the statutory exemption," that is exactly what the court did in *Garrett v. State*, 573 S.W.2d 543 (Tex. Crim. App. 1978), upon which appellant relies. The *Garrett* opinion, for the first time, engaged in a wholesale adoption of the merger doctrine as a limitation on the felony murder rule in Texas. It concluded that the underlying felony, aggravated assault, and the act in the homicide were one and the same, an indivisible transaction, and the murder conviction under section 19.02(a)(3) could not stand. "There must be a showing of felonious criminal conduct other than the assaults causing the homicide." The *Garrett* court based its "judicial adoption" in 1978 on *People v. Moran*, 158 N.E. 35 (N.Y. 1927), although it acknowledged that *Moran* was based on New York statutes and case law then in effect.

If the merger doctrine in Texas seemed settled after *Garrett*, it was only a mirage. Almost four years later, *Ex parte Easter*, 615 S.W.2d 719, 721 (Tex. Crim. App. 1981), held that not every "assaultive" offense, if alleged as an underlying felony, will merge with the homicide in a felony murder indictment under section 19.02(a)(3), noting that "the language carefully chosen in Garrett should not be given an overly broad meaning." *Easter* was a post-conviction proceeding wherein the petitioner challenged his felony murder conviction based on the underlying felony of injury to a child which had resulted in death. Petitioner relied upon *Garrett* because injury to a child was an assaultive offense. The *Easter* court disagreed, noting that the felony murder rule in the 1974 Penal Code dispensed with the inquiry into the *mens rea* accompanying the homicide itself, and that the underlying felony—injury to a child—supplied the necessary culpable mental state.

The felony murder rule in Texas has prevailed in Texas for many years. Any limitation of the rule took forms other than the merger doctrine. After the advent of the 1974 Penal Code, *Garrett* adopted the merger doctrine despite the wording of section 19.02(a)(3). *Ex parte Easter* contended that *Garrett* should not be read too broadly and that not every assaultive offensive merged with the alleged homicide. Since then, in case after case, the courts have so chipped away and undermined the *Garrett* decision that its continued viability is highly questionable. Moreover, the legislature has now enacted the 1994 Penal Code, which controls the instant case.

The legislature is invested with the law-making power of the people and may define crimes and fix penalties. A power which has been granted to one department of government by the state constitution may be exercised only by that branch to the exclusion of others. Any attempt by one department to interfere with the powers of another is null and void.

"It is the duty of the court to administer the law as it is written, and not to make law; and however harsh a statute may seem to be, or whatever may seem to be its omission, courts cannot . . . make it apply to cases to which it does not apply, without assuming functions that pertain to the legislative department of the government." The legislature is constitutionally entitled to expect that the judiciary will faithfully follow the specific text that was adopted.

In divining legislative intent, we look first to the language of the statute. When the meaning is plain, we look no further. We focus on the text of the statute and interpret it in a literal manner to discern a fair, objective meaning of the text. If the meaning of the statutory text, when read using the established canons of statutory construction relating to such text, should have been plain to the legislators who voted on it, courts will ordinarily give effect to that plain meaning.

There is, of course, a legitimate exception to this plain meaning rule: where application of the rule would lead to absurd consequences that the legislature could not possibly have intended, courts should not apply the language literally. There is no basis for the application of this exception to section 19.02(b). The language of section 19.02(b) is clear and the meaning plain. The legislature created three modes of first degree felony murder, each a separate and distinct offense. A conviction under section 19.02(b)(3) may stand alone. It may be a valid conviction without the need to be tied to section 19.02(b)(1) or section 6.04 of the 1994 Penal Code in order to convert it into an intent-to-kill murder by the transferred intent doctrine.

The courts sometimes explain felony murder by stating that the felon's intent to commit the [underlying] felony supplies the intent to kill, so that the felon intended to kill, resulting in a plain case of intent-to-kill murder. This sort of talk is pure fiction and it is better to recognize felony murder as a category of murder separate from intent-to-kill murder.

This is exactly what our legislature did in enacting the third mode of first degree murder in section 19.02(b)(3). In doing so it designed its own unique statute exempting only manslaughter as a predicate or underlying felony. If it had intended to exempt other felony offenses or lesser included felony offenses or to embrace the merger doctrine as a limitation on felony murder, it could easily have done so. The maxim *expresio unius est exclusio alterius* is often employed in the construction of statutes. In general, it means that a statute's inclusion of a specific limitation excludes all other limitations of that type. As applied to the instant case, it means that inclusion of the limitation as to manslaughter excludes all other limitations.

Our legislature within its constitutional role remains free to abolish felony murder or limit its application or effect to other felonies. It is not the role of courts to abolish or judicially limit or expand a constitutionally valid statutory offense clearly defined by the legislature.

The legislature has not expressly adopted the merger doctrine or implicitly approved of the *Garrett* decision. Appellant's conviction for felony murder under section 19.02(b)(3) with the underlying felony being deadly conduct (section 22.05) by repeatedly shooting a firearm into an automobile known to be occupied, an act clearly dangerous to human life, was proper. The trial court did not err in overruling the objection to the jury charge based on *Garrett* and the merger doctrine. The sole point of error is overruled.

The judgment is affirmed.

Notes

1.   Is it "bootstrapping" to allow "deadly conduct" to serve as the underlying felony for felony murder?

2.   In this case, the jury was given the option to find the defendant guilty of any of the three modes of committing murder as well as manslaughter. Do the facts support each of these options? Why do you think the jury found the defendant guilty of felony murder? Is it necessary to have a felony-murder doctrine to find a defendant guilty of a homicide under facts like those in Rodriguez?

Duration of Felony

The felony murder statute requires that the death must occur "during" the felony or in "immediate flight" from it. Analyzing a defense claim that the death did not occur while the offense was occurring requires a consideration of the nature of the felony as well as the degree of temporal and spatial separation from the commission of the felony. For example, had the arson in the *Torres* case ended when the defendants left the building after starting the fire? Not surprisingly, courts have often ruled that the offense is ongoing if the effect of the crime is occurring, such as the still-burning fire when the firefighters died.

Sometimes it is claimed that the death occurred *too soon*. If the defendant kills the victim and later decides to steal something from the body, the death may not occur during the commission of the felony. Continuous pursuit from the scene of the crime clearly qualifies as continuous flight from the commission the felony, but if the defendant has reached a place of temporary safety, the crime may be at an end. Of course, that does not eliminate the possibility of a homicide conviction for a death to which the defendant may be causally connected, but it may prevent the use of the felony-murder doctrine. The *Rodriguez* case, which follows, deals with a duration of the felony issue.

Rodriguez v. State

548 S.W.2d 26 (Tex. Crim. App. 1977)

Reynolds, Commissioner.

Indicted and prosecuted for murder, appellants were convicted of the offense of voluntary manslaughter. The punishment of each was fixed by the jury at confinement for twelve years. The prosecution was under [Texas Penal Code section} 19.02(a)(3), which reads:

(a) A person commits an offense if he:

. . . .

(3) commits or attempts to commit a felony other than voluntary or involuntary manslaughter, and in the course of and in furtherance of the commission or attempt, or in immediate flight from the commission or attempt, he commits or attempts to commit an act clearly dangerous to human life that causes the death of an individual.

Omitting its formal parts, the indictment charges that appellants

did, then and there commit a felony, to-wit: did then and there intentionally and knowingly carry on and about their persons a handgun while on certain premises licensed and issued a permit by the State of Texas for the sale and service of alcoholic beverages, to-wit: El Dandy Club Bar, 2619 Guatemozin, situated in Laredo, Webb County, Texas, and while in immediate flight from the commission of said offense the said JOSE GUTIERREZ RODRIQUEZ and LUIS MANI, then and there acting together, did commit an act clearly dangerous to human life, to-wit: did then and there discharge a handgun into the said El Dandy Club Bar, a business establishment at the time of the shooting, and did thereby cause the death of Jose T. Ramos by shooting him with the said handgun, ...

An evidential summary is that appellants entered the El Dandy Club Bar owned by Jose Trinidad Ramos, the deceased, and ordered beer. Sixteen or seventeen persons, including Ramos, were present. Appellant Rodriquez displayed a pistol, pointing it out the door and clicking it. Appellants were told to leave. They left and, once outside, called for Ramos to come out and talk with them. When Ramos started toward the door, the barmaid and a customer caused him to remain inside. Sounds of shots were heard. A bullet penetrated the bar building, striking Ramos in the head and killing him instantly. The pistol from which the fatal shot was fired was found under the front seat of a pickup truck appellant Rodriquez drove to a nearby bar owned by Mani. In a statement given by appellant Rodriquez after his arrest and introduced by him in evidence, he reported that the shot was fired by appellant Mani. Neither appellant testified during the guilt-innocence stage of the trial.

Appellants' first ground is that the possession of a weapon on premises licensed for the sale of alcoholic beverages is not the type of felony that will support an act of murder because it does not involve intentional violence. Suffice it to state, without an academic discussion of the

254

views of courts of other states as presented in the briefs that the legislature has seen fit to exempt only the felonies of voluntary and involuntary manslaughter, and we will not add to the statutory exemption. The first ground is overruled.

We now arrive at appellants' second ground which challenges, for three reasons, the sufficiency of the evidence to support the convictions. The first of these is that there is insufficient evidence to show flight. To establish the offense charged, it was necessary for the State to prove its essential allegation that the killing occurred "while (appellants were) in immediate flight from the commission of" the felony offense alleged. The court charged the jury that "'Flight' is the evading of the course of justice by voluntarily withdrawing one's self in order to avoid arrest or detention the act of fleeing or escaping from danger."

The definition is substantially the one appearing in Black's Law Dictionary, Revised Fourth Edition. Tested by the definition, the evidence is insufficient to prove an immediate flight from the commission of the underlying felony. The barmaid denied that she told appellants to leave and she did not notice that Ramos did. She said there was no kind of disagreement between Ramos and either one, or both, of the appellants. A customer testified that the barmaid did tell appellants to leave because they could not carry a gun there, and that Ramos told appellants it was his place of business and for them to move out. He said the appellants left immediately; they were not running and were not chased by anybody. When they were outside, appellants called for Ramos to come outside to talk with them, but, according to the barmaid, she stood in the door to stop Ramos from going out and, as the customer testified, another customer got hold of Ramos "so everything was all right." The shooting then occurred.

It is obvious that neither an arrest nor a detention of appellants was ever mentioned and that no overt act of either was threatened. No legitimate inference that appellants were fleeing from any danger can arise from the testimony about the acts of, or the conversations between, appellants and Ramos. Indeed, the testimonial facts are that appellants' departure was normal and that thereafter "everything was all right." In short, the evidence negates rather than establishes an immediate flight. To this extent, the second ground of error is sustained.

For the failure of the State to establish an essential element of the offense charged, the judgments must be reversed.

Causation, Agency

The felony murder statute provides that the act clearly dangerous to human life committed during the felony must cause the death of another for the offense of murder to be committed. Causation of death is an element of all homicide offenses, including felony murder. Clearly it is not sufficient that someone dies simultaneously with a felony. It would be absurd to think that a death by heart attack of a person unknown to the defendant a mile away from the scene of a burglary of an unoccupied home could cause the offense to become murder merely because it happened simultaneously with the burglary. A slightly less absurd case would be presented if the heart attack victim was the homeowner whose house was burglarized and who died of fright when the defendant entered the home. Such a case presents an issue of causation, a subject that will be considered in the next chapter. The pre-existing weakness of the victim's heart probably would cut the chain of causation in the example given. However, it is fair to say that the felony murder doctrine reduces the connection needed to show causation in some jurisdictions to a degree that rivals the diminution of the required showing of *mens rea*.

The prime example of a broad conception of causation in felony-murder cases occurs when neither the defendant nor an accomplice is responsible for the death. If X and Y burglarize the home of Z, and X shoots Z during the burglary (either intentionally or accidently), Y is guilty of felony murder as a party to the homicide. We will discuss principles of vicarious liability in the last chapter of the book, but it is sufficient for our current purposes to say that Y is guilty of felony murder for the death of Z because he intentionally committed a felony, committed a dangerous act by participating with an armed accomplice, and a death resulted. What if X and Y burglarize Z, and Z succeeds in killing X? Can Y be held responsible for the felony murder of his partner in crime? A similar issue is raised if neither the defendant or an agent of the defendant causes the death of another victim. Suppose X or Z accidently kill an innocent bystander, or a police officer responding to the report of burglary shoots at X and Y and accidently kills Z. In the *Miers* case, which follows below, the defendant claimed the victim accidently killed himself while trying to stop the crime.

Some courts confronting these scenarios refuse to hold the defendant responsible for a felony murder if no dangerous act of the defendant or an agent of the defendant directly caused the death. Other courts take a broader view of causation by maintaining that the defendant caused the death by putting into motion a dangerous criminal enterprise that foreseeably led to the death of the victim (or a bystander, police officer, or co-defendant).

Miers v. State

251 S.W.2d 404 (Tex. Crim. App. 1952)

Morrison, Judge.

Four witnesses present at the filling station on the night of the robbery testified for the State. They said that appellant and his companion Thorbus held them up with pistols and searched the establishment for money, the owner having refused to disclose where he had his money hidden.

Appellant corroborated the State's version of the robbery, except that he stated that he had fired to one side of deceased hoping to scare him, but that this failed to deter deceased who continued to come at him; that deceased grabbed his coat, and that he tried to hit deceased with the pistol in order to get loose from him. Appellant stated that at this juncture the deceased got the pistol out of his hand and hit him over the head with the same, causing the pistol to be discharged.

No State witness testified that they actually saw appellant pull the trigger that caused the death of deceased and because appellant testified that he did not shoot deceased, but that deceased shot himself accidentally in the scuffle. Bill of exception No. 8 complains of the failure of the court to give his requested charge as follows: "If you believe that the shot that was fired, if any, which killed the deceased . . . was not fired by the Defendant, Robert Ernest Miers, or if you have a reasonable doubt thereof, you should acquit the Defendant and say to the verdict, 'not guilty.'"

The requested charge is too restrictive. This is true because the facts of this case show that appellant and Thorbus entered the place of business for the purpose of committing the act of robbery. They then became principals and amenable under the law for acts of the other in the furtherance of their criminal enterprise.

Appellant now contends that the requested charge, though incorrect, put the trial court on notice that he wanted a charge on the claimed defense as testified to by him. We must first determine whether the facts testified to by appellant constituted a defense at all. He stated that he did not fire the fatal shot, but that the same was fired accidentally by the deceased while deceased was endeavoring to thwart his act of robbery.

In *Taylor v. State*, 55 S.W. 961, 964 (Tex. Crim. App. 1900), one of the robbers, while in the act of robbing a train, took the fireman from the engine to the express car. At this juncture, one Buchanan, a passenger on the train, came out of the rear and began firing. There was a return of Buchanan's fire, and in the progress thereof the fireman was killed. The robber was tried for the murder of the fireman.

One of the objections to the court's charge was that it authorized a conviction even if the fireman came to his death by an outside, independent and unexpected force, by a mere passenger who was under no obligation to shoot. Judge Henderson, in discussing the same, made this profound statement of law: "The whole question here is one of causal connection. If the appellant here set in motion the cause which occasioned the death of deceased, we hold it to be a sound doctrine that he would be as culpable as if he had done the deed with his own hands."

We hold here that appellant set in motion the cause which occasioned the death of deceased, and therefore his testimony did not present a defense.

Finding no reversible error, the judgment of the trial court is affirmed.

dispositive: relating to or bringing abt the settlement of an issue

Chapter 13: Causation

Introduction

When crimes are defined in a manner that requires a particular result for criminal liability, the element of causation must be proved beyond a reasonable doubt by the prosecution. Because some criminal offenses do not require a result, the issue of causation does not arise in the prosecution of every criminal case. It is appropriate to discuss this issue in our consideration of homicide offenses because proving that the defendant caused death is the *sine qua non* of *absolutely necessary* homicide. Many of the famous causation cases involve an issue concerning the cause of death in homicides.

Section 6.04(a) of the Texas Penal Code provides a classical statement of the causation requirement for result crimes:

A person is criminally responsible if the result would not have occurred but for his conduct, operating either alone or concurrently with another cause, unless the concurrent cause was clearly sufficient to produce the result and the conduct of the actor clearly insufficient.

The "but for" test is a traditional part of causation analysis in both tort and criminal law. However, "but for" is not dispositive of all causation questions. Even when it could be said that "but for" the action of the defendant, the harmful result would not have occurred, there is no causation if the result is too *reduced* attenuated from the defendant's act. For example, if "but for" the defendant's assaultive conduct, the defendant would not have taken the route home that he did in an attempt to evade the defendant, and he is struck by lightning and killed, there is no causation, despite the "but for" relationship, between criminal act and result. *must have some relation or connection*

On the other hand, even when "but for" is not satisfied, such as when there are two concurrent causes that are sufficient, there may not be causation. For example, consider the case of the unfortunate Mr. Geller in *People v. Dluglash*, 363 N.E. 1155 (1977), who is shot by two different assailants, acting separately, within minutes of each other's attack. There is no "but for" causation because, even if Dluglash had not attacked Geller, his death would have been secured by the actions of the other attacker. Nonetheless, Dluglash's act was considered to be the proximate cause of the death because his actions were sufficient to cause death, and the existence of another sufficient cause from an independent actor does not cut off the causative link for Dlugash. Had the defendant been acting in concert with the other actor, our concern with whether the actions of both would have been sufficient to cause death would be less important because, under principles of party liability, each would be responsible for the foreseeable death. (We will take up the subject of party liability in the last chapter of the text.)

In homicide cases, one of the increasingly difficult issues is whether the requirement of causation can be established when there is a long temporal gap between the defendant's assaultive act and the death of the victim. The *Govan* case is an example.

Paralyzed wife

State v. Govan

744 P.2d 712 (Ariz. Ct. App. 1987)

Greer, Judge.

On May 13, 1985, appellant was indicted on one count of second degree murder. Following a jury trial, he was convicted on October 18, 1985, of the lesser-included offense of manslaughter. He was sentenced to a mitigated term of imprisonment of six years.

The incident which gave rise to the criminal charges in this case occurred on April 5, 1980. The appellant and S.K., with whom he had been living for three years, argued over the appellant's alleged molestation of the victim's teenage daughter. The victim eventually fired a shot at the appellant. The appellant then left the scene, but later that day returned and was observed again arguing with the victim. The victim borrowed a neighbor's telephone and attempted to call the police. While the victim was attempting to dial the phone, the appellant pulled a gun out of his pocket and shot at the victim, striking her in the neck. As a result she was paralyzed from the neck down. The appellant told police that he had not intended to shoot the victim, but had drawn his gun and fired behind him without taking aim.

On May 1, 1980, the state charged appellant with aggravated assault for shooting S.K. During S.K.'s hospitalization, appellant visited her and they were subsequently married. The aggravated assault charge was dismissed without prejudice on March 11, 1981. Due to her quadriplegia S.K. suffered from several ailments and needed constant care. In January 1985, the victim contracted pneumonia and died. Appellant was subsequently charged with second degree murder and convicted of manslaughter.

A's Arguments

The appellant argues that he cannot be convicted of anything because there was no evidence to show that the shot he fired caused the quadriplegia of the victim. Defense counsel argued that the state needed to bring in a doctor from every institution that treated S.K. to show that the quadriplegia was the direct result of the gunshot wound. He then concluded that, "as to the rest of it, I would just say there is insufficient evidence." In denying the motion, the trial court properly noted that there was uncontroverted evidence that the victim had been taken immediately to a hospital in the Phoenix area and remained a quadriplegic until her death. In addition, both of the doctors who testified at trial said, without objection, that the cause of death was pneumonia stemming from the quadriplegia, which was caused by a gunshot wound to the neck.

In this case, there was substantial, if not overwhelming, evidence that the gunshot to the victim's neck resulted in her immediate paralysis and quadriplegia. It was not error to deny the motion for judgment of acquittal.

The appellant also argues, based on *State v. Hall*, 129 Ariz. 589 (1981), that the death was not the natural result of his having shot the victim. In *Hall*, the court first distinguished between cases where an intervening event was a coincidence and those where it was a response to the defendant's prior actions. It then stated that a defendant's actions may still be a proximate cause of death regardless of the type of intervening act that occurred, but as "common sense would suggest, the perimeters of legal cause are more closely drawn when the intervening cause was a matter of coincidence rather than response."

Thus, an intervening cause that was a coincidence will be a superseding [*takes the place of*] cause when it was unforeseeable. Alternatively, an intervening cause that was a response will be a superseding cause only where it was abnormal and unforeseeable. Appellant's action would not be a proximate cause of S.K.'s death if the chain of natural effects and causes was either non-existent because of or broken by intervening events which were unforeseeable and hence were superseding events. Here there were no intervening events which could be characterized as superseding. In this case, it is clear that the gunshot wound resulted in the quadriplegia. Furthermore, medical testimony proved that the quadriplegia, including the complications caused by the tracheostomy, eventually resulted in a "response" to that condition, which resulted in the victim's death. Thus, the appellant's conduct was a proximate cause of the victim's death and he is criminally liable for it.

The appellant refines his argument on appeal to contend that the victim simply gave up her will to live, and this broke the chain of causation between the shooting and her death. He points out that the victim did not seek medical attention for at least two weeks after she knew that she was ill.

This argument was never presented to the trial court. Ordinarily we would not review a matter not argued below, but to allow a conviction to stand that is not supported by the evidence would be fundamental error. However, we do not find appellant's argument persuasive. Although a victim may break the chain of causation by voluntarily doing harm to himself, this should not be so when an individual causes the victim to commit suicide or lose the will to live because of extreme pain from wounds inflicted by the appellant, or when the wound has rendered the victim irresponsible. The impact of quadriplegia on a person's physical and mental well-being may be equated with the effects of extreme pain. Thus, the rationale in *Hall, supra*, applies also to the relationship between the gunshot wound and the alleged loss of will to live. The appellant's conduct could be regarded as a proximate cause of the victim's death, and he would still be criminally liable for it.

Judgment and sentence affirmed. [*Holding*]

Notes

1.   The issue of causation in cases of lingering death were easier to resolve under the common law "year and a day rule," which provided that there was no causation if the death occurred more than a year and a day after the defendant's act. Modern medical advancements have made the rule obsolete. As the United States Supreme Court noted in *Rogers v. Tennessee*, 532 U.S. 451, 462 (2001):

> The year and a day rule is widely viewed as an outdated relic of the common law. . . .
> [T]he rule is generally believed to date back to the 13th century, when it served as a
> statute of limitations governing the time in which an individual might initiate a private

action for murder known as an "appeal of death;" that by the 18th century the rule had been extended to the law governing public prosecutions for murder; that the primary and most frequently cited justification for the rule is that 13th century medical science was incapable of establishing causation beyond a reasonable doubt when a great deal of time had elapsed between the injury to the victim and his death; and that, as practically every court recently to have considered the rule has noted, advances in medical and related science have so undermined the usefulness of the rule as to render it without question obsolete.

2.   In Texas, the year and a day rule was explicitly eliminated with the adoption of the 1974 Penal Code. Although the abolition of this outdated rule makes sense, it eliminates a clear but arbitrary line. Is there a danger of abuse if there is no fixed time limit? Consider the following newspaper article.

Δ asserted that trial ct erred in denying his motion for mistrial, by instructing the jury on the lesser- included offense

It was not error bc substantial evidence that the gunshot resulted in victim's paralysis + quadriplegia. Δ's conduct regarded as proximate cause of victim's death.

Medical Examiner Rules James Brady's Death a Homicide

By Peter Hermann and Michael E. Ruane, The Washington Post, August 8, 2014.

Monday's death of President Ronald Reagan's press secretary James S. Brady has been ruled a homicide resulting from the gunshot wound he suffered in the assassination attempt on Reagan in 1981, more than three decades ago. *30+ yrs ago*

The ruling was made by the medical examiner's office in Virginia, where Brady, 73, died in an Alexandria retirement community, and was announced Friday by Gwendolyn Crump, the D.C. police department's chief spokeswoman.

There was no immediate word on whether the shooter, John W. Hinckley Jr., who has been treated at St. Elizabeth's psychiatric hospital since his trial, could face new criminal charges. Hinckley, 59, was found not guilty by reason of insanity after he shot Reagan and three others on March 30, 1981.

Bill Miller, a spokesman for the U.S. Attorney's Office, said Friday that prosecutors are reviewing the ruling and that his office would have "no further comment at this time."

Mark MacDougall, a former federal prosecutor, said "the real hurdle for the government would seem to be proving, beyond a reasonable doubt, that Hinckley actually caused Mr. Brady's death 33 years after the shooting."

But such cases are becoming more common as advances in medical care help people live longer.

In 2007, a Pennsylvania man who had served 16 years for shooting a police officer in 1966 was arrested again and charged with murder after the officer's death, which was ruled a homicide based on the bullet wound 41 years earlier. The man was tried by a jury and acquitted. *no conviction*

And in 2012, there was a shooting case in the District that was ruled a homicide when the victim died 23 years later. In that case, the shooter was serving an 85-year prison sentence. New charges were not filed.

Brady was shot some 69 days into the Reagan presidency. Brady was hit first, above the left eye. The bullet that entered his head shattered into more than two-dozen fragments. Reagan was hit by a bullet that ricocheted off the limousine. Secret Service agent Timothy McCarthy and D.C. police officer Thomas Delahanty were also wounded.

Brady's recovery was marked by ups and downs. Within several months, he underwent two surgeries to stop spinal fluid from leaking from his cranial cavity, had an operation for a pulmonary embolism, and had epileptic seizures, pneumonia and persistent fevers.

He was discharged from the hospital but needed continuous nursing care at home. He also required extensive outpatient physical therapy. A year later, he was back in the hospital because of a blood clot in his left leg, which had been partially paralyzed, along with his left arm.

Intervening Cause

The *Govan* decision mentioned the concepts of coincidence and response. This analytical framework is helpful with cases where there is an intervening act that the defense claims cuts off criminal liability. *Kibbe v. Henderson*, which follows, is a case in which the question is whether intervening forces relieve the defendants of responsibility for the victim's death. As is typical of these cases, there is clearly criminal liability for some crime, in this case a robbery, but the question is whether the vulnerable victim's death after being abandoned by the robbers can be established or whether intervening acts cut off the responsibility for the death. Two *Kibbe* decisions follow. The first from the Second Circuit Court of Appeals deals with whether the jury instruction on causation was deficient, and a second from the United States Supreme Court says more about whether the claim was properly reached in a habeas corpus proceeding than the merits of the causation issue.

Kibbe v. Henderson

534 F.2d 493 (2d Cir. 1976)

Lumbard, Circuit Judge.

Kibbe and his codefendant, Roy Krall, met the decedent, George Stafford, at a bar in Rochester, New York on the evening of December 30, 1970. Stafford had been drinking heavily and by about 9:00 p.m. he was so intoxicated that the bartender refused to serve him further. Apparently the defendants saw Stafford offer a one hundred dollar bill for payment, which the bartender refused. At some point during the evening, Stafford began soliciting a ride to Canandaigua from the other patrons in the bar. Kibbe and Krall, who confessed to having already decided to rob Stafford, offered a ride and the three men left the bar together. Before starting out for Canandaigua, the three visited a second bar. When the bartender at this bar also refused to serve Stafford because of his inebriated condition, the three proceeded to a third bar, where each was served additional drinks.

Kibbe, Krall and Stafford left for Canandaigua in Kibbe's car about 9:30 that evening. According to statements of the defendants, as Krall was driving the car, Kibbe demanded Stafford's money and, upon receiving it, forced Stafford to lower his trousers and remove his boots to prove he had no more. At some time between 9:30 and 9:40 p.m., Stafford was abandoned on the side of an unlit, rural two-lane highway. His boots and jacket were also placed on the shoulder of the highway; Stafford's eyeglasses, however, remained in the car. There was testimony that it was "very cold" that night and that strong winds were blowing recently fallen snow across the highway, although the night was clear and the pavement was dry. There was an open and lighted service station in the general vicinity, but testimony varied as to its precise distance from the place where Stafford was abandoned. In any case, the station was no more than one-quarter of a mile away.

About half an hour after Kibbe and Krall had abandoned Stafford, Michael Blake, a college student, was driving his pickup truck northbound on the highway at 50 miles an hour, ten miles per hour in excess of the posted speed limit. A car passed Blake in a southbound direction and the driver flashed his headlights at Blake. Immediately thereafter, Blake saw Stafford sitting in the middle of the northbound lane with his hands in the air. Blake testified that he "went into a kind of shock" as soon as he saw Stafford, and that he did not apply his brakes. Blake further testified that he did not attempt to avoid hitting Stafford because he "didn't have time to react." After the collision, Blake stopped his truck and returned to assist Stafford, whereupon he found the decedent's trousers were around his ankles and his shirt was up to his chest. Stafford was wearing neither his jacket nor his boots.

Stafford suffered massive head and body injuries as a result of the collision and died shortly thereafter. An autopsy revealed a high alcohol concentration of .25% in his blood. The Medical Examiner testified that these injuries were the direct cause of death.

Kibbe and Krall were apprehended on December 31, 1970. They were tried for robbery and for the murder of Stafford under New York Penal Law § 125.25(2) which provides:

266

A person is guilty of murder in the second degree when:

(2) Under circumstances evincing a depraved indifference to human life, he recklessly engages in conduct which creates a grave risk of death to another person, and thereby causes the death of another person.

In his charge to the jury, the judge failed to define or explain the issue of causation as that term is used in § 125.25(2). No mention was made of the legal effect of intervening or supervening cause. Nevertheless, defense counsel failed to take any exception whatsoever to this omission. The jury returned guilty verdicts on the charges of second degree murder, second degree robbery, and third degree grand larceny. Kibbe was sentenced to concurrent terms of imprisonment of 15 years to life on the murder conviction, 5 to 15 years on the robbery conviction, and up to 4 years on the grand larceny conviction.

The Appellate Division affirmed the conviction on finding that there was sufficient evidence that Stafford's death was caused by appellant's acts "as well as by the acts of Blake." The court stated that while the trial judge's charge concerning causation was "lacking in detail" appellant had not questioned the sufficiency of the charge on appeal and no exceptions to or requests for a charge on causation had been made at trial. The New York Court of Appeals also found sufficient evidence of causation and unanimously affirmed the convictions.

Kibbe then petitioned for *habeas corpus* in the District Court for the Northern District. Judge Foley denied the petition and, on the question of the jury charge, noted that the correctness of instructions does not raise a constitutional claim cognizable on habeas corpus. Appeal to this court followed.

In this case, by the language of the statute, the state was bound to prove to the jury beyond a reasonable doubt that appellant evinced a depraved indifference to Stafford's life, recklessly engaged in conduct that created a grave risk of Stafford's death, and thereby caused Stafford's death. The court scrupulously instructed the jury with respect to the meaning of "recklessly", "depraved", "grave", and "indifferent" as used in Penal Law § 125.25(2). The omission of any definition of causation, however, permitted the jury to conclude that the issue was not before them or that causation could be inferred merely from the fact that Stafford's death succeeded his abandonment by Kibbe and Krall. *since causation wasn't mentioned jury automatically assumed it*

Even if the jury were aware of the need to determine causation,[1] the court's instruction did not provide the tools necessary to that task. The possibility that jurors, as laymen, may misconstrue the evidence before them makes mandatory in every case instruction as to the legal standards they must apply. Error in the omission of an instruction is compounded where the legal standard is complex and requires that fine distinctions be made. That is most assuredly the situation in this case. It has been held that where death is produced by an intervening force, such

---

1. The trial judge made brief mention of the term "causation" to his charge when he stated: "You will not consider either (first degree manslaughter or second degree manslaughter) unless you feel that these defendants or either of them, was guilty of causing the death of George Stafford recklessly." This instruction, however, was given in the context of explaining the relation between reckless conduct and manslaughter rather than in the context of a definition of causation. In fact, by emphasizing "recklessly", the judge may have implied that the jury could assume causation and had only to determine whether recklessness was involved.

intervening cause Rule.

as Blake's operation of his truck, the liability of one who put an antecedent force into action will depend on the difficult determination of whether the intervening force was a sufficiently independent or supervening cause of death. *See* W. LaFave & A. Scott, Criminal Law 257–63 (1972) (collecting cases).[2] The few cases that provide similar factual circumstances suggest that the controlling questions are whether the ultimate result was foreseeable to the original actor and whether the victim failed to do something easily within his grasp that would have extricated him from danger.[3]

The New York appellate courts applied these standards and found that there was sufficient evidence to uphold the convictions. We have no reason to doubt that conclusion.

Issue

The sufficiency of the evidence, however, is not the subject of our inquiry. Our sole concern is whether the jury was adequately instructed in order to make the same finding beyond a reasonable doubt. As this function was within the exclusive province of the jury, the appellate courts may not substitute their own findings for the jury's possible failure to consider the issue.

If the jury had been cognizant of the proper legal standards, this evidence, if believed, could have injected an element of reasonable doubt into the jury's deliberations as to whether defendants foresaw or could have foreseen that about one-half hour after they abandoned Stafford he would be struck in the middle of a highway lane by the driver of a speeding truck who failed to react in such a way to avoid a collision.

We are convinced that the trial judge's incomplete instructions took a necessary determination of causation of death from the jury and thereby deprived appellant of his right to due process.

---

2. The complexity of the definition of legal causation in LaFave and Scott, *supra*, demonstrates that an explanation of the concept of intervening and supervening cause would have been not merely helpful (as contended by Judge Mansfield), but essential to the jury's determination here. Given the proper standard for causation, the jury could have found that Blake had been so reckless as to absolve defendants of legal responsibility for Stafford's death:

> As might be expected, courts have tended to distinguish cases in which the intervening act was a coincidence from those in which it was a *response* to the defendant's prior action. An intervening act is a *coincidence* when the defendant's act merely put the victim at a certain place at a certain time, and because the victim was so located it was possible for him to be acted upon by the intervening cause. The case put earlier in which B, after being fired upon by A, changed his route and then was struck by lightning is an illustration of a coincidence. However, it is important to note that there may be a coincidence even when the subsequent act is that of a human agency, as where A shoots B and leaves him lying in the roadway, resulting in B being struck by C's car; or where A shoots at B and causes him to take refuge in a park, where B is then attacked and killed by a gang of hoodlums.
>
> By contrast, an intervening act may be said to be a *response* to the prior actions of the defendant when it involves a reaction to the conditions created by the defendant.
>
> Thus—though the distinction is not carefully developed in many of the decided cases—it may be said that a coincidence will break the chain of legal cause unless it was foreseeable, while a response will do so only if it is abnormal (and, if abnormal, also unforeseeable).

People v. Fowler, 178 P. 892 (Cal. 1918).

3. *See State v. Preslar*, 48 N.C. 421 (1856) (deliberate choice of victim to forego place of safety exonerates defendant of liability for victim's subsequent death from exposure).

Not every element was proven beyond a reasonable doubt be of trial judge's incomplete instructions took a necessary determination of causation from jury & deprived △ of his right to due process.

Henderson v. Kibbe

431 U.S. 145 (1977)

The Court, per Stevens, J., reversed.

Rule

The burden of demonstrating that an erroneous instruction was so prejudicial that it will support a collateral attack on the constitutional validity of a state court's judgment is even greater than the showing required to establish plain error on direct appeal. The question in such a collateral proceeding is "whether the ailing instruction by itself so infected the entire trial that the resulting conviction violates due process," not merely whether "the instruction is undesirable, erroneous, or even 'universally condemned.'" *did the instruction actually effect trial?*

In this case, the respondent's burden is especially heavy because no erroneous instruction was given; his claim of prejudice is based on the failure to give any explanation beyond the reading of the statutory language itself of the causation element. An omission, or an incomplete instruction, is less likely to be prejudicial than a misstatement of the law.

Because respondent did not submit a draft instruction on the causation issue to the trial judge, and because the New York courts apparently had no previous occasion to construe this aspect of the murder statute, we cannot know with certainty precisely what instruction should have been given as a matter of New York law. We do know that the New York Court of Appeals found no reversible error in this case; and its discussion of the sufficiency of the evidence gives us guidance about the kind of causation instruction that would have been acceptable.

The New York Court of Appeals concluded that the evidence of causation was sufficient because it can be said beyond a reasonable doubt that the "ultimate harm" was "something which should have been foreseen as being reasonably related to the acts of the accused." It is not entirely clear whether the court's reference to "ultimate harm" merely required that Stafford's death was foreseeable, or, more narrowly, that his death by speeding vehicle was foreseeable. In either event, the court was satisfied that the "ultimate harm" was one which "should have been foreseen." Thus, an adequate instruction would have told the jury that if the ultimate harm should have been foreseen as being reasonably related to defendants' conduct, that conduct should be regarded as having caused the death of Stafford. *causation + ultimate harm*

The significance of the omission of such an instruction may be evaluated by comparison with the instructions that were given. One of the elements of respondent's offense is that he acted "recklessly." By returning a guilty verdict, the jury necessarily found, in accordance with its instruction on recklessness, that respondent was "aware of and consciously disregard[ed] a substantial and unjustifiable risk" that death would occur. A person who is "aware of and consciously disregards" a substantial risk must also foresee the ultimate harm that the risk entails. Thus, the jury's determination that the respondent acted recklessly necessarily included a determination that the ultimate harm was foreseeable to him. *" Δ knew ultimate harm"*

In a strict sense, an additional instruction on foreseeability would not have been cumulative because it would have related to an element of the offense not specifically covered in the instructions given. But since it is logical to assume that the jurors would have responded to an instruction on causation consistently with their determination of the issues that were comprehensively explained, it is equally logical to conclude that such an instruction would not have affected their verdict.[1] Accordingly, we reject the suggestion that the omission of more complete instructions on the causation issue so infected the entire trial that the resulting conviction violated due process. Even if we were to make the unlikely assumption that the jury might have reached a different verdict pursuant to an additional instruction, that possibility is too speculative to justify the conclusion that constitutional error was committed.

Notes

1.   The analytical framework provided by the federal circuit court provides a useful template for discussing the causation issues, but it doesn't mean that it provides easy answers, particularly when there are a number of actors and transactions. Is the action of the driver of the truck a coincidence because he hit the victim in the road near where the crime ended? Or is it a response, or more accurately a non-response, of failing to brake when he was speeding on the highway? What about the victim? Is moving from the relative safety of the snow bank on the side of the road to the dangerous location in the middle of the road a reasonable response? Is someone that intoxicated able to be reasonable? Who is responsible for his extreme intoxication?

2.   Would this be an easier case if the victim had died of exposure on the side of the road on a cold night? Does the fact that the victim died in a less foreseeable way make the defendants less responsible for the death?

3.   The intervening act is often a response by the crime victim. If the victim dies in a desperate attempt to flee the crime committed by the defendant, the reaction of attempting to escape is deemed natural and reasonable. On the other hand, if the defendant refuses medical care that could have saved his or her life, is that response reasonable? Should it break the chain of causation?

Consider a Texas case from 1899, *Franklin v. State*, 51 S.W. 951 (1899). The defendant shot the victim in the leg, and the victim died nine days later. On appeal from his manslaughter conviction, the defendant argued there was insufficient evidence of causation based upon medical testimony from the treating physician. The doctor testified that the gunshot wound should not have been fatal, but the victim had refused his advice to permit his leg to be amputated. The doctor further testified the cause of death was gangrene or blood poisoning. The

---

1. In fact, it is not unlikely that a complete instruction on the causation issue would actually have been favorable to the prosecution. For example, an instruction might have been patterned after the following example:

> A, with intent to kill B, only wounds B, leaving him lying unconscious in the unlighted road on a dark night, and then C, driving along the road, runs over and kills B. Here C's act is a matter of coincidence rather than a response to what A has done, and thus the question is whether the subsequent events were foreseeable, as they undoubtedly were in the above illustration.

Such an instruction would probably have been more favorable to the prosecution than the instruction on recklessness which the court actually gave.

Court of Criminal Appeals affirmed the conviction, stating, "It is sufficient to say in this case that death resulted from a disease brought on directly by the wound which was inflicted by appellant[,] and . . . appellant cannot say that his act was not the proximate cause of the death of the deceased."

4.   As the *Franklin* case demonstrates, courts are reluctant to label a decision not to permit treatment involving something as horrific as an amputation an "unreasonable response" when the decision about treatment was made necessary by the defendant's criminal act. In a controversial English case, *Regina v. Blaue*, 1 W.L.R. 1411 (1975), the medical treatment that was refused by a victim who had been stabbed by the defendant was a routine blood transfusion. The medical testimony at the defendant's murder trial was that the transfusion would have saved the victim's life, but she refused it due to the fact she was a Jehovah's Witness and her religion would not permit her to accept the proposed medical care.

The appellate court affirmed the murder conviction by making reference to the tort law doctrine of "take your victim as you find him." The *Blaue* Court held that the doctrine applies not only to physical conditions that causes a victim to be unusually vulnerable to injury but the moral or religious beliefs of the victim as well. The court even suggested a higher standard applies in criminal law than tort law by reasoning that the requirement that a civil litigant must mitigate damages if possible might require the transfusion, but there is no such requirement in a criminal case.

Was the victim's response in *Blaue* unreasonable? If the family of the victim brought a wrongful death action against the defendant, would the court reduce the award because of the failure to mitigate damages? Would the civil court deny relief because of a lack of causation? Should causation be the same, more difficult, or easier in a criminal case?

5.   What if the victim in *Blaue* had agreed to the transfusion, but died because of medical malpractice during the operation? Would the defendant still be guilty on the theory advanced in *Franklin*, that the wound caused by the defendant's crime made the operation necessary? What if the transfusion is successful, but the stabbing victim dies because she contracted scarlet fever from another patient in the recovery room?

6.   Consider the case of *United Sates v. Feinberg*, 253 A.2d 636 (1969). Feinberg owned a cigar store in a skid row section of Philadelphia. Feinberg sold sterno that is used as a heating element often placed under chafing dishes at buffets. Some of the clients of the cigar store extracted alcohol from the sterno for drinking. Feinberg received a shipment of sterno from a different supplier than his usual source that contained a higher concentration of toxic methanol. The shipping boxes contained warnings saying "Institutional Sterno, Danger. Poison. For Use Only as a Fuel. For Industrial and Commercial Use. Not for Home Use." Feinberg sold 400 cans of the sterno and then returned the rest of it to the supplier. During a one-week period, thirty-one people died in the skid-row area as a result of methanol poisoning. No other industrial sterno had been sold in the area.

Concurrence

To be guilty of crimes requiring a particular result, like homicide, there must be a concurrence of the mental state and the act that causes the harm. For example, suppose X forms the intent to kill Y and drives to a store to buy a gun to kill Y, but does not arrive at the store because of a traffic accident. Unbeknownst to X, the driver of the other car in the accident is Y, who is killed. In this unlikely scenario, X is not guilty of murder. Although it could be said the defendant had the required mental state for murder, and the defendant's actions in driving caused the death, the two elements did not concur or coincide. If X was driving in a grossly negligent manner, it might be possible to convict her of manslaughter or criminally negligent homicide but, if the collision was an accident, there is no crime.

Concurrence problems sometimes arise in homicide cases when the defendant erroneously believes he or she has killed the victim and then disposes of body in a manner that in fact causes death. In this situation, it might be said that the defendant had the required mental state for murder when the victim was rendered unconscious, but there is no causation; whereas the defendant caused the death when disposing of the body without having an intent to kill. Not surprisingly, courts have generally taken a broader view by characterizing all of the events as part of the same transaction.

The issue of whether the mental state existed at the time of the criminal act arises in two cases that follow. In both *Bailey* and in *Decina*, it is claimed that the defendant lacked the mental state when the harm was caused.

Bailey v. State

304 S.W.3d 544 (Court of Appeals of Texas—San Antonio, 2009)

Opinion by Steven C. Hilbig, Justice.

Appellant, Joe Don Bailey, appeals his conviction for obstructing a highway. Bailey complains the evidence is legally and factually insufficient to support a finding he intentionally, knowingly, or recklessly obstructed the roadway. We reverse the judgment of the trial court and render a judgment of acquittal.

Background

At approximately 1:45 a.m. on November 23, 2007, Bailey had a single-vehicle accident while driving his three-quarter ton Dodge crew cab truck on Bear Springs Road in Bandera County, Texas. After the accident, Bailey's truck was lying on its side, straddling the road, and partially blocking both lanes of travel. Bailey immediately called a friend, William Wyman, and told him about the accident. Wyman drove to the accident scene. Wyman then called his sister Rachael and she and her friend Jerald Alex Donaldson went to the scene. Donaldson testified he never saw Bailey at the accident site. Wyman returned to Rachael's house, and Donaldson called Frank Roller, a friend who operated a tow truck, to come remove Bailey's truck from the road.

When Roller arrived with his wrecker at approximately 3:30 a.m., Bailey was not present, but Donaldson was still there. Using his tow truck, Roller righted Bailey's truck and moved it to the side of the road. About this time, Bandera County deputy sheriffs arrived and began an investigation. Collectively, the deputies testified they were concerned whether the driver of the truck had been injured and wanted to locate him. The deputies described the people at the scene as somewhat uncooperative, and testified they told the deputies that the driver was uninjured.

Several witnesses testified Bailey's truck created a hazardous condition on the road. Witnesses described the road as a two-lane, unlit, small, winding, and dangerous road, and that a person could not see the truck until nearly "on top" of it. The deputies identified Bailey as the owner of the truck through insurance papers found in the vehicle.

Bailey was subsequently charged with obstructing a highway. The jury found him guilty and the trial judge imposed a sentence of a $1,000 fine and 180 days in jail. The jail sentence was suspended and Bailey was placed on probation for six months. Bailey complains the evidence is legally and factually insufficient to support a finding he intentionally, knowingly, or recklessly obstructed the roadway.

Discussion

Bailey was charged with obstructing a highway pursuant to section 42.03 of the Texas Penal Code. The information filed in this case tracked the language of section 42.03, which provides in part:

(a) A person commits an offense if, without legal privilege or authority, he intentionally, knowingly, or recklessly:

273

(1) obstructs a highway, street, sidewalk, railway, waterway, elevator, aisle, hallway, entrance, or exit to which the public or a substantial group of the public has access, or any other place used for the passage of persons, vehicles, or conveyances, regardless of the means of creating the obstruction and whether the obstruction arises from his acts alone or from his acts and the acts of others.

(b) For purposes of this section, "obstruct" means to render impassable or to render passage unreasonably inconvenient or hazardous.

TEX. PENAL CODE ANN. § 42.03 (Vernon 2003).

The parties disagree on the mental state or *mens rea* required by the statute. Bailey contends the State was required to prove he acted intentionally, knowingly, or recklessly at the time his truck blocked the roadway. The State contends Bailey acted "recklessly," thereby supplying the requisite *mens rea*, when he left the vehicle in the roadway without either removing the truck or taking precautions to warn motorists the road was blocked.

We must consider the nature of the crime in order to apply the *mens rea* requirement of section 42.03. Based on a plain reading of the statute, we conclude obstructing a highway is a conduct-oriented crime, *i.e.*, a person must engage in the conduct with the requisite mental state. Accordingly, the State was required to show Bailey intentionally, knowingly, or recklessly engaged in the act or acts that caused his truck to obstruct the highway. Contrary to the State's argument, it would not be an offense if Bailey formed the "intent" to obstruct the highway at a later time because generally, the *mens rea* must exist at the time the act is performed. *See, e.g., Cook v. State*, 884 S.W.2d 485, 487 (Tex. Crim. App. 1994) (holding "in order to constitute a crime, the act or *actus reus* must be accompanied by a criminal mind or *mens rea*"); *Hobbs v. State,* 175 S.W.3d 777, 782 n.3 (Tex. Crim. App. 2005) (holding "intent to commit the felony or crime of theft, essentially necessary to constitute the crime of burglary, must exist at the time of and accompany the entry into the house"); *Peterson v. State*, 645 S.W.2d 807, 811 (Tex. Crim. App. 1983) (holding that to constitute theft, intent to deprive owner must exist at time property is taken).

There is no evidence to support the jury's determination Bailey intentionally, knowingly, or recklessly obstructed the road. The State consistently referred to Bailey's wreck as an accident and nothing in the record contradicts that characterization. There is no evidence upon which a rational jury could have found all the essential elements of the offense beyond a reasonable doubt. The evidence is therefore legally insufficient to support the trial court's judgment.

Notes

1.   The appellate court seems to find that *Bailey* both committed the *actus reus* and possessed the *mens rea* of the charged offense, just not at the same time. When did he commit the *actus reus*? When did he possess the *mens rea*?

People v. Decina

138 N.E.2d 799 (N.Y. App. 1956)

Froessel, Judge.

At about 3:30 p. m. on March 14, 1955, a bright, sunny day, defendant was driving, alone in his car, in a northerly direction on Delaware Avenue in the city of Buffalo. The portion of Delaware Avenue here involved is 60 feet wide. At a point south of an overhead viaduct of the Erie Railroad, defendant's car swerved to the left, across the center line in the street, so that it was completely in the south lane, traveling 35 to 40 miles per hour.

It then veered sharply to the right, crossing Delaware Avenue and mounting the easterly curb at a point beneath the viaduct and continued thereafter at a speed estimated to have been about 50 or 60 miles per hour or more. During this latter swerve, a pedestrian testified that he saw defendant's hand above his head; another witness said he saw defendant's left arm bent over the wheel, and his right hand extended towards the right door.

A group of six schoolgirls were walking north on the easterly sidewalk of Delaware Avenue, two in front and four slightly in the rear, when defendant's car struck them from behind. One of the girls escaped injury by jumping against the wall of the viaduct. The bodies of the children struck were propelled northward onto the street and the lawn in front of a coal company, located to the north of the Erie viaduct on Delaware Avenue. Three of the children, 6 to 12 years old, were found dead on arrival by the medical examiner, and a fourth child, 7 years old, died in a hospital two days later as a result of injuries sustained in the accident.

After striking the children, defendant's car continued on the easterly sidewalk, and then swerved back onto Delaware Avenue once more. It continued in a northerly direction, passing under a second viaduct before it again veered to the right and remounted the easterly curb, striking and breaking a metal lamppost. With its horn blowing steadily apparently because defendant was 'stooped over' the steering wheel the car proceeded on the sidewalk until if finally crashed through a 7 1/4-inch brick wall of a grocery store, injuring at least one customer and causing considerable property damage.

When the car came to a halt in the store, with its horn still blowing, several fires had been ignited. Defendant was stooped over in the car and was "bobbing a little." To one witness he appeared dazed, to another unconscious, lying back with his hands off the wheel. Various people present shouted to defendant to turn off the ignition of his car, and "within a matter of seconds the horn stopped blowing and the car did shut off."

Defendant was pulled out of the car by a number of bystanders and laid down on the sidewalk. To a policeman who came on the scene shortly he appeared "injured, dazed"; another witness said that "he looked as though he was knocked out, and his arm seemed to be bleeding." An injured customer in the store, after receiving first aid, pressed defendant for an explanation of the accident and he told her: "I blacked out from the bridge."

When the police arrived, defendant attempted to rise, staggered and appeared dazed and unsteady. When informed that he was under arrest, and would have to accompany the police to the station house, he resisted and, when he tried to get away, was handcuffed. The foregoing evidence was adduced by the People, and is virtually undisputed. Defendant did not take the stand nor did he produce any witnesses.

From the police station defendant was taken to the E. J. Meyer Memorial Hospital. Dr. Wechter, a resident physician in the hospital and a member of its staff, came to his room. He asked defendant how he felt and what had happened. Defendant, who still felt a little dizzy or blurry, said that as he was driving he noticed a jerking of his right hand, which warned him that he might develop a convulsion, and that as he tried to steer the car over to the curb he felt himself becoming unconscious, and he thought he had a convulsion. He was aware that children were in front of his car, but did not know whether he had struck them.

Defendant then proceeded to relate to Dr. Wechter his past medical history, namely, that at the age of 7 he was struck by an auto and suffered a marked loss of hearing. In 1946 he was treated in this same hospital for an illness during which he had some convulsions. Several burr holes were made in his skull and a brain abscess was drained. Following this operation defendant had no convulsions from 1946 through 1950. In 1950 he had four convulsions, caused by scar tissue on the brain. From 1950 to 1954 he experienced about 10 or 20 seizures a year, in which his right hand would jump although he remained fully conscious. In 1954, he had 4 or 5 generalized seizures with loss of consciousness, the last being in September 1954, a few months before the accident. Thereafter he had more hospitalization, a spinal tap, consultation with a neurologist, and took medication daily to help prevent seizures.

On the basis of this medical history, Dr. Wechter made a diagnosis of Jacksonian epilepsy, and was of the opinion that defendant had a seizure at the time of the accident. Other members of the hospital staff performed blood tests and took an electroencephalogram during defendant's three-day stay there. The testimony of Dr. Wechter is the only testimony before the trial court showing that defendant had epilepsy, suffered an attack at the time of the accident, and had knowledge of his susceptibility to such attacks.

Defendant was indicted and charged with violating section 1053-a of the Penal Law. Following his conviction, after a demurrer to the indictment was overruled, the Appellate Division held that the demurrer was properly overruled. Defendant appealed.

The defendant argues that his demurrer should have been sustained, since the indictment here does not charge a crime. The indictment states essentially that defendant, knowing "that he was subject to epileptic attacks or other disorder rendering him likely to lose consciousness for a considerable period of time," was culpably negligent "in that he consciously undertook to and did operate his Buick sedan on a public highway" and "while so doing" suffered such an attack which caused said automobile "to travel at a fast and reckless rate of speed, jumping the curb and driving over the sidewalk" causing the death of 4 persons. In our opinion, this clearly states a violation of section 1053-a of the Penal Law. The statute does not require that a defendant must deliberately intend to kill a human being, for that would be murder. Nor does the statute require that he knowingly and consciously follow the precise path that leads to death and destruction. It

276

is sufficient, we have said, when his conduct manifests a "disregard of the consequences which may ensue from the act, and indifference to the rights of others."

Assuming the truth of the indictment, as we must on a demurrer, this defendant knew he was subject to epileptic attacks and seizures that might strike at any time. He also knew that a moving motor vehicle uncontrolled on public highway is a highly dangerous instrumentality capable of unrestrained destruction. With this knowledge, and without anyone accompanying him, he deliberately took a chance by making a conscious choice of a course of action, in disregard of the consequences which he knew might follow from his conscious act, and which in this case did ensue. How can we say as a matter of law that this did not amount to culpable negligence within the meaning of section 1053-a?

To hold otherwise would be to say that a man may freely indulge himself in liquor in the same hope that it will not affect his driving, and if it later develops that ensuing intoxication causes dangerous and reckless driving resulting in death, his unconsciousness or involuntariness at that time would relieve him from prosecution under the statute. His awareness of a condition which he knows may produce such consequences as here, and his disregard of the consequences, renders him liable for culpable negligence, as the courts below have properly held. To have a sudden sleeping spell, an unexpected heart or other disabling attack, without any prior knowledge or warning thereof, is an altogether different situation, and there is simply no basis for comparing such cases with the flagrant disregard manifested here.

[Rule.]

Accordingly, the Appellate Division properly sustained the lower court's order overruling the demurrer, as well as its denial of the motion in arrest of judgment on the same ground.

[Holding]

Notes

1.   If *Decina* was suffering a seizure during the time that he lost control of his car, how could he have had the mental state required for recklessness? How can it be said that he committed a voluntary act?

2.   In crimes like *Decina* involving recklessness, the issue of mental state and causation are virtually the same. If the *mens rea* is supplied at an earlier point—when he got behind the wheel of the car—recklessness is arguably established by ignoring the risk of a seizure knowing the possible consequences. In other words, the common question to mental state and causation is whether the actual result that occurred was foreseeable.

[mental state + causation issue]

277

Chapter 14: Capital Punishment

Historical Background.

Sentencing and punishment issues are beyond the scope of this text that is intended as an introductory course about substantive criminal law. However, the death penalty is an important and specialized area of the law that is deserving of attention especially in a course that features Texas law. Capital sentencing is a highly controversial and important topic, particularly in Texas, which by almost every measure is the leading death penalty state in the nation. For example, in the period following the reinstatement of the death penalty after a moratorium period that ended in 1977, Texas has executed more than a third of all those who have been executed in the United States.

Capital punishment is a fitting subject to take up as part of a discussion of homicide because the only offense in Texas that can result in the death penalty is the highest homicide offense of capital murder. This chapter deals with the life and death question of the penalty to be imposed after a defendant has been convicted of capital murder. After such a conviction, only two penalties are possible under Texas law: a death sentence or a penalty of life imprisonment without the possibility of parole.

Capital cases are criminal cases, and most of the legal principles discussed in this text apply to capital cases. However, as the United States Supreme Court has often stated, "death is different." This chapter will provide a brief overview of some of the leading principles of the unique law of capital punishment.

Perhaps more than any other area of criminal procedure, the penalty phase of capital trials have been guided by federal constitutional principles since the quintet of decisions in 1976 reinstating the death penalty in the United States and establishing the ground rules for a constitutional capital procedure. Since 1976, the Texas procedures have been significantly altered in response to constitutional rulings from the United States Supreme Court, many of which arose in Texas cases. While constitutional guidelines predominate in this area, they allow a great deal of variation, and Texas procedure remains unusual among the states. To understand the current state of the law of capital punishment, it is necessary to return to cases that have established the constitutional foundation for the modern death penalty in Texas and in America.

Anglo-American law has a long tradition of capital penalties. In 18th century England, hundreds of crimes were punished with the death penalty, including property crimes, which accounted for the overwhelming majority of capital convictions and executions. The English tradition was carried over into colonial America, but because each colony developed its own laws, there were considerable variations. Southern colonies where black slaves outnumbered their masters typically maintained harsher codes reflecting disparate treatment of blacks and whites. At the time of the adoption of the United States Constitution, capital punishment was a common penalty found in all of the states, and its existence was tacitly acknowledged by the reference to "capital and other infamous crimes" in a clause of the Fifth Amendment recognizing the right to a grand jury indictment and by a similar reference in the Due Process Clause of that Amendment.

By the mid-19th century, a movement to abolish the death penalty achieved some success when Michigan eliminated capital punishment, except for the crime of treason, in 1847, followed by Rhode Island in 1852, Wisconsin in 1853, and Maine in 1887. However, efforts to abolish capital punishment in the legislative arena had only sporadic success. Maine abolished the penalty in 1876, restored it in 1883, and re-abolished it in 1887. Iowa abolished the penalty for a six-year period in 1872, but restored it in 1878. A period of abolition in Colorado was even shorter, from 1897 to 1901. While outright abolition remained a minority position in the states, the use of the death penalty typically was limited to fewer crimes in most jurisdictions. For example, in 1897, Congress reduced the number of federal capital offenses from sixty to three (murder, treason, and rape), and there was jury discretion as to whether to impose the penalty in murder and rape cases.

By 1960, while the number of executions in America was on the decline, only eight states had actually abolished capital punishment. In the 1960's, the movement to reform or abolish capital punishment moved from the legislative arena, where abolitionists had been unsuccessful, to the judicial arena. Two groups were particularly important in the judicial assault on the death penalty: The American Civil Liberties Union (ACLU) and the Legal Defense Fund (LDF), a litigation arm of the National Association for the Advancement of Colored People. The LDF was also active in the early cases attacking capital punishment in part because the mounting evidence of discrimination in capital sentencing helped to overcome opposition from some of the organization's members who did not regard the death penalty as a civil rights issue.

Because of the long history of acceptance of capital punishment in the Anglo-American legal tradition, the approach taken in cases in the 1960's was to attack the death penalty collaterally by challenging the processes by which the conviction and sentence was obtained rather than directly attacking its constitutional validity. An example of an early success in attacking the procedures used in capital cases was the decision in *Witherspoon v. Illinois*, 391 U.S. 510 (1968), which struck down the common practice of allowing blanket exclusion of all potential jurors who indicated any opposition to the death penalty, resulting in a jury "uncommonly willing to impose the penalty of death."

The increasingly aggressive appellate review strategy of civil rights groups, the growing trend of juries refusing to return death penalty verdicts, the reluctance of state penal authorities to schedule and perform executions in light of doubts about the procedures used in the capital cases, and the constitutional legitimacy of the death penalty itself led to a period of a moratorium on executions in America. Between 1960 and 1968 the annual number of executions declined steadily from 56 in 1960 to zero in 1968. By the time of the *Furman* decision in 1972, there had been no executions in the United States for four years, and none were performed for five years after the *Furman* decision until the moratorium period ended with the execution of Gary Gilmore in Utah on January 17, 1977, following the issuance of five opinions by the United States Supreme Court in 1976 that initiated the modern era of capital punishment.

Furman v. Georgia

The landmark decision in *Furman v. Georgia*, 408 U.S. 238 (1972), is the longest collective opinion ever written by the United States Supreme Court, consisting of over 230 pages and more than 50,000 words, all to interpret the meaning of four words of the Eighth Amendment of the United States Constitution: "cruel and unusual punishment." Although many commentators at the time of *Furman* believed it was the beginning of the end of the death penalty in America, the Supreme Court did not definitively rule the use of capital punishment in all circumstances constitutes cruel and unusual punishment in violation of the Eighth Amendment. The immediate effect of the *Furman* decision was to invalidate the death sentences of over 600 condemned persons on the death rows of 32 states. However, because each member of the court wrote a separate opinion and no two justices joined in any one opinion, the court plurality ruled only that capital punishment as it was currently administered was unconstitutional, but there were no clear guidelines as to how laws could be revised to meet constitutional standards.

Despite the long acceptance of capital punishment in America, Justices Brennan and Marshall found that the "cruel and unusual" language "must draw its meaning from the evolving standards of decency that mark the progress of a maturing society." The steady decline in the number of executions in America in the years preceding *Furman* was a strong inference for Justices Brennan and Marshall that the punishment is not being regularly and fairly applied and serves no valid legislative purpose. Justice Brennen remarked, "the likelihood is great that the punishment is tolerated only because of its disuse." Justice Marshall found that the death penalty had not been shown to be a deterrent to capital crimes, and retributive justifications were rejected with a declaration that vengeance is an impermissible societal goal inconsistent with the Eighth Amendment.

Justice Douglas rejected the statutes before the Court in *Furman* because of their discriminatory administration, enabling the death penalty to be selectively applied against the poor and racial minorities. Justice Douglas stated,

> A law that stated that anyone making more than $50,000 would be exempt from the death penalty would plainly fail, as would a law that would in turn say, that Blacks, those who never went beyond the fifth grade in school, those who made less than $3,000 a year, or those who were unpopular or unstable should be the only people executed. A law in which the overall view reaches that result in practice has no more sanctity than a law which in terms provide the same.

Although the analysis by Justice Douglas did not explicitly declare that the death penalty could never be administered in a constitutional manner, his systemic attack on the criminal justice system as it was administered appeared to doom in his eyes any attempt to remedy such deep-seated defects by mere legislative tinkering.

The four dissenting judges were the most recent appointments to the Supreme Court, all made by Republican President Richard Nixon: Chief Justice Burger, and Associate Justices Blackmun, Powell and Rehnquist. The dissenters argued that the five separate opinions constituting the plurality erroneously invalidated a historically acceptable penalty. Although many of the dissenters expressed personal opposition to capital punishment, they maintained that a decision to abolish a penalty of such long-standing acceptance and application would have to be a legislative. The dissenters argued the Court was overstepping its sphere of authority. As Justice Powell put it, "Legislative judgments as to the efficiency of particular punishments are presumptively rational and may not be struck down under the Eighth Amendment because this Court may think that some alternative sanction would be more appropriate."

Unlike Justices Brennan and Marshall who rejected the constitutionality of the death penalty on a *per se* basis, Justices Stewart and White joined the plurality in opinions that emphasized capital punishment was cruel and unusual because of the manner of its administration, but they were not willing to hold that the death penalty would necessarily be cruel and unusual without regard to the nature of the crime or the process leading to the decision to impose a penalty of death. Because these two opinions were far narrower than the approach taken by Brennan, Marshall, and Douglass, these decisions were the crucial and controlling opinions of *Furman v. Georgia*.

Justice Stewart felt that, under current practices, death sentences that were left to the unbridled discretion of a judge or jury were imposed so infrequently that they were "unusual." According to Justice Stewart, death sentences were "cruel and unusual" in the way "being struck by lightning is cruel and unusual," and that the Eighth and Fourteenth Amendments cannot tolerate the infliction of a sentence so unique in its severity and irrevocability under legal systems that permit this penalty "to be so wantonly and so freakishly imposed."

The infrequency of the imposition of the death penalty, was critical to the analysis of Justice White, who reasoned that a penalty imposed so infrequently could not effectively contribute to the deterrence of crime or any other permissible goal of the criminal justice system. Under the circumstances of such infrequent imposition, the death penalty is a "pointless and needless extinction of life with only marginal contributions to any discernable social or public purpose," and therefore is cruel and unusual.

Legislative Responses to *Furman* and the 1976 Cases

While many viewed *Furman* as the beginning of the end of capital punishment in America, the position of Justices Brennan and Marshall that the death penalty is cruel and unusual punishment in all cases was not supported by a majority in *Furman*, holding open the possibility that legislatures could reenact new statutes in an attempt to deal with the problem of the arbitrary and standardless administration of the penalty of death condemned by Justices Stewart and White. By the time of the five decisions of 1976 that inaugurated the modern era of capital punishment guided by federal constitutional requirements, 36 jurisdictions had re-enacted death penalty statutes.

There were two major legislative responses to *Furman*. The first was to make the penalty of death mandatory for certain types of crimes in an effort to avoid the problem of unbridled and standardless discretion. The second approach, which was to take different forms, was an attempt to guide and channel the decision as to whether to impose the death penalty by establishing standards for the judge or jury.

In five decisions handed down on July 2, 1976, a majority of the United States Supreme Court conclusively resolved the issue left open in *Furman* by holding that the death penalty is not unconstitutional *per se*. The Court also indicated which of the legislative responses to *Furman* were consistent with the Eighth Amendment. In the five separate cases, each involving a different statutory scheme, there were a total of 24 opinions. Justices Stewart, Powell and Stevens were in the majority in all five cases. In upholding the death penalty's inherent constitutionality and in endorsing the constitutional regime of guided discretion, as represented by the laws of Georgia, Florida, and Texas, they were joined by Chief Justice Burger and Justices White, Blackman, and Rehnquist. In rejecting the laws of Louisiana and North Carolina which imposed mandatory death penalties, Stewart, Powell, and Stevens were joined by Justices Brennan and Marshall.

In the guided discretion cases, the majority rejected the argument that the death penalty was cruel and unusual punishment under "evolving standards of decency" in light of the fact that at least 35 states and Congress had enacted statutes providing for the death penalty in the wake of the board-clearing decision in *Furman*. By the end of 1974, at least 254 persons had been sentenced to death since *Furman*, and by the end of March 1976, more than 460 persons were subject to death sentences. The *Gregg* plurality ruled that a death sentence established by a democratically elected legislature must be presumed to be valid, and the legislature is not required "to select the least severe penalty possible so long as the penalty selected is not cruelly inhuman or disproportionate to the crime involved." Although death as a punishment is "unique in its severity and irrevocability," the majority ruled the punishment is not invariably disproportionate to a crime such as murder. According to the *Gregg* majority, the concern expressed in *Furman* that the death penalty must not be imposed arbitrarily or capriciously can be met by a carefully drafted statute that ensures the sentencing authority is given adequate information to guide and channel the exercise of discretion in deciding whether to impose the death penalty.

In rejecting mandatory death penalty statutes in from Louisiana and North Carolina, the Court reasoned that making the death penalty mandatory upon conviction removed sentencing discretion that should be exercised in the interest of "individualized" justice, and that the total absence of discretion in sentencing might cause the trial of guilt to be affected by considerations of punishment. Thus, although the mandatory requirement of the death penalty for anyone convicted of specified crimes might, at first blush, seem to meet *Furman*'s concern with arbitrary life and death decisions, the apparently mandatory statute merely "papered over" the standardless discretion given to prosecutors in deciding whether to charge capital offenses and the discretionary authority of juries to convict the defendant of the lesser crime in order to avoid a death sentence.

In the lead case of *Gregg v. Georgia* in 1976, a majority of the Supreme Court identified three important policy goals that a constitutional system of capital punishment must achieve and strongly hinted that three procedures present in the Georgia system would help to assure the constitutional imprimatur of the Court. The three overlapping policy goals of *Gregg* are: (1) to narrow the class of individuals who are subject to the death penalty to make sure that the ultimate penalty is reserved for those who are truly deserving of such a uniquely severe penalty; (2) to guide the exercise of discretion so that the jury's discretionary decision whether to impose the penalty of death is carried out in a rational and consistent manner; (3) to establish a system that allows the jury to focus on the individual characteristics of the offender and the offense.

Three procedures found in the Georgia system that won the approval of the majority are: (1) a bifurcated trial in which the question of guilt or innocence is tried separately from the question of death or life imprisonment; (2) jury instructions that guide the jury's exercise of discretion; and (3) automatic appellate review that helps to ensure the jury was given appropriate guidance and that the imposition of the death penalty is not disproportionate to the crime and the criminal.

By upholding the different capital statutes of Georgia, Florida, and Texas in three of the five cases decided on the same day in 1976, the Supreme Court demonstrated that several different forms of guided discretion containing varying limits on the authority of the sentencer would be constitutionally acceptable. However, all three states had bifurcated trials, guiding jury instructions, and appellate review. The majority in the cases of the three approved systems found that all provided sufficient efforts to narrow the class of those eligible for death and standards to guide the decision for or against death while allowing the jury to focus on the individual characteristics of the offender and the offense. The differing methods approved demonstrated that states were free to experiment within the framework of required guided discretion. Thus, it was permissible that in Texas, the narrowing of the class of those eligible for the death penalty occurred primarily at the guilt/innocence phase by adding aggravating factors that elevated murder to capital murder as part of the definition of the offense rather than the system of aggravating factors at the sentencing stage in Georgia and Florida. It was acceptable that the jury decision in Florida was only advisory for a trial judge who ultimately decided whether to impose the death penalty, while the jury decision was binding in Texas and Georgia. As long as there was a sufficient opportunity to narrow and guide the decision-maker, it did not matter that the methods of guiding and narrowing varied in all three states: Florida requiring a weighing of statutorily provided aggravating factors against statutorily defined mitigators; Georgia merely specified aggravating factors and required the jury to find at least one such factor was present, but allowed the jury the authority to vote against the death penalty without legislative specification of possible reasons for extending mercy; and Texas had the most unusual of the approved systems with aggravated factors built into the definition of the only capital crime of capital murder and a penalty phase in which the jury answered special issues that would determine whether the death penalty would be imposed. The court's treatment of the Texas capital punishment scheme in *Jurek v. Texas* follows in the text.

Jurek v. Texas

428 U.S. 262 (1976)

Opinion by Justice Stevens.

The issue in this case is whether the imposition of the sentence of death for the crime of murder under the law of Texas violates the Eighth and Fourteenth Amendments to the Constitution.

The petitioner in this case, Jerry Lane Jurek, was charged by indictment with the killing of Wendy Adams "by choking and strangling her with his hands, and by drowning her in water by throwing her into a river in the course of committing and attempting to commit kidnapping of and forcible rape upon the said Wendy Adams."

Texas law requires that if a defendant has been convicted of a capital offense, the trial court must conduct a separate sentencing proceeding before the same jury that tried the issue of guilt. Any relevant evidence may be introduced at this proceeding, and both prosecution and defense may present argument for or against the sentence of death. The jury is then presented with two (sometimes three) questions, the answers to which determine whether a death sentence will be imposed.

The jury . . . considered the two statutory questions relevant to this case: (1) whether the evidence established beyond a reasonable doubt that the murder of the deceased was committed deliberately and with the reasonable expectation that the death of the deceased or another would result, and (2) whether the evidence established beyond a reasonable doubt that there was a probability that the defendant would commit criminal acts of violence that would constitute a continuing threat to society. The jury unanimously answered "yes" to both questions, and the judge, therefore, in accordance with the statute, sentenced the petitioner to death. The Court of Criminal Appeals of Texas affirmed the judgment.

We granted certiorari to consider whether the imposition of the death penalty in this case violates the Eighth and Fourteenth Amendments of the United States Constitution.

The petitioner argues that the imposition of the death penalty under any circumstances is cruel and unusual punishment in violation of the Eighth and Fourteenth Amendments. We reject this argument.

After this Court held Texas' system for imposing capital punishment unconstitutional in *Branch v. Texas*, decided with *Furman v. Georgia*, 408 U.S. 238 (1972), the Texas Legislature narrowed the scope of its laws relating to capital punishment. The new Texas Penal Code limits capital homicides to intentional and knowing murders committed in five situations: murder of a peace officer or fireman; murder committed in the course of kidnaping, burglary, robbery, forcible rape, or arson; murder committed for remuneration; murder committed while escaping or attempting to escape from a penal institution; and murder committed by a prison inmate when the victim is a prison employee.

In addition, Texas adopted a new capital-sentencing procedure. That procedure requires the jury to answer three questions in a proceeding that takes place subsequent to the return of a verdict finding a person guilty of one of the above categories of murder. The questions the jury must answer are these:

> (1) whether the conduct of the defendant that caused the death of the deceased was committed deliberately and with the reasonable expectation that the death of the deceased or another would result;

> (2) whether there is a probability that the defendant would commit criminal acts of violence that would constitute a continuing threat to society; and

> (3) if raised by the evidence, whether the conduct of the defendant in killing the deceased was unreasonable in response to the provocation, if any, by the deceased.

TEX. PENAL CODE ANN. Art. 37.071(b).

If the jury finds that the State has proved beyond a reasonable doubt that the answer to each of the three questions is yes, then the death sentence is imposed. If the jury finds that the answer to any question is no, then a sentence of life imprisonment results. The law also provides for an expedited review by the Texas Court of Criminal Appeals.

The Texas Court of Criminal Appeals has thus far affirmed only two judgments imposing death sentences under its post-*Furman* law in this case and in *Smith v. State*. In the present case the state appellate court noted that its law "limits the circumstances under which the State may seek the death penalty to a small group of narrowly defined and particularly brutal offenses. This insures that the death penalty will only be imposed for the most serious crimes [and] . . . that [it] will only be imposed for the same type of offenses which occur under the same types of circumstances."

While Texas has not adopted a list of statutory aggravating circumstances the existence of which can justify the imposition of the death penalty as have Georgia and Florida, its action in narrowing the categories of murders for which a death sentence may ever be imposed serves much the same purpose. In fact, each of the five classes of murders made capital by the Texas statute is encompassed in Georgia and Florida by one or more of their statutory aggravating circumstances. For example, the Texas statute requires the jury at the guilt-determining stage to consider whether the crime was committed in the course of a particular felony, whether it was committed for hire, or whether the defendant was an inmate of a penal institution at the time of its commission. Thus, in essence, the Texas statute requires that the jury find the existence of a statutory aggravating circumstance before the death penalty may be imposed. So far as consideration of aggravating circumstances is concerned, therefore, the principal difference between Texas and the other two States is that the death penalty is an available sentencing option even potentially for a smaller class of murders in Texas. Otherwise the statutes are similar. Each requires the sentencing authority to focus on the particularized nature of the crime.

But a sentencing system that allowed the jury to consider only aggravating circumstances would almost certainly fall short of providing the individualized sentencing determination that we today have held in *Woodson v. North Carolina*, 428 U.S. 280 (1976), to be required by the Eighth and Fourteenth Amendments. For such a system would approach the mandatory laws that we today hold unconstitutional in *Woodson* and *Roberts v. Louisiana*, 428 U.S. 325 (1976). A jury must be allowed to consider on the basis of all relevant evidence not only why a death sentence should be imposed, but also why it should not be imposed.

Thus, in order to meet the requirement of the Eighth and Fourteenth Amendments, a capital-sentencing system must allow the sentencing authority to consider mitigating circumstances. In *Gregg v. Georgia*, we today hold constitutionally valid a capital-sentencing system that directs the jury to consider any mitigating factors, and in *Proffitt v. Florida* we likewise hold constitutional a system that directs the judge and advisory jury to consider certain enumerated mitigating circumstances. The Texas statute does not explicitly speak of mitigating circumstances; it directs only that the jury answer three questions. Thus, the constitutionality of the Texas procedures turns on whether the enumerated questions allow consideration of particularized mitigating factors.

The second Texas statutory question asks the jury to determine "whether there is a probability that the defendant would commit criminal acts of violence that would constitute a continuing threat to society" if he were not sentenced to death. The Texas Court of Criminal Appeals has yet to define precisely the meanings of such terms as "criminal acts of violence" or "continuing threat to society." In the present case, however, it indicated that it will interpret this second question so as to allow a defendant to bring to the jury's attention whatever mitigating circumstances he may be able to show:

> In determining the likelihood that the defendant would be a continuing threat to society, the jury could consider whether the defendant had a significant criminal record. It could consider the range and severity of his prior criminal conduct. It could further look to the age of the defendant and whether or not at the time of the commission of the offense he was acting under duress or under the domination of another. It could also consider whether the defendant was under an extreme form of mental or emotional pressure, something less, perhaps, than insanity, but more than the emotions of the average man, however inflamed, could withstand.

In the only other case in which the Texas Court of Criminal Appeals has upheld a death sentence, it focused on the question of whether any mitigating factors were present in the case. *See Smith v. State*, No. 49,809 (Feb. 18, 1976). In that case the state appellate court examined the sufficiency of the evidence to see if a "yes" answer to question 2 should be sustained. In doing so it examined the defendant's prior conviction on narcotics charges, his subsequent failure to attempt to rehabilitate himself or obtain employment, the fact that he had not acted under duress or as a result of mental or emotional pressure, his apparent willingness to kill, his lack of remorse after the killing, and the conclusion of a psychiatrist that he had a sociopathic personality and that his patterns of conduct would be the same in the future as they had been in the past.

Thus, Texas law essentially requires that one of five aggravating circumstances be found before a defendant can be found guilty of capital murder, and that in considering whether to impose a death sentence the jury may be asked to consider whatever evidence of mitigating circumstances the defense can bring before it. It thus appears that, as in Georgia and Florida, the Texas capital-sentencing procedure guides and focuses the jury's objective consideration of the particularized circumstances of the individual offense and the individual offender before it can impose a sentence of death.

Focusing on the second statutory question that Texas requires a jury to answer in considering whether to impose a death sentence, the petitioner argues that it is impossible to predict future behavior and that the question is so vague as to be meaningless. It is, of course, not easy to predict future behavior. The fact that such a determination is difficult, however, does not mean that it cannot be made. Indeed, prediction of future criminal conduct is an essential element in many of the decisions rendered throughout our criminal justice system. The decision whether to admit a defendant to bail, for instance, must often turn on a judge's prediction of the defendant's future conduct. And any sentencing authority must predict a convicted person's probable future conduct when it engages in the process of determining what punishment to impose. For those sentenced to prison, these same predictions must be made by parole authorities. The task that a Texas jury must perform in answering the statutory question in issue is thus basically no different from the task performed countless times each day throughout the American system of criminal justice. What is essential is that the jury have before it all possible relevant information about the individual defendant whose fate it must determine. Texas law clearly assures that all such evidence will be adduced.

We conclude that Texas' capital-sentencing procedures, like those of Georgia and Florida, do not violate the Eighth and Fourteenth Amendments. By narrowing its definition of capital murder, Texas has essentially said that there must be at least one statutory aggravating circumstance in a first-degree murder case before a death sentence may even be considered. By authorizing the defense to bring before the jury at the separate sentencing hearing whatever mitigating circumstances relating to the individual defendant can be adduced, Texas has ensured that the sentencing jury will have adequate guidance to enable it to perform its sentencing function. By providing prompt judicial review of the jury's decision in a court with statewide jurisdiction, Texas has provided a means to promote the evenhanded, rational, and consistent imposition of death sentences under law. Because this system serves to assure that sentences of death will not be "wantonly" or "freakishly" imposed, it does not violate the Constitution. *Furman v. Georgia*, 408 U.S. at 310, (Stewart, J., concurring). Accordingly, the judgment of the Texas Court of Criminal Appeals affirmed.

Notes

1.   If one were writing a headline describing what the Supreme Court did in its five death penalty decisions of 1976, clearly the choice of "structured discretion necessary for a constitutional death penalty" would have been a more logical choice than "jury discretion required for a constitutional death penalty." However, the decision in *Woodson* striking down the North Carolina mandatory-death statute referenced individualized justice as a subsidiary theme. The majority in *Woodson* did say that mandatory death penalty statutes failed "to allow the

particularized consideration of relevant aspects of the character in record of each convicted defendant before the imposition upon him of a sentence of death."

The major thrust of *Woodson* was similar to the approach taken in *Jurek* and *Gregg* by emphasizing that the seemingly discretionless mandatory penalty obscured many discretionary decisions, such as the prosecutor's initial decision to seek the death sentence and the decision of the jury to convict of a capital offense rather than a lesser included offense. The *Woodson* majority failed to recognize any tension between the goals of guided discretion and individualization. To the extent there is a tension between the goals of guidance and individualization, the cases of 1976 emphasize guidance; but much of the later history of the treatment of the death penalty in the decades following *Greg* and *Woodson* focus on the expansion of individualization and the contraction of guidance.

2.   In addition to some type of jury instructions or standards, the most striking change in the procedures used in administering the death penalty in the years since *Furman* has been the use of a bifurcated or two-stage trial, in which the question of the defendant's guilt or innocence is tried in the first phase, and the question of imposing the death penalty or some lesser sanction is considered in a second stage. All states that have capital punishment now provide a bifurcated trial system.

Although the court indicated in the cases affirming the capital punishment systems of Georgia, Florida, and Texas that each system must be examined on an individual basis and that the procedures endorsed in those states are not necessarily essential to a constitutional system of capital punishment, given the uniformity of the practice of a two-part trial and the broad scope of evidence a defendant is now constitutionally entitled to introduce at the sentencing phase, the bifurcated trial appears to be an inevitable part of the system of capital punishment in America.

If guilt/innocence and sentencing are decided in a unitary proceeding, much of the information relevant to the sentencing decision would be inadmissible under typical rules of evidence. A bifurcated trial, therefore, is beneficial for both the prosecution and the defense. For example, when the question is whether the defendant is guilty of the offense charged, a defendant's past criminal record is not generally admissible to show that the defendant is predisposed to commit criminal activity. At the punishment stage, a whole range of information that would not be relevant to the question of guilt or innocence can be introduced to determine the appropriate punishment. In a number of cases since 1976, the Supreme Court has made clear that the defendant has a nearly absolute right to present any potentially mitigating evidence to the jury in a capital case. Dividing a capital trial into two separate hearings allows the defendant to present evidence concerning a host of factors—such as his age, his role in the offense, whether he acted under pressure from another individual, his mental capacity, and whether he was acting under the influence of an intoxicant or an extreme emotional disturbance—even if the evidence of these factors would not be sufficient to provide a defense to the criminal charge. A unitary trial would force a defendant to abandon any chance of winning on the question of guilt or innocence of the charged offense or forego presenting evidence that might persuade the jury to impose a sentence of life imprisonment rather than the death penalty.

3.	In upholding the constitutionality of the Georgia, Texas, and Florida capital punishment statutes, the United States Supreme Court placed particular emphasis on the fact that there was automatic appellate review in each state following a death sentence verdict. Although automatic appellate review remains a common feature, its efficacy in achieving the goals of the 1976 cases is questionable. Despite the emphasis in the 1976 opinions on the protection against arbitrariness through appellate review, appellate courts rarely have conducted a careful review of the proportionality of the death penalty in a particular case as compared with its imposition with others. Particularly when it comes to the sentence imposed rather than the question of guilt or innocence, the law has traditionally left the question of the appropriate sentence to the discretion of the trial court. Appellate courts have been characteristically unwilling to intervene and overturn decisions and, thus, have not functioned as an institution that reviews all cases to help ensure consistency and proportionality in the application of the death penalty, as the Supreme Court appeared to envision in 1976. Appellate review to ensure proportionality over a range of cases was explicitly abandoned as a constitutional imperative in *Pulley v. Harris*, 465 U.S. 43 (1984), in which the Supreme Court affirmed a death penalty despite the refusal of the California Supreme Court to conduct appellate proportionality review.

4.	The Texas capital statute upheld in *Jurek v. Texas* had a number of features in common with other approved systems, such as a bifurcated trial, jury instructions to guide the decision for life or death, and automatic appellate review. The Texas system also had a number of distinct features. Unlike Georgia, which had enumerated aggravated factors from which the jury had to choose at least one at the penalty stage of a bifurcated trial, and, unlike Florida, which required a weighing of aggravating and mitigating factors both of which were legislatively enumerated, the Texas statute narrowed the scope of those eligible for the death penalty at the first stage of trial. The Texas legislature added statutory aggravating requirements to the definition of capital murder, at least one of which had to be proven beyond a reasonable doubt to obtain a death-eligible conviction of capital murder. Thus, much of the narrowing accomplished by considering aggravating and mitigating factors at the punishment phase was already accomplished by a guilty verdict in the first stage in Texas.

5.	If the defendant was convicted of capital murder, the guided punishment phase of trial in Texas took the form of requiring the jury to answer special issues rather than to weigh aggravating and mitigating evidence. An affirmative answer to all three questions resulted in a death sentence. To result in a sentence of life imprisonment, one of the following must occur: (1) a negative answer to any one of the three issues, (2) if the jury was unable to reach a unanimous affirmative conclusion, (3) or if there was a ten-vote negative decision.

Because the same jury that decided the defendant committed some form of aggravated murder in the first stage of trial would decide these punishment issues at the second stage on the basis of all of the evidence presented in both stages, it is apparent that special issues one and three would be unlikely to provide any assistance to a jury in deciding whether to impose the penalty of death because they duplicated questions that had already been resolved adversely to the defendant at the guilt/innocence stage of trial. If there had been any substantial doubt the defendant had not committed the murder intentionally and knowingly, the jury would have acquitted the defendant of capital murder, perhaps, instead finding the defendant guilty of one of the lesser forms of homicide such as involuntary manslaughter, as it was known at that time, which only required proof of a reckless state of mind with regard to the risk of death. Any chance that the jury would convict the defendant of capital murder but answer the first special issue in the negative depended upon a jury finding that, while the defendant killed intentionally and knowingly, he or she did not act "deliberately and with a reasonable expectation that the death of the deceased or another would result."

Special issue number three, which was only submitted if the evidence at trial raised a question about whether the deceased was killed as a result of the defendant's unreasonable response to the provocation of the deceased, suffered from a similar problem of duplicating issues that would have already been decided adversely to the defense. At the time of the *Jurek* decision, the separate crime known as "voluntary manslaughter" was often raised as a lesser-include offense of capital murder or murder. Thus, a jury finding in favor of the defendant on the third special issue at the penalty stage of a capital murder trial would have to be persuaded that, while the defendant's response to provocation was not sufficiently reasonable to find the defendant guilty of voluntary manslaughter rather than murder, it was sufficient to find that the defendant's actions were not an "unreasonable in response" to any provocation.

The duplicative nature of special issues one and three created momentum for a death sentence by placing two of the three special issues in the prosecution's favor in almost every case. The result of these repetitive issues was that the question of whether life imprisonment or the death penalty should be imposed depended entirely on the second special issue, dealing with a defendant's future dangerousness. Whether the Texas system provided constitutionally sufficient guidance of jury discretion in sentencing an opportunity for individualized assessment of mitigating evidence also depended upon the adequacy of the second special issue to achieve these goals.

Mitigating Evidence

To ask the jury to determine life or death beyond a reasonable doubt based upon the highly speculative issue of whether there was a "probability" the defendant would "commit criminal acts of violence that would constitute a continuing threat to society" is a daunting task. Coupling "beyond a reasonable doubt" with the "probability" of future conduct was an oxymoronic pairing that would confuse conscientious and intelligent jurors and merely baffle jurors of lesser diligence. A plausible and dictionary-supported definition of probability includes "any chance of occurrence," an interpretation that would apply to all. On the other hand, to conclude that someone would be dangerous in the future might well be regarded as a conclusion that could never be reached by the high level of certainty required by a beyond a reasonable doubt standard. A standard that arguably could apply to all or to none depending upon interpretation was not a promising vehicle for avoiding the arbitrariness, one of the core problems with capital punishment identified in *Furman*.

Substantial doubts about the Texas special issues would come to fruition in the *Penry* case that will appear below. First, a brief discussion of some of the constitutional law developments that set the table for *Penry* and the Texas legislative response that modified, but did not abandon, the Texas special issues.

Between the *Jurek* decision in 1976 and the *Penry* decision in 1989, developments in constitutional death penalty law reflected the tension between two stated goals from the cases of 1976 concerning capital punishment: (1) the need for guided discretion to achieve consistency in imposing the death penalty and (2) the goal of individualized consideration of the offender and the offense, which has a tendency to promote its opposite.

The rise of individualization was due in part with disenchantment with the enterprise of finding fair and comprehensive standards for deciding who should live and who should die. For example, in *Walton v. Arizona*, 497 U.S. 639 (1990), the Court upheld an aggravating factor that the murder had to be especially heinous, atrocious, cruel, or depraved, although similar types of standards had been found constitutionally inadequate on the theory these words could describe any murder. Although the majority in *Walton* admitted this language was unconstitutionally vague by itself, by a five to four vote the Court found the narrowing instruction by the Arizona Supreme Court defining "especially cruel" to mean the infliction of mental anguish or physical abuse before the victim's death, and mental anguish to include the victim's uncertainty about his or her fate, was sufficient to save the statute from unconstitutional vagueness as applied in Walton's case.

A similar minimal narrowing construction of an Idaho statute using "utter disregard for human life" was found sufficient in *Arave v. Creech*, 507 U.S. 463 (1993). The vagueness of this aggravating factor was cured by a judicial construction of a "cold-blooded, pitiless slayer." "Pitiless" it was conceded added little but "cold-blooded" was found to be sufficiently clarifying by the majority.

Constitutional doubts about the sufficiency of the guidance provided by the Texas system were eased by the cases tolerating vague standards, allowing non-statutory and non-uniform standards to be used and by allowing duplication of issues already determined in the first stage of a capital trial to be repeated in instructing a jury about deciding whether to impose the death penalty. However, constitutional doubts about the Texas statute were growing because of its claimed deficiency with regard to another goal—the required individualized of the capital sentencing decision based upon a consideration of any possibly mitigating evidence.

The seeds of the requirement of individualization were planted in the 1976 cases in *Woodson* and *Roberts*, which rejected a mandatory death penalty. Those cases established that, even if a state accomplishes narrowing the class of those eligible for the death penalty in the guilt/innocence stage of trial, there must be a punishment hearing to allow the jury to give individual consideration to the character and circumstances of the defendant and the defendant's offense. If uniformity of treatment is to be achieved, consistency with regard to the relevant criteria would appear to be necessary, and the allowance of the consideration of every individual factor that a defendant might wish to raise threatens that consistency. The tension between the uniformity of treatment required to avoid arbitrary infliction and the required individualization highlighted in *Woodson* has been the subject of much debate by commentators and by members of the United States Supreme Court. Justice Scalia in his concurrence in *Walton v. Arizona* found the two goals incompatible and urged the court to eliminate the individualization requirement in favor of the avoidance of arbitrariness, stating:

> Pursuant to *Furman*, and in order "to achieve a more rational and more equitable administration of the death penalty," we require that States "channel the sentencer's discretion by 'clear and objective standards' that provide 'specific and detailed guidance.' In the next breath, however, we say that "the State *cannot* channel the sentencer's discretion . . . to consider any relevant [mitigating] information offered by the defendant," and that the sentencer must enjoy unconstrained discretion to decide whether any sympathetic factors bearing on the defendant or the crime indicate that he does not "deserve to be sentenced to death." The latter requirement quite obviously destroys whatever rationality and predictability the former requirement was designed to achieve.

> Since the individualized determination is a unitary one (does this defendant deserve death for this crime?) once one says each sentencer must be able to answer "no" for whatever reason it deems morally sufficient, . . . it becomes impossible to claim that the Constitution requires consistency and rationality among sentencing determinations to be preserved by strictly limiting the reasons for which each sentencer can say "yes."

Justice Blackmun, in a well-publicized opinion to the denial of certiorari in *Callins v. Collins*, agreed with Justice Scalia's analysis, but not his solution. Blackmun maintained that both consistency and individualized consideration were required by the Court's prior decisions and that the two goals were incompatible. However, Justice Blackmun concluded, in one of his last opinions before his retirement that the solution was to strike down all death penalty statutes.

Neither the approach of Justice Scalia nor that of Justice Blackmun have prevailed. In fact, the requirement of individualization that Justice Scalia would abandon has risen as the prime constitutional prerequisite in capital cases. Accommodating the tension between individualization and consistency has been accomplished in part by envisioning two distinct stages of the death penalty process: eligibility and selection. Unlike, Justice Scalia, who said in *Walton* that there is only one question—whether the defendant will be sentenced to death—

Justice Stevens in his *Walton* dissent discounted the tension between what others had called competing goals. He explained that the narrowing function for identifying statutory aggravating circumstances operates at an eligibility stage to promote consistency while the individualized consideration requirement operates at the subsequent punishment stage when the decision whether to impose death penalty on a particular convicted defendant is made.

The rise of the requirement of individualized consideration of any mitigating evidence begins with *Lockett v. Ohio*, 438 U.S. 586 (1978). Sandra Lockett was only 21 years of age when she helped plan a pawnshop robbery. Lockett's role in the crime was merely to drive the get-away vehicle from the robbery. Because one of her accomplice's killed the pawn shop owner, under principles of criminal law, Lockett was also responsible for the homicide as a party to the crime of felony murder. Although Lockett could not have been convicted of capital murder in Texas (because only an intentional murder can be the predicate for a capital conviction under the Texas capital murder statute), Ohio law lacked this eligibility limitation.

The Ohio capital statute recognized three mitigating factors that the jury could find was a reason to vote against the death penalty: victim participation; the influence of duress, coercion, or strong provocation on the defendant; or that the offense was primarily the product of defendant's psychosis or mental deficiency. None of these factors applied to Lockett. Lockett was convicted and sentenced to death. The Supreme Court reversed the conviction, holding that in all but the rarest capital cases, "the sentencer [may] . . . not be precluded from considering, as a mitigating factor, any aspect of a defendant's character or record and any of the circumstances of the offense that the defendant proffers as a basis for sentence less than death." This passage provided a definition of the term mitigating evidence that has been used in death penalty cases ever since and has been incorporated into the revised Texas death penalty statute. Although the death penalty criteria were reasonable, to the extent that the Ohio system left no room to allow Lockett to raise the mitigating circumstances of her youth and minor role in the offense, the system as applied to Lockett was unconstitutional.

In *Eddings v. Oklahoma*, 455 U.S. 104 (1982), and *Skipper v. South Carolina*, 476 U. S.1 (1986), the court made clear that *Lockett* required more than the right to present mitigating evidence. In *Eddings*, the sixteen-year-old defendant pleaded guilty to capital murder before a judge and introduced evidence relating to his background, including the fact that he had been neglected by his mother, beaten by his father, and he was a product of a broken home. At the conclusion of the evidence, the judge found the aggravating circumstances outweighed the mitigating circumstances and imposed the death penalty. In reaching this decision, the judge specifically stated that, under Oklahoma law, he could not "consider the fact of this young man's violent background." The United States Supreme Court reversed the conviction, holding that the imposition of the death penalty was in violation of the principle established in *Lockett* because the sentencer refused to consider, as a matter of law, "relevant mitigating evidence."

In *Skipper*, the defendant was prevented from presenting testimony at the penalty stage of trial by two jailers and one regular visitor to the prison that Skipper had "made a good adjustment" during his time in jail. The Supreme Court again reversed the death sentence, holding that the exclusion of the evidence was in violation of the Eighth Amendment as defined in *Lockett*. The evidence of Skipper's adjustment in jail was said to be relevant to his "probable future conduct if sentenced to life imprisonment," and that his "disposition to make a well-behaved and peaceful adjustment to life in prison is itself an aspect of his character that is by its nature relevant to the sentencing determination." *Skipper* takes a very broad view of what is considered "mitigating evidence." The evidence in *Eddings* looked to the past of the accused while the evidence in *Skipper* looked to the future. The opinion in *Skipper* stated that any evidence that "might serve as a basis for a sentence less than death" was admissible, and the defendant could not be refused the opportunity to present such evidence to the jury.

The *Lockett* case established the important principle that the defense could not be precluded from introducing any mitigating evidence, a term that was broadly defined to include "any aspect of a defendant's character or record and any of the circumstances of the offense." *Eddings* held that the defendant is entitled to a fact-finder who is willing to consider the mitigating evidence. Required consideration does not mean that the judge or jury who decides whether the death penalty will be imposed has to be persuaded by the mitigating evidence but the decision-maker must not refuse to consider the mitigating evidence. In a case that was to change the Texas system of capital punishment, the United States Supreme Court provided in *Penry v. Lynaugh* that the instructions given to the jury must provide the jury with an opportunity to give meaningful consideration, or a "reasoned moral response" to mitigating evidence. Although Penry was permitted to introduce evidence at the punishment phase of his Texas capital murder trial that he suffered from organic brain damage and moderate retardation, and despite the fact that the Texas death penalty statute had been upheld as facially constitutional in the 1976 decision of *Jurek v. Texas*, the Supreme Court reversed Penry's conviction in a landmark decision that appears below.

Penry v. Lynaugh

492 U.S. 302 (1989)

Justice O'Connor delivered the opinion of the Court.

In this case, we must decide whether petitioner, Johnny Paul Penry, was sentenced to death in violation of the Eighth Amendment because the jury was not instructed that it could consider and give effect to his mitigating evidence in imposing its sentence. We must also decide whether the Eighth Amendment categorically prohibits Penry's execution because he is mentally retarded.

On the morning of October 25, 1979, Pamela Carpenter was brutally raped, beaten, and stabbed with a pair of scissors in her home in Livingston, Texas. She died a few hours later in the course of emergency treatment. Before she died, she described her assailant. Her description led two local sheriff's deputies to suspect Penry, who had recently been released on parole after conviction on another rape charge. Penry subsequently gave two statements confessing to the crime and was charged with capital murder.

At a competency hearing held before trial, a clinical psychologist, Dr. Jerome Brown, testified that Penry was mentally retarded. As a child, Penry was diagnosed as having organic brain damage, which was probably caused by trauma to the brain at birth. Penry was tested over the years as having an IQ between 50 and 63, which indicates mild to moderate retardation. Dr. Brown's own testing before the trial indicated that Penry had an IQ of 54. Dr. Brown's evaluation also revealed that Penry, who was 22 years old at the time of the crime, had the mental age of a 6½-year-old, which means that "he has the ability to learn and the learning or the knowledge of the average 6½ year old kid." Penry's social maturity, or ability to function in the world, was that of a 9 or 10-year-old. Dr. Brown testified that "there's a point at which anyone with [Penry's] IQ is always incompetent, but, you know, this man is more in the borderline range."

The jury found Penry competent to stand trial. The guilt-innocence phase of the trial began [and the] . . . trial court determined that Penry's confessions were voluntary, and they were introduced into evidence. At trial, Penry raised an insanity defense and presented the testimony of a psychiatrist, Dr. Jose Garcia. Dr. Garcia testified that Penry suffered from organic brain damage and moderate retardation, which resulted in poor impulse control and an inability to learn from experience. Dr. Garcia indicated that Penry's brain damage was probably caused at birth but may have been caused by beatings and multiple injuries to the brain at an early age. In Dr. Garcia's judgment, Penry was suffering from an organic brain disorder at the time of the offense which made it impossible for him to appreciate the wrongfulness of his conduct or to conform his conduct to the law.

Penry's mother testified at trial that Penry was unable to learn in school and never finished the first grade. Penry's sister testified that their mother had frequently beaten him over the head with a belt when he was a child. Penry was also routinely locked in his room without access to a toilet for long periods of time. As a youngster, Penry was in and out of a number of

295

state schools and hospitals, until his father removed him from state schools altogether when he was 12. Penry's aunt subsequently struggled for over a year to teach Penry how to print his name.

The State introduced the testimony of two psychiatrists to rebut the testimony of Dr. Garcia. Dr. Kenneth Vogtsberger testified that although Penry was a person of limited mental ability, he was not suffering from any mental illness or defect at the time of the crime, and that he knew the difference between right and wrong and had the potential to honor the law. In his view, Penry had characteristics consistent with an antisocial personality, including an inability to learn from experience and a tendency to be impulsive and to violate society's norms. He testified further that Penry's low IQ scores underestimated his alertness and understanding of what went on around him.

Dr. Felix Peebles also testified for the State that Penry was legally sane at the time of the offense and had a "full-blown anti-social personality." In addition, Dr. Peebles testified that he personally diagnosed Penry as being mentally retarded in 1973 and again in 1977, and that Penry "had a very bad life generally, bringing up." In Dr. Peebles' view, Penry "had been socially and emotionally deprived and he had not learned to read and write adequately." Although they disagreed with the defense psychiatrist over the extent and cause of Penry's mental limitations, both psychiatrists for the State acknowledged that Penry was a person of extremely limited mental ability, and that he seemed unable to learn from his mistakes.

The jury rejected Penry's insanity defense and found him guilty of capital murder. The following day, at the close of the penalty hearing, the jury decided the sentence to be imposed on Penry by answering three "special issues":

> (1) whether the conduct of the defendant that caused the death of the deceased was committed deliberately and with the reasonable expectation that the death of the deceased or another would result;

> (2) whether there is a probability that the defendant would commit criminal acts of violence that would constitute a continuing threat to society; and

> (3) if raised by the evidence, whether the conduct of the defendant in killing the deceased was unreasonable in response to the provocation, if any, by the deceased.

TEX. CODE CRIM. PROC. ANN. Art. 37.071(b) (West).

Defense counsel raised a number of objections to the proposed charge to the jury. With respect to the first special issue, he objected that the charge failed to define the term "deliberately." With respect to the second special issue, he objected that the charge failed to define the terms "probability," "criminal acts of violence," and "continuing threat to society." Defense counsel also objected to the charge because it failed to "authorize a discretionary grant of mercy based upon the existence of mitigating circumstances" and because it "fail[ed] to require as a condition to the assessment of the death penalty that the State show beyond a reasonable doubt that any aggravating circumstances found to exist outweigh any mitigating circumstances." In addition, the charge failed to instruct the jury that it may take into consideration all of the evidence whether aggravating or mitigating in nature which was submitted in the full trial of the case. Defense counsel also objected that, in light of Penry's mental retardation, permitting the jury to assess the death penalty in this case amounted to cruel and unusual punishment prohibited by the Eighth Amendment.

The jury answered "yes" to all three special issues, and Penry was sentenced to death. The Texas Court of Criminal Appeals affirmed his conviction and sentence on direct appeal. That court held that terms such as "deliberately," "probability," and "continuing threat to society" used in the special issues need not be defined in the jury charge because the jury would know their common meaning. The court concluded that Penry was allowed to present all relevant mitigating evidence at the punishment hearing, and that there was no constitutional infirmity in failing to require the jury to find that aggravating circumstances outweighed mitigating ones or in failing to authorize a discretionary grant of mercy based upon the existence of mitigating circumstances. The court also held that imposition of the death penalty was not prohibited by virtue of Penry's mental retardation. This Court denied certiorari on direct review.

Penry then filed this federal habeas corpus petition challenging his death sentence. The District Court denied relief, [and] the Court of Appeals for the Fifth Circuit affirmed the District Court's judgment.

Penry does not challenge the facial validity of the Texas death penalty statute, which was upheld against an Eighth Amendment challenge in *Jurek v. Texas*. Nor does he dispute that some types of mitigating evidence can be fully considered by the sentencer in the absence of special jury instructions. See *Franklin v. Lynaugh*, 487 U.S. 164 (1988). Instead, Penry argues that, on the facts of this case, the jury was unable to fully consider and give effect to the mitigating evidence of his mental retardation and abused background in answering the three special issues.

Underlying *Lockett* and *Eddings* is the principle that punishment should be directly related to the personal culpability of the criminal defendant. If the sentencer is to make an individualized assessment of the appropriateness of the death penalty, "evidence about the defendant's background and character is relevant because of the belief, long held by this society, that defendants who commit criminal acts that are attributable to a disadvantaged background, or to emotional and mental problems, may be less culpable than defendants who have no such excuse." Moreover, *Eddings* makes clear that it is not enough simply to allow the defendant to present mitigating evidence to the sentencer. The sentencer must also be able to consider and give effect to that evidence in imposing sentence. Only then can we be sure that the sentencer has treated the defendant as a "uniquely individual human being" and has made a reliable determination that death is the appropriate sentence. "Thus, the sentence imposed at the penalty stage should reflect a reasoned moral response to the defendant's background, character, and crime."

Although Penry offered mitigating evidence of his mental retardation and abused childhood as the basis for a sentence of life imprisonment rather than death, the jury that sentenced him was only able to express its views on the appropriate sentence by answering three questions: Did Penry act deliberately when he murdered Pamela Carpenter? Is there a probability that he will be dangerous in the future? Did he act unreasonably in response to provocation? The

297

jury was never instructed that it could consider the evidence offered by Penry as mitigating evidence and that it could give mitigating effect to that evidence in imposing sentence.

Like the petitioner in *Franklin v. Lynaugh*, Penry contends that in the absence of his requested jury instructions, the Texas death penalty statute was applied in an unconstitutional manner by precluding the jury from acting upon the particular mitigating evidence he introduced. *Franklin* was the first case considered by this Court since *Jurek* to address a claim concerning the treatment of mitigating evidence under the Texas special issues. Like *Jurek* itself, *Franklin* did not produce a majority opinion for the Court. The Franklin plurality, and the two concurring Justices, concluded that Franklin was not sentenced to death in violation of the Eighth Amendment because the jury was free to give effect to his mitigating evidence of good behavior in prison by answering "no" to the question on future dangerousness.

In *Franklin*, however, the five concurring and dissenting Justices did not share the plurality's categorical reading of *Jurek*. In the plurality's view, *Jurek* had expressly and unconditionally upheld the manner in which mitigating evidence is considered under the special issues. In contrast, five Members of the Court read *Jurek* as not precluding a claim that, in a particular case, the jury was unable to fully consider the mitigating evidence introduced by a defendant in answering the special issues. Indeed, both the concurrence and the dissent understood *Jurek* as resting fundamentally on the express assurance that the special issues would permit the jury to fully consider all the mitigating evidence a defendant introduced that was relevant to the defendant's background and character and to the circumstances of the offense. Moreover, both the concurrence and the dissent stressed that "the right to have the sentencer consider and weigh relevant mitigating evidence would be meaningless unless the sentencer was also permitted to give effect to its consideration" in imposing sentence.

The concurrence in *Franklin* concluded that there was no Eighth Amendment violation in that case because Franklin's evidence of his good prison behavior had no clear relevance to his character other than to demonstrate his ability to live in a highly structured prison environment without endangering others. Thus, the jury was able to give effect to the mitigating force of this evidence in answering the second special issue. The concurrence noted, however:

> If . . . petitioner had introduced mitigating evidence about his background or character or the circumstances of the crime that was not relevant to the special verdict questions, or that had relevance to the defendant's moral culpability beyond the scope of the special verdict questions, the jury instructions would have provided the jury with no vehicle for expressing its "reasoned moral response" to that evidence. If this were such a case, then we would have to decide whether the jury's inability to give effect to that evidence amounted to an Eighth Amendment violation.

Penry argues that his mitigating evidence of mental retardation and childhood abuse has relevance to his moral culpability beyond the scope of the special issues, and that the jury was unable to express its "reasoned moral response" to that evidence in determining whether death was the appropriate punishment. We agree. Thus, we reject the State's contrary argument that the jury was able to consider and give effect to all of Penry's mitigating evidence in answering the special issues without any jury instructions on mitigating evidence.

The first special issue asks whether the defendant acted "deliberately and with the reasonable expectation that the death of the deceased . . . would result." Neither the Texas Legislature nor the Texas Court of Criminal Appeals have defined the term "deliberately," and the jury was not instructed on the term, so we do not know precisely what meaning the jury gave to it. Assuming, however, that the jurors in this case understood "deliberately" to mean something more than that Penry was guilty of "intentionally" committing murder, those jurors may still have been unable to give effect to Penry's mitigating evidence in answering the first special issue.

Penry's mental retardation was relevant to the question whether he was capable of acting "deliberately," but it also "had relevance to [his] moral culpability beyond the scope of the special verdict question." Personal culpability is not solely a function of a defendant's capacity to act "deliberately." A rational juror at the penalty phase of the trial could have concluded, in light of Penry's confession, that he deliberately killed Pamela Carpenter to escape detection. Because Penry was mentally retarded, however, and thus less able than a normal adult to control his impulses or to evaluate the consequences of his conduct, and because of his history of childhood abuse, that same juror could also conclude that Penry was less morally "culpable than defendants who have no such excuse," but who acted "deliberately" as that term is commonly understood.

In the absence of jury instructions defining "deliberately" in a way that would clearly direct the jury to consider fully Penry's mitigating evidence as it bears on his personal culpability, we cannot be sure that the jury was able to give effect to the mitigating evidence of Penry's mental retardation and history of abuse in answering the first special issue. Without such a special instruction, a juror who believed that Penry's retardation and background diminished his moral culpability and made imposition of the death penalty unwarranted would be unable to give effect to that conclusion if the juror also believed that Penry committed the crime "deliberately." Thus, we cannot be sure that the jury's answer to the first special issue reflected a "reasoned moral response" to Penry's mitigating evidence.

The second special issue asks "whether there is a probability that the defendant would commit criminal acts of violence that would constitute a continuing threat to society." The mitigating evidence concerning Penry's mental retardation indicated that one effect of his retardation is his inability to learn from his mistakes. Although this evidence is relevant to the second issue, it is relevant only as an aggravating factor because it suggests a "yes" answer to the question of future dangerousness. The prosecutor argued at the penalty hearing that there was "a very strong probability, based on the history of this defendant, his previous criminal record, and the psychiatric testimony that we've had in this case, that the defendant will continue to commit acts of this nature." Even in a prison setting, the prosecutor argued, Penry could hurt doctors, nurses, librarians, or teachers who worked in the prison.

Penry's mental retardation and history of abuse is thus a two-edged sword: it may diminish his blameworthiness for his crime even as it indicates that there is a probability that he will be dangerous in the future. As Judge Reavley wrote for the Court of Appeals below:

> What was the jury to do if it decided that Penry, because of retardation, arrested emotional development and a troubled youth, should not be executed? If anything, the

evidence made it more likely, not less likely, that the jury would answer the second question yes. It did not allow the jury to consider a major thrust of Penry's evidence as mitigating evidence.

The second special issue, therefore, did not provide a vehicle for the jury to give mitigating effect to Penry's evidence of mental retardation and childhood abuse.

The third special issue asks "whether the conduct of the defendant in killing the deceased was unreasonable in response to the provocation, if any, by the deceased." On this issue, the State argued that Penry stabbed Pamela Carpenter with a pair of scissors not in response to provocation, but "for the purpose of avoiding detection." Penry's own confession indicated that he did not stab the victim after she wounded him superficially with a scissors during a struggle, but rather killed her after her struggle had ended and she was lying helpless. Even if a juror concluded that Penry's mental retardation and arrested emotional development rendered him less culpable for his crime than a normal adult that would not necessarily diminish the "unreasonableness" of his conduct in response to "the provocation, if any, by the deceased." Thus, a juror who believed Penry lacked the moral culpability to be sentenced to death could not express that view in answering the third special issue if she also concluded that Penry's action was not a reasonable response to provocation.

The State contends, notwithstanding the three interrogatories, that Penry was free to introduce and argue the significance of his mitigating circumstances to the jury. In fact, defense counsel did argue that if a juror believed that Penry, because of the mitigating evidence of his mental retardation and abused background, did not deserve to be put to death, the juror should vote "no" on one of the special issues even if she believed the State had proved that the answer should be "yes." Thus, Penry's counsel stressed the evidence of Penry's mental retardation and abused background, and asked the jurors, "[C]an you be proud to be a party to putting a man to death with that affliction?" He urged the jury to answer the first special issue "no" because "it would be the just answer, and I think it would be a proper answer." As for the prediction of the prosecution psychiatrist that Penry was likely to continue to get into trouble, the defense argued:

> That may be true. But, a boy with this mentality, with this mental affliction, even though you have found that issue against us as to insanity, I don't think that there is any question in a single one of your juror's [sic] minds that there is something definitely wrong, basically, with this boy. And I think there is not a single one of you that doesn't believe that this boy had brain damage.

In effect, defense counsel urged the jury to "think about each of those special issues and see if you don't find that we're inquiring into the mental state of the defendant in each and every one of them."

In rebuttal, the prosecution countered by stressing that the jurors had taken an oath to follow the law, and that they must follow the instructions they were given in answering the special issues:

> You've all taken an oath to follow the law and you know what the law is. In answering these questions based on the evidence and following the law, and that's all that I asked

you to do, is to go out and look at the evidence. The burden of proof is on the State as it has been from the beginning, and we accept that burden. And I honestly believe that we have more than met that burden, and that's the reason that you didn't hear Mr. Newman [defense attorney] argue. He didn't pick out these issues and point out to you where the State had failed to meet this burden. He didn't point out the weaknesses in the State's case because, ladies and gentlemen, I submit to you we've met our burden . . . [Y]our job as jurors and your duty as jurors is not to act on your emotions, but to act on the law as the Judge has given it to you, and on the evidence that you have heard in this courtroom, then answer those questions accordingly.

In light of the prosecutor's argument, and in the absence of appropriate jury instructions, a reasonable juror could well have believed that there was no vehicle for expressing the view that Penry did not deserve to be sentenced to death based upon his mitigating evidence.

The State conceded at oral argument in this Court that if a juror concluded that Penry acted deliberately and was likely to be dangerous in the future, but also concluded that because of his mental retardation he was not sufficiently culpable to deserve the death penalty, that juror would be unable to give effect to that mitigating evidence under the instructions given in this case. The State contends, however, that to instruct the jury that it could render a discretionary grant of mercy, or say "no" to the death penalty, based on Penry's mitigating evidence, would be to return to the sort of unbridled discretion that led to *Furman v. Georgia*, 408 U.S. 238 (1972).

We disagree. To be sure, *Furman* held that "in order to minimize the risk that the death penalty would be imposed on a capriciously selected group of offenders, the decision to impose it had to be guided by standards so that the sentencing authority would focus on the particularized circumstances of the crime and the defendant." But as we made clear in *Gregg*, so long as the class of murderers subject to capital punishment is narrowed, there is no constitutional infirmity in a procedure that allows a jury to recommend mercy based on the mitigating evidence introduced by a defendant.

It is precisely because the punishment should be directly related to the personal culpability of the defendant that the jury must be allowed to consider and give effect to mitigating evidence relevant to a defendant's character or record or the circumstances of the offense. Rather than creating the risk of an unguided emotional response, full consideration of evidence that mitigates against the death penalty is essential if the jury is to give a "reasoned moral response to the defendant's background, character, and crime." In order to ensure "reliability in the determination that death is the appropriate punishment in a specific case," the jury must be able to consider and give effect to any mitigating evidence relevant to a defendant's background and character or the circumstances of the crime.

In this case, in the absence of instructions informing the jury that it could consider and give effect to the mitigating evidence of Penry's mental retardation and abused background by declining to impose the death penalty, we conclude that the jury was not provided with a vehicle for expressing its "reasoned moral response" to that evidence in rendering its sentencing decision. Our reasoning in *Lockett* and *Eddings* thus compels a remand for resentencing so that we do not "risk that the death penalty will be imposed in spite of factors which may call for a

301

less severe penalty." "When the choice is between life and death, that risk is unacceptable and incompatible with the commands of the Eighth and Fourteenth Amendments."

Notes

1.   The most immediate effect of the decision in *Penry* was a flood of litigation by defendants who had been convicted under Texas procedures that had been in place for over a decade. Because *Jurek* had not been overruled, the Texas capital punishment scheme was still facially constitutional, but courts were now required to decide whether the application of the Texas statute had been applied unconstitutionally under the facts of the particular case as it had been in the *Penry* case, because the mitigating evidence in that case had a mitigating aspect that could not be adequately considered under the Texas special issues.

Because the Texas statute was only unconstitutional as applied to someone like Penry, the question was whether the litigant was like him or more like the defendant in *Franklin v. Lynaugh*, 487 U.S. 164 (1988), whose claimed mitigating evidence was his good prison disciplinary record. Unlike the two-edged sword of *Penry* where his evidence was both mitigating but aggravating to the future dangerousness special issue, Franklin's good prison record could be fully considered under the future dangerousness special issue.

2.   The *Penry* decision created a dilemma for trial courts concerning whether to continue to administer the Texas death penalty statutes in the same manner as before *Penry* or whether the application of this system in a particular case would constitute an applied constitutional violation. For those who had not yet been tried, trial courts had to decide how to cope with the new dictates of *Penry* in the absence of legislative guidance in the interim between the *Penry* decision in 1989 and the legislative modification of the Texas system in response that did not occur until 1991.

One common response was for the trial court to inform the jury that it should answer one of the special issues in the negative even if evidence supported a yes answer if the jury believed there was mitigating evidence that suggested a sentence of less than death was appropriate. This attempt to place a band-aid on the gaping wound of the Texas capital procedures after *Penry* essentially required court-sponsored jury nullification to achieve a life sentence. This approach was rejected as inadequate by the United States Supreme Court in several cases, including John Paul Penry's own case upon retrial for capital murder in *Penry v. Johnson*, 532 U.S. 782 (2001). In *Penry II*, the Court found that the "ambiguous" and "internally inconsistent" nullification instruction failed to afford the jury an adequate vehicle by which to consider the proffered mitigating evidence of mental retardation.

3.   To address the concerns raised in *Penry*, the legislature made several statutory revisions to place broad consideration of mitigating circumstances into Texas capital sentencing. The former system developed in the wake of *Furman* and facially approved in *Jurek* remains in effect for offenses committed prior to September 1, 1999, the effective date of a more extensively revised system discussed more fully in the next section. Although the number of cases subject to the former system has declined, it is possible that the old statute could still be used in a case

because of the absence of a statute of limitation for the offense of capital murder. In cases tried under the former statute, the three special issues dealing with deliberateness, future dangerousness, and provocation are used as before, but, in addition, a fourth issue is submitted to the jury, often referred to as the *Penry* issue. The jury is instructed that, if it unanimously agrees that the answer to the other special issues is "yes," that the defendant acted deliberately, without provocation, and that there is a probability that the defendant will be dangerous in the future, the court instructs the jury to consider the following question:

> Whether, taking into consideration all of the evidence, including the circumstances of the offense, the defendant's character and background, and the personal moral culpability of the defendant, there is a sufficient mitigating circumstance or circumstances to warrant that a sentence of life imprisonment rather than a death sentence be imposed.

4.   The heart of the change to the Texas system established by the legislature for offenses committed after September 1, 1999, is the addition of the *Penry* issue that is added to the other special issues for offense committed prior to this date. However, for offenses committed after September 1, 1999, more extensive revisions to the Texas procedures apply. The former special issues dealing with deliberateness and provocation are eliminated, although future dangerousness is retained with the same wording as in the earlier statute. In capital cases in which the jury charge at the guilt/innocence stage permits the jury to find the defendant guilty as a party to the offense under Sections 7.01 and 7.02, Texas Penal Code (but not in cases where no such instruction is given because the indictment and proof only show a basis for finding the defendant guilty as the principal actor), the jury is instructed to consider "[w]hether the defendant actually caused the death of the deceased or did not actually cause the death of the deceased but intended to kill the deceased or another or anticipated that a human life would be taken."

As with the previous procedure, an affirmative response to this question (and the future dangerousness inquiry) requires a unanimous jury finding. Ten or more jurors must agree to enter a negative response, but the legislature added a provision that jurors need not agree on what particular evidence supports a negative response to this issue. Thus, the future dangerousness special issue is submitted in every case in which the jury has found the defendant guilty of capital murder and requires a unanimous "yes" vote for the jury to consider other issues, while the issue concerning the defendant's intent or awareness that human life would be taken is submitted only in cases where there is evidence the defendant is guilty as a party to the offense. Again, a unanimous jury finding of "yes" to this inquiry is necessary for the jury to consider the *Penry* issue while ten votes of no for either the future dangerousness or party's intent question are needed for the jury to return a verdict for life imprisonment.

This new special issue concerning the intent or awareness of death when a party liability theory was involved probably was designed to resolve any potential problems associated with imposing a death sentence on a "non-triggerman" capital defendant which was identified by the United States Supreme Court in cases such as *Enmund v. Florida*, 458 U.S. 782 (1982), which overturned a death sentence for a getaway driver in a robbery that turned deadly even though the defendant himself did not kill, attempt to kill or intend that a killing take place. However, unlike many other states that do not filter out those convicted of murder on a felony murder theory, Texas only permits a conviction of capital murder if the type of murder proved is one that involves intent to kill or knowledge that death will occur. The felony-murder doctrine allows a defendant to be convicted of a killing if the death occurred during the commission or immediate flight from the felony, even if the death was unintentional or accidental. In a state like Florida, the constitutionally required limitation of death to those who had either an intent to kill or a form of "reckless indifference to the value of human life" must occur at punishment stage of trial because felony murder may serve as a predicate for capital murder. However, in Texas, the issue of whether the defendant intended or anticipated death would occur must have been resolved in favor of the State beyond a reasonable doubt or there would not be a capital sentence punishment stage.

The new special issue given only in cases in which guilt as a party is possible is not responsive to the *Penry* concerns about full consideration of mitigating evidence, but other new provisions directly address this problem. The legislature expanded the previous definition of the evidentiary scope regarding "any matter" the court "deems relevant" to sentence expressly to "include evidence of the defendant's background or character or the circumstances of the offense that mitigates against the imposition of the death penalty." The legislature also added a required instruction that, in determining the special issues of future dangerousness and the new party's intent inquiry, the jury should consider all evidence admitted at the guilt and punishment stages, "including evidence of the defendant's background or character or the circumstances of the offense that militates for or mitigates against the imposition of the death penalty."

The most significant change added by the legislature was a new mitigating circumstances special issue which the capital jury must answer if it has unanimously, affirmatively answered the other special issues. This new required instruction is the same *Penry* instruction now required even for offenses committed before the effective date of the new statute:

> Whether, taking into consideration all of the evidence, including the circumstances of the offense, the defendant's character and background, and the personal moral culpability of the defendant, there is a sufficient mitigating circumstance or circumstances to warrant that a sentence of life imprisonment rather than a death sentence be imposed.

The statute makes clear that the jurors are not required to agree on what particular evidence supports an affirmative response to the issue, however, ten or more jurors must agree in order to answer this inquiry affirmatively. A negative response requires unanimous jury agreement. "Mitigating evidence" regarding this special issue is defined as evidence that "a juror might regard as reducing the defendant's moral blameworthiness." If the jury returns unanimous affirmative findings regarding the other special issues and a unanimous negative finding regarding the mitigating circumstances issue, the trial court "shall" sentence the defendant to death.

5.   Not all of the changes to the Texas system of capital punishment have been amendments in response to the decision of the United States Supreme Court in *Penry*. In addition to the legislative revisions to procedures designed to deal with the requirements of *Penry*, the substantive scope of the capital murder statute has undergone some expansion that is unrelated to that case's dictates. Capital murder in section 19.03 of the Texas Penal Code remains predicated on the first type of murder in the murder statute, section 19.02, which requires an intentional or knowing killing. The other forms of murder—killing with the intent to cause serious bodily injury but not death and felony murder—remain insufficient.

The five aggravating methods of elevating murder to capital murder that existed in the statute upheld in *Jurek* also remain: (1) murder of a person known by the defendant to be a peace officer or fireman who is acting in the lawful discharge of an official duty; (2) an intentional murder in the course of committing or attempting to commit kidnapping, burglary, robbery, aggravated rape, or arson; (3) committing murder either by employing another to commit the offense for remuneration or the promise of remuneration or murdering for remuneration or its promise; (4) committing murder while escaping or attempting to escape from a penal institution; or (5) the commission of a murder by a person incarcerated in a penal institution against an employee in of the penal institution. However, an "intentional murder during enumerated crimes" has been expanded to include the renamed offense of aggravated sexual assault, obstruction or retaliation, and some forms of terroristic threat. Murder by an incarcerated person has been expanded beyond an employee victim to any victim if the murder was committed with "the intent to establish, maintain, or participate in a combination or in the profits of a combination" or if the murder is committed against any victim without proof of the criminal combination circumstances if the inmate was serving a sentence of life imprisonment or a term of 99 years for the crimes of aggravated sexual assault, aggravated robbery, or injury to a child or an elderly or disabled person. It is now capital murder if a murder victim was under the age of six or the murder is in retaliation for the victim's service as a judge from the level of municipal court to the highest appellate courts in the state. Finally, killing multiple victims in the same transaction or in different transactions connected by a common plan or scheme can now result in a penalty of death.

6.   Most of the cases in the United States Supreme Court during the modern era of capital punishment have dealt with the extra procedures necessary in capital cases, particularly those required to narrow and guide the decision whether to impose the death penalty and those requiring that any possible mitigating evidence be considered by the sentencing authority. This super-due-process use of the Eighth Amendment's protection against cruel and unusual punishment is not the only line of important Eighth Amendment death penalty cases.

Another important development has been to create categorical exclusions from the death penalty for certain types of offenders for whom it has been held that a sentence of death would be a disproportionate penalty. These offenders are held to be immune from the death penalty and no amount of procedural protections save the death penalty from being ruled unconstitutional for those who are excluded under this more traditional form of Eighth Amendment protection. The first such case involved a defendant charged with rape rather than murder. *Coker v. Georgia*, 433 U.S. 584 (1977). Although *Coker* did not explicitly state a crime that does not involve the loss of life is immune from the death penalty, *Coker* has been widely regarded as achieving this result. *Kennedy v. Louisiana*, 534 U.S. 407 (2008) (following *Coker*'s precedent in a case involving the rape of a child).

Other disproportionality cases have excluded from the death penalty offenders whose role in the offense is minor, *Enmund v. Florida*, 458 U.S. 72 (1982); defendants who are severely mentally retarded, *Atkins v. Virginia*, 536 U.S. 304 (2002); and defendants who were younger than 18 years of age at the time of the offense, *Roper v. Simmons*, 543 U.S. 551 (2005).

Chapter 15: Burden of Proof

Introduction

So far, we have examined substantive criminal law primarily from the side of the prosecution by examining issues the prosecution must establish beyond a reasonable doubt to earn a conviction: mental state, voluntary act or omission, and causation of harm. Starting with the next chapter, we will begin looking at the other side of the coin by examining defenses that may be brought forward by the defendant in the hope of winning an acquittal.

What makes an issue an element the state must prove? What makes a factor defensive? It is not the content of the relevant factor as we have already seen in our discussion of mistake of fact, a defense that we discussed in the chapters related to mental state. The reason for taking up mistake of fact in relation to an essential element rather than with other defenses is that a mistake of fact is simply a specific way in which a defendant can be found to lack the mental state required for the crime. A person who takes the property of another under the mistaken belief that it belongs to her does not intend to deprive the owner of the property; or, stated from a defense perspective, the person has the defense of a mistake of fact. If there were a requirement the defendant prove a mistake of fact beyond a reasonable doubt, doesn't that mean the state is required to prove the mental state element beyond a reasonable doubt? In fact, the mistake of fact defense only requires the defendant meet a burden of production. This means that the defendant needs to produce some evidence of mistake to put the question of mistake at issue in the case. Once the production burden is met and the issue is joined, the state must disprove the claimed defense of mistake of fact beyond a reasonable doubt. Thus, this issue, relevant to whether a defendant will be convicted or acquitted, can either be part of the offense or part of the defense or both.

What we mean by calling something a defense is that the defendant is given some role in bringing the issue forward. If the issue is an element, the state must allege it in an indictment or other charging instrument, bring forward proof concerning the issue, and prove its existence to the satisfaction of the jury (or the judge in a bench trial) beyond a reasonable doubt. If it is considered a defense, the state is not required to allege it in the indictment and it is not an issue in the case unless the defendant puts it at issue by presenting some evidence that meets the burden of production. With some defenses, like mistake of fact, once the issue is in the case, the state must disprove it beyond a reasonable doubt. With other defenses, like insanity, the defendant has a burden both of production and persuasion.

It should be apparent that the burden of proof—the generic term that encompasses the burden of production and the burden of persuasion—is intrinsic to the concept of criminal defenses. This chapter provides the bridge between the prosecution's elements we have discussed and the defenses we will discuss in the next several chapters. Our focus in this chapter will be on the question of whether there are any constitutional principles that effect the allocation of the burdens of proof that determine elements and defenses.

Generally, the allocation of a burden of production to the defendant presents no constitutional difficulty. It makes sense to ask the defendant to bring forward defensive issues. It would not be efficient to require the state to disprove insanity, self-defense, or duress when there is no reason to think these potential issues are involved in the case. With a negating defense, like mistake of fact, the defendant can argue the lack of mental state, but if the defendant wants to argue this issue under the rubric of a mistake of fact, the defendant must bring forward some evidence there was a mistake during the relevant events that are the subject of the criminal trial.

The question of who has the burden of persuasion presents greater difficulties. While the legislature decides which party will carry this burden, the legislative prerogative is limited by constitutional constraints. The two principal cases in this chapter will focus on the question of whether a legislative allocation of the burden of proof to the defendant offends the requirement of proof beyond a reasonable doubt in criminal cases.

It was not until 1970 in the case of *In re Winship*, 397 U.S. 358 (1970), that the United States Supreme Court held due process of law includes the requirement of proof beyond a reasonable doubt in criminal cases. One of the reasons the declaration of this fundamental principle of due process came so late was that there was little opportunity for the issue to arise. Every state and the federal system followed a proof beyond a reasonable doubt standard in keeping with a centuries-old common law tradition. The *Winship* issue arose as part of a fundamental shift in the jurisprudence of juvenile law that began a couple of years earlier in the landmark decision of *In re Gault*, 387 U.S. 1 (1967).

The *Gault* decision recognized that, even though the juvenile court purported to have a less punitive approach than the adult criminal system, the delinquency jurisdiction of the juvenile court resembled the stigma and potential loss of liberty of the adult criminal system. Although a juvenile was found to be delinquent rather than convicted of a crime, sent to reform school instead of prison, and released on "after care" instead of parole, juvenile delinquency adjudications were essentially criminal convictions. Juvenile proceedings were denominated as civil and used the usual civil standard of proof of a preponderance of the evidence. *Gault* had declared that at least some fundamental protections of due process are required in juvenile delinquency adjudications. *Winship* followed *Gault* in ruling that proof beyond a reasonable doubt was one of these necessary fundamental protections.

What was not clear from *Winship* was exactly what had to be proved beyond a reasonable doubt. The *Winship* case had said "every fact necessary for conviction." What did that mean? Was the state required to prove every disputed issue beyond a reasonable doubt? Or, was the requirement more modest, such as every statutory element of the offense as defined by the legislature? Five years after *Winship*, a unanimous court (with two concurrences) gave *Winship* a broad reading in the case which follows in the text, *Mullaney v. Wilbur*, 421 US 684 (1975). The case involved a classic distinction in the criminal law that we have previously discussed—the difference between provoked and unprovoked murders. Under the common law, the decision as to which category applied was a life and death determination. (In Maine the stakes were only a bit lower: between a maximum life sentence or a maximum prison sentence of 20 years). At the time of the *Mullaney* opinion, a majority of states required the state to prove beyond a reasonable doubt that the murder was not the product of reasonable provocation. However, the state of Maine was one of a significant minority of states that placed this burden on the defense.

Mullaney, with no dissents, struck down the Maine statute on the ground it violated *Winship*. Yet two years later, in *Patterson v. New York*, 432 U.S. 197 (1977), which follows after *Mullaney* in the text, the Supreme Court upheld a New York statute that required the defendant bear the risk of non-persuasion as to whether the offense was murder or qualified as a mitigated form of homicide because of the existence of reasonable provocation (or extreme emotional disturbance as the New York statue put it in defining a mitigation that was a modern equivalent of common law heat of passion). The *Patterson* Court distinguished *Mullaney*; it did not overrule it. Understanding how these two opinions can co-exist is critical to understanding criminal defenses and fundamental issues that continue to be discussed in criminal law.

Mullaney v. Wilbur ~~gay guy~~

421 U.S. 684 (1975)

Justice Powell delivered the opinion of the Court.

The State of Maine requires a(defendant)charged with murder to prove that he acted "in the heat of passion on sudden provocation" in order to reduce the homicide to manslaughter. We must decide whether this rule comports with the due process requirement, as defined in *In re Winship*, 397 U.S. 358 (1970), that the prosecution prove beyond a reasonable doubt every fact necessary to constitute the crime charged.

In June 1966 a jury found respondent Stillman E. Wilbur, Jr., guilty of murder. The case against him rested on his own pretrial statement and on circumstantial evidence showing that he fatally assaulted Claude Hebert in the latter's hotel room. Respondent's statement, introduced by the prosecution, claimed that he had attacked Hebert in a frenzy provoked by Hebert's homosexual advance. The defense offered no evidence, but argued that the homicide was not unlawful since respondent lacked criminal intent. Alternatively, Wilbur's counsel asserted that at most the homicide was manslaughter rather than murder, since it occurred in the heat of passion provoked by the homosexual assault.

The trial court instructed the jury that Maine law recognizes two kinds of homicide, murder and manslaughter, and that these offenses are not subdivided into different degrees. The common elements of both are that the homicide be unlawful—*i.e.*, neither justifiable nor excusable—and that it be intentional. The prosecution is required to prove these elements by proof beyond a reasonable doubt, and only if they are so proved is the jury to consider the distinction between murder and manslaughter.

In view of the evidence the trial court drew particular attention to the difference between murder and manslaughter. After reading the statutory definitions of both offenses the court charged that "malice aforethought is an essential and indispensable element of the crime of murder," without which the homicide would be manslaughter. The jury was further instructed, however, that if the prosecution established that the homicide was both intentional and unlawful, malice aforethought was to be conclusively implied unless the defendant proved by a fair preponderance of the evidence that he acted in the heat of passion on sudden provocation. The court emphasized that "malice aforethought and heat of passion on sudden provocation are two inconsistent things," thus, by proving the latter the defendant would negate the former and reduce the homicide from murder to manslaughter.

The Maine murder statute provides: "Whoever unlawfully kills a human being with malice aforethought, either express or implied, is guilty of murder and shall be punished by imprisonment for life."

The manslaughter statute, in relevant part provides: "Whoever unlawfully kills a human being in the heat of passion, on sudden provocation, without express or /implied malice aforethought . . . shall be punished by a fine of not more than $1,000 or by imprisonment for not more than 20 years . . . ."

After retiring to consider its verdict, the jury twice returned to request further instruction. It first sought reinstruction on the doctrine of implied malice aforethought, and later on the definition of "heat of passion." Shortly after the second reinstruction, the jury found respondent guilty of murder.

Respondent appealed to the Maine Supreme Judicial Court, arguing that he had been denied due process because he was required to negate the element of malice aforethought by proving that he had acted in the heat of passion on sudden provocation. He claimed that under Maine law malice aforethought was an essential element of the crime of murder—indeed that it was the sole element distinguishing murder from manslaughter. Respondent contended, therefore, that this Court's decision in *Winship* requires the prosecution to prove the existence of that element beyond a reasonable doubt.

The Maine Supreme Judicial Court rejected this contention, holding that in Maine murder and manslaughter are not distinct crimes but, rather, different degrees of the single generic offense of felonious homicide. The Court further stated that for more than a century it repeatedly had held that the prosecution could rest on a presumption of implied malice aforethought and require the defendant to prove that he had acted in the heat of passion on sudden provocation in order to reduce murder to manslaughter. With respect to *Winship*, which was decided after respondent's trial, the court noted that it did not anticipate the application of the *Winship* principle to a factor such as the heat of passion on sudden provocation.

Accordingly, if the prosecution proves a felonious homicide the burden shifts to the defendant to prove that he acted in the heat of passion on sudden provocation in order to receive the lesser penalty prescribed for manslaughter.

This Court . . . repeatedly has held that state courts are the ultimate expositors of state law, and that we are bound by their constructions except in extreme circumstances not present here. Accordingly, we accept as binding the Maine Supreme Judicial Court's construction of state homicide law.

The Maine law of homicide, as it bears on this case, can be stated succinctly: Absent justification or excuse, all intentional or criminally reckless killings are felonious homicides. Felonious homicide is punished as murder—*i.e.*, by life imprisonment—unless the defendant proves by a fair preponderance of the evidence that it was committed in the heat of passion on sudden provocation, in which case it is punished as manslaughter—*i.e.*, by a fine not to exceed $1,000 or by imprisonment not to exceed 20 years. The issue is whether the Maine rule requiring the defendant to prove that he acted in the heat of passion on sudden provocation accords with due process.

Our analysis may be illuminated if this issue is placed in historical context.

At early common law only those homicides committed in the enforcement of justice were considered justifiable; all others were deemed unlawful and were punished by death. Gradually, however, the severity of the common-law punishment for homicide abated. Between the 13th and 16th centuries the class of justifiable homicides expanded to include, for example, accidental homicides and those committed in self-defense. Concurrently, the widespread use of capital punishment was ameliorated further by extension of the ecclesiastic jurisdiction. Almost any person able to read was eligible for "benefit of clergy," a procedural device that effected a transfer from the secular to the ecclesiastic jurisdiction. And under ecclesiastic law a person who committed an unlawful homicide was not executed; instead he received a one-year sentence, had his thumb branded and was required to forfeit has goods. At the turn of the 16th century, English rulers, concerned with the accretion of ecclesiastic jurisdiction at the expense of the secular, enacted a series of statutes eliminating the benefit of clergy in all cases of "murder of malice prepensed." Unlawful homicides that were committed without such malice were designated "manslaughter," and their perpetrators remained eligible for the benefit of clergy.

Even after ecclesiastic jurisdiction was eliminated for all secular offenses the distinction between murder and manslaughter persisted. It was said that "manslaughter, when voluntary, arises from the sudden heat of the passions, murder from the wickedness of the heart." 4 W. BLACKSTONE, COMMENTARIES. Malice aforethought was designated as the element that distinguished the two crimes, but it was recognized that such malice could be implied by law as well as proved by evidence. Absent proof that an unlawful homicide resulted from "sudden and sufficiently violent provocation," the homicide was "presumed to be malicious." In view of this presumption, the early English authorities, relying on the case of *The King v. Oneby*, 92 Eng.Rep. 465 (K.B. 1727), held that once the prosecution proved that the accused had committed the homicide, it was "incumbent upon the prisoner to make out, to the satisfaction of the court and jury" "all . . . circumstances of justification, excuse, or alleviation." 4 W. BLACKSTONE, COMMENTARIES. *See* M. FOSTER, CROWN LAW 255 (1762). Thus, at common law the burden of proving heat of passion on sudden provocation appears to have rested on the defendant.

In this country the concept of malice aforethought took on two distinct meanings: in some jurisdictions it came to signify a substantive element of intent, requiring the prosecution to prove that the defendant intended to kill or to inflict great bodily harm; in other jurisdictions it remained a policy presumption, indicating only that absent proof to the contrary a homicide was presumed not to have occurred in the heat of passion. In a landmark case, *Commonwealth v. York*, 50 Mass. 93 (1845), Chief Justice Shaw of the Massachusetts Supreme Judicial Court held that the defendant was required to negate malice aforethought by proving by a preponderance of the evidence that he acted in the heat of passion. Initially, 1888 York was adopted in Maine as well as in several other jurisdictions. In 1895, however, in the context of deciding a question of federal criminal procedure, this Court explicitly considered and unanimously rejected the general approach articulated in York. And, in the past half century, the large majority of States have abandoned York and now require the prosecution to prove the absence of the heat of passion on sudden provocation beyond a reasonable doubt.

This historical review establishes two important points. First, the fact at issue here—the presence or absence of the heat of passion on sudden provocation—has been, almost from the inception of the common law of homicide, the single most important factor in determining the degree of culpability attaching to an unlawful homicide. And, second, the clear trend has been toward requiring the prosecution to bear the ultimate burden of proving this fact.

Petitioners, the warden of the Maine Prison and the State of Maine, argue that despite these considerations *Winship* should not be extended to the present case. They note that as a formal matter the absence of the heat of passion on sudden provocation is not a "fact necessary to constitute the crime" of felonious homicide in Maine. This distinction is relevant, according to petitioners, because in *Winship* the facts at issue were essential to establish criminality in the first instance, whereas the fact in question here does not come into play until the jury already has determined that the defendant is guilty and may be punished at least for manslaughter. In this situation, petitioners maintain, the defendant's critical interests in liberty and reputation are no longer of paramount concern since, irrespective of the presence or absence of the heat of passion on sudden provocation, he is likely to lose his liberty and certain to be stigmatized. In short, petitioners would limit *Winship* to those facts which, if not proved, would wholly exonerate the defendant.

This analysis fails to recognize that the criminal law of Maine, like that of other jurisdictions, is concerned not only with guilt or innocence in the abstract but also with the degree of criminal culpability. Maine has chosen to distinguish those who kill in the heat of passion from those who kill in the absence of this factor. Because the former are less blameworthy, they are subject to substantially less severe penalties. By drawing this distinction, while refusing to require the prosecution to establish beyond a reasonable doubt the fact upon which it turns, Maine denigrates the interests found critical in *Winship*.

The safeguards of due process are not rendered unavailing simply because a determination may already have been reached that would stigmatize the defendant and that might lead to a significant impairment of personal liberty. The fact remains that the consequences resulting from a verdict of murder, as compared with a verdict of manslaughter, differ significantly. Indeed, when viewed in terms of the potential difference in restrictions of personal liberty attendant to each conviction, the distinction established by Maine between murder and manslaughter may be of greater importance than the difference between guilt and innocence for many lesser crimes.

Moreover, if *Winship* were limited to those facts that constitute a crime as defined by state law, a State could undermine many of the interests that decision sought to protect without effecting any substantive change in its law. It would only be necessary to redefine the elements that constitute different crimes, characterizing them as factors that bear solely on the extent of punishment. An extreme example of this approach can be fashioned from the law challenged in this case. Maine divides the single generic offense of felonious homicide into three distinct punishment categories—murder, voluntary manslaughter, and involuntary manslaughter. Only the first two of these categories require that the homicidal act either be intentional or the result of criminally reckless conduct. But under Maine law these facts of intent are not general elements of the crime of felonious homicide. Instead, they bear only on the appropriate punishment category. Thus, if petitioners' argument were accepted, Maine could impose a life sentence for any felonious homicide—even one that traditionally might be considered involuntary manslaughter—unless the defendant was able to prove that his act was neither intentional nor criminally reckless.[1]

Winship is concerned with substance rather than this kind of formalism. The rationale of that case requires an analysis that looks to the "operation and effect of the law as applied and enforced by the state," and to the interests of both the State and the defendant as affected by the allocation of the burden of proof.

In *Winship* the Court emphasized the societal interests in the reliability of jury verdicts: "The requirement of proof beyond a reasonable doubt has (a) vital role in our criminal procedure for cogent reasons. The accused during a criminal prosecution has at stake interests of immense importance, both because of the possibility that he may lose his liberty upon conviction and because of the certainty that he would be stigmatized by the conviction . . . ."

Moreover, use of the reasonable-doubt standard is indispensable to command the respect and confidence of the community in applications of the criminal law. It is critical that the moral force of the criminal law not be diluted by a standard of proof that leaves people in doubt whether innocent men are being condemned.

These interests are implicated to a greater degree in this case than they were in *Winship* itself. Petitioner there faced an 18-month sentence, with a maximum possible extension of an additional four and one-half years, whereas respondent here faces a differential in sentencing ranging from a nominal fine to a mandatory life sentence. Both the stigma to the defendant and the community's confidence in the administration of the criminal law are also of greater consequence in this case, since the adjudication of delinquency involved in *Winship* was "benevolent" in intention, seeking to provide "a generously conceived program of compassionate treatment."

Not only are the interests underlying *Winship* implicated to a greater degree in this case, but in one respect the protection afforded those interests is less here. In *Winship* the ultimate burden of persuasion remained with the prosecution, although the standard had been reduced to proof by a fair preponderance of the evidence. In this case, by contrast, the State has affirmatively shifted the burden of proof to the defendant. The result, in a case such as this one where the defendant is required to prove the critical fact in dispute, is to increase further the likelihood of an erroneous murder conviction.

It has been suggested that because of the difficulties in negating an argument that the homicide was committed in the heat of passion the burden of proving this fact should rest on the defendant. No doubt this is often a heavy burden for the prosecution to satisfy. The same may be said of the requirement of proof beyond a reasonable doubt of many controverted facts in a criminal trial. But this is the traditional burden which our system of criminal justice deems essential.

---

1. Many States impose different statutory sentences on different degrees of assault. If *Winship* were limited to a State's definition of the elements of a crime, these States could define all assaults as a single offense and then require the defendant to disprove the elements of aggravation—*e.g.*, intent to kill or intent to rob.

Indeed, the Maine Supreme Judicial Court itself acknowledged that most States require the prosecution to prove the absence of passion beyond a reasonable doubt.[2] Moreover, the difficulty of meeting such an exacting burden is mitigated in Maine where the fact at issue is largely an "objective, rather than a subjective, behavioral criterion." In this respect, proving that the defendant did not act in the heat of passion on sudden provocation is similar to proving any other element of intent; it may be established by adducing evidence of the factual circumstances surrounding the commission of the homicide. And although intent is typically considered a fact peculiarly within the knowledge of the defendant, this does not, as the Court has long recognized, justify shifting the burden to him.

Nor is the requirement of proving a negative unique in our system of criminal jurisprudence. Maine itself requires the prosecution to prove the absence of self-defense beyond a reasonable doubt. Satisfying this burden imposes an obligation that, in all practical effect, is identical to the burden involved in negating the heat of passion on sudden provocation. Thus, we discern no unique hardship on the prosecution that would justify requiring the defendant to carry the burden of proving a fact so critical to criminal culpability.

Maine law requires a defendant to establish by a preponderance of the evidence that he acted in the heat of passion on sudden provocation in order to reduce murder to manslaughter. Under this burden of proof a defendant can be given a life sentence when the evidence indicates that it is as likely as not that he deserves a significantly lesser sentence. This is an intolerable result in a society where, to paraphrase Mr. Justice Harlan, it is far worse to sentence one guilty only of manslaughter as a murderer than to sentence a murderer for the lesser crime of manslaughter. We therefore hold that the Due Process Clause requires the prosecution to prove beyond a reasonable doubt the absence of the heat of passion on sudden provocation when the issue is properly presented in a homicide case.

Justice Rehnquist, with whom Chief Justice Burger joins, concurring.

Respondent made no objection to the trial court's instruction respecting the burden of proof on the issue of whether he had acted in the heat of passion on sudden provocation. Nonetheless, on his appeal to the Supreme Judicial Court of Maine, that court considered his objection to the charge on its merits and held the charge to be a correct statement of Maine law. It neither made any point of respondent's failure to object to the instruction in the trial court, nor did it give any consideration to the doctrine long approved by this Court that the instructions to the jury are not to be judged in artificial isolation, but must be viewed in the context of the overall charge. It likewise expressed no view on whether, even though the instruction might have amounted to constitutional error, that error could have been harmless. Its reason for not treating the possibility that the error was harmless may have been because, as this Court's opinion points out the jury came back in the midst of its deliberations and requested further instructions on the doctrine of implied malice aforethought and the definition of "heat of passion."

---

2. Many States do require the defendant to show that there is "some evidence" indicating that he acted in the heat of passion before requiring the prosecution to negate this element by proving the absence of passion beyond a reasonable doubt. Nothing in this opinion is intended to affect that requirement.

I agree with the Court that *In re Winship* does require that the prosecution prove beyond a reasonable doubt every element which constitutes the crime charged against a defendant. I see no inconsistency between that holding and the holding of *Leland v. Oregon*, 343 U.S. 790 (1952). In the latter case this Court held that there was no constitutional requirement that the State shoulder the burden of proving the sanity of the defendant.

The Court noted in *Leland* that the issue of insanity as a defense to a criminal charge was considered by the jury only after it had found that all elements of the offense, including the *mens rea*, if any, required by state law, had been proved beyond a reasonable doubt. Although as the state court's instructions in *Leland* recognized, evidence relevant to insanity as defined by state law may also be relevant to whether the required *mens rea* was present, the existence or nonexistence of legal insanity bears no necessary relationship to the existence or nonexistence of the required mental elements of the crime. For this reason, Oregon's placement of the burden of proof of insanity on Leland, unlike Maine's redefinition of homicide in the instant case, did not affect an unconstitutional shift in the State's traditional burden of proof beyond a reasonable doubt of all necessary elements of the offense. Having once met that rigorous burden of proof that, for example, in a case such as this, the defendant not only killed a fellow human being, but did it with malice aforethought, the State could quite consistently with such a constitutional principle conclude that a defendant who sought to establish the defense of insanity, and thereby escape any punishment whatever for a heinous crime, should bear the laboring oar on such an issue.

Rule: It is the prosecution's duty to prove the absence of heat of passion beyond reasonable doubt if it is properly presented. △ had no burden

Issue: whether the Maine rule that requires a △ to prove that he acted in the heat of passion by a preponderance of the evidence is a violation of due process.

Holding: The prosecution must prove beyond a reasonable doubt the absence of the heat of passion when issue is properly presented.

Concurrence: Not unconstitutional to impose the burden of proving heat of passion on △ bc vital elements of crime had already been proven.

Could violate winship but distinguished from that case

Patterson v. New York

432 U.S. 197 (1977)

Justice White delivered the opinion of the Court.

The question here is the constitutionality under the Fourteenth Amendment's Due Process Clause of burdening the defendant in a New York State murder trial with proving the affirmative defense of extreme emotional disturbance as defined by New York law.

After a brief and unstable marriage, the appellant, Gordon Patterson, Jr., became estranged from his wife, Roberta. Roberta resumed an association with John Northrup, a neighbor to whom she had been engaged prior to her marriage to appellant. On December 27, 1970, Patterson borrowed a rifle from an acquaintance and went to the residence of his father-in-law. There, he observed his wife through a window in a state of semi-undress in the presence of John Northrup. He entered the house and killed Northrup by shooting him twice in the head.

Patterson was charged with second-degree murder. In New York there are two elements of this crime: (1) "intent to cause the death of another person;" and (2) "caus[ing] the death of such person or of a third person." Malice aforethought is not an element of the crime. In addition, the State permits a person accused of murder to raise an affirmative defense that he "acted under the influence of extreme emotional disturbance for which there was a reasonable explanation or excuse."

New York also recognizes the crime of manslaughter. A person is guilty of manslaughter if he intentionally kills another person "under circumstances which do not constitute murder because he acts under the influence of extreme emotional disturbance." Appellant confessed before trial to killing Northrup, but at trial he raised the defense of extreme emotional disturbance.

The jury was instructed as to the elements of the crime of murder. Focusing on the element of intent, the trial court charged:

> Before you, considering all of the evidence, can convict this defendant or any-one of murder, you must believe and decide that the People have established beyond a reasonable doubt that he intended, in firing the gun, to kill either the victim himself or some other human being . . . .

> Always remember that you must not expect or require the defendant to prove to your satisfaction that his acts were done without the intent to kill. Whatever proof he may have attempted, however far he may have gone in an effort to convince you of his innocence or guiltlessness, he is not obliged, he is not obligated to prove anything. It is always the People's burden to prove his guilt, and to prove that he intended to kill in this instance beyond a reasonable doubt.

The jury was further instructed, consistently with New York law, that the defendant had the burden of proving his affirmative defense by a preponderance of the evidence. The jury was

316

told that if it found beyond a reasonable doubt that appellant had intentionally killed Northrup but that appellant had demonstrated by a preponderance of the evidence that he had acted under the influence of extreme emotional disturbance, it had to find appellant guilty of manslaughter instead of murder.

The jury found appellant guilty of murder. Judgment was entered on the verdict, and the Appellate Division affirmed. While appeal to the New York Court of Appeals was pending, this Court decided *Mullaney v. Wilbur*, in which the Court declared Maine's murder statute unconstitutional. Under the Maine statute, a person accused of murder could rebut the statutory presumption that he committed the offense with "malice aforethought" by proving that he acted in the heat of passion on sudden provocation. The Court held that this scheme improperly shifted the burden of persuasion from the prosecutor to the defendant and was therefore a violation of due process. In the Court of Appeals appellant urged that New York's murder statute is functionally equivalent to the one struck down in *Mullaney* and that therefore his conviction should be reversed.

The Court of Appeals rejected appellant's argument, holding that the New York murder statute is consistent with due process. The Court distinguished *Mullaney* on the ground that the New York statute involved no shifting of the burden to the defendant to disprove any fact essential to the offense charged since the New York affirmative defense of extreme emotional disturbance bears no direct relationship to any element of murder. This appeal ensued, and we noted probable jurisdiction. We affirm. Holding

It goes without saying that preventing and dealing with crime is much more the business of the States than it is of the Federal Government and that we should not lightly construe the Constitution so as to intrude upon the administration of justice by the individual States. Among other things, it is normally "within the power of the State to regulate procedures under which its laws are carried out, including the burden of producing evidence and the burden of persuasion," and its decision in this regard is not subject to proscription under the Due Process Clause unless "it offends some principle of justice so rooted in the traditions and conscience of our people as to be ranked as fundamental." Rule:

In determining whether New York's allocation to the defendant of proving the mitigating circumstances of severe emotional disturbance is consistent with due process, it is therefore relevant to note that this defense is a considerably expanded version of the common-law defense of heat of passion on sudden provocation and that at common law the burden of proving the latter, as well as other affirmative defenses indeed, "all . . . circumstances of justification, excuse or alleviation" rested on the defendant. This was the rule when the Fifth Amendment was adopted, and it was the American rule when the Fourteenth Amendment was ratified ¬onoviolation

In 1895 the common-law view was abandoned with respect to the insanity defense in federal prosecutions. *Davis v. United States*, 160 U.S. 469 (1895). This ruling had wide impact on the practice in the federal courts with respect to the burden of proving various affirmative defenses, and the prosecution in a majority of jurisdictions in this country sooner or later came to shoulder the burden of proving the sanity of the accused and of disproving the facts constituting other affirmative defenses, including provocation. *Davis* was not a constitutional ruling, however, as *Leland v. Oregon* made clear.

At issue in *Leland v. Oregon* was the constitutionality under the Due Process Clause of the Oregon rule that the defense of insanity must be proved by the defendant beyond a reasonable doubt. Noting that *Davis* "obviously establish[ed] no constitutional doctrine," the Court refused to strike down the Oregon scheme, saying that the burden of proving all elements of the crime beyond reasonable doubt, including the elements of premeditation and deliberation, was placed on the State under Oregon procedures and remained there throughout the trial. To convict, the jury was required to find each element of the crime beyond a reasonable doubt, based on all the evidence, including the evidence going to the issue of insanity. Only then was the jury "to consider separately the issue of legal sanity per se . . . ." This practice did not offend the Due Process Clause even though among the 20 States then placing the burden of proving his insanity on the defendant, Oregon was alone in requiring him to convince the jury beyond a reasonable doubt.

In 1970, the Court declared that the Due Process Clause "protects the accused against conviction except upon proof beyond a reasonable doubt of every fact necessary to constitute the crime with which he is charged." Five years later, in *Mullaney v. Wilbur*, the Court further announced that under the Maine law of homicide, the burden could not constitutionally be placed on the defendant of proving by a preponderance of the evidence that the killing had occurred in the heat of passion on sudden provocation. The Chief Justice and Mr. Justice Rehnquist, concurring, expressed their understanding that the *Mullaney* decision did not call into question the ruling in *Leland v. Oregon* with respect to the proof of insanity.

Subsequently, the Court confirmed that it remained constitutional to burden the defendant with proving his insanity defense when it dismissed, as not raising a substantial federal question, a case in which the appellant specifically challenged the continuing validity of *Leland v. Oregon*. This occurred in *Rivera v. Delaware*, 429 U.S. 877 (1976), an appeal from a Delaware conviction which, in reliance on *Leland*, had been affirmed by the Delaware Supreme Court over the claim that the Delaware statute was unconstitutional because it burdened the defendant with proving his affirmative defense of insanity by a preponderance of the evidence. The claim in this Court was that *Leland* had been overruled by *Winship* and *Mullaney*. We dismissed the appeal as not presenting a substantial federal question.

We cannot conclude that Patterson's conviction under the New York law deprived him of due process of law. The crime of murder is defined by the statute, which represents a recent revision of the state criminal code, as causing the death of another person with intent to do so. The death, the intent to kill, and causation are the facts that the State is required to prove beyond a reasonable doubt if a person is to be convicted of murder. No further facts are either presumed or inferred in order to constitute the crime. The statute does provide an affirmative defense that the defendant acted under the influence of extreme emotional disturbance for which there was a reasonable explanation which, if proved by a preponderance of the evidence, would reduce the crime to manslaughter, an offense defined in a separate section of the statute. It is plain enough that if the intentional killing is shown, the State intends to deal with the defendant as a murderer unless he demonstrates the mitigating circumstances.

Here, the jury was instructed in accordance with the statute, and the guilty verdict confirms that the State successfully carried its burden of proving the facts of the crime beyond a reasonable doubt. Nothing in the evidence, including any evidence that might have been offered with respect to Patterson's mental state at the time of the crime, raised a reasonable doubt about his guilt as a murderer; and clearly the evidence failed to convince the jury that Patterson's affirmative defense had been made out. It seems to us that the State satisfied the mandate of *Winship* that it prove beyond a reasonable doubt "every fact necessary to constitute the crime with which [Patterson was] charged."

In convicting Patterson under its murder statute, New York did no more than *Leland* and *Rivera* permitted it to do without violating the Due Process Clause. Under those cases, once the facts constituting a crime are established beyond a reasonable doubt, based on all the evidence including the evidence of the defendant's mental state, the State may refuse to sustain the affirmative defense of insanity unless demonstrated by a preponderance of the evidence.

The New York law on extreme emotional disturbance follows this pattern. This affirmative defense, which the Court of Appeals described as permitting "the defendant to show that his actions were caused by a mental infirmity not arising to the level of insanity, and that he is less culpable for having committed them," does not serve to negative any facts of the crime which the State is to prove in order to convict of murder. It constitutes a separate issue on which the defendant is required to carry the burden of persuasion; and unless we are to overturn Leland and Rivera, New York has not violated the Due Process Clause, and Patterson's conviction must be sustained.

2 seperate issues

We are unwilling to reconsider *Leland* and *Rivera*. But even if we were to hold that a State must prove sanity to convict once that fact is put in issue, it would not necessarily follow that a State must prove beyond a reasonable doubt every fact, the existence or nonexistence of which it is willing to recognize as an exculpatory or mitigating circumstance affecting the degree of culpability or the severity of the punishment. Here, in revising its criminal code, New York provided the affirmative defense of extreme emotional disturbance, a substantially expanded version of the older heat-of-passion concept; but it was willing to do so only if the facts making out the defense were established by the defendant with sufficient certainty. The State was itself unwilling to undertake to establish the absence of those facts beyond a reasonable doubt, perhaps fearing that proof would be too difficult and that too many persons deserving treatment as murderers would escape that punishment if the evidence need merely raise a reasonable doubt *dangerous* about the defendant's emotional state. It has been said that the new criminal code of New York contains some 25 affirmative defenses which exculpate or mitigate but which must be established by the defendant to be operative. The Due Process Clause, as we see it, does not put New York to the choice of abandoning those defenses or undertaking to disprove their existence in order to convict of a crime which otherwise is within its constitutional powers to sanction by substantial punishment.

The requirement of proof beyond a reasonable doubt in a criminal case is "bottomed on a fundamental value determination of our society that it is far worse to convict an innocent man than to let a guilty man go free." The social cost of placing the burden on the prosecution to prove guilt beyond a reasonable doubt is thus an increased risk that the guilty will go free. While it is clear that our society has willingly chosen to bear a substantial burden in order to protect the innocent, it is equally clear that the risk it must bear is not without limits; and Mr. Justice Harlan's aphorism provides little guidance for determining what those limits are. Due process does not require that every conceivable step be taken, at whatever cost, to eliminate the possibility of convicting an innocent person. Punishment of those found guilty by a jury, for example, is not forbidden merely because there is a remote possibility in some instances that an innocent person might go to jail.

It is said that the common-law rule permits a State to punish one as a murderer when it is as likely as not that he acted in the heat of passion or under severe emotional distress and when, if he did, he is guilty only of manslaughter. But this has always been the case in those jurisdictions adhering to the traditional rule. It is also very likely true that fewer convictions of murder would occur if New York were required to negative the affirmative defense at issue here. But in each instance of a murder conviction under the present law New York will have proved beyond a reasonable doubt that the defendant has intentionally killed another person, an act which it is not disputed the State may constitutionally criminalize and punish. If the State nevertheless chooses to recognize a factor that mitigates the degree of criminality or punishment, we think the State may assure itself that the fact has been established with reasonably certainty. To recognize at all a mitigating circumstance does not require the State to prove its nonexistence in each case in which the fact is put in issue, if in its judgment this would be too cumbersome, too expensive, and too inaccurate.[1]

We thus decline to adopt as a constitutional imperative, operative countrywide, that a State must disprove beyond a reasonable doubt every fact constituting any and all affirmative defenses related to the culpability of an accused. Traditionally, due process has required that only the most basic procedural safeguards be observed; more subtle balancing of society's interests against those of the accused have been left to the legislative branch. We therefore will not disturb the balance struck in previous cases holding that the Due Process Clause requires the prosecution to prove beyond a reasonable doubt all of the elements included in the definition of the offense of which the defendant is charged. Proof of the nonexistence of all affirmative defenses has never been constitutionally required; and we perceive no reason to fashion such a rule in this case and apply it to the statutory defense at issue here.

This view may seem to permit state legislatures to reallocate burdens of proof by labeling as affirmative defenses at least some elements of the crimes now defined in their statutes. But there are obviously constitutional limits beyond which the States may not go in this regard. "([I]t

---

1. The drafters of the Model Penal Code would, as a matter of policy, place the burden of proving the nonexistence of most affirmative defenses, including the defense involved in this case, on the prosecution once the defendant has come forward with some evidence that the defense is present. The drafters recognize the need for flexibility, however, and would, in "some exceptional situations," place the burden of persuasion on the accused.

"Characteristically these are situations where the defense does not obtain at all under existing law and the Code seeks to introduce a mitigation. Resistance to the mitigation, based upon the prosecution's difficulty in obtaining evidence, ought to be lowered if the burden of persuasion is imposed on the defendant. Where that difficulty appears genuine and there is something to be said against allowing the defense at all, we consider it defensible to shift the burden in this way."

is not within the province of a legislature to declare an individual guilty or presumptively guilty of a crime." The legislature cannot "validly command that the finding of an indictment, or mere proof of the identity of the accused, should create a presumption of the existence of all the facts essential to guilt."

Long before *Winship*, the universal rule in this country was that the prosecution must prove guilt beyond a reasonable doubt. At the same time, the long-accepted rule was that it was constitutionally permissible to provide that various affirmative defenses were to be proved by the defendant. This did not lead to such abuses or to such widespread redefinition of crime and reduction of the prosecution's burden that a new constitutional rule was required. This was not the problem to which *Winship* was addressed. Nor does the fact that a majority of the States have now assumed the burden of disproving affirmative defenses for whatever reasons mean that those States that strike a different balance are in violation of the Constitution.

It is urged that *Mullaney v. Wilbur* necessarily invalidates Patterson's conviction. In *Mullaney* the charge was murder, which the Maine statute defined as the unlawful killing of a human being "with malice aforethought, either express or implied." The trial court instructed the jury that the words "malice aforethought" were most important because "malice aforethought is an essential and indispensable element of the crime of murder." Malice, as the statute indicated and as the court instructed, could be implied and was to be implied from "any deliberate, cruel act committed by one person against another suddenly . . . or without a considerable provocation," in which event an intentional killing was murder unless by a preponderance of the evidence it was shown that the act was committed "in the heat of passion, on sudden provocation." The instructions emphasized that "'malice aforethought and heat of passion on sudden provocation are two inconsistent things;' thus, by proving the latter the defendant would negate the former."

Mullaney's holding, it is argued, is that the State may not permit the blameworthiness of an act or the severity of punishment authorized for its commission to depend on the presence or absence of an identified fact without assuming the burden of proving the presence or absence of that fact, as the case may be, beyond a reasonable doubt. In our view, the *Mullaney* holding should not be so broadly read. The concurrence of two Justices in *Mullaney* was necessarily contrary to such a reading; and a majority of the Court refused to so understand and apply *Mullaney* when *Rivera* was dismissed for want of a substantial federal question.

Mullaney surely held that a State must prove every ingredient of an offense beyond a reasonable doubt, and that it may not shift the burden of proof to the defendant by presuming that ingredient upon proof of the other elements of the offense. This is true even though the State's practice, as in Maine, had been traditionally to the contrary. Such shifting of the burden of persuasion with respect to a fact which the State deems so important that it must be either proved or presumed is impermissible under the Due Process Clause.

It was unnecessary to go further in *Mullaney*. The Maine Supreme Judicial Court made it clear that malice aforethought, which was mentioned in the statutory definition of the crime, was not equivalent to premeditation and that the presumption of malice traditionally arising in intentional homicide cases carried no factual meaning insofar as premeditation was concerned.

Even so, a killing became murder in Maine when it resulted from a deliberate, cruel act committed by one person against another, "suddenly without any, or without a considerable provocation." Premeditation was not within the definition of murder; but malice, in the sense of the absence of provocation, was part of the definition of that crime. Yet malice, *i.e.*, lack of provocation, was presumed and could be rebutted by the defendant only by proving by a preponderance of the evidence that he acted with heat of passion upon sudden provocation. In *Mullaney* we held that however traditional this mode of proceeding might have been, it is contrary to the Due Process Clause as construed in *Winship*.

As we have explained, nothing was presumed or implied against Patterson; and his conviction is not invalid under any of our prior cases. The judgment of the New York Court of Appeals is affirmed.

Justice Powell, with whom Justice Brennan and Justice Marshall join, dissenting.

In the name of preserving legislative flexibility, the Court today drains *In re Winship* of much of its vitality. Legislatures do require broad discretion in the drafting of criminal laws, but the Court surrenders to the legislative branch a significant part of its responsibility to protect the presumption of innocence.

An understanding of the import of today's decision requires a comparison of the statutes at issue here with the statutes and practices of Maine struck down by a unanimous Court just two years ago in *Mullaney v. Wilbur*.

Maine's homicide laws embodied the common-law distinctions along with the colorful common-law language. Murder was defined in the statute as the unlawful killing of a human being "with malice aforethought, either express or implied." Manslaughter was a killing "in the heat of passion, on sudden provocation, without express or implied malice aforethought." Although "express malice" at one point may have had its own significant independent meaning, in practice a finding that the killing was committed with malice aforethought had come to mean simply that heat of passion was absent. Indeed, the trial court in *Mullaney* expressly charged the jury that "malice aforethought and heat of passion on sudden provocation are two inconsistent things." And the Maine Supreme Judicial Court had held that instructions concerning express malice (in the sense of premeditation) were unnecessary. The only inquiry for the jury in deciding whether a homicide amounted to murder or manslaughter was the inquiry into heat of passion on sudden provocation.

Our holding in *Mullaney* found no constitutional defect in these statutory provisions. Rather, the defect in Maine practice lay in its allocation of the burden of persuasion with respect to the crucial factor distinguishing murder from manslaughter. In Maine, juries were instructed that if the prosecution proved that the homicide was both intentional and unlawful, the crime was to be considered murder unless the defendant proved by a preponderance of the evidence that he acted in the heat of passion on sudden provocation. Only if the defendant carried this burden would the offense be reduced to manslaughter.

New York's present homicide laws had their genesis in lingering dissatisfaction with certain aspects of the common-law framework that this Court confronted in *Mullaney*. Critics charged that the archaic language tended to obscure the factors of real importance in the jury's decision. Also, only a limited range of aggravations would lead to mitigation under the common-law formula, usually only those resulting from direct provocation by the victim himself. It was thought that actors whose emotions were stirred by other forms of outrageous conduct, even conduct by someone other than the ultimate victim, also should be punished as manslaughterers rather than murderers. Moreover, the common-law formula was generally applied with rather strict objectivity. Only provocations that might cause the hypothetical reasonable man to lose control could be considered. And even provocations of that sort were inadequate to reduce the crime to manslaughter if enough time had passed for the reasonable man's passions to cool, regardless of whether the actor's own thermometer had registered any decline.

The American Law Institute took the lead in moving to remedy these difficulties. As part of its commendable undertaking to prepare a Model Penal Code, it endeavored to bring modern insights to bear on the law of homicide. The result was a proposal to replace "heat of passion" with the moderately broader concept of "extreme mental or emotional disturbance." The proposal first appeared in a tentative draft published in 1959, and it was accepted by the Institute and included as s 210.3 of the 1962 Proposed Official Draft.

At about this time the New York Legislature undertook the preparation of a new criminal code, and the Revised Penal Law of 1967 was the ultimate result. The new code adopted virtually word for word the ALI formula for distinguishing murder from manslaughter. Under current New York law, those who kill intentionally are guilty of murder. But there is an affirmative defense left open to a defendant: If his act was committed "under the influence of extreme emotional disturbance for which there was a reasonable explanation or excuse," the crime is reduced to manslaughter. The supposed defects of a formulation like Maine's have been removed. Some of the rigid objectivity of the common law is relieved, since reasonableness is to be determined "from the viewpoint of a person in the defendant's situation under the circumstances as the defendant believed them to be." The New York law also permits mitigation when emotional disturbance results from situations other than direct provocation by the victim. And the last traces of confusing archaic language have been removed. There is no mention of malice aforethought, no attempt to give a name to the state of mind that exists when extreme emotional disturbance is not present. The statute is framed in lean prose modeled after the ALI approach, giving operative descriptions of the crucial factors rather than attempting to attach the classical labels.

Despite these changes, the major factor that distinguishes murder from manslaughter in New York "extreme emotional disturbance" is undeniably the modern equivalent of "heat of passion." The ALI drafters made this abundantly clear. They were not rejecting the notion that some of those who kill in an emotional outburst deserve lesser punishment; they were merely refining the concept to relieve some of the problems with the classical formulation. Both the majority and the dissenters in the New York Court of Appeals agreed that extreme emotional disturbance is simply "a new formulation" for the traditional language of heat of passion.

But in one important respect the New York drafters chose to parallel Maine's practice precisely, departing markedly from the ALI recommendation. Under the Model Penal Code the prosecution must prove the absence of emotional disturbance beyond a reasonable doubt once the issue is properly raised. In New York, however, extreme emotional disturbance constitutes an affirmative defense rather than a simple defense. Consequently the defendant bears not only the burden of production on this issue; he has the burden of persuasion as well.

Mullaney held invalid Maine's requirement that the defendant prove heat of passion. The Court today, without disavowing the unanimous holding of *Mullaney*, approves New York's requirement that the defendant prove extreme emotional disturbance. The Court manages to run a constitutional boundary line through the barely visible space that separates Maine's law from New York's. It does so on the basis of distinctions in language that are formalistic rather than substantive.

This result is achieved by a narrowly literal parsing of the holding in *Winship*: "[T]he Due Process Clause protects the accused against conviction except upon proof beyond a reasonable doubt of every fact necessary to constitute the crime with which he is charged." The only "facts" necessary to constitute a crime are said to be those that appear on the face of the statute as a part of the definition of the crime. Maine's statute was invalid, the Court reasons, because it "defined [murder] as the unlawful killing of a human being 'with malice aforethought, either express or implied.'" "[M]alice," the Court reiterates, "in the sense of the absence of provocation, was part of the definition of that crime." *Winship* was violated only because this "fact" malice was "presumed" unless the defendant persuaded the jury otherwise by showing that he acted in the heat of passion. New York, in form presuming no affirmative "fact" against Patterson, and blessed with a statute drafted in the leaner language of the 20th century, escapes constitutional scrutiny unscathed even though the effect on the defendant of New York's placement of the burden of persuasion is exactly the same as Maine's.

This explanation of the *Mullaney* holding bears little resemblance to the basic rationale of that decision. But this is not the cause of greatest concern. The test the Court today establishes allows a legislature to shift, virtually at will, the burden of persuasion with respect to any factor in a criminal case, so long as it is careful not to mention the nonexistence of that factor in the statutory language that defines the crime. The sole requirement is that any references to the factor be confined to those sections that provide for an affirmative defense.

Perhaps the Court's interpretation of *Winship* is consistent with the letter of the holding in that case. But little of the spirit survives. Indeed, the Court scarcely could distinguish this case from *Mullaney* without closing its eyes to the constitutional values for which *Winship* stands. As Mr. Justice Harlan observed in *Winship*, "a standard of proof represents an attempt to instruct the factfinder concerning the degree of confidence our society thinks he should have in the correctness of factual conclusions for a particular type of adjudication." Explaining *Mullaney*, the Court says today, in effect, that society demands full confidence before a Maine factfinder determines that heat of passion is missing a demand so insistent that this Court invoked the Constitution to enforce it over the contrary decision by the State. But we are told that society is willing to tolerate far less confidence in New York's factual determination of precisely the same functional issue. One must ask what possibly could explain this difference in societal demands.

According to the Court, it is because Maine happened to attach a name "malice aforethought" to the absence of heat of passion, whereas New York refrained from giving a name to the absence of extreme emotional disturbance.

With all respect, this type of constitutional adjudication is indefensibly formalistic. A limited but significant check on possible abuses in the criminal law now becomes an exercise in arid formalities. What *Winship* and *Mullaney* had sought to teach about the limits a free society places on its procedures to safeguard the liberty of its citizens becomes a rather simplistic lesson in statutory draftsmanship. Nothing in the Court's opinion prevents a legislature from applying this new learning to many of the classical elements of the crimes it punishes.[2] It would be preferable, if the Court has found reason to reject the rationale of *Winship* and *Mullaney*, simply and straightforwardly to overrule those precedents.

The Court understandably manifests some uneasiness that its formalistic approach will give legislatures too much latitude in shifting the burden of persuasion. And so it issues a warning that "there are obviously constitutional limits beyond which the States may not go in this regard." The Court thereby concedes that legislative abuses may occur and that they must be curbed by the judicial branch. But if the State is careful to conform to the drafting formulas articulated today, the constitutional limits are anything but "obvious." This decision simply leaves us without a conceptual framework for distinguishing abuses from legitimate legislative adjustments of the burden of persuasion in criminal cases.

It is unnecessary for the Court to retreat to a formalistic test for applying *Winship*. Careful attention to the *Mullaney* decision reveals the principles that should control in this and like cases. In *Mullaney* we concluded that heat of passion was one of the "facts" described in *Winship* that is, a factor as to which the prosecution must bear the burden of persuasion beyond a reasonable doubt. We reached that result only after making two careful inquiries. First, we noted that the presence or absence of heat of passion made a substantial difference in punishment of the offender and in the stigma associated with the conviction. Second, we reviewed the history, in England and this country, of the factor at issue. Central to the holding in *Mullaney* was our conclusion that heat of passion "has been, almost from the inception of the common law of homicide, the single most important factor in determining the degree of culpability attaching to an unlawful homicide."

Implicit in these two inquiries are the principles that should govern this case. The Due Process Clause requires that the prosecutor bear the burden of persuasion beyond a reasonable doubt only if the factor at issue makes a substantial difference in punishment and stigma. The

---

2. For example, a state statute could pass muster under the only solid standard that appears in the Court's opinion if it defined murder as mere physical contact between the defendant and the victim leading to the victim's death, but then set up an affirmative defense leaving it to the defendant to prove that he acted without culpable *mens rea*. The State, in other words, could be relieved altogether of responsibility for proving anything regarding the defendant's state of mind, provided only that the fact of the statute meets the Court's drafting formulas.

To be sure, it is unlikely that legislatures will rewrite their criminal laws in this extreme form. The Court seems to think this likelihood of restraint is an added reason for limiting review largely to formalistic examination. But it is completely foreign to this Court's responsibility for constitutional adjudication to limit the scope of judicial review because of the expectation however reasonable that legislative bodies will exercise appropriate restraint.

requirement of course applies *a fortiori* if the factor makes the difference between guilt and innocence. But a substantial difference in punishment alone is not enough. It also must be shown that in the Anglo-American legal tradition the factor in question historically has held that level of importance. If either branch of the test is not met, then the legislature retains its traditional authority over matters of proof. But to permit a shift in the burden of persuasion when both branches of this test are satisfied would invite the undermining of the presumption of innocence, "that bedrock 'axiomatic and elementary' principle whose 'enforcement lies at the foundation of the administration of our criminal law.'"

I hardly need add that New York's provisions allocating the burden of persuasion as to "extreme emotional disturbance" are unconstitutional when judged by these standards. "Extreme emotional disturbance" is, as the Court of Appeals recognized, the direct descendant of the "heat of passion" factor considered at length in *Mullaney*. I recognize, of course, that the differences between Maine and New York law are not unimportant to the defendant; there is a somewhat broader opportunity for mitigation. But none of those distinctions is relevant here. The presence or absence of extreme emotional disturbance makes a critical difference in punishment and stigma, and throughout our history the resolution of this issue of fact, although expressed in somewhat different terms, has distinguished manslaughter from murder.

The Court beats its retreat from *Winship* apparently because of a concern that otherwise the federal judiciary will intrude too far into substantive choices concerning the content of a State's criminal law. The concern is legitimate but misplaced. *Winship* and *Mullaney* are no more than what they purport to be: decisions addressing the procedural requirements that States must meet to comply with due process. They are not outposts for policing the substantive boundaries of the criminal law.

The *Winship/Mullaney* test identifies those factors of such importance, historically, in determining punishment and stigma that the Constitution forbids shifting to the defendant the burden of persuasion when such a factor is at issue. *Winship* and *Mullaney* specify only the procedure that is required when a State elects to use such a factor as part of its substantive criminal law. They do not say that the State must elect to use it. For example, where a State has chosen to retain the traditional distinction between murder and manslaughter, as have New York and Maine, the burden of persuasion must remain on the prosecution with respect to the distinguishing factor, in view of its decisive historical importance. But nothing in *Mullaney* or *Winship* precludes a State from abolishing the distinction between murder and manslaughter and treating all unjustifiable homicide as murder. In this significant respect, neither *Winship* nor *Mullaney* eliminates the substantive flexibility that should remain in legislative hands.

Moreover, it is unlikely that more than a few factors although important ones for which a shift in the burden of persuasion seriously would be considered will come within the *Mullaney* holding. With some exceptions, then, the State has the authority "to recognize a factor that mitigates the degree of criminality or punishment" without having "to prove its nonexistence in each case in which the fact is put in issue." New ameliorative affirmative defenses, which the Court expresses concern, generally remain undisturbed by the holdings in *Winship* and *Mullaney* and need not be disturbed by a sound holding reversing Patterson's conviction.

Furthermore, as we indicated in *Mullaney*, even as to those factors upon which the prosecution must bear the burden of persuasion, the State retains an important procedural device to avoid jury confusion and prevent the prosecution from being unduly hampered. The State normally may shift to the defendant the burden of production, that is, the burden of going forward with sufficient evidence "to justify [a reasonable] doubt upon the issue." If the defendant's evidence does not cross this threshold, the issue be it malice, extreme emotional disturbance, self-defense, or whatever will not be submitted to the jury.

To be sure, there will be many instances when the *Winship/Mullaney* test as I perceive it will be more difficult to apply than the Court's formula. Where I see the need for a careful and discriminating review of history, the Court finds a bright line standard that can be applied with a quick glance at the face of the statute. But this facile test invites tinkering with the procedural safeguards of the presumption of innocence, an invitation to disregard the principles of *Winship* that I would not extend.

Notes

1.   Isn't Justice Powell right that the majority in *Patterson* has created an indefensibly formalistic rule? If the drafters of legislation are careful to avoid colorful words like malice aforethought in favor of a lean modern approach, the requirement of proof beyond a reasonable doubt can be evaded. Justice White says there are obvious limits beyond which the legislature cannot go in playing the game of creating a minimal legislative crime and passing all of the issues that make the offense serious to the defense. Justice White's example of a limit that would exceed legislative authority is that it would be unconstitutional to declare a defendant presumptively guilty based upon the filing of the allegations of criminality in the indictment and require the defendant to prove innocence. Of course, that would violate procedural due process because we require a trial with many procedural protections including proof beyond a reasonable doubt. However, that example does not speak to the substantive due process question raised by Justice Powell that the substantive crime could be reduced to almost nothing.

In footnote 8 (renumbered above as footnote 2) in the Powell concurrence, Justice Powell refers to the hypothetical possibility that the state could pass a minor assault statute (an unconsented touching that could be regarded as offensive) and then require the defendant to (1) disprove an intent to kill or harm and (2) prove lack of causation of death or serious harm in order to win an acquittal or be convicted of a less-serious offense. If such a statute were carefully worded to conform to the drafting lessons of *Patterson*, wouldn't the statute be constitutional?

2.   A question for those with an undergraduate degree in English: After *Patterson*, who should you hire to draft statutes—Ernest Hemingway or William Faulkner?

3.   Is Justice Powell's position weakened by his concession that the legislature would be free to eliminate the historically important factor of provocation in homicide offenses? We don't offer a discount to reasonably provoked arsonists or embezzlers. If you were on trial for murder, would you prefer the law to be that reasonable provocation is irrelevant or to be able to argue for a provocation discount even if you bear the burden of production? Isn't Justice White right that

the New York legislature made a reasonable decision to liberalize the provocation discount to remove the rigidity of the common-law tradition, but to allow this broader defense only if the defendant is required to prove it by a preponderance of the evidence? Isn't Justice White correct in his footnote 8 in the majority opinion (renumbered as footnote 1 above) in *Patterson* that a rule that requires the state to prove any issue that makes a difference beyond a reasonable doubt instead of just the elements of the offense as drafted by the legislature will result in chilling the development of ameliorative new defenses that might benefit defendants?

4.   After *Mullaney* and *Patterson*, what is it that the State must prove beyond a reasonable doubt in a criminal case?

5.   A question that we will raise in cases dealing with defenses in the next chapters is whether there is a *Mullaney/Patterson* problem. Answering this question will require a two-step analysis: (1) Is there only a burden of production on the defendant or is there both a burden of production <u>and</u> a burden of persuasion on the defendant? (2) If it is the latter, is that defensive matter independent of the statutory elements or does it negate the statutory elements?

If the answer to the first question is that there is only a burden of production for the defendant, the analysis is at an end because there can be no *Mullaney/Patterson* violation merely from a production burden. Proof beyond a reasonable doubt speaks to persuasion, not merely a requirement of coming forward with evidence.

6.   Apply the two-part *Mullaney/Patterson* test to the two offenses we have already discussed: mistake of fact and mistake of law. The second step in the analysis can only be conducted with reference to a particular statutory offense. How else can you decide whether the defense is independent of the elements of the offense or whether the defense, if proved, negates one of the elements?

Assume that a statute provides that it is an offense intentionally or knowingly to operate the motor vehicle of another without the owner's consent. In one case, the claim is mistake of fact. The defendant claims he thought he had consent from the owner, but it turned out the person consenting was not the owner. In a second case, the defense is mistake of law by a police officer who is the defendant. The defendant's claim is that he knew he did not have the consent of the owner, but that he was lawfully entitled to take the car in an emergency due to his reliance on a written opinion of the attorney general that law enforcement officers can commandeer cars in an emergency.

7.   Is it a violation of *Mullaney/Patterson* for a legislature to put the burden of persuasion on the defense for self-defense? A definitive answer can be given without examining the charged criminal statute. In *Ohio v. Martin*, the Supreme Court upheld a statute that placed the burden of persuasion on the defense. In *Holloway v. McElroy*, 632 F.2d 605 (5th Cir. 1980), the Fifth Circuit Court of Appeals held that a Louisiana statute placing the burden of persuasion on the defendant was unconstitutional. The statute was unconstitutional as applied to a murder statute that stated the crime was committed if the defendant, "intentionally or knowingly and unlawfully caused the death of another." Can you guess how the wording of the Ohio statute differed from the one in Louisiana?

8.   What is the significance of the history of heat of passion manslaughter? Justice Powell, dissenting in *Patterson*, says only historically recognized defenses and mitigations are given the constitutional protection of proof beyond a reasonable doubt. Does history support the Powell analysis? As Justice Powell conceded in his majority opinion for the court in *Patterson*, the common law for centuries placed the burden of persuasion on the defendant to prove that an intentional killing occurred in the heat of passion.

        Is it significant that the modern trend is to put the burden on the prosecution (as a majority of states now do)? A significant minority, including New York, as discussed in *Patterson*, place the burden on the defendant. Unless there is a constitutional mandate, aren't states free to devise their own laws? Can the constitutional mandate be derived simply from what a majority of the states do? Justice White clearly says otherwise in *Patterson* in discounting the importance of the modern trend to the constitutional issue.

9.   Counting what the trend is in the state courts is an unstable proposition. Consider that Texas at the time of both *Mullaney* and *Patterson* was correctly counted among the states that put the burden of persuasion for provocation on the State once the defense has met a production burden. Where is the burden allocated now? Is the decision of the Texas legislature to shift the burden of the issue of provocation to the defendant impermissible under *Mullaney* or permissible under *Patterson*?

Rule: The state has the power to regulate procedures under which its laws are carried out, including the burden of producing evidence and the burden of persuasion, and its decision in this regard is not subject to proscription under the Due process clause unless it offends some principle of justice -> to be ranked fundamental.
The Δ who raises an affirmative defense shall bear the burden of persuasion unless the affirmative defense is "presumed element of the offense under the statute.

Issue: Were the Δ's rights violated when he was required under state law to bear the burden of persuasion for his affirmative defense to murder?

NO. 2 elements to crime & Malice not one of them

Dissent: Ct ignores holding in Mullaney + approves NY's requirement that Δ bear burden of persuasion. Language difference formalistic "fact" presumes none / factor at issue must make substantial difference in punishment & stigma

329

Texas Definitions Related to Burdens of Proof

The reduction of the penalty for murder (a first-degree felony carrying a maximum of life imprisonment) to the level of a second-degree murder (maximum of 20 years' imprisonment) is not a defense or an affirmative defense, terms that are generally used to refer issues that result in exoneration. The provocation issue that is now consigned to the punishment phase of trial could be described as a partial defense or a mitigation. In the next several chapters, we will encounter issues that are given the name defense or affirmative defense.

These two terms are used interchangeably in many jurisdictions. However, Texas has given the terms "defense" and "affirmative defense" separate specific definitions in Sections 2.03 and 2.04 of the Texas Penal Code. The difference between the two terms relates to the issues of burden of production and persuasion. This is very helpful in analyzing *Mullaney/Patterson* issues because the first step in the analysis is determining what burden is allocated to the defense. If only a burden of production is given to the defendant, the analysis is at an end because a *Mullaney/Patterson* violation only arises in cases in which a burden of persuasion is placed on the defendant's shoulders.

Under Section 2.03, a jury instruction on a "defense" is required to "charge that a reasonable doubt on the issue requires that the defendant be acquitted." Thus, a "defense" requires a defendant to meet a production burden of "some evidence" in order to inject the defensive issue into the case. Once this low threshold is passed, the judge instructs the jury that the State must disprove the proffered defense beyond a reasonable doubt.

Under Section 2.04, a jury instruction on an affirmative defense is required to "charge that the defendant must prove the affirmative defense by a preponderance of evidence." Thus, for an affirmative defense, the defendant must do more than meet a production burden; the defendant must persuade the jury of the existence of a valid defense by a preponderance of the evidence.

The full definition of defense and affirmative defense is set out below in the text of sections 2.03 and 2.04:

Sec. 2.03. Defense.

(a) A defense to prosecution for an offense in this code is so labeled by the phrase: "It is a defense to prosecution . . . ."

(b) The prosecuting attorney is not required to negate the existence of a defense in the accusation charging commission of the offense.

(c) The issue of the existence of a defense is not submitted to the jury unless evidence is admitted supporting the defense.

(d) If the issue of the existence of a defense is submitted to the jury, the court shall charge that a reasonable doubt on the issue requires that the defendant be acquitted.

(e) A ground of defense in a penal law that is not plainly labeled in accordance with this chapter has the procedural and evidentiary consequences of a defense.

Sec. 2.04. Affirmative Defense.

(a) An affirmative defense in this code is so labeled by the phrase: "It is an affirmative defense to prosecution . . . ."

(b) The prosecuting attorney is not required to negate the existence of an affirmative defense in the accusation charging commission of the offense.

(c) The issue of the existence of an affirmative defense is not submitted to the jury unless evidence is admitted supporting the defense.

(d) If the issue of the existence of an affirmative defense is submitted to the jury, the court shall charge that the defendant must prove the affirmative defense by a preponderance of evidence.

Chapter 16: Necessity and Duress

Introduction

The defense of necessity is a choice of evils claim in which a defendant admits a violation of a criminal statute but argues that the violation was preferable to the harm that would have resulted had the offense not occurred. A classic example is to destroy a building by pulling it down to create a fire break that prevents greater destruction. At one time, the defense of necessity was characterized as applying only to emergencies created by natural forces. This limitation has since disappeared and would apply to a situation involving human actors, such as a decision to operate an automobile at a speed faster than the posted limit in order to get a heart attack victim to a hospital.

Under the common law, the defense of necessity generally required:

- An imminent danger;
- No reasonable legal way to avoid the danger;
- The offense is the lesser harm;
- No contrary legislative enactment;
- Reasonable belief that the offense would effectively avoid the danger; and
- The defendant did not create the danger ("clean hands" doctrine).

The defense of duress can be characterized as a more specific type of necessity in which the evil to be avoided is an imminent threat of death or serious bodily injury. The statutory codification of the common-law defense of duress in Section 8.05 of the Texas Penal Code recognizes a defense to the commission of an offense less than a felony if there is an imminent threat of force or use of force. The duress statute creates a choice of evils affirmative defense, similar to the defense of necessity, by excusing criminal conduct because it is a lesser harm than the threatened infliction of force. Like necessity, there is a reasonableness requirement expressed in the duress statute as "force or threat of force [that] would render a person of reasonable firmness incapable of resisting the pressure."

Despite the similarity between the two defenses, necessity is considered a justification and duress is considered an excuse. The distinction between these two types of defenses is often elusive, and the drafters of the Model Penal Code advocated moving away from these concepts. The distinction persists in some jurisdictions. The primary difference is that justified actions cannot be lawfully resisted, and a person could aid another who is justified but not one who is merely excused. Insanity is an excuse defense. A sane person who aided an insane person to commit a crime would not be excused, and the criminal acts of the insane person could be resisted by the victims of those acts. In contrast, a person could aid a person who is acting in self-defense, which is generally considered a justification.

Imminence and Legislative Preclusion

There is little controversy about whether some type of necessity defense should be recognized by the law, but there are stringent limitations on its availability. The *Roy* case that follows demonstrates two of the important limitations on the defense.

Fake cop (margin annotation)

Roy v. State

552 S.W.2d 827 (Tex. Crim. App. 1977)

Onion, Presiding Judge.

This is an appeal from a conviction for unlawfully carrying a handgun. TEX. PENAL CODE ANN. § 46.02 (Vernon 1977). Punishment of one hundred twenty (120) days in jail and a fine of $300.00 was assessed by the jury.

The record discloses that around 1 a.m., April 2, 1975, police officers Townsend and Fergerson were on routine patrol in the 5th Ward area of Houston. They observed a 1974 Dodge pickup truck driven by appellant leave the parking lot of Scorpio's Lounge and proceed slowly near the intersection of 76th Street and Avenue P. The officers noticed a passenger slumped down alongside appellant in the pickup cab. Townsend testified that he decided to stop appellant because of his slow rate of speed and because he thought appellant had just picked up a prostitute. Both Townsend and Fergerson testified that they had difficulty stopping the pickup, even after turning on their flashing lights. Appellant finally stopped only after the police car pulled directly in front of his truck.

Townsend further testified that appellant was abusive and arrogant when questioned and that he claimed to be a deputy constable entitled to carry a weapon. As proof of his alleged peace officer status, appellant displayed a printed card and badge which purported to identify him as a deputy constable of Harris County. Since the card contained no photograph or fingerprint identification, Townsend was suspicious and radioed his supervisor, Sergeant Chebret. Chebret arrived shortly thereafter and after examining the identification card, concluded that appellant was not a law enforcement officer and directed that he be arrested. Immediately after the arrest, Townsend conducted an inventory of the pickup and discovered a loaded .38 caliber revolver in the side compartment of the left door.

A's argument / *Holding* (margin annotations)

Appellant contends that the trial court erred in refusing to allow him to establish the defense of necessity by testimony of the arresting officers on the issue of inadequate police patrols and appellant's alleged need to carry the pistol for self-protection. We hold that the error, if any, in excluding this testimony was harmless.

The defense of necessity was only recently established in Texas with the 1973 enactment of Texas Penal Code § 9.22. The statute makes availability of the defense dependent on three conditions: (1) the actor must reasonably believe the conduct is immediately necessary to avoid imminent harm; (2) the harm sought to be avoided must clearly be greater than the harm actually caused (*i.e.*, the offense); and (3) a legislative purpose to exclude the justification claimed for the conduct must not otherwise plainly appear. Without considering the second condition, we conclude that the first and third conditions were not satisfied, that the defense of necessity was not raised by the evidence, and that there was no harm in the trial court's exclusion of the proffered testimony.

Appellant's bills of exception reveal that the officers would have testified before the jury as follows:

> Officer Townsend: that the site of the offense is adjacent to an area where an officer was shot 2 weeks before; that this area was one involving "quite a few robberies of people and burglaries and mugging . . .;" that the officer did not know whether sufficient police protection existed in the area to guarantee the personal safety of all the residents; and that this "beat" was no tougher than the others.

> Officer Fergerson: that an estimated 3 police patrol vehicles at a time were patrolling an estimated 30 square mile area near the site of the offense; that there were approximately 30 or 40 taverns in the area; that this was what the officers considered to be a "high crime" area; that in the officer's opinion, "with the manpower that we have, we can get out there and try" to adequately protect the area.

Even construing this testimony favorably to appellant, we fail to see any circumstances which made it immediately necessary for appellant to possess a weapon. Nor does it appear elsewhere in the record that appellant had been threatened or that he was in any conceivable danger of imminent harm. Although appellant testified that his truck had been burglarized sometime in the past and that someone had once "used a firearm on him," such testimony fails to establish an immediate necessity to avoid imminent harm. Therefore, the first condition under § 9.22 could not have been satisfied.

The third condition makes the defense of necessity unavailable if a legislative purpose to exclude it is expressed elsewhere in the law. PRACTICE COMMENTARY, § 9.22. We find such purpose to be expressed in V.T.C.A., Penal Code, § 46.02, which seeks to prohibit carrying deadly weapons. The Legislature has not deprived citizens of the right to bear arms; rather, § 46.02 is an attempt to insure that certain types of weapons readily capable of and specifically designed for inflicting serious injury are removed from the public domain. To allow any person to carry a weapon prohibited under § 46.02 anytime he felt he was in a "high crime" area would openly thwart the purpose of the statute.

For these reasons, we hold that appellant's proffered evidence did not raise a fact issue entitling him to the defense of necessity and that the trial court committed no error in excluding it.

A did not meet 2 conditions

NO imminent harm
You need reason to believe

The judgment is affirmed.

Notes

1.   The defendant in *Armstrong v. State*, 653 S.W.2d 810 (Tex. Crim. App. 1983), argued it was reversible error for the trial court to refuse to submit a requested necessity defense instruction to justify a violation of the same gun statute as the one involved in *Roy*. The holding in *Roy* was distinguished on the theory that the threat in *Roy* was a remote and generalized fear whereas, in *Armstrong*, the defendant had been (1) raped two weeks before the gun offense and (2) threatened with death by her rapist one week before the gun offense if she informed the

police of the rape. With the aid of a gun, Armstrong had managed to turn her attacker into the police, but he'd been released on bond. He subsequently intimidated Armstrong's mother before Armstrong was arrested for illegally carrying a handgun. The *Armstrong* Court stated:

> We decline to hold that, as a matter of law, specific threats by a specific person who has committed violent acts directed against the threatened person cannot raise the defense of necessity if the person so threatened is then charged with carrying a weapon which she believes to have been necessary, in the circumstances, to her defense.

Armstrong, 653 S.W.2d at 811.

The difference between the more specific threat as opposed to the more generalized fear in *Roy* is a valid distinction with regard to imminent need to violate a penal statute. But to the extent that the greater immediacy was prompted by a threat of death or serious injury from a human actor, the proper defense would appear to be the more specific offense of duress rather than the more easily established defense of necessity. However, the *Armstrong* Court made no reference to the more appropriate, but more onerous, defense of duress in ruling the trial court erred by not granting the defense request for a necessity instruction.

If defense counsel is able to obtain a necessity instruction, it is preferable to a duress instruction because duress is an affirmative defense and necessity is a defense, as are all of the justifications found in Chapter 9 of Texas Penal Code. Affirmative defenses require a defendant to meet a preponderance of the evidence persuasion burden with regard to the defense, but defenses require only that a defendant meet a burden of production. Once the production burden is met, the State must disprove the defense beyond a reasonable doubt. Duress requires a threat of serious bodily injury or death in a felony case. Necessity merely requires that the harm of the criminal violation be outweighed by the threatened harm.

2.   Did the greater imminence in the *Armstrong* case cause the legislative preclusion problem to disappear as well?

3.   The importance of the imminence of the harm is illustrated by *Armstrong* and *Roy.* Speculative future fear is often found to be insufficient. If the threatened harm is clearly too remote, the trial court may decide the issue as a matter of law by refusing the requested instruction. The Third Court of Appeals found that the harm allegedly avoided was too remote to justify the necessity instruction granted by the trial court. The defendant, fighting the charge of possession of marijuana over four ounces, argued that as a matter of law, the State's evidence did not rebut his defense. He'd presented expert testimony that his use of marijuana was necessary to combat post-traumatic stress disorder brought on when he was required to terminate his wife's life support system. The Court of Appeals stated:

> According to the uncontested testimony, smoking marihuana was appellant's preferred coping mechanism. However, appellant himself testified that during a five-month period when he did not smoke marihuana, he was able to avoid causing serious injury to himself and others. While we do not doubt that appellant's post-traumatic stress disorder may have made this task difficult, the imminent harm component contemplates more than this; it necessitates an immediate, non-deliberative action made without hesitation or thought of the

legal consequence. Appellant's marihuana possession resulted from a considered decision to cultivate fifteen marihuana plants. Appellant's "medicinal" use of marihuana to manage his post-traumatic stress disorder symptoms is not the type of imminent harm to which the necessity defense applies. Accordingly, the district court erred by instructing the jury on the defense of necessity.

Stefanoff v. State, 78 S.W.3d 496 (Tex. App.—Austin 2002, pet. ref'd).

Continuing Necessity

Defenses of necessity and duress only last for as a long as the threatened harm. In *Duson v. State*, 559 S.W.2d 807 (1977), for example, a defendant's claim that driving while intoxicated was necessary because he was escaping from threatened violence in a tavern was rejected because his arrest occurred many blocks from the scene of the alleged assault. Assuming his claim about the attack was true, his continued driving was no longer justified. Limitations of this sort have been criticized by some commentators as creating unrealistic requirements, particularly if the result is a decision not to give a jury instruction that would allow the jury to judge the validity of the claim. In a number of jurisdictions, claims of a necessity or duress justifying a prison escape because of fear of assault or a fire in the prison have been refused without a jury instruction on the ground of a lack of continuing necessity. The justification for denying the defendant the opportunity to present such a claim has been that because escape is a continuing offense; even if the initial escape is justified, the failure of the defendant to turn himself in as soon as the immediate danger has passed prevents any possible defense. In Texas, a more generous approach has been taken, as the *Spakes* case illustrates.

Spakes v. State *escaped jail*

891 S.W.2d 7 (Tex. App—Amarillo 1994)

Boyd, Justice.

In this appeal, appellant Harry Jack Spakes attacks his conviction for the offense of escape, a third degree felony. The ensuing punishment, enhanced by virtue of two previous felony convictions, was assessed by the trial jury at sixty (60) years confinement in the Institutional Division of the Texas Department of Criminal Justice. Appellant contends the trial Δ's court erred in excluding the defense of necessity in its jury charge. For reasons later expressed, *argument* we reverse the judgment of the trial court. *Holding*

Appellant testified that while he was confined in the Potter County jail in 1991, he successfully filed a grievance against a corrections officer who was thereafter demoted. Appellant was transferred to the Randall County jail in November 1992. Prior to his transfer, appellant was told by a Potter County corrections officer that the demoted officer had friends in the Randall County jail and, if appellant were transferred there, "he (appellant) wouldn't make it out of here alive."

Appellant said he expressed his fears about being transferred to his wife, attorney, and the officer transferring him from Potter County who assured him he would have an audience with Sergeant Sluder, the Randall County jail supervisor. Two days after his transfer, appellant met with Sluder and informed him of his fear that he might be killed in the Randall County jail. Sluder responded that appellant would be placed in a jail section which housed more inmates as the risk of an incident would be less and so that Sluder could keep an eye on him better.

For four weeks after appellant's conversation with Sluder, no incidents occurred while he was being held in section DM–15. However, during that period, appellant filed writs against Randall County, a lawsuit against Randall and Potter Counties, and assisted other prisoners with their legal matters. This practice, he noted, was frowned upon by the corrections officers. On December 4, 1992, without warning or explanation, correction officers entered his cell after "lights out" and transferred him to cell D–4, which contained three capital murder suspects.

Appellant believed he was being punished by this cell transfer and cites testimony by Sluder that during the four-week period prior to the move, no disciplinary reports had been filed against him by corrections officers, nor had any grievances been filed against him by other inmates. On December 4, 1992, as a result of the cell transfer, appellant filed a grievance. Although such grievances are ordinarily answered within seventy-two hours, Sluder did not reply to this grievance until seven or eight days later. According to appellant, other than the grievance procedure, there was no other practical way to communicate his fears because, although the cells have emergency communication buttons, he was afraid his cell mates could overhear any attempt he made to talk to the authorities by use of the emergency communication.

Three days before the escape giving rise to this prosecution, appellant was told by his cell mates of the planned escape. The cell mates threatened to cut his throat if he did not accompany them because they feared he would inform the corrections officers of their escape. Because of the crimes with which his cell mates were charged (one of his cell mates having bragged about chopping up his girlfriend with an axe), appellant believed they would not fail to carry out their threat.

After the escape, and after separating from the other escapees, appellant approached the Suburban Bible Church between Amarillo and Canyon. He testified that he asked a woman waiting in the church parking lot "if [he] could get some help" and some water. She replied that there were people in the church that would help him and that he could get some water inside.

Coincidentally, there were two off-duty police officers in the church who recognized appellant and arrested him. Under cross-examination, when asked why he did not turn himself in to the authorities during the twelve-hour period he was separated from the others, appellant's only explanation was "I don't trust them. This was when I didn't trust anybody."

There is a paucity of cases in Texas considering if, when, and how the necessity defense is applicable to the offense of escape. In *Branson v. State*, the Texas Court of Criminal Appeals, without specifically discussing whether the defense of necessity is available in an escape case, rejected the contention that sordid jail conditions and the desire to seek the aid of counsel entitles an escapee to a charge on the necessity defense. En route to that conclusion, the court noted that the common law "appears to have recognized that there was a possible defense to the crime of escape" in extreme cases. The court did not expressly deny that a necessity defense might be one of those possible defenses. Therefore, even if it did not do so explicitly, inferentially the court recognized that in a proper case, the defense of necessity might be available.

In *Fitzgerald v. State*, an escape case in which the necessity defense was raised, the court noted that Texas formerly did not have a statute recognizing the general principle of the necessity defense except in special limited circumstances. However, the court commented that section 9.22 of the Texas Penal Code had now firmly established its existence and spelled out the details of its application. Even so, the court noted "it is still a general principle, admitting its application on an ad hoc determination of 'the myriad variety of harms to avoid which a person is justified in committing an offense.'" Significantly, the court went on to say that it "seems to have accepted that in compelling enough circumstances an escape may be justified." Thus, by a process of gradual evolution, it now appears to be established that in a proper escape case, the necessity defense of section 9.22 is available.

It is well established that a defendant is entitled to an affirmative defensive instruction on every issue raised by the evidence regardless of whether it is strong, feeble, unimpeached or contradicted and even if the trial court is of the opinion that the testimony is not entitled to belief. The defendant's testimony alone may be sufficient to raise a defensive theory requiring a charge.

Thus, having made the decision that the necessity defense is available in an escape case, it next becomes necessary for us to decide if the evidence in this case was sufficient to require the submission of that defense in the charge. Our review of the evidence convinces us that appellant's testimony was sufficient to require the submission of the defense to the jury. A proper objection having been made, the failure to submit the question presents reversible error.

340

Holding

Accordingly, the judgment of the trial court is reversed and the cause remanded to that court.

Spakes v. State

913 S.W.2d 597 (Tex. Crim. App. 1996)

Per Curiam.

A jury convicted Appellant of escape and assessed his punishment at sixty years imprisonment after finding that he was a habitual offender. This conviction was reversed because the trial court failed to submit a requested instruction on the defense of necessity.

The State's petition was granted to determine whether a predicate to the defense of necessity, as applicable to the offense of escape, includes an attempt to surrender once the immediate threat justifying the escape has ceased. The State notes that numerous other jurisdictions have imposed this requirement based on an analysis conducted in *People v. Lovercamp,* 43 Cal. App. 3d 823, 118 Cal. Rptr. 110 (1975).

Texas adopted the current penal code in 1973, incorporating within it several common law defenses, including necessity and duress. TEX. PENAL CODE ANN. § 9.22 (Necessity) provides that conduct is justified if:

(1) the actor reasonably believes the conduct is immediately necessary to avoid imminent harm;

(2) the desirability and urgency of avoiding the harm clearly outweigh, according to ordinary standards of reasonableness, the harm sought to be prevented by the law prescribing the conduct; and

(3) a legislative purpose to exclude the justification claimed for the conduct does not otherwise plainly appear.

Texas Penal Code § 38.07, at the time this offense was committed provided:

(a) A person commits an offense if he escapes from custody when he is:

(1) Under arrest for, charged with, or convicted of an offense; or

(2) In custody pursuant to a lawful order of a court.

As can be seen, "a legislative purpose to exclude the justification claimed for the conduct does not otherwise plainly appear." Although the State presents several cogent arguments as to why an attempt to surrender should be a prerequisite to applying a necessity defense to the offense of escape, these arguments are appropriate for the legislature, not for the judiciary. The plain language codifying the necessity defense evinces a legislative intent that the defense apply to all offenses unless the legislature has specifically excluded it from them. We therefore conclude that a person accused of escape need not present evidence of an attempted surrender before a necessity instruction is required, if some evidence otherwise complying with § 9.22 has been presented.

The judgment of the Court of Appeals is affirmed.

Keller, Judge, dissenting.

The majority holds that an attempt to surrender is not a predicate to the necessity defense in a prosecution for the offense of escape. The majority reaches this conclusion by reasoning that, because escape is not a continuing offense, an inmate's departure may be justified merely by the circumstances that exist at the time he initially leaves custody, regardless of whether he attempts to return to custody after those circumstances dissipate. Under the majority's analysis, a convict is free to stay at large forever, so long as his initial departure was immediately necessary to avoid imminent harm. I disagree.

The necessity defense consists of three elements, all of which must be satisfied. While the majority opinion clearly addresses the first and third elements, I believe that it has failed to properly take into account the second element. The second element requires an assessment of the policy reasons for taking a particular action and balances the interests of society versus those of the individual. In balancing these competing interests, I would submit that the harm the individual seeks to avoid in escaping custody never outweighs the harm the law seeks to prevent unless the individual returns (or attempts to return) to custody after the danger motivating his departure has passed.

The majority apparently believes that the balancing of interests can take into account only the facts that exist at the time the escape is complete. But, nothing in the language of the second element requires that the balancing of interests be limited to the timeframe in which the offense occurs. There exist examples in the Penal Code that expressly contemplate a defense being established by events occurring after the completion of an offense. The renunciation defense to solicitation must occur after all the elements of the solicitation offense are satisfied. Moreover, the provision reducing the punishment for kidnapping if the victim is released in a "safe place" has been analyzed like a defense. Obviously, the "release in a safe place" must occur after the elements of the kidnapping are complete.

The necessity defense is really the ultimate catch-all provision for criminal defenses. It is used to judge extreme situations that ought to constitute a defense but have not been specifically provided for by the legislature. While it may not always be appropriate to look beyond the timeframe of the offense itself when assessing competing interests, when it is appropriate, we should not hesitate to do so. I believe that this case presents the latter situation.

Although the issue appears to be one of first impression in Texas, the Court's opinion is at odds with the majority of jurisdictions that have addressed the issue. Most jurisdictions (thirty) require an attempt to surrender or report to the authorities (assuming there is time to do so) as a precondition for asserting justification-type defenses.

Admittedly, several jurisdictions have held that the surrender requirement turns upon whether or not escape is a continuing offense. But aside from the continuing offense distinction, there is another rationale for incorporating into the necessity defense a requirement to report to the authorities: considerations of public policy warrant imposing this requirement in order to balance adequately the interests of the individual against the interests of society. When a Texas statute is unambiguous, an appellate court must interpret it in accordance with the plain meaning of its words unless that interpretation would lead to absurd results. But, even if we were to hold § 9.22 to be unambiguous, subsection (2) plainly requires the balancing of the individual's interests against those of society. Unlike any other provision of the Penal Code, the necessity defense expressly mandates the application of public policy considerations.

Because I believe that the harm the escapee seeks to avoid never clearly outweighs the harm the law seeks to prevent unless the escapee subsequently surrenders or attempts to do so (as long as he has the opportunity), I would reverse and remand accordingly.

I respectfully dissent.

Notes

1.   The holding in *Spakes*—that an escaped prisoner need not surrender in order to claim the defense of necessity—is not the rule followed in most jurisdictions. In most other jurisdictions, escape is considered to be a continuing offense. The United States Supreme Court addressed the issues of prison escape, the defense of necessity, and the requirement of surrender in *United States v. Bailey*, 444 U.S.394 (1980). The Court concluded that, because under federal law escape is a continuing offense, the defense of necessity is available only to a defendant who surrendered or who offered evidence that his failure to surrender was justified:

> [S]everal considerations lead us to conclude that, in order to be entitled to an instruction on duress or necessity as a defense to the crime charged, an escapee must first offer evidence justifying his continued absence from custody as well as his initial departure and that an indispensable element of such an offer is testimony of a bona fide effort to surrender or return to custody as soon as the claimed duress or necessity had lost its coercive force.

> [W]e think it clear beyond peradventure that escape from federal custody as defined in § 751(a) is a continuing offense and that an escapee can be held liable for failure to return to custody as well as for his initial departure. Given the continuing threat to society posed by an escaped prisoner, "the nature of the crime involved is such that Congress must assuredly have intended that it be treated as a continuing one."

Judge Keller, dissenting in the *Spakes* case, argued that in Texas, the surrender requirement should apply even if escape is not a continuing offense. She would so rule for policy reasons. Do you agree? Is there a difference between:

(a) finding the evidence sufficient on appeal if a duress or necessity escape defense is rejected at trial, and
(b) denying the defendant a jury instruction in this kind of case at trial?

2.   Holdings like the one in *Bailey* create categorical exclusions for the defenses of duress and necessity and prevent jury consideration of situations where defendants have been under enormous pressure. One such categorical exclusion is the common-law rule that duress and necessity are never available to justify a homicide. A typical case is *United States v. LaFleur*, 971 F.2d 200 (9th Cir. 1991), where the refusal to instruct the jury occurred in a case in which the defendant claimed that he was forced to participate in a murder at gunpoint. Several justifications have been given for the rule. The fact that the co-defendant claimed the same defense and both defendants pointed fingers at the other helps to explain the reluctance of the law to recognize claims of duress and necessity for murder. It has also been argued that taking a life can never be the lesser evil because the threat of death to the defendant can only be at best an equal evil.

The Model Penal Code takes a different approach by recommending that the restriction against homicide offenses should be removed so that the issue becomes a jury issue. An example of a possibly appropriate case is the 19th century case of *United States v. Holmes*, 26 F. Cas. 360 C.C.E.D. Pa. (1842), which involved an overloaded life raft following the collision of a ship with an iceberg. Because it appeared that the small boat might sink with its 31 passengers, the surviving crew members threw 14 single men to their deaths in the ocean (women, children, and married men who were with their families were spared). The seamen were convicted and sentenced to six months' imprisonment.

The Model Penal Code drafters felt that the arbitrary restriction for homicide offenses could possibly yield if the jury agrees in extraordinary circumstances, like the life raft case, on the theory that some dying is better than all perishing. Many states have retained the common-law barrier that maintains a firm line against justifying any homicide. The language of the Texas statutes closely tracks the Model Penal Code provisions on duress and necessity. No Texas court has addressed the question of whether the Texas statutes are designed to liberalize the common law rule to make duress potentially available in homicide cases.

3.   It is clear that Texas has repudiated one common-law doctrine. The Texas duress statute explicitly rejects the archaic common law doctrine of "coverture," which presumed that a woman committing a crime in the presence of her husband was acting under duress. Section 8.05(e) provides: "It is no defense that a person acted at the command or persuasion of his spouse, unless he acted under compulsion that would establish a defense under this section."

4.   A common category of defendants who pursue a defense of necessity are political protesters. Often these defendants seek to be arrested, often for a criminal trespass, by refusing to move from a nuclear power plant, an abortion clinic, a defense installation, or a foreign embassy to protest some social or political issue. The protestors engage in civil disobedience and then raise a choice of evils claim that their actions are a lesser evil than what they are protesting. These claims usually run aground on the shoals of the legislative preclusion doctrine, but courts often allow the protestors to present their claims. Because public exposure of the issue is the goal, the trial often achieves the purpose of the protestors, even though the defendants are convicted usually of minor offenses.

Clean Hands

A common limitation of the defenses of duress and necessity is that the defendant asserting the claim must be free from fault in bringing about the situation in which resort to the violation of the law became necessary. This doctrine, often referred to as the "clean hands" doctrine, is designed to prevent the defenses to those whose conduct would foreseeably lead to the need to commit crimes. This issue is explored in the duress case of *Tyner*.

Tyner v. State

No. 05-99-00310-CR, 2001 WL 683638 (Tex. App.—Dallas, June 19, 2001)

Bridges, J.

Rayland Ladon Tyner appeals his aggravated robbery conviction. The jury convicted appellant and sentenced him to fifty-five years' confinement and a $1645.50 fine. In a single point of error, appellant argues the trial court erred in denying his request for an instruction on the law of duress. We reverse the trial court's judgment and remand for further proceedings.

We note appellant does not challenge the sufficiency of the evidence to support his conviction. Thus, only a brief recitation of the facts is necessary. On September 27, 1998, appellant robbed a Sonic restaurant at gunpoint. At trial, appellant testified and admitted committing the robbery but claimed he did so under duress. Specifically, appellant testified he was at an apartment complex prior to the robbery when three men, members of a rival gang, drove up and confronted him. The driver of the car pointed a gun at appellant and told him to get in the car. Appellant refused. The driver told appellant "we got your baby mama around the corner pregnant and she can deliver any time, any time." At the time, appellant's wife was pregnant, and he testified he got in the car because he was afraid for her. Appellant had seen his wife earlier that day but had not seen her since. In the car, appellant told the men they had him, but he asked them to leave his wife alone. Appellant testified he had been selling drugs in some apartments on the men's turf, and they said he had caused a shortage in their money.

Appellant thought the men were going to kill him, so to help himself survive, appellant took out a mirror and snorted $200 to $300 worth of cocaine that he had. Appellant believed the cocaine would make his heart keep pumping and allow him to live longer if the men shot him.

The men drove appellant around Dallas and finally stopped and told appellant to give them everything in his pockets. The driver of the car pointed at a Sonic restaurant and told appellant, "I want you to bring me the money." Appellant understood this to mean they wanted him to rob the Sonic. One of the men threw appellant a black hat, but appellant stayed in the car. Appellant asked for a gun, and one of the men hit him in the back of the head with a gun. One of the men asked appellant if he thought it was a game and said, "Didn't you buy that pistol from Kevin the other day?" In fact, appellant had a pistol tucked in his waistband under his shirt. Appellant got out of the car and approached the Sonic. One of the men told appellant to "think about your baby mama while you're in there. She can still go into labor at any time." Appellant pulled the hat over his face and went into the Sonic and told a woman, "I need your money." The Sonic employees put money in a bag that appellant took outside. The men who had brought appellant to the Sonic drove away, and police arrived and arrested appellant.

In his sole point of error, appellant argues the trial court erred in failing to include his requested instruction on the law of duress. It is an affirmative defense to prosecution that a person engaged in proscribed conduct because he was compelled to do so by threat of imminent death or serious bodily injury to himself or another. An accused is entitled to an affirmative defense instruction on every issue raised by the evidence, regardless of whether such evidence is strong, feeble, unimpeached or contradicted, and even if the trial court is of the opinion that the testimony is not entitled to belief. However, the claim of duress must have an objective, reasonable basis. Compulsion within the meaning of section 8.05 exists only if the force or threat of force would render a person of reasonable firmness incapable of resisting the pressure. The defense of duress is unavailable if the actor intentionally, knowingly, or recklessly placed himself in a situation in which it was probable that he would be subjected to compulsion.

At trial, appellant requested that the trial court charge the jury on the defense of duress. The trial court refused, stating the defense of duress is not available if the actor intentionally, knowingly, or recklessly placed himself in a situation in which it was probable that he would be subjected to compulsion. The trial court explained the evidence showed appellant engaged in drug selling activities in an area controlled by a gang of which he was not a member. For that reason, appellant testified, he was taken in a vehicle and forced to commit a robbery. The trial court concluded appellant's testimony effectively took away the defense of duress. We disagree.

Follow the trial court's rationale in denying appellant's request, no defendant would ever be entitled to a charge on duress if the defendant placed himself in a situation where it was probable he would be subjected to any compulsion. In this case, appellant was aware he was selling drugs in an area controlled by a rival gang, and he also testified he was aware his activity could put him and his wife in danger. However, we cannot conclude appellant thereby placed himself in a situation in which it was probable that he would be subject to being taken by armed men, who threatened his pregnant wife's safety, and compelled to rob a restaurant. Accordingly, the trial court erred refusing to charge the jury on this issue.

Notes

1.   It is unsettled whether defendants who choose to engage in drug-dealing or to join street gangs thereby place themselves in situations where threats of death or serious bodily injury are to be expected, in effect forfeiting the defense of duress. Compare the court's decision in *Tyner* to these statements from cases ruling that the defendant could not present the defense of duress:

> "Varnado made a voluntary decision to place himself in a perilous position in the drug trade, thereby subjecting himself to the inherent dangers of his chosen vocation." *Varnado v. State*, 05-95-01542-CR, 1998 WL 10218 (Tex. App. Jan. 14, 1998).

> "Scott knowingly associated himself with the selling of drugs, a criminal activity, and with a gang noted for violence." *State v. Scott*, 827 P.2d 733, 741 (Kan. 1992).

> "By becoming involved with this drug ring, Williams through his own recklessness made others aware of his connection with Eubanks, including his abductors. Williams was readily identifiable to those in the organization, including his abductors, and the abductors acted accordingly. This was a situation

that would not have occurred but for Williams's association with the drug organization." *Williams v. State*, 646 A.2d 1101, 1110 (Md. App. 1994).

2.   *Tyner* is a duress case. Does a person who is forced to commit a crime by threat of death or serious bodily injury have a claim that any criminal act is involuntary? As we discussed in the chapter dealing with the act requirement, the concept of a required voluntary act is quite limited. A person acting out of duress or necessity has a claim that the lesser harm was chosen from an array of bad choices. Nonetheless the person does choose. Thus, while the decision may be coerced, it is not involuntary in the limited sense that this term is used in substantive criminal law.

3.   If a defendant claims he or she only agreed to drive the get-away car from the scene of a Texas robbery because he or she was threatened at gun point by the perpetrator of the robbery, the judge will instruct the jury about the duress defense under Section 8.05 of the Texas Penal Code, which is affirmative defense. This means the jury will be told that the defendant must establish the defense by a preponderance of the evidence. What result if the defendant objects to the instruction on grounds that the placement of the burden of persuasion violated due process under *Mullaney* and *Patterson*?

Chapter 17: Self-Defense

Introduction

Self-defense contains many of the requirements applicable to necessity and duress, such as an objective or reasonable person standard as to the imminent necessity to defend and in a manner reasonably proportional to the need. Like the clean hands doctrine with duress and necessity, one who provokes the need to resort to self-defense may not claim the defense.

The goal of the self-defense doctrine is to allow people to protect themselves when the state cannot, but not to allow vigilantism. A defendant may have a valid claim of self-defense even if she was mistaken in believing her use of force was necessary to respond to an imminent threat, so long as his belief was reasonable. Deadly force may not be used unless the actor reasonably believes a lethal degree of force is necessary to protect herself against imminent death or infliction of serious bodily harm by the other person.

Reasonable Belief

The reasonableness of a defendant's belief in the need to use self-defense has both a subjective and an objective component. The defendant must honestly believe that force was necessary. However, most of the debate in self-defense cases surrounds whether that defendant's subjective belief is reasonable. The question is whether a reasonable person in the defendant's circumstances would have believed that it was imminently necessary to resort to a reasonable degree of force to defend against an unlawful use of force by another. As with the objective standard used with the partial defense or mitigation of heat of passion in murder cases, there is a tension between the concept of examining the issue from the defendant's situation and the objective reasonableness standard. *Johnson v. State*, which follows, provides an example of a case raising difficult questions in applying the objective standard of reasonableness.

Johnson v. State

271 S.W.3d 359 (Tex. App—Beaumont 2008)

Charles Kreger, Justice.

In February 2002, a grand jury returned a three-count indictment charging appellant, Naomi Loutricia Johnson, with the offenses of murder, manslaughter, and criminally negligent homicide. The case proceeded to trial in April 2004, with appellant apparently testifying in her own defense. This trial ended with the jury unable to reach a verdict necessitating the trial court's declaring a mistrial. Retrial commenced in October 2006, with the State announcing it was proceeding only on the murder charge and abandoning the remaining counts. Appellant did not testify in her retrial. The jury found appellant guilty and the trial court assessed punishment at confinement in the Institutional Division of the Texas Department of Criminal Justice for a term of thirty-five years. Appellant [contends that] the trial court committed reversible error when it refused to give a jury instruction on the issue of self-defense.

With one significant exception, that being the question of self-defense, the basic facts are not in dispute. In the early morning hours of December 15, 2001, appellant stabbed T.L.B., her boyfriend of five years, in the chest with a pocket knife she carried in her purse. The stabbing took place in the front yard of appellant's home in which T.L.B. had also resided since 1996. T.L.B. sustained a three-quarter inch stab wound to the chest which pierced the pulmonary artery and continued on into the aorta causing his death.

Instruction on Self-Defense

Prior to commencing deliberations, the jury in a criminal case must be provided with "a written charge distinctly setting forth the law applicable to the case." For example, under the proper circumstances, a trial judge is required to instruct the jury on any statutory defense, including justification, whenever it is raised by the evidence. Thus, a defendant has the right to an instruction on every defensive issue raised by the evidence, regardless of whether the evidence is strong, feeble, unimpeached, or contradicted, and even when the trial court thinks that the testimony raising the defense is not worthy of belief. This statutory mandate is designed to insure that the jury, not the trial judge, will decide the relative credibility of all the evidence. *Granger v. State*, 3 S.W.3d 36, 38 (Tex. Crim. App. 1999) ("When a judge refuses to give an instruction on a defensive issue because the evidence supporting it is weak or unbelievable, he effectively substitutes his judgment on the weight of the evidence for that of the jury."). Furthermore, when inconsistent evidence elicited at trial supports more than one defensive theory, the defendant is still entitled to an instruction on every theory raised, even if the defenses are themselves inconsistent or contradictory.

A defendant need not testify in order for a defensive issue to be sufficiently raised. Defensive issues may be raised by the testimony of any witness, even one called by the State.

At the time of the incident in question, the applicable law governing self-defense read as follows:

351

§ 9.31. Self–Defense.

(a) Except as provided in Subsection (b), a person is justified in using force against another when and to the degree he reasonably believes the force is immediately necessary to protect himself against the other's use or attempted use of unlawful force.

§ 9.32. Deadly Force in Defense of Person.

(a) A person is justified in using deadly force against another:

> (1) if he would be justified in using force against the other under Section 9.31;

> (2) if a reasonable person in the actor's situation would not have retreated; and

> (3) when and to the degree he reasonably believes the deadly force is immediately necessary:

>> (A) to protect himself against the other's use or attempted use of unlawful deadly force; or

>> (B) to prevent the other's imminent commission of aggravated kidnapping, murder, sexual assault, aggravated sexual assault, robbery, or aggravated robbery.

On the day of the stabbing, appellant provided a written statement to the police. This statement was introduced into evidence before the jury as State's Exhibit No. 87. The more pertinent portions of appellant's statement appear in the record as follows:

> This all started on Friday, December 14, 2001. I came home at 5:53 PM. I remember looking at the clock in my car. [T.L.B.] got home at 6:13 PM. I know because I looked at the clock on the TV. [T.L.B.] went off on me about not cooking pork chops. He was cussing at me and calling me "b* * * *," "sorry motherf* * * * ", and "a* *hole." He said I wasn't looking for a job and that no other motherf* * * * * 'n* * * * * would put up with my sh* *. [T.L.B.] was all up in my face and wanted to know where I'd been. I told him to get out of my face and leave me alone. He tried to suck on my neck but I told him to stop. He smelled my perfume and wanted to know where I went since I wasn't working. I said I took my momma to The White House 'cause there was a sale. [T.L.B.] went off about my momma not paying for gas and he wanted to know why we went in the Lincoln instead of my momma's Cadillac. He grabbed my purse and dug around in it. He took the tops off my perfumes and spit on my shoes. I was watching Family Feud on channel 161 and he took the remote control from my hand and changed the channel. I just ignore him. When he took a shower, I turned the channel back to 161. After [T.L.B.] took a shower, he got up in my face again and asked me if I loved him. He was getting ready to go to Silsbee to get a haircut. That's where he's from and he goes there every Friday to get a haircut and shave. I told him that I didn't want to go with him, I just wanted to look at TV, but he insisted that I go.

> [T.L.B.] drove us to Silsbee in the Lincoln. We left about 8:00 PM. I didn't want to talk to him so he was all upset and said that he ain't gonna talk to himself. At the barber, [T.L.B.] said I was trying to show my cleavage. He's always accusing me of messing

around. After the haircut, [T.L.B.] drove us to a house on Harriet in Beaumont. A chick named Wilma lived there. [T.L.B.]'s sister . . . . and two guys named Chris and Leon. We got there sometime between 9:30 and 10:00 PM. We were all there conversating and after a while, [T.L.B.'s sister] got up and left 'cause she thought I was making eyes at Chris. Then [T.L.B.] got mad and was thinking me and Chris was trying to be on cool, but we were just talking. [T.L.B.] said we were leaving or I had to walk. We got in the car and [T.L.B.] drove us home. He was steady saying that he was gonna beat my a* * and calling me a b* * * *. We got home around 11:00 PM. We were still arguing. When we got in the house, [T.L.B.] was cussing and clowning and raising hell. I left the front door open so everybody could hear. I don't have a phone, so I was thinking somebody might call the police. He said he was gonna bust me in the head and his fist was all balled. This was all in the living room. [T.L.B.] was grabbing and pulling on me. I took my pocket knife out of my purse. I was holding it in my left hand. Somehow we ended up back outside and he was coming at me and I stabbed him in the chest. It was just reflex 'cause I wasn't gonna let him hit me. I stabbed him just one time. [T.L.B.] fell and started doing convulsions and stuff. I was hysterical. I tried to help him. I dragged him into the driveway and tried to do CPR, but it didn't work. He died. I didn't know what to do. I dragged [T.L.B.] to the back yard so I could go call for help. I drove the Lincoln to my sister's house at Calder West Apartments. My sister [S.P.] lives there. I told her what happened. She drove me to my momma's house on Woodway 'cause she didn't have a phone at her apartment. When we got there, my sister, [T.N.], called 911. After that, [S.P.] drove us to my house on Amarillo.

Detective Bryan Skinner of the Beaumont Police Department was involved in investigating the incident and initially interviewed appellant at the scene of the offense. Skinner testified that appellant admitted stabbing T.L.B. "so he wouldn't jump on her, I believe, is the way she phrased it." Later on that day, Skinner took appellant's statement, set out above, at the police station. During cross-examination, Skinner was asked if anything in appellant's written statement triggered the belief that appellant had been defending herself during her altercation with T.L.B., with Skinner replying, "That is what I believe she was trying to convey, and you can take it at face value. I do not believe the facts substantiated what she was saying." Moments later, the following exchange took place:

[Trial Counsel:] She also told you that she wasn't going to let him hit her, correct?

[Detective Skinner:] That was what she said.

[Trial Counsel:] Does that sound like self-defense?

[Detective Skinner:] That is what she was claiming.

[Trial Counsel:] You believed everything else of her statement, correct?

[Detective Skinner:] No, sir. I said that's what she wanted to say and you can look at it at face value and believe what you want. I said the facts don't substantiate everything that she said.

While appellant chose not to testify, the defense called two of her friends as witnesses. Both witnesses were female and both had observed the relationship between appellant and T.L.B.

over the course of several years. They each also testified to having witnessed T.L.B. physically assault appellant on separate occasions. One defense witness who observed T.L.B. grab appellant by the throat, choke, and shove her was of the opinion that T.L.B. was capable of causing appellant serious injury. Each witness also stated that T.L.B. verbally abused appellant on a regular basis.

At the close of the evidence, the trial court submitted its proposed charge to each side. When asked for objections, appellant's trial counsel responded with the following:

> [Trial Counsel:] There is, Your Honor. The objection is to the failure to include an instruction on self-defense in the charge. I would proffer that it would be proper based on the testimony to provide the jury with the self-defense instruction that's followed by force and then deadly force as justification secondary to self-defense, Your Honor.

Without elaboration, the trial court denied the request for a self-defense instruction. On appeal, appellant's position is that she did present evidence which entitled her to the self-defense instruction requested. The State's reply brief concedes that appellant both properly requested the self-defense instruction and preserved the issue for review, but argues that the evidence presented failed to raise the issue in that there was no evidence indicating appellant was facing deadly force or the threat of death at the time she stabbed T.L.B. As framed, the issue we must decide is whether the evidence adduced at trial by either party, when viewed in the light most favorable to appellant, is sufficient to raise the issue of self-defense.

At the outset, we note that in *Hamel v. State*, the Court reaffirmed its holding that it is not necessary for a jury to find the deceased was using or attempting to use unlawful deadly force against a defendant in order for the defendant's right of self-defense to exist. A person has the right to defend himself from "apparent danger" to the same extent as he would if the danger were real. In the instant case, trial counsel's requested instruction specifically included wording on apparent danger. As noted above, section 9.32(a)(1) provides that a person is justified in using deadly force against another if he would be justified in using non-deadly force against the other under section 9.31. Section 9.31(a) justifies the use of force against another "when and to the degree he reasonably believes the force is immediately necessary to protect himself against the other's use or attempted use of unlawful force." This language in section 9.31(a) constitutes the "apparent danger" portion of a self-defense instruction.

Appellant's Self-Defense Evidence

In a homicide prosecution, a defendant who raises self-defense may introduce evidence of the decedent's violent character. "Specific, violent acts of misconduct may be admitted to show the reasonableness of the defendant's fear of danger, or to show that the deceased was the first aggressor."

In the instant case, to establish her "fear" (apparent danger from her standpoint) at the time of the stabbing, appellant introduced testimony from two of her friends who had personally witnessed past physical violence and verbal abuse directed toward appellant by T.L.B. The Court of Criminal Appeals has recognized this type of evidence as "an established method of proof in self-defense cases, because the law recognizes the fact that future conduct may be reasonably inferred from past conduct." Additional evidence of appellant's "fear" at the time of the stabbing

354

was also before the jury in the form of appellant's written statement, which described the continuing conflict between appellant and T.L.B. from the time both arrived home, with the abusive conduct on T.L.B.'s part escalating throughout the night and into the early morning hours of December 15. When a jury considers whether a defendant acted in self-defense, it must "view the reasonableness of the defendant's actions solely from the defendant's standpoint." As the Court noted in *Bennett*, the reasonableness of the defendant's fear "must be judged from the standpoint of the accused at the instant he responds to the attack." Viewed in the light most favorable to appellant, and under the appropriate standards of review, appellant presented sufficient evidence of apparent danger to warrant such an instruction.

[handwritten margin note: How to judge S.D.]

Along with her description of the escalating threats and verbal abuse by T.L.B. throughout the evening, appellant's written statement factually asserts that in the moments just before she stabbed him, T.L.B. had clenched his fist and had verbally threatened to "beat [appellant's] a* *," and "bust" appellant's head. Moreover, it is important to note that appellant perceived T.L.B. advancing toward her the moment she stabbed him; she explained that she "wasn't gonna let him hit me." As noted previously, for appellant to be entitled to a self-defense instruction, there must also be some evidence that, at the moment it became necessary for her to use deadly force, it was not reasonable for appellant to have retreated from the immediate situation.[1] The "retreat" provision in section 9.32(a)(2) requires the jury deciding the self-defense issue "to determine whether the appellant had the ability and opportunity to retreat considered as a part of all of the circumstances of the moment." Indeed, appellant's duty to retreat under section 9.32 did not arise until she believed deadly force was immediately necessary to protect herself against T.L.B.'s use or attempted use of unlawful deadly force. To undertake a retreat without a reasonable belief that one can escape the imminent threat of the perceived harm is not required. Thus, the duty to retreat encompasses something more than merely leaving the scene of the confrontation.

Taking the above-described evidence in the light most favorable to the defense, we find evidence of T.L.B.'s threats and verbal abuse directed at appellant throughout their relationship, including the day in question; evidence of the prior instances of physical assaults perpetrated on appellant by T.L.B.; appellant's statement that moments before the stabbing, T.L.B. clenched his fist and threatened to "beat [appellant's] a* *," and "bust" her head; and that as T.L.B. advanced toward appellant, she inflicted the single, albeit fatal, stab-wound to prevent T.L.B. from hitting her, combine to raise the issue that retreat was not a viable or reasonable alternative for appellant at the moment her duty to retreat arose.

In addressing appellant's [claim the trial court erred in not instructing the jury on the issue of self-defense], we do not apply the usual rule of appellate deference to the trial court's ruling denying a requested defensive instruction; instead, we view the evidence in the light most favorable to the defensive issue requested. In examining the trial evidence in the light most favorable to appellant's self-defense theory, we find the trial court erred in denying her the jury instruction.

Harm Analysis

---

1. *Schmolesky:* Note that Texas law no longer requires retreat. I have retained the discussion of retreat in this opinion because many other jurisdictions still require retreat before using deadly force, if retreat is possible.

Having found error in the trial court's denial of the requested self-defense instruction, we must now determine whether that error requires reversal. If the charge contains error, and that error has been properly preserved by an objection or requested instruction, reversal is required if the error is "calculated to injure the rights of defendant," meaning there must be some harm. "Unless all harm was abated, appellant suffered 'some' harm."

Because appellant admitted that she intentionally stabbed T.L.B. to stop him from jumping on her or hitting her, and the jury was not instructed to consider appellant's statutory defensive theory that was sufficiently raised by the evidence, the jury had no choice but to convict appellant of murder. The trial court's error prevented the jury from giving consideration to acquitting appellant by reason of her immediate need to defend herself from what she reasonably perceived to be an attempt by T.L.B. to cause her serious bodily injury or death. We therefore find the trial court's error was calculated to injure appellant's rights. From the error in question, appellant suffered some harm.

Holding We reverse the judgment of the trial court and remand for a new trial on the merits.

Horton, Justice, dissenting.

In my opinion, the majority does not properly place the burden of producing evidence on each of the elements of Johnson's claim of self-defense. Because Johnson did not meet her burden of production on two of the elements of her claim of self-defense, the trial court did not err in refusing her requested instruction. As a result, I dissent.

With respect to a claim of self-defense, the defendant bears the burden to "produce some evidence to support the particular defense." If the defendant meets that burden, the State would then shoulder the burden of persuasion to disprove the defense.

While there is certainly evidence that Johnson reasonably feared that the victim might strike her with his fists, there is no evidence to show that Johnson feared she might suffer any serious bodily injury or death at the time she stabbed the victim or that Johnson reasonably believed the victim's fists were deadly weapons. There is no evidence that Johnson thought the use of deadly force (in contrast to using non-deadly force) was immediately necessary to protect herself from the victim's impending assault. The evidence in the record does not show that Johnson subjectively believed that deadly force was necessary to meet the threat that the victim posed to her. The necessity of her proof on this element is illustrated by *Werner v. State*, where the Texas Court of Criminal Appeals held that "in absence of evidence of use or attempted use of deadly force by the deceased, the statutory defense permitted by § 9.32 is not available, and a defendant is not entitled to a jury instruction." On this record, I cannot infer that Johnson, when she stabbed the victim, reasonably thought that he was about to kill or seriously injure her. While it is possible that she might have formed such a subjective belief, there is no evidence that she did. Moreover, we do not know what Johnson subjectively believed at the time because she did not testify. The majority errs when it infers that Johnson believed she was facing deadly force based upon the victim's clenching of his fists and threats of assault. Consequently, I cannot determine that the trial court erred in refusing the requested instruction.

Finally, there is no testimony from any witness that the victim had ever threatened to kill Johnson, or that Johnson had previously expressed fear that the victim might kill her. Nor is there testimony that the victim on prior occasions had caused Johnson to suffer a serious bodily injury. I acknowledge that one of Johnson's friends testified that she believed that the victim caused Johnson to suffer a black eye on two prior occasions and that she saw the victim hit Johnson in the head on one occasion. Another of Johnson's friends saw the victim on a prior occasion choke Johnson. Nevertheless, even with the testimony of these two witnesses, the record is devoid of any evidence that the victim had previously caused Johnson any serious bodily injury or that Johnson feared that she might suffer a serious bodily injury on the evening that she stabbed the victim in the heart.

To support a claim of self-defense that justified her use of deadly force, Johnson bore the burden of producing evidence to show her subjective belief that deadly force was immediately necessary to avoid her suffering death or serious bodily injury. On this record, the trial court correctly refused the instruction because Johnson did not met her burden of production on that element of her self-defense claim. Because the majority finds that Johnson was entitled to the defense when on this record she was not, I dissent.

Notes

1. A defendant who reasonably believes force is necessary is not deprived of the defense of self-defense if it turns out he was mistaken. For example, if the gun that was pointed at the actor was unloaded, or if the person the defendant thought was breaking into his house turns out to be his next-door neighbor returning a borrowed item.

Texas courts commonly refer to the rule that self-defense can be justified by a mistaken but reasonable belief as the "apparent danger" doctrine. For example, the Texas Court of Criminal Appeals explained in a case in which the defendant claimed that he mistakenly thought he was being attacked:

> In the instant case, since appellant used deadly force, there must be some evidence to satisfy the requisites of Sections 9.31 and 9.32 [of the Texas Penal Code]. Thus there must be some evidence to show that appellant reasonably believed that use of deadly force was immediately necessary to protect himself against his brother's use or attempted use of unlawful force. That appellant was not in fact attacked by his brother is immaterial. A person has a right to defend from apparent danger to the same extent as he would had the danger been real; provided he acted upon a reasonable apprehension of danger as it appeared to him at the time.

Dyson v. State, 672 S.W.2d 460, 463 (Tex. Crim. App. 1984).

2. Compare the evidence of self-defense presented in *Johnson* to the evidence presented in *Samuel v. State*, another case in which the appellant argued on appeal that the trial court erred in not instructing the jury on the defense of self-defense:

Alonzo Samuel appeals a conviction for manslaughter on the grounds that the trial court erred by failing to instruct the jury on the use of deadly force in self-defense. Appellant stated that burglars had stolen the stereo and VCR from his apartment just a day before the incident (but he had not reported the burglary because he believed that doing so would be useless). On the day of the offense, appellant returned home at 10:40 p.m. Afraid that burglars might have come back to steal more of his property, he turned on the lights in the apartment to check for possible intruders. After determining that no one was in the living room and kitchen, he went to his bedroom to get his shotgun and check the rest of the apartment. While appellant was checking the bathroom, he heard the front door open and feared that the burglars had returned. As he was running to the living room, he saw a movement coming directly toward him. Appellant claimed that he and the complainant bumped into each other as he was trying to run out of the apartment and that, in a reflex reaction, he then tightened his grip on the gun and it went off. Appellant testified that he definitely did not intend to pull the trigger. [Appellant and the complainant were co-workers who car pooled to work together. Appellant claimed that he did not know why the complainant had come to his apartment but speculated that she probably came to pay him back $15 she borrowed a week earlier.]

Samuel v. State, No. 14-01-00255-CR, 2002 WL 58891 (Tex. App.—Houston Jan. 17, 2002).

In this case, was there any evidence to support the claim of self-defense? Is this case different from *Johnson v. State*?

3.　　What ought to be taken into account as part of the situation of the defendant which provides the setting for making the determination of reasonableness? In *Johnson*, neither the majority nor the dissenting opinion explicitly emphasize the defendant was female and the other person male. Should the analysis be gender neutral or should it be part of the relevant "situation"?

Most courts consider physical characteristics such as the relative size and strength of the actors to be relevant factors when assessing reasonableness, but there is a much greater reluctance to consider cultural background or psychological make-up as part of the defendant's situation. Would it be appropriate to include the defendant's unusually nervous nature as part of the defendant's "situation," or would that destroy the objectivity of the standard?

An example of the policy debate about this issue is the controversial case of Bernard Goetz, who shot four young black men on a subway car when one of them approached Goetz asking him for $5. The court ruled the jury could consider Goetz's prior experience of being robbed when assessing whether he reasonably believed the young men in the subway car were threatening him with death or serious bodily injury. As the court explained:

> [W]e have frequently noted that a determination of reasonableness must be based on the "circumstances" facing a defendant or his "situation." Such terms encompass more than the physical movements of the potential assailant. . . . [T]hese terms include any relevant knowledge the defendant had about that person. They also necessarily bring in the physical attributes of all persons involved, including the defendant. Furthermore, the defendant's circumstances encompass any prior experiences he had which could provide a reasonable basis for a belief that another person's intentions were to injure or rob him or that the use of deadly force was necessary under the circumstances.

People v. Goetz, 497 N.E.2d 41, 52 (N.Y. 1986).

A contrary result was reached in the Texas case of *Werner v. State*, 711 S.W.2d 639 (Tex. Crim. App. 1986), in which the trial court excluded testimony of a psychiatrist who would have testified the defendant exhibited the signs of a "Holocaust syndrome" by virtue of having been raised by parents who were survivors of Nazi death camps. Because of this background, the defendant "had a state of mind to defend because he comes from a family that did not." The Texas Court of Criminal Appeals upheld excluding the evidence because it "only tended to show that possibly appellant was not an ordinary and prudent person with respect to self-defense. This did not entitle appellant to an enlargement of the statutory defense on account of his psychological peculiarities."

4.   A history of assaultive or abusive treatment against the defendant by the person killed by the defendant is relevant in a case of a claim of self-defense, but the requirement of a reasonable belief in the imminent necessity to resort to self-defense remains. In a number of cases involving battered women, the issue is whether a self-defense instruction is appropriate for a defendant who killed the victim at the wrong time. While there might clearly have been entitlement to a self-defense instruction if the defensive force had been used during one of the beatings, is a self-defense instruction appropriate in a case in which the defendant killed her long time abuser when no abuse was occurring? Or even while he slept?

The use of battered women's syndrome evidence in self-defense cases is controversial, and some courts have ruled the evidence inadmissible for any purpose. Other courts have found that the evidence is admissible for at least some purposes. Texas law broadly allows evidence of battered women's syndrome under a provision of the Texas Code of Criminal Procedure that specifically permits expert testimony relating to family violence in murder cases when a defendant asserts a justification defense.

Section 38.36(b) of the Texas Code of Criminal Procedure provides:

(a) In a prosecution for murder, if a defendant raises as a defense a justification provided by Section 9.31, 9.32, or 9.33, Penal Code, the defendant, in order to establish the defendant's reasonable belief that use of force or deadly force was immediately necessary, shall be permitted to offer:

(1) Relevant evidence that the defendant had been the victim of acts of family violence committed by the deceased, as family violence is defined by Section 71.004, Family Code; and

(2) Relevant expert testimony regarding the condition of the mind of the defendant at the time of the offense, including those relevant facts and circumstances relating to family violence that are the basis of the expert's opinion.

The following brief summary of expert testimony from *State v. Richardson*, 525 N.W.2d 378 (Wis. Ct. App. 1994), is typical of the type of testimony offered:

Battered woman's syndrome has two main components—"cycle of violence" and "learned helplessness." The cycle of violence is a three-stage circular process—a tension-building phase erupting into violence followed by a honeymoon stage where the batterer often apologizes and the victim forgives the batterer. The expert testified that the honeymoon phase is very seductive to the battered woman for staying in the abusive relationship. Over time, this cycle often "gets more intense, more repetitive, more frequent and more violent" and consequently more lethal.

The expert also testified that certain characteristics of battered women along with "learned helplessness" and fear of the unknown explain why battered women often do not leave their batterers. "Learned helplessness" is the theory that victims of repeated abuse will eventually abandon any efforts to leave the abusive situation. Common characteristics of battered women are low self-esteem, denial of anger and fear, feelings of guilt, social isolation, depression and the belief that no one can help them.

5.   In Texas, a defendant is not entitled to a jury instruction on self-defense unless she "essentially admits to every element of the offense." As the Court of Criminal Appeals explained:

We have said with respect to defenses such as necessity and self-defense that when the defensive evidence merely negates the necessary culpable mental state, it will not suffice to entitle the defendant to a defensive instruction. Rather, a defensive instruction is only appropriate when the defendant's defensive evidence essentially admits to every element of the offense including the culpable mental state, but interposes the justification to excuse the otherwise criminal conduct.

Shaw v. State, 243 S.W.3d 647, 659 (Tex. Crim. App. 2007).

6.   Self-defense is almost always raised in a case in which an assaultive crime or homicide is alleged. At one time the Court of Criminal Appeals held the defense could not be raised in property crime cases, *Johnson v. State*, 650 S.W.2d 414 (Tex. Crim. App. 1983), but this holding was overruled in *Boget v. State*, 74 S.W.3d 23 (Tex. Crim. App. 2002). Presiding Judge Keller explained the court's rationale:

The duty of this Court is to effectuate the intent of the statute. In this case, that means encouraging the use of restraint in defensive situations. A rule that allows a charge on self-defense where a person kills another, but prohibits the defense when a person merely damages the other's property is inconsistent with the purposes of the statute.

For instance, assume a person is about to be run down by a speeding car. If she brandishes her pistol and fires at the front tires of the car to stop the vehicle, she will not receive a charge on self-defense should she be indicted for criminal mischief? On the other hand, if she shoots the driver she is entitled to a charge on self-defense in a murder prosecution. This result is contrary to the object of the statute because it punishes the individual who used the least force possible in self-preservation.

In Boget's case, had his flashlight gone through the window and hit Palacios [the driver of the damaged vehicle], he would be entitled to a charge on self-defense in an assault prosecution. It would be illogical to deny him the instruction simply because his force didn't actually land on Palacios. The relevant inquiry is whether he directed his force against another. We find that under Boget's version of the facts, his force was directed against Palacios.

Provoker Limitation

Self-defense is not available to those who provoke a situation in which it becomes necessary to use defensive force. The Texas Court of Criminal Appeals, in *Smith v. State*, 965 S.W.2d 509 (Tex. Crim. App. 1998), stated the classic common law theory in applying the doctrine in Texas law:

> Provoking the difficulty, as the doctrine of provocation is commonly referred to in our jurisprudence, is a concept in criminal law which acts as a limitation or total bar on a defendant's right to self-defense. The phrase "provoking the difficulty" is a legal term of art, and more accurately translates in modern usage to "provoked the attack." The rule of law is that if the defendant provoked another to make an attack on him, so that the defendant would have a pretext for killing the other under the guise of self-defense, the defendant forfeits his right of self-defense. Although we address the issue in terms of intent to kill the victim, the law equally applies to a forfeiture of right to self-defense of any degree of harm the defendant intends to inflict upon the victim. For instance, if the defendant employs provocation with intent to assault the victim, and provokes an attack and makes an assault, then self-defense is lost as to the assault.

The provoker rule is an important limitation to the availability of defensive force claims. The rule can have harsh results for defendants who become embroiled in confrontations of their own making that later face dangerous circumstances, as the *Peterson* case illustrates.

United States v. Peterson

483 F.2d 1222 (D.C. Cir.1983)

Robinson, Circuit Judge.

The events immediately preceding the homicide are not seriously in dispute. The version presented by the Government's evidence follows. Charles Keitt, the deceased, and two friends drove in Keitt's car to the alley in the rear of Peterson's house to remove the windshield wipers from the latter's wrecked car.[1] While Keitt was doing so, Peterson came out of the house into the back yard to protest. After a verbal exchange, Peterson went back into the house, obtained a pistol, and returned to the yard. In the meantime, Keitt had reseated himself in his car, and he and his companions were about to leave.

Upon his reappearance in the yard, Peterson paused briefly to load the pistol. "If you move," he shouted to Keitt, "I will shoot." He walked to a point in the yard slightly inside a gate in the rear fence and, pistol in hand, said, "If you come in here I will kill you." Keitt alighted from his car, took a few steps toward Peterson and exclaimed, "What the hell do you think you are going to do with that?" Keitt then made an about-face, walked back to his car and got a lug wrench. With the wrench in a raised position, Keitt advanced toward Peterson, who stood with the pistol pointed toward him. Peterson warned Keitt not to "take another step" and, when Keitt continued onward shot him in the face from a distance of about ten feet. Death was apparently instantaneous. Shortly thereafter, Peterson left home and was apprehended 20-odd blocks away.

This description of the fatal episode was furnished at Peterson's trial by four witnesses for the Government. Peterson did not testify or offer any evidence, but the Government introduced a statement which he had given the police after his arrest, in which he related a somewhat different version. Keitt had removed objects from his car before, and on the day of the shooting he had told Keitt not to do so. After the initial verbal altercation, Keitt went to his car for the lug wrench, so he, Peterson, went into his house for his pistol. When Keitt was about ten feet away, he pointed the pistol "away of his right shoulder;" adding that Keitt was running toward him, Peterson said he "got scared and fired the gun. He ran right into the bullet." "I did not mean to shoot him," Peterson insisted, "I just wanted to scare him."

At trial, Peterson moved for a judgment of acquittal on the ground that as a matter of law the evidence was insufficient to support a conviction. The trial judge denied the motion. The jury returned a verdict finding Peterson guilty of manslaughter. Judgment was entered conformably with the verdict, and this appeal followed.

More than two centuries ago, Blackstone, best known of the expositors of the English common law, taught that "all homicide is malicious, and of course, amounts to murder, unless . . . *justified* by the command or permission of the law; *excused* on the account of accident or self-preservation; or *alleviated* into manslaughter, by being either the involuntary consequence

---

[1]

of some act not strictly lawful, or (if voluntary) occasioned by some sudden and sufficiently violent provocation."

Tucked within this greatly capsulized schema of the common law of homicide is the branch of law we are called upon to administer today. No issue of justifiable homicide, within Blackstone's definition is involved. But Peterson's consistent position is that as a matter of law his conviction of manslaughter—alleviated homicide—was wrong, and that his act was one of self-preservation—excused homicide. The Government, on the other hand, has contended from the beginning that Keitt's slaying fell outside the bounds of lawful self-defense. The questions remaining for our decision inevitably track back to this basic dispute.

Self-defense, as a doctrine legally exonerating the taking of human life, is as viable now as it was in Blackstone's time, and in the case before us the doctrine is invoked in its purest form. But "[t]he law of self-defense is a law of necessity;" the right of self-defense arises only when the necessity begins, and equally ends with the necessity; and never must the necessity be greater than when the force employed defensively is deadly. The "necessity must bear all semblance of reality, and appear to admit of no other alternative, before taking life will be justifiable as excusable." Hinged on the exigencies of self-preservation, the doctrine of homicidal self-defense emerges from the body of the criminal law as a limited though important exception to legal outlawry of the arena of self-help in the settlement of potentially fatal personal conflicts.

all elements must be met for S.D.

So it is that necessity is the pervasive theme of the well-defined conditions which the law imposes on the right to kill or maim in self-defense. There must have been a threat, actual or apparent, of the use of deadly force against the defender. The threat must have been unlawful and immediate. The defender must have believed that he was in imminent peril of death or serious bodily harm, and that his response was necessary to save himself therefrom. These beliefs must not only have been honestly entertained, but also objectively reasonable in light of the surrounding circumstances. It is clear that no less than a concurrence of these elements will suffice.

Here the parties' opposing contentions focus on the roles of two further considerations. One is the provoking of the confrontation by the defender. The other is the defendant's failure to utilize a safe route for retreat from the confrontation. The essential inquiry, in final analysis, is whether and to what extent the rule of necessity may translate these considerations into additional factors in the equation. To these questions, in the context of the specific issues raised, we now proceed.

The trial judge's charge authorized the jury, as it might be persuaded, to convict Peterson of second-degree murder or manslaughter, or to acquit by reason of self-defense. On the latter phase of the case, the judge instructed that with evidence of self-defense present, the Government bore the burden of proving beyond a reasonable doubt that Peterson did not act in self-defense; and that if the jury had a reasonable doubt as to whether Peterson acted in self-defense, the verdict must be not guilty. The judge further instructed that the circumstances under which Peterson acted, however, must have been such as to produce a reasonable belief that Keitt was then about to kill him or do him serious bodily harm, and that deadly force was necessary to repel him. In determining whether Peterson used excessive force in defending himself, the judge said, the jury could consider all of the circumstances under which he acted.

These features of the charge met Peterson's approval, and we are not summoned to pass on them. There were, however, two other aspects of the charge to which Peterson objected, and which are now the subject of vigorous controversy. The first of Peterson's complaints centers upon an instruction that the right to use deadly force in self-defense is not ordinarily available to one who provokes a conflict or is the aggressor in it. Mere words, the judge explained, do not constitute provocation or aggression; and if Peterson precipitated the altercation but thereafter withdrew from it in good faith and so informed Keitt by words or acts, he was justified in using deadly force to save himself from imminent danger or death or grave bodily harm. And, the judge added, even if Keitt was the aggressor and Peterson was justified in defending himself, he was not entitled to use any greater force than he had reasonable ground to believe and actually believed to be necessary for that purpose. Peterson contends that there was no evidence that he either caused or contributed to the conflict, and that the instructions on that topic could only misled the jury.

It has long been accepted that one cannot support a claim of self-defense by a self-generated necessity to kill. The right of homicidal self-defense is granted only to those free from fault in the difficulty; it is denied to slayers who incite the fatal attack, encourage the fatal quarrel or otherwise promote the necessitous occasion for taking life. The fact that the deceased struck the first blow, fired the first shot or made the first menacing gesture does not legalize the self-defense claim if in fact the claimant was the actual provoker. In sum, one who is the aggressor in a conflict culminating in death cannot invoke the necessities of self-preservation. Only in the event that he communicates to his adversary his intent to withdraw and in good faith attempts to do so is he restored to his right of self-defense.

This body of doctrine traces its origin to the fundamental principle that a killing in self-defense is excusable only as a matter of genuine necessity. Quite obviously, a defensive killing is unnecessary if the occasion for it could have been averted.

In the case at bar, the trial judge's charge fully comported with these governing principles. The remaining question, then, is whether there was evidence to make them applicable to the case. A recapitulation of the proofs shows beyond peradventure that there was. Should the last info have been said

It was not until Peterson fetched his pistol and returned to his back yard that his confrontation with Keitt took on a deadly cast. Prior to his trip into the house for the gun, there was, by the Government's evidence, no threat, no display of weapons, no combat. There was an exchange of verbal aspersions and a misdemeanor against Peterson's property was in progress but, at this juncture, nothing more. Even if Peterson's post-arrest version of the initial encounter were accepted—his claim that Keitt went for the lug wrench before he armed himself—the events which followed bore heavily on the question as to who the real aggressor was.

The evidence is uncontradicted that when Peterson reappeared in the yard with his pistol, Keitt was about to depart the scene. Richard Hilliard testified that after the first argument, Keitt reentered his car and said "Let's go." This statement was verified by Ricky Gray, who testified that Keitt "got in the car and . . . they were getting ready to go;" he, too, heard Keitt give the direction to start the car. The uncontroverted fact that Keitt was leaving shows plainly that so far as he was concerned the confrontation was ended. It demonstrates just as plainly that even if he had previously been the aggressor, he no longer was.

Not so with Peterson, however, as the undisputed evidence made clear. Emerging from the house with the pistol, he paused in the yard to load it, and to command Keitt not to move. He then walked through the yard to the rear gate and, displaying his pistol, dared Keitt to come in, and threatened to kill him if he did. While there appears to be no fixed rule on the subject, the cases hold, and we agree, that an affirmative unlawful act reasonably calculated to produce an affray foreboding injurious or fatal consequences is an aggression which, unless renounced, nullifies the right of homicidal self-defense. We cannot escape the abiding conviction that the jury could readily find Peterson's challenge to be a transgression of that character.

We think the evidence plainly presented an issue of fact as to whether Peterson's conduct was an invitation to and provocation of the encounter which ended in the fatal shot. We sustain the trial judge's action in remitting that issue for the jury's determination.

The second aspect of the trial judge's charge as to which Peterson asserts error concerned the undisputed fact that at no time did Peterson endeavor to retreat from Keitt's approach with the lug wrench. The judge instructed the jury that if Peterson had reasonable grounds to believe and did believe that he was in imminent danger of death or serious injury, and that deadly force was necessary to repel the danger, he was required neither to retreat nor to consider whether he could safely retreat. Rather, said the judge, Peterson was entitled to stand his ground and use such force as was reasonably necessary under the circumstances to save his life and his person from pernicious bodily harm. But, the judge continued, if Peterson could have safely retreated but did not do so, that failure was a circumstance which the jury might consider, together with all others, in determining whether he went further in repelling the danger, real or apparent, than he was justified in going.

Peterson contends that this imputation of an obligation to retreat was error, even if he could safely have done so. He points out that at the time of the shooting he was standing in his own yard, and argues he was under no duty to move. We are persuaded to the conclusion that in the circumstances presented here, the trial judge did not err in giving the instruction challenged.

Within the common law of self-defense there developed the rule of "retreat to the wall," which ordinarily forbade the use of deadly force by one to whom an avenue for safe retreat was open. This doctrine was but an application of the requirement of strict necessity to excuse the taking of human life, and was designed to insure the existence of that necessity. Even the innocent victim of a vicious assault had to elect a safe retreat, if available, rather than resort to defensive force which might kill or seriously injure.

In a majority of American jurisdictions, contrarily to the common law rule, one may stand his ground and use deadly force whenever it seems reasonably necessary to save himself. While the law of the District of Columbia on this point is not entirely clear, it seems allied with the strong minority adhering to the common law. In 1856, the District of Columbia Criminal

Court ruled that a participant in an affray "must endeavor to retreat, . . . that is, he is obliged to retreat, if he can safely." The court added that "[a] man may, to be sure, decline a combat when there is no existing or apparent danger, but the retreat to which the law binds him is that which is the consequence." In a much later era this court, adverting to necessity as the soul of homicidal self-defense, declared that "no necessity for killing an assailant can exist, so long as there is a safe way open to escape the conflict." Moreover, the common law rule of strict necessity pervades the District concept of pernicious self-defense, and we cannot ignore the inherent inconsistency of an absolute no-retreat rule. Until such time as the District law on the subject may become more definitive, we accept these precedents as ample indication that the doctrine of retreat persists.

That is not to say that the retreat rule is without exceptions. Even at common law it was recognized that it was not completely suited to all situations. Today it is the more so that its precept must be adjusted to modern conditions nonexistent during the early development of the common law of self-defense. One restriction on its operation comes to the fore when the circumstances apparently foreclose a withdrawal with safety. The doctrine of retreat was never intended to enhance the risk to the innocent; its proper application has never required a faultless victim to increase his assailant's safety at the expense of his own. On the contrary, he could stand his ground and use deadly force otherwise appropriate if the alternative were perilous, or if to him it reasonably appeared to be. A slight variant of the same consideration is the principle that there is no duty to retreat from an assault producing an imminent danger of death or grievous bodily harm. "Detached reflection cannot be demanded in the presence of an uplifted knife," nor is it "a condition of immunity that one in that situation should pause to consider whether a reasonable man might not think it possible to fly with safety or to disable his assailant rather than to kill him."

The trial judge's charge to the jury incorporated each of these limitations on the retreat rule. Peterson, however, invokes another—the so-called "castle" doctrine. It is well settled that one who through no fault of his own is attacked in his home is under no duty to retreat therefrom. The oft-repeated expression that "a man's home is his castle" reflected the belief in olden days that there were few if any safer sanctuaries than the home. The "castle" exception, moreover, has been extended by some courts to encompass the occupant's presence within the curtilage outside his dwelling. Peterson reminds us that when he shot to halt Keitt's advance, he was standing in his yard and so, he argues, he had no duty to endeavor to retreat.

Despite the practically universal acceptance of the "castle" doctrine in American jurisdictions wherein the point has been raised, its status in the District of Columbia has never been squarely decided. But whatever the fate of the doctrine in the District law of the future, it is clear that in absolute form it was inapplicable here. The right of self-defense, we have said, cannot be claimed by the aggressor in an affray so long as he retains that unmitigated role. It logically follows that any rule of no-retreat which may protect an innocent victim of the affray would, like other incidents of a forfeited right of self-defense, be unavailable to the party who provokes or stimulates the conflict. Accordingly, the law is well settled that the "castle" doctrine can be invoked only by one who is without fault in bringing the conflict on. That, we think, is the critical consideration here.

We need not repeat our previous discussion of Peterson's contribution to the altercation which culminated in Keitt's death. It suffices to point out that by no interpretation of the evidence could it be said that Peterson was blameless in the affair. And while, of course, it was for the jury to assess the degree of fault, the evidence well-nigh dictated the conclusion that it was substantial.

The only reference in the trial judge's charge intimating an affirmative duty to retreat was the instruction that a failure to do so, when it could have been done safely, was a factor in the totality of the circumstances which the jury might consider in determining whether the force which he employed was excessive. We cannot believe that any jury was at all likely to view Peterson's conduct as irreproachable. We conclude that for one who, like Peterson, was hardly entitled to fall back on the "castle" doctrine of no retreat, that instruction cannot be just cause for complaint.

The judgment of conviction appealed from is accordingly affirmed.

Notes

1.   Didn't Keitt initiate the confrontation by trespassing and stealing Peterson's property? The decision in Peterson reflects the typical attitude taken by the courts when a gun is introduced. At one time, Texas law allowed a person to carry arms to the scene of an incident when seeking a settlement of a disagreement without forfeiting the right of self-defense. The current statute provides that the use of force is not justified if the actor sought an explanation from or discussion with the other person concerning the actor's differences with the other person while the actor was carrying a weapon in violation of Penal Code Section 46.02 or possessing or transporting a weapon in violation of Penal Code Section 46.05. However, the mere possession of a weapon by a defendant does not disallow a claim of self-defense if, for example, a person has a gun on premises under his or her control.

2.   In *Smith v. State*, 965 S.W.2d 509 (Tex. Crim. App. 1998), the Texas Court of Criminal Appeals held that a jury instruction on self-defense should contain language about the provoker limitation when there is sufficient evidence: (1) the defendant did some act or used some words which provoked the attack, (2) such act or words were reasonably calculated to provoke the attack, and (3) the act was done or the words were used for the purpose and with the intent that the defendant would have a pretext for inflicting harm upon the other. Although the language about having a pretext for inflicting harm is not in the self-defense statute, the majority opinion of Judge Richardson in *Elizondo v. State*, 487 S.W.3d 185 (Tex. Crim. App. 2016), stated that this concept is an important common law aspect of the provoker limitation that remains part of the law.

In *Elizondo*, the evidence showed that, after an altercation in a nightclub, the defendant left the scene and went to a pick-up truck parked about 70 yards away. Three men involved in the prior altercation followed, and a physical altercation ensued while the defendant held a gun in his hand. Although there was disputed evidence concerning many aspects of the events, including whether the defendant went to his truck to avoid his attackers or to retrieve his gun, it was undisputed that both the defendant and the decedent were pointing guns at each other at the time of the killing. The trial court instructed the jury on self-defense, but the jury convicted the defendant of murder. On appeal, the defendant argued the trial court erred by including in the self-defense charge an instruction stating that self-defense is unavailable to one who provokes the encounter.

Although the Court in *Elizondo* was able to point to evidence to support the finding that the defendant intended to provoke the encounter with words and actions, the court found no evidence that the defendant had planned these actions in order to have a pretext for inflicting harm. The court considered the spontaneous nature of the final fatal encounter and actions of others that could not be foreseen, such as some of the participants following the defendant to his vehicle. The court reversed and remanded for a new trial because of the inclusion of the provoker limitation when that aspect of self-defense law was not raised by the evidence.

Would Peterson have prevailed under the approach taken in *Elizondo*? Although introducing a gun into the encounter escalated tensions and may be regarded as provocative, wasn't this a spontaneous decision that resulted in reactions by another that could not be foreseen? (In *Elizondo*, the actions of the group following Elizondo to his car; in *Peterson*, the action of Keitt getting out of the car and confronting Peterson rather than remaining a passenger in an exiting car.) In *Elizondo*, the parties disputed the question of whether the defendant went to his car to get the gun or whether he intended to drive away and obtained the gun only when he was attacked. In contrast, it was clear Peterson entered his home to obtain a gun before returning to confront the thieves. Nonetheless, under one view of the evidence, the defendant went to his car to get a weapon to confront his antagonists. If there is reasonable evidence to support this view, shouldn't the provoker limitation be given to allow the jury to decide the question? In both cases, the jury was given the choice to decide whether the defendant should forfeit the right of self-defense as a provoker and, in both cases, the jury decided against the defendant. Can you reconcile the contrary appellate holdings or are they inconsistent?

3.   A provoker can regain the right of self-defense under Texas law if: (1) the defendant abandons the encounter, or clearly communicates to the assailant his or her intent to do so in the reasonable belief that he or she cannot safely abandon the encounter; and (2) the assailant nevertheless continues or attempts to use unlawful force against the defendant.

While the defendant's intent is a crucial consideration, it is not sufficient for the State to simply prove that the defendant intended to provoke the victim in order to show that provocation defeats a claim of self-defense. Provocation includes both the intent and some particular action to provoke the victim Thus, the defendant's mere presence in a location with an intent to provoke is insufficient to require a charge on provoking the difficulty.

4.   The court in *Peterson* acknowledges that, under the common law duty to retreat doctrine, retreat was not required in one's home. This rule was known as the "castle doctrine." The *Peterson* Court did not reach the question of whether the castle exception to the duty to retreat applied because Peterson was not entitled to self-defense as the provoker who escalated the encounter. If the castle doctrine was relevant and it applied in Peterson's yard, his claim would be that he had no duty to retreat and was privileged to stand his ground.

4.   Not all jurisdictions recognized the castle doctrine, including Texas. Prior to the 2007 amendments to the self-defense statute, the Texas rule provided no duty to retreat before the use of defensive, non-deadly force, but there was a duty to retreat before the use of deadly force. The same rule applied in one's castle as when not at home.

The legislature amended the self-defense statute in 1995 to provide that a duty to retreat "does not apply to an actor who uses force against a person who is at the time of the use of force committing an offense of unlawful entry in the habitation of the actor." In 2007, the legislature again amended the duty to retreat provisions of the self-defense statute. The amendments of 2007 present a murky picture with regard to the duty to retreat and the castle doctrine. The statute elevates the protection of the home to create a strong stand-your-ground position. If someone enters another's home by force and without consent, the homeowner no longer has any duty to retreat. On the other hand, it is less clear if there is a duty to retreat or a castle exception if an altercation develops that arguably allows the use of force between a home owner and someone who has been invited to home. It would seem odd that a castle exception not recognized by Texas law before the 2007 amendments would arise from a statute that does not specifically address the castle doctrine. More fundamentally, any castle doctrine exception to the duty to retreat is influenced by the question of whether there is a duty to retreat that survives in Texas law.

Consider the following opinion in *Whitney*, which is one of the few to discuss these self-defense issues after the 2007 amendments.

Whitney v. State

396 S.W.3d 696 (Tex. App—Fort Worth 2013)

Lee Gabriel, Justice.

Background Facts and Procedural History

Appellant killed her daughter Tashira's boyfriend with a hammer. Tashira and the deceased often quarreled, at times violently. During their last argument, Tashira called Appellant, who then drove to Tashira's apartment. A neighbor saw Appellant climb out of her van and walk to the apartment holding a yellow handled hammer.

The deceased was gathering his belongings in the bedroom when the Appellant came through the unlocked apartment door. She and the deceased started arguing and continued to do so after Tashira closed the bedroom door between them. When the door reopened the deceased approached Appellant. It is unclear from the record whether he intended to attack Appellant or to escape past her out the front door. Before he could do either, Appellant threw a cup of bleach-water into his face. He fell facedown to the floor, and Appellant struck him in the back of the head with the hammer.

The deceased died from his injuries shortly thereafter, and the State charged Appellant with murder. The jury convicted Appellant of murder and, after the punishment phase, assessed punishment at fifteen years' confinement, finding that she had acted under the immediate influence of sudden passion arising from an adequate cause. The trial court sentenced Appellant accordingly.

No-Duty-to-Retreat Instruction   *Issue:*

Appellant contends that the trial court erred by including in its charge to the jury an instruction that Appellant concedes tracks a penal code provision regarding a duty to retreat. She complains of the following instruction:

> A defendant who has a right to be present at the location where the force is used, who has not provoked the person against whom the force is used, and who is not engaged in criminal activity at the time the force is used is not required to retreat before using force in self-defense.

Although Appellant concedes that this instruction tracks the penal code, see TEX. PENAL CODE ANN. § 9.31(e) (West 2011), she argues that because the legislature eliminated the statutory duty to retreat in 2007, the trial court erred by including this instruction in the charge because it implies that there is a duty to retreat. In other words, Appellant argues that the charge was erroneous because it "implied the existence of a non-existent duty."

Prior to September 1, 2007, section 9.32 of the penal code provided that the use of deadly force was justified only "if a reasonable person in the actor's situation would not have retreated." However, effective September 1, 2007, the 80th Legislature amended the statute to delete existing language regarding a general duty to retreat and to add new language specifying the circumstances under which a person does not have a duty to retreat. The legislature deleted from

371

penal code section 9.32(a)(2) the language "if a reasonable person in the actor's situation would not have retreated; and," and it added the following that now appears in section 9.32(c):

> A person who has a right to be present at the location where the deadly force is used, who has not provoked the person against whom the deadly force is used, and who is not engaged in criminal activity at the time the deadly force is used is not required to retreat before using deadly force as described by this section.

Section 9.31(e) was added at the same time and differs from section 9.32(c) only by omitting "deadly" before each of the four appearances of the word "force." It reads as follows:

> A person who has a right to be present at the location where the force is used, who has not provoked the person against whom the force is used, and who is not engaged in criminal activity at the time the force is used is not required to retreat before using force as described by this section.

Appellant's characterization of the duty to retreat as "non-existent" may be too strong. In Morales, the court of criminal appeals addressed the changes made to the self-defense statute by the 80th Legislature, specifically, the no-duty-to-retreat provisions at issue here. One of Morales's grounds for review asked, "Whether the 2007 amendment to the self-defense statute eliminated the duty to retreat in a self-defense case." Although the opinion does not specifically address this question, it implies that the duty to retreat is not, in Appellant's words, "non-existent." First, the court acknowledged that when the provisions apply, the defendant has no duty to retreat. Then, in discussing the "no duty to retreat provisions," the court stated that when "these provisions do not apply, the failure to retreat may be considered in determining whether a defendant reasonably believed that his conduct was immediately necessary to defend himself or a third person." Further, the court wrote, when the provisions do not apply, the prosecutor may argue the failure to retreat as a factor in determining whether the defendant's conduct really was immediately necessary. Or if a fact issue is raised regarding the applicability of the provisions that specifically negate a duty to retreat, the prosecutor can argue that the facts do not satisfy the provisions and then argue the failure to retreat as a factor relevant to the defensive issue.

We conclude, therefore, that the report of the death of the duty to retreat is exaggerated.

And as the State points out, Appellant cites no authority for her position. But even if an instruction setting out the circumstances under which a person using force (or deadly force) has no duty to retreat necessarily implies the existence of such a duty, we do not hold it error for the trial court to have included the instruction in its charge. The court of criminal appeals has held that a trial court will not be held to have erred in its jury charge by tracking the law as set out by the legislature. As stated above, Appellant concedes that the complained-of instruction tracked the law as set out by the legislature.

Moreover, the legislature added the language of which Appellant complains in the very same act in which it deleted the language that she calls the statutory basis for a duty to retreat. What we take from that is that the legislature intended to eliminate a defendant's burden to affirmatively establish that he or she retreated before employing force (or deadly force) and to stress the set of circumstances under which a defendant could not be held to have such a duty. We refuse to infer,

372

therefore, that the legislature intended to abolish the duty to retreat while at the same time implying its continued existence. Absent any controlling authority to the contrary, Appellant's position is not persuasive.

The 2007 Texas Statute: Duty to Retreat and Defense Presumptions

Traditionally, Texas law has not required a person to retreat before using non-deadly force, even if a safe avenue of retreat was available. However, prior to a legislative amendment, effective September 1, 2007, an actor was not justified in using deadly force if a reasonable person in the actor's situation would have retreated. The retreat requirement applied even in the defendant's home, although the jury could consider the location of the defendant at the time of the incident in determining whether the defendant had the ability and a safe opportunity for retreat. However, effective September 1, 2007, the legislature amended the self-defense statute, Section 9.31 of the Texas Penal Code, to provide:

> (e) A person who has a right to be present at the location where the force is used, who has not provoked the person against whom the force is used, and who is not engaged in criminal activity at the time the force is used is not required to retreat before using force as described by this section.
>
> (f) For purposes of Subsection (a), in determining whether an actor described by Subsection (e) reasonably believed that the use of force was necessary, a finder of fact may not consider whether the actor failed to retreat.

This provision would appear to have little impact on self-defense law for non-deadly force since prior to the amendment, there was no duty to retreat before resorting to non-deadly self-defense. However, these provisions are incorporated by reference into the statute dealing with deadly force in self-defense, Section 9.32 of the Texas Penal Code. That statute was also amended to provide a corresponding right to use deadly force when such a degree of force is otherwise justified without requiring retreat in nearly identical language to the provisions of section 9.31.

The statutory exemption from a duty to retreat and the irrelevance of the existence of a safe avenue of retreat to the determination of whether the actor's use of force was reasonable is supported by the creation of an unusual defense presumption in both the self-defense and deadly force in self-defense statutes. Section 9.31 (a) of the Texas Penal Code provides:

> The actor's belief that the force was immediately necessary as described by this subsection is presumed to be reasonable if the actor:
>
> (1) Knew or had reason to believe that the person against whom the force was used:
>
> > (A) Unlawfully and with force entered, or was attempting to enter unlawfully and with force, the actor's occupied habitation, vehicle, or place of business or employment;

(B) Unlawfully and with force removed, or was attempting to remove unlawfully and with force, the actor from the actor's habitation, vehicle, or place of business or employment; or

(C) Was committing or attempting to commit aggravated kidnapping, murder, sexual assault, aggravated sexual assault, robbery, or aggravated robbery;

(2) Did not provoke the person against whom the force was used; and

(3) Was not otherwise engaged in criminal activity, other than a Class C misdemeanor that is a violation of a law or ordinance regulating traffic at the time the force was used.

The likely legislative intent in creating this presumption and apparently eliminating a duty to retreat was to allow Texas citizens threatened or attacked with unlawful force to "stand their ground," using a proportionate level of force without regard to the possible existence of a safe avenue of retreat. However, it is possible that the statue could be interpreted as accomplishing this purpose only when the statutory prerequisites pertain: (1) when the actor did not provoke the person against whom the force was used; (2) when the actor was not committing a crime (or at least was not committing a crime above the level of a Class C misdemeanor); and (3) the actor reasonably believed that the person against whom force was used was illegally entering or attempting to remove the defendant from his or her home, car, or office or the person against whom the defendant used force was committing or attempting to commit aggravated kidnapping, murder, sexual assault, aggravated sexual assault, robbery, or aggravated robbery in the actor's home, vehicle, or place of business.

It could be argued that there remains a duty to retreat before using deadly force, even for the victim of one of the enumerated offenses, if it does not occur in the home or office or involve a car belonging to the defendant. Such an interpretation would actually increase the duty to retreat requirement when non-deadly force is used in self-defense because there was previously no duty to retreat before the legislative amendment. A similar expansion could arguably apply to defense of third parties that has been historically exempt from the duty to retreat requirement.

It is also unclear how the unusual defense presumption will operate. All other presumptions in Texas law benefit the State and are intended only to be a permissive invitation for the jury to find the presumed fact upon proof of the fact giving rise to the presumption under Section 2.05 of the Texas Penal Code. However, the constitutional considerations prohibiting shifts in the burden of proof on essential elements of the crime that make conclusive or mandatory presumptions unacceptable for the more customary prosecution presumptions do not apply to the self-defense presumption because it benefits the state. It is the criminal accused who is entitled to constitutional protections against state actions but the legislature is free to impose any burden that it deems appropriate for the state.

Defense of Others

The traditional rule of the defense of third parties is that the use of force in the defense of others is allowed to the same extent as "others" would be allowed to act in their own self-defense. Thus, if X has a right to use force in self-defense to counter the unlawful assault of Y, then bystander, Z, has the right to enter the fray by using a reasonable degree of force to protect X. Section 9.33 of the Texas Penal Code entitled, "Defense of Third Person" codifies this common law defense. The statute states:

> A person is justified in using force or deadly force against another to protect a third person if:

> (2) Under the circumstances as the actor reasonably believes them to be, the actor would be justified under Section 9.31 or 9.32 in using force or deadly force to protect himself against the unlawful force or unlawful deadly force he reasonably believes to be threatening the third person he seeks to protect; and

> (2) The actor reasonably believes that his intervention is immediately necessary to protect the third person.

If a person acts to protect himself, the doctrine of self-defense applies if the person reasonably believes the use of force is imminently necessary, even if the actor is mistaken. Should the same rule apply with the defense of a third person? For example, suppose X is a provoker and lacks a valid claim of self-defense for that reason against Y. Can Z act on X's behalf with a defense of third party justification because Z did not see the first part of the encounter in which X provoked Y? Assume that based upon what Z observed, Z reasonably believes that use of defensive force is imminently necessary. If the answer is no, Z is punished despite his reasonable belief in the necessity to use defensive force. If the answer is yes, there is a broader justification for use of force vicariously than would pertain directly.

The two approaches to this problem have been called the "alter-ego" rule and the "reasonable person" rule. As a Massachusetts court of appeals recently explained:

> One group of State courts holds that one who comes to the defense of another does so at his or her own risk: if the third person in retrospect would not have been permitted to use force, the intervening defendant is not permitted to claim defense of another. This is known as the "alter ego" rule. A second group of State courts, including Massachusetts, holds that the intervening defendant need only reasonably believe that the third party is being unlawfully attacked; the question whether that belief was correct in retrospect does not enter the analysis.

Com. v. Young, 959 N.E.2d 943, 952 (Mass. 2012).

A Texas case dealing with the defense of third parties, *Morales*, which follows, discusses the impact of the 2007 statutory changes.

Morales v. State

357 S.W.3d 1 (Tex. Crim. App. 2011)

Keller, P.J., delivered the opinion of the Court in which Meyers, Price, Womack, Keasler, Hervey, Cochran and Alcala, J.J. joined.

In 2007, the legislature made significant amendments to the self-defense statute, including adding provisions that allow a person, under certain circumstances, to stand his ground while defending himself and that, under certain circumstances, create a presumption that a defendant's conduct was reasonable. We are now called upon to construe some of those amendments and to determine what instructions should be given in the jury charge in such cases.

Background

On December 2, 2007, a fight broke out between the Kirby Block gang and the Manett Boys gang. During the altercation, Enil Lopez and appellant's brother Juan fought each other. At some point, appellant shot and killed Lopez. Testimony about what transpired was conflicting. Some witnesses said Lopez was unarmed, and some said that he had a metal pipe (possibly a tire iron) and was beating Juan with it. One witness said that Juan helped pull some baseball bats out of a car and then participated with several others in beating Lopez. Other witnesses testified that Juan was lying helplessly on the ground while Lopez attacked him with a pipe. Appellant was indicted and went to trial for murder.

The jury charge contained instructions on defense of a third person. These instructions incorporated some instructions on self-defense. Originally, the charge included language regarding whether "a reasonable person in the defendant's situation would not have retreated." Appellant objected to this instruction as not consistent with the current statute. After studying the matter and consulting with staff attorneys, the trial judge modified the instructions. Appellant maintained that his objection still applied to the modified charge, and he requested that the italicized portions of the charge as set out below be deleted. The trial judge denied his request. The modified jury charge provided in relevant part:

A person is justified in using deadly force against another if he could be justified in using force against the other in the first place, as set out above, and when he reasonably believes that such deadly force is immediately necessary to protect himself against the other person's use or attempted use of unlawful deadly force *and if a person in the defendant's situation would not have had a duty to retreat.*

. . . .

Therefore a person may act against another in defense of a third person, provided he acted upon a reasonable apprehension of danger to such third person, as it appeared to him from his standpoint at the time, and that he reasonably believed such deadly force by his intervention on behalf of such third person was immediately necessary to protect such person from another's use or attempted use of unlawful deadly force, *and provided it reasonably appeared to such person, as seen from his viewpoint alone, that a person in the situation of the person being defended would not have had a duty to retreat.*

A person who has a right to be present at the location where the force is used, who has not provoked the person against whom the force is used, and who is not engaged in criminal activity at the time the force is used is not required to retreat before using force as described herein.

. . . .

[If] it reasonably appeared to defendant that the life or person of Juan Carlos Morales was in danger, and there was created in defendant's mind a reasonable expectation or fear of Juan Carlos Morales' death or serious bodily injury from the use of unlawful deadly force at the hands of Enil Lopez *and that defendant reasonably believed that, under the circumstances then existing, a person in Juan Carlos Morales' situation would not have had a duty to retreat before using deadly force in his own defense*, and that the defendant, acting under such apprehension and reasonably believing that the use of deadly force, by his intervention, was immediately necessary to protect Juan Carlos Morales against Enil Lopez's use or attempted use of unlawful deadly force, then you will find the defendant not guilty, or, if you should have a reasonable doubt as to whether the defendant was acting in defense of Juan Carlos Morales on said occasion under the foregoing circumstances, then you should give the defendant the benefit of the doubt and find him "not guilty."

The jury charge did not contain any instructions regarding a presumption of reasonable conduct in the self-defense context, nor did appellant request any such instructions. Appellant was convicted and sentenced to twenty-five years' imprisonment.

On appeal, appellant contended that the trial judge erred in failing to delete the complained-of references to a duty to retreat and that the trial judge erred in failing to include instructions regarding a presumption of reasonable conduct. With respect to the duty to retreat, the court of appeals held that there was no error in the charge because "the language of the charge states the penal code's language regarding when a person does not have a duty to retreat almost verbatim." The court of appeals held that the trial judge did not err in failing to submit instructions on the presumption of reasonableness because it "was undisputed that more than seven persons, including Juan, were involved in the fight" and that the fight constituted a riot, which would negate entitlement to the presumption. Appellant now claims that the court of appeals erred in disposing of his complaints with respect to the defense-of-others instructions in the jury charge.

Analysis

A defendant is justified in defending a third person if, under the circumstances as the defendant reasonably believes them to be, the third person would be justified in defending himself. The self-defense statute provides that deadly force is justified if, among other things, the actor "reasonably believes the deadly force is immediately necessary . . . to protect himself against the other's use or attempted use of unlawful deadly force." Before 2007, the self-defense statute also imposed a requirement that "a reasonable person in the actor's situation would not have retreated." Incorporating this retreat provision with respect to the defense of a third person meant instructing the jury that the defendant must have "reasonably believed that a reasonable person in the third person's situation would not have retreated."

But this retreat provision was deleted in 2007. With respect to situations involving deadly force, the legislature added provisions specifying when a person does not have a duty to retreat, namely:

> (c) A person who has a right to be present at the location where the deadly force is used, who has not provoked the person against whom the deadly force is used, and who is not engaged in criminal activity at the time the deadly force is used is not required to retreat before using deadly force as described by this section.

> (d) For purposes of Subsection (a)(2), in determining whether an actor described by Subsection (c) reasonably believed that the use of deadly force was necessary, a finder of fact may not consider whether the actor failed to retreat.

These "no duty to retreat" provisions are not all-encompassing. By their language, they do not apply if the defendant provoked the person against whom force or deadly force was used or if the defendant was engaged in criminal activity at the time. But when these provisions do apply, the defendant has no duty to retreat.

In an attempt to take the new version of the statute into account, the trial judge modified his original instructions. Instead of asking the jury to determine whether "a reasonable person would not have retreated," the instructions asked the jury to determine whether a person "would not have had a duty to retreat." But no language in the current self-defense statutes calls for determining, as a general matter, whether a duty to retreat exists. There are only provisions that say, under specified circumstances, that a person is not required to retreat. The court of appeals' statement that the trial judge's instructions tracked the current statute was only half right: The trial judge submitted an instruction that tracked the current statute, but as can be seen from the italicized portions of the jury instructions set out above, he also submitted additional instructions, which did not conform to the statute.

We conclude that the trial court erred in submitting the italicized portions of the jury charge set out above because those instructions were not authorized by statute and they constituted comments on the weight of the evidence.

With the 2007 amendments, the Legislature added provisions that required the jury to presume that deadly force was reasonable under certain circumstances. According to appellant, the following presumption should have been submitted:

> The actor's belief under Subsection (a)(2) that the deadly force was immediately necessary as described by that subdivision is presumed to be reasonable if the actor:

> (1) knew or had reason to believe that the person against whom the deadly force was used . . . . was committing or attempting to commit an offense described by Subsection (a)(2)(B);

> (2) did not provoke the person against whom the force was used; and

> (3) was not otherwise engaged in criminal activity, other than a Class C misdemeanor that is a violation of a law or ordinance regulating traffic at the time the force was used.

The Penal Code requires that a presumption that favors the defendant be submitted to the jury "if there is sufficient evidence of the facts that give rise to the presumption . . . unless the court is satisfied that the evidence as a whole clearly precludes a finding beyond a reasonable doubt of the presumed fact."

As we observed earlier, the court of appeals concluded that there was insufficient evidence to submit the presumption because the fight constituted a riot, due to its consisting of more than seven persons, and because Juan was involved in the fight. If Juan were guilty of violating the riot statute, then he would be "otherwise engaged in criminal activity," and the presumption would not apply to any force or deadly force used by him.

Under the riot statute, a riot exists if, among other things, an "assemblage of seven or more persons" results in conduct that "creates an immediate danger of damage to property or injury to persons." A person commits an offense "if he knowingly participates in a riot." We will assume, without deciding, that the fight constituted a riot. The court of appeals pointed to several acts that showed Juan's participation in the riot: fighting Lopez, pulling baseball bats out of a car, and participating with seven to nine other individuals in beating Lopez. But while the court of appeals says that Juan's involvement in the riot was undisputed, it does not say whether his commission of all of these acts was undisputed. If the evidence that Juan pulled baseball bats out of a car and participated in the beating is undisputed, then his participation in the riot would be unquestionably established. But this evidence appears to be disputed; it seems to be inconsistent with the testimony of other witnesses who suggested that Lopez was beating Juan with a pipe while Juan lay helplessly on the ground. We do not hold that this evidence is inconsistent. We merely note the possibility of inconsistency and leave it to the court of appeals to address on remand (if necessary) whether there is an actual conflict in the evidence.

Although it appears to be undisputed that Juan was fighting Lopez during the riot, the question remains whether Juan's fighting was justified as self-defense. The self-defense and defense of third person statutes are not limited to particular crimes; they simply provide that a person's use of force or deadly force is justified if certain circumstances are met. These defenses logically apply to the crime of participating in a riot, so long as *all* of the actor's actions that would otherwise constitute participation are justified under one or more of these defenses. Not only is this interpretation consistent with the plain language of the self-defense and defense-of-others statutes, it avoids the absurd result of penalizing someone simply because his attackers are numerous. A person who legitimately defends himself against attack should not be open to criminal liability simply because, instead of being faced with one attacker, he is faced with seven. We also point out that the focus of the defense-of-third-persons defense is upon what the actor reasonably believes concerning the situation of the third person. If appellant reasonably believed that Juan's participation in the riot was limited to legitimately defending himself, then appellant would be entitled to the presumption, even if appellant's belief was actually incorrect.

In this case, the court of appeals did not address whether there was some evidence to support a finding that appellant reasonably believed the facts to be such that, if the belief were accurate, all of Juan's actions would be justified by self-defense. If there is a conflict in the evidence on the relevant matters, then there may be a fact issue supporting the submission of the presumption to the jury, "unless the court is satisfied that the evidence as a whole clearly precludes a finding beyond a reasonable doubt of the presumed fact." We conclude that the court of appeals' analysis on whether appellant was entitled to a presumption charge was incomplete.

Disposition

The court of appeals has some flexibility in proceeding, so long as it does not proceed in a manner inconsistent with holdings set out above. It may address singly, or in combination, any error or harm issue(s) that would logically dispose of the case. The court of appeals is free to make alternate holdings if it so desires. We reverse the judgment of the court of appeals and remand the case for proceedings consistent with this opinion.

Notes

1.　　The Texas Court of Criminal Appeals opinion in *Morales* states:

> We also point out that the focus of the defense-of-third-persons defense is upon what the actor reasonably believes concerning the situation of the third person. If appellant reasonably believed that Juan's participation in the riot was limited to legitimately defending himself, then appellant would be entitled to the presumption, even if appellant's belief was actually incorrect.

From this passage it is clear Texas follows the reasonable-person approach to defense of third parties.

At one time, New York was in the opposing alter ego camp. The following excerpt from *People v. Young*, 183 N.E.2d 319, 319–20 (N.Y. Ct. App. 1962), explains the opposing view:

> Whether one, who in good faith aggressively intervenes in a struggle between another person and a police officer in civilian dress attempting to effect the lawful arrest of the third person, may be properly convicted of assault in the third degree is a question of law of first impression here.

> The opinions in the court below in the absence of precedents in this State carefully expound the opposing views found in other jurisdictions. The majority in the Appellate Division have adopted the minority rule in the other States that one who intervenes in a struggle between strangers under the mistaken but reasonable belief that he is protecting another who he assumes is being unlawfully beaten is thereby exonerated from criminal liability. The weight of authority holds with the dissenters below that one who goes to the aid of a third person does so at his own peril.

> While the doctrine espoused by the majority of the court below may have support in some States, we feel that such a policy would not be conducive to an orderly society. We agree with the settled policy of law in most jurisdictions that the right of a person to defend another ordinarily should not be greater than such person's right to defend himself.

> In this case there can be no doubt that the defendant intended to assault the police officer in civilian dress. The resulting assault was forceful. Hence motive or mistake of

fact is of no significance as the defendant was not charged with a crime requiring such intent or knowledge. To be guilty of third degree assault "It is sufficient that the defendant voluntarily intended to commit the unlawful act of touching." Since in these circumstances the aggression was inexcusable the defendant was properly convicted.

2.   The current New York penal code, the defense of persons statute provides, "A person may . . . use physical force upon another person when and to the extent he or she reasonably believes such to be necessary to defend himself, herself or a third person from what he or she reasonably believes to be the use or imminent use of unlawful physical force by such other person . . . ." N.Y. PENAL LAW § 35.15. New York courts have interpreted this statute as superseding the decision in *Young*. The "alter ego" rule is the traditional common law approach, but the reasonable person doctrine is now the law in most jurisdictions.

3.   The *Young* case involved a police officer victim where special rules apply. The use of force in self-defense or in defense of a third person is generally not justified to resist an arrest or search the actor knows is being made by a peace officer or the agent of a peace officer, even if the arrest or search is unlawful. An exception to the prohibition against the use of force exists if the peace officer or agent uses or attempts to use excessive force in making the arrest or search. The rationale for these rules is to require persons who are being falsely arrested to seek legal remedies later, but a person should not have to endure bodily injury if excessive force is used. A defendant must show the officer's use of excessive force occurred before the defendant offered resistance. The limitation of self-defense in this situation exists only if the actor knew the person using excessive force was a peace officer or the agent of a peace officer acting in the presence of the officer. The defendant may use force only when and to the degree the defendant reasonably believes the force is immediately necessary to protect himself or herself against the excessive force of the officer or person acting at the officer's direction.

4.   Are the statements of the *Morales* Court concerning effect of the 2007 Texas amendments regarding the duty to retreat consistent with the interpretation given to *Morales* by the court in *Whitney*?

Chapter 18: Other Use of Force Defenses

Defense of Property

Although self-defense is the most frequently litigated use of force defense, there are other defenses that authorize the use of force recognized by the common law that have, in some cases, been codified and expanded. These defenses sometimes overlap. The use of force in law enforcement may authorize action by a law enforcement official or someone acting at the direction of an officer, but an officer retains a personal right of self-defense. Both defenses may be available in some circumstances. Frequently, self-defense and defense of property overlap. This is particularly true in Texas after the amendment of the self-defense statute, which:

- eliminated a duty to retreat
- created a presumption of reasonableness when
  - a person enters a home or office forcibly and without consent or
  - someone attempts to dispossess an owner of his or her home or car.

Whether the best strategic approach for a criminal defense attorney will be one of these defenses or both will require careful attention to the authorizations and limitations of the two defenses. In many respects, the two defenses are similar: the need for an objectively reasonable belief in the imminent necessity to use a reasonable degree of force to prevent the harm to the person, another person, or property depending upon the defense. One traditional advantage of a defense-of-property claim is that there is no duty to retreat, but as we discussed in the last chapter, it is questionable whether much of the duty to retreat doctrine remains for self-defense in Texas.

Another factor that brings defense of property doctrine close to self-defense is that the traditional justification for the use of deadly force in defense of property is the reasonable belief that a person is about to enter a home in order to commit a crime with an assaultive element or the threat of personal danger such as murder, rape, robbery or arson. The offense of burglary is often included, although not without controversy. There is debate about whether burglary should be regarded as a personal or property crime, as the opinion later in the chapter in *Tennesee v. Garner* illustrates. Which designation is more appropriate depends upon the facts of the particular case. Because a burglary is a preemptive crime, complete at the moment of unconsented-to entry with the intent to commit a theft or a felony, it can range from breaking into an abandoned house to steal something to a forcible entry with a machine gun to commit murder. Most burglaries are more similar to the former, but burglary is listed in most statutes authorizing deadly force in the defense of property, including the Texas statute. The *Drinkert* case that follows involves a defense of property claim where the defendant's argued he had a reasonable belief that a burglary was occurring. Although there was a substantial question at trial about whether there was a burglary, the opinion emphasizes that it is the defendant's belief and what a reasonable person in the defendant's situation which controls, not the actual situation.

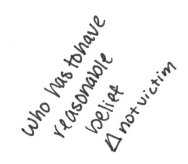
Who has to have reasonable belief ∆ not victim

Ex parte Drinkert

821 SW 2d 953 (Tex. Crim. App. 1991)

Maloney, Judge.

This is a post conviction application for writ of habeas corpus filed pursuant to article 11.07, V.A.C.C.P.

The jury convicted applicant of murder following his plea of not guilty and the court sentenced him to fifteen years in prison. The Thirteenth Court of Appeals affirmed the conviction in an unpublished opinion.

The record reflects that applicant and Dirk, his teenage son, lived in separate trailers on applicant's land. A partially constructed A-frame house was also located on the tract of land. Tommy Mason and Mike Piper, two of Dirk's friends, decided to take gasoline from a large drum in the A-frame house. Dirk testified in a prior proceeding that he told Piper not to go into the house, but that he could take gasoline from a bus, also located on the property. Piper testified that he and Mason believed that they had permission to enter the house. Applicant had no knowledge of this, nor did he give them permission to enter the house.

Applicant was inside the A-frame house working on plans for its completion and eating lunch when Mason and Piper tried to enter the house through a locked door. Applicant heard the door rattle and someone say that the door was locked. He also heard someone run by the house saying, "I know how to get in." Thinking that someone was breaking into the house, applicant got his rifle.

Mason entered the home through a loose panel on the exterior of the house. Applicant ordered Mason, whom he knew, to kneel down and place his hands on his head. According to applicant, Mason made a dive for the gun and applicant fired. He fired a total of three shots. One hit Mason in the chest and another bounced off the floor and hit him in the leg. Another shot hit Piper, who was standing at the entrance of the panel opening with a hammer.

Applicant testified that Mason was like a son to him, but on that day Mason was not acting normal. Mason was an 18 year old, high school dropout, 6' 1" tall, and 200 lbs. Applicant, on the other hand, was 69 years old, 165 lbs, hard of hearing, and in poor health.

Applicant's fourth ground is that he was denied effective assistance of counsel at trial. "To establish ineffective assistance of counsel . . . applicant must show that: (1) counsel's performance was deficient, and (2) the deficient performance prejudiced the defense so [much that it deprived applicant] of a fair trial." We now "determine whether, in light of all the circumstances, the trial counsel's acts or omissions were outside the range of professional competent assistance, and if so, whether there is a reasonable probability that the result of the trial would have been different absent the deficient conduct." *Issue*

Applicant . . . contends that his trial counsel's performance was deficient because he did not object to the prosecutor's argument that the jury should consider the deceased's state of mind in determining whether applicant had the right to defend his property. This argument was not only contrary to the court's charge, which instructed the jury to consider self-defense and defense of property from applicant's standpoint, but it was also a misstatement of the applicable law. The law of self-defense and defense of property requires the jury to view the reasonableness of the defendant's actions solely from the defendant's standpoint.

Trial counsel stated that he did not object to the jury charge. He did not know why he failed to object to the jury argument "other than it just slipped by me," and, "[i]n retrospect . . . it appears that I should have objected to the indictment and jury charge as well as to the prosecutor's argument concerning the state of mind of the deceased."

Trial counsel's omissions were outside the realm of professional competent assistance. "[A] criminal defense lawyer must have a firm command of the . . . governing law before [the lawyer] can render reasonably effective assistance." Trial counsel's failure to object to the jury charge, and jury argument were not the result of a reasonable professional judgment, but rather of ignorance of criminal procedure. We conclude that the performance of applicant's trial counsel fell below an objective standard of reasonableness and, as such, was deficient.

We now determine whether the trial counsel's deficient performance prejudiced applicant's defense so much so that it deprived him of a fair trial. To prove that he was prejudiced by the ineffective assistance, applicant must show: "[A] reasonable probability that but for counsel's unprofessional errors, the result of the proceeding would have been different. A reasonable probability is a probability sufficient to undermine confidence in the outcome."

The court instructed the jury that if it found that applicant reasonably believed that the deceased was entering applicant's habitation, building, or premises without his effective consent with the intent to commit a theft, and that applicant reasonably believed, *viewing the circumstances from his standpoint alone*, that deadly force was immediately necessary to prevent the burglary, and that applicant further reasonably believed, *from his standpoint at the time*, that the use of nondeadly force to protect the premises would expose him or his family, or both, to a substantial risk of death or serious bodily injury, then applicant had the right to use deadly force.

Despite the court's charge, the prosecutor argued the following to the jury without objection:

> You never heard Dirk Drinkert say anything about talking to Tommy Mason about being in that house. He talked to Michael Piper at that time. Never talked to Tommy Mason, and we are not concerned here with Mike Piper, because Mike Piper is alive. Tommy Mason is dead, and that is who we are concerned with, and that is who you should concern yourself with.

> And in doing so, consider that, consider whether Tommy Mason reasonably believed he had consent and permission to be in that property. Did Tommy Mason reasonably believe that?

384

You know, they talk about—they said this was a burglary. I didn't hear about any property being taken; didn't hear anything about that. They talk about a burglary. Well, let's turn that about. Turn about is fair play in a case. They want you to do all this reasonable doubt and everything like that. Well let's look at Tommy Mason. Did he reasonably believe they had consent to be there, and if he reasonably believed that, then he thought he had effective consent when he went in there, didn't he, and if he had consent to be in there, it wasn't a burglary, so think about Tommy Mason. You have to think about Tommy Mason because that is who we are talking about.

Proper jury argument falls within one of four categories: (1) summation of the evidence; (2) reasonable deductions from the evidence; (3) responses to argument of opposing counsel; and, (4) pleas for law enforcement. Here, the prosecutor responded to defense counsel's argument that a burglary had occurred. However, prosecutorial jury argument which contains a statement of law contrary to that presented in the court's charge is error. The instant case involves an argument which is not only contrary to the court's charge, but also a misstatement of the applicable law.

incorrect charge

The jury could reasonably infer from the prosecutor's argument that since the deceased reasonably believed that he had consent to enter applicant's house, he did not commit a burglary, therefore applicant had no right to defend his person or property. Had applicant's trial counsel objected to the prosecutor's argument, the trial judge should have sustained the objection and instructed the jury to disregard the argument. There is a reasonable probability that but for trial counsel's failure to object to the prosecutor's argument the result of the proceeding would have been different.

Trial counsel's failure to object to the prosecutor's argument undermine[s] confidence in the outcome of applicant's trial. We have reviewed the record and find that the evidence of applicant's guilt is not so overwhelming as to conclude otherwise. We find that there is a reasonable probability that the outcome of applicant's trial would have been different absent applicant's counsel's deficient performance.

Accordingly, the relief sought is granted. The trial court's judgment is vacated, and applicant is remanded to the custody of the Sheriff of Bee County to answer the indictment.

Notes

1.   The decision of the court is not that the defendant in *Drinkert* established a valid defense of property, but that he was entitled to a lawyer who would object to an argument by the prosecution that misstates the law on a point crucial to the claimed defense. Nonetheless, the fact that the court granted the writ of habeas corpus rather than finding harmless error is indicative of the importance of the opportunity to allow the jury to consider a possible defense. The jury instruction provided a correct statement, and it was only in argument that the misstatement occurred. Based upon what you know from the facts, would you vote to convict or acquit if you were on the jury in a new trial?

2.   Is this a case of an overlap of defense of property and self-defense? At the time the fatal shots were fired, was the defendant in imminent danger of serious bodily harm?

Deadly Force in Defense of Property

Texas includes burglary on the list of offenses that can justify the use of deadly force in the protection of property, as do many other states. However, by including theft during the nighttime and criminal mischief during the nighttime, the Texas statute on the use of deadly force in defense of property uniquely goes far beyond the typical list of crimes that can trigger the justification of deadly force. In fact, far from requiring a duty to retreat before using deadly force, the statute authorizes pursuit of a person who has committed theft during the nighttime. If the *Peterson* case in the last chapter had occurred in Texas, it would appear that he would have a credible claim he could pursue and kill the thief who took the windshield wipers from his junk car, even if he didn't have a lug wrench in his hand (but not during the day). The curious nighttime requirement is perhaps a vestige of the common law standard of burglary, which required an entry at night, an element that has been universally eliminated by modern statutes, including Texas.

Many people would be surprised to learn that Peterson would not have a valid claim of self-defense because getting and displaying a gun is considered provoking the difficulty; but pursuing a misdemeanant thief with a gun at night appears to be authorized by the Texas defense of property statutes. Of course, it would be ill advised to provide that legal advice to someone who keeps a shotgun at the ready, as a careful examination of Sections 9.41 and 9.42 of the Texas Penal Code reveals.

Sec. 9.41. Defense of a person's own property. *Non deadly*

(a) A person in lawful possession of land or tangible, movable property is justified in using force against another when and to the degree the actor reasonably believes the force is immediately necessary to prevent or terminate the other's trespass on the land or unlawful interference with the property.

(b) A person unlawfully dispossessed of land or tangible, movable property by another is justified in using force against the other when and to the degree the actor reasonably believes the force is immediately necessary to reenter the land or recover the property if the actor uses the force immediately or in fresh pursuit after the dispossession and:

> (1) the actor reasonably believes the other had no claim of right when he dispossessed the actor; or

> (2) the other accomplished the dispossession by using force, threat, or fraud against the actor.

Sec. 9.42. Deadly force to protect property.

A person is justified in using deadly force against another to protect land or tangible, movable property:

(1) if he would be justified in using force against the other under Section 9.41; and

(2) when and to the degree he reasonably believes the deadly force is immediately necessary:

> (A) to prevent the other's imminent commission of arson, burglary, robbery, aggravated robbery, theft during the nighttime, or criminal mischief during the nighttime; or

> (B) to prevent the other who is fleeing immediately after committing burglary, robbery, aggravated robbery, or theft during the nighttime from escaping with the property; and

(3) he reasonably believes that:

> (A) the land or property cannot be protected or recovered by any other means; or

> (B) the use of force other than deadly force to protect or recover the land or property would expose the actor or another to a substantial risk of death or serious bodily injury.

The statutory direction concerning deadly force provides contrasting permissions and limitations that make easy assessment of what is authorized difficult. On the one hand, the statute contains many cautions to those who might use deadly force when property, but not life or limb, is at risk. For example, in addition to the standard use of force requirements of a reasonable belief in the imminent necessity to use reasonable force to protect property, the statute contains a last resort provision that justifies deadly force to protect property when "the land or property cannot be protected by any other means" and the use of lesser force "would expose the actor or another to a substantial risk of death or serious bodily injury." Some of the enumerated crimes also suggest that deadly force should not be routinely used because they contain an assaultive or dangerous component that also might trigger other defenses such as self-defense or use of force for law enforcement such as arson and aggravated robbery. On the other hand, the inclusion of theft during the night and criminal mischief during the night on the list of those offenses for which deadly force may be used when it is imminently necessary to prevent the commission of these offenses sends another message. Similarly, including theft during the night on the list of offenses that authorize deadly force to prevent the flight of the perpetrator immediately after its commission authorizes the use of lethal force when no bodily harm has been threatened or inflicted.

Theft and criminal mischief may be misdemeanors depending upon the value of the items involved without regard to whether the offenses are committed in the daylight or at night. To include these offenses in a list authorizing lethal force appears to declare open season on vagrants and juvenile delinquents who create minor disturbances to the security of property. Deadly force to prevent one from fleeing clearly contemplates that there is no duty to retreat before using deadly force. It may be all too easy to justify dispensing with the last resort cautions in the statute based upon the belief that property being stolen is unlikely to be recovered or protected by other means. The apprehension by the police of every vandal and thief in modern urban society is impossible.

Such apparent permission to shoot and kill may not be beneficial to a nervous home owner with a gun because the reasonableness of the imminent necessity of using deadly force as a last resort will appear far less reasonable in retrospect if a meter reader, neighbor, or investigating police officer is mistakenly killed instead of the thief or vandal. This is so even though, in theory, it is the actor's reasonable belief concerning the need to use deadly force that should control, rather than the actual situation. The *Law* case that follows dramatically illustrates this problem.

Law v. State

318 A.2d 859 (Md. App. 1974)

Lowe, J., delivered the opinion of the Court.

When James Cecil Law, Jr. purchased a thirty-nine dollar shot gun for "house protection," he could not possibly have conceived of the ordeal it would cause him to undergo.

Mr. Law, a 32 year old black man, had recently married and moved to a predominantly white middle-class neighborhood. Within two weeks his home was broken into and a substantial amount of clothing and personal property was taken. The investigating officer testified that Mr. Law was highly agitated following the burglary and indicated that he would take the matter in his own hands. The officer quoted Mr. Law as saying: "I will take care of the job. I know who it is." The officer went on to say that Law told him "he knew somebody he could get a gun from in D.C. and he was going to kill the man and he was going to take care of it." Two days later he purchased a 12 gauge shotgun and several "double ought" shells.

The intruder entered the Law's home between 6:30 and 9:00 in the evening by breaking a windowpane in the kitchen door which opened onto a screened back porch. The intruder then apparently reached in and unlocked the door. Law later installed "double locks" which required the use of a key both inside and outside. He replaced the glass in the door window in a temporary manner by holding it in place with a few pieces of molding, without using the customary glazing compound to seal it in.

One week after the break-in a well-meaning neighbor saw a flickering light in the Law's otherwise darkened house and became suspicious. Aware of the previous burglary, he reported to the police that someone was breaking into the Law's home. Although the hour was 8:00 p.m., Mr. Law and his bride had retired for the evening. When the police arrived, a fuse of circumstances ignited by fear exploded into a tragedy of errors.

The police did not report to or question the calling neighbor. Instead they went about routinely checking the house seeking the possible illegal point of entry. They raised storm windows where they could reach them and shook the inside windows to see if they were locked. They shined flashlights upon the windows out of reach, still seeking evidence of unlawful entry. Finding none, two officers entered the back screened porch to check the back door, whereupon they saw the windowpane which appeared to have been temporarily put in place with a few pieces of molding. These officers apparently had not known of the repair or the cause of damage.

Upstairs Mr. and Mrs. Law heard what sounded like attempts to enter their home. Keenly aware of the recent occurrence, Mr. Law went downstairs, obtained and loaded his newly acquired shotgun and, apparently facing the rear door of the house, listened for more sounds.

In the meantime, the uniformed officers found what they thought to be the point of entry of a burglar, and were examining the recently replaced glass. While Officer Adams held the flashlight on the recently replaced pane of glass, Officer Garrison removed the molding and the glass, laid them down and stated that he was going to reach in and unlock the door from the inside to see if entry could be gained. Officer Adams testified that they "were talking in a tone a little lower than normal at this point." Officer Adams stated that Officer Garrison then tested the inside lock, discovered it was a deadlock and decided no one could have gotten in the door without a key. A law enforcement student, riding with Officer Garrison that evening, testified that he then heard a rattling noise and someone saying "if there was somebody here, he's still in there." As Officer Garrison removed his hand from the window he was hit by a shotgun blast which Law fired through the door. Officer Garrison was dead on arrival at the hospital.

Officer Potts, the officer next to arrive at the scene, saw Officer Adams running to his car to call for reinforcements. He heard another shot and Officer Adams yell "they just shot at me."

The tragedy of errors had only begun. The officers, having obtained reinforcements and apparently believing they had cornered a burglar, subjected the house to a fusillade of gun fire evinced by over forty bullet holes in the bottom of the kitchen door and the police department transcription of a telephone conversation during the ensuing period of incomprehensible terror.

Mr. Law testified that while he stood listening to the sounds and voices at the door, fearful that someone was about to come in "the gun went off, like that, and when it went off like that it scared me and I was so scared because I had never shot a shotgun before and then I heard a voice on the outside say that someone had been shot." Mr. Law was not able to hear who had been shot but he then "hollered up to my wife, call a police officer, I think I shot a burglar." His wife called the police and most of her conversation was recorded.

The appellant, James Cecil Law, Jr. was found guilty of murder in the second degree and of assault with intent to murder. He was convicted by a jury in the Circuit Court for Charles County following removal from Prince George's County. Judge James C. Mitchell sentenced him to concurrent ten year terms.

Issue

The appellant's first question assigning error for failure to grant his motion for judgment of acquittal is a request for our review of the trial court's constitutional responsibility to pass upon the sufficiency of the evidence. In doing so we are not permitted to substitute our judgment of whether there was reasonable doubt of the defendant's guilt for that exercised by the jury. The limit of our review is to determine whether there was relevant and legally sufficient evidence, properly before the jury, to sustain a conviction.

There is a dearth of Maryland authority upon the question of what constitutes justifiable homicide in the defense of one's home. We hasten to note, however, that the single case directly meeting the question does so concisely and clearly. In 1962, the Court of Appeals in *Crawford v. State*, 190 A.2d 538 (Md. App. 1963), reversed a conviction of manslaughter against a 42 year old man, suffering from a nervous condition and ulcers, whose home was being broken into by a 23 year old man and a partner. The decedent had knocked out a piece of masonite replacing one of four glass panes in the door. Crawford fired a shotgun through the door killing the attacker before he was able to enter.

Certain of the circumstances of that case coincide remarkably with the case at bar. It is as remarkably distinguished, however, by the character and purpose of the decedent, who had previously beaten Crawford and was returning to rob and beat him again after threatening to do so. Without digression on tangential issues, Chief Judge Brune noted with little discussion, as we do here, the appropriateness of the holding of *Gunther v. State,* 179 A.2d 880 (Md. App. 1962), that one not seeking a fight may arm himself in anticipation of a violent attack.

The defense of habitation is explained by text writers and treated in *Crawford* as an extension of the right of self-defense. The distinction between the defense of home and the defense of person is primarily that in the former there is no duty to retreat. "A man in his own home was treated as 'at the wall' and could not, by another's assault, be put under any duty to flee therefrom."

The regal aphorism that a man's home is his castle has obscured the limitations on the right to preserve one's home as a sanctuary from fear of force or violence.

Crawford articulates the rule well, distilling it from a review or cases in many jurisdictions:

> Most American jurisdictions in which the question has been decided have taken the view that if an assault on a dwelling and an attempted forcible entry are made under circumstances which would create *a reasonable apprehension* that it is the design of the assailant *to commit a felony* or to inflict on the inhabitants injury which may result in loss of life or great bodily harm, and that the danger that the design will be carried into effect is imminent, a lawful occupant of the dwelling may prevent the entry even by the taking of the intruder's life.

The felonies the prevention of which justifies the taking of a life "are such and only such as are committed by forcible means, violence, and surprise such as murder, robbery, burglary, rape or arson." Wharton goes on to say that it is "essential that killing is *necessary* to prevent the commission of the felony in question. If other methods would prevent its commission, a homicide is not justified; all other means of preventing the crime must first be exhausted."

The right thus rests upon real or apparent necessity. It is this need for caution in exercising the right that has been relegated to obscurity. The position espoused by appellant typifies the misunderstanding of the extent of the right to defend one's home against intrusion. He says:

> The defendant is not required to act as a reasonable, prudent and cautious individual, nor was he required to limit his force to only that that was required under the circumstances—not when the defendant was in his own home, and believed he was being set upon, or about to be set upon by would be robbers or burglars who were in the act of breaking into his home at the time.

The judgment which must usually be made precipitously under frightening conditions nevertheless demands a certain presence of mind and reasonableness of judgment. Although one is "not obliged to retreat . . . but . . . may even pursue the assailant until he finds himself or his property out of danger . . . this will not justify a person['s] firing upon everyone who forcibly enters his house, even at night." Harris, *Principles of Criminal Law* (adapted by M.F. Force), at 127.

In 1894 Mr. Justice Harlan redefined the scope of the rule within its permissible limits:

> In East's Pleas of the Crown, the author, considering what sort of an attack it was lawful and justifiable to resist, even by the death of the assailant, says: "A man may repel force by force, in defense of his person, habitation, or property, against one who manifestly intends and endeavors, *by violence or surprise*, to commit a known felony, such as murder, rape, robbery, arson, burglary, and the like, upon either. In these cases he is not obliged *to retreat*, but may pursue his adversary until he has secured himself from all danger; and if he kill him in so doing it is called justifiable self-defense; as, on the other hand, the killing by such felon of any person so lawfully defending himself will be murder. But *a bare fear of any of these offenses, however well grounded*, as that another lies in wait to take away the party's life, *unaccompanied with any overt act indicative of such an intention, will not warrant in killing that other by way of prevention.*"

Beard v. United States, 158 U.S. 550 (1895).

Did the trial judge err in instructing the jury that the defense of justifiable homicide was available only if the Appellant acted as a reasonable, prudent and cautious man under the circumstances, and that he used no more force than was necessary under the circumstances?

The same authorities answer appellant's [this] assignment of error that answered his first. Appellant argues that in defense of his home he "is not subject to the standards of a reasonable, prudent and cautious person, nor is his degree of force limited only to that required under the circumstances to repel the intruder." Quite the contrary, we do not find the right to defend one's habitation to be so absolute as to sanction promiscuous shooting upon a baseless apprehension by an unreasonable person. The permissible degree of force used to repel an intruder must not be excessive. *Wharton* emphasizes that "all other means of preventing the crime must first be exhausted." The question of excessive force to resist the intrusion, in most instances, as in *Crawford*, is the most difficult problem the jury has to cope with when death of the intruder was the result. Apropos of the appellant's question is the statement in *State v. Sorrentino*, that a defendant is not justified in taking a life "[i]f a cautious and prudent man, under the same circumstances, would not believe the danger to have been real."

Notes

1.   After noting a dearth of state authority upon the question of what constitutes justifiable homicide in the defense of one's home, the Court cites the case of *Crawford v. State*, 190 A.2d 538 (Md. App. 1963), which "concisely and clearly" deals with this issue. The Court states this with regard to *Crawford*: "Certain of the circumstances of that case coincide remarkably with the case at bar. It is as remarkably distinguished, however, by the character and purpose of the decedent, who had previously beaten Crawford and was returning to rob and beat him again after threatening to do so."

In both *Law* and *Crawford*, a recent crime victim heard signs of an attempted entry through a recently repaired door that had been the point of entry in the previous crime. In both, the defendant fired a gun through the closed door before an entry could occur. And in both cases, the gunshot killed a person on the other side of the door. Isn't the remarkably distinguishing difference between the two cases the identity of the decedent? Crawford killed his previous attacker; Law killed a police officer. What does that fact have to do with the reasonable belief in the imminent necessity to use deadly force? Is the rule of law (and *Law*) that if you are right you have a defense, but if you're wrong you are going to prison?

2.   One of the requirements of the deadly force in defense of property statute is that there must be no reasonable alternative to the use of lethal force. In many circumstances, an argument can be made that if there is not yet a personal threat, an available option is to call the police. If a defendant resorts to self-help, would it be relevant that police departments in large urban areas do not always send an officer to the scene if a home or a car for property crimes (without personal injuries)?

3.   Even if deadly force would be justifiable under the Texas deadly force in defense of property statute, the use of a mechanical device, such as a spring gun, is not justifiable if the device is "designed to cause, or known by the actor to create a substantial risk of causing death or serious bodily injury under Section 9.44 of the Texas Penal Code."

4.   Under Section 9.43, force and, when appropriate, deadly force may be used in the defense of a third party's property if the actor would be justified in protecting the property were it his own and:

> (1) the actor reasonably believes the unlawful interference constitutes attempted or consummated theft of or criminal mischief to the tangible, movable property; or
>
> (2) the actor reasonably believes that:
>
>> (A) the third person has requested his protection of the land or property;
>>
>> (B) he has a legal duty to protect the third person's land or property; or
>>
>> (C) the third person whose land or property he uses force or deadly force to protect is the actor's spouse, parent, or child, resides with the actor, or is under the actor's care.

Use of Force in Law Enforcement

Law enforcement officers have recognized the right to use reasonable force to make arrests and to prevent harm to citizens from criminal offenders. As was discussed in the self-defense chapter, even if a person is falsely arrested, there is no entitlement to use force to resist that arrest unless, without first offering any resistance, the officer uses excessive force. Not surprisingly, there is a great deal of controversy that arises over claims that police officers used force without justification and used excessive force whether or not there was a basis for an arrest. *Tennessee v. Garner*, which follows, is the most important decision of the United States Supreme Court dealing with law enforcement use of deadly force.

Tennessee v. Garner

471 U.S. 1 (1985)

Justice White delivered the opinion of the Court.

z

This case requires us to determine the constitutionality of the use of deadly force to prevent the escape of an apparently unarmed suspected felon. We conclude that such force may not be used unless it is necessary to prevent the escape and the officer has probable cause to believe that the suspect poses a significant threat of death or serious physical injury to the officer or others.

At about 10:45 p.m. on October 3, 1974, Memphis Police Officers Elton Hymon and Leslie Wright were dispatched to answer a "prowler inside call." Upon arriving at the scene they saw a woman standing on her porch and gesturing toward the adjacent house. She told them she had heard glass breaking and that "they" or "someone" was breaking in next door. While Wright radioed the dispatcher to say that they were on the scene, Hymon went behind the house. He heard a door slam and saw someone run across the backyard. The fleeing suspect, who was appellee-respondent's decedent, Edward Garner, stopped at a 6-feet-high chain link fence at the edge of the yard. With the aid of a flashlight, Hymon was able to see Garner's face and hands. He saw no sign of a weapon, and, though not certain, was "reasonably sure" and "figured" that Garner was unarmed. He thought Garner was 17 or 18 years old and about 5'5" or 5'7" tall. While Garner was crouched at the base of the fence, Hymon called out "police, halt" and took a few steps toward him. Garner then began to climb over the fence. Convinced that if Garner made it over the fence he would elude capture, Hymon shot him. The bullet hit Garner in the back of the head. Garner was taken by ambulance to a hospital, where he died on the operating table. Ten dollars and a purse taken from the house were found on his body.

In using deadly force to prevent the escape, Hymon was acting under the authority of a Tennessee statute and pursuant to Police Department policy. The statute provides that "[i]f, after notice of the intention to arrest the defendant, he either flee or forcibly resist, the officer may use all the necessary means to effect the arrest." The Department policy was slightly more restrictive than the statute, but still allowed the use of deadly force in cases of burglary. The incident was reviewed by the Memphis Police Firearm's Review Board and presented to a grand jury. Neither took any action.

Garner's father then brought this action in the Federal District Court for the Western District of Tennessee, seeking damages under 42 U.S.C. § 1983 for asserted violations of Garner's constitutional rights. The complaint alleged that the shooting violated the Fourth, Fifth, Sixth, Eighth, and Fourteenth Amendments of the United States Constitution. It named as defendants Officer Hymon, the Police Department, its Director, and the Mayor and city of Memphis. After a 3-day bench trial, the District Court entered judgment for all defendants. It dismissed the claims against the Mayor and the Director for lack of evidence. It then concluded that Hymon's actions were authorized by the Tennessee statute, which in turn was constitutional. Hymon had employed the only reasonable and practicable means of preventing Garner's escape.

Garner had "recklessly and heedlessly attempted to vault over the fence to escape, thereby assuming the risk of being fired upon."

The Court of Appeals for the Sixth Circuit affirmed with regard to Hymon, finding that he had acted in good-faith reliance on the Tennessee statute and was therefore within the scope of his qualified immunity.

The Court of Appeals reversed and remanded. It reasoned that the killing of a fleeing suspect is a "seizure" under the Fourth Amendment, and is therefore constitutional only if "reasonable." The Tennessee statute failed as applied to this case because it did not adequately limit the use of deadly force by distinguishing between felonies of different magnitudes—"the facts, as found, did not justify the use of deadly force under the Fourth Amendment." Officers cannot resort to deadly force unless they "have probable cause . . . to believe that the suspect [has committed a felony and] poses a threat to the safety of the officers or a danger to the community if left at large."

The State of Tennessee, which had intervened to defend the statute, appealed to this Court.

Whenever an officer restrains the freedom of a person to walk away, he has seized that person. While it is not always clear just when minimal police interference becomes a seizure, there can be no question that apprehension by the use of deadly force is a seizure subject to the reasonableness requirement of the Fourth Amendment.

A police officer may arrest a person if he has probable cause to believe that person committed a crime. Petitioners and appellant argue that if this requirement is satisfied the Fourth Amendment has nothing to say about how that seizure is made. This submission ignores the many cases in which this Court, by balancing the extent of the intrusion against the need for it, has examined the reasonableness of the manner in which a search or seizure is conducted. To determine the constitutionality of a seizure "[w]e must balance the nature and quality of the intrusion on the individual's Fourth Amendment interests against the importance of the governmental interests alleged to justify the intrusion." balancing test

The same balancing process applied in the cases cited above demonstrates that, notwithstanding probable cause to seize a suspect, an officer may not always do so by killing him. The intrusiveness of a seizure by means of deadly force is unmatched. The suspect's fundamental interest in his own life need not be elaborated upon. The use of deadly force also frustrates the interest of the individual, and of society, in judicial determination of guilt and punishment. Against these interests are ranged governmental interests in effective law enforcement. It is argued that overall violence will be reduced by encouraging the peaceful submission of suspects who know that they may be shot if they flee. Effectiveness in making arrests requires the resort to deadly force, or at least the meaningful threat thereof. "Being able to arrest such individuals is a condition precedent to the state's entire system of law enforcement."

Without in any way disparaging the importance of these goals, we are not convinced that the use of deadly force is a sufficiently productive means of accomplishing them to justify the killing of nonviolent suspects. The use of deadly force is a self-defeating way of apprehending a suspect and so setting the criminal justice mechanism in motion. If successful, it guarantees that that mechanism will not be set in motion. And while the meaningful threat of deadly force might be thought to lead to the arrest of more live suspects by discouraging escape attempts, the presently available evidence does not support this thesis. The fact is that a majority of police departments in this country have forbidden the use of deadly force against nonviolent suspects. If those charged with the enforcement of the criminal law have abjured the use of deadly force in arresting nondangerous felons, there is a substantial basis for doubting that the use of such force is an essential attribute of the arrest power in all felony cases. Petitioners and appellant have not persuaded us that shooting nondangerous fleeing suspects is so vital as to outweigh the suspect's interest in his own life.

The use of deadly force to prevent the escape of all felony suspects, whatever the circumstances, is constitutionally unreasonable. It is not better that all felony suspects die than that they escape. Where the suspect poses no immediate threat to the officer and no threat to others, the harm resulting from failing to apprehend him does not justify the use of deadly force to do so. It is no doubt unfortunate when a suspect who is in sight escapes, but the fact that the police arrive a little late or are a little slower afoot does not always justify killing the suspect. A police officer may not seize an unarmed, nondangerous suspect by shooting him dead. The Tennessee statute is unconstitutional insofar as it authorizes the use of deadly force against such fleeing suspects.

It is not, however, unconstitutional on its face. Where the officer has probable cause to believe that the suspect poses a threat of serious physical harm, either to the officer or to others, it is not constitutionally unreasonable to prevent escape by using deadly force. Thus, if the suspect threatens the officer with a weapon or there is probable cause to believe that he has committed a crime involving the infliction or threatened infliction of serious physical harm, deadly force may be used if necessary to prevent escape, and if, where feasible, some warning has been given. As applied in such circumstances, the Tennessee statute would pass constitutional muster.

It is insisted that the Fourth Amendment must be construed in light of the common-law rule, which allowed the use of whatever force was necessary to effect the arrest of a fleeing felon, though not a misdemeanant. As stated in Hale's posthumously published Pleas of the Crown:

> [I]f persons that are pursued by these officers for felony or the just suspicion thereof . . . shall not yield themselves to these officers, but shall either resist or fly before they are apprehended or being apprehended shall rescue themselves and resist or fly, so that they cannot be otherwise apprehended, and are upon necessity slain therein, because they cannot be otherwise taken, it is no felony.

2 M. HALE, HISTORIA PLACITORUM CORONAE 85 (1736).

Most American jurisdictions also imposed a flat prohibition against the use of deadly force to stop a fleeing misdemeanant, coupled with a general privilege to use such force to stop a fleeing felon.

The State and city argue that because this was the prevailing rule at the time of the adoption of the Fourth Amendment and for some time thereafter, and is still in force in some States, use of deadly force against a fleeing felon must be "reasonable." It is true that this Court has often looked to the common law in evaluating the reasonableness, for Fourth Amendment purposes, of police activity. On the other hand, it "has not simply frozen into constitutional law those law enforcement practices that existed at the time of the Fourth Amendment's passage." Because of sweeping change in the legal and technological context, reliance on the common-law rule in this case would be a mistaken literalism that ignores the purposes of a historical inquiry.

It has been pointed out many times that the common-law rule is best understood in light of the fact that it arose at a time when virtually all felonies were punishable by death. "Though effected without the protections and formalities of an orderly trial and conviction, the killing of a resisting or fleeing felon resulted in no greater consequences than those authorized for punishment of the felony of which the individual was charged or suspected." Courts have also justified the common-law rule by emphasizing the relative dangerousness of felons.

Neither of these justifications makes sense today. Almost all crimes formerly punishable by death no longer are or can be. And while in earlier times "the gulf between the felonies and the minor offences was broad and deep," today the distinction is minor and often arbitrary. Many crimes classified as misdemeanors, or nonexistent, at common law are now felonies. These changes have undermined the concept, which was questionable to begin with, that use of deadly force against a fleeing felon is merely a speedier execution of someone who has already forfeited his life. They have also made the assumption that a "felon" is more dangerous than a misdemeanant untenable. Indeed, numerous misdemeanors involve conduct more dangerous than many felonies.

There is an additional reason why the common-law rule cannot be directly translated to the present day. The common-law rule developed at a time when weapons were rudimentary. Deadly force could be inflicted almost solely in a hand-to-hand struggle during which, necessarily, the safety of the arresting officer was at risk. Handguns were not carried by police officers until the latter half of the last century. Only then did it become possible to use deadly force from a distance as a means of apprehension. As a practical matter, the use of deadly force under the standard articulation of the common-law rule has an altogether different meaning—and harsher consequences—now than in past centuries.

One other aspect of the common-law rule bears emphasis. It forbids the use of deadly force to apprehend a misdemeanant, condemning such action as disproportionately severe.

In short, though the common-law pedigree of Tennessee's rule is pure on its face, changes in the legal and technological context mean the rule is distorted almost beyond recognition when literally applied.

Nor do we agree with petitioners and appellant that the rule we have adopted requires the police to make impossible, split-second evaluations of unknowable facts. We do not deny the practical difficulties of attempting to assess the suspect's dangerousness. However, similarly difficult judgments must be made by the police in equally uncertain circumstances. Nor is there any indication that in States that allow the use of deadly force only against dangerous suspects, the standard has been difficult to apply or has led to a rash of litigation involving inappropriate second-guessing of police officers' split-second decisions. Moreover, the highly technical felony/misdemeanor distinction is equally, if not more, difficult to apply in the field. An officer is in no position to know, for example, the precise value of property stolen, or whether the crime was a first or second offense. Finally, as noted above, this claim must be viewed with suspicion in light of the similar self-imposed limitations of so many police departments.

The District Court concluded that Hymon was justified in shooting Garner because state law allows, and the Federal Constitution does not forbid, the use of deadly force to prevent the escape of a fleeing felony suspect if no alternative means of apprehension is available. This conclusion made a determination of Garner's apparent dangerousness unnecessary. The court did find, however, that Garner appeared to be unarmed, though Hymon could not be certain that was the case. Restated in Fourth Amendment terms, this means Hymon had no articulable basis to think Garner was armed.

In reversing, the Court of Appeals accepted the District Court's factual conclusions and held that "the facts, as found, did not justify the use of deadly force." We agree. Officer Hymon could not reasonably have believed that Garner—young, slight, and unarmed—posed any threat. Indeed, Hymon never attempted to justify his actions on any basis other than the need to prevent an escape. The District Court stated in passing that "[t]he facts of this case did not indicate to Officer Hymon that Garner was 'non-dangerous.'" This conclusion is not explained, and seems to be based solely on the fact that Garner had broken into a house at night. However, the fact that Garner was a suspected burglar could not, without regard to the other circumstances, automatically justify the use of deadly force. Hymon did not have probable cause to believe that Garner, whom he correctly believed to be unarmed, posed any physical danger to himself or others.

The dissent argues that the shooting was justified by the fact that Officer Hymon had probable cause to believe that Garner had committed a nighttime burglary. While we agree that burglary is a serious crime, we cannot agree that it is so dangerous as automatically to justify the use of deadly force. The FBI classifies burglary as a "property" rather than a "violent" crime. Although the armed burglar would present a different situation, the fact that an unarmed suspect has broken into a dwelling at night does not automatically mean he is physically dangerous. This case demonstrates as much. In fact, the available statistics demonstrate that burglaries only rarely involve physical violence. During the 10-year period from 1973–1982, only 3.8% of all burglaries involved violent crime. Bureau of Justice Statistics.

We hold that the statute is invalid insofar as it purported to give Hymon the authority to act as he did. As for the policy of the Police Department, the absence of any discussion of this issue by the courts below, and the uncertain state of the record, preclude any consideration of its validity.

The judgment of the Court of Appeals is affirmed, and the case is remanded for further proceedings consistent with this opinion. Holding

Notes

1.   Because the restrictions of the Fourth Amendment do not generally apply to private individuals, it would appear that a private party would not be constrained by the holding in *Tennessee v. Garner*. Does that mean a private person has more authority to provide vigilante justice under defense-of-third-party provisions in self-defense and defense-of-property provisions than police officers who are constrained by the Fourth Amendment limitations of *Garner*?

Under Section 9.51 of the Texas Penal Code, restrictions on the use of deadly force announced by Garner apply to law enforcement officers and private citizens. Deadly force is justifiable in an effort to make an arrest only if all of the usual requirements of this defense are satisfied and:

> (1) the actor reasonably believes the conduct for which arrest is authorized included the use or attempted use of deadly force; or

> (2) the actor reasonably believes there is a substantial risk that the person to be arrested will cause death or serious bodily injury to the actor or another if the arrest is delayed.

The statute essentially codifies the standards of *Garner* and appears to apply them equally to private citizen and law enforcement officer. While the statute corrects the anomaly created by *Garner*'s applicability only to state actors, the average person would be surprised by the relative equality of the authority of the private citizen and the law enforcement officer to use force for the enforcement of the law. In fact, while the power of citizen arrest is surprisingly broad, the authority of the police officer is greater. The authority to use force under Section 9.51 is limited to arrest for the private citizen, but it extends to arrest or search for the officer.

Arrest authority is also broader for the law enforcement officer under Article 14.01 of the Texas Code of Criminal Procedure, which restricts the power of private citizens to make arrests to only felonies or breaches of the peace committed in the presence or view of the person. Law enforcement officers may arrest for any offense committed in the presence or view of the officers. Also, law enforcement officers possess a broader authority to arrest based upon probable cause even if the offense was not committed in the presence or view of the officer.

2.   A number of Texas statutes provide authority to use force for the purpose of law enforcement even if the actor or his or her property is not threatened. The self-defense statute provides a justification to use a reasonable degree of force to prevent the imminent commission of enumerated offenses that contain an assaultive component justifying the use of force or deadly force when the actor reasonably believes that it is imminently necessary to prevent the commission of aggravated kidnapping, murder, sexual assault, aggravated sexual assault, robbery, or aggravated robbery. TEX. PENAL CODE ANN. §§ 9.31(a)(3) and 9.32(a)(2)(B). The use of force on behalf of third parties defense impliedly carries the justification to use force to prevent the imminent commission of these offenses against third parties. TEX. PENAL CODE ANN. § 9.33.

This law enforcement aspect of self-defense and defense of others are complemented by Section 9.51 of the Texas Penal Code. Section 9.51 governs the use of force by law enforcement officers and those acting in the presence of and at the direction of law enforcement officers to secure a lawful arrest or search. Section 9.52 addresses the use of force to prevent an escape from custody. Section 9.53 governs the use of force in maintaining security in a correctional facility. All of these defenses follow the familiar pattern of necessity, self-defense, and other justifications in Chapter 9 of the Texas Penal Code by requiring a reasonable belief in the imminent necessity to use a reasonable degree of force, which may include deadly force under appropriate circumstances. Section 9.53 provides a significantly broader authority for officers and employees of penal institutions to use reasonable force to maintain safety and security without a required showing of imminence.

3.   The Texas Penal Code has defenses related to law enforcement that do not relate to the use of force. The public duty defense codified at Section 9.21 of the Texas Penal Code expressly states that the defense is not available to justify the use of force and more specific statutory defenses such as self-defense and defense of property control in such cases. An example of an application of the statute not involving the use of force occurred in *Rosalez v. State*, 875 S.W.2d 705 (Tex. App.—Dallas 1993, pet. ref'd), in which the Dallas Court of Appeals upheld the actions of the peace officers under a public duty theory. The court held that the peace officers "reasonably believed their entry onto appellant's property was required to carry out their statutory duty to suppress crime and prevent offenses against the property of another." At issue in the case was whether a conviction should be upheld when the police entered an owner's property without his consent to investigate suspected burglars, but after finding no burglary, arrested the property owner for possession of marijuana. The court affirmed the marijuana possession conviction even after concluding the officers entered the home without probable cause. The court held the officers acted pursuant to a statutory duty to suppress crime and prevent offenses against the property of another, and, therefore, acted reasonably.

The public duty defense is not restricted to public officials. Although the title of the offense suggests an actor must have an affirmative obligation to carry out some publically mandated duty, the wording of the statutory defense uses the language of a reasonable belief that the conduct engaged in was required or authorized. Thus, the statute would seem to overlap significantly with the mistake of law defense discussed earlier in the text, but without several of the significant limitations of that defense. Comparing Section 9.21, Public Duty, to Section 8.03, Mistake of Law, reveals a number of important advantages for the defense under Section 9.21. The Public Duty defense is established if reliance upon the legality of conduct is reasonable in contrast to the requirement in Section 8.03 that the authorization be in writing or issued by an official charged by law with interpreting the law in question, as is the case with mistake of law. The Public Duty statute specifically provides that reliance may be reasonable, "even though the court or government tribunal lacks jurisdiction or the process is unlawful," and does not specify that authorization must be in writing. A further advantage is that, unlike the affirmative defense of mistake of law, public duty is a defense. This means that the defendant need only meet a production burden to be entitled to an instruction, and the State must disprove the validity of the public duty claim beyond a reasonable doubt.

Entrapment

4.   The Texas Penal Code also contains an offense related to law enforcement misconduct known as entrapment. The theory of the entrapment defense is that—while law enforcement officers may engage in undercover work and pretend to be willing to violate the law in order to catch offenders who commit crimes where there is no complainant—police should not create crimes through inducements that would cause a normally law-abiding citizen to commit a crime. A defendant may be entitled to a jury instruction on the defense of entrapment, codified at Section 8.06 of the Texas Penal Code, if the defendant affirmatively provides some evidence that he "was induced to [engage in the conduct charged] by a law enforcement agent using persuasive or other means likely to cause persons to commit the offense."

One of the most unusual procedural aspects of entrapment is that the defense can have two opportunities to present it. In addition to seeking a jury decision regarding the defense through the normal mechanism of jury instructions, the defense may raise the issue of whether there was entrapment as a matter of law at a pre-trial hearing. However, the court in *Hernandez v. State*, 161 S.W.3d 491, 494 (Tex. Crim. App. 2005) held that at a pre-trial hearing, a trial judge is not required to believe a defendant's version of events supporting an entrapment instruction, even if the defendant's account is largely uncontested. If the facts are undisputed and the question is only one of law, whether the conduct of the law enforcement officials constitutes entrapment may be decided by the judge before trial. If there is a factual dispute concerning what took place, the trial court will deny the pre-trial motion and allow the jury to decide the issue.

In contrast to a jury instruction at the close of the case, in the pre-trial determination, the burden lies upon the defendant to prove the entrapment defense as a matter of law. Although it is difficult for the defense to win a pretrial determination of entrapment as a matter of law, a successful pre-trial motion will result in a dismissal that the State cannot appeal. See *Taylor v. State*, 886 S.W.2d 262, 265–266 (Tex. Crim. App. 1994) (statute authorizing state appeals does not include trial court dismissal based upon sufficiency of evidence showing entrapment). At a pre-trial entrapment hearing, the State has no burden other than to raise a fact issue for the jury to resolve. At trial, however, entrapment is a "defense," and the State has the burden of disproving the factual defense by a showing beyond a reasonable doubt once the defendant has met a production burden.

Courts have historically approached entrapment from two different perspectives. The subjective approach focuses on the defendant's predisposition to commit the offense charged, whereas the objective approach focuses only on the conduct of law enforcement officers in inducing the defendant to commit the offense. Based on the interpretation of the statutory language in Section 8.06(a) of the Texas Penal Code—that the defendant was induced commit the offense "by a law enforcement agent using persuasion or other means likely to cause persons to commit the offense"—the Court of Criminal Appeals held, at one time, that the Texas statute embodies an objective test for entrapment, one that assesses the nature of the police activity without reference to the predisposition of the particular defendant.

However, the Court of Criminal Appeals altered this view in *England v. State*, 887 S.W.2d 902 (Tex. Crim. App. 1994), holding that the two-pronged test of the entrapment defense in Texas contains both subjective and objective elements. The defendant must have been the target of police persuasion that subjectively induced him or her to commit the offense, and the

[handwritten margin note: Pretrial v. jury instruction]

[handwritten note: Test for entrapment in TX]

403

inducement must be sufficient to cause a hypothetical law abiding person of average resistance to commit the offense.

An important procedural consequence of this change relates to the question of admissibility of prior offenses and bad acts committed by the defendant. Under the previous objective view, prior offenses were inadmissible because they were irrelevant when the focus was on the police conduct and whether officers would have induced a hypothetical reasonable person to commit the offense. However, in *England v. State*, the Court of Criminal Appeals held that evidence the defendant readily agreed to sell LSD to an officer on two occasions before the charged offense was admissible because it tended to make it more probable the defendant's later sale was not because of an officer's persuasion.

Whether the defense is subjective, objective, or some combination of the two, entrapment is a difficult defense to establish. The Penal Code provides that, "conduct merely affording a person an opportunity to commit an offense does not constitute entrapment." Thus, most of the implicit encouragement to criminality involved in undercover police activities, such as drug purchases by undercover officers, fall far short of entrapment.

Rule: The use of deadly force to prevent the escape of all felony suspects whatever the circumstances, is constitutionally unreasonable. It is not better that all felony suspects die than that escape. Where the suspect poses no immediate threat to the officer and no threat to others, the harm resulting from failing to apprehend him does not justify the use of deadly force to do so.

Issue: Is a statute authorizing a police officer to use all necessary means in effecting an arrest unconstitutional?

Holding: YES.

The apprehension of a suspect is a seizure for the purposes of the constitution and the use of deadly force to achieve a seizure is only permitted under certain circumstances. The 4th Amendment allows the use of deadly force to apprehend felons who the police have probable cause to believe are dangerous to them or to the public. The shooting of appellee's son, who was a suspect in a burglary, was not an acceptable use of deadly force.

Special Relationship Use of Force

The authority of parents over their children under the age of 18 is recognized by Section 9.61 of the Texas Penal Code, which authorizes parents to use reasonable force "when and to the degree the actor reasonably believes the force is necessary to discipline the child or to safeguard or promote his welfare." There is no imminence requirement for parental authority use of force. However, only the use of force is justified by the statute, never the infliction of serious bodily injury or deadly force.

The use of force is not limited to biological parents; it applies to step-parents and others acting "in loco parentis," including a "grandparent and guardian, any person acting by, through, or under the direction of a court with jurisdiction over the child, and anyone who has express or implied consent of the parent or parents." Although this language might be broad enough to include teachers and guardians of those judged incompetent, there are special statutes justifying the use of reasonable non-deadly force for such actors as well as others who act in loco parentis in Sections 9.62 and 9.63 of the Texas Penal Code. The justification to use force applies more broadly than the caption to the statute referring to "Educator-Student" in Section 9.62 would suggest. It is available to an actor who "is entrusted with the care, supervision, or administration of the person for a special purpose . . . when and to the degree the actor reasonably believes the force is necessary to further the special purpose or to maintain discipline in a group." The justification is not based upon the actor's subjective belief that the use of force is appropriate, but is judged by a reasonable person standard.

The use of force authorized by the statute is limited to appropriate purposes. The *Hogenson* case that follows was a civil suit to recover for alleged assault after a school football coach struck a seventh grader "for the purpose of instruction and encouragement."

Hogenson v. Williams

542 S.W.2d 456 (1976)

Cornelius, Justice.

Appellants brought suit to recover damages for an assault they alleged appellee committed upon Rory Melvin Hogenson. Appellee was Rory's football coach at Terrell Middle School in Denison, Texas. During a practice session of the 7th grade football team, appellee became displeased with Rory's performance of blocking assignments, and as a result started yelling at Rory, then struck the boy's helmet with force sufficient to cause him to stumble and fall to the ground, and then grabbed his face mask. Shortly thereafter Rory was admitted to the hospital complaining of weakness of his left hand, left forearm and elbow region and spasms of the left neck muscles. His condition was diagnosed as a severe cervical sprain and bruising of the brachial plexus. He was discharged from the hospital after eight days and completely recovered within several months. Appellee was twenty-eight years old, was 5'11" tall and weighed 195 pounds. Rory was twelve years of age and weighed 115 pounds.

In response to special issues and instructions the jury found that appellee did not commit an assault upon Rory and that appellee's contact with Rory was done for instruction and encouragement without any intent to injure him. Based upon such answers, the trial court rendered judgment that appellants recover nothing.

The appeal first contends that the trial court erred in instructing the jury, in connection with . . . Special Issue No. 2 and its accompanying instruction which read as follows:

SPECIAL ISSUE NO. 2.
Do you find from a preponderance of the evidence that any contact, if there was, between Defendant Gary L. Williams and Plaintiff Rory Melvin Hogenson was done for instruction and encouragement and without any intent to injure or harm him?

ANSWER "WE DO" OR "WE DO NOT"

ANSWER: We do

You are further instructed that you may take into consideration a teacher of a physical contact sport would not commit an assault where he makes physical contact with a student for the purpose of encouragement and instruction and without any intent to injure him. In determining whether or not there was such an intent, you may take into consideration the relative size and strength of the parties and the amount and degree of force and violence, if any, used. Any force or violence used under such circumstances other than that necessary for instruction and encouragement, taking into consideration the relative size and strength of the parties, would be an assault if the other conditions under the definitions thereof are present.

Appellee argues that the issue and instruction were proper under the general rule that school teachers have the right to discipline their pupils, and the use of reasonable force or physical contact to accomplish that purpose is privileged and does not constitute an assault. Although appellee testified that the physical contact he used was not for the purpose of

406

disciplining the child, he stated it was administered for the purpose of "firing him up" or "instilling spirit in him." He thus contends that the phrase "for the purpose of instruction and encouragement," as used in the instruction and issue, properly applied the law to the facts of this case. We do not agree. The wording of the issue and the instruction gives an incorrect and incomplete statement of the law of privileged force. The phrase "for instruction and encouragement" comes close to expressing the legitimate purposes of privileged force, but it is neither entirely accurate nor complete, and in our opinion it is conducive to misunderstanding. Moreover, the instruction repeated the error of requiring that an intent to injure be present in order for the physical contact to constitute an assault.

Texas cases have long recognized the rule that public school teachers and others standing *in loco parentis* may use reasonable force to discipline their charges. The former Penal Code defined that right as one of "moderate restraint or correction." See Article 1142, subparagraph (1), Penal Code of 1925. The present Code acknowledges that the right exists:

> (1) if the actor is entrusted with the care, supervision, or administration of the person for a special purpose; and
>
> (2) when and to the degree the actor reasonably believes the force is necessary to further the special purpose or to maintain discipline in a group.

TEX. PENAL CODE ANN. § 9.62.

Both of those enactments are generally expressive of the common law majority rule. See Ann. 43 A.L.R.2d 469. The Restatement of Torts, Second Edition, in Sections 147, 150, 151 and 155, articulates the rule in somewhat more detail. It provides that:

> (1) One standing *in loco parentis* is privileged to use reasonable force as he reasonably believes necessary for the child's proper control, training or education;
>
> (2) In determining if the force is reasonable for those purposes the following factors are to be considered:
>
> > (a) The age, sex and condition of the child,
> >
> > (b) The nature of his offense or conduct and his motives,
> >
> > (c) The influence of his example upon other students,
> >
> > (d) Whether the force was reasonably necessary to compel obedience to a proper command, and
> >
> > (e) Whether the force was disproportionate to the offense, is unnecessarily degrading, or is likely to cause serious injury.
>
> (3) Force applied for any purpose other than the proper training or education of the child or for the preservation of discipline, as judged by the above standards, is not privileged.

The Texas Statutes and the Restatement appear to be in harmony. The "special purpose" mentioned in Section 9.62 of the Penal Code, in the case of a public school teacher, is that of controlling, training and educating the child. Those factors which the Restatement provides are to be considered in judging the reasonableness of the force have also been recognized by the Texas cases construing the former Article 1142. Although the language found in the Restatement and the Texas cases suggests that it is *punishment* for wrongful or contumacious conduct that is primarily contemplated by the rule, a liberal construction of the Restatement language, as well as some decisions from other states, indicate that reasonable force may also be applied to enforce compliance with *instructional* commands. Such a construction is consistent with the public policy of our state to give school teachers the necessary support to enable them to efficiently discharge their responsibilities. But we do not accept the proposition that a teacher may use physical violence against a child merely because the child is unable or fails to perform, either academically or athletically, at a desired level of ability, even though the teacher considers such violence to be "instruction and encouragement." In our opinion, the proper construction of the rule of privileged force as expressed by the above statutes and authorities, and as the rule is applied in a civil assault case against a school teacher, is that any force used must be that which the teacher *reasonably* believes necessary (1) to enforce compliance with a *proper* command issued for the purpose of controlling, training or educating the child, or (2) to punish the child for prohibited conduct; and in either case, the force or physical contact must be reasonable and not disproportionate to the activity or the offense. In the event of a retrial, defensive issues based upon privileged force should be accompanied with instructions clearly enunciating these principles.

For the errors noted, the judgment of the trial court is reversed and the cause is remanded for a new trial.

Holding

Notes

Fair Warning! Better Behave!

The commentary to the legislative committee that drafted the Penal Code that became effective in 1974 noted that section 9.61 (parent-child) applies only to children under the age of 18 but that no age limit applies to the Educator-Student domestic authority to use force. The commentary to proposed Penal Code explained: "Unlike Section 9.61, Section 9.62 sets no age limit for the student because a university instructor with a class of 25-year-old graduate students may need the justification as much as the elementary school teacher with a class of 7-year-olds."

Chapter 19: Miscellaneous Defenses

This chapter deals with three topics: intoxication, consent, and youth. It is somewhat misleading to refer to these topics as defenses. The Texas intoxication statute, Section 8.04(a) of the Texas Penal Code, begins by saying that voluntary intoxication is not a defense. Consent is not a general defense, but is a defense to specific, limited offenses. Most of our discussion about age does not provide for exoneration, but rather, whether an adult criminal court or the juvenile court has jurisdiction over a criminal law issue. However, there is a defense of involuntary intoxication and a potential punishment mitigation for "temporary insanity" caused by voluntary intoxication. Consent may exculpate completely if lack of consent is an element of the offense. There is also an infancy defense that would exonerate those who are below the minimum age for juvenile court jurisdiction.

Intoxication

Intoxication raises difficult policy problems in criminal law. A person may voluntarily ingest enough liquor or other intoxicating substance to lack the capacity to intend or know. On the other hand, such extreme intoxication is dangerous not only to the person who is intoxicated, but also to others. Isn't the decision to consume alcohol or other drugs itself reckless? If undesired possible harms occur, isn't the outcome foreseeable when an individual experiences an extreme loss of control? Research has consistently confirmed that more than half of those convicted of violent crimes had been consuming alcohol at or near the time of the crime. Does that suggest crimes committed by intoxicated persons should be strict liability? Does it matter that some people are victims of an addiction and are hindered in their ability to control their conduct and their consumption of an intoxicant?

The conflicting policy issues have produced a variety of methods of handling the problem of intoxicated criminal offenders. The common law rule, which is still followed in some states, is that intoxication as operates as a defense can only if it negates intent in specific intent crimes. C L
The Model Penal Code found the common law treatment of specific intent crimes to be illogical in general, and it eliminated special rules for such crimes with regard to mistake of fact and voluntary intoxication. Under the Model Penal Code, intoxication may negate the mental state required for the crime, but not for crimes requiring a reckless mental state. This approach, which is followed in many states, makes the reckless act the ingestion of the intoxicant leading to foreseeable, albeit unintended, harms.

Some states, like Texas, do not allow voluntary intoxication as a criminal defense. This approach has been challenged on due process grounds, relying on cases like *Winship*, *Mullaney*, and *Patterson*. If it is impermissible to require the defendant to bear a burden of persuasion of an issue that is an element of a crime, isn't it also a violation of due process to forbid to allow the defense to present evidence of intoxication that negates that mental state, and to require the jury to be instructed in a way that allows a finding that the mental state was not proved by the prosecution? A divided United States Supreme Court confronted this difficult question in *Montana v. Egelhoff*, which follows.

Montana v. Egelhoff

518 U.S. 37 (1996)

Justice Scalia announced the judgment of the Court and delivered an opinion, in which The Chief Justice, Justice Kennedy, and Justice Thomas join.

We consider in this case whether the Due Process Clause is violated by Montana Code Annotated § 45-2-203, which provides, in relevant part, that voluntary intoxication "may not be taken into consideration in determining the existence of a mental state which is an element of [a criminal] offense."

In July 1992, while camping out in the Yaak region of northwestern Montana to pick mushrooms, respondent made friends with Roberta Pavola and John Christenson, who were doing the same. On Sunday, July 12, the three sold the mushrooms they had collected and spent the rest of the day and evening drinking, in bars and at a private party in Troy, Montana. Some time after 9 p.m., they left the party in Christenson's 1974 Ford Galaxy station wagon. The drinking binge apparently continued, as respondent was seen buying beer at 9:20 p.m. and recalled "sitting on a hill or a bank passing a bottle of Black Velvet back and forth" with Christenson.

At about midnight that night, officers of the Lincoln County, Montana, sheriff's department, responding to reports of a possible drunk driver, discovered Christenson's station wagon stuck in a ditch along U.S. Highway 2. In the front seat were Pavola and Christenson, each dead from a single gunshot to the head. In the rear of the car lay respondent, alive and yelling obscenities. His blood-alcohol content measured 0.36 percent over one hour later. On the floor of the car, near the brake pedal, lay respondent's .38-caliber handgun, with four loaded rounds and two empty casings; respondent had gunshot residue on his hands.

Respondent was charged with two counts of deliberate homicide, a crime defined by Montana law as "purposely" or "knowingly" causing the death of another human being. MONT. CODE ANN. § 45-5-102 (1995). Respondent's defense at trial was that an unidentified fourth person must have committed the murders; his own extreme intoxication, he claimed, had rendered him physically incapable of committing the murders, and accounted for his inability to recall the events of the night of July 12. Although respondent was allowed to make this use of the evidence that he was intoxicated, the jury was instructed, pursuant to MONT. CODE ANN. § 45-2-203 (1995), that it could not consider respondent's "intoxicated condition . . . in determining the existence of a mental state which is an element of the offense." The jury found respondent guilty on both counts, and the court sentenced him to 84 years' imprisonment.

The Supreme Court of Montana reversed. It reasoned (1) that respondent "had a due process right to present and have considered by the jury all relevant evidence to rebut the State's evidence on all elements of the offense charged," and (2) that evidence of respondent's voluntary intoxication was "clear[ly] . . . relevant to the issue of whether [respondent] acted knowingly and purposely." Because § 45-2-203 prevented the jury from considering that evidence with regard to that issue, the court concluded that the State had been "relieved of part of its burden to prove

410

beyond a reasonable doubt every fact necessary to constitute the crime charged," and that respondent had therefore been denied due process. We granted certiorari.

In re Winship, 397 U.S. 358 (1970), announced the proposition that the Due Process Clause requires proof beyond a reasonable doubt of every fact necessary to constitute the charged crime, and *Sandstrom v. Montana*, 442 U.S. 510 (1979), established a corollary, that a jury instruction which shifts to the defendant the burden of proof on a requisite element of mental state violates due process. These decisions simply are not implicated here because, as the Montana court itself recognized, "[t]he burden is not shifted" under § 45-2-203. The trial judge instructed the jury that "[t]he State of Montana has the burden of proving the guilt of the Defendant beyond a reasonable doubt," and that "[a] person commits the offense of deliberate homicide if he purposely or knowingly causes the death of another human being." Thus, failure by the State to produce evidence of respondent's mental state would have resulted in an acquittal. That acquittal did not occur was presumably attributable to the fact, noted by the Supreme Court of Montana, that the State introduced considerable evidence from which the jury might have concluded that respondent acted "purposely" or "knowingly." For example, respondent himself testified that, several hours before the murders, he had given his handgun to Pavola and asked her to put it in the glove compartment of Christenson's car. That he had to retrieve the gun from the glove compartment before he used it was strong evidence that it was his "conscious object" to commit the charged crimes; as was the execution-style manner in which a single shot was fired into the head of each victim.

"The doctrines of *actus reus*, *mens rea*, insanity, mistake, justification, and duress have historically provided the tools for a constantly shifting adjustment of the tension between the evolving aims of the criminal law and changing religious, moral, philosophical, and medical views of the nature of man. This process of adjustment has always been thought to be the province of the States." *Powell v. Texas*, 392 U.S. 514, 535–36 (1968) (plurality opinion). The people of Montana have decided to resurrect the rule of an earlier era, disallowing consideration of voluntary intoxication when a defendant's state of mind is at issue. Nothing in the Due Process Clause prevents them from doing so, and the judgment of the Supreme Court of Montana to the contrary must be reversed.

Justice Ginsburg, concurring in the judgment (opinion omitted).

Justice O'Connor, with whom Justice Stevens, Justice Souter, and Justice Breyer join, dissenting.

Due process demands that a criminal defendant be afforded a fair opportunity to defend against the State's accusations. Meaningful adversarial testing of the State's case requires that the defendant not be prevented from raising an effective defense, which must include the right to present relevant, probative evidence. To be sure, the right to present evidence is not limitless; for example, it does not permit the defendant to introduce any and all evidence he believes might work in his favor, nor does it generally invalidate the operation of testimonial privileges. Nevertheless, "an essential component of procedural fairness is an opportunity to be heard. That opportunity would be an empty one if the State were permitted to exclude competent, reliable evidence" that is essential to the accused's defense. Section 45-2-203 forestalls the defendant's

411

ability to raise an effective defense by placing a blanket exclusion on the presentation of a type of evidence that directly negates an element of the crime, and by doing so, it lightens the prosecution's burden to prove that mental-state element beyond a reasonable doubt. *See* MONT. CODE ANN. § 45-2-203.

Justice Souter, dissenting (opinion omitted).

Justice Breyer, with whom Justice Stevens joins, dissenting (opinion omitted).

Notes

1.   Was Eggelhoff too intoxicated to "purposely" or "knowingly" cause the death of another human being? Is it fair to preclude him from presenting evidence of his intoxication for the purpose of raising a reasonable doubt he lacked the *mens rea* to be convicted of deliberate homicide? Note Eggelhoff's blood-alcohol content was 0.36 percent when tested more than an hour after he and the victims were found by the police.

Consider these estimates of the effects of alcohol intoxication:

- 0.02-0.03 BAC: No loss of coordination, slight euphoria and loss of shyness. Depressant effects are not apparent. Mildly relaxed and maybe a little lightheaded.

- 0.04-0.06 BAC: Feeling of well-being, relaxation, lower inhibitions, sensation of warmth. Euphoria. Some minor impairment of reasoning and memory, lowering of caution. Your behavior may become exaggerated and emotions intensified (good emotions are better, bad emotions are worse).

- 0.07-0.09 BAC: Slight impairment of balance, speech, vision, reaction time, and hearing. Euphoria. Judgment and self-control are reduced, and caution, reason and memory are impaired, 0.08 is legally impaired and it is illegal to drive at this level. You will probably believe that you are functioning better than you really are.

- 0.10-0.125 BAC: Significant impairment of motor coordination and loss of good judgment. Speech may be slurred; balance, vision, reaction time and hearing will be impaired. Euphoria.

- 0.13-0.15 BAC: Gross motor impairment and lack of physical control. Blurred vision and major loss of balance. Euphoria is reduced and dysphoria (anxiety, restlessness) is beginning to appear. Judgment and perception are severely impaired.

- 0.16-0.19 BAC: Dysphoria predominates, nausea may appear. The drinker has the appearance of a "sloppy drunk."

- 0.20 BAC: Feeling dazed, confused or otherwise disoriented. May need help to stand or walk. If you injure yourself you may not feel the pain. Some people experience nausea and vomiting at this level. The gag reflex is impaired and you can choke if you do vomit. Blackouts are likely at this level so you may not remember what has happened.

- 0.25 BAC: All mental, physical and sensory functions are severely impaired. Increased risk of asphyxiation from choking on vomit and of seriously injuring yourself by falls or other accidents.

- 0.30 BAC: Stupor. You have little comprehension of where you are. You may pass out suddenly and be difficult to awaken.

- 0.35 BAC: Coma is possible. This is the level of surgical anesthesia.

- 0.40 BAC and up: Onset of coma, and possible death due to respiratory arrest.

Be Responsible About Drinking, Inc., Effects at Specific B.A.C. Levels, at http://www.brad21.org/effects_at_specific_bac.html.

Compare Egelhoff's level of intoxication to the much more typical level of 0.08, which is commonly used as the threshold of "legally intoxicated." With a BAC of 0.08, is there any mental state that would be negated? What is the minimum BAC at which a defendant could plausibly claim his intoxication negated the *mens rea* of a charged offense?

2.   Justice Scalia seems to suggest that, under the common law, intoxication should actually be considered an aggravating factor that has no mitigating aspect. Do you agree? Does your agreement extend to all offenses regardless of the penalty? Would you vote to give Eglehoff the death penalty if it was an option?

3.   Texas is a state that, like Montana, does not allow voluntary intoxication to be considered as a defense to crime. Section 8.04(a) says simply that voluntary intoxication is not a defense. However, Subsection (b) of the statute establishes that "[e]vidence of temporary insanity caused by intoxication may be introduced by the actor in mitigation of the penalty attached to the offense for which he is being tried."

The right of a defendant to a mitigation instruction is available only at the punishment stage of trial and only if there is evidence to support the view that, as a result of the intoxication, the defendant temporarily met the standards of insanity under Section 8.01 of the Texas Penal Code as a result of the intoxication. This requires a showing that the defendant did not know right from wrong. This reference to the insanity defense standards adds a confusing criterion. Would Eglehoff have met this standard if the case had been tried in Texas? Certainly it is arguable that he was so intoxicated that he did not know what he was doing and, therefore, did not know right from wrong. But others might think his impairment had nothing to do with his cognitive ability to know what was legally right and wrong.

Even if the defense can make a sufficient showing of temporary insanity under the insanity defense standard, the instruction is of dubious benefit. The jury is not required to regard the intoxication as mitigating, and there is no direction as to how the mitigation should be considered nor is the degree of mitigation specified. Jurors who might otherwise be inclined to give some mitigating weight to the defendant's intoxication may even believe that they are not authorized to do so if they are unable to find that the defendant's impairment reached the level required by the insanity defense standard.

4.   Is the State entitled to an instruction at the guilt/innocence stage of trial that voluntary intoxication is not a defense? In *Taylor v. State*, 885 S.W.2d 154 (Tex. Crim. App. 1994), an instruction that intoxication is not a defense was deemed permissible even though the evidence of intoxication was that the defendant "started feeling funny" after ingesting what was described as a "not substantial" amount of marijuana. The decision of the trial court to instruct the jury at the guilt/innocence stage of trial that intoxication is not a defense was upheld in *Sakil v. State*, 287 S.W.3d 23 (Tex. Crim. App. 2009). Even without a request for an instruction and despite evidence that the defendant was not intoxicated on the day of the alleged assault, the instruction was not error because the trial judge apparently believed the jury might link the evidence of the defendant's unusual behavior on the date of the assault with his history of substance abuse. Unlike the punishment phase mitigation instruction, there is no required showing of intoxication giving rise to temporary insanity. Thus, it appears to require little evidentiary foundation for an instruction that voluntary intoxication is not an offense.

Rule: allowing evidence of voluntary intoxication is not a traditional well founded principle of American Law that would constitute a violation of Δ's 14th Amend. rights under the constitution.

Issue: whether voluntary intoxication may negate a requisite mental state for the crime of homicide?
—NO

Holding: Mont. Sup. Ct. reversed. State can be shown to jury to help asses whether Δ acted in heat of passion.
although a rule allowing a jury to consider evidence of Δ's voluntary intoxication where relevant t' mens rea has gained considerable acceptance, it is too recent and not fundamental to constitute the prohibition of allowing evidence of voluntary intoxication is not a violation of Δ's 14th Amend rights.

Dissent: Due process demands that a criminal Δ be given a fair opportunity to defend against the State's accusations. Key to this opportunity to present evidence that would relate to the mental state required for the crime.

Involuntary Intoxication

In contrast to voluntary intoxication, which is not a defense by explicit statutory declaration, involuntary intoxication has been declared a common law defense applicable in Texas, despite not having statutory authorization. In *Torres v. State*, which follows, the Court of Criminal Appeals created the defense of involuntary intoxication by analogy to the insanity defense. The court established the important principle that, while criminal offenses must be grounded in a statute, and common law crimes are not possible in Texas, *defenses* to criminal liability may be court-created.

lady on drugs aggravated robbery

Torres v. State

585 S.W.2d 746 (Tex. Crim. App. 1979)

Tom G. Davis, Judge.

Issue: Appeal is taken from a conviction for aggravated robbery. Appellant contends that the trial court erred in refusing to submit her requested instruction on involuntary intoxication.

Appellant and Robert Miranda broke into the house of Margaret Garcia at 3:00 a.m. on the morning of July 18, 1975. Mrs. Garcia was first awakened by voices. When the lights in the room were turned on she saw Miranda standing in the room with a gun and the appellant nearby holding a knife. Both intruders threatened to kill Mrs. Garcia if she did not comply with their demands.

Mrs. Garcia was forced to go throughout her house gathering almost every item of value and then load them into her car. The car was ultimately loaded to capacity with rugs, pictures, furniture, appliances, and other household goods. The next morning Mrs. Garcia was forced to accompany appellant and Miranda to Garcia's bank to cash two checks they had forced her to write. They first went to a drive-in window. The teller refused to cash the checks as Mrs. Garcia did not have any identification. Mrs. Garcia suggested that she could cash the checks inside the bank. Miranda allowed Mrs. Garcia to go inside the bank.

Mrs. Garcia notified a police officer inside the bank of the robbery in progress. The officer went outside to investigate. Upon seeing the officer, Miranda ran from the scene. The officer pursued, and after an exchange of gunfire Miranda was wounded and apprehended.

Some ten minutes later other officers summoned to the scene found the appellant asleep in Mrs. Garcia's car. The car was still on the parking lot of the bank.

Mrs. Garcia testified that the appellant was taking the initiative and guiding the actions of Miranda when they first came into her house. Later, on the way to the bank, Mrs. Garcia noticed that the appellant seemed to be going to sleep. Although Mrs. Garcia did not see the appellant or Miranda take any pills, she stated that their actions during the episode led her to believe that both were on drugs.

The only defense witness was Robert Miranda. The record reflects that Miranda had already been convicted and sent to prison for his part in the robbery. Miranda testified that on the night of the offense he and the appellant had been at a bar until about 2:00 a.m. Miranda stated that he had been drinking and taking "pills" while there. From the bar he and the appellant went home.

According to Miranda, appellant had complained to him because he had not found a job. Appellant finally asked Miranda to take her home as she had a headache. Once at the house, Miranda mixed water, "Alka-Seltzer," and "4 or 5" 250-milligram tablets of Thorazine for the appellant. Appellant was not told that the Thorazine tablets had been included in the mixture.

Miranda testified that Thorazine tablets were "downers, depressers and makes you drowsy and go to sleep." When asked why he drugged the appellant's medication, Miranda replied, "Well, we had been arguing about me not having a job and I wanted her to quit complaining about it." Appellant did not testify.

Appellant requested a charge directing the jury to acquit her if they found that she was involuntarily intoxicated and further found that she did not act voluntarily in the commission of the offense because of this intoxication. The trial court refused to give this charge. In *Hanks v. State*, this Court reviewed a trial court's failure to charge on temporary insanity due to involuntary intoxication. This Court stated:

> Aside from the question of temporary insanity resulting from involuntary intoxication as a defense to crime, this evidence was not sufficient to raise the issue of involuntary intoxication. If appellant was aware that a suspected drug had been placed in his drink, as he testified, and in spite of such knowledge he drank the beverage, any intoxication resulting therefrom could not be classified as Involuntary. To constitute involuntary intoxication, there must be an absence of an exercise of independent judgment and volition on the part of the accused in taking the intoxicant.

In the present case, there is evidence that the appellant did not know that any intoxicant was included in the preparation she drank. Although she voluntarily drank the preparation, unless she knew it contained the drug her actions were not a volitional consumption of the intoxicant. We find the evidence was sufficient to show involuntary consumption of the intoxicant under *Hanks*.

2 issues to address!

This conclusion leaves us with two issues. First, does the defense of involuntary intoxication exist in this jurisdiction, and second, did the evidence entered at trial raise this defense and entitle appellant to a defensive charge.

As can be drawn from *Hanks v. State*, no prior case in this jurisdiction has spoken directly to the issue of involuntary intoxication. No statute in this jurisdiction is directly controlling. Texas Penal Code section 8.04 provides that voluntary intoxication is no defense to the commission of crime. Section 8.04 does provide that the temporary insanity caused by intoxication can be evidence in mitigation of punishment, and if raised, the court must charge the jury on this law. This statute does not speak to involuntary intoxication.

The common law disfavor with the defense of intoxication is that it would allow a person to avoid criminal responsibility because of his voluntary act in rendering himself of unsound mind. This consideration does not exist when the intoxication is not self-induced.

Texas Penal Code section 8.01 relieves a person of criminal culpability if as the result of mental disease or defect he "did not know that his conduct was wrong or was incapable of conforming his conduct to the requirements of law." It would be inconsistent to deny this defense to a person who loses his ability to conform his conduct or perceive its culpability because of involuntary intoxication. We find that the defense of involuntary intoxication is well founded in the common law and implicit in our statutory scheme.

We perceive of no reason to stray from the test already codified as the level of mental dysfunction necessary to relieve a defendant from the criminal consequences of his acts. We hold that involuntary intoxication is a defense to criminal culpability when it is shown that: (1) the accused has exercised no independent judgment or volition in taking the intoxicant; and (2) as a result of his intoxication the accused did not know that his conduct was wrong or was incapable of conforming his conduct to the requirements of the law he allegedly violated.

[handwritten margin note: elements of invol. intox.]

[handwritten above line: Δ has burden of persuasion]

Appellant is entitled to a charge on affirmative defenses raised by the evidence. As noted above, we find the evidence sufficient to raise the issue of whether the intoxicant was administered to the appellant without her knowledge. Although the evidence of appellant's state of mind at the time of the offense is meager, it is sufficient to raise the issue for submission to the jury. The victim testified that appellant seemed "drugged," and the circumstances surrounding her arrest are some evidence of her mental state. We find that the appellant was entitled to have the issue of involuntary intoxication submitted to the jury.

The judgment is reversed and the cause remanded. *[handwritten: Holding]*

Notes

1. The involuntary intoxication defense is not limited to the unknowing or forcible ingestion of illicit drugs, but also applies to prescription drugs if the effect of the substance is unknown to the defendant. For example, in *Mendenhall v. State*, 15 S.W.3d 560 (Tex. App.—Waco 2000), *aff'd*, 77 S.W.3d 815 (Tex. Crim. App. 2002), the defendant presented evidence that his assault of prison employees was not consistent with his unusual behavior and was explained by his ingesting insulin, a prescription medication, on an empty stomach the morning of his divorce trial, causing a hypoglycemic reaction. The defendant's testimony combined with medical testimony that a hypoglycemic reaction could cause an individual to meet the then-applicable standards of being unable to conform his or her conduct to the requirements of law meant that the trial court erred by not submitting an involuntary intoxication defense to the jury. However, the error was found harmless in light of testimony by physicians that the defendant's blood-sugar level was normal when he was taken to the emergency room after his outburst in the divorce trial and the transcript of the divorce hearing demonstrated that Mendenhall was not confused moments before his outburst.

2. To prove the affirmative defense of involuntary intoxication in Texas, a defendant must show that he or she was intoxicated; that the intoxication was involuntary; and that because of this involuntary intoxication, the defendant did not know that what he or she was doing was wrong. Consider Torres, who presented evidence she was involuntarily intoxicated because, unbeknownst to her, someone mixed Thorazine (a major depressant) with her Alka-Seltzer. Assuming the jury credits this evidence of involuntary intoxication, how might the Thorazine have caused her to not know that aggravated robbery is wrong? *[handwritten: Exactly!!]*

418

Consent

Consent is a criminal law chameleon. It is irrelevant in some crimes, like murder, because mercy killing is still murder. It is an element of some offenses, like sexual assault, in which consent by an adult victim prevents the State from obtaining a conviction. It is not an element, but a limited defense under Texas law only to the offenses of assault, aggravated assault, and deadly conduct, under section 22.06 of the Texas Penal Code. Consent as a defense is discussed in *Bufkin*, which follows.

"love bites"

Bufkin v. State

207 S.W.3d 779 (2006)

Keller, P.J., delivered the opinion of the Court.

Whether the defendant in this case was entitled to a defensive instruction on consent depends upon whether or not the evidence supporting that instruction related to an instance of conduct upon which the State relied for conviction or to a different instance of conduct that simply happened to also conform to the indictment's allegations. We conclude that the defendant's evidence related to an instance of conduct upon which the State relied for conviction, and as a result, we affirm the judgment of the court of appeals.

Appellant was charged by information with family-violence assault. The information alleged that the assault occurred "on or about August 9, 2003," and specified in separate paragraphs two different factual methods of committing the assault:

Paragraph A.

[The defendant did] intentionally, knowingly, or recklessly cause bodily injury to Shelby Hooper by striking her with the defendant's hand.

Paragraph B.

[The defendant did] intentionally, knowingly, or recklessly cause bodily injury to Shelby Hooper by biting her.

At trial, the State introduced evidence that the police were dispatched to a hotel room that had recently been the scene of an altercation between appellant and Hooper. Hysterical and crying, Hooper told the officers that appellant had struck her with his fists and bitten her. Consistent with Hooper's statements, officers observed a cut on her lip and bite marks on her back and buttocks. After admitting, during questioning, that he had hit Hooper in the head with a closed fist, appellant was arrested.

Hooper testified for the defense. She stated that she had provided the police with a misleading picture of what really occurred on the evening of the alleged assault. With regard to the allegation that appellant hit her with his hand, she claimed that she was the aggressor that evening and that appellant was simply defending himself. With regard to the bite allegation, she denied that she was bitten on August 9th and claimed that the bite marks on her body were actually the result of "love bites" that were a part of consensual sexual activity occurring on the prior evening (August 8th).

At the jury charge conference, appellant requested consent instructions in connection with both the alleged striking and the alleged biting. The trial court denied these requests. The court did, however, submit an instruction on self-defense. With regard to the elements of the offense, the charge's application paragraph instructed the jury to find appellant guilty if it found "from the evidence beyond a reasonable doubt that on or about August 9, 2003, in Fort Bend

420

County, Texas, the defendant did intentionally, knowingly, or recklessly cause bodily injury to Shelby Hooper by striking her with his hand or by biting her." The jury found appellant guilty.

The court of appeals reversed, holding that Hooper's testimony that the bite was consensual was sufficient to raise the defense of consent as to the biting allegation, and consequently, appellant was entitled to the consent instruction as to that allegation. The appellate court subsequently decided it could not find the error harmless under the standard applicable to non-constitutional error because it could not determine whether the jury convicted on the basis of biting or striking (or both) and because "whether Hooper was assaulted was a determination for the jury to make."

The State's position is that Hooper's testimony concerning "love bites" occurring on August 8th and the police testimony regarding unwanted biting occurring on August 9th described separate instances of conduct. Appellant contends that the same instance of conduct was described, and there was simply a dispute about the timing and nature of that single instance of conduct. It is certainly true that the defendant cannot foist upon the State a crime the State did not intend to prosecute in order to gain an instruction on a defensive issue or a lesser included offense. But it is also true that the defendant has the right to controvert the facts upon which the prosecution intends to rely, and that right includes claiming that events unfolded in a way different than the State has alleged.

In resolving the issue before us, we must first keep in mind that we do not apply the usual rule of appellate deference to trial court rulings when reviewing a trial court's decision to deny a requested defensive instruction (whether for the submission of a defense or for a lesser-included offense). Quite the reverse, we view the evidence in the light most favorable to the defendant's requested submission.

The question here is whether we are dealing with distinct instances of conduct or alternative versions of the same instance of conduct. That inquiry must, of course, be conducted within the proper standard of review: in the light most favorable to the defendant's requested instruction. Consequently, the inquiry is whether, viewed in the light most favorable to the defendant's requested submission, the evidence is sufficient for a rational jury to conclude that the State and the defendant are proposing alternate versions of the same instance of conduct rather than separate instances of conduct. In other words, a rational factfinder must have reason to believe that the defendant's scenario competes, rather than coexists, with the State's scenario. For the former to occur, it seems to be generally, perhaps always, true that the evidence must reveal some sort of connection between the two described instances that suggests that they are, in fact, only one instance. Our "on or about" jurisprudence has often focused on when and under what circumstances the State is required to elect between *multiple* instances of conduct that appear to conform to the allegations of the charging instrument. But, if there is evidence that the parties' respective scenarios compete, then there is no occasion for the State to elect: the parties are not presenting multiple instances of conduct but are presenting alternate versions of the same instance, at least for the purpose of determining whether to grant the submission of the defendant's requested charge.

A classic situation in which the parties may dispute the timing of an offense is in a murder prosecution. Obviously, a person cannot be killed twice, so a claim by the defense that the victim was killed on a different day than alleged by the State's evidence amounts to proposing an alternate version of the offense rather than a separate offense. A defendant might, for example, claim that the killing was with "sudden passion" so as to obtain the sudden passion mitigating instruction at the punishment phase of trial, or under older law, a voluntary manslaughter instruction at the guilt phase of trial. Perhaps this hypothetical defendant produces evidence that on the day before the alleged date of the offense, the victim and the defendant had a heated argument of a nature that raised sudden passion, and that the argument was witnessed by a third person. In that scenario, the defendant might claim the victim was killed the same day as the argument, under sudden passion, but the State might claim that the killing occurred a day later, after the passion should have cooled. Both parties' claims are connected by the evidence that the victim is dead. Each party is trying to explain the fact of the death, and those explanations involve the offense occurring at different points in time.

In the present case, appellant's proffered instance of conduct was temporally separated by a day from the instance of conduct relied upon by the State. But the defensive story presented here is similar to the murder example because: (1) the defensive evidence in this case denied that the State's proffered "unwanted biting" incident ever occurred, claiming *instead* that a "love bites" incident occurred, and (2) the bite marks supplied an evidentiary connection between the two proffered instances that suggested they were one. The State claimed that the bite marks were produced during a non-consensual assault occurring on August 9th while appellant claimed that those very same marks were produced, *instead*, during a consensual sexual encounter occurring on August 8th.

We observe that appellant's case would have been like *Campbell* if appellant had claimed that he gave Hooper "love bites" on August 8th and that *someone else* bit Hooper on August 9th, and for whatever reason, Hooper decided to blame the incident on appellant.

The bite marks in the present case supplied a reason for the factfinder to believe that the parties were in fact referring to the same incident. Without the bite marks in this case, there would be no basis, apart from appellant's bare denial of the State's version of events, for concluding that the evidence described one incident instead of two. As with the dead body in the hypothetical murder defendant's case, the bite marks here served to tie the two scenarios together, making them alternative versions of one event. Appellant's scenario was an alternate explanation for the appearance of those marks: giving the jury the task of deciding whether the marks were produced by "love bites" on August 8th or by an assault on August 9th. The bite marks were used by the State as evidence that the crime was committed; the alternate story supplied by the defense was an attempt to explain that evidence away.

Because the instances of conduct respectively supported by the parties were in competition, the defendant was entitled to his defensive instruction. Without the consent instruction, the jury charge authorized conviction for biting even if the jury believed the defense's scenario. This is so because the "love bites" incident satisfied the elements of assault that were outlined in the submitted jury instructions. "Lack of consent" is not an element of assault under § 22.01; rather, "consent" is set up as a defense to assault under § 22.06: "The

422

victim's effective consent . . . is a defense to prosecution under Section 22.01 (Assault) . . . if . . . the conduct did not threaten or inflict serious bodily injury."[1] The jury charge tracked the language of § 22.01 but did not include the language of § 22.06. And because the jury charge included the standard "on or about" language in its application paragraph giving the State leeway (as it should) in proving when the offense occurred conduct consisting of "consensual biting on August 8th" was encompassed by the application paragraph's allegations. The consent instruction is what would have given the jury a vehicle to effectuate any belief in the defendant's claim that the biting incident, and the bite marks that resulted, were a product of consensual conduct that was not against the law.

It is true that the State also prosecuted appellant for striking Hooper with his hand. But the jury charge submitted the biting and striking allegations in the disjunctive, so the defendant's proposed instruction was needed to rebut a theory of liability upon which the jury could have decided to solely rely.[2] We conclude that the court of appeals was correct in holding that the trial court erred in denying the defendant's requested instruction. *Holding*

Notes

1. 	In this case the testimony raising the consent issue came from the "victim" who told the police on the night of the defendant's arrest a version of events that she recanted at trial. This is a good example of the fact that the prosecution represents the State and not the victim. Prosecutors are often influenced in their chargingdecisions based on by the willingness of witnesses to testify, especially in a case like *Bufkin* where only two people are present. However, the wishes of the victim are not controlling.

It is not uncommon in domestic violence cases for complainants to call the police to complain about a partner and later reconcile, not wishing to testify at trial. Many prosecutors have a policy of following through with domestic violence prosecutions despite the contrary wishes of the complainant. If the complainant, Hooper, had testified that the defendant was the aggressor and that there was no consent to the biting, should she be prosecuted for perjury? In a perjury prosecution, it is not necessary to prove which statement is false if it can be shown that two inconsistent statements were given under oath.

2. 	The defense of consent in section 22.06 of the Texas Penal Code is not available if the defendant's conduct threatened or inflicted serious bodily injury or if the conduct was an implicit risk of the victim's occupation, recognized medical treatment, or a scientific experiment conducted by recognized methods. The defense is not available if the offense was committed "as a condition of the defendant's or the victim's initiation or continued membership in a criminal street gang."

---

1. Contrast with the offense of sexual assault, which, at least in some cases, incorporates lack of consent as an element. TEX. PENAL CODE ANN. § 22.011(a)(1)(A)–(C).

2. Had the jury instructions charged the hitting and biting theories *conjunctively*, an argument could be made that the "love bites" incident, which did not include hitting, could not have served as a basis for conviction, even under the charges "on or about" language. But that is not the case before us.

Infancy and Youth Related Issues

Under the common law, children under the age of seven were conclusively presumed not to be responsible for their criminal acts. There was a rebuttable presumption of incapacity for children between the ages of seven and fourteen. This infancy prohibition and possible defense ended at age fourteen, when offenders would be treated like any adult offender. The institution of the juvenile court arose in the early 20th century, and it created an alternate legal system for youthful offenders.

Section 8.07 of the Texas Penal Code, entitled "Age Affecting Criminal Responsibility" gives a misleading impression when it states, "A person may not be prosecuted for or convicted of any offense that the person committed when younger than 15 years of age . . . ." What the statute does not say is that there is a juvenile system that may find delinquent offenders as young as ten years old. The true infancy defense, or more appropriately jurisdictional bar, is to children under the age of 10 who may not be tried for criminal conduct in either adult or juvenile court.

For youthful offenders who commit acts that would be crimes if committed by an adult, there is exclusive juvenile court jurisdiction for crimes committed when the individual was at least age ten, but less than fifteen. For offenders aged fifteen to seventeen, there is original exclusive jurisdiction in the juvenile court, but that jurisdiction may be waived for felony offenses and the juvenile transferred to adult court. Such a transfer of jurisdiction to the adult court can only occur if there is a transfer hearing under Section 54.02 of the Texas Family Code. Whether to treat the person as an adult subject to adult penalties or retain jurisdiction in the juvenile court is based upon a consideration of the following factors:

- Whether the alleged offense is a personal or property crime;

- Whether the offense was committed in an aggressive and premeditated manner;

- Whether the grand jury would likely return an indictment;

- The sophistication and maturity of the juvenile;

- The juvenile's record and previous history; and

- Prospects of adequate public protection and prospects of rehabilitation through the juvenile court jurisdiction (which ends for purposes of disposition at age 18).

The *Bannister* case that follows involves an interesting manipulation of the jurisdictional rules between adult and juvenile courts.

juvenile liar

Bannister v. State

552 S.W.2d 124 (Tex. Crim. App. 1977)

Onion, Presiding Judge.

This is an appeal from an order revoking probation.

On July 8, 1974 the appellant, Donna Kay Bannister, entered a guilty plea in the Criminal District Court of Dallas County under the false name of Tasha Diane Williams to the offense of burglary of a habitation, a first degree felony. The record before us reflects that she gave her age as 19 or 20 and led her court-appointed counsel to believe she was 22 years of age. It appears, however, at the time she was only 15 years of age and was an escapee from the Gainesville State Training School. After receiving a five (5) year probated sentence, she and a friend, who also received probation, decided not to report to the probation officer as required. Apparently they were later returned to Gainesville and only subsequently was she brought before the court for revocation of probation. Then for the first time she claimed she was in fact Donna Kay Bannister and at the time of her guilty plea she was only 15 years of age. Her appointed counsel offered a birth certificate reflecting February 2, 1959 as her birth date and claimed the District Court was without jurisdiction and never acquired the same as there was never a discretionary transfer of jurisdiction from the Juvenile Court and won a stipulation from the State that such transfer had never occurred. The District Court overruled the jurisdictional plea and revoked probation. This appeal followed.

In view Family Code, § 54.02, § 51.08 and § 51.09, Penal Code, § 8.07, it appears that the appellant has played the game of "courts" and won. It does not appear that under these statutes the appellant waived her rights to be tried as a juvenile, despite her actions in misleading the trial court at the time of her conviction.

Consistently through these prior opinions the court has held that the rights of a juvenile defendant to be tried as a juvenile may be waived. The determination of whether a defendant should be tried as a juvenile has been termed a question "of preliminary character" which, if not raised during or before trial, was lost. In each of the progression of statutes and amendments, the defendant or some other person was required to raise the issue before the announcement of ready for trial, or later in Article 2338-1, supra, the determinant of waiver was whether "during the pendency of a criminal charge or indictment" it was "ascertained" that a person should be not tried as an adult.

The present statute, effective September 1, 1973, reads as follows:

Sec. 51.08. Transfer from Criminal Court.

If the defendant in a criminal proceeding is a child who is charged with an offense other than perjury or a traffic offense, unless he has been transferred to criminal court under Section 54.02 of this code (dealing with waiver of jurisdiction by the juvenile court and transfer to a district court), the court exercising criminal jurisdiction shall transfer the case to the juvenile court, together with a copy of the accusatory pleading and other

425

papers, documents, and transcripts of testimony relating to the case, and shall order that the child be taken to the place of detention designated by the juvenile court, or shall release him to the custody of his parent, guardian, or custodian, to be brought before the juvenile court at a time designated by that court.

This statute was in effect when the appellant herein entered her guilty plea to the burglary of a habitation in 1974. The statute is silent as to the procedure for raising the question of age "in a criminal proceeding" and no longer mentions the "if . . . it be ascertained" provision of the former statute.

Family Code, § 51.09, also in effect at the time of appellant's guilty plea, sets forth the requirements for a waiver if a child or juvenile wishes to waive rights enumerated in the Family Code. It provided:

Unless a contrary intent clearly appears elsewhere in this title, any right granted to a child by this title or by the constitution or laws of this state or the United States may be waived in proceedings under this title if:

(1) the waiver is made by the child and the attorney for the child;

(2) the child and the attorney waiving the right are informed of and understand the right and the possible consequences of waiving it;

(3) the waiver is voluntary; and

(4) the waiver is made in writing or in court proceedings that are recorded.

The appellant by not informing her attorney or the court of her actual age at the time of her guilty plea would have "waived" her right to be tried as a juvenile under past decisional laws. However, this "waiver" was not in accordance with, Family Code, § 51.09.

At the time of the guilty plea, appellant was within the definition of a "child" as defined by V.T.C.A., Family Code, § 51.02, which provides in part:

In this title:

(1) a "Child" means a person who is:

(A) ten years of age or older and under 17 years of age; or

(B) seventeen years of age or older and under 18 years of age who is alleged or found to have engaged in delinquent conduct or conduct indicating a need for supervision as a result of acts committed before becoming 17 years of age.

Moreover the juvenile court is given exclusive original jurisdiction over proceedings under Title 3 of the Family Code. Family Code, § 51.04. And Family Code, § 54.02, provides for the procedure for waiver of juvenile court jurisdiction and discretionary transfer to criminal court.

Most important to the decision before this court are the provisions of Penal Code, § 8.07 (Age Affecting Criminal Responsibility), in effect at the time of appellant's guilty plea. It provided:

(a) Except as provided by Subsection (c) of this section, a person may not be prosecuted or convicted for any offense that he committed when younger than 15 years.

(b) Except as provided by Subsection (c) of this section, a person who is younger than 17 years may not be prosecuted or convicted for any offense, unless the juvenile court waives jurisdiction and certifies him for criminal prosecution.

(c) Subsections (a) and (b) of this section shall not apply to prosecutions for:

(1) aggravated perjury, when it appears by proof that the actor had sufficient discretion to understand the nature and obligation of an oath;

(2) a violation of a penal statute cognizable under Chapter 302, Acts of the 55th Legislature, Regular Session, 1957, as amended; or

(3) a violation of a motor vehicle traffic ordinance of an incorporated city or town.

(d) No person who has been adjudged a delinquent child may be convicted of any offense alleged in the petition to adjudge him a delinquent child or any offense within the knowledge of the juvenile proceeding.

(e) No person may, in any case, be punished by death for an offense committed while he was younger than 17 years.

It is clear when the foregoing provisions of the Family Code are read with said § 8.07 of the Penal Code that the district court did not have jurisdiction to try appellant for burglary of a habitation in view of her age despite her deliberate action in misleading the court. Such action under the foregoing statutes did not constitute waiver. The fact that appellant's age was not discovered until the time of revocation of probation proceedings does not change the situation. The district court simply did not acquire jurisdiction over the appellant, and we need not, in my opinion, determine whether the revocation proceedings are criminal proceedings for the purpose of determining the question before us.

The trial court should have transferred the case to the juvenile court upon learning appellant's true age.

Since it now appears that the appellant became eighteen years of age on February 2, 1977, even the juvenile courts cannot exercise jurisdiction over her. V.T.C.A., Family Code, s 54.05(b).

Whether the drafters of the Family Code and Penal Code intended to allow "a child" to benefit from a fraud upon the court the statutes had such effect in the case at bar.

427

The judgment is reversed and the cause remanded.

Notes

1.   After the opinion in *Bannister*, the Texas Legislature amended the Texas Family Code to provide that a juvenile court has jurisdiction to consider the transfer of jurisdiction to adult court for individuals who are over the age of 18 for crimes committed when the individual was within the age range for exclusive original jurisdiction of the juvenile court. In some circumstances, Family Code Section 54.02(j)(4) provides that such a transfer may occur if the juvenile court finds from a preponderance of the evidence that:

> (A) for a reason beyond the control of the state it was not practicable to proceed in juvenile court before the 18th birthday of the person; or

> (B) after due diligence of the state it was not practicable to proceed in juvenile court before the 18th birthday of the person because:

>> (i) the state did not have probable cause to proceed in juvenile court and new evidence has been found since the 18th birthday of the person;

>> (ii) the person could not be found; or

>> (iii) a previous transfer order was reversed by an appellate court or set aside by a district court

This provision apparently would prevent a defendant from benefiting from a fraud on the court and absconding, as in the *Bannister* case. However, in *Moore v. State*, 446 S.W.3d 47 (Tex. App.—Houston [1st Dist.] 2014), the State was unsuccessful in its attempt to invoke the statutory exception to the usual limit of juvenile court jurisdiction of age 18. In *Moore*, a 12-year-old complainant reported that her then 16-year-old cousin had been sexually assaulting her for several years prior to her outcry. A police investigation began soon after the outcry, but because the investigating detective had a heavy caseload, it was almost two years before the case was forwarded to the district attorney's office. Due to an error in one of the reports, the detective believed the alleged perpetrator was 17-years-old when the case was forwarded but, in fact, he had already turned 18, and he was 19 before the juvenile court conducted a transfer hearing. The juvenile court found that, for a reason beyond the control of the State, it was not practicable to proceed in juvenile court before the defendant's 18th birthday. At age 19, the defendant pleaded guilty to Aggravated Sexual Assault of a Child in criminal district court was placed on deferred-adjudication probation for five years.

The court of appeals vacated the judgment of conviction on the ground that the juvenile court lacked jurisdiction to transfer the case in *Moore v. State*, 446 S.W.3d 47 (Tex. App.—Houston [1st Dist.] 2014). The Court of Criminal Appeals affirmed, agreeing with the appellate court that the State did not meet its burden under Family Code Section 54.02(j)(4)(A) because the detective's heavy caseload and mistake as to the defendant's age were not reasons beyond the State's control. Although the prosecutor did not receive the case until the defendant was already

428

past his 18th birthday, the statutory reference to "the state" was held to include both law enforcement and the prosecution.

2.   The *Bannister* opinion mentions that Section 8.07 prevents the imposition of the death penalty to persons under the age of 17. This provision was changed to age 18 after the decision of the United States Supreme Court in *Roper vs. Simmons*, 543 U.S. 551 (2005), which held that the death penalty is cruel and unusual punishment under the Eighth Amendment when applied to an offender who was younger than 18 at the time of the commission of the offense.

3.   Waiver to adult court becomes more likely the closer the offender is to the age of 17 because of the limited jurisdictional authority of the court for adjudication is 17 and for purposes of disposition jurisdiction ends at age 18.

Chapter 20: Insanity Defense

Introduction

Criminal law is premised on the concept that people have free will and choose to commit criminal acts. The emphasis on *mens rea* in criminal law underscores this premise. Retributive and deterrent theories of punishment are premised on the understanding that people should be punished for criminal acts that they chose to commit. General and specific deterrence depend upon people sane enough to make rational decisions to avoid criminal penalties. What about those who are unable to make rational choices because of a mental disease or defect? Is it fair and effective to punish those who commit crimes without the capacity to make free and informed choices? The insanity defense has been the uneasy concession to the principle that it is not just to hold some mentally ill persons responsible for acts that are the result of their involuntary illness. However, the defense has been beset by doubts about its fairness and efficacy. Can we define what types of impairments provide an excuse, and can we identify correctly those who fit the definition? How can this be done when mental impairment is a continuum of impairment while the law must make the binary decision that the defendant is either responsible or not? Has science advanced to the point that experts can give meaningful assistance while maintaining the decision in the justice system on moral and legal principles? Despite doubts and controversy about the insanity defense, it remains a part of the law of most American jurisdictions.

In Texas, under Texas Penal Code Section 8.01, insanity is an affirmative defense if, at the time of the conduct charged, the actor, as a result of severe mental disease or defect, did not know that his conduct was wrong. Insanity is regarded as a classic defense of excuse rather than justification. Unlike defenses such as mistake of fact or self-defense, which deny the criminality of the conduct, an insanity defense usually involves an admission of the criminal conduct but asks that that the defendant be excused from criminal liability based upon mental disease or defect at the time of the conduct charged.

As the language of the statute indicates, Texas utilizes a "right/wrong" test for insanity. This test is a variation of an old English formulation known as the *M'Naghten* test. The test was first promulgated in 1863 in response to a decision in the case of Daniel M'Naghten, who was prosecuted by the British government for the murder of Edward Drummond, the private secretary of Sir Robert Peel, the Prime Minister of England. M'Naghten, suffering from delusions of persecution, set out to kill the Prime Minister, but due to unforeseen circumstances, missed his intended target and killed an aide instead. M'Naghten was found not guilty by reason of insanity. Queen Victoria summoned the House of Lords to "take the opinion of the Judges on the law governing such cases." A general inquiry was conducted whereby the judges of the Queen's Bench were asked a number of questions regarding the matter of the insanity defense. The combined answers to the questions have come to be known as the *M'Naghten* test which provides that a defendant is not guilty by reason of insanity if:

> 1. At the time of the committing of the act, the party accused was labouring under such a defect of reason, from disease of the mind, as not to know the nature and quality of the act he was doing;

2. Or if he did know it, that he did not know that he was doing what was wrong.

See *M'Naghten's Case*, 8 Eng. Rep. at 719; *See also United States v. Freeman*, 357 F.2d 606, 617 (2d Cir. 1966) (providing additional history of *M'Naghten*).

The *M'Naghten* test has been criticized for its narrow cognitive focus on what the defendant knew to the exclusion of volitional or emotional impairments that might affect the normative judgment of the jury or judge about whether the accused should be excused from criminal responsibility. Texas briefly expanded the apparently narrow cognitive confines of *M'Naghten* when the insanity defense was modified in 1973 to conform to a variation of the American Law Institute's (ALI) 1962 Model Penal Code Section 4.01(1) which provides that:

(1) A person is not responsible for criminal conduct if at the time of such conduct as a result of mental disease or defect he lacks substantial capacity either to appreciate the criminality [wrongfulness] of his conduct or to conform his conduct to the requirements of law.

(2) As used in this Article, the terms "mental disease or defect" do not include an abnormality manifested only by repeated criminal or otherwise antisocial conduct.

In 1973, the Texas Legislature adopted an approach influenced by the Model Penal Code by adding a "volitional" prong to the *M'Naghten* analysis that asked, in addition to whether the defendant knew right from wrong, whether the defendant was capable of conforming his conduct to the requirements of the law. This variation of the Model Penal Code test allowed for both a cognitive inquiry under the *M'Naghten* test as well as a possible defense that one could not control his or her conduct, similar to the so called "irresistible impulse test" used in several jurisdictions. The broadened view of the insanity defense was short lived because in 1983, the Texas Legislature once again narrowed the scope of the insanity defense and returned the statute to a type of *M'Naghten* test in the wake of the controversy following the acquittal of John Hinckley, the would-be assassin of President Reagan.

Despite the wording of the statute requiring a "mental disease or defect," the ultimate inquiry is not solely based on the medical aspects of the defendant's case. It requires a jury determination of the ethical and legal propriety of excusing the defendant. In the words of an early decision of the Court of Criminal Appeals, insanity must have controlled the will and taken away the freedom of moral action. *Witty v. State*, 171 S.W. 229 (Tex. Crim. App. 1914). The actual existence of a mental disease by itself is not sufficient to establish legal insanity unless that disease made the defendant so ill that he did not know that his conduct was wrong.

From a medical standpoint, a defendant may be suffering from some mental disease or defect, but not be relieved of criminal responsibility for that crime unless the mental condition reached the point where the defendant was unable to distinguish right from wrong. For example, in *Torres v. State*, 976 S.W.2d 345 (Tex. App.—Corpus Christi 2008, no pet.), the court held that the evidence was legally and factually sufficient to support a finding that the defendant, accused of murdering one son and the attempted murder of another, knew the difference between right and wrong and, thus, was not entitled to insanity defense. The court referred to the record that reflected that a person affected by depression could still know right from wrong; that the defendant denied having any delusions, hallucinations, or other symptoms of losing touch with reality; that the defendant exhibited signs of organizational skills at the time of the offense; that the defendant was worried that, because of her father's failing health, she would be unable to provide for her sons and her ex-husband might obtain custody of them; that the defendant believed her sons got what they deserved; and that, when the defendant's father went to call for help, the defendant tried to dissuade him.

Assuming the defendant can meet the threshold requirement of producing "competent evidence" of insanity, the court is required to instruct the jury regarding the insanity defense. Section 8.01 of the Texas Penal Code provides that insanity is an affirmative defense, which means the defendant is required to carry both the burden of production of evidence and the burden of persuasion. The defendant must produce and prove by a preponderance of the evidence that as a result of mental disease or defect at the time of the charged conduct he did not know what he was doing was wrong.

The insanity defense is broader than the mental state required for the crime. For example, an intentional killing of a victim that the defendant believes is necessary in self-defense because of an insane delusion that the victim was trying to kill the defendant might qualify for an insanity defense, even though the mental state required for the murder could be proved. However, if insanity causes the defendant not to understand the nature of his or her conduct, evidence of the defendant's mental disease or defect might be relevant to the question of whether the defendant had the required mental state for the crime. Such a claim was presented in *Arizona v. Clark*, which follows.

crazy guvy

Clark v. Arizona

548 U.S. 735 (2006)

Justice Souter delivered the opinion of the Court.

issue:

The case presents two questions: whether due process prohibits Arizona's use of an insanity test stated solely in terms of the capacity to tell whether an act charged as a crime was right or wrong; and whether Arizona violates due process in restricting consideration of defense evidence of mental illness and incapacity to its bearing on a claim of insanity, thus eliminating its significance directly on the issue of the mental element of the crime charged (known in legal shorthand as the *mens rea*, or guilty mind). We hold that there is no violation of due process in either instance.

Holding:

In the early hours of June 21, 2000, Officer Jeffrey Moritz of the Flagstaff Police responded in uniform to complaints that a pickup truck with loud music blaring was circling a residential block. When he located the truck, the officer turned on the emergency lights and siren of his marked patrol car, which prompted petitioner Eric Clark, the truck's driver (then 17), to pull over. Officer Moritz got out of the patrol car and told Clark to stay where he was. Less than a minute later, Clark shot the officer, who died soon after but not before calling the police dispatcher for help. Clark ran away on foot but was arrested later that day with gunpowder residue on his hands; the gun that killed the officer was found nearby, stuffed into a knit cap.

Clark was charged with first-degree murder . . . for intentionally or knowingly killing a law enforcement officer in the line of duty. In March 2001, Clark was found incompetent to stand trial and was committed to a state hospital for treatment, but two years later the same trial court found his competence restored and ordered him to be tried. Clark waived his right to a jury, and the case was heard by the court.

At trial, Clark did not contest the shooting and death, but relied on his undisputed paranoid schizophrenia at the time of the incident in denying that he had the specific intent to shoot a law enforcement officer or knowledge that he was doing so, as required by the statute. Accordingly, the prosecutor offered circumstantial evidence that Clark knew Officer Moritz was a law enforcement officer. The evidence showed that the officer was in uniform at the time, that he caught up with Clark in a marked police car with emergency lights and siren going, and that Clark acknowledged the symbols of police authority and stopped. The testimony for the prosecution indicated that Clark had intentionally lured an officer to the scene to kill him, having told some people a few weeks before the incident that he wanted to shoot police officers. At the close of the State's evidence, the trial court denied Clark's motion for judgment of acquittal for failure to prove intent to kill a law enforcement officer or knowledge that Officer Moritz was a law enforcement officer.

In presenting the defense case, Clark claimed mental illness, which he sought to introduce for two purposes. First, he raised the affirmative defense of insanity, putting the burden on himself to prove by clear and convincing evidence, that "at the time of the commission of the criminal act [he] was afflicted with a mental disease or defect of such severity that [he] did not

433

know the criminal act was wrong."[1] Second, he aimed to rebut the prosecution's evidence of the requisite *mens rea*, that he had acted intentionally or knowingly to kill a law enforcement officer.

The trial court ruled that Clark could not rely on evidence bearing on insanity to dispute the *mens rea*. The court cited *State v. Mott*, 931 P.2d 1046 (Ariz. 1997) (en banc), which "refused to allow psychiatric testimony to negate specific intent," and held that "Arizona does not allow evidence of a defendant's mental disorder short of insanity . . . to negate the *mens rea* element of a crime." As to his insanity, then, Clark presented testimony from classmates, school officials, and his family describing his increasingly bizarre behavior over the year before the shooting. Witnesses testified, for example, that paranoid delusions led Clark to rig a fishing line with beads and wind chimes at home to alert him to intrusion by invaders, and to keep a bird in his automobile to warn of airborne poison. There was lay and expert testimony that Clark thought Flagstaff was populated with "aliens" (some impersonating government agents), the "aliens" were trying to kill him, and bullets were the only way to stop them. A psychiatrist testified that Clark was suffering from paranoid schizophrenia with delusions about "aliens" when he killed Officer Moritz, and he concluded that Clark was incapable of luring the officer or understanding right from wrong and that he was thus insane at the time of the killing. In rebuttal, a psychiatrist for the State gave his opinion that Clark's paranoid schizophrenia did not keep him from appreciating the wrongfulness of his conduct, as shown by his actions before and after the shooting (such as circling the residential block with music blaring as if to lure the police to intervene, evading the police after the shooting, and hiding the gun).

At the close of the defense case consisting of this evidence bearing on mental illness, the trial court . . . issued a special verdict of first-degree murder, expressly finding that Clark shot and caused the death of Officer Moritz beyond a reasonable doubt and that Clark had not shown that he was insane at the time. The judge noted that though Clark was indisputably afflicted with paranoid schizophrenia at the time of the shooting, the mental illness "did not . . . distort his perception of reality so severely that he did not know his actions were wrong." For this conclusion, the judge expressly relied on "the facts of the crime, the evaluations of the experts, [Clark's] actions and behavior both before and after the shooting, and the observations of those that knew [Clark]." The sentence was life imprisonment without the possibility of release for 25 years.

Clark moved to vacate the judgment and sentence, arguing, among other things, that Arizona's insanity test and its *Mott* rule each violate due process. As to the insanity standard,

---

1. The Arizona insanity statute provides that:

> A person may be found guilty except insane if at the time of the commission of the criminal act the person was afflicted with a mental disease or defect of such severity that the person did not know the criminal act was wrong. A mental disease or defect constituting legal insanity is an affirmative defense. Mental disease or defect does not include disorders that result from acute voluntary intoxication or withdrawal from alcohol or drugs, character defects, psychosexual disorders or impulse control disorders. Conditions that do not constitute legal insanity include but are not limited to momentary, temporary conditions arising from the pressure of the circumstances, moral decadence, depravity or passion growing out of anger, jealousy, revenge, hatred or other motives in a person who does not suffer from a mental disease or defect or an abnormality that is manifested only by criminal conduct.

434

Clark claimed (as he had argued earlier) that the Arizona Legislature had impermissibly narrowed its standard in 1993 when it eliminated the first part of the two-part insanity test announced in *M'Naghten's Case*. The court denied the motion.

The Court of Appeals of Arizona affirmed Clark's conviction . . . and the Supreme Court of Arizona denied further review.

We granted certiorari to decide whether due process prohibits Arizona from thus narrowing its insanity test or from excluding evidence of mental illness and incapacity due to mental illness to rebut evidence of the requisite criminal intent. We now affirm.

Holding of Sup.Ct.

Clark first says that Arizona's definition of insanity, being only a fragment of the Victorian standard from which it derives, violates due process. The landmark English rule in *M'Naghten's Case*, states that "the jurors ought to be told . . . that to establish a defence on the ground of insanity, it must be clearly proved that, at the time of the committing of the act, the party accused was laboring under such a defect of reason, from disease of the mind, as not to know the nature and quality of the act he was doing; or, if he did know it, that he did not know he was doing what was wrong." The first part asks about cognitive capacity: whether a mental defect leaves a defendant unable to understand what he is doing. The second part presents an ostensibly alternative basis for recognizing a defense of insanity understood as a lack of moral capacity: whether a mental disease or defect leaves a defendant unable to understand that his action is wrong.

When the Arizona Legislature first codified an insanity rule, it adopted the full *M'Naghten* statement (subject to modifications in details that do not matter here):

> A person is not responsible for criminal conduct if at the time of such conduct the person was suffering from such a mental disease or defect as not to know the nature and quality of the act or, if such person did know, that such person did not know that what he was doing was wrong.

In 1993, the legislature dropped the cognitive incapacity part, leaving only moral incapacity as the nub of the stated definition. Under current Arizona law, a defendant will not be adjudged insane unless he demonstrates that "at the time of the commission of the criminal act [he] was afflicted with a mental disease or defect of such severity that [he] did not know the criminal act was wrong." moral

Clark challenges the 1993 amendment excising the express reference to the cognitive incapacity element. He insists that the side-by-side *M'Naghten* test represents the minimum that a government must provide in recognizing an alternative to criminal responsibility on grounds of mental illness or defect, and he argues that elimination of the *M'Naghten* reference to nature and quality "offends [a] principle of justice so rooted in the traditions and conscience of our people as to be ranked as fundamental."

The claim entails no light burden and Clark does not carry it. History shows no deference to *M'Naghten* that could elevate its formula to the level of fundamental principle, so as to limit the traditional recognition of a State's capacity to define crimes and defenses.

Even a cursory examination of the traditional Anglo-American approaches to insanity reveals significant differences among them, with four traditional strains variously combined to yield a diversity of American standards. The main variants are the cognitive incapacity, the moral incapacity, the volitional incapacity, and the product-of-mental-illness tests. The first two emanate from the alternatives stated in the *M'Naghten* rule. The volitional incapacity or irresistible-impulse test, which surfaced over two centuries ago (first in England, then in this country), asks whether a person was so lacking in volition due to a mental defect or illness that he could not have controlled his actions. And the product-of-mental-illness test was used as early as 1870, and simply asks whether a person's action was a product of a mental disease or defect. Seventeen States and the Federal Government have adopted a recognizable version of the *M'Naghten* test with both its cognitive incapacity and moral incapacity components. One State has adopted only *M'Naghten's* cognitive incapacity test and 10 (including Arizona) have adopted the moral incapacity test alone. Fourteen jurisdictions, inspired by the Model Penal Code, have in place an amalgam of the volitional incapacity test and some variant of the moral incapacity test, satisfaction of either (generally by showing a defendant's substantial lack of capacity) being enough to excuse. Three States combine a full *M'Naghten* test with a volitional incapacity formula. And New Hampshire alone stands by the product-of-mental-illness test. The alternatives are multiplied further by variations in the prescribed insanity verdict: a significant number of these jurisdictions supplement the traditional "not guilty by reason of insanity" verdict with an alternative of "guilty but mentally ill." Finally, four States have no affirmative insanity defense, though one provides for a "guilty and mentally ill" verdict. These four, like a number of others that recognize an affirmative insanity defense, allow consideration of evidence of mental illness directly on the element of *mens rea* defining the offense.

With this varied background, it is clear that no particular formulation has evolved into a baseline for due process, and that the insanity rule, like the conceptualization of criminal offenses, is substantially open to state choice. Indeed, the legitimacy of such choice is the more obvious when one considers the interplay of legal concepts of mental illness or deficiency required for an insanity defense, with the medical concepts of mental abnormality that influence the expert opinion testimony by psychologists and psychiatrists commonly introduced to support or contest insanity claims. For medical definitions devised to justify treatment, like legal ones devised to excuse from conventional criminal responsibility, are subject to flux and disagreement. There being such fodder for reasonable debate about what the cognate legal and medical tests should be, due process imposes no single canonical formulation of legal insanity.

Nor does Arizona's abbreviation of the *M'Naghten* statement raise a proper claim that some constitutional minimum has been shortchanged. Clark's argument of course assumes that Arizona's former statement of the *M'Naghten* rule, with its express alternative of cognitive incapacity, was constitutionally adequate (as we agree). That being so, the abbreviated rule is no less so, for cognitive incapacity is relevant under that statement, just as it was under the more extended formulation, and evidence going to cognitive incapacity has the same significance under the short form as it had under the long.

Though Clark is correct that the application of the moral incapacity test (telling right from wrong) does not necessarily require evaluation of a defendant's cognitive capacity to appreciate the nature and quality of the acts charged against him, his argument fails to recognize that cognitive incapacity is itself enough to demonstrate moral incapacity. Cognitive incapacity, in other words, is a sufficient condition for establishing a defense of insanity, albeit not a necessary one. As a defendant can therefore make out moral incapacity by demonstrating cognitive incapacity, evidence bearing on whether the defendant knew the nature and quality of his actions is both relevant and admissible. In practical terms, if a defendant did not know what he was doing when he acted, he could not have known that he was performing the wrongful act charged as a crime. Indeed, when the two-part rule was still in effect, the Supreme Court of Arizona held that a jury instruction on insanity containing the moral incapacity part but not a full recitation of the cognitive incapacity part was fine, as the cognitive incapacity part might be "treated as adding nothing to the requirement that the accused know his act was wrong."

The Court of Appeals of Arizona acknowledged as much in this case, too, ("It is difficult to imagine that a defendant who did not appreciate the 'nature and quality' of the act he committed would reasonably be able to perceive that the act was 'wrong'"), and thus aligned itself with the long-accepted understanding that the cognitively incapacitated are a subset of the morally incapacitated within the meaning of the standard *M'Naghten* rule.[2]

Clark, indeed, adopted this very analysis himself in the trial court: "[I]f [Clark] did not know he was shooting at a police officer, or believed he had to shoot or be shot, even though his belief was not based in reality, this would establish that he did not know what he was doing was wrong." The trial court apparently agreed, for the judge admitted Clark's evidence of cognitive incapacity for consideration under the State's moral incapacity formulation. And Clark can point to no evidence bearing on insanity that was excluded. His psychiatric expert and a number of lay witnesses testified to his delusions, and this evidence tended to support a description of Clark as lacking the capacity to understand that the police officer was a human being. There is no doubt that the trial judge considered the evidence as going to an issue of cognitive capacity, for in finding insanity not proven he said that Clark's mental illness "did not . . . distort his perception of reality so severely that he did not know his actions were wrong." We are satisfied that neither in theory nor in practice did Arizona's 1993 abridgment of the insanity formulation deprive Clark of due process.

Clark's second claim of a due process violation challenges the rule adopted by the Supreme Court of Arizona in *State v. Mott*, 931 P.2d 1046 (en banc), *cert. denied*, 520 U.S. 1234 (1997). This case ruled on the admissibility of testimony from a psychologist offered to show

---

2. The *M'Naghten* test is a sequential test, first asking the factfinder to conduct the easier enquiry whether a defendant knew the nature and quality of his actions. If not, the defendant is to be considered insane and there is no need to pass to the harder and broader enquiry whether the defendant knew his actions were wrong. And, because, owing to this sequence, the factfinder is to ask whether a defendant lacks moral capacity only when he possesses cognitive capacity, the only defendants who will be found to lack moral capacity are those possessing cognitive capacity. *Cf.* 2 C. TORCIA, WHARTON'S CRIMINAL LAW § 101 (15th ed.1994). Though, before 1993, Arizona had in place the full *M'Naghten* test with this sequential enquiry, *see, e.g., Schantz*, 403 P.2d, at 525, it would appear that the legislature eliminated the cognitive capacity part not to change the meaning of the insanity standard but to implement its judgment that a streamlined standard with only the moral capacity part would be easier for the jury to apply, *see* ARIZONA HOUSE OF REPRESENTATIVE JUDICIARY COMMITTEE NOTES 3 (Mar. 18, 1993); 1 R. GERBER, CRIMINAL LAW OF ARIZONA 502–6, 502–11 (2d ed.1993 and Supp.2000). This is corroborated by the State's choice for many years against revising the applicable recommended jury instruction (enumerating the complete *M'Naghten* test) in order to match the amended statutory standard. See 1 GERBER, *supra*, at 502–6.

that the defendant suffered from battered women's syndrome and therefore lacked the capacity to form the *mens rea* of the crime charged against her. The opinion variously referred to the testimony in issue as "psychological testimony," and "expert testimony," and implicitly equated it with "expert psychiatric evidence." The state court held that testimony of a professional psychologist or psychiatrist about a defendant's mental incapacity owing to mental disease or defect was admissible, and could be considered, only for its bearing on an insanity defense; such evidence could not be considered on the element of *mens rea*, that is, what the State must show about a defendant's mental state (such as intent or understanding) when he performed the act charged against him.

Understanding Clark's claim requires attention to the categories of evidence with a potential bearing on *mens rea*. First, there is "observation evidence" in the everyday sense, testimony from those who observed what Clark did and heard what he said; this category would also include testimony that an expert witness might give about Clark's tendency to think in a certain way and his behavioral characteristics. This evidence may support a professional diagnosis of mental disease and in any event is the kind of evidence that can be relevant to show what in fact was on Clark's mind when he fired the gun. Observation evidence in the record covers Clark's behavior at home and with friends, his expressions of belief around the time of the killing that "aliens" were inhabiting the bodies of local people (including government agents), his driving around the neighborhood before the police arrived, and so on. Contrary to the dissent's characterization, observation evidence can be presented by either lay or expert witnesses.

Second, there is "mental-disease evidence" in the form of opinion testimony that Clark suffered from a mental disease with features described by the witness. As was true here, this evidence characteristically but not always comes from professional psychologists or psychiatrists who testify as expert witnesses and base their opinions in part on examination of a defendant, usually conducted after the events in question. The thrust of this evidence was that, based on factual reports, professional observations, and tests, Clark was psychotic at the time in question, with a condition that fell within the category of schizophrenia.

Third, there is evidence we will refer to as "capacity evidence" about a defendant's capacity for cognition and moral judgment (and ultimately also his capacity to form *mens rea*). This, too, is opinion evidence. Here, as it usually does, this testimony came from the same experts and concentrated on those specific details of the mental condition that make the difference between sanity and insanity under the Arizona definition.[3] In their respective testimony on these details the experts disagreed: the defense expert gave his opinion that the symptoms or effects of the disease in Clark's case included inability to appreciate the nature of

---

3. Arizona permits capacity evidence, *see, e.g., State v. Sanchez*, 573 P.2d 60, 64 (1977); see also ARIZ. RULE EVID. 704 (2006) (allowing otherwise admissible evidence on testimony "embrac[ing] an ultimate issue to be decided by the trier of fact"), though not every jurisdiction permits such evidence on the ultimate issue of insanity. *See, e.g.,* FED. RULE EVID. 704(b) ("No expert witness testifying with respect to the mental state or condition of a defendant in a criminal case may state an opinion or inference as to whether the defendant did or did not have the mental state or condition constituting an element of the crime charged or a defense thereto. Such ultimate issues are matters for the trier of fact alone."); *United States v. Dixon*, 185 F.3d 393, 400 (5th Cir. 1999) (in the face of mental-disease evidence, Rule 704(b) prohibits an expert "from testifying that [the mental-disease evidence] does or does not prevent the defendant from appreciating the wrongfulness of his actions").

his action and to tell that it was wrong, whereas the State's psychiatrist was of the view that Clark was a schizophrenic who was still sufficiently able to appreciate the reality of shooting the officer and to know that it was wrong to do that.

It is clear that *Mott* itself imposed no restriction on considering evidence of the first sort, the observation evidence. We read the *Mott* restriction to apply, rather, to evidence addressing the two issues in testimony that characteristically comes only from psychologists or psychiatrists qualified to give opinions as expert witnesses: mental-disease evidence (whether at the time of the crime a defendant suffered from a mental disease or defect, such as schizophrenia) and capacity evidence (whether the disease or defect left him incapable of performing or experiencing a mental process defined as necessary for sanity such as appreciating the nature and quality of his act and knowing that it was wrong).

Mott was careful to distinguish this kind of opinion evidence from observation evidence generally and even from observation evidence that an expert witness might offer, such as descriptions of a defendant's tendency to think in a certain way or his behavioral characteristics; the Arizona court made it clear that this sort of testimony was perfectly admissible to rebut the prosecution's evidence of *mens rea*. Thus, only opinion testimony going to mental defect or disease, and its effect on the cognitive or moral capacities on which sanity depends under the Arizona rule, is restricted.

In this case, the trial court seems to have applied the *Mott* restriction to all evidence offered by Clark for the purpose of showing what he called his inability to form the required *mens rea*, (that is, an intent to kill a police officer on duty, or an understanding that he was engaging in the act of killing such an officer. Thus, the trial court's restriction may have covered not only mental-disease and capacity evidence as just defined, but also observation evidence offered by lay (and expert) witnesses who described Clark's unusual behavior. Clark's objection to the application of the *Mott* rule does not, however, turn on the distinction between lay and expert witnesses or the kinds of testimony they were competent to present.

There is some, albeit limited, disagreement between the dissent and ourselves about the scope of the claim of error properly before us. To start with matters of agreement, all Members of the Court agree that Clark's general attack on the *Mott* rule covers its application in confining consideration of capacity evidence to the insanity defense.

In sum, the trial court's ruling, with its uncertain edges, may have restricted observation evidence admissible on *mens rea* to the insanity defense alone, but we cannot be sure.[4] But because a due process challenge to such a restriction of observation evidence was, by our measure, neither pressed nor passed upon in the Arizona Court of Appeals, we do not consider it.

---

4. We therefore have no reason to believe that the courts of Arizona would have failed to restrict their application of *Mott* to the professional testimony the *Mott* opinion was stated to cover, if Clark's counsel had specified any observation evidence he claimed to be generally admissible and relevant to *mens rea*. Nothing that we hold here is authority for restricting a factfinder's consideration of observation evidence indicating state of mind at the time of a criminal offense (conventional *mens rea* evidence) as distinct from professional mental-disease or capacity evidence going to ability to form a certain state of mind during a period that includes the time of the offense charged. And, of course, nothing held here prevents Clark from raising this discrete claim when the case returns to the courts of Arizona, if consistent with the State's procedural rules.

What we . . . now consider, is Clark's claim that *Mott* denied due process because it "*preclude[d] Eric from contending that . . . factual inferences*" of the "mental states which were necessary elements of the crime charged" "*should not be drawn* because the behavior was explainable, instead, as a manifestation of his chronic paranoid schizophrenia." We consider the claim, as Clark otherwise puts it, that "Arizona's prohibition of 'diminished capacity' evidence by criminal defendants violates" due process.

Clark's argument that the *Mott* rule violates the Fourteenth Amendment guarantee of due process turns on the application of the presumption of innocence in criminal cases, the presumption of sanity, and the principle that a criminal defendant is entitled to present relevant and favorable evidence on an element of the offense charged against him.

The first presumption is that a defendant is innocent unless and until the government proves beyond a reasonable doubt each element of the offense charged, *Patterson*, 432 U.S., at 210–211; *In re Winship*, 397 U.S. 358, 361–364 (1970), including the mental element or *mens rea*. Before the last century, the *mens rea* required to be proven for particular offenses was often described in general terms like "malice," but the modern tendency has been toward more specific descriptions, as shown in the Arizona statute defining the murder charged against Clark: the State had to prove that in acting to kill the victim, Clark intended to kill a law enforcement officer on duty or knew that the victim was such an officer on duty. As applied to *mens rea* (and every other element), the force of the presumption of innocence is measured by the force of the showing needed to overcome it, which is proof beyond a reasonable doubt that a defendant's state of mind was in fact what the charge states.

The presumption of sanity is equally universal in some variety or other, being (at least) a presumption that a defendant has the capacity to form the *mens rea* necessary for a verdict of guilt and the consequent criminal responsibility. This presumption dispenses with a requirement on the government's part to include as an element of every criminal charge an allegation that the defendant had such a capacity. The force of this presumption, like the presumption of innocence, is measured by the quantum of evidence necessary to overcome it; unlike the presumption of innocence, however, the force of the presumption of sanity varies across the many state and federal jurisdictions, and prior law has recognized considerable leeway on the part of the legislative branch in defining the presumption's strength through the kind of evidence and degree of persuasiveness necessary to overcome it.

There are two points where the sanity or capacity presumption may be placed in issue. First, a State may allow a defendant to introduce (and a factfinder to consider) evidence of mental disease or incapacity for the bearing it can have on the government's burden to show *mens rea*. In such States the evidence showing incapacity to form the guilty state of mind, for example, qualifies the probative force of other evidence, which considered alone indicates that the defendant actually formed the guilty state of mind. If it is shown that a defendant with mental disease thinks all blond people are robots, he could not have intended to kill a person when he shot a man with blond hair, even though he seemed to act like a man shooting another man. In jurisdictions that allow mental-disease and capacity evidence to be considered on par with any other relevant evidence when deciding whether the prosecution has proven *mens rea* beyond a reasonable doubt, the evidence of mental disease or incapacity need only support what the factfinder regards as a reasonable doubt about the capacity to form (or the actual formation of) the *mens rea*, in order to require acquittal of the charge. Thus, in these States the strength of the presumption of sanity is no greater than the strength of the evidence of abnormal mental state that the factfinder thinks is enough to raise a reasonable doubt.

The second point where the force of the presumption of sanity may be tested is in the consideration of a defense of insanity raised by a defendant. Insanity rules like *M'Naghten* and the variants discussed in Part II, are attempts to define, or at least to indicate, the kinds of mental differences that overcome the presumption of sanity or capacity and therefore excuse a defendant from customary criminal responsibility. The burden that must be carried by a defendant who raises the insanity issue, again, defines the strength of the sanity presumption. A State may provide, for example, that whenever the defendant raises a claim of insanity by some quantum of credible evidence, the presumption disappears and the government must prove sanity to a specified degree of certainty (whether beyond reasonable doubt or something less). Or a jurisdiction may place the burden of persuasion on a defendant to prove insanity as the applicable law defines it, whether by a preponderance of the evidence or to some more convincing degree. In any case, the defendant's burden defines the presumption of sanity, whether that burden be to burst a bubble or to show something more.

The third principle implicated by Clark's argument is a defendant's right as a matter of simple due process to present evidence favorable to himself on an element that must be proven to convict him. As already noted, evidence tending to show that a defendant suffers from mental disease and lacks capacity to form *mens rea* is relevant to rebut evidence that he did in fact form the required *mens rea* at the time in question; this is the reason that Clark claims a right to require the factfinder in this case to consider testimony about his mental illness and his incapacity directly, when weighing the persuasiveness of other evidence tending to show *mens rea*, which the prosecution has the burden to prove.

As Clark recognizes, however, the right to introduce relevant evidence can be curtailed if there is a good reason for doing that. "While the Constitution . . . prohibits the exclusion of defense evidence under rules that serve no legitimate purpose or that are disproportionate to the ends that they are asserted to promote, well-established rules of evidence permit trial judges to exclude evidence if its probative value is outweighed by certain other factors such as unfair prejudice, confusion of the issues, or potential to mislead the jury." And if evidence may be kept out entirely, its consideration may be subject to limitation, which Arizona claims the power to impose here. State law says that evidence of mental disease and incapacity may be introduced and considered, and if sufficiently forceful to satisfy the defendant's burden of proof under the insanity rule it will displace the presumption of sanity and excuse from criminal responsibility. But mental-disease and capacity evidence may be considered only for its bearing on the insanity defense, and it will avail a defendant only if it is persuasive enough to satisfy the defendant's burden as defined by the terms of that defense. The mental-disease and capacity evidence is thus being channeled or restricted to one issue and given effect only if the defendant carries the burden to convince the factfinder of insanity; the evidence is not being excluded entirely, and the question is whether reasons for requiring it to be channeled and restricted are good enough to satisfy the standard of fundamental fairness that due process requires. We think they are.

441

The first reason supporting the *Mott* rule is Arizona's authority to define its presumption of sanity (or capacity or responsibility) by choosing an insanity definition, as discussed in Part II, and by placing the burden of persuasion on defendants who claim incapacity as an excuse from customary criminal responsibility. No one, certainly not Clark here, denies that a State may place a burden of persuasion on a defendant claiming insanity. And Clark presses no objection to Arizona's decision to require persuasion to a clear and convincing degree before the presumption of sanity and normal responsibility is overcome.

But if a State is to have this authority in practice as well as in theory, it must be able to deny a defendant the opportunity to displace the presumption of sanity more easily when addressing a different issue in the course of the criminal trial. Yet, as we have explained, just such an opportunity would be available if expert testimony of mental disease and incapacity could be considered for whatever a factfinder might think it was worth on the issue of *mens rea*. As we mentioned, the presumption of sanity would then be only as strong as the evidence a factfinder would accept as enough to raise a reasonable doubt about *mens rea* for the crime charged; once reasonable doubt was found, acquittal would be required, and the standards established for the defense of insanity would go by the boards.

Now, a State is of course free to accept such a possibility in its law. After all, it is free to define the insanity defense by treating the presumption of sanity as a bursting bubble, whose disappearance shifts the burden to the prosecution to prove sanity whenever a defendant presents any credible evidence of mental disease or incapacity. In States with this kind of insanity rule, the legislature may well be willing to allow such evidence to be considered on the *mens rea* element for whatever the factfinder thinks it is worth. What counts for due process, however, is simply that a State that wishes to avoid a second avenue for exploring capacity, less stringent for a defendant, has a good reason for confining the consideration of evidence of mental disease and incapacity to the insanity defense.

It is obvious that Arizona's *Mott* rule reflects such a choice. The State Supreme Court pointed out that the State had declined to adopt a defense of diminished capacity (allowing a jury to decide when to excuse a defendant because of greater than normal difficulty in conforming to the law).[5] The court reasoned that the State's choice would be undercut if evidence of incapacity could be considered for whatever a jury might think sufficient to raise a reasonable doubt about *mens rea*, even if it did not show insanity. In other words, if a jury were free to decide how much evidence of mental disease and incapacity was enough to counter evidence of *mens rea* to the point of creating a reasonable doubt, that would in functional terms be analogous to allowing

---

5. Though the term "diminished capacity" has been given different meanings. *See, e.g.,* Morse, *Undiminished Confusion in Diminished Capacity*, 75 J.CRIM. L. & C. 1 (1984) ("The diminished capacity doctrine allows a criminal defendant to introduce evidence of mental abnormality at trial either to negate a mental element of the crime charged, thereby exonerating the defendant of that charge, or to reduce the degree of crime for which the defendant may be convicted, even if the defendant's conduct satisfied all the formal elements of a higher offense.") California, a jurisdiction with which the concept has traditionally been associated, understood it to be simply a "'showing that the defendant's mental capacity was reduced by mental illness, mental defect or intoxication.'" *People v. Berry*, 556 P.2d 777, 781 (Cal. 1976) (in banc) (quoting *People v. Castillo*, 449 P.2d 449, 452 (Cal. 1969); emphasis deleted), *abrogated by* CAL.PENAL CODE ANN. §§ 25(a), 28(a)-(b), 29 (West 1999 and Supp.2006).

jurors to decide upon some degree of diminished capacity to obey the law, a degree set by them, that would prevail as a stand-alone defense.

A State's insistence on preserving its chosen standard of legal insanity cannot be the sole reason for a rule like *Mott*, however, for it fails to answer an objection the dissent makes in this case. An insanity rule gives a defendant already found guilty the opportunity to excuse his conduct by showing he was insane when he acted, that is, that he did not have the mental capacity for conventional guilt and criminal responsibility. But, as the dissent argues, if the same evidence that affirmatively shows he was not guilty by reason of insanity (or "guilty except insane" under Arizona law), also shows it was at least doubtful that he could form *mens rea*, then he should not be found guilty in the first place; it thus violates due process when the State impedes him from using mental-disease and capacity evidence directly to rebut the prosecution's evidence that he did form *mens rea*.

Are there, then, characteristics of mental-disease and capacity evidence giving rise to risks that may reasonably be hedged by channeling the consideration of such evidence to the insanity issue on which, in States like Arizona, a defendant has the burden of persuasion? We think there are: in the controversial character of some categories of mental disease, in the potential of mental-disease evidence to mislead, and in the danger of according greater certainty to capacity evidence than experts claim for it.

To begin with, the diagnosis may mask vigorous debate within the profession about the very contours of the mental disease itself. *See, e.g.*, AMERICAN PSYCHIATRIC ASSOCIATION, DIAGNOSTIC AND STATISTICAL MANUAL OF MENTAL DISORDERS xxxiii (4th ed. text rev. 2000) (hereinafter DSM-IV-TR) ("DSM-IV reflects a consensus about the classification and diagnosis of mental disorders derived at the time of its initial publication. New knowledge generated by research or clinical experience will undoubtedly lead to an increased understanding of the disorders included in DSM-IV, to the identification of new disorders, and to the removal of some disorders in future classifications. The text and criteria sets included in DSM-IV will require reconsideration in light of evolving new information."). And Members of this Court have previously recognized that the end of such debate is not imminent.

Next, there is the potential of mental-disease evidence to mislead jurors (when they are the factfinders) through the power of this kind of evidence to suggest that a defendant suffering from a recognized mental disease lacks cognitive, moral, volitional, or other capacity, when that may not be a sound conclusion at all. Even when a category of mental disease is broadly accepted and the assignment of a defendant's behavior to that category is uncontroversial, the classification may suggest something very significant about a defendant's capacity, when in fact the classification tells us little or nothing about the ability of the defendant to form *mens rea* or to exercise the cognitive, moral, or volitional capacities that define legal sanity. See DSM-IV-TR xxxii-xxxiii ("When the DSM-IV categories, criteria, and textual descriptions are employed for forensic purposes, there are significant risks that diagnostic information will be misused or misunderstood. These dangers arise because of the imperfect fit between the questions of ultimate concern to the law and the information contained in a clinical diagnosis. In most situations, the clinical diagnosis of a DSM-IV mental disorder is not sufficient to establish the existence for legal purposes of . . . 'mental disease' or 'mental defect.' In determining whether an individual meets a specified legal standard (*e.g.*, for . . . criminal responsibility . . .), additional information is usually required beyond that contained in the DSM-IV diagnosis."). The limits of the utility of a professional disease diagnosis are evident in the dispute between the two testifying experts in this case; they agree that Clark was schizophrenic, but they come to opposite conclusions on whether the mental disease in his particular case left him bereft of cognitive or moral capacity. Evidence of mental disease, then, can easily mislead; it is very easy to slide from evidence that an individual with a professionally recognized mental disease is very different, into doubting that he has the capacity to form *mens rea*, whereas that doubt may not be justified. And of course, in the cases mentioned before, in which the categorization is doubtful or the category of mental disease is itself subject to controversy, the risks are even greater that opinions about mental disease may confuse a jury into thinking the opinions show more than they do. Because allowing mental-disease evidence on *mens rea* can thus easily mislead, it is not unreasonable to address that tendency by confining consideration of this kind of evidence to insanity, on which a defendant may be assigned the burden of persuasion.

There are, finally, particular risks inherent in the opinions of the experts who supplement the mental-disease classifications with opinions on incapacity: on whether the mental disease rendered a particular defendant incapable of the cognition necessary for moral judgment or *mens rea* or otherwise incapable of understanding the wrongfulness of the conduct charged. Unlike observational evidence bearing on *mens rea*, capacity evidence consists of judgment, and judgment fraught with multiple perils: a defendant's state of mind at the crucial moment can be elusive no matter how conscientious the enquiry, and the law's categories that set the terms of the capacity judgment are not the categories of psychology that govern the expert's professional thinking. Although such capacity judgments may be given in the utmost good faith, their potentially tenuous character is indicated by the candor of the defense expert in this very case. Contrary to the State's expert, he testified that Clark lacked the capacity to appreciate the circumstances realistically and to understand the wrongfulness of what he was doing, but he said that "no one knows exactly what was on [his] mind" at the time of the shooting. And even when an expert is confident that his understanding of the mind is reliable, judgment addressing the basic categories of capacity requires a leap from the concepts of psychology, which are devised for thinking about treatment, to the concepts of legal sanity, which are devised for thinking about criminal responsibility. *See* Insanity Defense Work Group, American Psychiatric Association Statement on the Insanity Defense, 140 AM. J. PSYCHIATRY 681, 686 (1983), reprinted in 2 The Role of Mental Illness in Criminal Trials 117, 122 (J. Moriarty ed. 2001) ("The American Psychiatric Association is not opposed to legislatures restricting psychiatric testimony about the . . . ultimate legal issues concerning the insanity defense . . . . When . . . . 'ultimate issue' questions are formulated by the law and put to the expert witness who must then say 'yea' or 'nay,' then the expert witness is required to make a leap in logic. He no longer addresses himself to medical concepts but instead must infer or intuit what is in fact unspeakable, namely, the *probable relationship* between medical concepts and legal or moral constructs such as free will. These impermissible leaps in logic made by expert witnesses confuse the jury . . . . This state of affairs does considerable injustice to psychiatry and, we believe, possibly to criminal defendants. These psychiatric disagreements . . . cause less than fully understanding juries or the public to conclude that psychiatrists cannot agree."). In sum, these empirical and conceptual problems add up to a real risk that an expert's judgment in giving capacity evidence will come with an apparent authority that psychologists and psychiatrists do not claim to have. We think that this risk, like the difficulty in assessing the significance of mental-disease evidence, supports the State's decision to channel such expert testimony to consideration on the insanity defense, on which the party seeking the benefit of this evidence has the burden of persuasion.

It bears repeating that not every State will find it worthwhile to make the judgment Arizona has made, and the choices the States do make about dealing with the risks posed by mental-disease and capacity evidence will reflect their varying assessments about the presumption of sanity as expressed in choices of insanity rules. The point here simply is that Arizona has sensible reasons to assign the risks as it has done by channeling the evidence.[6]

Arizona's rule serves to preserve the State's chosen standard for recognizing insanity as a defense and to avoid confusion and misunderstanding on the part of jurors. For these reasons, there is no violation of due process . . . and no cause to claim that channeling evidence on mental disease and capacity offends any "principle of justice so rooted in the traditions and conscience of our people as to be ranked as fundamental." *Patterson*, 432 U.S. at 202.

The judgment of the Court of Appeals of Arizona is, accordingly, affirmed.

Justice <u>Breyer</u>, concurring in part and dissenting in part. [Omitted.]

Justice Kennedy, with whom Justice Stevens and Justice Ginsburg join, dissenting.

In my submission the Court is incorrect in holding that Arizona may convict petitioner Eric Clark of first-degree murder for the intentional or knowing killing of a police officer when Clark was not permitted to introduce critical and reliable evidence showing he did not have that intent or knowledge.

Since I would reverse the judgment of the Arizona Court of Appeals on this ground, and the Arizona courts might well alter their interpretation of the State's criminal responsibility statute were my rationale to prevail, it is unnecessary for me to address the argument that Arizona's definition of insanity violates due process.

Clark claims that the trial court erred in refusing to consider evidence of his chronic paranoid schizophrenia in deciding whether he possessed the knowledge or intent required for first-degree murder. Seizing upon a theory invented here by the Court itself, the Court narrows Clark's claim so he cannot raise the point everyone else thought was involved in the case. The

---

6. Arizona's rule is supported by a further practical reason, though not as weighty as those just considered. As mentioned before, if substantial mental-disease and capacity evidence is accepted as rebutting *mens rea* in a given case, the affirmative defense of insanity will probably not be reached or ruled upon; the defendant will simply be acquitted (or perhaps convicted of a lesser included offense). If an acquitted defendant suffers from a mental disease or defect that makes him dangerous, he will neither be confined nor treated psychiatrically unless a judge so orders after some independent commitment proceeding. But if a defendant succeeds in showing himself insane, Arizona law (and presumably that of every other State with an insanity rule) will require commitment and treatment as a consequence of that finding without more. It makes sense, then, to channel capacity evidence to the issue structured to deal with mental incapacity when such a claim is raised successfully. *See, e.g., Jones*, 463 U.S. at 368 ("The purpose of commitment following an insanity acquittal . . . is to treat the individual's mental illness and protect him and society from his potential dangerousness.").

Court says the only issue before us is whether there is a right to introduce mental-disease evidence or capacity evidence, not a right to introduce observation evidence. This restructured evidentiary universe, with no convincing authority to support it, is unworkable on its own terms. Even were that not so, however, the Court's tripartite structure is something not addressed by the state trial court, the state appellate court, counsel on either side in those proceedings, or the briefs the parties filed with us. The Court refuses to consider the key part of Clark's claim because his counsel did not predict the Court's own invention. It is unrealistic, and most unfair, to hold that Clark's counsel erred in failing to anticipate so novel an approach. If the Court is to insist on its approach, at a minimum the case should be remanded to determine whether Clark is bound by his counsel's purported waiver.

The Court's error, of course, has significance beyond this case. It adopts an evidentiary framework that, in my view, will be unworkable in many cases. The Court classifies Clark's behavior and expressed beliefs as observation evidence but insists that its description by experts must be mental-disease evidence or capacity evidence. These categories break down quickly when it is understood how the testimony would apply to the question of intent and knowledge at issue here. The most common type of schizophrenia, and the one Clark suffered from, is paranoid schizophrenia. The existence of this functional psychosis is beyond dispute, but that does not mean the lay witness understands it or that a disputed issue of fact concerning its effect in a particular instance is not something for the expert to address. Common symptoms of the condition are delusions accompanied by hallucinations, often of the auditory type, which can cause disturbances of perception. Clark's expert testified that people with schizophrenia often play radios loudly to drown out the voices in their heads. Clark's attorney argued to the trial court that this, rather than a desire to lure a policeman to the scene, explained Clark's behavior just before the killing. The observation that schizophrenics play radios loudly is a fact regarding behavior, but it is only a relevant fact if Clark has schizophrenia.

Even if this evidence were, to use the Court's term, mental-disease evidence, because it relies on an expert opinion, what would happen if the expert simply were to testify, without mentioning schizophrenia, that people with Clark's symptoms often play the radio loudly? This seems to be factual evidence, as the term is defined by the Court, yet it differs from mental-disease evidence only in forcing the witness to pretend that no one has yet come up with a way to classify the set of symptoms being described. More generally, the opinion that Clark had paranoid schizophrenia—an opinion shared by experts for both the prosecution and defense—bears on efforts to determine, as a factual matter, whether he knew he was killing a police officer. The psychiatrist's explanation of Clark's condition was essential to understanding how he processes sensory data and therefore to deciding what information was in his mind at the time of the shooting. Simply put, knowledge relies on cognition, and cognition can be affected by schizophrenia. The mental-disease evidence at trial was also intertwined with the observation evidence because it lent needed credibility. Clark's parents and friends testified Clark thought the people in his town were aliens trying to kill him. These claims might not be believable without a psychiatrist confirming the story based on his experience with people who have exhibited similar behaviors. It makes little sense to divorce the observation evidence from the explanation that makes it comprehensible.

Assuming the Court's tripartite structure were feasible, the Court is incorrect when it narrows Clark's claim to exclude any concern about observation evidence. Clark's claim goes well beyond an objection to *Mott*. In fact, he specifically attempted to distinguish *Mott* by noting that the trial court in this case refused to consider all evidence of mental illness. The Court notices these arguments but criticizes Clark's counsel for not being specific about the observation evidence he wanted the trial court to consider. There was no reason, though, for Clark's counsel to believe additional specificity was required, since there was no evident distinction in Arizona law between observation evidence and mental-disease testimony.

Second, *Mott*'s holding was not restricted to mental-disease evidence. The Arizona Supreme Court did not refer to any distinction between observation and mental-disease evidence, or lay and expert testimony. Its holding was stated in broad terms: "Arizona does not allow evidence of a defendant's mental disorder short of insanity either as an affirmative defense or to negate the *mens rea* element of a crime." Even if, as the Court contends, *Mott* is limited to expert testimony, the Court's categories still do not properly interpret *Mott*, because the Court's own definition of observation evidence includes some expert testimony.

It makes no difference that in the appeals court Clark referred to the issue as inability to form knowledge or intent. He did not insist on some vague, general incapacity. He stated, instead, that he "suffered from a major mental illness and was psychotic at the time of the offense."

Before this Court Clark framed the issue in broad terms that encompass the question whether the evidence of his mental illness should have been considered to show he did not at the time of the offense have the knowledge or intent to shoot a police officer. In the end we must decide whether he had the right to introduce evidence showing he lacked the intent or knowledge the statute itself sets forth in describing a basic element of the crime. Clark has preserved this issue at all stages, including in this Court.

Clark challenges the trial court's refusal to consider any evidence of mental illness, from lay or expert testimony, in determining whether he acted with the knowledge or intent element of the crime. States have substantial latitude under the Constitution to define rules for the exclusion of evidence and to apply those rules to criminal defendants. This authority, however, has constitutional limits. "Whether rooted directly in the Due Process Clause of the Fourteenth Amendment or in the Compulsory Process or Confrontation Clauses of the Sixth Amendment, the Constitution guarantees criminal defendants 'a meaningful opportunity to present a complete defense.'" "This right is abridged by evidence rules that infringe upon a weighty interest of the accused and are arbitrary or disproportionate to the purposes they are designed to serve."

The central theory of Clark's defense was that his schizophrenia made him delusional. He lived in a universe where the delusions were so dominant, the theory was, that he had no intent to shoot a police officer or knowledge he was doing so. It is one thing to say he acted with intent or knowledge to pull the trigger. It is quite another to say he pulled the trigger to kill someone he knew to be a human being and a police officer. If the trier of fact were to find Clark's evidence sufficient to discount the case made by the State, which has the burden to prove knowledge or intent as an element of the offense, Clark would not be guilty of first-degree murder under Arizona law.

The Court attempts to diminish Clark's interest by treating mental-illness evidence as concerning only "judgment," rather than fact. This view appears to derive from the Court's characterization of Clark's claim as raising only general incapacity. This is wrong for the reasons already discussed. It fails to recognize, moreover, the meaning of the offense element in question here. The *mens rea* element of intent or knowledge may, at some level, comprise certain moral choices, but it rests in the first instance on a factual determination. That is the fact Clark sought to put in issue. Either Clark knew he was killing a police officer or he did not.

The issue is not, as the Court insists, whether Clark's mental illness acts as an "excuse from customary criminal responsibility," but whether his mental illness, as a factual matter, made him unaware that he was shooting a police officer. If it did, Clark needs no excuse, as then he did not commit the crime as Arizona defines it. For the elements of first-degree murder, where the question is knowledge of particular facts—that one is killing a police officer—the determination depends not on moral responsibility but on empirical fact. Clark's evidence of mental illness had a direct and substantial bearing upon what he knew, or thought he knew, to be the facts when he pulled the trigger; this lay at the heart of the matter.

Arizona's rule is problematic because it excludes evidence no matter how credible and material it may be in disproving an element of the offense. The Court's cases have noted the potential arbitrariness of *per se* exclusions and, on this rationale, have invalidated various state prohibitions.

This is not to suggest all general rules on the exclusion of certain types of evidence are invalid. If the rule does not substantially burden the defense, then it is likely permissible. *See Scheffer*, 523 U.S. at 316–17 (upholding exclusion of polygraph evidence in part because this rule "does not implicate any significant interest of the accused"). Where, however, the burden is substantial, the State must present a valid reason for its *per se* evidentiary rule.

The risk of jury confusion also fails to justify the rule. The State defends its rule as a means to avoid the complexities of determining how and to what degree a mental illness affects a person's mental state. The difficulty of resolving a factual issue, though, does not present a sufficient reason to take evidence away from the jury even when it is crucial for the defense. "We have always trusted juries to sort through complex facts in various areas of law." Even were the risk of jury confusion real enough to justify excluding evidence in most cases, this would provide little basis for prohibiting all evidence of mental illness without any inquiry into its likely effect on the jury or its role in deciding the linchpin issue of knowledge and intent.

The Court undertakes little analysis of the interests particular to this case. By proceeding in this way it devalues Clark's constitutional rights. The reliability rationale has minimal applicability here. The Court is correct that many mental diseases are difficult to define and the subject of great debate. Schizophrenia, however, is a well-documented mental illness, and no one seriously disputes either its definition or its most prominent clinical manifestations. The State's own expert conceded that Clark had paranoid schizophrenia and was actively psychotic at the time of the killing. The jury-confusion rationale, if it is at all applicable here, is the result of the Court's own insistence on conflating the insanity defense and the question of intent. Considered on its own terms, the issue of intent and knowledge is a straightforward factual question. A trier of fact is quite capable of weighing defense testimony and then determining whether the accused did or did not intend to kill or knowingly kill a human being who was a police officer. True, the issue can be difficult to decide in particular instances, but no more so than many matters juries must confront.

The fact that mental-illness evidence may be considered in deciding criminal responsibility does not compensate for its exclusion from consideration on the *mens rea* elements of the crime. The evidence addresses different issues in the two instances. Criminal responsibility involves an inquiry into whether the defendant knew right from wrong, not whether he had the *mens rea* elements of the offense. While there may be overlap between the two issues, "the existence or nonexistence of legal insanity bears no necessary relationship to the existence or nonexistence of the required mental elements of the crime."

Even if the analyses were equivalent, there is a different burden of proof for insanity than there is for *mens rea*. Arizona requires the defendant to prove his insanity by clear and convincing evidence. The prosecution, however, must prove all elements of the offense beyond a reasonable doubt. *See Mullaney, supra*, at 703−04. The shift in the burden on the criminal responsibility issue, while permissible under our precedent, cannot be applied to the question of intent or knowledge without relieving the State of its responsibility to establish this element of the offense. *See Sandstrom v. Montana*, 442 U.S. 510, 524 (1979) (jury instruction that had the effect of placing the burden on the defendant to disprove that he had the requisite mental state violates due process). While evidentiary rules do not generally shift the burden impermissibly, where there is a right to have evidence considered on an element of the offense, the right is not respected by allowing the evidence to come in only on an issue for which the defendant bears the burden of proof. *See Cool v. United States*, 409 U.S. 100, 103 (1972) (per curiam) (jury instruction that allowed jury to consider accomplice's testimony only if it was true beyond a reasonable doubt "places an improper burden on the defense and allows the jury to convict despite its failure to find guilt beyond a reasonable doubt"); *Martin v. Ohio*, 480 U.S. 228, 233−34 (1987) (State can shift the burden on a claim of self-defense, but if the jury were disallowed from considering self-defense evidence for purposes of deciding the elements of the offense, it "would relieve the State of its burden and plainly run afoul of *Winship*'s mandate"). By viewing the Arizona rule as creating merely a "presumption of sanity (or capacity or responsibility)," rather than a presumption that the *mens rea* elements were not affected by mental illness, the Court fails to appreciate the implications for *Winship*.

The State attempts to sidestep the evidentiary issue entirely by claiming that its mental-illness exclusion simply alters one element of the crime. The evidentiary rule at issue here, however, cannot be considered a valid redefinition of the offense. Under the State's logic, a person would be guilty of first-degree murder if he knowingly or intentionally killed a police officer or committed the killing under circumstances that would show knowledge or intent but for the defendant's mental illness. To begin with, Arizona law does not say this. And if it did, it would be impermissible. States have substantial discretion in defining criminal offenses. In some instances they may provide that the accused has the burden of persuasion with respect to affirmative defenses. *See Patterson v. New York*, 432 U.S. 197, 210 (1977). "But there are obviously constitutional limits beyond which the States may not go in this regard." If it were otherwise, States could label all evidentiary exclusions as redefinitions and so evade constitutional requirements. There is no rational basis, furthermore, for criminally punishing a person who commits a killing without knowledge or intent only if that person has a mental illness. The State attempts to bring the instant case within the ambit of *Montana v. Egelhoff*, 518 U.S. 37 (1996), but in *Egelhoff* the excluded evidence concerned voluntary intoxication, for which a person can be held responsible. Viewed either as an evidentiary rule or a redefinition of the offense, it was upheld because it "comports with and implements society's moral perception that one who has voluntarily impaired his own faculties should be responsible for the consequences." An involuntary mental illness does not implicate this justification.

Future dangerousness is not, as the Court appears to conclude, a rational basis for convicting mentally ill individuals of crimes they did not commit. Civil commitment proceedings can ensure that individuals who present a danger to themselves or others receive proper treatment without unfairly treating them as criminals. The State presents no evidence to the contrary, and the Court ought not to imply otherwise.

Putting aside the lack of any legitimate state interest for application of the rule in this case, its irrationality is apparent when considering the evidence that is allowed. Arizona permits the defendant to introduce, for example, evidence of "behavioral tendencies" to show he did not have the required mental state. While defining mental illness is a difficult matter, the State seems to exclude the evidence one would think most reliable by allowing unexplained and uncategorized tendencies to be introduced while excluding relatively well-understood psychiatric testimony regarding well-documented mental illnesses. It is unclear, moreover, what would have happened in this case had the defendant wanted to testify that he thought Officer Moritz was an alien. If disallowed, it would be tantamount to barring Clark from testifying on his behalf to explain his own actions. If allowed, then Arizona's rule would simply prohibit the corroboration necessary to make sense of Clark's explanation. In sum, the rule forces the jury to decide guilt in a fictional world with undefined and unexplained behaviors but without mental illness. This rule has no rational justification and imposes a significant burden upon a straightforward defense: He did not commit the crime with which he was charged.

These are the reasons for my respectful dissent.

Notes

1.   Five states—Idaho, Kansas, Montana, North Dakota, and Utah—have abolished insanity as an affirmative defense. The Nevada Legislature also amended that state's penal code to eliminate insanity as an affirmative defense, but the Nevada Supreme Court ruled that "legal insanity is a well-established and fundamental principle of the law of the United States. It is therefore protected by the Due Process Clauses of both the United States and Nevada Constitutions. The Legislature may not abolish insanity as a complete defense to a criminal offense." *Finger v. State*, 27 P.3d 66, 84 (Nev. 2001). The United States Supreme Court has not ruled on the question whether the insanity defense is constitutionally required.

Was the Nevada Supreme Court right? If a state decides to have an insanity defense or decides that one is constitutionally required, which of the various tests reviewed by the *Clark* Court is the best? If Clark had been tried in one of the states that have abolished the insanity defense, could the defense have presented the expert evidence that they wished to introduce on the question of mental state?

2.   Most jurisdictions that provide for an affirmative insanity defense have adopted some version of the *M'Naughten* test. Most jurisdictions require the defendant to prove insanity by a preponderance of the evidence, or, in a few states, by clear and convincing evidence, or even beyond a reasonable doubt. During the 1960's and 1970's, most jurisdictions adopted the Model Penal Code test, and most placed the burden of proof on the government to disprove insanity. However, after John Hinckley was found not guilty by reason of insanity on charges of attempting to assassinate President Reagan, many states as well as the federal government revised their insanity defense statutes, narrowing the definition of insanity, placing the burden of proof on defendants, and adopting a heightened burden.

3.   An unusual procedural aspect of presenting an insanity defense is the requirement, under Article 46C.051 of the Texas Code of Criminal Procedure, that the defendant must provide notice of an intent to raise the defense at least 20 days prior to trial or at the time of a pretrial hearing if it is set earlier than the twenty-day period prior to trial. The apparent purpose of requiring notice is to allow time for a possible mental health examination by a neutral expert, appointed by the court. That expert may then file a report concerning his or her findings with regard to insanity and, possibly, a separate report with regard to the question of competency to stand trial, which is judged by a different standard. The failure to comply with the notice requirement prevents the defense from admitting evidence of insanity, unless the judge finds "good cause exists for failure to provide notice." TEX. CODE CRIM. PROC. ANN. art. 46C.052 (West 2015).

4.   Mental disease or defect is not within the experience or knowledge of most jurors. While the insanity defense does not require expert testimony as a prerequisite for raising it, the importance of expert testimony in the typical insanity defense case cannot be overstated. Although expert witness testimony is critical with regard to the foundation requirement of establishing mental disease or defect, the caselaw on the insanity defense makes clear that, ultimately, the decision as to whether the weight of both the medical testimony as well as the nonmedical testimony establishes that the defendant should be found not guilty by reason of insanity is a legal and moral conclusion for the jury, or the judge in a bench trial, and not a medical question. As the discussion in *Clark* indicated, one of the primary reasons that the majority gave for allowing the prohibition of expert witness testimony on insanity on the question of mental state is the desire to contain the role of the experts in order to prevent jurors from merely deferring to the expert witnesses. Texas courts have made it clear that expert witnesses do not have a monopoly on testimony concerning the sanity of a defendant of the defendant. Lay testimony is also admissible.

5.   The case of *DeRusse v. State*, 579 SW2d 224 (1979), presents a familiar scenario of dueling mental health experts in a case raising the insanity defense. The evidence established that

the defendant and his wife fatally beat their three-year-old son with their hands, a board, a belt, and an electric cord. The child was pronounced dead on arrival at the hospital. Two of the nurses on duty in the emergency room at the time testified that the child appeared to have been run over by a car.

The County Medical Examiner testified that:

the child was severely beaten. I estimated that about seventy-five percent of the body surface was covered with contusions and bruises and that the bruising was from the top of the head to the tops of the feet. There was literally no area spared of the bruising.

In support of the defendant's defense of insanity, the defense presented the testimony of Dr. Henry Hammer, a clinical psychologist, who had examined the defendant. He testified:

I saw Mr. DeRusse as suffering from a paranoid state which is transitory, psychotic episode of indeterminate length. This means that for a specific part of his life, Mr. DeRusse was out of contact with reality. The greater portion of his life he was in contact with reality and continues to be in contact with reality. That is, he would be perceived by most reasonable people to be okay, to not be crazy. However, when you get into that segment of his life that encapsulates a delusional belief system, his perception of the situation and yours might be very radically different. His area of interest, which was delusional, happened to be in the sphere of religion.

He believed . . . very deeply in possession by demons. This gets into a religious area that is tricky to deal with because a significant portion of the population, maybe small in terms of percentage but large in terms of numbers, also believe in possession by spirits. Where it gets to be important to distinguish is his particular elaboration of those beliefs, how they were in his mind. He had a very concrete belief that his son was possessed by a spirit, by a demon, that his son was acting not on his own but at the behest of a spirit, a demon.

Now, insofar as you and I would not agree that that is in fact what has been happening, he was out of contact with reality. Now that is very superficially what went on. What we are dealing with here is a whole complex personality on which superimposed is this basic disorder. This disorder which is of indeterminant length but of serious proportion.

Dr. Hammer testified that appellant did not intend to harm his son when he beat him:

He was busy attacking the behavior of a demon, in his own mind, he was. As extra baggage to that, as something that happened inadvertently, he—undesirably, perhaps, undesirably is a better term, he was also causing physical harm to his son. He saw that as very undesirable. He did not want to cause harm to the son. He did want to correct this demonic behavior he perceived.

Dr. Hammer testified that, in his opinion, appellant's delusional belief that his son was possessed by a demon was a mental disease or defect and appellant, as a result, did not know that his conduct was wrong.

In rebuttal, the State called Dr. Joel Kutnick, a psychiatrist who had been appointed by the trial court to examine the defendant as to his competence to stand trial and his sanity at the time of the offense. Dr. Kutnick testified that the defendant had not beaten his son to get rid of a demon, but as means of discipline:

> [A]s I see the case, the religious issue, in one way, is kind of a red herring because Mr. DeRusse himself doesn't feel or doesn't in any way say that the reason he was disciplining his child was because he was trying to get rid of the demon. He was doing it as a way of trying to teach his boy the correct way of behaving and in his own mind felt that he was doing the right kind of thing in terms of bringing up his son. The religious issue is kind of, wasn't the kind of thing that motivated him to act in terms of delivering punishment to his son at all.

Dr. Kutnick testified that he did not believe that appellant's religious beliefs constituted a mental disease or defect. He expressed his disagreement with Dr. Hammer as follows:

> Dr. Hammer feels . . . that because his religious beliefs are such that a majority of the population don't have the strong conviction or as a bizarre kinds of things, like demon possession and seeing smoke arise from the boy's body, at one time, that this represents a psychosis, a mental illness, a paranoid state. I don't see this as a mental illness. I think one has to be very careful when one gets into the area of religion and calling people mentally ill. Many, many people have all kinds of religious beliefs . . . . They are not sick in the psychiatric sense, they are only caught up in their own cultural beliefs. I feel that the way Mr. DeRusse presents with his rational thinking and being able to explain, if you accept his basic premises that there is a good and evil in the world and that the evil is because of Satan and his henchmen demons and good comes out of the world because of God . . ., if you accept all of those basic tenets, that what he says and how he views things makes perfect sense and is not illogical at all, if you accept those tenets. That to me is not mental illness.

As a basis for his testimony, Dr. Kutnick described the history of the case as related to him by the defendant during the course of his examination. Specifically, Dr. Kutnick testified that the defendant had told him that he had burned the soles of his son's feet with matches; that appellant and his wife had poured jalapeno pepper juice in the boy's eyes; and that on the night he died, the child had been left tied to a door so that he could not raid the refrigerator, a habit which his parents were trying to break.

Is the battle of the experts in this case helpful in resolving the question of sanity or insanity? Should DeRusse be held responsible for causing the death of his son? Was DeRusse mad or bad?

6.   Under current Texas law, a finding of the not guilty by reason of insanity means that the defendant stands acquitted of the offense charged and may not be considered a person charged with an offense and double jeopardy protections prevent another attempt by the prosecution to convict the defendant of the same offense. However, an acquittal based on a finding of not guilty by reason of insanity does not function as a typical acquittal. In many cases, a verdict of not guilty by reason of insanity will not result in the release of the defendant but the result is another form of involuntary deprivation of liberty—in a mental health institution rather than a penal

institution. Nonetheless, neither the judge nor the parties may inform the jury of the consequences to the defendant if a verdict of not guilty by reason of insanity is returned under Article 46C.154 of the Texas Code of Criminal Procedure.

If the jury returns a verdict of not guilty by reason of insanity, the court must make a determination as to whether "the offense of which the person was acquitted involved conduct that:

(1) caused serious bodily injury to another person;

(2) placed another person in imminent danger of serious bodily injury; or

(3) consisted of a threat of serious bodily injury to another person through the use of a deadly weapon.

TEX. CODE CRIM. PROC. art. 46C.155.

If the court finds that the offense does not involve these elements, the court must make a determination as to whether the defendant suffers from a mental illness or is mentally retarded. If so, the defendant will be referred to the appropriate court for civil commitment proceedings. If, however, the court finds that the offense involved the threat or infliction of serious bodily under the above criteria, the criminal trial court maintains jurisdiction over the defendant. The court is than required to order the acquitted person to be committed for evaluation of his present mental condition and for treatment to the maximum-security unit of any facility designated by the department. The period of the initial commitment may not exceed 30 days. The court is required to order the acquitted person committed to a mental hospital or other appropriate facility for inpatient treatment or residential care if the state establishes by clear and convincing evidence that:

(1) the person has a severe mental illness or mental retardation;

(2) the person, as a result of that mental illness or mental retardation, is likely to cause serious bodily injury to another if the person is not provided with treatment and supervision; and

(3) inpatient treatment or residential care is necessary to protect the safety of others.

TEX. CODE CRIM. PROC. art. 46C.256.

This order for commitment expires the 181st day following the date the order is issued, but is subject to renewal as provided by Article 46C.261, subject to an indefinite number of annual renewals of the commitment order on an annual basis. Most defendants who are found not guilty by reason of insanity are committed to mental institutions for a considerable time.

Incompetency

The insanity defense is firmly established in public consciousness because it is often at issue in cases that receive a great deal of publicity. However, it is a defense of last resort that is infrequently raised and, when it is raised, it is usually in trials of very serious offenses. Juror hostility to the defense, the difficulty of establishing the mental process of seriously disordered defendants on an issue for which the defense must carry the burden of persuasion, and the consequence of involuntary commitment for an indefinite term if the defense is successful contribute to the infrequent use of the defense. Thus, while the insanity defense has been the subject of much scholarly and political debate, this level of attention is entirely out of proportion to the practical impact in the criminal justice system. Studies of the use of the insanity defense report that less than one percent of criminal defendants plead insanity, and of those who do plead insanity, only about 25 percent are found to be not guilty by reason of insanity.

A far more common issue than the insanity defense that is raised in criminal cases is the question of whether the defendant is incompetent to stand trial. Incompetency is a cousin to the insanity defense. The question of whether the defendant is competent concerns the mental capability of the defendant that often involves experts who are often appointed to examine the defendant and report on the competency of the defendant to stand trial and also to examine the defendant with regard to insanity defense issues.

A very important similarity is that a finding of incompetency is often the mechanism by which a person is transferred from the criminal justice system to the mental health system. An individual who is found incompetent can be temporarily detained in a mental health facility to see if the defendant can attain competency. If the defendant is not likely to attain competency, and in any case, if he or she has not attained competency after a commitment that is limited to 120 days, the defendant may no longer be detained on basis of incompetency to stand trial under Article 46B.073 Texas Code of Criminal Procedure. One extension of 60 additional days is allowed only if the head of the mental health facility asserts that the defendant is making progress towards attaining competency. If the defendant remains incompetent to stand trial, the individual must be released or be involuntarily committed in a mental health facility, which can occur only after a due process hearing at which it is found by clear and convincing evidence that the person is mentally ill and a danger to self or others or without treatment will continue to suffer mental or physical deterioration. Any commitment is also for a limited time, but subject to renewals of the continued need for involuntary civil commitment at intervals that can become as infrequent as occurring annually. Thus, incompetency is the mechanism by which many defendants move from charges in the criminal justice system to a potentially long-term mental health commitment.

Despite the similarities between incompetency to stand trial and the insanity defense there are significant differences. Incompetency is not a defense. Criminal charges may remain, and the statute of limitations is tolled during incompetency confinement. Advance notice of an intended insanity claim must be provided by the defense in advance of trial, and the insanity defense could be forfeited if notice is not timely provided. Incompetency, by contrast, can be raised at any time by the defense or the court *sua sponte*. The issue of whether the defendant was incompetent when tried has been raised successfully for the first time on appeal. The reason that incompetency is unwaivable is that it is a due process right of fundamental fairness that a trial cannot be conducted if the defendant is unable to rationally understand the proceedings and consult with counsel. An incompetent defendant is incompetent to waive his or her incompetency. Thus, the standard for competency, unlike the right/wrong insanity defense, relates to the ability of the defendant to understand the proceedings and to rationally consult with defense counsel. Note that the competency inquiry is concerned with the defendant's present capabilities at the time of trial while the insanity defense is concerned with the defendant's state of mind at the time of the offense. Unlike the infrequently raised insanity defense, questions concerning a defendant's competency often arise.

Either party may suggest there is a question concerning the competency of the defendant or the court may raise the issue on its own motion. If a bona fide doubt about incompetency, the trial court has a duty to conduct a hearing inquire into the defendant's ability to meet the following standard codified at Article 46B.003 of the Texas Code of Criminal Procedure:

> (a) A person is incompetent to stand trial if the person does not have:
>
>> (1) sufficient present ability to consult with the person's lawyer with a reasonable degree of rational understanding; or
>>
>> (2) a rational as well as factual understanding of the proceedings against the person.

If the inquiry reveals a "bona fide doubt" about the defendant's competency, the trial court must conduct a hearing, which in Texas, may be before a separate jury from the jury selected to determine guilt or innocence. Texas is unique in requiring a jury determination of this issue upon request. It is important to remember that while a finding of incompetency prevents a criminal conviction while the defendant is incompetent, a finding of incompetency is not a defense (unlike insanity), and the criminal charges may be tried if the defendant attains competency. A temporary commitment to a mental health facility for an incompetent defendant is permitted only if there is a finding of a reasonable likelihood that the defendant will attain competency in the foreseeable future. *See Jackson v. Indiana*, 406 U.S. 715 (1972) (finding due process and equal protection violations in the indefinite commitment of a defendant charged with criminal offenses until the defendant attained competency when such a commitment on the basis of unproven charges was a likely life sentence due to the unlikelihood the defendant would ever attain competency).

In Texas, a temporary commitment to attain competency may be ordered if the defendant cannot be treated on an out-patient basis, limited to a period of 60 days if the pending charges are misdemeanors or 120 days if the pending charges are felonies. TEX. CODE CRIM. PROC. art. 46B.073(b). One extension of 60 additional days may be sought by the head of the mental health facility only if "the defendant has not attained competency; and an extension of the initial restoration period will likely enable the facility or program to restore the defendant to competency within the period of the extension." TEX. CODE CRIM. PROC. art. 46B.080(b). If the mental health facility is of the opinion that the defendant has attained competency, the trial proceeds if, after a hearing requested by either party, the court finds the defendant now meets the "rational understanding and ability to rationally consult with counsel" standard of competency.

If the defendant has not attained competency at the end of the period of permitted commitment, or if the court determines the defendant will not attain competency in the foreseeable future during the period of commitment, the defendant must either be released or be given a hearing to determine whether he or she meets the standard for involuntary civil commitment. Thus, like the far less common insanity defense, a finding of incompetency is a mechanism by which a person who has come to the attention of authorities by virtue of an arrest and the filing of criminal charges is transferred from the criminal justice system to the mental health system. Whether a person is brought to the commitment hearing with or without the referral from the criminal justice system based upon findings of incompetency to stand trial or a verdict of not guilty by reason of insanity, a person may be committed involuntarily to a mental health facility only if a court finds by clear and convincing evidence that the person is mentally ill and, as a result is likely to cause: serious harm to self; serious harm to others; or, is experiencing severe and abnormal distress, experiencing substantial deterioration of his ability to function independently, and is unable to make a rational and informed decision as to whether or not to submit to treatment. TEX. HEALTH AND SAFETY CODE §§ 574.034 and 574.035.

Issue: Does a state violate due process of law by preventing the introduction of evidence showing diminished capacity by a criminal Δ?

Holding: NO. A state's prohibition of the introduction of diminished mental capacity by the Δ does not violate due process. The state prohibition applies only to evidence regarding mental capacity & mental disease, rather than observation. Evidence regarding mental disease and capacity presents risks which can be limited by allowing only the insanity issue to be considered, upon which the burden of evidence rests on Δ. The diagnosis does not reveal the uncertainty about what actually defines mental illness. Second the evidence of mental disease may lead jurors to mistakenly suppose that the Δ lacks reasoning thought, willpower or moral discrimination bc of his mental illness when such may not be the case.

The court said while not every state will find it necessary to exclude mental capacity or mental disease evidence it is still a sensible choice by AZ.

A state does not violate due process by preventing the intro of evidence showing diminishe capacity by Δ.

Diss: No logic in strictly enforcing a seperation of the observational evidence from the scientific explanation which makes it understandable the element at issue is mensrea bears directly on the quilty mind.

457

Chapter 21: Inchoate Crimes: Mental State, Agreement, and Act

Introduction

If the police are able to apprehend a person just before she was poised to commit a dangerous crime, or officers uncover a well-planned conspiracy to commit a terrorist act before a bomb explodes, should the reward for this work be that no criminal conviction is possible because no offense has occurred? Inchoate or incomplete crimes allow criminal convictions when the complete offense defined by the penal code has not been accomplished. While there is little controversy about the need for criminal sanctions for individuals who have manifested their dangerousness sufficiently, there are difficult problems with prosecuting persons based not on what they did, but what they intended to do. Of course, what people intended is an important issue with completed crimes as well, but the infliction of harm or the achievement of some criminal objective provides an important basis for inferring mental state that is absent in inchoate offenses.

This chapter will examine some of the particular problems of the inchoate crimes of attempt, conspiracy, and solicitation. These three offenses, found in Sections 15.01 through 15.05 of the Texas Penal Code, define offenses with several common features including: a required specific intent that the object crime be committed; completion of the crime intended is not required, but completion is not a defense; and the penalty for the offense is one penalty level lower than would apply if the intended offense had been committed. All three of the offenses are auxiliary statutes that do not stand alone. There is no such thing in Texas law of criminal conspiracy or criminal attempt by itself. Rather the inchoate offense requires a pairing with an offense defined by a statute as a completed crime. Thus, inchoate crimes are a combination of two statutes, such as solicitation of murder, conspiracy to possess and deliver controlled substances, and attempted arson.

There are also important differences among the three inchoate offenses. Under Texas law, an attempt of both felonies and misdemeanors (Class B or higher) may be prosecuted. The object crime must be a felony for a criminal conspiracy in Texas, and only the solicitation of capital felonies and felonies of the first degree constitute crimes. (This is true of the general inchoate statutes of attempt, conspiracy, and solicitation. Some completed penal statutes have a solicitation element, such as solicitation of prostitution).

An attempt is considered to be a lesser-included offense of a completed crime. Thus, while a defendant cannot defend against an attempt crime on the ground the defendant actually committed the completed offense (because completion is no defense), there cannot be a conviction of the completed crime *and* an attempt to commit the same crime when there is only one criminal act. This is not true for conspiracy and solicitation because most crimes can be committed by a single actor, and the agreement with or solicitation of another can constitute a separate offense.

An attempt can be undertaken by a single actor whereas solicitation and conspiracy at least contemplate the participation of others. Particular emphasis is placed on whether the act went far enough to demonstrate the defendant's intent to commit an attempt. With conspiracy and solicitation, the offense contemplates the participation of others. Because offenses of greater scale and danger can be committed by criminal groups, solicitation and conspiracy become complete sooner than an attempt, which requires an act of perpetration, not merely one of preparation. In contrast, the solicitation itself is sufficient, and any overt act by any conspirator is sufficient to have an indictable conspiracy. For this reason, the section of this chapter dealing with the act requirement will be focused on attempt cases because an overt act is not required for solicitation. It isalso rarely an issue in conspiracy cases because any act by any conspirator is sufficient.

Mental State

The desire to punish persons who have clearly shown their desire to commit serious crimes without requiring law enforcement officers to wait until harm has occurred is the purpose of inchoate crimes. Allowing the state this power is fraught with the concern that innocent people and those whose thoughts about criminal activity never go forward may be subject to substantial penalties without having caused harm and without presenting a serious public danger. Tort law differs from criminal law in this regard because unsuccessful attempts do not give rise to liability. Because the criminal law punishes for a criminal intent divorced from causation of harm, the subject of mental state is particularly important with inchoate crimes. This is especially true under modern statutes like the inchoate offenses in the Texas Penal Code that provide for much more severe penalties than was true of common law attempt. Attempted crimes were considered relatively minor offenses, usually misdemeanors.

Inchoate crimes are specific-intent offenses—requiring proof that the defendant intended to commit the target offense. Even if the target offense does not require an intent to cause a prohibited result, an attempt, conspiracy, or solicitation to commit that offense does. The fact that attempt requires specific intent, even when the particular crime attempted does not, sometimes results in confusion about what evidence is sufficient to prove a defendant's intent. This problem is aggravated by the need to combine the inchoate statute with a particular completed offense. As the *Flanagan* case that follows illustrates, the fit between the auxiliary inchoate offense and the completed crime may not be possible for some statutory offenses.

Flanagan v. State

675 S.W.2d 734 (Tex. Crim. App. 1982)

Miller, Judge.

Opinion on State's motion for rehearing and on court's own motion for rehearing.

On original submission, a panel of this Court held that the evidence in the instant cause was insufficient to show that the appellant, who was convicted of attempted murder, had the specific intent to kill.

The State argues in its motion for rehearing en banc that since the offense of murder under Texas Penal Code § 19.02(a)(2) does not require that a person have the specific intent to kill, the panel was incorrect in engrafting such intent into the offense of attempted murder. As authority for its argument, the State refers us to *Baldwin v. State*, 538 S.W.2d 615 (Tex. Crim. App. 1976), and *Garcia v. State*, 541 S.W.2d 428 (Tex. Crim. App. 1976). After careful reconsideration, we find the *Baldwin* analysis to be incorrect and will accordingly deny the State's Motion for Rehearing. Nevertheless, although the State did not directly attack the holding of the panel opinion that the evidence was insufficient to show an intent to kill, we will en banc on our own motion also reconsider that holding, find it erroneous, and affirm the judgment of the trial court.

Trial ct affirmed evidence insufficient

Issue 1

I. Intent Required to Commit Attempted Murder

We will first address the issue raised by the State on rehearing.

Prior to the 1973 enactment of the new penal code, Texas had neither a general attempt statute similar to Texas Penal Code § 15.01 nor a statute which authorized a conviction for murder when only an intent to cause serious bodily injury exists as is now found in Texas Penal Code § 19.02(a)(2). Although a specific intent to kill had been an essential element of the old penal code offense of assault with intent to murder, the question which arose in *Baldwin* was whether the new penal code's enactment of § 19.02(a)(2) now permitted a conviction for attempted murder when a person acts with only the intent to cause serious bodily injury.

In *Baldwin*, in an opinion approved by the Court, Commissioner Brown found that a specific intent to kill was no longer a necessary element of attempted murder.

No specific intent necessary

We initially note that § 15.01 plainly requires that a person must act "with specific intent to commit an offense." *Baldwin* attempts to construe that language to mean that a person may be convicted of an attempted offense when he acts "with the same intent required by the attempted offense." If that were the language of the statute, then it would follow that the intent necessary to support a conviction for attempted murder could be the same as that required by § 19.02(a)(2)—the intent to cause serious bodily injury. The statute, however, is not so worded.

Can we infer Δ had intent to kill off duty cop?

Indeed, § 15.01 defines the elements of criminal attempt in traditional terms. The element "with specific intent to commit an offense" has traditionally been interpreted to mean that the actor must have the intent to bring about the desired result, which in the case of attempted murder is the death of the individual.

Thus, a specific intent to kill is a necessary element of attempted murder. The authorities in support of this interpretation are numerous and convincing. Furthermore, if we were to apply the *Baldwin* interpretation of § 15.01 to the remaining subsection of § 19.02, other offenses would potentially overlap, such as attempted murder and robbery. For instance, is a person who is in the immediate flight from the commission of a robbery and who commits an act that is clearly dangerous to human life such as driving his "getaway" car the wrong way down a one-way street guilty of attempted murder even though no one is killed or even injured? According to the *Baldwin* analysis, the only intent necessary to commit attempted murder would be the intent required by § 19.02(a)(3) which in this instance would be the intent required to commit the robbery. We contend the Legislature did not intend for § 15.01 to have such absurd results. ~~Transferred Intent~~

For the reasons discussed and contrary to the State's contention, attempted murder can only be committed by a person who has the intent to commit or complete the offense of murder, viz., the intent to kill. The State's motion for rehearing is denied.

II. Sufficiency of the Evidence

We next address the issue which was not raised in the State's brief on rehearing but which will be considered on our own motion en banc. We find the panel opinion incorrectly held the evidence was insufficient to prove that the appellant had the specific intent to kill.

Was evidence sufficient?

The complainant, Dallas Police Officer Jerry M. Rhodes, testified that on the morning of April 18, 1977, around 1:00 a.m., he was driving his pickup truck down R.L. Thornton Freeway in Dallas when he observed the car in the lane just ahead of him weaving in and out of its lane. He next observed the front seat passenger stick part of his body out of the window and fire a shotgun toward the front of the car. Rhodes then testified:

Q. What happened after that?

A. Shortly thereafter we continued eastbound. I was behind the vehicle, I noticed the subject I believed had done the firing turn around and look at me. He stuck his body outside of the car.

Q. When he turned to look at you was he looking through the rear glass while inside the car or what?

A. No, sir. He stuck his body, his upper part of his body outside of the car hanging from the passenger window and turned around and looked at the vehicle behind him which was me.

Q. How much of his body was protruding out of the passenger window?

A. Probably about a third of it.

461

Q. The area around the navel or above?

A. Right, yes, sir.

Q. What did you then see him do?

A. I saw him sit back down in the vehicle and reach in the back seat, pick up something that I didn't know what it was. I was approximately fifty feet behind him. I saw him again stick part of his body out of his car and I noticed that he had a gun in his hand and the gun was fired at me.

Q. What type of gun was this?

A. This was a shotgun.

Q. When you say he fired a gun at you, you mean fired it directly at you?

A. Yes, sir. He fired it directly at me.

Q. It wasn't like he was trying to shoot your tire or anything like that?

A. No, sir.

Q. This is how great a distance?

A. Approximately fifty feet.

Q. When the shots were fired were they fired directly at you or at another part of the pickup?

A. They were fired directly at me.

Q. The muzzle of the shotgun was pointed directly at you when the blast was fired?

A. Yes, sir.

After the second shotgun blast, Rhodes passed the car, which had slowed down to about thirty-five miles per hour. He eventually exited the freeway at a spot where he felt he could drive into a service station and call the police if the other car attempted to follow him off the freeway. The other car, however, continued to travel down the freeway after Rhodes exited. Rhodes testified that while he was still on the freeway he wrote the license plate number of the car on his hand, mistaking one of the six digits. After exiting, he called the Mesquite Police Department to report the incident, describe the car and the two individuals in the car, and relay the license plate number. The next morning, Rhodes went to the Mesquite Police Department, where he had been told two suspects had been arrested, and identified appellant as the person who had fired the shotgun.

The appellant testified that although he was in the car on the night in question, he was the driver of the car. His brother, who was the passenger, was drunk and was firing a shotgun out the window of the car in an attempt to hit the lights. Appellant testified he had no knowledge of any attempt to shoot at Rhodes' pickup. His brother did not testify at trial.

The specific intent to kill may be inferred from the use of a deadly weapon, and a shotgun is a deadly weapon *per se*, unless in the manner of its use it is reasonably apparent that death or serious bodily injury could not result. For example, in *Scott v. State*, 81 S.W. 952 (Tex. Crim. App. 1904), where the defendant fired a shotgun loaded with bird or squirrel shot at the complainant who was some 125 to 200 yards away, this Court held that it was not possible that any serious injury could have been inflicted and thus the shotgun was not in the manner of its use a deadly weapon.

Applying the above rules to the facts in the instant case, the panel opinion found that the "firing of the shotgun did not occur with the capacity and under such circumstances as are reasonably calculated to produce the death of the other person," and that the evidence was insufficient to prove beyond a reasonable doubt that the appellant had the specific intent to kill. On rehearing, we find that the panel opinion failed to consider the totality of the facts before reaching its conclusion.

Rhodes specifically testified that the appellant saw him, picked up the shotgun, and aimed the shotgun directly at him before pulling the trigger. Accordingly, the question of appellant's intent to kill, under a traditional sufficiency of the evidence analysis, should be: whether any rational trier of fact could find beyond a reasonable doubt that Dennis LaFaine Flanagan had the intent to kill Jerry Rhodes when he reached into the backseat of the car he was traveling in and picked up a shotgun, leaned out the window of the car as it traveled between 50 and 60 miles per hour, aimed the shotgun muzzle directly at Jerry Rhodes who was driving a pickup truck about 50 feet behind him, and pulled the trigger of the shotgun causing it to fire?

Real Q to ask

Under this analysis, there is clearly sufficient evidence to support the trial court's finding. Appellant's act of pointing and firing the shotgun directly at Rhodes, who was driving a car only 50 feet behind him, demonstrates that it was his "conscious objective or desire" to cause the death of his target.

The judgment of the trial court is affirmed. *Holding*

Agreement

Under the common law, conspiracy required an agreement of two or more people to accomplish a criminal act (or a lawful act by unlawful means) and an overt act by one or more co-conspirators in furtherance of the conspiracy. What if someone feigned agreement, such as an undercover officer or a person who has reported a criminal overture to the police and who has been informed to play along to acquire more evidence? Because there was no meeting of the minds in this situation, there was no conspiracy under the common law. The Model Penal Code worded its conspiracy statute to focus on whether the defendant agreed, avoiding the common law approach of an agreement of two or more people. Under this "unilateral" view, a conviction becomes possible if the defendant agrees with someone who has no intention of actually committing the object crime.

The Texas conspiracy statute, 15.02 of the Texas Penal Code, uses the Model Penal Code language: "A person commits criminal conspiracy if, with intent that a felony be committed: (1) he agrees with one or more persons that they or one or more of them engage in conduct that would constitute the offense." Despite avoiding the bilateral common law language of "an agreement of two or more persons," the Court of Criminal Appeals retained the requirement of an actual agreement in *Williams v. State*, 646 S.W.2d 221 (1983), which follows in the text.

Williams v. State

646 S.W.2d 221 (Tex. Crim. App. 1983)

McCormick, Judge.

This is an appeal from a conviction for conspiracy to commit aggravated kidnapping. Punishment, enhanced by one prior conviction, was assessed at life.

Appellant argues that since the evidence shows that the appellant's only co-conspirator was feigning participation the evidence is insufficient to support a conspiracy conviction.

V.T.C.A., Penal Code, Section 15.02(a), sets out the elements of a conspiracy. They are:

(1) a person

(2) with intent that a felony be committed

(3) *agrees* with one or more persons that they or one or more of them engage in conduct that would constitute the offense; and

(4) he or one or more of them performs an overt act in pursuance of the agreement.

Thus, one of the essential elements that must be proven is an agreement between the co-conspirators to commit the offense. The *corpus delicti* of conspiracy must contain a showing of *agreement* to commit a crime. Black's Law Dictionary defines agreement as follows: "A coming or knitting together of minds; . . . the coming together in accord of two minds on a given proposition; . . . a mutual assent to do a thing . . . ."

If an indictment alleges a conspiracy between only two individuals, but the evidence at trial shows that there was no actual, positive agreement to commit a crime, then the evidence is insufficient to support a conviction for conspiracy.

The evidence adduced at the trial of this cause shows that in June of 1977 Steve Jennings, appellant's alleged co-conspirator, was asked by Lt. David Golden of the Dallas Police Department to cultivate a friendship with appellant. Jennings was to report any suspicious activity to Lt. Golden. Around August 1, 1977, appellant asked Jennings if he was interested in making big money. Jennings replied affirmatively. During the next two weeks, appellant asked Jennings if kidnapping would bother him. When Jennings replied "no", appellant told Jennings he was setting up a kidnapping whereby a ransom of $100,000 would be paid and they would make a sixty-forty split of the ransom money. Through the month of August the plans for the kidnapping were formulated. The victim was to be the son of appellant's former employer. Appellant told Jennings his job was to stay with the boy until after the money was picked up. They were to keep the boy in a vacant apartment in the apartment building which appellant managed. Appellant told Jennings that after the ransom had been paid they would kill the boy and bury him in the river bottoms off Military Parkway. Other plans and preparations were made.

465

On Friday, September 16, 1977, two days before the kidnapping was to occur, Jennings contacted Lt. Golden and told him of the plans. Jennings was wired for sound by police officers and Jennings met with the appellant for further discussion of the kidnapping. This conversation was recorded by the police. Jennings' telephone was also tapped and, at the police officers' request, he phoned appellant on Saturday and talked with appellant further about the kidnapping plan. Appellant was arrested later that day at his place of business.

At trial, Jennings testified that it was never his intention to go along with the kidnapping. Rather, he was involved merely to get information for Lt. Golden.

In *Woodworth v. State,* 20 Tex.App. 375 (1886), the defendant was charged with conspiring to commit burglary with intent to steal. At trial, defendant's sole co-conspirator testified that his only purpose in going along with the plan was to expose the defendant and in fact he did report the plan to the sheriff. This Court found that the transaction between the defendant and his alleged co-conspirator did not constitute a conspiracy in that the co-conspirator never intended to commit, or to assist in the commission of the burglary. He merely feigned his assent, and thus the evidence was insufficient to support the defendant's conviction for conspiracy.

> Our Penal Code defines the offense of conspiracy to be a positive agreement entered into between two or more persons to commit one of certain named offenses, burglary being one of the offenses named. PENAL CODE, Arts. 800, 802, 804. An "agreement," as defined by Webster, is "the union of two or more minds in a thing done or to be done. A coming or knitting together of minds." One of the definitions of the term given by Bouvier is: "A coming together of parties in opinion or determination; the union of two or more minds in a thing done or to be done; a mutual assent to do a thing." Another definition quoted by the last named author is, that it "consists of two persons being of the same mind, intention, or meaning, concerning the matter agreed upon." 1 BOUV. LAW DIC., title "Agreement."

Woodworth v. State, supra, at 381, 382.

In the case at bar, we find there was no meeting of the minds between the alleged co-conspirators. There was no criminal intent in the minds of both individuals. Thus, there could be no conspiracy.

The State argues that Section 15.02, *supra,* was written so as to adopt a unilateral approach and thus each individual's culpability should be determined without regard to the disposition of the other alleged co-conspirators. And to a certain extent, we agree.[37] However,

---

37. We believe this is why the Legislature was so careful in its wording of Section 15.02(c), which provides:
> (c) It is no defense to prosecution for criminal conspiracy that:
> > (1) one or more of the coconspirators is not criminally responsible for the object offense;
> > (2) one or more of the coconspirators has been acquitted so long as two or more coconspirators have not been acquitted;
> > (3) one or more of the coconspirators has not been prosecuted or convicted, has been convicted of a different offense, or is immune from prosecution;
> > (4) the actor belongs to a class of persons that by definition of the object offense is legally incapable of committing the object offense in an individual capacity; or

the essence of the conspiracy statute is aimed directly at the increased danger to society presented by criminal combinations.

Because we have found the evidence insufficient to show an agreement as required by Section 15.02, the judgment is reversed and the cause is reformed to show an acquittal.

---

(5) the object offense was actually committed.

Special Intent for Conspiracy

A conspiracy creates two separate bases of criminal liability: first, for the agreement that constitutes the conspiracy itself; and second, for any crimes committed by coconspirators that are reasonably foreseeable. Conspiracy is punished as a separate offense because of the dangers of people acting together to accomplish a criminal purpose. One of the critical questions in conspiracy law is how specific the agreement must be. An express agreement that fully establishes all the details is not necessary. Few criminal conspiracy agreements are written or comprehensive. An agreement can be sufficient for criminal liability even if it is contingent upon future events and all of the details about what will be expected to occur are vague. Nonetheless, as the *Garcia* case demonstrates, some agreements may be insufficient to meet the specific-intent requirement for inchoate offenses. The sometimes ambiguous nature of conspiracy is illustrated by the *James* case, after *Garcia* in the text. However, *James* shows that the conspiratorial objective can be ambiguous, contingent on other events, and involve spontaneous acts without preventing a finding of a criminal agreement.

United States v. Garcia

151 F.3d 1243 (9th Cir. 1998)

Reinhardt, Circuit Judge.

In this case, we consider whether testimony regarding the existence of an implicit, general agreement among gang members to support one another in fights against rival gangs can constitute sufficient evidence to support a conviction of conspiracy to commit assault when the conduct of the alleged conspirators is otherwise insufficient.

One evening, a confrontation broke out between rival gangs at a party on the Pasqua Yaqui Indian reservation. The resultant gunfire injured four young people, including appellant Cody Garcia. Two young men involved in the shooting, Garcia and Noah Humo, were charged with conspiracy to assault three named individuals with dangerous weapons. A jury acquitted Humo but convicted Garcia. Because there is no direct evidence of an agreement to commit the criminal act which was the alleged object of the conspiracy, and because the circumstances of the shootings do not support the existence of an agreement, implicit or explicit, the government relied heavily on the gang affiliation of the participants to show the existence of such an agreement. We hold that gang membership itself cannot establish guilt of a crime, and a general agreement, implicit or explicit, to support one another in gang fights does not provide substantial proof of the specific agreement required for a conviction of conspiracy to commit assault. The defendant's conviction therefore rests on insufficient evidence, and we reverse.

Background

The party at which the shootings occurred was held in territory controlled by the Crips gang. The participants were apparently mainly young Native Americans. While many of the attendees were associated with the Crips, some members of the Bloods gang were also present. Appellant Cody Garcia arrived at the party in a truck driven by his uncle, waving a red bandanna out the truck window and calling out his gang affiliation: "ESPB Blood!" Upon arrival, Garcia began "talking smack" to (insulting) several Crips members. Prosecution witnesses testified that Garcia's actions suggested that he was looking for trouble and issuing a challenge to fight to the Crips at the party.

Meanwhile, Garcia's fellow Bloods member Julio Baltazar was also "talking smack" to Crips members, and Blood Noah Humo bumped shoulders with one Crips member and called another by a derogatory Spanish term. Neither Baltazar nor Humo had arrived with Garcia, nor is there any indication that they had met before the party to discuss plans or that they were seen talking together during the party.

At some point, shooting broke out. Witnesses saw both Bloods and Crips, including Garcia and Humo, shooting at one another. Baltazar was seen waving a knife or trying to stab a Crip. The testimony at trial does not shed light on what took place immediately prior to the shooting, other than the fact that one witness heard Garcia ask, "Who has the gun?" There is some indication that members of the two gangs may have "squared off" before the shooting

469

began. No testimony establishes whether the shooting followed a provocation or verbal or physical confrontation.

Four individuals were injured by the gunfire: the defendant, Stacy Romero, Gabriel Valenzuela, and Gilbert Baumea. Stacy Romero who at the time was twelve years old was the cousin both of Garcia's co-defendant Humo and his fellow Blood, Baltazar. No evidence presented at trial established that any of the injured persons was shot by Garcia, and he was charged only with conspiracy. The government charged both Garcia and Humo with conspiracy to assault Romero, Valenzuela, and Baumea with dangerous weapons under 18 U.S.C. §§ 371, 113(a)(3) and 1153; Humo alone was charged with two counts of assault resulting in serious bodily injury under 18 U.S.C. §§ 113(a)(6) and 1153.

After a jury trial, Humo was acquitted on all counts. Garcia was convicted of conspiracy to assault with a dangerous weapon and sentenced to 60 months in prison. He appeals on the ground that there was insufficient evidence to support his conviction.

Sufficiency of the Evidence

In order to prove a conspiracy, the government must present sufficient evidence to demonstrate both an overt act and an agreement to engage in the specific criminal activity charged in the indictment. While an implicit agreement may be inferred from circumstantial evidence, proof that an individual engaged in illegal acts with others is not sufficient to demonstrate the existence of a conspiracy. Both the existence of and the individual's connection to the conspiracy must be proven beyond a reasonable doubt.

The government claims that it can establish the agreement to assault in two ways: first, that the concerted provocative and violent acts by Garcia, Humo and Baltazar are sufficient to show the existence of a prior agreement; and second, that by agreeing to become a member of the gang, Garcia implicitly agreed to support his fellow gang members in violent confrontations.

However, no inference of the existence of any agreement could reasonably be drawn from the actions of Garcia and other Bloods members on the night of the shooting. An inference of an agreement is permissible only when the nature of the acts would logically require coordination and planning. The government presented no witnesses who could explain the series of events immediately preceding the shooting, so there is nothing to suggest that the violence began in accordance with some prearrangement. The facts establish only that perceived insults escalated tensions between members of rival gangs and that an ongoing gang-related dispute erupted into shooting. Testimony presented at trial suggest more chaos than concert. Such evidence does not establish that parties to a conspiracy "worked together understandingly, with a single design for the accomplishment of a common purpose." *United States v. Melchor–Lopez*, 627 F.2d 886, 890 (9th Cir. 1980).

Given that this circumstantial evidence fails to suggest the existence of an agreement, we are left only with gang membership as proof that Garcia conspired with fellow Bloods to shoot the three named individuals. The government points to expert testimony at the trial by a local gang unit detective, who stated that generally gang members have a "basic agreement" to back one another up in fights, an agreement which requires no advance planning or coordination. This testimony, which at most establishes one of the characteristics of gangs but not a specific objective of a particular gang—let alone a specific agreement on the part of its members to accomplish an illegal objective—is insufficient to provide proof of a conspiracy to commit assault or other illegal acts.

Recent authority in this circuit establishes that "membership in a gang cannot serve as proof of intent, or of the facilitation, advice, aid, promotion, encouragement or instigation needed to establish aiding and abetting." *Mitchell v. Prunty*, 107 F.3d 1337, 1342 (9th Cir. 1997). In overturning the state conviction of a gang member that rested on the theory that the defendant aided and abetted a murder by "fanning the fires of gang warfare," the *Mitchell* opinion expressed concern that allowing a conviction on this basis would "smack of guilt by association." *Id.* at 1342. The same concern is implicated when a conspiracy conviction is based on evidence that an individual is affiliated with a gang which has a general rivalry with other gangs, and that this rivalry sometimes escalates into violent confrontations.

The *Mitchell* court reasoned that the conviction in that case necessarily rested on the faulty assumption that gang members typically act in a concerted fashion. Such an assumption would be particularly inappropriate here. Acts of provocation such as "talking smack" or bumping into rival gang members certainly does not prove a high level of planning or coordination. Rather, it may be fairly typical behavior in a situation in which individuals who belong to rival gangs attend the same events. At most, it indicates that members of a particular gang may be looking for trouble, or ready to fight. It does not demonstrate a coordinated effort with a specific illegal objective in mind. The fact that gang members attend a function armed with weapons may prove that they are prepared for violence, but without other evidence it does not establish that they have made plans to initiate it. And the fact that more than one member of the Bloods was shooting at rival gang members also does not prove a prearrangement—the Crips, too, were able to pull out their guns almost immediately, suggesting that readiness for a gunfight requires no prior agreement. Such readiness may be a sad commentary on the state of mind of many of the nation's youth, but it is not indicative of a criminal conspiracy.

Finally, as the *Mitchell* panel warned, allowing gang membership to serve as evidence of aiding and abetting "would invite absurd results. Any gang member could be held liable for any other gang member's act at any time so long as the act was predicated on the common purpose of 'fighting the enemy.'" *Mitchell*, 107 F.3d at 1341. Similarly, allowing a general agreement among gang members to back each other up to serve as sufficient evidence of a conspiracy would mean that any time more than one gang member was involved in a fight it would constitute an act in furtherance of the conspiracy and all gang members could be held criminally responsible—whether they participated in or had knowledge of the particular criminal act, and whether or not they were present when the act occurred. Indeed, were we to accept "fighting the enemy" as an illegal objective, all gang members would probably be subject to felony prosecutions sooner rather than later, even though they had never personally committed an improper act. This is contrary to fundamental principles of our justice system. "[T]here can be no conviction for guilt by association . . . ." *Melchor–Lopez*, 627 F.2d at 891.

Because of these concerns, evidence of gang membership cannot itself prove that an individual has entered a criminal agreement to attack members of rival gangs. Moreover, here the conspiracy allegation was even more specific: the state charged Garcia with conspiracy to assault three specific individuals—Romero, Baumea and Valenzuela—with deadly weapons. Even if the testimony presented by the state had sufficed to establish a general conspiracy to assault Crips, it certainly did not even hint at a conspiracy to assault the three individuals listed in the indictment. Of course, a more general indictment would not have solved the state's problems in this case. In some cases, when evidence establishes that a particular gang has a specific illegal objective such as selling drugs, evidence of gang membership may help to link gang members to that objective. However, a general practice of supporting one another in fights, which is one of the ordinary characteristics of gangs, does not constitute the type of illegal objective that can form the predicate for a conspiracy charge.

Conclusion

Because the government introduced no evidence from which a jury could reasonably have found the existence of an agreement to engage in any unlawful conduct, the evidence of conspiracy was insufficient as a matter of law. A contrary result would allow courts to assume an ongoing conspiracy, universal among gangs and gang members, to commit any number of violent acts, rendering gang members automatically guilty of conspiracy for any improper conduct by any member. We therefore reverse Garcia's conviction and remand to the district court to order his immediate release.

Reversed and remanded.

United States v. James

528 F.2d 999 (5th Cir. 1976)

Brewster, District Judge.

This appeal involves seven appellants, each of whom was convicted for one or more of the offenses charged in a four court indictment.

Each of the seven appellants was convicted under Count I alleging a conspiracy in violation of 18 U.S.C. § 371, to commit the offenses of (1) assault on federal officers engaged in the performance of their duties, in violation of 18 U.S.C. § 111, (2) of using firearms to commit the assault in violation of 18 U.S.C. § 924(c), and (3) of unlawfully possessing unregistered firearms required by law to registered, in violation of 26 U.S.C. § 5861(d). The firearms were described as an automatic rifle, a fragmentation bomb and incendiary devices. Three overt acts hereinafter after discussed were alleged.

Henry, Shillingford, Norman and James were the only appellants named in Counts II and III charging respectively the substantive offenses above described as the first and second objects of the conspiracy. James was the only defendant named in Count IV, which charged him with the substantive offense above described as the third object of the conspiracy.

Each defendant was found guilty by a jury of all of the charges against him. Toni Austin and Ann Lockhart, the two female defendants, were each sentenced to three years on her Count I conviction. Henry, Shillingford, Norman and James each received a seven year sentence on his Count II conviction. The sentence on each of the other convictions was five years. By provision for concurrent and consecutive sentences on their convictions, Henry, Shillingford, Norman and James each had twelve years to serve.

The date of the commission of each of the substantive offenses was August 18, 1971. The conspiracy charged in Court I was claimed to have begun on or about July 15 and to have continued to and including August 18, when it culminated in a shoot-out at about 6:30a.m. between FBI Agents and members of the police force of Jackson, Mississippi, on the one hand, and the appellants on the other, at the "capitol" of the Republic of New Africa (RNA) in Jackson, resulting in the death of a Jackson policeman, the wounding of another and of an FBI Agent. The FBI was there to execute an arrest warrant on Jerry R. Steiner in pursuance of a complaint charging him with unlawful interstate flight to avoid prosecution on a first degree murder charge in Michigan. The Jackson police were participating to execute warrants on misdemeanor charges on three persons they had good reason to believe were in the house with Steiner and others. The warrant was not served on Steiner because, for some reason that was never satisfactorily explained, he left the house at 11:00p.m. on the night before the visit by the FBI to serve the warrant on him. The FBI had no knowledge of his departure until after the shoot-out.

A general knowledge of the RNA is necessary to an understanding of this case. The appellants claim that hostility of the FBI and the Jackson law enforcement officers toward the RNA caused such officers to use the arrest warrants as a pretext to intrude and search RNA

Core Issue: What is the agreement?

properties on August 18th. The government contends that the purposes and setup of the RNA furnished both the motive and the framework for the actions of the appellants that constituted the offenses here involved. The fugitive Steiner and all of the appellants, except Ann Lockhart, were "citizens" of the RNA; and some of the appellants were high officials of it.

The RNA claims that it is an independent foreign nation composed of "citizens" descended from Africans who were at one time slaves in this country.

The provisional "capitol" of the RNA on August 18 was a residential building at 1148 Lewis Street in Jackson, but the RNA was in the process of moving it to another residential building in Jackson at 1320 Lynch Street. The officers of the RNA worked and lived in the "capitol." Some "citizens" and a few potential "citizens" also stayed in the "capitol" for periods of time. An armed guard was usually stationed at or near the entrance of the "capitol," and persons not well known to them were searched before being allowed to enter. "Citizens" in the "capitol" had been seen to point weapons at police cars as they drove by.

"Security" was an uppermost concern of those who worked in the 'capitol'. A substantial part of the time of a three day RNA meeting known as "The People's Center Conference" (PCC), held in Jackson in mid-July, attended by "citizens" of RNA from Africa and throughout the United States, was devoted to discussion of security measures for its officials and "capitol." RNA "citizens" were "cautioned to be wary of bad faith arrest tactics which might come from local police." Military-type drills with weapons were held periodically from the time of such meeting until August 18. The "citizens" participating in those drills were taught that, upon the command, "jump," they should get their weapons and go to certain vantage points where they could fire at persons trying to "intrude" the "capitol." They kept their long guns stacked, military-style, in one of the rooms of the "capitol" where they would be readily accessible if a "jump" order were given.

Appellant Henry was President of the RNA during all of the period pertinent to this case.

The FBI kept advised of the developments of the RNA through a paid black informer who posed as a "citizen" of RNA and was on the "inside."

On the late evening of August 13, after regular business hours, a teletype message was received by the FBI office in Jackson, from the Detroit, Michigan FBI office on the exclusive wire for FBI communications that on that date a complaint had been filed in Grand Rapids, Michigan charging one Jerry R. Steiner, also known as Sylee Lagondele Omos, I., with violation of 18 U.S.C. § 1073, by unlawful flight to avoid prosecution on a first degree murder charge, and that an arrest warrant, a copy of which was enclosed, had been issued by United States District Judge Engel of Grand Rapids. Steiner was charged by the State of Michigan with the first degree murder of a 17 year old service station attendant, who was shot in the back of the head during a robbery of the station at which he was employed. A state warrant was outstanding against him on the murder charge. The teletype also advised the FBI that Steiner had in the past resisted arrest and should be considered extremely dangerous in view of that resistance and of the first degree murder charge.

In mid-July, Agent Holder of the Jackson office of the FBI received information from an unrecalled source that Steiner was in Jackson, and was later advised by a confidential informant "who had never been found to be unreliable" that on August 17 Steiner was present at the Lewis Street provisional "capitol" of the RNA and there was no reason to believe that he would soon be leaving that address. Agent Holder first knew that Steiner was a fugitive wanted for murder when he saw the teletype in FBI headquarters on Monday morning, August 16, at the time that matter was assigned to him. The teletype also gave a detailed description of Steiner.

The teletype was received and acted upon during the time the RNA was in the process of moving its "capitol" from 1148 Lewis Street to 1320 Lynch Street in Jackson.

In accordance with [a] prearranged plan, agents and officers took positions around the two buildings. At 6:30a.m. the occupants of 1148 Lewis Street were advised over a bullhorn or megaphone by Special Agent Amann that FBI agents and officers of the Jackson Police Department had the residence completely surrounded; that the officers had warrants for the arrest of four occupants at that address; and that within 60 seconds all residents were to surrender immediately through the front door with their arms extended over their heads. After the first 60 second announcement was made by Amann that they were there to arrest four fugitives, that everyone in the house was to come out; and that if they would, the officers would take the fugitives in custody and leave, the agents heard the sound of running footsteps inside the house. After the expiration of 60 seconds, there was a lapse of several more seconds at which time an announcement was made that if the occupants did not come out within 15 seconds, tear gas would be fired. At the end of those 15 seconds, there was no response from the occupants; and after several more seconds had elapsed, Linberg gave orders via walkie-talkie radios to fire tear gas cannisters into the rear windows of the building, which was done. Simultaneously with the firing of the tear gas, or instantaneously thereafter, a heavy barrage of automatic and other rifle fire came from inside the "capitol;" and shooting from there continued for about twenty minutes. Special Agents and police officers returned the fire. During the barrage, Jackson Police Detective Lt. Louis Skinner was killed by a rifle bullet through his head, Jackson Police Officer Billy Crowell was shot in the shoulder, and Special Agent Stringer of the FBI was seriously wounded by a rifle bullet through his thigh.

After about 20 minutes, seven occupants identified as Larry Jackson, and the appellants, James, Lockhart, Stalling, Toni Rene Austin, Norman, and Shillingford, emerged from the rear of the building and were taken into custody by FBI agents and placed under arrest for assaulting a federal officer. All of the individuals were immediately searched, and FBI Agent Agnew located a bullet clip containing live 7.62 millimeter rifle cartridges in the pistol pocket of appellant James. [Numerous weapons were found in the building.]

A's arguments

All of the appellants contend that the evidence is insufficient to support any conviction under the conspiracy count. The principal grounds urged in support of this contention are: (1) the evidence did not show (a) any agreement to assault, intimidate or interfere with anyone, or (b) any "knowledge that federal officers would come in conflict with the essentially defensive precautions;" or (2) any connection of any individual defendant with the conspiracy. In addition, they claim that the indictment fails to show any logical relationship between the offense alleged as the third object (unlawful possession of unregistered firearms required to be registered) of the conspiracy and the overt acts. We are of the opinion that there is no merit in any of the contentions except the one that the evidence is insufficient to show Ann Lockhart was a participant in the conspiracy.

All of the appellants except Ann Lockhart were "citizens" of the RNA. As such, they were working with and under the appellant Henry, the militant President of the RNA in the "capitol." They were members of his "underground army" and his "crack security guard." A poster on the wall in the "capitol" at the time of and for some time prior to the shoot-out stated: "Our most important gratuity is an intelligent underground army which, if the Republic is attacked will burn white America to the ground as mercilessly as a missile attack." Official pamphlets were also distributed among the "citizens" at the "capitol" on how to destroy city utility systems. The Jackson police served a warrant on Henry about a week before August 18; and he advised Police Lt. Skinner, the officer who was mortally wounded in the shootout, that the RNA would be ready for the officers the next time. An RNA official issued a press release stating that the RNA "heavily armed, crack security guard" could effectively slaughter several scores of officers. The "capitol" at Lewis Street was an armed fortress, with guns, ammunition, underground bunker, escape tunnel, holes in the foundations through which shots would be fired, and armed guards on duty at the entrance. Appellant Henry was 43 years old, but the other appellant RNA "citizens" were much younger. Most of them were around 20 and made eager members of the RNA "crack security guard." Preparations for a violent and deadly confrontation with law enforcement officers had been taking place for some time before the August 18 shoot-out. As has already been pointed out, much of the time of the three-day national meeting of the RNA in mid-July was devoted to "security" measures for RNA officers and property; and the caution was issued to be "warned of bad faith tactics which might come from local police." Henry sometimes carried a rifle with a scope on it while in the "capitol" and a .45 automatic pistol when on speaking engagements elsewhere. The members of the security guard were also given karate lessons. The preparations at the "capitol" included "jump" drills, wherein each "citizen" there was taught to take a designated position with a loaded gun at an opening and shoot at objectionable intruders, especially law enforcement officers. This evidence and much more leaves no doubt that the appellant RNA citizens were participants in a plan to defy, intimidate and shoot it out with any law enforcement officers, federal or state, when the opportunity presented itself. The federal government was the one which they thought was standing in the way of their acquisition of the five southern states they were claiming. When the notice was given over a bullhorn on the morning of August 18 that FBI Agents and local police were at the Lewis Street "capitol," the "jump" command was given, and the "crack security guard" engaged in "combat-win procedures" that resulted in killing one Jackson policeman, wounding another one and an FBI Agent.

The facts above stated, along with others included in the statement of the case at the beginning of the opinion, are adequate to establish a common plan among the appellants alleged as the basis of the conspiracy. The actions of the defendants themselves are always important circumstances from which to draw inferences of a conspiracy. *United States v. Warner*, 441 F.2d 821, 830 (5th Cir. 1971). The manner in which the appellants acted during the shoot-out on the morning of August 18 was strong evidence of a common plan and certainly showed concerted action. They did not go about things haphazardly in trying to carry out what some of the RNA "citizens" had called their "combat-win procedures." The evidence of a common plan or unlawful combination is much stronger in this case than it was in many of the cases cited under this heading, where the evidence was held to be sufficient. There is no doubt that there was a common plan to defy, intimidate and shoot it out with any law enforcement officers when the opportunity presented itself.

common plan does not have to be express agreement

The following legal principles support the Court's holding that the evidence is sufficient to show the existence of the agreement or common design which formed the basis for the conspiracy alleged in the indictment. To establish the common plan element of a conspiracy, it is not necessary for the government to prove an express agreement between the alleged conspirators to go forth and violate the law. The "common purpose and plan may be inferred from a 'development and collocation of circumstances.'" "A conspiracy is seldom born of 'open covenants openly arrived at.'" "The proof, by the very nature of the crime, must be circumstantial and therefore inferential to an extent varying with the conditions under which the crime may be committed." Knowledge by a defendant of all details or phases of a conspiracy is not required. It is enough that he knows the essential nature of it. "And, it is black letter law that all participants in a conspiracy need not know each other; all that is necessary is that each know that it has a 'scope' and that for its success it requires an organization wider than may be disclosed by his personal participation."

The appellants' claim that there is no evidence to show any "knowledge that federal officers would come in conflict with the essentially defensive precautions" is based upon the argument that some time before the shoot-out, the appellants claim that the "citizens" were instructed to avoid shooting at federal officers. The jury did not have to believe their claim; but even if it was true, inferences that such instructions were later abandoned or superseded could be drawn from the facts already detailed. The "combat-win procedures" were well planned and set up for the appellant RNA "citizens" to go into concerted violent action against any law enforcement officers when the "jump" command was given. They were eagerly awaiting the chance. A strong circumstance showing that federal officers were within the contemplation of the plan is that after the appellants at the Lewis Street "capitol" were advised in the loud tones of a bullhorn that FBI Agents were present to serve a federal warrant, the "jump" command was given and the "combat-win procedures" were put into action. If it had been a part of the plan not to use the "procedures" against federal officers, it is only logical to conclude that the command would not have been given and the plan would not have been put into effect when the appellants heard that FBI Agents were among the officers present and participating. There is no merit in this contention. *Contention not upheld*

Conspiracy = common scheme, small evidence

The claims of each of the appellants that the evidence is insufficient to connect him or her with the conspiracy, if it was established, must be judged in the light of the legal principles that follow in this paragraph. Once the existence of a common scheme of a conspiracy is shown, slight evidence is all that is required to connect a particular defendant with the conspiracy. The connection may be shown by circumstantial evidence. "A person may be held as a conspirator *Rule:* although he joins the criminal concert at a point in time far beyond the initial act of the conspirators. If he joins later, knowing of the criminal design, and acts in concert with the original conspirators, he may be held responsible, not only for everything which may be done thereafter, but also for everything which has been done prior to his adherence to the criminal design . . . ." The fact that a conspirator is not present at, or does not participate in, the commission of any of the overt acts does not, by itself, exonerate him.

A few conclusory comments based on the facts already set out will suffice in the discussion of the question of the sufficiency of the evidence to show the connection, or lack of it, of each defendant with the conspiracy. It would unduly lengthen this opinion to do otherwise.

Henry. He was the President of RNA. All of the "security" measures and "combat-win procedures" were planned and practiced under his direct supervision. He had made public threats of violence against law enforcement officers who might come to the "capitol." Within less than a month of the shoot-out, he held a meeting wherein instructions were given RNA "citizens" to shoot people, especially police officers and FBI Agents, who might try to intrude the "capitol." The shoot-out went according to the plan and procedure he had helped set up. While he was at the Lynch Street house to which the "capitol" was being moved, instead of the Lewis Street "capitol," at the time of the shoot-out, his presence and participation in the shoot-out were not necessary to support his conviction under the conspiracy count. *Posey v. United States*, 416 F.2d 545, 556 (5th Cir. 1969). In the Posey case, the killings within the contemplation of a conspiracy by members of the White Knights, "a self-styled militant organization," were carried out. The defendant who was the Imperial Wizard of the White Knights claimed that the evidence was insufficient to connect him with the conspiracy on the ground that he was not present at and did not participate in the killings. The court held that such proof was not necessary. So it is here. The overwhelming evidence shows that this tragedy would not have taken place except for the work of Henry.

Norman. He was Vice-President of RNA, and had been actively involved in RNA in Jackson for some time. He and President Henry designated the chain of command for the security forces. He assisted Henry in the RNA meeting in July when instructions were given to shoot intruders attempting to enter the "capitol," especially police and FBI Agents. He admitted just after the shoot-out that he was a participant in it. He said he was firing a British 303 gun from inside the house.

James. He held the title of Interior Minister of the RNA. He lived at the Lewis Street 'capitol' for most of six weeks before August 18. He was a participant in the 'combat-win procedure' drills. He was in charge of the arsenal of some 30 weapons and ammunition to be used in carrying out the common plan. It was his job to assign the weapons to members of the crack security guard. He discussed the bomb and the Molotov cocktails with such members and told them how to use them. He told the officers shortly after the shoot-out that he had shot at any white man he saw. His fingerprints were on the automatic rifle found under the house beside a pile of spent rounds after the shoot-out He was one of the main actors in the conspiracy.

Toni Rene Austin. As Minister of Finance of the RNA, she was in charge of the treasury. She lived with her husband, appellant James, in the room in the back part of the "capitol" where the arsenal and ammunition for the security guard were kept. She did guard duty at the "capitol," and participated in the "jump" drills. On July 27, she wrote out a list of ammunition to be bought for use by the security guard. The ammunition was not purchased until the night before the shoot-out. She was in the "capitol" when the officers made their announcements on the morning of August 18, but did not come out until forced by tear gas to do so after the shoot out.

Shillingford. He was a "citizen" of the RNA. He had come to Jackson a few days before the shoot-out to participate in the RNA activities at the "capitol." He stayed at the "capitol" and was an active "citizen" there. He was the one who went on the night of August 17 and got the ammunition which was on the list prepared by appellant Toni Austin on July 27. He was a member of the crack security guard, and fired an M—1 rifle from his station inside the west part of the "capitol" during the shoot-out.

Stalling. He was an active "citizen" of the RNA. He lived in the Lewis Street "capitol." He helped dig the escape tunnel which was to figure importantly in the security procedures when it was finished. He did active guard duty at the "capitol" and participated in the "jump" drills. He took the female defendants to the escape tunnel during the shooting.

Under the circumstances, a reasonably-minded jury could well conclude beyond a reasonable doubt that the conspiracy alleged actually existed, and that the appellants, Henry, Norman, James, Austin, Shillingford and Stalling, were each members of it. That leaves the question of the sufficiency of the evidence to connect Ann Lockhart with it.

Lockhart. Her residence was in Wisconsin. She was not a "citizen" of RNA, but she obviously sympathized with its objectives. Her husband was appellant Norman, the Vice-President of RNA. She had spent over a month of the summer in Africa, and was not in Jackson for the People's Center Council in July. She arrived at the Lewis Street "capitol" on August 16, and stayed with her husband until after the shoot-out. On August 16 and 17, she purchased groceries and prepared meals for the occupants of the "capitol." Her stopover there was intended to be very short, as her plans were to leave for North Carolina on the morning of August 18. The evidence is insufficient to show that she had any knowledge of the conspiracy or participation in it. There is nothing in the record to justify making her responsible for her husband's unlawful conduct. Mere presence at the scene of a crime or mere association with the members of a conspiracy is not enough to prove participation in it. In *United States v. Webb*, 359 F.2d 558, 562 (6th Cir. 1966), where circumstances similar to those involving Lockhart here were present, the Court said:

> Defendant Stokely's unexplained presence during such a series of suspicious events might well justify grave doubts about her role. But neither association with conspirators nor knowledge that something illegal is going on by themselves constitute proofs of participation in a conspiracy.

The able trial judge realized the seriousness of this question, for, in his discussion of the sufficiency of the evidence to take the case to the jury, he said:

> I determine that there is substantial evidence upon which a jury might reasonably base a finding that the defendants are guilty beyond a reasonable doubt of the charges against them in the indictment although I have some questions in my mind concerning defendant Ann Lockhart, a/k/a Tamu Sanna.

The conviction of Ann Lockhart on Count I is therefore reversed. Holding

Notes

1.   The *mens rea* for conspiracy involves two intents: first, the intent to agree; and second, the intent to accomplish the criminal act. Some completed offenses involve an agreement without creating a separate crime of conspiracy. For example, in a sale of illegal drugs, both the seller and buyer are committing a crime. Because the buyer and seller agreed to a sale, have they created a criminal conspiracy? A simple agreement between a buyer and seller to exchange something of value for cocaine is itself a substantive crime, but "something more" is necessary for the existence of a drug distribution conspiracy. There must be a further understanding between the buyer and seller, often implicit, that usually relates to the subsequent distribution of the narcotics, particularly if the volume of the transactions becomes so great that it raises the inference of further transactions.

2.   A street corner transaction for heroin is clearly illegal, whether it be a substantive offense alone or also part of a conspiracy. Another issue arises if a person who is engaged in a legal business does business with a criminal conspiracy. What if the person or company knows that a business transaction will result in the item sold being used in an illegal manner? Does knowledge of that use combined with continued sales equal an agreement to form or join a conspiracy? *Direct Sales Co. v. United States*, 319 U.S. 703 (1943), involved a corporate drug manufacturer that sold much of its wares by mail order. A regular postal customer of the company was a small-town physician, Dr. Tate, who frequently ordered massive quantities of morphine, far in excess of what he could lawfully dispense in the course of his practice. Even after the Bureau of Narcotics informed the company that it was being used as a source for illicit redistribution and that an average physician would not legitimately require the size lots that it offered for sale, the company continued to sell to Tate unusually large amounts of morphine at a deep discount. Eventually the company was convicted of conspiring with Dr. Tate to illegally distribute the drug. The Supreme Court unanimously upheld a challenge to the sufficiency of the evidence relying in large part on the economic benefit from the sales to the company in concluding that the leap from knowledge to agreement could be inferred.

3.   One of the best-known conspiracy cases dealing with a legitimate business with knowledge that the goods and services are being used for an illegal purpose is *People v. Lauria*, 251 Cal.App.2d 471, 59 Cal. Rptr.628 (Cal. App. 2 1967). During a prostitution investigation, an undercover police woman called Lauria, who ran a telephone answer service used by three suspected prostitutes who were under investigation. When the undercover officer hinted that she was a prostitute concerned with the secrecy of her activities and their concealment from the police, Lauria's office manager assured her that the operation of the service was discreet and "about as safe as you can get." The undercover officer later told Lauria that her business was modeling, and she had been referred to the answering service by Terry, one of the three prostitutes under investigation. She complained that because of the operation of the service she had lost two valuable customers, referred to as "tricks." Lauria defended his service, but he did not respond to the hints of the undercover officer that she needed customers in order to make money, saying that "his business was taking messages."

Lauria and the three prostitutes were indicted for conspiracy to commit prostitution, but the trial court set aside Lauria's indictment as having been brought without probable cause. The

State appealed, arguing that since only a tacit, mutual understanding is necessary to establish a conspiracy, Lauria's act of continuing to provide the answering service after becoming aware it was being used to help run an illegal business was sufficient. Lauria admitted he knew some of his customers were prostitutes, but the California appellate court affirmed the dismissal of the indictment. The court refused to equate providing a legal good or service combined with knowledge of another's criminal activity with conspiracy to further such criminal activity.

The *Lauria* Court distinguished *Direct Sales* (see the previous note) on the ground that the step from knowledge to intent and agreement could be taken in *Direct Sales* because there was more than "acquiescence, carelessness, indifference, lack of concern." Rather, the grossly inflated volume of sales demonstrated an "informed and interested cooperation, stimulation, instigation." The Direct Sales company had acquired a "stake in the venture," which made them a conspirator rather than merely a vendor indifferent to the use of the product. In the absence of evidence of charging higher prices to clients using the phone service for illegal purposes or an inflated volume that benefits the supplier, furnishing a legal service did not make Lauria a conspirator with intent to achieve the illegal purpose, despite his knowledge of the criminal enterprise.

The most controversial aspect of *Lauria* was its dicta suggesting the possibility of a different result for conspiracies involving more serious criminal objectives:

> A supplier who furnishes equipment which he *knows* will be used to commit a serious crime may be deemed from that knowledge alone to have intended to produce the result. . . . For instance, . . . the operator of a telephone answering service with positive knowledge that his service was being used to facilitate the extortion of ransom, the distribution of heroin, or the passing of counterfeit money who continued to furnish the service with knowledge of its use, might be chargeable on knowledge alone with participation in a scheme to extort money, to distribute narcotics, or to pass counterfeit money. The same result would follow the seller of gasoline who knew the buyer was using his product to make Molotov cocktails for terroristic use.

> With respect to misdemeanors, we conclude that positive knowledge of the supplier that his products or services are being used for criminal purposes does not, without more, establish an intent of the supplier to participate in the misdemeanors. With respect to felonies, we do not decide the converse, *viz.*, that in all cases of felony knowledge of criminal use alone may justify an inference of the supplier's intent to participate in the crime.

In Texas, the criminal objective must be a felony. Thus, the approach in *Lauria* would be less helpful to a Texas defendant. However, *Lauria* did not rule on the result in felony cases and even the dicta did not suggest that the refusal to take the step from knowledge to intent and agreement in all felony cases. The suggestion that a different inference of agreement from knowledge applies depending upon the gravity of the offense has been criticized as an expedient rule that lacks the consistency and notice required of penal statutes. However, in an area of law that is unclear and infrequently litigated, *Lauria* remains one of the most frequently cited and discussed cases.

The Act Requirement for Attempt

Persons convicted of a criminal attempt are punished for their *mens rea*, which has to be inferred without the benefit of a completed crime. Perhaps a helpful way to look at the act requirement for attempt crimes is that the role of the mental state and act are reversed from that in completed offenses. With completed crimes, we hope to deter and punish harmful acts, but the mental state requirement is the filter that prevents imposition of criminal penalties on those not deserving of blame. (I killed the victim but it was an accident.) In contrast, with attempt crimes, the harm has not occurred, and the defendant is punished for his guilty intention. The act requirement acts as the filter to make sure that someone in fact intends or to save from criminal convictions those who only contemplated criminal activity but never seriously advanced towards carrying out that intent. Thus, in attempt law, the question of whether the act has gone far enough to establish criminality is a difficult and important question.

The standard for determining whether there has been a sufficient act for attempt liability varies in different states, but the trend has been toward the approach taken in Model Penal Code. That approach asks whether the defendant has taken a substantial step towards completion. This approach is in contrast to the common law, which examined what remained to be done to complete the crime when it was interrupted. The test was sometimes stated in terms of whether the defendant's acts approached a "dangerous proximity" towards completion, and in some cases found an insufficient act if an "indispensable element" remained to be accomplished.

The "substantial step" standard of the Model Penal Code takes the position that it is better policy to look at what the defendant has done than to speculate about what remains to be done. Federal courts have generally adopted the "substantial step" approach, as does the Fifth Circuit Court of Appeals in *Mandujano*, a case that was based upon events occurring in San Antonio.

equivocality

United States v. Mandujano

499 F.2d 370 (5th Cir. 1974)

Rives, Circuit Judge.

Mandujano appeals from the judgment of conviction and fifteen-year sentence imposed by the district court, based upon the jury's verdict finding him guilty of attempted distribution of heroin. We affirm.

The government's case rested almost entirely upon the testimony of Alfonso H. Cavalier, Jr., a San Antonio police officer assigned to the Office of Drug Abuse Law Enforcement. Agent Cavalier testified that, at the time the case arose, he was working in an undercover capacity and represented himself as a narcotics trafficker. At about 1:30 P.M. on the afternoon of March 29, 1973, pursuant to information Cavalier had received, he and a government informer went to the Tally-Ho Lounge, a bar located on Guadalupe Street in San Antonio. Once inside the bar, the informant introduced Cavalier to Roy Mandujano. After some general conversation, Mandujano asked the informant if he was looking for "stuff." Cavalier said, "Yes." Mandujano then questioned Cavalier about his involvement in narcotics. Cavalier answered Mandujano's questions, and told Mandujano he was looking for an ounce sample of heroin to determine the quality of the material. Mandujano replied that he had good brown Mexican heroin for $650.00 an ounce, but that if Cavalier wanted any of it he would have to wait until later in the afternoon when the regular man made his deliveries. Cavalier said that he was from out of town and did not want to wait that long.

Mandujano offered to locate another source, and made four telephone calls in an apparent effort to do so. The phone calls appeared to be unsuccessful, for Mandujano told Cavalier he wasn't having any luck contacting anybody. Cavalier stated that he could not wait any longer. Then Mandujano said he had a good contact, a man who kept narcotics around his home, but that if he went to see this man, he would need the money "out front." To reassure Cavalier that he would not simply abscond with the money, Mandujano stated, "[Y]ou are in my place of business. My wife is here. You can sit with my wife I am not going to jeopardize her or my business for $650.00." Cavalier counted out $650.00 to Mandujano, and Mandujano left the premises of the Tally-Ho Lounge at about 3:30 P.M. About an hour later, he returned and explained that he had been unable to locate his contact. He gave back the $650.00 and told Cavalier he could still wait until the regular man came around. Cavalier left, but arranged to call back at 6:00 P.M. When Cavalier called at 6:00 and again at 6:30, he was told that Mandujano was not available. Cavalier testified that he did not later attempt to contact Mandujano, because, "Based on the information that I had received, it would be unsafe for either my informant or myself to return to this area."

The only other government witness was Gerald Courtney, a Special Agent for the Drug Enforcement Administration. Agent Courtney testified that, as part of a surveillance team in the vicinity of the Tally-Ho Lounge on March 29, 1973, he had observed Mandujano leave the bar around 3:15 or 3:30 P.M. and drive off in his automobile. The surveillance team followed

Mandujano but lost him almost immediately in heavy traffic. Courtney testified that Mandujano returned to the bar at about 4:30 P.M.

Mandujano urges that his conduct as described by agent Cavalier did not rise to the level of an attempt to distribute heroin. He claims that at most he was attempting to <u>acquire</u> a controlled substance, <u>not to distribute it</u>; that it is impossible for a person to attempt to distribute heroin which he does not possess or control; that his acts were only preparation, as distinguished from an attempt; and that the evidence was insufficient to support the jury's verdict.

In *United States v. Noreikis*, the court commented that,

> While it seems to be well settled that mere preparation is not sufficient to constitute an attempt to commit a crime, it seems equally clear that the semantical distinction between preparation and attempt is one incapable of being formulated in a hard and fast rule. The procuring of the instrument of the crime might be preparation in one factual situation and not in another. The matter is sometimes equated with the commission of an overt act, the "doing something directly moving toward, and bringing him nearer, the crime he intends to commit."

481 F.2d 1177, 1181 (7th Cir. 1973).

The courts in many jurisdictions have tried to elaborate on the distinction between mere preparation and attempt. See the Comment at 39-48 of Tent. Draft No. 10, 1960 of the Model Penal Code.[1]

Although the foregoing cases give somewhat varying verbal formulations, careful examination reveals fundamental agreement about what conduct will constitute a criminal attempt. First, the defendant must have been acting with the kind of culpability otherwise required for the commission of the crime which he is charged with attempting.

---

1. This comment to the Model Penal Code catalogues a number of formulations which have been adopted or suggested, including the following:

> (a) The physical proximity doctrine—the overt act required for an attempt must be proximate to the completed crime, or directly tending toward the completion of the crime, or must amount to the commencement of the consummation.

> (b) The dangerous proximity doctrine—a test given impetus by Mr. Justice Holmes whereby the greater the gravity and probability of the offense, and the nearer the act to the crime, the stronger is the case for calling the act an attempt.

> (c) The indispensable element test—a variation of the proximity tests which emphasizes any indispensable aspect of the criminal endeavor over which the actor has not yet acquired control.

> (d) The probable desistance test—the conduct constitutes an attempt if, in the ordinary and natural course of events, without interruption from an outside source, it will result in the crime intended.

> (e) The abnormal step approach—an attempt is a step toward crime which goes beyond the point where the normal citizen would think better of his conduct and desist.

> (f) The *res ipsa loquitur* or unequivocality test—an attempt is committed when the actor's conduct manifests an intent to commit a crime.

Second, the defendant must have engaged in conduct which constitutes a substantial step toward commission of the crime. A substantial step must be conduct strongly corroborative of the firmness of the defendant's criminal intent. The phrase "substantial step," rather than "overt act," is suggested by *Gregg v. United States, supra* ("a step in the direct movement toward the commission of the crime"); *United States v. Coplon, supra* ("before he has taken the last of his intended steps"); and *People v. Buffum, supra* ("some *appreciable fragment* of the crime"), and indicates that the conduct must be more than remote preparation.

The district court charged the jury in relevant part as follows:

> Now, the essential elements required in order to prove or to establish the offense charged in the indictment, which is, again, that the defendant knowingly and intentionally attempted to distribute a controlled substance, must first be a specific intent to commit the crime, and next that the accused willfully made the attempt, and that a direct but ineffectual overt act was done toward its commission, and that such overt act was knowingly and intentionally done in furtherance of the attempt.
>
> In determining whether or not such an act was done, it is necessary to distinguish between mere preparations on the one hand and the actual commencement of the doing of the criminal deed on the other. Mere preparation, which may consist of planning the offense or of devising, obtaining or arranging a means for its commission, is not sufficient to constitute an attempt, but the acts of a person who intends to commit a crime will constitute an attempt where they, themselves, clearly indicate a certain unambiguous intent to willfully commit that specific crime and in themselves are an immediate step in the present execution of the criminal design, the progress of which would be completed unless interrupted by some circumstances not intended in the original design.

These instructions, to which the defendant did not object, are compatible with our view of what constitutes an attempt.

After the jury brought in a verdict of guilty, the trial court propounded a series of four questions to the jury:

> (1) Do you find beyond a reasonable doubt that on the 29th day of March, 1973, Roy Mandujano, the defendant herein, knowingly, willfully and intentionally placed several telephone calls in order to obtain a source of heroin in accordance with his negotiations with Officer Cavalier which were to result in the distribution of approximately one ounce of heroin from the defendant Roy Mandujano to Officer Cavalier? **NO**
>
> (2) Do you find beyond a reasonable doubt that the telephone calls inquired about in question no? (1) Constituted overt acts in furtherance of the offense alleged in the indictment? **Yes**
>
> (3) Do you find beyond a reasonable doubt that on the 29th day of March, 1973, Roy Mandujano, the defendant herein, knowingly, willfully and intentionally requested and received prior payment in the amount of $650.00 for approximately one ounce of heroin that was to be distributed by the defendant Roy Mandujano to Officer Cavalier? **Yes**

(4) Do you find beyond a reasonable doubt that the request and receipt of a prior payment inquired about in question no? (3) Constituted an overt act in furtherance of the offense alleged in the indictment? *yes*

Neither the government nor the defendant objected to this novel procedure. After deliberating, the jury answered "No" to question (1) and "Yes" to questions (3) and (4). The jury's answers indicate that its thinking was consistent with the charge of the trial court.

The evidence was sufficient to support a verdict of guilty under section 846. Agent Cavalier testified that at Mandujano's request, he gave him $650.00 for one ounce of heroin, which Mandujano said he could get from a "good contact." From this, plus Mandujano's comments and conduct before and after the transfer of the $650.00, as described in Part I of this opinion, the jury could have found that Mandujano was acting knowingly and intentionally and that he engaged in conduct—the request for and the receipt of the $650.00—which in fact constituted a substantial step toward distribution of heroin. From interrogatory (4), it is clear that the jury considered Mandujano's request and receipt of the prior payment a substantial step toward the commission of the offense. Certainly, in the circumstances of this case, the jury could have found the transfer of money strongly corroborative of the firmness of Mandujano's intent to complete the crime. Of course, proof that Mandujano's "good contact" actually existed, and had heroin for sale, would have further strengthened the government's case; however, such proof was not essential.

 For the reasons stated in this opinion, the judgment is Affirmed.

Notes

1.   Many jurisdictions, including Texas have not adopted a particular test for determining when acts are sufficient to constitute an attempt, but rather, make an ad hoc determination based upon the facts of the case with only the general guidance provided by the attempt statute, Section 15.01 of Texas Penal Code, which requires that actions must have passed the point of "mere preparation."

2.   The problem of sufficient act for attempt can be complicated for crimes like burglary, which already have an anticipatory thrust. The crime is complete at the moment of entry with intent. In *McCravy v. State*, 642 S.W.2d 450 (Tex. Crim. App. 1980), the defendant claimed that his burglary indictment should be dismissed because it did not state an offense. The indictment alleged that the defendant's action in going to the roof of the building turning off electrical power were overt acts beyond preparation that constituted a sufficient act to be attempted burglary. On original submission the Court sustained the defendant's argument that the indictment did not state an offense:

> Though clearly an "act," "climbing to the roof" equally clearly is not an act which tends to effect an "intrusion" or "entry" to the building. The allegation of "turning off electrical power" informs neither that appellant did, or did not, do an act which tended to intrude any part of appellants body or any physical object connected with it. As such, the

indictment fails to allege that appellant committed an act which amounted to more than mere preparation which tended but failed to effect commission of an intended burglary.

On motion for rehearing, the Court changed its position and ruled in favor of the state's position that the allegations stated acts that go beyond mere preparation. The Court stated on rehearing:

> [O]ur earlier opinion requires an allegation of acts which [would require] the performance of a "last proximate act" . . . . As a practical matter, the question presented is at what point we will draw the imaginary line which separates the allegation of an act that amounts to no more than "mere preparation" from the allegation of an act which "tends . . . to effect the commission of the offense . . . ." We do not believe that the intent of Sec. 15.01 was to draw this line at the "last proximate act." There is necessarily a "gray area" between an allegation of a situation which is clearly no more than mere preparation, and an allegation of a situation in which the accused is discovered clearly engaged in the last act prior to a successful entry. It is this "gray area" into which the present case falls.

3. Consider the analysis of the issue in *People v. Coleman*, 86 N.W.2d 281, 285 (Mich. 1957) which appears to employ an equivocality approach:

> The purchase of a fountain pen intended for forgery would doubtless be deemed merely an act of preparation. Likewise, even the purchase of a hunting rifle, secretly intended for the murder of the neighbor, though equally useful for the hunting of deer. Not so, however, the placing of a bomb so connected that it would explode when the occupant of the house turned on his radio. An important difference between the acts is this: In the former cases, the acts of the defendant have never gone beyond acts of an ambiguous nature. The purchase . . . is as consistent with good as with evil. Not so the placing of the bomb, although in each case the ultimate result is not yet accomplished.

Chapter 22: Solicitation, Abandonment, and Impossibility

Solicitation

The issue of whether a sufficient act has occurred to warrant inchoate criminal liability is an important issue only in attempt cases. Little or no act is required with the offenses of solicitation and conspiracy impossibility because the act of seeking agreement is demonstration that the defendant is committed enough to carry out his criminal desires to involve others in the scheme. In contrast, attempt can be committed alone. The special dangerous of group criminality also help to justify finding a fully-baked inchoate crime early in the scheme. Any overt act committed by any conspirator is sufficient to achieve a fully-baked conspiracy. As the *Invatury* case illustrates, no act beyond the solicitation itself is required to qualify as the inchoate offense of solicitation. If the defendant in *Invatury* had been prosecuted for attempt, it might be a close case as to whether a sufficient act had been committed for attempt liability but no such question is raised with regard with regard to solicitation.

Ivatury v. State of Texas

792 S.W.2d 845 (Tex. App.—Dallas 1990)

Kinkeade, Justice.

Chandrasekhar Ivatury appeals his conviction of criminal solicitation of capital murder. After a jury found him guilty, it assessed punishment at twenty years' confinement in the Texas Department of Corrections[1] and a $10,000 fine. Ivatury argues: (1) that the evidence is insufficient to support his conviction; (2) that the State did not disprove Ivatury's theory of entrapment … [W]e affirm the judgment of the trial court.

Facts

Patrick Fahey, a United States Customs Service agent, first became aware of Ivatury during a December 1988 investigation of an illegal transfer of high technology to Communist Bloc countries. After Ivatury heard that Agent Fahey was asking questions about him, he called Agent Fahey to set up a meeting. Ivatury told Agent Fahey that in exchange for complete immunity and the right to carry a gun, he could guarantee an espionage conviction against the primary individuals under investigation based on a computer tape he possessed about the Stealth bomber. Ivatury also indicated he had information regarding the removal of technical data from a defense contractor, the December murder of the owner of the Million Dollar Saloon, and the production and sale of counterfeit United States passports and entry stamps. The government refused Ivatury's request for immunity and Agent Fahey obtained a grand jury subpoena to acquire the computer tape, which Ivatury never produced. Unable at this point to further pursue the espionage investigation of Ivatury, Agent Fahey proceeded to the next area of investigation, passport fraud.

In pursuit of this new investigation, Agent Fahey instructed Michael Borer, a confidential informant, to call Ivatury in an attempt to obtain a counterfeit passport. Borer and Ivatury exchanged numerous phone calls and finally agreed to meet. During one of the taped phone calls, Ivatury told Borer that if Agent Fahey kept pushing his buttons, Agent Fahey was going to get hurt. Later at the tape recorded meeting, they also discussed Agent Fahey. Ivatury stated to Borer that he had asked his lawyer what would happen if "he took Agent Fahey out." The lawyer told him that he would have about ten thousand FBI agents "standing on him." After reviewing these tapes, Agent Fahey's supervisor instructed Borer to continue the investigation of the passport fraud and to ask Ivatury at their next face-to-face meeting if he was serious about killing Agent Fahey. During that next meeting, Borer told Ivatury that he knew "a kid from the Philippines [who was in reality undercover agent Enrique Villarma] that would do him [Agent Fahey] in a heartbeat," to which Ivatury responded "How much?" and asked for his phone number. In a later phone conversation with Borer, Ivatury stated he had a photograph of Agent Fahey that Villarma could use to identify him.

Upon Villarma's arrival in Dallas, Ivatury met with him in Villarma's hotel room. Due to technical difficulties the agents were unable to tape this meeting, but Agent Fahey, who was in the next room, overheard the entire meeting through a connecting double door. Ivatury told

489

Villarma what he wanted done. After Villarma asked Ivatury if he knew who he was dealing with when he said the man he wanted to kill was a customs agent, Ivatury responded "Yes, this is no big deal. I have done it before." They then discussed how and when Villarma would make the hit and how much it would cost. In a subsequent phone conversation, Ivatury gave Villarma Agent Fahey's work address and telephone numbers. The two then arranged a second meeting. Ivatury missed the meeting because he said he lacked transportation. The two then arranged for Villarma to pick Ivatury up for another meeting. At this meeting Ivatury offered to provide a computer, a high power rifle, portable telephone, or anything else Villarma might need to make the hit. After this meeting, Agent Fahey placed Ivatury under arrest.

Agent Fahey obtained a search warrant for Ivatury's house and safety deposit box. Although not specifically listed as an item sought in the search warrant, Agent Fahey discovered a computer tape, of the special type used in the defense industry, in the safety deposit box. However, neither of the searches conducted pursuant to the warrants produced a rifle, picture of Agent Fahey, or money.

Entrapment

Ivatury contends that a rational trier of fact could not have found that the State disproved the theory of entrapment beyond a reasonable doubt. He argues that the United States Customs supervisor instructed Borer to pursue him and that Borer first mentioned murdering Agent Fahey. Section 8.06 of the Texas Penal Code provides:

> (a) It is a defense to prosecution that the actor engaged in the conduct charged because he was induced to do so by a law enforcement agent using persuasion or other means likely to cause persons to commit the offense. Conduct merely affording a person an opportunity to commit an offense does not constitute entrapment.

TEX. PENAL CODE ANN. § 8.06 (Vernon 1974). The entrapment defense becomes available if the officer specifically instructed his agent or informant to use an improper procedure to "make a case" against a particular defendant. *Rangel v. State*, 585 S.W.2d 695, 699 (Tex. Crim. App. 1979). Section 8.06 adopts an objective test for entrapment, and once the court makes a determination that an inducement occurred, its only consideration becomes the nature of the police activity involved, without reference to the predisposition of the particular defendant. *Johnson v. State*, 650 S.W.2d 784, 788 (Tex. Crim. App.1983).

In the instant case, Ivatury told Borer that if Agent Fahey kept pushing his buttons, Agent Fahey was going to get hurt. Ivatury also told Borer that he had asked his lawyer what would happen if he took Agent Fahey out. Ivatury made both of these statements prior to the customs supervisor instruction to Borer to ask Ivatury at their next face-to-face meeting if he was serious about killing Agent Fahey. At that next meeting, after Ivatury continued to complain about Agent Fahey, Borer told Ivatury, "You ought to quit . . . fuckin' with him. I got a kid from the Philippines who would do him in a heartbeat." Ivatury immediately responded, "How much?" and asked for the hit man's phone number.

Further, Borer testified at trial that he did not bring up the idea of killing Agent Fahey with Ivatury and that he never indicated to Ivatury that he would like to see Agent Fahey killed.

This evidence shows that Ivatury originated the idea of harming Agent Fahey and that no inducement occurred. Because Ivatury failed to prove that the customs agents induced him to commit the offense, no entrapment occurred. We overrule his third point of error.

Sufficiency of the Evidence

Ivatury contends that the evidence is insufficient to support the conviction. Ivatury argues that the State failed to prove that he acted with the intent that a capital murder be committed. He further argues that the alleged solicitation was not made under circumstances "strongly corroborative" of his intent that the other person act on the solicitation. When determining whether the evidence is sufficient to support the conviction, we view the evidence in the light most favorable to the verdict to determine whether any rational trier of fact could have found the essential elements of the crime beyond a reasonable doubt. In evaluating whether sufficient evidence of corroboration exists, this court eliminates from consideration the accomplice testimony and then determines whether other incriminating evidence remains, which tends to connect the defendant with the crime. To support a conviction for criminal solicitation pursuant to section 15.03 of the Texas Penal Code, the evidence must establish that the defendant acted knowingly and with a specific intent that a capital murder be committed. *See* TEX. PENAL CODE ANN. § 15.03(a). Although the statute requires conduct of an active and positive nature, no requirement exists that the offense occur at the beginning of an actor's involvement in a criminal enterprise. The statute disallows a conviction for criminal solicitation based solely on the uncorroborated testimony of the person allegedly solicited. The circumstances surrounding the solicitation must strongly corroborate both the solicitation itself and the actor's intent that the other person act on the solicitation. *See* TEX. PENAL CODE ANN. § 15.03(b).

In the instant case, Ivatury first brought up the idea of harming Agent Fahey during a taped phone conversation with Borer. Ivatury affirmatively stated to Borer, "The way I look at it, he's gonna push one too many buttons as it is and the boy's gonna get hurt." During a subsequent tape recorded meeting with Borer, Ivatury relayed a conversation he had with his lawyer stating, "I told my lawyer that, okay, I said what if I take Fahey out, okay?" He further asked his lawyer, "I said Denver, what happens if Patric [sic] Fahey disappears?"

Agent Fahey testified that when he played these tapes for his supervisor, his supervisor became concerned for Agent Fahey's safety and instructed Borer at his next face-to-face meeting with Ivatury to ask him if he was serious about killing Agent Fahey and having him disappear. Pursuant to these instructions, after Ivatury continued to complain about Agent Fahey, Borer said, "You ought to quit . . . fuckin' with him. I, I got a kid from the Phillipeans [sic] that would do him in a heartbeat." Ivatury immediately responded, "How much?" He later asked for the hit man's phone number.

Agent Fahey also testified to what he overheard at the first meeting between Ivatury and the hit man, Villarma. When Villarma asked Ivatury what he wanted, Ivatury responded, "I need to get someone taken care of." After Ivatury identified the person as a customs agent, Villarma said, "Do you know who you're ... fuckin' with?" Ivatury replied, "Yes, this is no big deal. I have done it before." When Villarma quoted Ivatury a price of $10,000, Ivatury responded, "Fine." In a subsequent taped phone conversation between Ivatury and Villarma, Ivatury furnished the hit man with Agent Fahey's name, work address, and phone numbers. He also agreed to bring the money and a photograph of Agent Fahey to their next meeting. Although Ivatury failed to appear for that meeting, he gave Villarma a plausible excuse for his nonappearance and set up a third meeting where he did appear.

Ivatury's words and conduct reflect an active and positive desire that a capital murder be committed. They indicate that he acted knowingly and with a specific intent to solicit Villarma to commit the capital murder of Agent Fahey. Even with the elimination of Villarma's testimony, sufficient incriminating evidence remains, which tends to connect Ivatury with the offense and strongly corroborates the seriousness of his intent. There remains Borer's testimony, the intended victim, Agent Fahey's testimony, and the tape recordings of Ivatury's communications with Borer and Villarma, which clearly evidence his intent. The tape recordings alone sufficiently corroborate Ivatury's intent.

Abandonment

Under the common law, once one had committed a sufficient act to be considered an attempt, or once one had agreed to form or join a criminal conspiracy and an overt act had been performed by any conspirator, the defendant had reached the point of no return with regard to inchoate crime liability. The actor or actors could think better of their criminal desires at the eleventh hour and avoid criminal liability for the completed crime, but such an abandonment did not undo the inchoate offense, just as putting back the property taken in a completed theft did not prevent a theft conviction.

The drafters of the Model Penal Code took the position that it would be sound policy to create an incentive for those far down the road of a criminal plan to renounce that objective even if the point of a full-blown attempt or conspiracy had been reached. Following the Model Penal Code, many states, including Texas, now allow renunciation as a defense to an attempted crime. Other jurisdictions—including the federal courts—do not. However, the defense is not easy to establish in those jurisdictions that do recognize it. The typical renunciation defense is available only to those who chose to renounce the object crime rather than those who get cold feet because of a fear that the criminal plan will not succeed. It is difficult to determine whether the actors withdrew out of motive to shun criminal activity or were prevented from committing the crime by external forces. The *Scott* case that follows addresses this issue.

burned ex's house & car

Scott v. State

No. 2-06-335-CR, 2007 WL 2460254 (Tex. App—Fort Worth, Aug. 31, 2007)

Anne Gardner, Justice.

Appellant David Scott appeals from his convictions for attempted arson of a habitation and attempted arson of a vehicle. In two points, he argues the evidence is legally and factually insufficient to support the trial court's rejection of his renunciation defense. We affirm.

Background

A grand jury indicted Appellant for attempted capital murder, arson of a habitation, and arson of a vehicle by pouring gasoline on the home and vehicle of complainants Carol Alruwaili and Najjma Alruwaili and starting a fire. Pursuant to a plea agreement, the State abandoned the attempted capital murder charge, Appellant entered an open plea of guilty to attempted arson of a habitation and attempted arson of a vehicle, and the trial court found him guilty.

The issue of punishment was tied to the court. Appellant testified in his defense. The record shows that in the early morning hours of November 6, 2005, Appellant got drunk and high on cocaine and marijuana. Walking part of the way and riding a bicycle part of the way, he went to the home of his fifteen-year-old ex-girlfriend, Najjma, who lived with her parents. Once there, he attempted to call her on his cell phone. Najjma hung up on him the first time he called; the second and third times he called, one of Najjma's friends cursed at him. Appellant testified that he became "real angry" and described his mood as "storming" and "raging."

He found a gasoline can lying near the house, and he poured gasoline on the house and the car in the driveway. Appellant testified, "I wanted to light it on fire. But every time I lit a piece of paper, it just, like, kept going out. I'd try to find something else. It kept going out." Appellant denied that the gasoline ever ignited. The following colloquy then occurred between him and his counsel:

Q. At some point did you change your mind about what you were doing?

A. Yes, sir, I did.

Q. And what were you thinking at that time as far as what you were doing?

A. By then, like, the-you know, the drugs and alcohol was, like, wearing off. I was sobering up. It was kind of chilly outside, too. And I just started thinking, you know, saying I'm tripping, you know. Like, I just threw the gasoline can on the ground, threw the piece of paper on the ground. I didn't try to cover nothing or hide nothing up. And I walked off, you know.

Q. So you decided to abandon your effort.

A. Yes, sir.

494

Q. Is that right?

A. Yes, sir.

. . . .

Q. [A]t what point did you decide that you weren't going to proceed with this crime?

A. Just standing there, you know, I was thinking like-you know what I'm saying? . . . I don't even need to be doing this. So I threw the gasoline can on the ground, threw the paper on the ground, and I walked off . . . .

Q. Was it voluntary on your part?

A. Yes, sir . . . .

Q. There wasn't anything, anything outside—any other factors involved other than your decision that you weren't going to do that?

A. No, sir. It was just me. It was dark. There was nobody coming down the streets or neighbors looking out windows. There was nothing like that.

The State also introduced into evidence Appellant's written statement to police, in which he stated that he threw burning paper on the car in an attempt to set the gasoline on fire.

Fire Marshal Ricky Jones, who examined the scene later that morning, found several pieces of charred paper that appeared to have been set on fire. Although Appellant testified that the gasoline never ignited, Jones testified that gasoline on both the car and the house ignited and burned briefly.

Carol Alruwaili, Najjma's mother, testified that she awoke between 4:00 and 5:00 a.m. on the morning in question and noticed the very strong odor of gasoline in the house. Following the odor through the house, she determined that it was coming from outside the garage. She opened the door and thought that she saw a person crouched in the bushes. Alruwaili went back into the house, turned on an exterior light, went back outside, and found a gas can in the bushes. She immediately called 911.

During punishment-phase argument, Appellant's counsel argued that Appellant had renounced his criminal objective and was entitled to a one-grade reduction in punishment under penal code section 15.04(d). The trial court sentenced Appellant to ten years' confinement for attempted arson of a vehicle and seventeen years' confinement for attempted arson of a habitation.

Attempted Arson

A person commits arson if the person starts a fire, regardless of whether the fire continues after ignition, with intent to destroy or damage any habitation or vehicle. *Id.* at § 28.02(a)(2) (Vernon Supp. 2006). Arson of a habitation is a first degree felony, and arson of a vehicle is a second degree felony. *Id.* at § 28.02(d). A person commits attempted arson if, with specific intent to commit arson, he does an act that amounts to more than mere preparation but fails to effect the commission of arson. *Id.* at § 15.01(a). Attempted arson is one punishment grade lower than arson, *i.e.*, attempted arson of a habitation is a second degree felony and attempted arson of a vehicle is a state jail felony. *See id.* at § 15.01(d).

Renunciation

Penal Code section 15.04(d) allows admission of evidence of renunciation in mitigation of punishment for inchoate offenses. Evidence that a defendant renounced his criminal objective by abandoning his criminal conduct before the criminal offense was committed and that he made a substantial effort to prevent commission of the object offense is admissible as mitigation evidence at the hearing on punishment if he has been found guilty of criminal attempt. If the factfinder finds that the defendant renounced his criminal objective, the punishment shall be one grade lower than that provided for the offense committed.

Renunciation of an inchoate offense under section 15.04(d) is a punishment-phase affirmative defense. The defendant has the burden of proving an affirmative defense by a preponderance of the evidence. TEX. PENAL CODE ANN. § 2.04(d) (Vernon 2003).

Discussion

Applying the appropriate standards of review, we hold that the evidence is legally and factually sufficient to support the trial court's implicit rejection of Appellant's renunciation defense. Appellant testified that he tried but failed to ignite the gasoline, but Fire Marshal Jones testified that the gasoline was ignited on both the house and the car but failed to sustain combustion. Under section 28.02's definition of arson—starting a fire, regardless of whether the fire continues after ignition, with the intent to destroy or damage a habitation or vehicle—this testimony not only supports the rejection of Appellant's renunciation defense, but tends to show that he actually succeeded in committing the offense of arson before he left the scene. See TEX. PENAL CODE ANN. § 28.02(a). A reasonable factfinder could also conclude from Carol Alruwaili's testimony that Appellant was hiding in the bushes outside her door and abandoned his attempt to burn down the house only when she turned on the outside light. Thus, the evidence is legally sufficient to support the trial court's rejection of the renunciation defense. Further, considering all the evidence relevant to renunciation, we cannot say that the trial court's rejection of the defense is so against the great weight and preponderance of the evidence as to be manifestly unjust; thus, the evidence is factually sufficient.

We overrule Appellant's two points, and we affirm the trial court's judgment.

Holding

Notes

1.   The renunciation defense applies to all three inchoate crimes in Texas, but there are different considerations depending on which of the inchoate crimes is involved. The defense requires that the commission of the crime must be avoided. Merely walking away from a

conspiracy may be insufficient to prevent completion because the other conspirators may continue. On the other hand, prevention can be achieved with a single actor abandoning attempting a crime. However, discerning the motivation of the actor who silently quits the criminal enterprise may be difficult.

2.	Assume a person decides to shoplift and conceals an item, but thinks better of it before walking out of the store. Is this a voluntary renunciation if the person's decision if it was prompted by a sign that said: "shoplifting is wrong"? What if the sign said "shoplifting is a crime," or "shoplifters will be prosecuted"? Would the defendant qualify for the defense in any of these circumstances, in all, or in none?

3.	Federal law does not recognize renunciation as a defense to conspiracy, but does allow the defense of withdrawal. Unlike the defense of renunciation, withdrawal is not a complete defense—it ends future liability, but it does not undo past liability. However, withdrawal can become a complete defense if the defendant withdraws from the conspiracy and the statute of limitations then runs before charges are filed.

Impossibility in Attempt Crimes

The question of whether one can be convicted of an attempt to commit a crime that was impossible to commit is a difficult question to which courts have frequently given contradictory answers. The question is one that arises in attempt crimes because, both by common law tradition and statutory codification, impossibility is not a bar to a conviction of solicitation and conspiracy. For example, Section 15.03 of the Texas Penal Code, the Texas solicitation statute, prohibits the solicitation of a qualifying crime with intent to commit an act that "under the circumstances surrounding his conduct as the actor believes them to be, would constitute the felony." The conspiracy statute has similar language. This language means, for example, that the fact the intended victim of your solicitation or conspiracy to murder has already died (unbeknownst to the actor) makes no difference. The fact that the actor can no longer cause the death of the victim does not prevent soliciting or conspiring to accomplish this impossible objective. This is not always the case with attempt. The difference in treatment has been explained by the dangerousness associated with the willingness to engage in organized criminal activity.

The guiding principle with attempt is that impossibility does not bar criminal liability for attempt if it is only factually impossible to commit the offense, but that if commission of the offense is legally impossible, no criminal liability is possible. Some cases of impossibility in attempt are easier than others. All agree that if the defendant falsely believes the intended act is criminal and it is not, there is no crime. If the drinking age is lowered again to 18, but the defendant who is 20 didn't get the memo, engaging in drinking that the person falsely thinks is illegal does not make that act a crime.

If the defendant is a pickpocket and he puts his hand into the intended victim's empty pocket instead of the one with the victim's wallet, the fortuity of the empty pocket saves the defendant from a completed theft, but not an attempted theft. This is an example of factual impossibility. However, some types of impossibility are hybrids of fact and law and have produced confusion that's caused the drafters of the Model Penal Code to eliminate the impossibility bar.

The classic case of legal impossibility that is based upon a factual mistake is the *Jaffe* case. The defendant bought fabric at a very low price; so low that Jaffe believed the cloth was stolen. Clearly he was not guilty of receiving stolen goods because he did not receive anything that was stolen. Had the facts been as he believed, however, he would have received stolen goods and he could be convicted of attempted receiving stolen goods under the Model Penal Code. In the majority of states that still distinguish legal and factual impossibility, Jaffe would not be guilty of attempt because it is considered to be legally impossible to be guilty of the offense when there are no stolen goods involved.

The fact and law distinction is not easy to maintain in a consistent manner. Consider our previous example of the defendant who wants to kill someone who is deceased. This is like *Jaffe* because there is no live victim to be killed, just as there were no stolen goods. However, if the defendant fires a gun into a room where he mistakenly thinks the intended victim is located, that is only factual impossibility. Are you satisfied with a rule that allows one person to engage in similar conduct with dissimilar liability? Furthermore, the distinction is often unsatisfactory. The attempt to bribe a juror is overturned as legal impossibility because the person that the defendant attempted to bribe was not a juror. *See Booth v. State*, 398 P.2d 863 (Okla. 1964). Like *Jaffe* where there were no stolen goods, there is no juror. But there are other jurors, and the next time the defendant might get to one and undermine the legal system.

A majority of the Texas Court of Criminal Appeals in *Lawhorn v. State*, 898 S.W.2d 886 (Tex. Crim. App. 1995), stated that legal impossibility is a valid defense in Texas attempt law, while factual impossibility is not. Judge Meyers dissented, advocating the Model Penal Code position. The *Hair, Chen*, and *Oviedo* cases that follow assume that the legal and factual impossibility distinction remains the law, and the courts grapple with making the distinction.

Stolen TV

United States v. Hair

356 F. Supp. 339 (D.D.C. 1973)

Flannery, District Judge.

Officer James E. Blackburn of the Metropolitan Police Department was advised by a previously reliable informer that the defendant had expressed an interest in buying a stolen television set. The informer also advised Officer Blackburn that he had sold stolen merchandise to the defendant on more than five occasions within the past year and on at least two occasions within the past month. On at least four of the occasions, the sale of the stolen merchandise was consummated in a grocery store operated by the defendant.

Officer Blackburn then secured a new color television which he gave to the informer with instructions to sell it to the defendant and to advise the defendant that it was a stolen set. The informer proceeded to follow the Officer's directions and sold the television set to the defendant at his grocery store, advising him that it had been stolen.

Issue

The core question in this case is whether the defendant committed a crime when he received the color television set from the informer with intent to defraud, believing the property to be stolen, when, in fact, the property had not been stolen. The government contends that the defendant had committed the crime of attempted receiving stolen property and that the applicable statutes, 22 D.C. CODE §§ 22-1031 and 22-22052, permit the construction that an attempt to receive stolen property is a crime even though the property is not stolen. The defendant on the other hand asserts the defense of impossibility, maintaining that the act of attempted or actual receipt of property which was not, in fact, stolen is not a crime in the District of Columbia.

There is no statutory or case law in the District of Columbia dealing with this question, but the subject has been discussed in other jurisdictions. In *People v. Jaffe*, 78 N.E. 169 (N.Y. 1906), the Court of Appeals for New York held that where the property was not stolen, there can be no attempted receipt of stolen property. In *Jaffe* a clerk stole goods from his employer under an agreement to sell them to the accused, but before delivery of the goods, the theft was discovered and the goods were recovered. Later, the employer redelivered the goods to the clerk to sell to the accused who purchased them for about half of their value believing them to be stolen. The court held that the goods had lost their character as stolen goods at the time the defendant had purchased them and that his criminal intent was insufficient to sustain a conviction for an attempt to receive stolen property knowing it to have been stolen. In *People v. Rollino*, 233 N.Y.S.2d 580 (1962), the Supreme Court of New York followed the holding in the Jaffe case and found that an unsuccessful attempt to do that which is not a crime, when effectuated, cannot be held to be an attempt to commit the crime specified. Since the completed act did not and could not, as a matter of law, constitute larceny, the court held that it was legally impossible for the defendant to be guilty of attempted larceny. The rationale of the *Jaffe* case has been followed in other jurisdictions.

The California courts have held that there may be the crime of attempt to receive stolen property even though the property is not stolen. *See e. g., People v. Parker*, 31 Cal.Rptr. 716

(1963); *People v. Meyers*, 28 Cal. Rptr. 753 (1963); *People v. Rojas*, 358 P.2d 921 (1961); *People v. Camodeca*, 338 P.2d 903 (1959); *Faustina v. Superior Court*, 345 P.2d 543 (1959); *People v. Siu*, 271 P.2d 575 (1954). In *Rojas* and *Faustina*, stolen goods were recovered by police, unknown to the defendants, whereupon the police delivered them to defendants who received them believing them to be stolen. Both cases rejected *Jaffe*, distinguishing between what a person actually does and what he intends to do. The courts found that the fact a person is mistaken regarding the external realities does not alter his intention, but simply makes it impossible to effectuate that intention. Other jurisdictions adhere to the California position that a person be charged with attempt to commit a crime even though the crime itself cannot be fully consummated due to an extrinsic fact unbeknown to that person.

Added to the lack of uniformity among other jurisdictions on this issue is the morass of commentary surrounding the defense of impossibility in attempt crimes. Many courts compartmentalize fact patterns into the category of "factual impossibility" and legal impossibility. This court agrees with the position taken by the court in Moretti, supra, that the defense is "so fraught with intricacies and artificial distinctions that it has little value as an analytical method for reaching substantial justice." However, this court respectfully disagrees with the Moretti court's position that the place to remedy the problem is in the courts. Rather, this court believes that the issue must be resolved through legislation.

However, until the statutes are revised, this court is persuaded that the rationale of *Jaffe* and *Rollino* is the more logical and should be followed. Because the television set received by the defendant was not stolen, this court, after careful review of the authorities, finds that no crime was committed since an unsuccessful attempt to do that which is not a crime cannot be held to be an attempt to commit the crime specified. No crime committed

501

attempted sex w/ fake kid

factual impossibility

Chen v. State

42 S.W.3d 926 (Tex. Crim. App. 2001)

Holland, J., delivered the opinion of the unanimous Court.

Appellant was convicted in a bench trial of attempted sexual performance by a child, and he was sentenced to seven years confinement and a fine of $1000. *See* TEX. PENAL CODE ANN.§ 15.01, 43.25(b). Imposition of the seven years confinement was suspended and appellant was placed on seven years community supervision. The court of appeals affirmed the conviction. We granted appellant's petition for discretionary review to determine "whether a 47 year old male undercover officer posing as a 13 year old female for the purposes of internet communications established evidence that was sufficient, as a matter of law, to support a conviction for the offense of attempted sexual performance by a child." We will affirm the judgment of the court of appeals. *affirmed*

The evidence presented at appellant's bench trial showed that on December 13, 1996, appellant placed an advertisement on an America Online computer bulletin board stating, "A nude dancer needed for discreet pleasure. I am generous and rich. You must be very attractive and young." Detective Steve Nelson, a Dallas Police Officer working on a specialized crime task involving child exploitation, discovered the advertisement. On December 16, 2001, he e-mailed appellant back representing himself as J. Cirello and asking appellant "how young of a nude dancer [he was] looking for." Appellant replied, "I will say between 20 and 30 or as long as you have a young looking face and tender body." Detective Nelson responded that there was no one in that age range and signed the email "J. Cirello."

Appellant e-mailed again and asked, "What age are you in?" Posing as J. Cirello, Detective Nelson wrote, "If you don't care about age I am 13, looking for independence. What are you looking for?" Appellant replied that he was looking for a girl who "dares to be nude and watched by me while I am masturbating." He asked to "get together" and requested her name and location. Detective Nelson e-mailed, stating "My name is Julie." He also wrote that "Julie" had never seen a man masturbate and did not want "her" parents to find out.

During the next few e-mails, appellant asked where Julie lived and when they could get together. He expressed a desire to exchange telephone numbers. He stated that they could get to know each other first and assured Julie that he would not hurt her. "Julie" asked for his description and his phone number and stated that "it might be better if [she] calls [appellant]." "Julie" wrote that "she" had never had sex before and was a little scared. Appellant responded that "sex [a] is wonderful thing." He also later wrote that "sex is not my major object." "Julie" then expressed that "she" was possibly interested in sex "if the right person came along to explain things and help [her]." For a few more weeks, Appellant and "Julie" e-mailed each other, discussing appellant's sexual history, "Julie's" nervousness, and plans to meet in person. Appellant described his van as champagne colored. ??

On February 6, 1997, appellant and "Julie" began their plan to meet. Appellant assured "Julie" that he would bring protection and lubrication, so that he would not hurt her or get her

502

pregnant. After a series of e-mails, they decided to meet at a Best Western on a Tuesday afternoon (February 11, 1997). Appellant informed Julie that he had a room reserved for that day. "Julie" wrote appellant, stating that she would be outside the lobby between 3:30 and 4:00 p.m. and described herself as "5-foot one inch tall with long blond hair."

The Garland Police Department set up surveillance at the Best Western. Appellant arrived at the motel in a champagne colored minivan. He initially sat in the minivan for about ten minutes. Eventually, he went in the lobby, stayed for two minutes, then came back out to his vehicle. When he got back into his minivan, the police arrested him. Appellant had a package of condoms and a tube of KY Jelly on the console of his minivan. He later gave a voluntary statement in which he admitted that he was going to show a girl how to have sex. WTF?

Δ's arguments

Detective Nelson admitted on cross-examination that he was a white male and had never been known by the name of Julie Cirello. "Julie" did not exist, and he was the author of the e-mails signed by "Julie." Appellant asked the trial court to render a verdict of "not guilty" because the State failed to prove the elements contained in the indictment. Specifically, appellant argued that the State failed to prove he attempted to induce the named complainant, Julie Cirello, to commit any acts alleged in the indictment. Additionally, he asserted that the State failed to prove that Julie Cirello was a person under the age of 18 and that the proof presented at trial was a fatal variance with the allegation in the indictment. The trial court found appellant guilty beyond a reasonable doubt as charged in the indictment.

On appeal, appellant argued that because Julie Cirello did not exist, it was impossible for the State to prove a "completed" offense. The court of appeals rejected appellant's argument, stating that "[t]he State did . . . prove appellant attempted to induce a person, whom he knew as Julie Cirello, a thirteen-year-old child, to have sexual intercourse with him." *Chen*, slip op. at 4. There was not a variance between the allegations in the indictment and the proof at trial. *See id.* This Court granted appellant's petition for discretionary review.

In his brief, appellant argues that the court of appeals erred by equating the intent element of the criminal intent statute (Texas Penal Code section 15.01) with the specific intent requirement of the underlying offense (Texas Penal Code section 43.25). Appellant asserts that the crucial issue in this case is that it is "legally impossible" to commit the underlying offense. Therefore, the evidence in the record is insufficient as a matter of law to support the verdict.

In response, the State argues that this Court should reject the doctrine of legal impossibility as a defense. It states that the defense is not in the Penal Code and has been questioned by members of this Court in the past. Alternatively, the State asks this Court to hold that the impossibility doctrine does not apply to attempt crimes. Even if legal impossibility is a valid defense, the State asserts that appellant's circumstances present a factual impossibility claim, which is not a recognized defense.

The relevant portion of Texas Penal Code section 43.25(b) states, "A person commits an offense if, knowing the character and content thereof, he employs, authorizes, or induces a child younger than 18 years of age to engage in sexual conduct or a sexual performance." TEX. PENAL CODE ANN. § 43.25(b). "A person commits an offense, if with specific intent to commit an offense, he does an act amounting to more than mere preparation that tends but fails to effect the commission of the offense intended." TEX. PENAL CODE ANN. § 15.01. Therefore, the offense of attempted sexual performance by a child is committed if: 1) the defendant; 2) with specific intent to commit sexual performance by a child; 3) does an act amounting to more than mere preparation; 4) that tends but fails to effect the commission of sexual performance by a child.

This Court discussed the doctrine of legal impossibility and factual impossibility at length in *Lawhorn v. State*, 898 S.W.2d 886 (Tex. Crim. App., 1995). At that time, we stated that legal impossibility was a valid defense, while factual impossibility was not. In his dissent, Judge Meyers asserted that neither legal nor factual impossibility should be a valid defense to a crime because neither defense is listed in the Texas Penal Code and older common law cases discussing legal impossibility should not survive the enactment of the Texas Penal Code. We find it unnecessary to dispose of the legal impossibility doctrine at this time. While we acknowledge that the line between legal and factual impossibility is sometimes difficult to draw, appellant's case does not involve a legal impossibility scenario. Rather, it presents factual impossibility.

"The distinction between factual and legal impossibility has been characterized as turning on whether the goal of the actor was deemed by the law to be a crime." 21 AM.JUR.2D CRIMINAL LAW § 178 (1999). Legal impossibility exists "where the act if completed would not be a crime, although what the actor intends to accomplish would be a crime." *Lawhorn*, 898 S.W.2d at 891. It has also been described as "existing [when] what the actor intends to do would not constitute a crime, or at least the crime charged." *Id.* On the other hand, factual impossibility exists when "due to a physical or factual condition unknown to the actor, the attempted crime could not be completed." *Id.* In other words, factual impossibility "refers to a situation in which the actor's objective was forbidden by the criminal law, although the actor was prevented from reaching that objective due to circumstances unknown to him." 21 AM.JUR.2D CRIMINAL LAW § 178.

This Court has very few cases raising the issues of factual or legal impossibility—especially in the context of attempt crimes. The concept of factual impossibility is well-illustrated in *People v. Grant*, 233 P.2d 660 (Cal. App. 1951). In Grant, the defendant placed a homemade bomb in his suitcase for a family trip to San Diego. The defendant apparently intended for his family to be on the plane when it exploded, leaving him to collect the insurance money on their lives. The bomb discharged before the plane had been filled with people, but it was extinguished before it harmed anyone. At trial, evidence was admitted that showed if the bomb had worked properly, the plane would have crashed into the ocean. In discussing the factual impossibility of the crime, the court noted that the defendant intended to cause the destruction of his family's airplane. Even though the bomb exploded early, the defendant was still guilty of attempted murder. "[W]here a defendant is charged with an attempt to commit a crime it is immaterial whether the attempted crime is impossible of completion if, as in the present case, completion was apparently possible to the defendant who was acting with the intent to commit the crime of murder."

In applying these concepts to the instant case, we initially note that if Julie Cirello had been an actual thirteen year old, then what appellant intended to accomplish (sexual performance by a child) constituted an actual crime. Appellant's goal was to commit the offense of sexual performance by a child. Because that goal is a crime by law, the doctrine of legal impossibility is not at issue in this case. Rather, this case presents a factual impossibility scenario. Due to a factual condition unknown to appellant (that Julie Cirello did not actually exist), the offense of sexual performance by a child could not be completed. It is true that, as appellant claims, the actual offense of sexual performance by a child would have been impossible for appellant to complete; the complainant, Julie Cirello, did not physically exist. But completion of the crime was apparently possible to appellant. He had specific intent to commit the offense of sexual performance by a child, and he committed an act amounting to more than mere preparation that tended but failed to effect the commission of the offense. The State presented evidence for each of the necessary elements of attempted sexual performance by a child.

In conclusion, appellant's case does not present the doctrine of legal impossibility. The evidence presented at trial, reviewed in the light most favorable to the verdict, was sufficient for the trier of fact to reasonably conclude that appellant was guilty of attempted sexual performance by a child.

The judgment of the court of appeals is affirmed.

United States v. Oviedo

525 F.2d 881 (5th Cir. 1976)

Dyer, Circuit Judge.

Oviedo appeals from a judgment of conviction for the attempted distribution of heroin, in violation of 21 U.S.C.A. § 846.1 Oviedo contends that under the facts of this case, he is not guilty of any criminal offense. We agree and reverse.

Oviedo was contacted by an undercover agent, who desired to purchase narcotics. Arrangements were made for the sale of one pound of heroin. The agent met Oviedo at the appointed time and place. Oviedo transferred the substance to the agent, and asked for his money in return. However, the agent informed Oviedo that he would first have to test the substance. A field test was performed with a positive result. Oviedo was placed under arrest.

Subsequent to the arrest, a search warrant was issued for Oviedo's residence. When the search was executed, two pounds of a similar substance was found hidden in a television set. Up to this point, the case appeared unexceptional.

A chemical analysis was performed upon the substances seized, revealing that the substances were not in fact heroin, but rather procaine hydrochloride, an uncontrolled substance.[1] Since any attempt to prosecute for distribution of heroin would have been futile, the defendant was charged with an attempt to distribute heroin.

At trial, Oviedo took the stand and stated that he knew the substance was not heroin, and that he, upon suggestion of his cohorts, was merely attempting to "rip off" the agent. It was, in his view, an easy way to pocket a few thousand dollars.

The court instructed the jury that they could find Oviedo guilty of attempted distribution if he delivered the substance thinking it to be heroin.[2] The jury rejected Oviedo's claimed knowledge of the true nature of the substance, and returned a verdict of guilty. Although Oviedo argues on appeal that there was insufficient evidence to establish that he thought the substance was heroin, this contention is without merit.[3] We thus take as fact Oviedo's belief that the substance was heroin.

---

1. Although not an opium derivative, procaine hydrochloride will give a positive reaction to the Marquis Reagent Field Test.

2. The court charged the jury on this issue:

> In other words, if you find beyond a reasonable doubt that Mr. Oviedo did knowingly and unlawfully and intentionally attempt to distribute what you have found beyond a reasonable doubt . . . he believed to be one pound of heroin . . . it would be no defense that the substance involved was not actually heroin. On the other hand, if you do not find beyond a reasonable doubt that the Defendant believed the substance involved to be heroin, even though you might find all of the other elements of the offense present beyond a reasonable doubt, then it would be your duty to acquit the Defendant.

3. The fact that the procaine was secreted inside a television set, together with the discussions between Oviedo and the undercover agent, lead to the reasonable inference that Oviedo thought the substance to be heroin, and support

The facts before us are therefore simple—Oviedo sold a substance he thought to be heroin, which in reality was an uncontrolled substance. The legal question before us is likewise simple—are these combined acts and intent cognizable as a criminal attempt under 21 U.S.C.A. § 846. The answer, however, is not so simple. Issue

Oviedo and the government both agree the resolution of this case rests in an analysis of the doctrines of legal and factual impossibility as defenses to a criminal attempt. Legal impossibility occurs when the actions which the defendant performs or sets in motion, even if fully carried out as he desires, would not constitute a crime. *United States v. Conway*, 507 F.2d 1047 (5th Cir. 1975). Factual impossibility occurs when the objective of the defendant is proscribed by the criminal law but a circumstance unknown to the actor prevents him from bringing about that objective. *Id.* at 1050. The traditional analysis recognizes legal impossibility as a valid defense, but refuses to so recognize factual impossibility. *United States v. Berrigan*, 482 F.2d 171 (3d Cir. 1973).

These definitions are not particularly helpful here, for they do nothing more than provide a different focus for the analysis. In one sense, the impossibility involved here might be deemed legal, for those *acts* which Oviedo set in motion, the transfer of the substance in his possession, were not a crime. In another sense, the impossibility is factual, for the *objective* of Oviedo, the sale of heroin, was proscribed by law, and failed only because of a circumstance unknown to Oviedo.

Although this issue has been the subject of numerous legal commentaries,6 federal cases reaching this question are few, and no consensus can be found. In *United States v. Heng Awkak Roman*, 356 F.Supp. 434 (S.D.N.Y. 1973), *aff'd*, 484 F.2d 1271 (2d Cir. 1973), the defendants were transporting a suitcase containing heroin. Through the aid of an informer and unknown to the defendants, the contents of the suitcase were replaced with soap powder. The defendants were arrested when they attempted to sell the contents of the suitcase, and were subsequently charged with *attempted* possession with intent to distribute. The court rejected defendants' contention that they could not be charged with attempted possession, since it was impossible for them to possess heroin. Recognizing the difficulty in distinguishing between legal and factual impossibility, the court never so categorized the case. Nevertheless, the court concluded that since the objective of the defendants was criminal, impossibility would not be recognized as a defense.

The defendants in *United States v. Berrigan*, 482 F.2d 171 (3d Cir. 1973), were charged with attempting to violate 18 U.S.C. § 1791, prohibiting the smuggling of objects into or out of a federal correctional institution. Since the evidence established that the warden had knowledge of the smuggling plan, and since lack of knowledge was a necessary element of the offense, the defendants could not be found guilty of violating the statute. The court held that such knowledge by the warden would also preclude conviction for the attempt, since "attempting to do that which is not a crime is not attempting to commit a crime." *Berrigan*, at 190.

---

the jury's conclusion.

intent not sufficient
objective acts
performed = criminal
in nature

The *Berrigan* court rested its determination on a strict view of legal impossibility. According to the court, such impossibility exists when there is an intention to perform a physical act, the intended physical act is performed, but the consequence resulting from the intended act does not amount to a crime. In this analysis, the intent to perform a physical act is to be distinguished from the motive, desire or expectation to violate the law.

The application of the principles underlying these cases leads to no clearer result than the application of our previous definitions of legal and factual impossibility. Applying *Roman*, we would not concern ourselves with any theoretical distinction between legal and factual impossibility, but would affirm the conviction, since the objective of Oviedo was criminal. Applying *Berrigan*, we would look solely to the physical act which Oviedo "intended," the transfer of the procaine in his possession, and we would conclude that since the transfer of procaine is not criminal, no offense is stated. The choice is between punishing criminal intent without regard to objective acts, and punishing objective acts, regarding intent as immaterial.

In our view, both *Roman* and *Berrigan* miss the mark, but in opposite directions. A strict application of the *Berrigan* approach would eliminate any distinction between factual and legal impossibility, and such impossibility would *always* be a valid defense, since the "intended" physical acts are never criminal. The *Roman* approach turns the attempt statute into a new substantive criminal statute where the critical element to be proved is *mens rea simpliciter*. It would allow us to punish one's thoughts, desires, or motives, through indirect evidence, without reference to any objective fact. The danger is evident.

We reject the notion of *Roman,* adopted by the district court, that the conviction in the present case can be sustained since there is sufficient proof of intent, not because of any doubt as to the sufficiency of the evidence in that regard, but because of the inherent dangers such a precedent would pose in the future.

When the question before the court is whether certain conduct constitutes mere preparation which is not punishable, or an attempt which is, the possibility of error is mitigated by the requirement that the objective acts of the defendant evidence commitment to the criminal venture and corroborate the *mens rea. United States v. Mandujano*, 499 F.2d 370 (5th Cir. 1974). To the extent that this requirement is preserved it prevents the conviction of persons engaged in innocent acts on the basis of a *mens rea* proved through speculative inferences, unreliable forms of testimony, and past criminal conduct.

Courts could have approached the preparation—attempt determination in another fashion, eliminating any notion of particular objective facts, and simply could have asked whether the evidence at hand was sufficient to prove the necessary intent. But this approach has been rejected for precisely the reasons set out above, for conviction upon proof of mere intent provides too great a possibility of speculation and abuse.

In urging us to follow *Roman,* which found determinative the criminal intent of the defendants, the government at least implicitly argues that we should reject any requirement demanding the same objective evidentiary facts required in the preparation—attempt determination. We refuse to follow that suggestion.

508

When the defendant sells a substance which is actually heroin, it is reasonable to infer that he knew the physical nature of the substance, and to place on him the burden of dispelling that inference. However, if we convict the defendant of attempting to sell heroin for the sale of a non-narcotic substance, we eliminate an objective element that has major evidentiary significance and we increase the risk of mistaken conclusions that the defendant believed the goods were narcotics.[4]

Thus, we demand that in order for a defendant to be guilty of a criminal attempt, the objective acts performed, without any reliance on the accompanying *mens rea*, mark the defendant's conduct as criminal in nature. The acts should be unique rather than so commonplace that they are engaged in by persons not in violation of the law.

[handwritten margin note: Rule:]

Here we have only two objective facts. First, Oviedo told the agent that the substance he was selling was heroin, and second, portions of the substance were concealed in a television set. If another objective fact were present, if the substance were heroin, we would have a strong objective basis for the determination of criminal intent and conduct consistent and supportative of that intent. The test set out above would be met, and, absent a delivery, the criminal attempt would be established. But when this objective basis for the determination of intent is removed, when the substance is not heroin, the conduct becomes ambivalent, and we are left with a sufficiency-of-the-evidence determination of intent rejected in the preparation—attempt dichotomy. We cannot conclude that the objective acts of Oviedo apart from any indirect evidence of intent mark his conduct as criminal in nature. Rather, those acts are consistent with a noncriminal enterprise. Therefore, we will not allow the jury's determination of Oviedo's intent to form the sole basis of a criminal offense.

The government also argues that *United States v. Mandujano, supra*, although involving a preparation—attempt determination, compels a contrary result. In *Mandujano,* the defendant negotiated a sale of heroin with an undercover agent. After taking the agent's money, the defendant set about to find his source. He was unsuccessful, and returned a few hours later with the money and without the heroin. We found the evidence sufficient to take the case beyond preparation, and to support his conviction for attempted distribution.

In making that determination, we recognized that in order to be guilty of an attempt, the objective conduct of the defendant must strongly corroborate the firmness of the defendant's criminal intent. The objective acts must not be equivocal in nature. In that case, we had as objective facts defendant's act of taking money and his personal statements that he would purchase heroin with that money. Importantly, there were no objective facts which made these acts equivocal.

---

4. Enker, *Impossibility in Criminal Attempts—Legality and the Legal Process*, 53 MINN. L.R. 665, 680 (1969). *Mens rea* is within one's control but, as already seen, it is not subject to direct proof. More importantly, perhaps, it is not subject to direct refutation either. It is the subject of inference and speculation. The act requirement with its relative fixedness, its greater visibility and difficulty of fabrication, serves to provide additional security and predictability by limiting the scope of the criminal law to those who have engaged in conduct that is itself objectively forbidden and objectively verifiable. Security from officially imposed harm comes now only from the knowledge that one's thoughts are pure but that one's acts are similarly pure. So long as a citizen does not engage in forbidden conduct, he has little need to worry about possible erroneous official conclusions about his guilty mind. *Id.* at 688.

The situation in *Mandujano* is distinguishable from that now before us. Just as it is reasonable to infer a person's knowledge and criminal intent from the possession of a substance which is in fact narcotics, it is also reasonable to infer that same knowledge and intent from an individual's statements of future intention. However, just as it is impossible to infer that intent when the substance possessed is not in fact narcotics, it is also impossible to infer that intent when objective facts indicate that the person did not carry out his self-proclaimed intention.

Thus, when Mandujano stated that he would purchase heroin, we could infer that he intended to purchase heroin since there were no objective facts to the contrary. But here, Oviedo stated he would sell heroin and then sold procaine. Based on these objective facts, we cannot infer that he intended to do that which he said he was going to do, because he in fact did something else.

Reversed.

Notes

1.   The court in *United States v. Hair* ruled that the defendant could not be guilty of attempted receiving stolen property when the property was not stolen. The court in *Chen v. State* ruled that the defendant could be guilty of attempted sexual performance by a child when the victim was not a child. Are the rulings inconsistent?

2.   Most federal courts have ruled that impossibility is not a defense to an attempted crime under federal law. Would the federal courts allow attempt liability even in cases of inherent factual impossibility? For example, where the defendant, wishing to kill an enemy, stabs a voodoo doll with a needle? Is the evil mental state and this act enough for criminal liability?

3.   Consider whether the factual and legal impossibility distinction should be applied in the following cases:

a. The defendant obtains a packet of white powder he believes to be a narcotic, but it is in fact talcum powder. Defendant is charged with attempted possession of a controlled substance. See *People v. Siu*, 271 P.2d 575 (Cal. 1954).

b. A week before hunting season opens, the defendant stops on the side of the highway and shoots at what he believes to be a live deer, but in fact is a stuffed deer placed in a field by wildlife officials. The defendant is charged with attempting to shoot a deer out of season. See *State v. Guffey*, 262 S.W.2d 152 (Mo. 1953).

c. The defendant fires a gun at the White House after he sees a man who resembles—but in fact is not—President Clinton standing on the White House grounds. The defendant is charged with the attempted assassination of the President. See *United States v. Duran*, 884 F.Supp. 577 (D.D.C.1995).

d. "Lady Eldon, when traveling with her husband on the Continent, bought what she supposed to be a quantity of French lace, which she hid, concealing it from Lord Eldon in one of the pockets of the coach. The package was brought to light by a custom officer at Dover. The lace turned out to be an English manufactured article . . . not subject to duty. Lady Eldon had bought it at a price vastly above its value, believing it to be genuine, intending to smuggle it into England." Lady Eldon was charged with attempted smuggling of French lace. Quoted in J. C. Smith, *Two Problems in Criminal Attempts*, 70 HARV. L. REV. 422 (1957).

Chapter 23: Party Liability

Introduction

The topic of this chapter is vicarious criminal liability when individuals who do not personally cause the harm that is the object of a statutory criminal offense are subject to the same conviction and penalty as the principal actor who does cause harm.

Like party liability, inchoate crimes allow for criminal liability without causation of harm but party liability is a theory of complicity in a crime not a type of crime. Inchoate crimes either must be charged or enter the case as a lesser included offense alternative to the charged offense. It is not necessary to allege a party theory in the indictment and it does not provide an alternative to the charged offense but a theory of complicity or manner of commission of the offense charged. However, there are some important similarities between parties and inchoate crimes. Because inchoate crimes allow conviction without completion, causation of harm is not required and an intention to cause the harm is paramount. Similarly, a party does not have to cause harm personally but the actor's intent to aid others to cause the harm is paramount. Conspiracy is an inchoate crime but the concept of conspiracy reappears in this chapter as a theory of involvement in crimes rather than the separate crime of conspiracy. Causation of harm is not required for guilt of an inchoate offense and an act of a party need not have a crucial or causative role in the offense for there to be party liability.

Several titles have been given to actors who are vicariously connected to crimes: aiders and abettors, accessories, or the term that the Texas Penal Code uses: parties. Consolidating different types of accessories under the heading of "parties" signals an intention to eliminate common law distinctions based upon the method of complicity and, instead, to treat all who are legally implicit in the same category as the principal with independent legal liability.

The common law had four categories of complicity in crime. There were principals in the first and second degree and accessories before and after the fact. The difference between principals and accessories was presence. Principals were present at the scene of the crime; accessories were not. The principal in the first degree was present and committed the criminal act. A principal in the second degree was present and intentionally assisted but did not personally commit the criminal act. Accessories were not present but provided assistance either before or after the crime, which determined the type of accessory. These distinctions were important in the common law. Liability hinged on the principal in the first degree. Other principals and accessories could not be convicted of a different offense than the principal in the first degree and could not be convicted at all unless and until this actor was convicted. Trials could be won or lost based upon alleging and proving the proper theory of complicity.

It was sometimes difficult to characterize the proper role in the offense. For example, suppose X gave poison to Y to put in Z's coffee in order to kill Z. If both X and Y knew the nature and consequences of their acts, both were guilty; X as an accessory before the fact and Y as the principal in the first degree. But what if X knew that he was giving Y poison but he told Y that it was prescription medicine and Y had no reason to believe otherwise. In this scenario, Y does not have the required intent to kill Z and is guilty of nothing. X is guilty as a principal in the first degree (every completed criminal offense must have one) because X is "constructively" present and caused Z's death.

Section 7.01 (c) of the Texas Penal Code provides: "All traditional distinctions between accomplices and principals are abolished by this section, and each party to an offense may be charged and convicted without alleging that he acted as a principal or accomplice." It no longer matters in Texas whether one is a principle in the first or second degree or an accomplice before the fact. Anyone who acts with intent to commit the crime can be convicted of the offense if it occurs without regard to the type of complicity or whether others have been convicted at all or convicted of a different offense. To make clear the independent nature of the method of complicity of each actor, the legislature enacted section 7.03 of the Texas Penal Code, which provides: "it is no defense . . . that the person for whose conduct the actor is criminally responsible has been acquitted, has not been prosecuted or convicted, has been convicted of a different offense or of a different type or class of offense, or is immune from prosecution."

The exception to the rule that each role in the offense is subject to the same conviction is the category of accessory after the fact. Someone in this role is not considered to be a party to the crime. A person who offers aid to the perpetrators of an offense in helping them to escape, destroy evidence, or other assistance may be guilty of a separate crime but the act post-crime does not make the actor a party to the commission of the previously committed crime. It is important to distinguish the situation of a person who had no involvement until after the crime's commission from a person who agrees prior to the crime to provide assistance after the crime. In the latter situation, the actor is an accessory before the fact because the willingness to help offers support and encouragement that furthers the criminal enterprise. In fact, even if plans change and the other parties to the crime are unable to use the help that had been offered, the person who offered the assistance remains an accessory before the fact even though no actual aid was given. The person who has no involvement but intentionally offers post-crime aid is not a party to the crime committed by those the actor aids; but he or she is subject to criminal prosecution under section 38.05 of the Texas Penal Code; "Hindering arrest or prosecution."

While all parties to a crime are subject to conviction for the same offense regardless of their role, comparative assessments of the degree of participation and responsibility are often the subject of argument at sentencing. All parties may be subject to the same penalties but differing punishment may be assessed. However, the elimination of common law categories has changed the rigidity of allocating criminal responsibility through the fountainhead of the principal in the first degree. The *Boyer* case that follows provides a dramatic illustration of this in a case in which a party to the crime is convicted even though the principal and all other parties will not or cannot be convicted.

cop + informant + drugs

Boyer v. State

801 S.W.2d 897 (Tex. Crim. App. 1991)

McCormick, Presiding Judge.

Appellant was convicted by a jury of delivery of amphetamine, less than twenty-eight grams. The trial court, finding two enhancement paragraphs to be true, sentenced the appellant to twenty-five years in prison. The Court of Appeals, in an unpublished opinion, held that there was insufficient evidence to sustain the conviction of delivery, by actual transfer, under the law of parties and entered a judgment of acquittal. *Boyer v. State*, No. 2-88-088-CR (Fort Worth, August 31, 1989). We reverse. no act to constitute delivery

The transfer of the amphetamine occurred in a parked car. James Brumley, an undercover Department of Public Safety Narcotics Investigator, and his informant sat in the front seat. The appellant sat in the back. Appellant ordered the informant to hand Brumley the drugs. After the transfer was made, Brumley tried to give appellant one hundred dollars. Appellant refused the money and told Brumley to give it to the informant. Brumley did, and appellant was later convicted.

The gist of the Court of Appeals' holding is that, since neither Brumley nor the informant could be convicted of an offense, then neither could the appellant. Specifically, the Court of Appeals found that Brumley was acting in his official capacity as a law enforcement officer and participated in the transfer of the drugs solely for the purpose of apprehending appellant. Because of this, the lower court found that Brumley did not become a party to the crime and could not be held criminally responsible. The Court of Appeals also found that the informant could not become a party to the crime, and could not be held criminally responsible. When an individual serves as an intermediary and acts as an agent for a law enforcement officer in carrying out his official duties, the intermediary cannot be held criminally responsible for his conduct. The Court of Appeals is correct to the extent that neither Brumley nor his informant could be held criminally responsible for their actions. However, the Court of Appeals also found that since neither Brumley nor the informant could be held criminally responsible no offense was committed. Finding that no offense was committed between Brumley and the informant, the Court of Appeals reasoned that appellant's conviction could not stand under the law of parties. We disagree.

The proper focus is on the *conduct* of the informant, not whether he is criminally responsible. Texas Penal Code, Section 7.03(2), states:

> In a prosecution in which an actor's criminal responsibility is based on the *conduct* of another, the actor may be convicted on proof of commission of the offense and that he was a party to its commission, and it is no defense: . . . (2) that the person for whose conduct the actor is criminally responsible has been acquitted, has not been prosecuted or convicted, has been convicted of a different offense or of a different type or class of offense, or is immune from prosecution.

(Emphasis added).

D had specific intent   514
    so does not matter abt informer

Under the law of parties, as long as the conduct of the informant results in the "commission of an offense," and appellant solicited that conduct, then a conviction may be had. The conduct of the informant which resulted in the commission of the offense does not require that he be "criminally responsible" for that offense.

Our holding is supported by the language of the statute itself. For example, Section 7.03(2) states that a person charged under the law of parties may not raise as a defense the fact that the person for whose conduct the actor is criminally responsible has been acquitted of the offense. A person who is acquitted of an offense obviously is not "criminally responsible" for his conduct. The same holds true when the person is immune from prosecution. Since the informant here was acting as an intermediary for Officer Brumley, he was immune from prosecution. Consequently, the Court of Appeals was incorrect when it found that the informant had to be criminally responsible before appellant could be convicted.

The Court of Appeals found that the informant "did knowingly or intentionally deliver amphetamine to Officer Brumley by actual transfer . . . ." The informant's conduct resulted in the commission of an offense. Since the delivery was done at the appellant's instruction, his conviction is proper.

Reversed and remanded to the Court of Appeals for consideration of appellant's remaining ground for review. Holding

Notes

1.   How can someone be a party to a crime when he is the only person who can be guilty of a crime? Is it appropriate for the state to provide a seller and a buyer for a drug transaction and then prosecutes the agent that the state has employed to facilitate the feigned sale? Should the entrapment defense apply to this situation? Entrapment was alleged in the similar case of *United States v. Russell*, 411 U.S. 423 (1973), which also involved a defendant who was convicted of transferring drugs from a government source to a government agent. The trial court held that this was not entrapment as a matter of law and put the question to the jury who voted to convict; a conviction that was affirmed by the United States Supreme Court.

2.   Texas law includes a requirement of corroboration of an accomplice's testimony in order for the State to meet its burden of proof. This evidentiary enhancement of the burden of proof in cases in which accomplice testimony is introduced against the defendant only applies to real accomplices. Because the defendant in *Boyer* only a pretended to be an accomplice, no corroboration was necessary. Although there was other corroborating evidence in the *Boyer* case, what do you think of the possibility of allowing a conviction based solely on the testimony of paid informant whose pay depends on providing evidence leading to arrest and whose information is derived from his or her own familiarity with drug trafficking?

Sufficient Conduct for Complicity

The most frequently quoted language in jury instructions comes from section 7.02 of the Texas Penal Code, which provides that a person is a party to a crime if: "(2) acting with intent to promote or assist the commission of the offense, he solicits, encourages, directs, aids, or attempts to aid the other person to commit the offense." This formulation allows conviction of individuals whose contribution to a criminal enterprise is slight so long as some act has been done with the intent that the crime be committed. Consider, for example, a case from the American west in an earlier era. A group of brothers, the Skeltons, were riding on horseback in pursuit of Ross, a man that the Skeltons wanted to kill because he had seduced the sister of the Skeltons. (The possibility that their sister may have wanted to be seduced either did not occur to them or did not matter.) Someone tried to warn Ross by sending a telegram which would have stated: "Four men on horseback. Look out." A relative of the Skeltons, Judge Talley, learned of the proffered warning telegram and knew the telegraph operator who was supposed to deliver it. Judge Talley persuaded him not to send it. The unwarned Ross was killed by the Skeltons. Is Judge Talley guilty of the crime (as an accessory before the fact under the common law terminology)? He is. It matters not that Ross might not have been able to escape even if he received the telegram. It is not necessary to show that the aid played a causative role. What matters is that with intent that the Skeltons kill Ross, the judge acted to aid the murder. The Texas statute, along with the Model Penal Code, have expanded party liability beyond that of the common law by adding "attempt to aid" as a basis for criminal liability. Under this provision, Judge Talley is a party to the murder even if the telegraph operator ignores Talley's request and delivers the warning telegraph.

The two cases that follow, *Valdez* and *Meyers* are cases in which the alleged complicity of the defendants is slight. It takes very little to infer an intent to aid or encourage but it requires more than association with knowledge that someone is committing a crime.

516

Valdez v. State

623 S.W.2d 317 (Tex. Crim. App. 1979)

Clinton, Judge.

This appeal arises from a jury verdict finding appellant guilty of burglary of a vehicle; the trial court assessed his punishment at five years confinement.

Appellant contends that the evidence is insufficient to support the finding of guilt.

The State presented the testimony of the complaining witness, Fermin Perez, who stated that on December 2, 1976, he left his 1957 Ford automobile unlocked with the windows down outside a bowling alley. Before Perez left his car, he engaged a warning device which would cause the horn to blow if the vehicle were entered. Upon hearing the warning device, Perez went outside, noticing the door to his car was open and saw his "C.B. head set" had been thrown over the front seat into the back. He replaced the C.B., closed the door and went back inside. The next morning, Perez noticed that a tape deck speaker box which had contained approximately fifteen tapes was missing and reported the burglary to the police. Ultimately, eleven tapes were returned to Perez and he was paid $60.00 for the unrecovered tapes and speaker box.

The defense evidence consisted of the testimony of appellant [age 21] and his neighbor, seventeen year old Lupe Gutierrez. According to these witnesses, on the day of the burglary they had gone "riding around" in appellant's car and then to the bowling alley where they stayed for half an hour. When they decided to leave, appellant walked out first and was almost to his car when he heard a "loud horn." According to appellant, he looked back, and "Lupe was coming to my car with the speaker box that the tapes were in." Gutierrez testified as follows:

A: I just saw the tapes in the car and I got in there and I took the tapes. I grabbed the tapes. And I guess it was wired or something and the alarm went off. I just ran to (appellant's) car.

Q: Now had you and (appellant), while you were inside the bowling alley, had you talked at all about doing this?

A: No . . .

Q: He had no knowledge that you were going to do this?

A: No sir. I don't think so.

Q: Had you indicated anything to him about this?

A: No, I didn't.

Q: Had you decided to do this when you went into the bowling alley?

A: I just saw them when I walked in, but I didn't tell him anything.

517

Q: What did you do with the speaker box?

A: I threw it. I threw it out.

Q: How about the tapes?

A: I kept the tapes.

Q: You kept all the tapes?

A: Yeah, I kept them all.

Q: Did you give any to Mr. Valdez?

A: No, I didn't.

Q: Did he at any time ask you for any of the tapes?

A: No, he didn't.

On cross-examination, Gutierrez was asked:

Q: So [appellant] did know you burglarized a car and he did help you, carry you away and the stolen goods away, didn't he?

A: Yes, sir. We left in his car.

Q: He aided you in getting away with the goods you had stolen, and he knew you had stole them because he was there, present when you stole them?

A: Yes, sir.

Q: And you were sixteen and he was twenty-one, is that correct?

A: That's correct.

Appellant gave virtually identical testimony. It was also brought out before the jury that on December 6th, Bee County Deputy Sheriff Eddie Hons spoke with Lupe Gutierrez and recovered about six eight track stereo tapes. On December 8th, Hons contacted appellant at work and asked him to come by the Sheriff's Office which appellant did. Hons informed appellant that he knew about the burglary and after discussing it for a while, appellant gave Hons a statement. Hons testified that he did not arrest appellant because "he indicated . . . that he was going to try to help to get the rest of the property back to the victim, Mr. Perez." On cross-examination appellant admitted that after talking with Hons he did not believe he was seriously implicated in the burglary, and in attempting to give Hons a full description of what happened, he included several things Gutierrez had told him, but of which he had no personal knowledge. According to Hons, he returned the six tapes recovered from Gutierrez to Perez; according to Perez, about a week after the burglary, appellant and Gutierrez returned four or five more tapes to the victim at

518

his home. It was also established that appellant and his father gave Perez a check for $60.00 in about May of 1977 to pay for any unrecovered tapes, as well as the speaker box.

The trial court charged the jury as to the law of parties pursuant to § 7.02(a)(2) and a verdict of guilty was returned.

The State contends that in appellant's written confession, he admitted his participation "with his juvenile companion in his carrying away of the stolen property and flight from the burglary scene. Further, appellant was found to have been in possession of property taken in the burglary shortly after the burglary occurred."

It is true that an inference or presumption of a defendant's guilt of a burglary or theft sufficient to sustain a conviction may arise from his possession of property stolen or taken in a recent burglary; however, to warrant such an inference or presumption of guilt from the circumstances of possession alone, such possession must be personal, recent, unexplained and must involve a distinct and conscious assertion of right to the property by the accused. In the instant case, both appellant and Gutierrez consistently denied that appellant's "taking"—as recited by his statement—was intentional, but rather, that Gutierrez had inadvertently "left" two of the stolen tapes in appellant's car.

Appellant's explanation of his possession of the recently stolen tapes was reasonable and un-contradicted; this, coupled with his action in returning the tapes in his possession to their rightful owner render his recent possession of the tapes insufficient to warrant an inference of guilt. If appellant is a party to the burglary, it is by virtue of § 7.02(a)(2), V.T.C.A. Penal Code. Therefore the question remains whether the evidence could reasonably be interpreted by the jury as showing participation in the event sufficient to render him guilty as a party. The provisions of § 7.01, V.T.C.A. Penal Code abolished the distinction formerly made between "principals" and "accomplices" by Articles 65 and 70, Vernon's Ann. P.C. 1925. Under the former Penal Code,

> [t]o be guilty of a felony offense as a principal, a defendant must be actually present at the time of its commission or if not present, . . . he must at the time the act is being done, be himself actively engaged in the furtherance of the common purpose and design at some other place.

Here, there is no showing whatever that appellant had any purpose or design in common with Gutierrez to enter Perez' vehicle with the intent to commit theft. "As to those situations in which one may be guilty as a principal when actually present, the very least that is required is, in addition to physical presence, encouragement by words or agreement to the commission of the offense. Such agreement must be prior to or contemporaneous with the criminal event." Here, it is un-contradicted that appellant's acts occurred after the commission of the burglary was completed by Gutierrez. The former Penal Code's provision that an "accessory" was a party to a crime has been eliminated; the conduct formerly constituting accessory acts is proscribed in the new Penal Code by § 38.05 which defines a separate and distinct crime of "hindering apprehension or prosecution."

It clearly follows that a person's "accessory" conduct is no longer recognized under Texas law as conduct making him a party to the crime with which the accused was here charged.

519

If chargeable at all, appellant's conduct would be more appropriately alleged pursuant to § 38.05, *supra*.

For the State's failure to prove both appellant's intent to promote or assist the commission of the burglary, as well as his solicitation, encouragement, direction, aid, or attempted aid of Gutierrez in the commission of the burglary, this cause is reversed and the prosecution is ordered dismissed.

Opinion on State's Motion for Rehearing

W. C. Davis, Judge.

On original submission, this case was reversed for insufficient evidence.

The State's evidence consisted of testimony from the complaining witness, Fermin Perez, that on the night of December 2, 1976, he left his car in the parking lot of a bowling alley. Later, Perez heard the warning device go off in his car. Perez went outside and saw that his car door was open and his CB radio had been pulled out. The next day, Perez noticed that his speaker box and approximately fifteen tapes were missing. The State also introduced the appellant's statement to the police. The statement recites:

> On 12/2/1976, Gutierriez came over to my house and asked me to go riding around. We left in my car and drove to the Bowling Alley in Beeville, Texas. I parked my car in the parking lot and we went inside. A short time later we walked back outside the bowling alley. As we walked by a black 1957 Ford four door car, parked in front of the bowling alley, Lupe opened the door on the drivers (sic) side and started taking some eight track stereo (sic) tapes from inside the car, the tapes were in a speaker box. The alarm went off in the car when Lupe tried to pull out the C.B. radio. We ran to my car, Lupe was carrying the tapes and the speaker, we got into my car and drove away. I took two of the tapes and Lupe took about ten tapes and Lupe threw the speaker out of the car window because he thought it wasn't any good. Lupe came to my house on 12/7/76 and told me that the man knew we stole his tapes, so I gave the two tapes I had to Lupe so he could return them to the owner.

It is well settled that the mere presence of an accused at the scene of an offense is not alone sufficient to support a conviction under the principles of V.T.C.A. Penal Code, § 7.02(a)(2); however, it is a circumstance tending to prove guilt which, combined with other facts, may suffice to show that the accused was a participant. Further, while flight alone will not support a guilty verdict, evidence of flight from the scene of a crime is a circumstance from which an inference of guilt may be drawn. In this case, the appellant was present at the scene of the crime; there was evidence that he and his companion fled the scene of the crime together, then later split the stolen proceeds. On appeal, the Court of Criminal Appeals must view the evidence in the light most favorable to the verdict. We find that the facts of this case are sufficient to support the jury's determination of guilt. In construing the sufficiency of the evidence presented in this case, it is unnecessary to apply the presumption of guilt arising from the unexplained possession of recently stolen property to sustain the conviction. However, since this subject was addressed on original submission, we need to rectify the stance taken by the panel majority concerning this presumption. The opinion on original submission stated:

> Appellant's explanation of his possession of the recently stolen tapes was reasonable and uncontradicted; this, coupled with his action in returning the tapes in his possession to the rightful owner render his recent possession of the tapes insufficient to warrant an inference of guilt.[1]

The explanation referred to above was the appellant's explanation tendered at the time of his trial. It is well settled that it is not the explanation given at the time of trial which controls whether or not the presumption arises, but the explanation given at the time an accused is first confronted with the possession of the stolen property. Further, we note that the fact that the appellant returned the stolen property after being confronted with its theft, has no bearing on the sufficiency of the evidence to show that the appellant committed the offense charged. The State's motion for rehearing is granted. The judgment is affirmed.

Teague, J. not participating.

Dissenting Opinion on State's Motion for Rehearing

Clinton, Judge, dissenting.

Not wishing to belabor the position of the unanimous panel opinion on original submission, but finding the treatment of this cause by the majority on rehearing so woefully inadequate to justify the conclusion, I am compelled to respond.

Viewing the evidence in a light most favorable to the verdict of guilt, it reveals that appellant's juvenile companion alone entered the vehicle, and obtained therefrom the tapes and speaker; that both appellant and Gutierrez fled the scene; and then—as the majority characterizes it—"split" the stolen proceeds. Assuming that the evidence clearly established a calculated "split" of the property obtained by Gutierrez from the vehicle, does the majority hold that this circumstance, coupled with "presence" and "flight," constitute sufficient direct proof of secondary facts which, by logical inference, demonstrate the ultimate fact to be proved: that appellant himself entered Perez' vehicle with the accompanying mental state charged? If not, the only circumstantial proof left is the inference of guilt this Court has held can arise from proof of the defendant's possession of recently stolen property. But the majority explicitly rejects the necessity to rely on this "presumption" in reaching the conclusion that the evidence is sufficient. While § 7.02(a)(2), is cited, plainly the majority result is in no manner dependent upon application of the law of "parties." Neither does the majority assail the panel's application of that body of law on original submission. Again, assuming unambiguous proof of a "split" of the property taken by Gutierrez, does the majority hold that the criminal conduct alleged against appellant can be committed by "adoption" or "ratification" of Gutierrez' act, after the fact? Does the majority hereby revive the old code concept of "accessory" conduct? The real problem with the State's evidence in this case is that it was merely amplified by the defensive testimony

---

1. If appellant had intended to keep any part of the burglarized property, his keeping only two of approximately fifteen tapes would prove him to be a self-sacrificing criminal indeed.

adduced; the latter clearly did not conflict with the State's evidence in any respect material to the offense charged. Granted, the jury had unlimited authority to disbelieve the testimony of appellant and Gutierrez that appellant neither knew of Gutierrez' intent nor acted with intent to assist it, but such rejection does not establish for the State the elements of the offense.

I respectfully dissent.

Notes

1.   The dissent states that the majority is not relying on the "law of parties" in reaching the conclusion that the evidence is sufficient to affirm the defendant's burglary conviction. Could the defendant be convicted of burglary without relying on the law of parties?

2.   Is it possible for a party who has provided aid before the offense to renounce the offense and avoid conviction? If there is such a defense, is it the same as the renunciation defenses recognized for inchoate offenses? Does Valdez have a valid renunciation defense, if there is one?

Meyers v. State

665 S.W.2d 590 (Tex. App. Corpus Christi 1984)

Gonzalez, Justice.

This is an appeal from a conviction for possession of a controlled substance, methamphetamine. The jury found appellant guilty but found the enhancement paragraphs not true. Punishment was assessed at fifteen years confinement. We reverse on the basis that the evidence is insufficient to support the conviction. Holding

On June 24, 1980, two narcotics detectives and a uniformed officer obtained a search warrant for the apartment where appellant was residing. The warrant was executed sometime between 8:00 and 9:00 o'clock in the morning. Appellant and a woman, Tammy Napolean, were ordered out of bed and escorted to the living room where the search warrant and their rights were read to them. A detective found a hypodermic syringe filled with a liquid, a bag containing two small packets of powdery substance, several empty syringes, and, on top of the refrigerator, a bottle containing a liquid substance. All of these substances were positively identified as methamphetamine.

At the trial on the merits, Tammy Napoleon testified that the methamphetamine was hers, that she pled guilty to the offense, and that she was assessed five years.

Appellant was indicted for possession of methamphetamine. The court's charge included an instruction on the law of parties. This charge may be given when supported by the evidence even though that manner of criminal responsibility is not pled in the indictment. Thus, if the evidence is sufficient to show that appellant either possessed the methamphetamine or was a party to Tammy Napolean's possession of methamphetamine, the conviction of appellant is valid.

law of parties

For one to be criminally responsible as a party, the State must prove that the defendant acted with the intent to promote or assist in the commission of the offense by soliciting, encouraging, directing, aiding, or attempting to aid the other person in its commission. TEX. PENAL CODE ANN. § 7.02(a)(2) (Vernon 1974). Although all traditional distinctions between accomplices and principals have been abolished, the statement of the Court of Criminal Appeals in *Forbes v. State*, 513 S.W.2d 72, (Tex. Crim. App. 1974), remains sound as a fundamental principle of the State's burden of proof when it seeks to rely on the law of parties to support a conviction. "To warrant a conviction of an accomplice, the State must prove the commission of the offense by the principal 'to the same certainty as if the principal were on trial, and therefore beyond a reasonable doubt.'" The State urges that, because appellant provided Tammy Napolean with food, lodging, and a "base of operation," he directly aided and encouraged Ms. Napolean in her possession of methamphetamine.

We reject the State's argument. "The mere presence of a defendant at the scene of an offense or even knowledge of an offense does not make one a party to joint possession." *Rhyne v. State*, 620 S.W.2d 599, 601 (Tex. Crim. App. 1981). "It has consistently been held in this state

523

that possession means more than just being where the action is . . . ." *Rhyne*, 572 S.W.2d at 540. We refuse to hold that providing another person with food or lodging is sufficient to make one a party to possession. Not enough—

There was also testimony from Ms. Napolean that, at about 2:00 a.m. on the morning of their arrest, appellant had driven her to her friend's house. She stated he left and that shortly before she returned to their apartment, she acquired the methamphetamine from the same person who gave her a ride back. Even if the jury disbelieved the story of how the witness claimed to have come into possession of the methamphetamine, there is no evidence in the record of appellant aiding or encouraging Ms. Napolean in possessing methamphetamine. We refuse to hold that the party statute extends criminal liability to the extent urged by the State. Absent other facts and circumstances besides providing Ms. Napolean a place to stay, we hold the evidence to be insufficient to show that appellant encouraged or aided the criminal conduct.

Holding

Notes

1.   Would it matter if Ms. Napolean was the wife of the defendant? What if Ms. Napolean were the daughter of the defendant? Consider Section 7.02(a)(3) of the Texas Penal Code, stating that it is no defense if: "having a legal duty to prevent commission of the offense and acting with intent to promote or assist its commission, he fails to make a reasonable effort to prevent commission of the offense."

2.   In this case, the jury charge included instructions on party liability as well as the defendant's guilt as a principal actor. If the evidence is insufficient to show that the defendant actually committed the offense but sufficient to show that defendant is guilty as a party, the evidence is sufficient so long as a party instruction has been included in the jury charge. If it hasn't, the conviction must be reversed for insufficient evidence. An instruction on party liability may be given along with an instruction alleging that the defendant was the principal actor. If the evidence is sufficient on either theory, after considering the evidence in a light most favorable to the verdict, the conviction is affirmed. Does this potentially deny the defendant of the right to a unanimous jury verdict? Party + principal actor instructions can go together

Conspiracy as a Theory of Complicity

Very often when there are multiple actors, a party to a crime will also be a conspirator for the separate crime of agreeing to commit the object offense. However, it is possible to be a party to a crime but not a conspirator. Recall the case of Judge Talley. It appears that Talley acted without any "preconcert" or prior agreement to prevent the warning telegram from being delivered. Talley wished to facilitate the crime and he acted without consulting with the Skeltons. However, most people who aid a criminal enterprise do so only with some express or implicit agreement.

Conspiracy may be a separate crime that can be charged if the offense is not completed but conspiracy is also a theory of complicity for completed crimes. Because the agreement constitutes a conspiracy that is separate from the criminal acts or assistance performed by the defendant, there can be a conviction of conspiracy and the completed crime in most jurisdictions. Each offense requires proof that the other does not under *Blockburger* because most completed crimes can be committed without an agreement and completion of the crime which is required for the object offense, is not required for conspiracy. Some states have prohibited convictions of conspiracy and the completed object of the conspiracy based upon statutory direction or judicial interpretation of the presumed legislative intent. However, most jurisdictions find no double jeopardy bar; notably the federal courts, where prosecutions for conspiracy and the completed crime that is the object of the conspiracy are common.

The use of conspiracy theory for party complicity in completed crimes undermines the principle that a person can only be convicted as a party if it was that person's intent that the crime should be committed. Conspiracy allows for vicarious responsibility for the acts of other conspirators that were committed in furtherance of the conspiracy and that were a foreseeable outcome of the conspiracy. Whether the acts of a co-conspirator were foreseeable and in furtherance of the conspiracy are often disputed issues in conspiracy prosecutions as well by virtue of the controversial conspiratorial method of party liability that is codified in Texas at Section 7.02 (b) of the Texas Penal Code, which provides:

> If, in the attempt to carry out a conspiracy to commit one felony, another felony is committed by one of the conspirators, all conspirators are guilty of the felony actually committed, though having no intent to commit it, if the offense was committed in furtherance of the unlawful purpose and was one that should have been anticipated as a result of the carrying out of the conspiracy.

The *Anderson* case, which follows, is an example of an application of this important theory of complicity.

Anderson v. State

416 S.W.3d 884 (Tex. Crim. App. 2013)

Meyers, J., delivered the opinion for a unanimous Court.

Appellant, Rodney Anderson, was charged with possession of methamphetamine with intent to deliver, over four grams but less than 200 grams, and aggravated assault of a public servant. The jury found him guilty, and he was sentenced to 40 years' imprisonment in the Texas Department of Criminal Justice—Correctional Institution Division for the possession offense, and life imprisonment for the aggravated assault. Appellant appealed, asserting that the evidence was legally insufficient to support his conviction of aggravated assault of a public servant. The court of appeals held that a rational jury could find that Appellant was guilty of aggravated assault of a public servant under the conspiracy theory of party liability. *Anderson v. State*, No. 09–10–00061–CR, 2011 WL 6743297 (Tex. App—Beaumont December 21, 2011). Appellant filed a petition for discretionary review, which we granted to consider whether the court of appeals erred in holding that the evidence was legally sufficient to support Appellant's conviction for aggravated assault under the law of parties in Texas Penal Code Section 7.02(b). We hold that the evidence is sufficient to support Appellant's conviction for the aggravated assault charge under the conspiracy theory of the law of parties. We will affirm the judgment of the court of appeals.

Facts

Appellant and Timothy Sherber had sold methamphetamine to Jeffery Harmon on numerous occasions. Harmon, who was acting as a paid confidential informant for the Texas Department of Public Safety, arranged to meet Appellant and Sherber in a parking lot to purchase methamphetamine. Appellant and Sherber arrived at the arranged location in Sherber's truck, and Harmon approached Appellant, who was sitting on the passenger side. When Appellant showed Harmon the drugs, Harmon removed his hat, which was a signal to the undercover officers waiting in the parking lot. On Harmon's signal, the undercover officers pulled their weapons, identified themselves as police, and yelled at Appellant and Sherber to get out of the vehicle. Instead, Sherber backed his truck out of the parking space before officers were able to block him in. One of the officers who approached Sherber's truck on foot struck the driver's side window with the barrel of his gun and repeatedly yelled at Sherber to stop.

As he attempted to flee, Sherber hit two unmarked patrol cars. One of the detectives fired his weapon several times, and Appellant suffered a gunshot wound to the chin. Sherber continued to drive forward and hit the side of a marked patrol car as he exited the parking lot. The officer driving the marked patrol car was injured in this collision. Another officer rammed the side of Sherber's truck to bring it to a stop, and Appellant and Sherber were arrested. Officers searched Sherber's truck and found a plastic bag containing methamphetamine on the passenger side of the floorboard. They also collected loose methamphetamine from inside Sherber's truck and on the ground outside the passenger door. Appellant was tried by a jury and found guilty of possession with intent to deliver four grams or more but less than 200 grams of methamphetamine and with aggravated assault on a public servant. He was sentenced to 40

526

years' imprisonment in the Texas Department of Criminal Justice-Correctional Institution Division for the possession charge, and life in prison for aggravated assault.

Court of Appeals

Appellant appealed, contending that the evidence was legally insufficient to sustain his conviction of aggravated assault of a public servant. The court of appeals noted that the jury charge in this case authorized the jury to convict Appellant of aggravated assault if the jury determined beyond a reasonable doubt that 1) Appellant intended to promote or assist Sherber in the aggravated assault of the officer; or 2) the aggravated assault was committed by Sherber in furtherance of a conspiracy to commit the felony offense of possession with intent to distribute a controlled substance, and that Appellant should have anticipated that an aggravated assault of a public servant could result from the parties' carrying out their conspiracy. The court of appeals evaluated whether Appellant's conviction could be affirmed under a conspiracy theory and determined that,

> [b]ased on the evidence, it was reasonable for the jury to infer from the circumstances that Sherber committed the aggravated assault in furtherance of his conspiracy with Anderson to commit the felony offense of possession with intent to deliver a controlled substance. The evidence is also sufficient to support the reasonable inference that Anderson should have anticipated that, under the circumstances of this case, police officers would face injury as a result of Sherber's attempt to flee.

The court of appeals concluded that a rational jury could have found Appellant guilty under the conspiracy theory of the law of parties. Appellant filed a petition for discretionary review, which we granted to determine whether the court of appeals erred in holding that the evidence was legally sufficient to support Appellant's aggravated assault conviction under the conspiracy theory of the law of parties.

Arguments of the Parties

Appellant's Arguments

Appellant argues that the court of appeals erred in holding that the evidence was legally sufficient under the law of parties' conspiracy prong because Appellant did not anticipate the second felony of aggravated assault of a public servant, and thus cannot be guilty under the conspiracy theory of party liability. Appellant argues that it is well settled law that co-conspirators are responsible only for conduct they anticipate. Appellant contends that he had no reason to anticipate violence or assault because he and Sherber were conducting "a drug transaction between old friends who always and repeatedly bought and sold drugs peaceably and amicably." He also could not anticipate that the truck would be used as a deadly weapon because its obvious intended and immediate purpose was merely a means of transporting the men and the drugs. Appellant argues that the truck "does not fall into the category of obvious, apparent, and innately understood deadly weapons in the same fashion as a firearm or switchblade."

Finally, Appellant asserts that the application paragraph of the jury charge failed to instruct the jury to find that he should have anticipated the aggravated assault, and no rational juror could have found beyond a reasonable doubt that Appellant anticipated Sherber's actions. Because Appellant "could not anticipate, as a 7.02(b) conspiracy requires, the truck's use as a deadly weapon, and the jury was not instructed to first find this fact in the application paragraph of the charge, his conviction under 7.02(b) for party liability fails for insufficient evidence."

State's Arguments

The State argues that the evidence is sufficient to establish that Appellant should have anticipated aggravated assault of a public servant as a result of his conspiracy to distribute methamphetamine. Although the application paragraph of the jury charge did not include the "should have anticipated" language from Penal Code Section 7.02(b), the State points out that a review of the sufficiency of the evidence is based on a hypothetically correct jury charge. *Malik v. State*, 953 S.W.2d 234, 240 (Tex. Crim. App.1997). Thus, the State contends that the court of appeals' analysis of the sufficiency of the evidence was correct.

The State says that case law supports a finding that Appellant should have anticipated violence as a result of his conspiracy to commit the felony offense of possession of a controlled substance with intent to distribute. *Ervin v. State*, 333 S.W.3d 187 (Tex. App.—Houston [1st Dist.] 2010, pet. ref'd); *Love v. State*, 199 S.W.3d 447 (Tex. App.—Houston [1st Dist.] 2006, pet. ref'd) (defendant should have anticipated that violence would occur when co-conspirator was armed with a deadly weapon); *Hernandez v. State*, 171 S.W.3d 347 (Tex. App.—Houston [14th Dist.] 2005, pet. ref'd); *Moore v. State*, 24 S.W.3d 444 (Tex. App.—Texarkana 2000, pet. ref'd) (even when co-conspirators were unarmed, a defendant should have anticipated that a deadly weapon might be acquired during the commission of the offense); *Rue v. State*, No. 05–97–00482–CR, 1998 WL 300911 (Tex. App.—Dallas, June 10, 1998, no pet.) (defendant should have anticipated that his co-conspirator would commit aggravated assault when he tried to flee the scene of the offense in his vehicle). The State contends that a jury may make reasonable inferences from the evidence to determine whether a particular offense should have been anticipated as a result of carrying out the conspiracy. The State says that it is well known that drug transactions include risks and that the jury made reasonable inferences from the evidence in determining that Appellant should have anticipated that his conspiracy to deliver drugs could result in the use of the truck in a violent effort to escape from law enforcement.

The State concludes that the question of whether Appellant should have anticipated the secondary felony is one for the jury and that the evidence, when viewed in the light most favorable to the verdict, is sufficient to establish Appellant's guilt as a party to the offense of aggravated assault under the conspiracy theory of the law of parties.

Law of Parties

Texas Penal Code Section 7.02(b) states that "if, in the attempt to carry out a conspiracy to commit one felony, another felony is committed by one of the conspirators, all conspirators are guilty of the felony actually committed, though having no intent to commit it, if the offense was committed in furtherance of the unlawful purpose and was one that should have been anticipated as a result of the carrying out of the conspiracy."

Should have been anticipated by quanity of drugs involved, value of drugs.

528

Analysis

For a defendant to be found guilty as a party to a secondary offense,[1] the jury must determine that the second felony was committed in furtherance of the unlawful purpose and was one that the co-conspirator should have anticipated as a result of carrying out the conspiracy. TEX. PENAL CODE § 7.02(b). Section 7.02(b) does not require the State to prove that Appellant actually anticipated the secondary felony, only that the crime is one that should have been anticipated.

The hypothetically correct jury charge in this case would have included the "should have been anticipated" language in the application paragraph. Thus, to find Appellant guilty of aggravated assault of a public servant under Section 7.02(b), the jury must have determined beyond a reasonable doubt that: (1) Appellant and Sherber engaged in an attempt to carry out a conspiracy to possess and deliver methamphetamine; (2) in that attempt, Appellant's co-conspirator committed aggravated assault of a public servant; (3) the aggravated assault was committed in furtherance of the conspiracy to possess and deliver methamphetamine; and (4) the aggravated assault was an offense that Appellant should have anticipated as a result of carrying out the conspiracy to commit the drug offense.

Issue

The question before us is whether it was rational for the jury to infer that Appellant should have anticipated the second offense. Because the party-conspirator theory of liability under which Appellant was convicted is similar to the federal rule of co-conspirator liability under *Pinkerton v. United States*, 328 U.S. 640 (1946), we will adopt the approach used by federal courts, which focuses on an examination of the totality of the circumstances to determine whether, on the facts of each case, a particular offense committed by a co-conspirator was "reasonably foreseeable" within the scope of the unlawful agreement.

In cases involving large-scale conspiracies to distribute drugs, federal courts have generally taken note of a link between the size of the drug operation and frequent use of weapons and violence. In such cases (for example, those involving tens of thousands of dollars' worth of illicit drugs and/or multiple kilograms being sold in a single transaction), federal courts have typically applied the *Pinkerton* rule to find that co-conspirators' crimes involving violence or weapons were reasonably foreseeable to other members of the conspiracy, thereby triggering co-conspirator liability. *See, e.g., United States v. Dean*, 59 F.3d 1479, 1490 n.20 (5th Cir. 1995) (taking note of "connection between the amount of drugs involved in a transaction, and hence the amount of money, and the foreseeability for Pinkerton purposes" of a co-conspirator's use of weapons or violence); *United States v. Gutierrez*, 978 F.2d 1463, 1468 (7th Cir. 1992) (noting that "the illegal drug industry is a dangerous and violent business," and holding that, because defendants agreed to sell two kilograms of cocaine for $60,000, it was "reasonably foreseeable that a gun would be carried" in relation to the transaction); *United States v. Diaz*, 864 F.2d 544, 549 (7th Cir.1988) (noting that "[w]hen an individual conspires to take part in a street transaction involving a kilogram of cocaine worth $39,000, it certainly is quite reasonable to assume that a weapon of some kind would be carried"); *but see United States v. Castaneda*, 9 F.3d 761, 767 (9th Cir. 1993) (reversing firearm-possession conviction under *Pinkerton* theory because

---

1. Under *Pinkerton*, co-conspirators are liable for the overt acts of every other conspirator done in furtherance of the conspiracy, but only if those acts were reasonably foreseeable.

defendant, wife of a high-level drug dealer, merely answered telephone and took messages, and thus played no more than a "passive role" in drug conspiracy), *overruled on other grounds*, *United States v. Nordby*, 225 F.3d 1053, 1059 (9th Cir. 2000).

On the other hand, in recognition of the fact that small-scale drug operations are less likely to lead to the use of weapons or violence, federal courts have frequently found that co-conspirators' violent acts in furtherance of a drug conspiracy were not reasonably foreseeable in situations involving small quantities of drugs, small amounts of money, small-time drug dealers, or minor participants in the conspiracy. *See, e.g., United States v. Bingham*, 653 F.3d 983, 997 (9th Cir. 2011) (defendants with "extremely minor roles in the conspiracy" not liable for firearm possessed by co-conspirator); *United States v. Wade*, 318 F.3d 698, 703–04 (6th Cir. 2003) (finding "scant evidence" to support finding of foreseeability as to co-conspirator's gun possession where defendant was "retail dealer" in $1,100 sale of crack); *United States v. Cochran*, 14 F.3d 1128, 1133 (6th Cir. 1994) (holding that co-conspirator's firearm possession was not reasonably foreseeable when gun was hidden from defendant's view and there was no evidence that conspiracy involved violence or large quantities of drugs). Among all relevant circumstances, federal courts have considered the quantity of the illegal narcotics, its value, the amount of money possessed by the conspirators, the degree of a defendant's involvement in the conspiracy, the prior relationship of the co-conspirators, the length of time that a defendant may have been involved in the drug trade, and the visibility of any weapons.

Considering the totality of the circumstances in this case, we conclude that Appellant and Sherber were acting together in a criminal business to sell moderate amounts of methamphetamine and that, given the volume of drugs involved, Sherber's assault of the officer in this case was one that should have been anticipated as a result of the carrying out of the conspiracy. The intended delivery to the informant in this case was for two ounces of methamphetamine, an amount that suggests more than personal use. From the 8.51 grams of methamphetamine that were strewn throughout the truck, it appears that Appellant and Sherber intended to sell smaller amounts of methamphetamine to other people in the future. On the six prior occasions when Appellant sold methamphetamine to the informant, the sales ranged from 3.8 grams to one ounce of methamphetamine, and Appellant told the informant that he was in the process of selling a total of one-half of a kilogram so that he could obtain another one-half of a kilogram to sell. Appellant had $3,500 cash in his possession when he was arrested in this case. These facts suggest that, although they were not likely engaged in the large-scale transfer of multiple kilograms and tens of thousands of dollars of drug money, Appellant and Sherber were more than just small-time dealers.

The prior and present relationship between Appellant and Sherber suggests that they were acting jointly to engage in the continuous operation of an enterprise to market and distribute methamphetamine in quantities of grams and ounces. On the six prior occasions when he sold methamphetamine to the informant, Appellant was usually accompanied by Sherber. Furthermore, on this occasion, Sherber drove Appellant across several Texas counties to deliver the drugs and sat in the driver's seat of the truck while Appellant discussed the sale with the informant. Because of the number of repeat transactions, the distance traveled to complete the sale, the quantity of drugs involved, and the amount of cash possessed, Appellant should have anticipated that he and Sherber might become the target of a thief or a police investigation, and that violence might be used either to protect the drugs or to escape.

As we stated in *Hooper*, juries are permitted to draw multiple reasonable inferences from direct or circumstantial evidence. *Hooper*, 214 S.W.3d at 16. It was reasonable for the jury to infer that Appellant should have anticipated that the police could bust the drug transaction, and reasonable for the jury to infer that Appellant should have anticipated that an officer could be injured while attempting to bust the drug transaction. The evidence supports the jury's finding that Appellant should have anticipated the aggravated assault of a public servant in furtherance of the conspiracy to commit the offense of possession of a controlled substance with intent to deliver. There is no indication that the jury engaged in speculation or guessing about the meaning of the evidence or facts to reach this conclusion.

Conclusion

We conclude that a rational jury could find beyond a reasonable doubt that Appellant should have anticipated his co-conspirator committing aggravated assault of a public servant as a result of carrying out their conspiracy to deliver methamphetamine. The court of appeals properly held that the evidence was sufficient to support Appellant's conviction for aggravated assault of a public servant under the conspiracy theory of the law of parties. The judgment of the court of appeals is affirmed.

Notes

1.   The evidence was found to be sufficient to support a conviction under the conspiracy theory of party liability even though the jury was not given this instruction. The reason that this occurred is that sufficiency of the evidence cases are reviewed under a hypothetically correct jury instruction rather than the instruction actually given under *Malik v. State*. Because an appellate decision reversing a conviction for insufficient evidence results in acquittal and a double jeopardy bar to retrial, the Court reasoned that prior caselaw that measured the sufficiency of the evidence based upon the actual jury instruction gave an unwarranted "windfall" to a defendant who would have been convicted if the jury had been properly instructed. Could the jury rationally have reached the verdict that it did on aggravated assault based upon the driver's conduct without the all foreseeable crimes in furtherance of the conspiracy instruction?

2.   Even greater criminal liability was assessed based upon the intersection of party liability and felony murder in *Enmund v. Florida*. Enmund drove the get-away car from a burglary in which his co-defendants did not carry weapons. During the burglary, one of the conspirators gained control of a gun that the victim produced and killed the victim. Although Enmund was not present when the death occurred, he was a party to the burglary during which the death occurred. It was not necessary to show that the shooting death was a foreseeable result of the burglary because the intent transferring crime of felony murder was involved. The United States Supreme Court reversed the death sentence on the ground that a death sentence was a grossly disproportionate penalty for someone whose role in the offense was as minor as Enmund's

participation in the crime. Nonetheless, the felony murder conviction was affirmed and a life sentence could be imposed. Is it appropriate that Anderson received life imprisonment for a non-lethal crime that does not have the unique intent transferring effect of felony murder?

3.   The "*Pinkerton* Rule," relied upon by the Court in *Anderson* is a famous United States Supreme Court opinion that deals with the scope of a conspiracy rather than the use of conspiracy as a theory of complicity. As *Anderson* demonstrates, the broad scope of conspiracy allowed under *Pinkerton* has been carried over to party liability. Under *Pinkerton*, once a person has been shown to be a part of a conspiracy, the rule allows for vicarious liability for the crimes of co-conspirators that fall within the scope of the criminal plan and, where the actions of a co-conspirator fall outside the scope of the criminal agreement, to all criminal acts that were "reasonably foreseeable." By virtue of the criminal agreement, the acts and intentions of one coconspirator become the acts and intentions of the others, and liability can be attributed to all conspirators.

4.   The *Enmund* case involved a felony murder but *Anderson* did not involve a homicide or felony murder theory. There is no mental state required for the death in a felony murder case; rather the mental state needed is only the one necessary for the underlying felony. By contrast, the aggravated assault statute requires a mental state with regard to the result of causing serious bodily injury. If the legislature makes the mental state part of the definition of the crime, doesn't the conspiracy theory of party liability reduce the mental state to negligence by the use of reasonably foreseeable language? Doesn't that violate the principle of *Mullaney/Patterson* that the state must prove every element of the offense as defined by the legislature?

Challenges have been made to the conspiracy method of party liability statute on *Mullaney/ Patterson* grounds but, so far, without success. A typical response to this claim came was provided by the Third Court of Appeals in case upholding a capital murder conviction and a sentence of life imprisonment without the possibility of parole in *Gravis v. State*, 982 S.W.2d 933, 938 (Tex.App.—Austin 1998, pet. ref'd). The Court reasoned that:

> While this section [7.02 (b) Texas Penal Code] allows criminal responsibility for the conduct of another, thereby eliminating the necessity for proof of intent to commit the felony actually committed [capital murder], it does not excuse the state from proving a culpable mental state. In fact, the statute requires the state to show that the defendant had *both* the *mens rea* to engage in a conspiracy and the culpable mental state to commit the underlying, *i.e.*, the intended felony. The mental state required for the underlying felony supplies the *mens rea* for the felony actually committed by the co-conspirator.

Accessory After the Fact: Hindering Apprehension or Prosecution

The common law crime of misprison of felony developed at a time before professional police forces. Anyone who knew of the existence of a felony but failed to report it, could be found guilty of misprison and was subject to a fine. The offense emphasized the communal obligation to enforce the law. With the development of professional police forces beginning in the 18th century, the crime of misprison began to change. It is doubtful that this English offense requiring an affirmative duty to report was ever transplanted to America.

Texas and most states have followed the lead of the Model Penal Code in eliminating party liability for a person who intentionally provides post-crime aid to the felons who committed the crime. However, most jurisdictions have some type of criminal statute providing separate penalties for those who would have been accessories after the fact under the common law. The Texas statute, Section 38.05 entitled "Hindering Apprehension or Prosecution," is a typical statute that requires some type of affirmative assistance. The *Stephens* case that follows is a Wyoming case that examines the nature of the aid that is needed for conviction under a law similar to the Texas statute.

Knew abt burglary

Stephens v. State

734 P.2d 555 (Wy. 1987)

Brown, Chief Justice.

issue

This is an appeal from a conviction of accessory after the fact to the commission of a burglary, in violation of § 6-5-202, W.S.1977. The issues raised by appellant are whether or not there was sufficient evidence of the element of "rendering assistance" and of the element of "intent" to sustain the conviction. We hold that there was not sufficient evidence of either element, and reverse the conviction. *Holding*

On December 1, 1985, appellant was at his ex-wife's residence with Harry Van Buren. Appellant agreed to let Van Buren stay with him that evening and in return Van Buren agreed to help appellant look for a part for appellant's truck the following morning. Appellant left the house about three o'clock that afternoon, while Van Buren remained. The next time appellant saw Van Buren was about 8:00 that evening. At that time, Van Buren informed appellant and appellant's girlfriend that he had burglarized Yellowstone Electric hours earlier. Appellant told Van Buren he "didn't want to hear about it." The next morning appellant and his girlfriend awoke to find Van Buren gone. He returned around 7:30 a.m., and went with appellant to look for the truck part, as previously arranged.

When appellant was unable to find the truck part he needed he asked Van Buren to give him some money to purchase a car. Van Buren complied, giving appellant $100. Thereafter, an automobile was purchased and the two traveled back to the home, appellant driving the recently purchased car while Van Buren drove the truck. Upon arriving home, appellant noticed that Van Buren, having arrived home already, was being questioned by police officers in a police car. Subsequently, appellant was approached by the police officers.

When the officers questioned appellant about the burglary and Van Buren's possible role in it, appellant replied that he did not know anything about it. Upon further questioning, appellant informed the officers that a few years earlier he had received money from Van Buren from a similar burglary. Appellant told the officers that he had learned his lesson after the earlier burglary and would not get involved in that situation again.

About fifteen minutes later the police confronted appellant with some information they had received from his girlfriend, and appellant then admitted that he knew of the burglary and of Van Buren's role in it. Appellant also told the officers that he had told Van Buren he did not want to know about it.

The statute under which appellant was convicted reads, in part:

(a) A person is an accessory after the fact if, with intent to hinder, delay or prevent the discovery, detection, apprehension, prosecution, detention, conviction or punishment of another for the commission of a crime, he renders assistance to the person.

The two elements that appellant contends are missing are the elements of intent and rendering assistance.

Rendering Assistance

"Render assistance" is defined in § 6-5-201 as follows:

(A) Harbor or conceal the person;

(B) Warn the person of impending discovery or apprehension, excluding an official warning given in an effort to bring the person into compliance with the law;

(D) By force, intimidation or deception, obstruct anyone in the performance of any act which might aid in the discovery, detection, apprehension, prosecution, conviction or punishment of the person.

The state contends that appellant rendered assistance by harboring or concealing Van Buren and by helping Van Buren to avoid discovery and apprehension. The facts that the state relies on are that appellant provided Van Buren a place to stay the night after the burglary and that he denied knowledge of Van Burens involvement in the burglary. Case law from other jurisdictions does not support this argument.

In the case of *State v. Clifford*, 502 P.2d 1371 (Ore. 1972), the defendant saw Douglas Wright a day after Wright murdered two people and kidnapped a five-year-old boy. After learning of the murder, defendant was arrested on other charges and asked by the police if he had seen Wright. Defendant told the police either that he had not seen Wright, or that he had not seen him in a long time. The Oregon Supreme Court, after reciting the common-law history of the offense of being an accessory after the fact, concluded that there was no sharp line between conduct which constituted aiding or concealing and that which does not. However, some type of line may be drawn from examples given.

> [T]he examples describing criminal conduct uniformly consist of an affirmative act from which the intention to aid an offender, to escape arrest, conviction or punishment is obvious. None of the examples indicate that a mere denial of knowledge of the whereabouts of an offender at some time in the past would amount to accessorial conduct.

State v. Clifford, supra, at 1374.

Furthermore, other cases uniformly support the conclusion reached by the Oregon Supreme Court, that is, merely denying knowledge of the principal's involvement in a crime will not give rise to a charge of accessory after the fact. *See Findley v. State*, 378 S.W.2d 850 (Tex. Crim. App. 1964); *Tipton v. State*, 72 S.W.2d 290 (Tex. Crim. App. 1934). A mere denial of knowledge is to be differentiated from an "affirmative statement of facts tending to raise any defense for (the principal), or a statement within itself indicating an effort to shield or protect (the principal)." *State v. Clifford, supra*, 502 P.2d at 1374, quoting from *Tipton v. State, supra*.

Such an affirmative statement would be such as supplying a false alibi. This amounts to more than passive nondisclosure.

In the case here, appellant did nothing more than passively deny knowledge of Van Buren's involvement in the burglary. When finally confronted by the statement made by his girlfriend, appellant relented and told the police what he really knew. This does not rise to the level of helping Van Buren avoid discovery and detection, especially in light of appellant's probable intent, which will be discussed later.

Further, we question whether appellant actually harbored Van Buren. Again, case law supports appellant. Here, the distinction is between active concealment and merely allowing a person to stay in one's home. This distinction is examined in the case of *United States v. Bissonette*, 586 F.2d 73 (8th Cir. 1978). There, the defendant kept several juveniles, including her grandson, in her basement following a shooting and jail break, of which she was aware. "She [the defendant] told [the juveniles] and the others to stay in the basement when she was out of the house, to keep the doors locked, and the blinds drawn. In the following days, she purchased food and cooked for [the juveniles] and cashed a check for [her grandson]."

The federal court found that the defendant's conduct went beyond merely offering the juveniles the comforts of her home. "She instructed the fugitives to stay in the basement when she was out of the house, to keep the blinds drawn, and the doors locked; she berated them when they tried to contact friends outside the house, lest their discovery result." This all resulted in an affirmative, continuing pattern of conduct establishing the intent of the defendant to prevent apprehension of her grandson by the authorities.

The *Bissonette* case is far different than the case before us. Here, appellant had agreed to let Van Buren spend the night at his home. This agreement was made before appellant had any knowledge of a burglary. Further, appellant did not keep Van Buren concealed, but rather, was accompanied by him in public to look for a truck part, and then to purchase a car. There was no active concealment.

[handwritten: simply denying knowledge] Intent *[handwritten: of the crime is not enough]*

Appellant also contends there was insufficient evidence of intent to uphold his conviction. The requisite intent, from a plain reading of the statute, is to hinder, prevent or delay the discovery or apprehension, etc., of the principal. Once more, case law is in appellant's favor.

> If, however, the act is a mere false denial of knowledge which may have been motivated by self-interest, there must also be evidence from which the jury could infer that the actor told the lie with the intent to aid the offender and that the lie was, under the existing circumstances, likely to aid the offender to escape arrest or punishment.

State v. Clifford, supra, at 1374−75.

The intent evident from the testimony presented at trial was clearly self-motivated. First, Van Buren had already been apprehended by the police when they questioned appellant. Second, appellant knew that he was guilty himself of receiving stolen property (the $100 that Van Buren

[handwritten: Gen rule: OK to lie to police (101)]

gave him to buy a car).[1] Further, appellant knew that four years ago when an almost identical situation arose, he ended up with a felony on his record and a two to four year sentence, suspended, with four years' probation. Appellant certainly had plenty of self-interest in denying any knowledge of Van Buren's activities in the present instance. Further, no other evidence presented at trial indicated any intent of appellant to benefit Van Buren.

[W]e are unable to find evidence sufficient to uphold appellant's conviction, either on the element of intent or of rendering assistance. The conviction is reversed and the charge of accessory after the fact is dismissed.

Notes

1.   The Texas cases cited in *Stephens* were decided before the 1974 Code in Texas when accessories after the fact were considered to be parties to the crime assisted. However, the Texas cases cited in *Stephens* both held that one who merely provided a false denial of knowledge without affirmative aid was not an accessory after the fact. *See Findley v. State*, 378 S.W.2d 850 (Tex. Crim. App. 1964); *Tipton v. State*, 72 S.W.2d 290 (Tex. Crim. App. 1934). This tradition is carried over to the hindering separate offense. Not every jurisdiction has exempted such false statements from criminal liability. The federal system, for example, makes it a crime to make a false statement to a federal officer.

2.   It is important to remember that a prior agreement to provide post-crime aid is sufficient to make one a party (an accessory <u>before</u> the fact in common law terminology). The issue of whether there was a prior agreement can be inferred circumstantially. For example, consider the case of *Guillory v. State*, 877 S.W. 2d 71 (Houston [1st Dist.] 1994):

> About 2:30 in the afternoon on Easter Sunday 1992, Betty Howard was in the parking lot of a Kroger store, loading groceries into the rear of her car, when she was accosted by a woman later identified as Jamie McBride. McBride grabbed Howard's arm, took her purse, shoved her against the car, and ran off. Howard called out for help, and several people ran after McBride; as they got close, a late model pickup truck drove up, and the man driving opened the door. As McBride got in, Paul Castillo grabbed onto the back of the pickup truck, and hung on for several seconds in a futile attempt to stop the truck. He let go as the truck sped off . . . .

> An hour or two later, McBride returned to the Kroger store, accompanied by Guillory, in a different vehicle. One of those who had chased McBride earlier, Willie Johnson, the store security guard, recognized Guillory and McBride, and called the Houston Police. Johnson also alerted the store manager, who then followed McBride and Guillory while they were inside. The pair were detained as they were emerging from the store, and both Howard and Castillo were called to come back; they both identified McBride as the person who had shoved Howard and stolen her purse. Castillo further identified Guillory as the driver of the pickup truck.

---

1. Appellant pled *nolo contendre* to the charge of receiving stolen property as a result of this incident. He received a sentence of four months in the county jail, with credit for time served, and with one month suspended.

Appellant contends that the charge required the jury to find that he had participated in the robbery as a principal, and that even in the light most favorable to the verdict, the evidence presented at trial showed, at most, only that he was a party to the offense, not a principal.

To sustain a conviction as a party to an offense, there must be evidence of a common purpose or design prior to, or contemporaneous with, the criminal event. . . . An appellate court may look, however, to events before, during, and after the commission of the offense in determining whether an individual is a party. If the evidence shows only the mere presence of an accused at the scene of an offense, or even his flight from the scene, without more, then it is insufficient to sustain a conviction as a party to the offense. Standing alone, proof that an accused assisted the primary actor in making his getaway is likewise insufficient—even though the accused's conduct may constitute the independent offense of hindering apprehension or prosecution under TEX. PENAL CODE ANN. § 38.05 (West). However, presence at, or flight from, the scene may combine with other facts to show that the accused was a participant in the offense.

[The state's witnesses] testified, without material difference, to what they saw of McBride's getaway: the pickup truck came up fast as those pursuing McBride got close to her, the driver opened the door, she jumped in, and they took off. Here, unlike in several other cases where the driver of a getaway vehicle unsuccessfully challenged the sufficiency of the evidence to support his or her conviction as a party to an offense, the State presented no evidence from any of its witnesses concerning where the getaway vehicle was, or what its driver was doing, before the robbery. Howard testified, however, that there were six or seven people in her immediate vicinity—within three or four car lengths—when McBride snatched her purse. In addition, Johnson testified, without objection, that when McBride and Guillory were detained as they were emerging from the store, each had items on his or her person that the store manager had seen them shoplift.

The jury could reasonably conclude from Howard's testimony, that McBride would not have undertaken a daytime robbery with so many people so close at hand unless she had planned in advance for a means of escape more reliable than spontaneous assistance from Guillory, and that McBride and Guillory had prearranged her getaway. The jury could also reasonably conclude . . . that McBride and Guillory acted pursuant to a common purpose or design; . . . the two of them lived together, were together before and after that offense, and they were in possession of stolen property at the time they were arrested . . . . Ultimately, from all the evidence before it, the jury could reasonably conclude that McBride and Guillory had acted pursuant to a common purpose or design in robbing Howard.

Appendix of Selected Texas Statutes

Texas Penal Code (Excerpts)

Sec.1.03. Effect of Code.
(a) Conduct does not constitute an offense unless it is defined as an offense by statute, municipal ordinance, order of a county commisioners court, or rule authorized by and lawfully adopted under a statute.
(b) The provisions of Titles 1, 2, and 3 apply to offenses defined by other laws, unless the statute defining the offense provides otherwise; however, the punishment affixed to an offense defined outside this code shall be applicable unless the punishment is classified in accordance with this code.
(c) This code does not bar, suspend, or otherwise affect a right or liability to damages, penalty, forfeiture, or other remedy authorized by law to be recovered or enforced in a civil suit for conduct this code defines as an offense, and the civil injury is not merged in the offense.

CHAPTER 2 BURDEN OF PROOF

Sec. 2.01. Proof Beyond a Reasonable Doubt.
All persons are presumed to be innocent and no person may be convicted of an offense unless each element of the offense is proved beyond a reasonable doubt. The fact that he has been arrested, confined, or indicted for, or otherwise charged with, the offense gives rise to no inference of guilt at his trial.

Sec. 2.02. Exception.
(a) An exception to an offense in this code is so labeled by the phrase: ``It is an exception to the application of ....''
(b) The prosecuting attorney must negate the existence of an exception in the accusation charging commission of the offense and prove beyond a reasonable doubt that the defendant or defendant's conduct does not fall within the exception.
(c) This section does not affect exceptions applicable to offenses enacted prior to the effective date of this code.

Sec. 2.03. Defense.
(a) A defense to prosecution for an offense in this code is so labeled by the phrase: ``It is a defense to prosecution ....''
(b) The prosecuting attorney is not required to negate the existence of a defense in the accusation charging commission of the offense.
(c) The issue of the existence of a defense is not submitted to the jury unless evidence is admitted supporting the defense.
(d) If the issue of the existence of a defense is submitted to the jury, the court shall charge that a reasonable doubt on the issue requires that the defendant be acquitted.

(e) A ground of defense in a penal law that is not plainly labeled in accordance with this chapter has the procedural and evidentiary consequences of a defense.

Sec. 2.04. Affirmative Defense.
(a) An affirmative defense in this code is so labeled by the phrase: ``It is an affirmative defense to prosecution ....''
(b) The prosecuting attorney is not required to negate the existence of an affirmative defense in the accusation charging commission of the offense.
(c) The issue of the existence of an affirmative defense is not submitted to the jury unless evidence is admitted supporting the defense.
(d) If the issue of the existence of an affirmative defense is submitted to the jury, the court shall charge that the defendant must prove the affirmative defense by a preponderance of evidence.

Sec. 2.05. Presumption.
When this code or another penal law establishes a presumption with respect to any fact, it has the following consequences:

(1) if there is sufficient evidence of the facts that give rise to the presumption, the issue of the existence of the presumed fact must be submitted to the jury, unless the court is satisfied that the evidence as a whole clearly precludes a finding beyond a reasonable doubt of the presumed fact; and
(2) if the existence of the presumed fact is submitted to the jury, the court shall charge the jury, in terms of the presumption and the specific element to which it applies, as follows:
> (A) that the facts giving rise to the presumption must be proven beyond a reasonable doubt;
> (B) that if such facts are proven beyond a reasonable doubt the jury may find that the element of the offense sought to be presumed exists, but it is not bound to so find;
> (C) that even though the jury may find the existence of such element, the state must prove beyond a reasonable doubt each of the other elements of the offense charged; and
> (D) if the jury has a reasonable doubt as to the existence of a fact or facts giving rise to the presumption, the presumption fails and the jury shall not consider the presumption for any purpose.

CHAPTER 6 CULPABILITY GENERALLY

Sec.6.01. Requirement of Voluntary Act or Omission.
(a) A person commits an offense only if he voluntarily engages in conduct, including an act, an omission, or possession.
(b) Possession is a voluntary act if the possessor knowingly obtains or receives the thing possessed or is aware of his control of the thing for a sufficient time to permit him to terminate his control.

(c) A person who omits to perform an act does not commit an offense unless a law as defined by Section 1.07 provides that the omission is an offense or otherwise provides that he has a duty to perform the act.

Sec. 6.02. Requirement of Culpability.

(a) Except as provided in Subsection (b), a person does not commit an offense unless he intentionally, knowingly, recklessly, or with criminal negligence engages in conduct as the definition of the offense requires.

(b) If the definition of an offense does not prescribe a culpable mental state, a culpable mental state is nevertheless required unless the definition plainly dispenses with any mental element.

(c) If the definition of an offense does not prescribe a culpable mental state, but one is nevertheless required under Subsection (b), intent, knowledge, or recklessness suffices to establish criminal responsibility.

(d) Culpable mental states are classified according to relative degrees, from highest to lowest, as follows:

> (1) intentional;
> (2) knowing;
> (3) reckless;
> (4) criminal negligence.

(e) Proof of a higher degree of culpability than that charged constitutes proof of the culpability charged.

Sec. 6.03. Definitions of Culpable Mental States.

(a) A person acts intentionally, or with intent, with respect to the nature of his conduct or to a result of his conduct when it is his conscious objective or desire to engage in the conduct or cause the result.

(b) A person acts knowingly, or with knowledge, with respect to the nature of his conduct or to circumstances surrounding his conduct when he is aware of the nature of his conduct or that the circumstances exist. A person acts knowingly, or with knowledge, with respect to a result of his conduct when he is aware that his conduct is reasonably certain to cause the result.

(c) A person acts recklessly, or is reckless, with respect to circumstances surrounding his conduct or the result of his conduct when he is aware of but consciously disregards a substantial and unjustifiable risk that the circumstances exist or the result will occur. The risk must be of such a nature and degree that its disregard constitutes a gross deviation from the standard of care that an ordinary person would exercise under all the circumstances as viewed from the actor's standpoint.

(d) A person acts with criminal negligence, or is criminally negligent, with respect to circumstances surrounding his conduct or the result of his conduct when he ought to be aware of a substantial and unjustifiable risk that the circumstances exist or the result will occur. The risk must be of such a nature and degree that the failure to perceive it constitutes a gross deviation from the standard of care that an ordinary person would exercise under all the circumstances as viewed from the actor's standpoint.

Sec. 6.04. Causation: Conduct and Results.

(a) A person is criminally responsible if the result would not have occurred but for his conduct, operating either alone or concurrently with another cause, unless the concurrent cause was clearly sufficient to produce the result and the conduct of the actor clearly insufficient.

(b) A person is nevertheless criminally responsible for causing a result if the only difference between what actually occurred and what he desired, contemplated, or risked is that:

>   (1) a different offense was committed; or

>   (2) a different person or property was injured, harmed, or otherwise affected.

CHAPTER 7 CRIMINAL RESPONSIBILITY FOR CONDUCT OF ANOTHER

SUBCHAPTER A COMPLICITY

Sec. 7.01. Parties to Offenses.

(a) A person is criminally responsible as a party to an offense if the offense is committed by his own conduct, by the conduct of another for which he is criminally responsible, or by both.

(b) Each party to an offense may be charged with commission of the offense.

(c) All traditional distinctions between accomplices and principals are abolished by this section, and each party to an offense may be charged and convicted without alleging that he acted as a principal or accomplice.

Sec. 7.02. Criminal Responsibility for Conduct of Another.

(a) A person is criminally responsible for an offense committed by the conduct of another if:

>   (1) acting with the kind of culpability required for the offense, he causes or aids an innocent or nonresponsible person to engage in conduct prohibited by the definition of the offense;

>   (2) acting with intent to promote or assist the commission of the offense, he solicits, encourages, directs, aids, or attempts to aid the other person to commit the offense; or

>   (3) having a legal duty to prevent commission of the offense and acting with intent to promote or assist its commission, he fails to make a reasonable effort to prevent commission of the offense.

(b) If, in the attempt to carry out a conspiracy to commit one felony, another felony is committed by one of the conspirators, all conspirators are guilty of the felony actually committed, though having no intent to commit it, if the offense was committed in furtherance of the unlawful purpose and was one that should have been anticipated as a result of the carrying out of the conspiracy.

Sec. 7.03. Defenses Excluded.

In a prosecution in which an actor's criminal responsibility is based on the conduct of another, the actor may be convicted on proof of commission of the offense and that he was a party to its commission, and it is no defense:

(1) that the actor belongs to a class of persons that by definition of the offense is legally incapable of committing the offense in an individual capacity; or

(2) that the person for whose conduct the actor is criminally responsible has been acquitted, has not been prosecuted or convicted, has been convicted of a different offense or of a different type or class of offense, or is immune from prosecution.

CHAPTER 8 GENERAL DEFENSES TO CRIMINAL RESPONSIBILITY

Sec.8.01. Insanity.

(a) It is an affirmative defense to prosecution that, at the time of the conduct charged, the actor, as a result of severe mental disease or defect, did not know that his conduct was wrong.

(b) The term ``mental disease or defect'' does not include an abnormality manifested only by repeated criminal or otherwise antisocial conduct.

Sec.8.02. Mistake of Fact.

(a) It is a defense to prosecution that the actor through mistake formed a reasonable belief about a matter of fact if his mistaken belief negated the kind of culpability required for commission of the offense.

(b) Although an actor's mistake of fact may constitute a defense to the offense charged, he may nevertheless be convicted of any lesser included offense of which he would be guilty if the fact were as he believed.

Sec. 8.03. Mistake of Law.

(a) It is no defense to prosecution that the actor was ignorant of the provisions of any law after the law has taken effect.

(b) It is an affirmative defense to prosecution that the actor reasonably believed the conduct charged did not constitute a crime and that he acted in reasonable reliance upon:

> (1) an official statement of the law contained in a written order or grant of permission by an administrative agency charged by law with responsibility for interpreting the law in question; or
>
> (2) a written interpretation of the law contained in an opinion of a court of record or made by a public official charged by law with responsibility for interpreting the law in question.

(c) Although an actor's mistake of law may constitute a defense to the offense charged, he may nevertheless be convicted of a lesser included offense of which he would be guilty if the law were as he believed.

Sec. 8.04. Intoxication.

(a) Voluntary intoxication does not constitute a defense to the commission of crime.

(b) Evidence of temporary insanity caused by intoxication may be introduced by the actor in mitigation of the penalty attached to the offense for which he is being tried.

(c) When temporary insanity is relied upon as a defense and the evidence tends to show that such insanity was caused by intoxication, the court shall charge the jury in accordance with the provisions of this section.

(d) For purposes of this section ``intoxication'' means disturbance of mental or physical capacity resulting from the introduction of any substance into the body.

Sec. 8.05. Duress.

(a) It is an affirmative defense to prosecution that the actor engaged in the proscribed conduct because he was compelled to do so by threat of imminent death or serious bodily injury to himself or another.

(b) In a prosecution for an offense that does not constitute a felony, it is an affirmative defense to prosecution that the actor engaged in the proscribed conduct because he was compelled to do so by force or threat of force.

(c) Compulsion within the meaning of this section exists only if the force or threat of force would render a person of reasonable firmness incapable of resisting the pressure.

(d) The defense provided by this section is unavailable if the actor intentionally, knowingly, or recklessly placed himself in a situation in which it was probable that he would be subjected to compulsion.

(e) It is no defense that a person acted at the command or persuasion of his spouse, unless he acted under compulsion that would establish a defense under this section.

Sec. 8.06. Entrapment.

(a) It is a defense to prosecution that the actor engaged in the conduct charged because he was induced to do so by a law enforcement agent using persuasion or other means likely to cause persons to commit the offense. Conduct merely affording a person an opportunity to commit an offense does not constitute entrapment.

(b) In this section "law enforcement agent"' includes personnel of the state and local law enforcement agencies as well as of the United States and any person acting in accordance with instructions from such agents.

Sec. 8.07. Age Affecting Criminal Responsibility.

(a) A person may not be prosecuted for or convicted of any offense that the person committed when younger than 15 years of age except:

    (1) perjury and aggravated perjury when it appears by proof that the person had sufficient discretion to understand the nature and obligation of an oath;

    (2) a violation of a penal statute cognizable under Chapter 729, Transportation Code, except for:

        (A) an offense under Section 521.457, Transportation Code;

        (B) an offense under Section 550.021, Transportation Code;

        (C) an offense punishable as a Class B misdemeanor under Section 550.022, Transportation Code;

        (D) an offense punishable as a Class B misdemeanor under Section 550.024, Transportation Code; or

(E) an offense punishable as a Class B misdemeanor under Section 550.025, Transportation Code;

(3) a violation of a motor vehicle traffic ordinance of an incorporated city or town in this state;

(4) a misdemeanor punishable by fine only other than public intoxication;

(5) a violation of a penal ordinance of a political subdivision;

(6) a violation of a penal statute that is, or is a lesser included offense of, a capital felony, an aggravated controlled substance felony, or a felony of the first degree for which the person is transferred to the court under Section 54.02, Family Code, for prosecution if the person committed the offense when 14 years of age or older; or

(7) a capital felony or an offense under Section 19.02 for which the person is transferred to the court under Section 54.02(j)(2)(A), Family Code.

(b) Unless the juvenile court waives jurisdiction under Section 54.02, Family Code, and certifies the individual for criminal prosecution or the juvenile court has previously waived jurisdiction under that section and certified the individual for criminal prosecution, a person may not be prosecuted for or convicted of any offense committed before reaching 17 years of age except an offense described by Subsections (a)(1)-(5).

(c) No person may, in any case, be punished by death for an offense committed while he was younger than 17 years.

CHAPTER 9 JUSTIFICATION EXCLUDING CRIMINAL RESPONSIBILITY

SUBCHAPTER A GENERAL PROVISIONS

Sec. 9.01. Definitions.
In this chapter:

(1) "Custody" has the meaning assigned by Section 38.01.

(2) "Escape'" has the meaning assigned by Section 38.01.

(3) "Deadly force'" means force that is intended or known by the actor to cause, or in the manner of its use or intended use is capable of causing, death or serious bodily injury.

Sec. 9.02. Justification as a Defense.
It is a defense to prosecution that the conduct in question is justified under this chapter.

Sec. 9.03. Confinement as Justifiable Force.
Confinement is justified when force is justified by this chapter if the actor takes reasonable measures to terminate the confinement as soon as he knows he safely can unless the person confined has been arrested for an offense.

Sec. 9.04. Threats as Justifiable Force.
The threat of force is justified when the use of force is justified by this chapter. For purposes of this section, a threat to cause death or serious bodily injury by the production of a weapon or

otherwise, as long as the actor's purpose is limited to creating an apprehension that he will use deadly force if necessary, does not constitute the use of deadly force.

Sec. 9.05. Reckless Injury of Innocent Third Person.

Even though an actor is justified under this chapter in threatening or using force or deadly force against another, if in doing so he also recklessly injures or kills an innocent third person, the justification afforded by this chapter is unavailable in a prosecution for the reckless injury or killing of the innocent third person.

Sec. 9.06. Civil Remedies Unaffected.

The fact that conduct is justified under this chapter does not abolish or impair any remedy for the conduct that is available in a civil suit.

SUBCHAPTER B JUSTIFICATION GENERALLY

Sec. 9.21. Public Duty.

(a) Except as qualified by Subsections (b) and (c), conduct is justified if the actor reasonably believes the conduct is required or authorized by law, by the judgment or order of a competent court or other governmental tribunal, or in the execution of legal process.

(b) The other sections of this chapter control when force is used against a person to protect persons (Subchapter C), to protect property (Subchapter D), for law enforcement (Subchapter E), or by virtue of a special relationship (Subchapter F).

(c) The use of deadly force is not justified under this section unless the actor reasonably believes the deadly force is specifically required by statute or unless it occurs in the lawful conduct of war. If deadly force is so justified, there is no duty to retreat before using it.

(d) The justification afforded by this section is available if the actor reasonably believes:

>   (1) the court or governmental tribunal has jurisdiction or the process is lawful, even though the court or governmental tribunal lacks jurisdiction or the process is unlawful; or
>   (2) his conduct is required or authorized to assist a public servant in the performance of his official duty, even though the servant exceeds his lawful authority.

Sec. 9.22. Necessity.

Conduct is justified if:

(1) the actor reasonably believes the conduct is immediately necessary to avoid imminent harm;

(2) the desirability and urgency of avoiding the harm clearly outweigh, according to ordinary standards of reasonableness, the harm sought to be prevented by the law proscribing the conduct; and

(3) a legislative purpose to exclude the justification claimed for the conduct does not otherwise plainly appear.

SUBCHAPTER C PROTECTION OF PERSONS

Sec. 9.31. SELF-DEFENSE.

(a) Except as provided in Subsection (b), a person is justified in using force against another when and to the degree the actor reasonably believes the force is immediately necessary to protect the actor against the other's use or attempted use of unlawful force. The actor's belief that the force was immediately necessary as described by this subsection is presumed to be reasonable if the actor:

    (1) knew or had reason to believe that the person against whom the force was used:

        (A) unlawfully and with force entered, or was attempting to enter unlawfully and with force, the actor's occupied habitation, vehicle, or place of business or employment;

        (B) unlawfully and with force removed, or was attempting to remove unlawfully and with force, the actor from the actor's habitation, vehicle, or place of business or employment; or

        (C) was committing or attempting to commit aggravated kidnapping, murder, sexual assault, aggravated sexual assault, robbery, or aggravated robbery;

    (2) did not provoke the person against whom the force was used; and

    (3) was not otherwise engaged in criminal activity, other than a Class C misdemeanor that is a violation of a law or ordinance regulating traffic at the time the force was used.

(b) The use of force against another is not justified:

    (1) in response to verbal provocation alone;

    (2) to resist an arrest or search that the actor knows is being made by a peace officer, or by a person acting in a peace officer's presence and at his direction, even though the arrest or search is unlawful, unless the resistance is justified under Subsection (c);

    (3) if the actor consented to the exact force used or attempted by the other;

    (4) if the actor provoked the other's use or attempted use of unlawful force, unless:

        (A) the actor abandons the encounter, or clearly communicates to the other his intent to do so reasonably believing he cannot safely abandon the encounter; and

        (B) the other nevertheless continues or attempts to use unlawful force against the actor; or

    (5) if the actor sought an explanation from or discussion with the other person concerning the actor's differences with the other person while the actor was:

        (A) carrying a weapon in violation of Section 46.02; or

        (B) possessing or transporting a weapon in violation of Section 46.05.

(c) The use of force to resist an arrest or search is justified:

    (1) if, before the actor offers any resistance, the peace officer (or person acting at his direction) uses or attempts to use greater force than necessary to make the arrest or search; and

    (2) when and to the degree the actor reasonably believes the force is immediately necessary to protect himself against the peace officer's (or other person's) use or attempted use of greater force than necessary.

(d) The use of deadly force is not justified under this subchapter except as provided in Sections 9.32, 9.33, and 9.34.

(e) A person who has a right to be present at the location where the force is used, who has not provoked the person against whom the force is used, and who is not engaged in criminal activity at the time the force is used is not required to retreat before using force as described by this section.

(f) For purposes of Subsection (a), in determining whether an actor described by Subsection (e) reasonably believed that the use of force was necessary, a finder of fact may not consider whether the actor failed to retreat.

Sec. 9.32. DEADLY FORCE IN DEFENSE OF PERSON.

(a) A person is justified in using deadly force against another:

    (1) if the actor would be justified in using force against the other under Section 9.31; and

    (2) when and to the degree the actor reasonably believes the deadly force is immediately necessary:

        (A) to protect the actor against the other's use or attempted use of unlawful deadly force; or

        (B) to prevent the other's imminent commission of aggravated kidnapping, murder, sexual assault, aggravated sexual assault, robbery, or aggravated robbery.

(b) The actor's belief under Subsection (a)(2) that the deadly force was immediately necessary as described by that subdivision is presumed to be reasonable if the actor:

    (1) knew or had reason to believe that the person against whom the deadly force was used:

        (A) unlawfully and with force entered, or was attempting to enter unlawfully and with force, the actor's occupied habitation, vehicle, or place of business or employment;

(B) unlawfully and with force removed, or was attempting to remove unlawfully and with force, the actor from the actor's habitation, vehicle, or place of business or employment; or

(C) was committing or attempting to commit an offense described by Subsection (a)(2)(B);

(2) did not provoke the person against whom the force was used; and

(3) was not otherwise engaged in criminal activity, other than a Class C misdemeanor that is a violation of a law or ordinance regulating traffic at the time the force was used.

(c) A person who has a right to be present at the location where the deadly force is used, who has not provoked the person against whom the deadly force is used, and who is not engaged in criminal activity at the time the deadly force is used is not required to retreat before using deadly force as described by this section.

(d) For purposes of Subsection (a)(2), in determining whether an actor described by Subsection (c) reasonably believed that the use of deadly force was necessary, a finder of fact may not consider whether the actor failed to retreat.

Sec. 9.33. Defense of Third Person.

A person is justified in using force or deadly force against another to protect a third person if:

(1) under the circumstances as the actor reasonably believes them to be, the actor would be justified under Section 9.31 or 9.32 in using force or deadly force to protect himself against the unlawful force or unlawful deadly force he reasonably believes to be threatening the third person he seeks to protect; and

(2) the actor reasonably believes that his intervention is immediately necessary to protect the third person.

Sec. 9.34. Protection of Life or Health.

(a) A person is justified in using force, but not deadly force, against another when and to the degree he reasonably believes the force is immediately necessary to prevent the other from committing suicide or inflicting serious bodily injury to himself.

(b) A person is justified in using both force and deadly force against another when and to the degree he reasonably believes the force or deadly force is immediately necessary to preserve the other's life in an emergency.

SUBCHAPTER D PROTECTION OF PROPERTY

Sec. 9.41. Protection of One's Own Property.

(a) A person in lawful possession of land or tangible, movable property is justified in using force against another when and to the degree the actor reasonably believes the force is immediately necessary to prevent or terminate the other's trespass on the land or unlawful interference with the property.

(b) A person unlawfully dispossessed of land or tangible, movable property by another is justified in using force against the other when and to the degree the actor reasonably believes the force is immediately necessary to reenter the land or recover the property if the actor uses the force immediately or in fresh pursuit after the dispossession and:

> (1) the actor reasonably believes the other had no claim of right when he dispossessed the actor; or
>
> (2) the other accomplished the dispossession by using force, threat, or fraud against the actor.

Sec. 9.42. Deadly Force to Protect Property.

A person is justified in using deadly force against another to protect land or tangible, movable property:

(1) if he would be justified in using force against the other under Section 9.41; and

(2) when and to the degree he reasonably believes the deadly force is immediately necessary:

> (A) to prevent the other's imminent commission of arson, burglary, robbery, aggravated robbery, theft during the nighttime, or criminal mischief during the nighttime; or
>
> (B) to prevent the other who is fleeing immediately after committing burglary, robbery, aggravated robbery, or theft during the nighttime from escaping with the property; and

(3) he reasonably believes that:

> (A) the land or property cannot be protected or recovered by any other means; or
>
> (B) the use of force other than deadly force to protect or recover the land or property would expose the actor or another to a substantial risk of death or serious bodily injury.

Sec. 9.43. Protection of Third Person's Property.

A person is justified in using force or deadly force against another to protect land or tangible, movable property of a third person if, under the circumstances as he reasonably believes them to be, the actor would be justified under Section 9.41 or 9.42 in using force or deadly force to protect his own land or property and:

> (1) the actor reasonably believes the unlawful interference constitutes attempted or consummated theft of or criminal mischief to the tangible, movable property; or
>
> (2) the actor reasonably believes that:
>
>> (A) the third person has requested his protection of the land or property;
>>
>> (B) he has a legal duty to protect the third person's land or property; or
>>
>> (C) the third person whose land or property he uses force or deadly force to protect is the actor's spouse, parent, or child, resides with the actor, or is under the actor's care.

Sec. 9.44. Use of Device to Protect Property.

The justification afforded by Sections 9.41 and 9.43 applies to the use of a device to protect land or tangible, movable property if:

(1) the device is not designed to cause, or known by the actor to create a substantial risk of causing, death or serious bodily injury; and

(2) use of the device is reasonable under all the circumstances as the actor reasonably believes them to be when he installs the device.

SUBCHAPTER E LAW ENFORCEMENT

Sec. 9.51. Arrest and Search.

(a) A peace officer, or a person acting in a peace officer's presence and at his direction, is justified in using force against another when and to the degree the actor reasonably believes the force is immediately necessary to make or assist in making an arrest or search, or to prevent or assist in preventing escape after arrest, if:

> (1) the actor reasonably believes the arrest or search is lawful or, if the arrest or search is made under a warrant, he reasonably believes the warrant is valid; and

> (2) before using force, the actor manifests his purpose to arrest or search and identifies himself as a peace officer or as one acting at a peace officer's direction, unless he reasonably believes his purpose and identity are already known by or cannot reasonably be made known to the person to be arrested.

(b) A person other than a peace officer (or one acting at his direction) is justified in using force against another when and to the degree the actor reasonably believes the force is immediately necessary to make or assist in making a lawful arrest, or to prevent or assist in preventing escape after lawful arrest if, before using force, the actor manifests his purpose to and the reason for the arrest or reasonably believes his purpose and the reason are already known by or cannot reasonably be made known to the person to be arrested.

(c) A peace officer is justified in using deadly force against another when and to the degree the peace officer reasonably believes the deadly force is immediately necessary to make an arrest, or to prevent escape after arrest, if the use of force would have been justified under Subsection (a) and:

> (1) the actor reasonably believes the conduct for which arrest is authorized included the use or attempted use of deadly force; or

> (2) the actor reasonably believes there is a substantial risk that the person to be arrested will cause death or serious bodily injury to the actor or another if the arrest is delayed.

(d) A person other than a peace officer acting in a peace officer's presence and at his direction is justified in using deadly force against another when and to the degree the person reasonably believes the deadly force is immediately necessary to make a lawful arrest, or to prevent escape after a lawful arrest, if the use of force would have been justified under Subsection (b) and:

> (1) the actor reasonably believes the felony or offense against the public peace for which arrest is authorized included the use or attempted use of deadly force; or

> (2) the actor reasonably believes there is a substantial risk that the person to be arrested will cause death or serious bodily injury to another if the arrest is delayed.

(e) There is no duty to retreat before using deadly force justified by Subsection (c) or (d).

(f) Nothing in this section relating to the actor's manifestation of purpose or identity shall be construed as conflicting with any other law relating to the issuance, service, and execution of an arrest or search warrant either under the laws of this state or the United States.

(g) Deadly force may only be used under the circumstances enumerated in Subsections (c) and (d).

Sec. 9.52. Prevention of Escape from Custody.
The use of force to prevent the escape of an arrested person from custody is justifiable when the force could have been employed to effect the arrest under which the person is in custody, except that a guard employed by a correctional facility or a peace officer is justified in using any force, including deadly force, that he reasonably believes to be immediately necessary to prevent the escape of a person from the correctional facility.

Sec. 9.53. Maintaining Security in Correctional Facility.
An officer or employee of a correctional facility is justified in using force against a person in custody when and to the degree the officer or employee reasonably believes the force is necessary to maintain the security of the correctional facility, the safety or security of other persons in custody or employed by the correctional facility, or his own safety or security.

SUBCHAPTER F SPECIAL RELATIONSHIPS

Sec. 9.61. Parent—Child.
(a) The use of force, but not deadly force, against a child younger than 18 years is justified:
> (1) if the actor is the child's parent or stepparent or is acting in loco parentis to the child; and
> (2) when and to the degree the actor reasonably believes the force is necessary to discipline the child or to safeguard or promote his welfare.

(b) For purposes of this section, ``in loco parentis'' includes grandparent and guardian, any person acting by, through, or under the direction of a court with jurisdiction over the child, and anyone who has express or implied consent of the parent or parents.

Sec. 9.62. Educator—Student.
The use of force, but not deadly force, against a person is justified:
(1) if the actor is entrusted with the care, supervision, or administration of the person for a special purpose; and
(2) when and to the degree the actor reasonably believes the force is necessary to further the special purpose or to maintain discipline in a group.

Sec. 9.63. Guardian—Incompetent.

The use of force, but not deadly force, against a mental incompetent is justified:
(1) if the actor is the incompetent's guardian or someone similarly responsible for the general care and supervision of the incompetent; and
(2) when and to the degree the actor reasonably believes the force is necessary:

(A) to safeguard and promote the incompetent's welfare; or

(B) if the incompetent is in an institution for his care and custody, to maintain discipline in the institution.

TITLE 4 INCHOATE OFFENSES
CHAPTER 15 PREPARATORY OFFENSES

Sec. 15.01. Criminal Attempt.

(a) A person commits an offense if, with specific intent to commit an offense, he does an act amounting to more than mere preparation that tends but fails to effect the commission of the offense intended.

(b) If a person attempts an offense that may be aggravated, his conduct constitutes an attempt to commit the aggravated offense if an element that aggravates the offense accompanies the attempt.

(c) It is no defense to prosecution for criminal attempt that the offense attempted was actually committed.

(d) An offense under this section is one category lower than the offense attempted, and if the offense attempted is a state jail felony, the offense is a Class A misdemeanor.

Sec. 15.02. Criminal Conspiracy.

(a) A person commits criminal conspiracy if, with intent that a felony be committed:

(1) he agrees with one or more persons that they or one or more of them engage in conduct that would constitute the offense; and

(2) he or one or more of them performs an overt act in pursuance of the agreement.

(b) An agreement constituting a conspiracy may be inferred from acts of the parties.

(c) It is no defense to prosecution for criminal conspiracy that:

(1) one or more of the coconspirators is not criminally responsible for the object offense;

(2) one or more of the coconspirators has been acquitted, so long as two or more coconspirators have not been acquitted;

(3) one or more of the coconspirators has not been prosecuted or convicted, has been convicted of a different offense, or is immune from prosecution;

(4) the actor belongs to a class of persons that by definition of the object offense is legally incapable of committing the object offense in an individual capacity; or

(5) the object offense was actually committed.

(d) An offense under this section is one category lower than the most serious felony that is the object of the conspiracy, and if the most serious felony that is the object of the conspiracy is a state jail felony, the offense is a Class A misdemeanor.

Sec.15.03. Criminal Solicitation.

(a) A person commits an offense if, with intent that a capital felony or felony of the first degree be committed, he requests, commands, or attempts to induce another to engage in specific conduct that, under the circumstances surrounding his conduct as the actor believes them to be, would constitute the felony or make the other a party to its commission.

(b) A person may not be convicted under this section on the uncorroborated testimony of the person allegedly solicited and unless the solicitation is made under circumstances strongly corroborative of both the solicitation itself and the actor's intent that the other person act on the solicitation.

(c) It is no defense to prosecution under this section that:

(1) the person solicited is not criminally responsible for the felony solicited;

(2) the person solicited has been acquitted, has not been prosecuted or convicted, has been convicted of a different offense or of a different type or class of offense, or is immune from prosecution;

(3) the actor belongs to a class of persons that by definition of the felony solicited is legally incapable of committing the offense in an individual capacity; or

(4) the felony solicited was actually committed.

(d) An offense under this section is:

(1) a felony of the first degree if the offense solicited is a capital offense; or

(2) a felony of the second degree if the offense solicited is a felony of the first degree.

Sec. 15.04. Renunciation Defense.

(a) It is an affirmative defense to prosecution under Section 15.01 that under circumstances manifesting a voluntary and complete renunciation of his criminal objective the actor avoided commission of the offense attempted by abandoning his criminal conduct or, if abandonment was insufficient to avoid commission of the offense, by taking further affirmative action that prevented the commission.

(b) It is an affirmative defense to prosecution under Section 15.02 or 15.03 that under circumstances manifesting a voluntary and complete renunciation of his criminal objective the actor countermanded his solicitation or withdrew from the conspiracy before commission of the object offense and took further affirmative action that prevented the commission of the object offense.

(c) Renunciation is not voluntary if it is motivated in whole or in part:

(1) by circumstances not present or apparent at the inception of the actor's course of conduct that increase the probability of detection or apprehension or that make more difficult the accomplishment of the objective; or

(2) by a decision to postpone the criminal conduct until another time or to transfer the criminal act to another but similar objective or victim.

(d) Evidence that the defendant renounced his criminal objective by abandoning his criminal conduct, countermanding his solicitation, or withdrawing from the conspiracy before the criminal offense was committed and made substantial effort to prevent the commission of the object offense shall be admissible as mitigation at the hearing on punishment if he has been found guilty of criminal attempt, criminal solicitation, or criminal conspiracy; and in the event of a finding of renunciation under this subsection, the punishment shall be one grade lower than that provided for the offense committed.

Sec. 15.05. No Offense.

Attempt or conspiracy to commit, or solicitation of, a preparatory offense defined in this chapter is not an offense.

TITLE 5 OFFENSES AGAINST THE PERSON
CHAPTER 19 CRIMINAL HOMICIDE

Sec. 19.01. Types of Criminal Homicide.

(a) A person commits criminal homicide if he intentionally, knowingly, recklessly, or with criminal negligence causes the death of an individual.

(b) Criminal homicide is murder, capital murder, manslaughter, or criminally negligent homicide.

Sec. 19.02. Murder.

(a) In this section:

(1) "Adequate cause" means cause that would commonly produce a degree of anger, rage, resentment, or terror in a person of ordinary temper, sufficient to render the mind incapable of cool reflection.

(2) "Sudden passion" means passion directly caused by and arising out of provocation by the individual killed or another acting with the person killed which passion arises at the time of the offense and is not solely the result of former provocation.

>   (b) A person commits an offense if he:
>   (1) intentionally or knowingly causes the death of an individual;
>   (2) intends to cause serious bodily injury and commits an act clearly dangerous to human life that causes the death of an individual; or
>   (3) commits or attempts to commit a felony, other than manslaughter, and in the course of and in furtherance of the commission or attempt, or in immediate flight from the commission or attempt, he commits or attempts to commit an act clearly dangerous to human life that causes the death of an individual.

(c) Except as provided by Subsection (d), an offense under this section is a felony of the first degree.

(d) At the punishment stage of a trial, the defendant may raise the issue as to whether he caused the death under the immediate influence of sudden passion arising from an adequate cause. If the defendant proves the issue in the affirmative by a preponderance of the evidence, the offense is a felony of the second degree.

Sec. 19.03. Capital Murder.

(a) A person commits an offense if the person commits murder as defined under Section 19.02(b)(1) and:

>   (1) the person murders a peace officer or fireman who is acting in the lawful discharge of an official duty and who the person knows is a peace officer or fireman;
>   (2) the person intentionally commits the murder in the course of committing or attempting to commit kidnapping, burglary, robbery, aggravated sexual assault, arson,

obstruction or retaliation, or terroristic threat under Section 22.07(a)(1), (3), (4), (5), or (6);

(3) the person commits the murder for remuneration or the promise of remuneration or employs another to commit the murder for remuneration or the promise of remuneration;

(4) the person commits the murder while escaping or attempting to escape from a penal institution;

(5) the person, while incarcerated in a penal institution, murders another:

    (A) who is employed in the operation of the penal institution; or

    (B) with the intent to establish, maintain, or participate in a combination or in the profits of a combination;

(6) the person:

    (A) while incarcerated for an offense under this section or Section 19.02, murders another; or

    (B) while serving a sentence of life imprisonment or a term of 99 years for an offense under Section 20.04, 22.021, or 29.03, murders another;

(7) the person murders more than one person:

    (A) during the same criminal transaction; or

    (B) during different criminal transactions but the murders are committed pursuant to the same scheme or course of conduct; or

(8) the person murders an individual under six years of age.

(b) An offense under this section is a capital felony.

(c) If the jury or, when authorized by law, the judge does not find beyond a reasonable doubt that the defendant is guilty of an offense under this section, he may be convicted of murder or of any other lesser included offense.

Sec. 19.04. Manslaughter.

(a) A person commits an offense if he recklessly causes the death of an individual.

(b) An offense under this section is a felony of the second degree.

Sec. 19.05. Criminally Negligent Homicide.

(a) A person commits an offense if he causes the death of an individual by criminal negligence.

(b) An offense under this section is a state jail felony.

Sec. 21.08. Indecent Exposure.

(a) A person commits an offense if he exposes his anus or any part of his genitals with intent to arouse or gratify the sexual desire of any person, and he is reckless about whether another is present who will be offended or alarmed by his act.

(b) An offense under this section is a Class B misdemeanor.

Sec. 22.06. Consent as Defense to Assaultive Conduct.

The victim's effective consent or the actor's reasonable belief that the victim consented to the actor's conduct is a defense to prosecution under Section 22.01 (Assault), 22.02 (Aggravated Assault), or 22.05 (Deadly Conduct) if:

    (1) the conduct did not threaten or inflict serious bodily injury; or
    (2) the victim knew the conduct was a risk of:
        (A) his occupation;
        (B) recognized medical treatment; or
        (C) a scientific experiment conducted by recognized methods.

Sec. 30.02. Burglary.

(a) A person commits an offense if, without the effective consent of the owner, the person:
    (1) enters a habitation, or a building (or any portion of a building) not then open to the public, with intent to commit a felony, theft, or an assault; or
    (2) remains concealed, with intent to commit a felony, theft, or an assault, in a building or habitation; or
    (3) enters a building or habitation and commits or attempts to commit a felony, theft, or an assault.
(b) For purposes of this section, "enter" means to intrude:
    (1) any part of the body; or
    (2) any physical object connected with the body.
(c) Except as provided in Subsection (c-1) or (d), an offense under this section is a:
    (1) state jail felony if committed in a building other than a habitation; or
    (2) felony of the second degree if committed in a habitation.
(c-1) An offense under this section is a felony of the third degree if:
    (1) the premises are a commercial building in which a controlled substance is generally stored, including a pharmacy, clinic, hospital, nursing facility, or warehouse; and
    (2) the person entered or remained concealed in that building with intent to commit a theft of a controlled substance.
(d) An offense under this section is a felony of the first degree if:
    (1) the premises are a habitation; and
    (2) any party to the offense entered the habitation with intent to commit a felony other than felony theft or committed or attempted to commit a felony other than felony theft.

Sec. 30.05. Criminal Trespass.

(a) A person commits an offense if he enters or remains on or in property, including an aircraft or other vehicle, of another without effective consent or he enters or remains in a building of another without effective consent and he:
    (1) had notice that the entry was forbidden; or
    (2) received notice to depart but failed to do so.
(b) For purposes of this section:
    (1) "Entry" means the intrusion of the entire body.
    (2) "Notice" means:

(A) oral or written communication by the owner or someone with apparent authority to act for the owner;

(B) fencing or other enclosure obviously designed to exclude intruders or to contain livestock;

(C)   a sign or signs posted on the property or at the entrance to the building, reasonably likely to come to the attention of intruders, indicating that entry is forbidden;

Sec. 36.05. Tampering With Witness.

(a)   A person commits an offense if, with intent to influence the witness, he offers, confers, or agrees to confer any benefit on a witness or prospective witness in an official proceeding or coerces a witness or prospective witness in an official proceeding:

(1)   to testify falsely;

(2)   to withhold any testimony, information, document, or thing;

(3)   to elude legal process summoning him to testify or supply evidence;

(4)   to absent himself from an official proceeding to which he has been legally summoned; or

(5)   to abstain from, discontinue, or delay the prosecution of another.

(b)   A witness or prospective witness in an official proceeding commits an offense if he knowingly solicits, accepts, or agrees to accept any benefit on the representation or understanding that he will do any of the things specified in Subsection (a).

(c) It is a defense to prosecution under Subsection (a)(5) that the benefit received was:

(1)   reasonable restitution for damages suffered by the complaining witness as a result of the offense; and

(2) a result of an agreement negotiated with the assistance or acquiescence of an attorney for the state who represented the state in the case.

(d) An offense under this section is a state jail felony.

Sec. 38.05. Hindering Apprehension or Prosecution.

(a) A person commits an offense if, with intent to hinder the arrest, prosecution, conviction, or punishment of another for an offense or, with intent to hinder the arrest, detention, adjudication, or disposition of a child for engaging in delinquent conduct that violates a penal law of the grade of felony, he:

(1) harbors or conceals the other;

(2) provides or aids in providing the other with any means of avoiding arrest or effecting escape; or

(3) warns the other of impending discovery or apprehension.

(b)   It is a defense to prosecution under Subsection (a)(3) that the warning was given in connection with an effort to bring another into compliance with the law.

(c)   Except as provided by subsection (d), an offense under this section is a Class A misdemeanor.

(d) An offense under this section is a felony of the third degree if the person who is harbored, concealed, provided with a means of avoiding arrest or effecting escape, or warned of discovery or apprehension is under arrest for, charged with, or convicted of a felony, including an offense under Section 62.102, Code of Criminal Procedure, or is in custody or detention for, is alleged in a petition to have engaged in, or has been adjudicated as having engaged in delinquent conduct that violates a penal law of the grade of felony, including an offense under Section 62.102, Code of Criminal Procedure, and the person charged under this section knew that the person they harbored, concealed, provided with a means of avoiding arrest or effecting escape, or warned of discovery or apprehension is under arrest for, charged with, or convicted of a felony, or is in custody or detention for, is alleged in a petition to have engaged in, or has been adjudicated as having engaged in delinquent conduct that violates a penal law of the grade of felony.

CHAPTER 48 CONDUCT AFFECTING PUBLIC HEALTH

Sec. 48.01. Smoking Tobacco.
(a) In this section, "e-cigarette" has the meaning assigned by Section 161.081, Health and Safety Code.
(a-1) A person commits an offense if the person is in possession of a burning tobacco product, smokes tobacco, or operates an e-cigarette in a facility of a public primary or secondary school or an elevator, enclosed theater or movie house, library, museum, hospital, transit system bus, intrastate bus, plane, or train which is a public place.
(b) It is a defense to prosecution under this section that the conveyance or public place in which the offense takes place does not have prominently displayed a reasonably sized notice that smoking is prohibited by state law in such conveyance or public place and that an offense is punishable by a fine not to exceed $500.
(c) All conveyances and public places set out in Subsection (a-1) shall be equipped with facilities for extinguishment of smoking materials and it shall be a defense to prosecution under this section if the conveyance or public place within which the offense takes place is not so equipped.
(d) It is an exception to the application of Subsection (a-1) if the person is in possession of the burning tobacco product, smokes tobacco, or operates the e-cigarette exclusively within an area designated for smoking tobacco or operating an e-cigarette or as a participant in an authorized theatrical performance.
(e) An area designated for smoking tobacco or operating an e-cigarette on a transit system bus or intrastate plane or train must also include the area occupied by the operator of the transit system bus, plane, or train.
(f) An offense under this section is punishable as a Class C misdemeanor.

Texas Code of Criminal Procedure (Excerpts)

Art. 37.071. PROCEDURE IN CAPITAL CASE

Sec. 1. If a defendant is found guilty in a capital felony case in which the state does not seek the death penalty, the judge shall sentence the defendant to life imprisonment or to life imprisonment without parole as required by Section 12.31, Penal Code.

Sec. 2. (a)(1) If a defendant is tried for a capital offense in which the state seeks the death penalty, on a finding that the defendant is guilty of a capital offense, the court shall conduct a separate sentencing proceeding to determine whether the defendant shall be sentenced to death or life imprisonment without parole. The proceeding shall be conducted in the trial court and, except as provided by Article 44.29(c) of this code, before the trial jury as soon as practicable. In the proceeding, evidence may be presented by the state and the defendant or the defendant's counsel as to any matter that the court deems relevant to sentence, including evidence of the defendant's background or character or the circumstances of the offense that mitigates against the imposition of the death penalty. This subdivision shall not be construed to authorize the introduction of any evidence secured in violation of the Constitution of the United States or of the State of Texas. The state and the defendant or the defendant's counsel shall be permitted to present argument for or against sentence of death. The introduction of evidence of extraneous conduct is governed by the notice requirements of Section 3(g), Article 37.07. The court, the attorney representing the state, the defendant, or the defendant's counsel may not inform a juror or a prospective juror of the effect of a failure of a jury to agree on issues submitted under Subsection (c) or (e).

(2) Notwithstanding Subdivision (1), evidence may not be offered by the state to establish that the race or ethnicity of the defendant makes it likely that the defendant will engage in future criminal conduct.

(b) On conclusion of the presentation of the evidence, the court shall submit the following issues to the jury:

(1) whether there is a probability that the defendant would commit criminal acts of violence that would constitute a continuing threat to society; and

(2) in cases in which the jury charge at the guilt or innocence stage permitted the jury to find the defendant guilty as a party under Sections 7.01 and 7.02, Penal Code, whether the defendant actually caused the death of the deceased or did not actually cause the death of the deceased but intended to kill the deceased or another or anticipated that a human life would be taken.

(c) The state must prove each issue submitted under Subsection (b) of this article beyond a reasonable doubt, and the jury shall return a special verdict of "yes" or "no" on each issue submitted under Subsection (b) of this Article.

(d) The court shall charge the jury that:

(1) in deliberating on the issues submitted under Subsection (b) of this article, it shall consider all evidence admitted at the guilt or innocence stage and the punishment stage, including evidence of the defendant's background or character or the circumstances of the offense that militates for or mitigates against the imposition of the death penalty;

(2) it may not answer any issue submitted under Subsection (b) of this article "yes" unless it agrees unanimously and it may not answer any issue "no" unless 10 or more jurors agree; and

(3) members of the jury need not agree on what particular evidence supports a negative answer to any issue submitted under Subsection (b) of this article.

(e)(1) The court shall instruct the jury that if the jury returns an affirmative finding to each issue submitted under Subsection (b), it shall answer the following issue:

Whether, taking into consideration all of the evidence, including the circumstances of the offense, the defendant's character and background, and the personal moral culpability of the defendant, there is a sufficient mitigating circumstance or circumstances to warrant that a sentence of life imprisonment without parole rather than a death sentence be imposed.

(2) The court shall:

(A) instruct the jury that if the jury answers that a circumstance or circumstances warrant that a sentence of life imprisonment without parole rather than a death sentence be imposed, the court will sentence the defendant to imprisonment in the Texas Department of Criminal Justice for life without parole; and

(B) charge the jury that a defendant sentenced to confinement for life without parole under this article is ineligible for release from the department on parole.

(f) The court shall charge the jury that in answering the issue submitted under Subsection (e) of this article, the jury:

(1) shall answer the issue "yes" or "no";

(2) may not answer the issue "no" unless it agrees unanimously and may not answer the issue "yes" unless 10 or more jurors agree;

(3) need not agree on what particular evidence supports an affirmative finding on the issue; and

(4) shall consider mitigating evidence to be evidence that a juror might regard as reducing the defendant's moral blameworthiness.

(g) If the jury returns an affirmative finding on each issue submitted under Subsection (b) and a negative finding on an issue submitted under Subsection (e)(1), the court shall sentence the defendant to death. If the jury returns a negative finding on any issue submitted under Subsection (b) or an affirmative finding on an issue submitted under Subsection (e)(1) or is unable to answer any issue submitted under Subsection (b) or (e), the court shall sentence the defendant to confinement in the Texas Department of Criminal Justice for life imprisonment without parole.

(h) The judgment of conviction and sentence of death shall be subject to automatic review by the Court of Criminal Appeals.

(i) This article applies to the sentencing procedure in a capital case for an offense that is committed on or after September 1, 1991. For the purposes of this section, an offense is committed on or after September 1, 1991, if any element of that offense occurs on or after that date.

Art. 37.0711. PROCEDURE IN CAPITAL CASE FOR OFFENSE COMMITTED BEFORE SEPTEMBER 1, 1991.

Sec. 1. This article applies to the sentencing procedure in a capital case for an offense that is committed before September 1, 1991, whether the sentencing procedure is part of the original trial of the offense, an award of a new trial for both the guilt or innocence stage and the punishment stage of the trial, or an award of a new trial only for the punishment stage of the trial.

For the purposes of this section, an offense is committed before September 1, 1991, if every element of the offense occurs before that date.

      Sec. 2. If a defendant is found guilty in a case in which the state does not seek the death penalty, the judge shall sentence the defendant to life imprisonment.

      Sec. 3. (a) (1) If a defendant is tried for a capital offense in which the state seeks the death penalty, on a finding that the defendant is guilty of a capital offense, the court shall conduct a separate sentencing proceeding to determine whether the defendant shall be sentenced to death or life imprisonment. The proceeding shall be conducted in the trial court and, except as provided by Article 44.29(c) of this code, before the trial jury as soon as practicable. In the proceeding, evidence may be presented as to any matter that the court deems relevant to sentence. This subdivision shall not be construed to authorize the introduction of any evidence secured in violation of the Constitution of the United States or of this state. The state and the defendant or the defendant's counsel shall be permitted to present argument for or against sentence of death.

      (2) Notwithstanding Subdivision (1), evidence may not be offered by the state to establish that the race or ethnicity of the defendant makes it likely that the defendant will engage in future criminal conduct.

      (b) On conclusion of the presentation of the evidence, the court shall submit the following three issues to the jury:

      (1) whether the conduct of the defendant that caused the death of the deceased was committed deliberately and with the reasonable expectation that the death of the deceased or another would result;

      (2) whether there is a probability that the defendant would commit criminal acts of violence that would constitute a continuing threat to society; and

      (3) if raised by the evidence, whether the conduct of the defendant in killing the deceased was unreasonable in response to the provocation, if any, by the deceased.

      (c) The state must prove each issue submitted under Subsection (b) of this section beyond a reasonable doubt, and the jury shall return a special verdict of "yes" or "no" on each issue submitted.

      (d) The court shall charge the jury that:

      (1) it may not answer any issue submitted under Subsection (b) of this section "yes" unless it agrees unanimously; and

      (2) it may not answer any issue submitted under Subsection (b) of this section "no" unless 10 or more jurors agree.

      (e) The court shall instruct the jury that if the jury returns an affirmative finding on each issue submitted under Subsection (b) of this section, it shall answer the following issue:

      Whether, taking into consideration all of the evidence, including the circumstances of the offense, the defendant's character and background, and the personal moral culpability of the defendant, there is a sufficient mitigating circumstance or circumstances to warrant that a sentence of life imprisonment rather than a death sentence be imposed.

      (f) The court shall charge the jury that, in answering the issue submitted under Subsection (e) of this section, the jury:

      (1) shall answer the issue "yes" or "no";

      (2) may not answer the issue "no" unless it agrees unanimously and may not answer the issue "yes" unless 10 or more jurors agree; and

(3) shall consider mitigating evidence that a juror might regard as reducing the defendant's moral blameworthiness.

(g) If the jury returns an affirmative finding on each issue submitted under Subsection (b) and a negative finding on the issue submitted under Subsection (e), the court shall sentence the defendant to death. If the jury returns a negative finding on any issue submitted under Subsection (b) or an affirmative finding on the issue submitted under Subsection (e) or is unable to answer any issue submitted under Subsection (b) or (e), the court shall sentence the defendant to confinement in the Texas Department of Criminal Justice for life.

(h) If a defendant is convicted of an offense under Section 19.03(a)(7), Penal Code, the court shall submit the issues under Subsections (b) and (e) of this section only with regard to the conduct of the defendant in murdering the deceased individual first named in the indictment.

(i) The court, the attorney for the state, or the attorney for the defendant may not inform a juror or prospective juror of the effect of failure of the jury to agree on an issue submitted under this article.

(j) The Court of Criminal Appeals shall automatically review a judgment of conviction and sentence of death not later than the 60th day after the date of certification by the sentencing court of the entire record, unless the Court of Criminal Appeals extends the time for an additional period not to exceed 30 days for good cause shown. Automatic review under this subsection has priority over all other cases before the Court of Criminal Appeals, and the court shall hear automatic reviews under rules adopted by the court for that purpose.

Art. 37.09. LESSER INCLUDED OFFENSE.

An offense is a lesser included offense if:
> (1) it is established by proof of the same or less than all the facts required to establish the commission of the offense charged;
> (2) it differs from the offense charged only in the respect that a less serious injury or risk of injury to the same person, property, or public interest suffices to establish its commission;
> (3) it differs from the offense charged only in the respect that a less culpable mental state suffices to establish its commission; or
> (4) it consists of an attempt to commit the offense charged or an otherwise included offense.

39198709R00315

Made in the USA
San Bernardino, CA
18 June 2019